Microsoft® Windows Server™ 2003 Administrator's Pocket Consultant, Second Edition

William R. Stanek

PUBLISHED BY
Microsoft Press
A Division of Microsoft Corporation
One Microsoft Way
Redmond, Washington 98052-6399

Library of Congress Control Number: 2005939170

Printed and bound in the United States of America.

5 6 7 8 9   QWE   0 9 8

Distributed in Canada by H.B. Fenn and Company Ltd.

A CIP catalogue record for this book is available from the British Library.

Microsoft Press books are available through booksellers and distributors worldwide. For further information about international editions, contact your local Microsoft Corporation office or contact Microsoft Press International directly at fax (425) 936-7329. Visit our Web site at www.microsoft.com/mspress. Send comments to *mspinput@microsoft.com*.

Acquisitions Editor: Martin DelRe
Project Editor: Denise Bankaitis
Technical Editor: Rozanne Whalen
Copy Editor: Joseph Gustaitis
Indexer: Jack Lewis

Body Part No. X11-74977

Contents at a Glance

Table of Contents

What do you think of this book? We want to hear from you!	Microsoft is interested in hearing your feedback about this publication so we can continually improve our books and learning resources for you. To participate in a brief online survey, please visit: *www.microsoft.com/learning/booksurvey/*

Acknowledgments

Writing *Microsoft Windows Server 2003 Administrator's Pocket Consultant 2nd Edition* was a lot of fun—and a lot of work. As you'll see, Windows Server 2003 is very different from its predecessors, and that meant a lot of research to ensure that the book was as accurate as it could be. When all was said and done with the first edition, I ended up with a book that was nearly 1,000 pages long, and that just isn't what a Pocket Consultant is meant to be. Pocket Consultants are meant to be portable and readable—the kind of book you use to solve problems and get the job done wherever you might be. With that in mind, I had to go back in and carefully review the text, making sure I focused on the core of Windows Server 2003 administration. Revising the book for the second edition was no less challenging. There's a wealth of changes for the latest service packs and R2, which meant a lot of research and a lot of digging into the operating system internals. The result is the book you hold in your hand, which I hope you'll agree is one of the best practical, portable guides to Windows Server 2003.

It's gratifying to see techniques I've used time and again to solve problems put into a printed book so that others may benefit from them. But, no man is an island, and this book couldn't have been written without help from some very special people. As I've stated in *Microsoft Windows XP Administrator's Pocket Consultant 2nd Edition* and in *Microsoft SQL Server 2005 Administrator's Pocket Consultant*, the team at Microsoft Press is top-notch. Throughout the writing process, Maureen Zimmerman and Denise Bankaitis were instrumental in helping me stay on track and getting the tools I needed to write this book. Both Maureen and Denise did a first-rate job managing the editorial process from the Microsoft Press side. Susan McClung headed up the editorial process for nSight, Inc. Their professionalism, thoroughness, and attention to every detail are much appreciated!

Unfortunately for the writer (but fortunately for readers), writing is only one part of the publishing process. Next came editing and author review. I must say, Microsoft Press has the most thorough editorial and technical review process I've seen anywhere—and I've written a lot of books for many publishers. Special thanks to Maureen, Denise, and Susan for helping me to meet review deadlines. Rozanne Whalen was the technical editor for the book. It was a great pleasure working with Rozanne. I'd also like to thank Joseph Gustaitis for his careful copyediting of this book. I believe Joe has been the copyeditor for every Pocket Consultant that I've written. His work is always top-notch!

I owe many thank yous to Martin DelRe and Lucinda Rowley. Thank you for believing in my work and for supporting my books. Thank you also to Linda Engelman. I truly enjoy working with all of you.

I thank you also to the many 3CRD reviewers at Microsoft who reviewed the final copy and to my agents at Studio B, David Rogelberg and Neil Salkind.

Hopefully, I haven't forgotten anyone, but if I have, it was an oversight. *Honest.;-)*

Introduction

Microsoft Windows Server 2003 Administrator's Pocket Consultant 2nd Edition is designed to be a concise and compulsively usable resource for Microsoft Windows Server 2003 administrators. This is the readable resource guide that you'll want on your desk at all times. The book covers everything you need to perform the core administrative tasks for servers running Windows Server 2003. Not only has this book been updated to incorporate the latest service packs and changes, but it has also been updated to cover the R2 version of Windows Server 2003.

Because the focus is on giving you maximum value in a pocket-sized guide, you don't have to wade through hundreds of pages of extraneous information to find what you're looking for. Instead, you'll find exactly what you need to get the job done. In short, the book is designed to be the one resource you turn to whenever you have questions regarding Windows Server 2003 administration. To this end, the book zeroes in on daily administration procedures, frequently used tasks, documented examples, and options that are representative while not necessarily inclusive.

One of the goals is to keep the content concise so that the book remains compact and easy to navigate while at the same time ensuring that it is packed with as much information as possible—making it a valuable resource. Thus, instead of a hefty 1000-page tome or a lightweight 100-page quick reference, you get a valuable resource guide that can help you quickly and easily perform common tasks, solve problems, and implement advanced Windows technologies like Active Directory directory service, Dynamic Host Configuration Protocol (DHCP), Windows Internet Name Service (WINS), and Domain Name System (DNS).

Who Is This Book For?

Microsoft Windows Server 2003 Administrator's Pocket Consultant covers the Standard, Enterprise, Web, and Datacenter Server editions of Windows Server 2003. The book is designed for:

- Current Windows Server 2003 system administrators
- Accomplished users who have some administrator responsibilities
- Administrators upgrading to Windows Server 2003 from previous versions
- Administrators transferring from other platforms

To pack in as much information as possible, I had to assume that you have basic networking skills and a basic understanding of Windows Server 2003 and that Windows Server 2003 is already installed on your systems. With this in mind, I don't devote entire chapters to comprehending Windows Server 2003 architecture, installing Windows Server 2003, or understanding Windows Server 2003 startup and shutdown. I do, however, cover Windows Server 2003 configuration, Group Policy, security, auditing, data backup, system recovery, and much more.

I also assume that you're fairly familiar with Windows commands and procedures as well as the Windows user interface. If you need help learning Windows basics, you should read the Windows documentation.

How Is This Book Organized?

Microsoft Windows Server 2003 Administrator's Pocket Consultant is designed to be used in the daily administration of Windows networks, and, as such, the book is organized by job-related tasks rather than by Windows Server 2003 features. If you're reading this book, you should be aware of the relationship between Pocket Consultants and Administrator's Companions. Both types of books are designed to be a part of an administrator's library. While Pocket Consultants are the down-and-dirty, in-the-trenches books, Administrator's Companions are the comprehensive tutorials and references that cover every aspect of deploying a product or technology in the enterprise.

Speed and ease of reference are an essential part of this hands-on guide. The book has an expanded table of contents and an extensive index for finding answers to problems quickly. Many other quick reference features are included as well. These features include quick step-by-step instructions, lists, tables with fast facts, and extensive cross-references.

Chapters 1 to 5 cover the fundamental tasks you need for Windows Server 2003 administration. Chapter 1 provides an overview of Windows Server 2003 administration tools, techniques, and concepts. The chapter also introduces the security and maintenance enhancements included in Service Pack 1 and R2. Chapter 2 explores the tasks you'll need to manage Windows Server 2003 systems. Chapter 3 covers monitoring Windows Server 2003 services, processes, and events. Chapter 4 discusses Group Policy and also explains how to automate common administrative tasks. Chapter 5 details how to work with support services and remote desktop connectivity through terminal services.

Chapters 6 to 10 cover the essential tasks for managing Active Directory and administering user, computer, and group accounts. Chapter 6 introduces Active Directory structures and explains how to work with Active Directory domains. Chapter 7 explores core Active Directory administration. You'll learn how to manage computer accounts, domain controllers, and organizational units. Chapter 8 describes how to use system accounts, built-in groups, user rights, built-in capabilities, and implicit groups. You'll find extensive tables that tell you exactly when you should use certain types of accounts, rights, and capabilities. The core administration tasks for creating user and group accounts are covered in Chapter 9, with a logical follow-up for managing existing user and group accounts covered in Chapter 10.

Chapters 11 to 15 cover data administration. Chapter 11 starts by explaining how to add hard disk drives to a system and how to partition drives. Then the chapter dives into common tasks for managing file systems and drives, such as defragmenting disks, compression, encryption, and more. In Chapter 12, you'll find tasks for managing volume sets and redundant array of independent disks (RAID) arrays, as well as detailed advice on repairing damaged arrays.

Chapter 13 focuses on managing files and folders and all the tasks that go along with it. You'll also find an extensive discussion of file screening, storage reporting, and combating malware. Chapter 14 details how to enable file, drive, and folder sharing for remote network and Internet users and then goes on to cover Active Directory object security and auditing. The chapter also examines both NTFS file system (NTFS) disk quotas and Storage Resource Manager disk quotas. Chapter 15 explores data backup and recovery. The chapter starts with a discussion of backup and recovery planning and then provides step-by-step procedures for implementing a backup plan and recovering systems.

Chapters 16 to 20 cover network infrastructure and advanced administation tasks. Chapter 16 provides the essentials for installing, configuring, and testing Transmission Control Protocol/Internet Protocol (TCP/IP) networking on Windows Server 2003 systems—covering everything from installing network adapter cards to actually connecting a computer to a Windows Server 2003 domain. Chapter 17 begins with a troubleshooting guide for common printer problems and then goes on to cover tasks for installing and configuring local printers and network print servers. Chapters 18, 19, and 20 focus on the key Windows Server 2003 services: DHCP, WINS, and DNS. DHCP is used to assign dynamic Internet Protocol (IP) addresses to network clients. WINS is used to resolve computer names to IP addresses. DNS is used to resolve host names to IP addresses.

Conventions Used in This Book

I've used a variety of elements to help keep the text clear and easy to follow. You'll find code terms and listings in monospace type, except when I tell you to actually type a command. In that case, the command appears in **bold** type. When I introduce and define a new term, I put it in *italics*.

Other conventions include:

Note   To provide details on a point that needs emphasis

Best Practices   To examine the best technique to use when working with advanced configuration and administration concepts

Caution   To warn you when there are potential problems you should look out for

More Info   To provide more information on the subject

Real World   To provide real-world advice when discussing advanced topics.

Tip   To offer helpful hints or additional information

I truly hope you find that *Microsoft Windows Server 2003 Administrator's Pocket Consultant* provides everything you need to perform essential administrative tasks on Windows Server 2003 systems as quickly and efficiently as possible. Your thoughts are welcome at williamstanek@aol.com or visit *http://www.williamstanek.com/*. Thank you.

Support

Every effort has been made to ensure the accuracy of this book and of the contents of the companion disc. Microsoft Press provides corrections for books through the World Wide Web at the following address:

http://www.microsoft.com/mspress/support/default.asp

If you have comments, questions, or ideas about this book or the companion disc, please send them to Microsoft Press using either of the following methods:

Postal Mail:

> Microsoft Press
> Attn: Editor, *Microsoft Windows Server 2003 Administrator's Pocket Consultant*
> One Microsoft Way
> Redmond, WA 98052-6399

E-mail:

> *mspinput@microsoft.com*

Please note that product support isn't offered through the mail addresses above. For support information, visit Microsoft's Web site at *http://www.microsoft.com/support.*

Chapter 1

Overview of Microsoft Windows Server 2003 System Administration

Microsoft Windows Server 2003 is a powerful, versatile, and fully featured version of Windows Server. As a server operating system, Windows Server 2003 is fundamentally different from Windows desktop editions, such as Windows Vista and Windows XP Professional. Beginning with Service Pack 1 (SP1), Windows Server 2003 has many security and maintenance enhancements that change the way the operating system works in domains and workgroups. These security enhancements are further complemented with the introduction of Release 2 of Windows Server 2003, referred to in this book as Windows Server 2003 R2.

As with earlier versions of Windows Server 2003, Service Pack 1, Release 2, and later versions of Windows Server 2003 build on and extend the underlying technology architecture introduced with Windows 2000, including the following:

Active Directory directory service An extensible and scalable directory service that uses a namespace based on the Internet standard Domain Name System (DNS).

IntelliMirror Change and configuration management features that support mirroring of user data and environment settings, as well as central management of software installation and maintenance.

Security Architecture Architecture that provides improvements for smart cards, public and private encryption keys, and security protocols. It also features tools for analyzing system security and for applying uniform security settings to groups of systems.

Terminal Services Services that allow you to remotely log on to and manage other Windows Server 2003 systems.

1

Windows Script Host   A scripting environment for automating common administration tasks, such as creating user accounts or generating reports from event logs.

Although Windows Server 2003 SP1 and R2 have dozens of other new features, each of the features just listed has far-reaching effects on how you perform administrative tasks. None has more effect than Active Directory technology. A sound understanding of Active Directory structures and procedures is essential to your success as a Windows Server 2003 systems administrator.

That said, the Windows Server 2003 security architecture also has a far-reaching effect on how you perform administrative tasks. Through Active Directory and administrative templates, you can apply security settings to workstations and servers throughout the organization. Thus, rather than managing security on a machine-by-machine basis, you can manage security on an enterprise-wide basis.

The focus of this book is on managing the Windows Server 2003 family of operating systems. If you want to learn more about managing Windows XP and Windows Vista, good resources are *Microsoft Windows XP Professional Administrator's Pocket Consultant 2nd Edition* (Microsoft Press, 2005) and *Microsoft Windows Vista Administrator's Pocket Consultant* (Microsoft Press, 2006).

Microsoft Windows Server 2003

The Windows Server 2003 family of operating systems consists of Windows Server 2003, Standard Edition; Windows Server 2003, Enterprise Edition; Windows Server 2003, Datacenter Edition; and Windows Server 2003, Web Edition. Each edition has a specific purpose, as follows:

Windows Server 2003, Standard Edition   Designed to provide services and resources to other systems on a network. It's a direct replacement for Windows NT 4.0 Server and Windows 2000 Server. The operating system has a rich set of features and configuration options. Windows Server 2003, Standard Edition supports two-way and four-way symmetric multiprocessing (SMP) and up to 4 gigabytes (GB) of memory on 32-bit systems and 32 GB on 64-bit systems.

Windows Server 2003, Enterprise Edition   Extends the features provided in Windows Server 2003, Standard Edition to include support for Cluster Service, metadirectory services, and Services for Macintosh. It also supports 64-bit systems, hot swappable RAM, and nonuniform memory access (NUMA). Enterprise servers can have up to 32 GB of RAM on x86 and 1 terabyte (TB) of RAM on 64-bit systems and eight CPUs.

Windows Server 2003, Datacenter Edition   The most robust Windows server. It has enhanced clustering features and supports very large memory configurations with up to 64 GB of RAM on x86 and 1 TB of RAM on 64-bit systems. It has a minimum CPU requirement of eight and can support up to 64 CPUs on Datacenter Itanium Edition (single partition).

Windows Server 2003, Web Edition   Designed to provide Web services for deploying Web sites and Web-based applications. As such, this server edition includes the Microsoft .NET Framework, Microsoft Internet Information Services (IIS), ASP.NET, and network load-balancing features but lacks many other features, including Active Directory. In fact, the only other key Windows features in this edition are the Distributed File System (DFS), Encrypting File System (EFS), and Remote Desktop for administration. Windows Server 2003, Web Edition supports up to 2 GB of RAM and two CPUs.

Note   The various server editions support the same core features and administration tools. This means you can use the techniques discussed in this book regardless of which Windows Server 2003 edition you're using. Note also that because you can't install Active Directory on the Web Edition, you can't make a server running Windows Server 2003, Web Edition a domain controller. The server can, however, be a part of an Active Directory domain.

When you install a Windows Server 2003 system, you configure the system according to its role on the network.

- Servers are generally assigned to be part of a workgroup or a domain.

- Workgroups are loose associations of computers in which each individual computer is managed separately.

- Domains are collections of computers that you can manage collectively by means of domain controllers, which are Windows Server 2003 systems that manage access to the network, to the directory database, and to shared resources.

Note   In this book "Windows Server 2003" and "Windows Server 2003 family" refer to the family of four products: Windows Server 2003, Standard Edition; Windows Server 2003, Enterprise Edition; Windows Server 2003, Datacenter Edition; and Windows Server 2003, Web Edition. The various server editions support the same core features and administration tools.

All versions of Windows Server 2003 allow you to configure different views for the Start Menu. The views for the Start Menu are:

Classic Start Menu   The view used in previous versions of Windows. With this view, clicking Start displays a pop-up dialog box with direct access to common menus and menu items.

With the Classic Start Menu, you access administrative tools by clicking Start, clicking Programs, and then clicking Administrative Tools. You access the Control Panel by clicking Start, pointing to Settings, and then clicking Control Panel.

Simple Start Menu   Allows you to directly access commonly used programs and directly execute common tasks. You can, for example, click Start and then click Log Off to log off the computer quickly.

With the Simple Start Menu, you access administrative tools by clicking Start and then clicking Administrative Tools. You access the Control Panel by clicking Start and then clicking Control Panel.

Domain Controllers and Member Servers

When you install Windows Server 2003 on a new system, you can configure the server to be a member server, a domain controller, or a stand-alone server. The differences between these types of servers are extremely important. Member servers are a part of a domain but don't store directory information. Domain controllers are distinguished from member servers because they store directory information and provide authentication and directory services for the domain. Stand-alone servers aren't a part of a domain and have their own user database. Because of this, stand-alone servers also authenticate logon requests themselves.

Windows 2000 and Windows Server 2003 don't designate primary or backup domain controllers. Instead, they support a multimaster replication model. In this model any domain controller can process directory changes and then replicate those changes to other domain controllers automatically. This differs from the Windows NT single master replication model in which the primary domain controller stores a master copy and backup controllers store backup copies of the master. In addition, Windows NT distributed only the Security Account Manager (SAM) database, but Windows 2000 and Windows Server 2003 distribute an entire directory of information called a *data store*. Inside the data store are sets of objects representing user, group, and computer accounts as well as shared resources, such as servers, files, and printers.

Domains that use Active Directory are referred to as *Active Directory domains*. This distinguishes them from Windows NT domains. Although Active Directory domains can function with only one domain controller, you can and should configure multiple domain controllers in the domain. This way, if one domain controller fails, you can rely on the other domain controllers to handle authentication and other critical tasks.

In an Active Directory domain, any member server can be promoted to a domain controller, and you don't need to reinstall the operating system as you had to in Windows NT. To promote a member server, all you need to do is install the Active Directory component on the server. You can also demote domain controllers to be member servers, provided that the server isn't the last domain controller on the network. You promote and demote domain controllers by using the Active Directory Installation Wizard and following these steps:

1. Click Start.

2. Select Run.

3. Type **dcpromo** in the Open field, and then click OK.

Understanding and Using Server Roles

Servers running Windows Server 2003 are configured based on the services they offer. You can add or remove services at any time by using the Configure Your Server Wizard and following these steps:

1. Click Start.

2. Select Programs or All Programs as appropriate.

3. Select Administrative Tools, and then select Configure Your Server Wizard.

4. Click Next twice. Windows Server 2003 gathers information about the server's current roles. The Server Role page displays a list of available server roles and specifies whether they're configured. Adding and removing roles is easy. Just perform the following steps:

   ❑ If a role isn't configured and you want to add the role, click the role in the Server Role column and then click Next. Follow the prompts.

   ❑ If a role is configured and you want to remove the role, click the role in the Server Role column and then click Next. Read any warnings displayed carefully and then follow the prompts.

Any server can support one or more of the following server roles:

Application server   A server that provides Extensible Markup Language (XML) Web services, Web applications, and distributed applications. When you configure a server with this role, IIS, COM+, and the Microsoft .NET Framework are installed automatically. You also have the option of adding Microsoft FrontPage Server Extensions and enabling or disabling ASP.NET.

DHCP server   A server that runs the Dynamic Host Configuration Protocol (DHCP) and can automatically assign Internet Protocol (IP) addresses to clients on the network. This option installs DHCP and starts the New Scope Wizard.

DNS server   A server that runs DNS resolves computer names to IP addresses and vice versa. This option installs DNS and starts the DNS Server Wizard.

Domain controller   A server that provides directory services for the domain and has a directory store. Domain controllers also manage the logon process and directory searches. This option installs DNS and Active Directory.

File server   A server that serves and manages access to files. This option enables you to quickly configure disk quotas and indexing. You can also install the Web-based file administration utility, which installs IIS and enables Active Server Pages (ASP).

Mail server (POP3, SMTP)   A server that provides basic Post Office Protocol 3 (POP3) and Simple Mail Transfer Protocol (SMTP) mail services so that POP3 mail clients can send and receive mail in the domain. Once you install this service, you define a default domain for mail exchange and then create and manage mailboxes. These basic services are best for small offices or remote locations where e-mail exchange is needed but you don't need the power and versatility of Microsoft Exchange Server.

Print server   A server that provides and manages access to network printers, print queues, and printer drivers. This option enables you to quickly configure printers and print drivers that the server should provide.

Remote access/VPN server   A server that routes network traffic and manages dial-up networking or virtual private networking (VPN). This option starts the Routing and Remote Access Setup Wizard. You can configure routing and remote access to allow outgoing connections only, incoming and outgoing connections, or no outside connections at all.

Server cluster node   A server that operates as part of a group of servers working together called a *cluster*. This option starts the New Server Cluster Wizard, which allows you to create a new cluster group, or the Add Nodes Wizard, which allows you to add the server to an existing cluster. (This server role is supported by the Enterprise and Datacenter versions only.)

Streaming media server   A server that provides streaming media content to other systems on the network or the Internet. This option installs Windows Media Services. (This server role is supported by the Standard and Enterprise versions only.)

Terminal Server   A server that processes tasks for multiple client computers running in terminal services mode. This option installs Terminal Server. You don't need to install Terminal Server to remotely manage this server. Remote Desktop is installed automatically with the operating system.

WINS server   A server that runs Windows Internet Name Service (WINS), resolves NetBIOS names to IP addresses, and vice versa. This option installs WINS.

Once installed, you can manage server roles using Manage Your Server. This enhanced utility in Windows Server 2003 might just become your command and control center. As shown in Figure 1-1, the current role(s) of the server are displayed in Manage Your Server. You access this tool from the Administrative Tools menu. Click Start, Program or All Programs, and then select Manage Your Server. Use the quick links provided to manage the installed server roles and related information.

> **Tip**   Use the arrow icons to the left of the role name to shrink or expand the role information provided. Don't overlook Tools And Updates and See Also. Under these headings you'll find links for quick access to Administrative Tools, Windows Update, the System Properties dialog box, Help And Support, and more. As a final note, although you might be tempted to select the Don't Display This Page At Logon check box (it's in the lower-left corner of the dialog box), I don't suggest doing it. I've found that most of the tools I routinely work with and the tasks I regularly perform can be quickly accessed from this dialog box. It really is a good command and control center.

Figure 1-1   Manage Your Server provides quick access to frequently used tools and information.

Frequently Used Tools

Many utilities are available for administrating Windows Server 2003 systems. The tools you'll use the most include:

Control Panel   A collection of tools for managing system configuration. With Classic Start Menu, you can access these tools by selecting Start, choosing Settings, and then selecting Control Panel. With Simple Start Menu, you can access these tools by selecting Start and then selecting Control Panel.

Graphical administrative tools   The key tools for managing network computers and their resources. You can access these tools by selecting them individually on the Administrative Tools submenu.

Administrative wizards   Tools designed to automate key administrative tasks. Unlike in Windows NT, there's no central place for accessing wizards. Instead, you access wizards by selecting the appropriate menu options in other administrative tools.

Command-line utilities   You can launch most administrative utilities from the command line. In addition to these utilities, Windows Server 2003 provides others that are useful for working with Windows Server 2003 systems.

The following sections provide brief introductions to these administrative utilities. Additional details for key tools are provided throughout this book. Keep in mind that to use these utilities you might need an account with administrator privileges.

Using Control Panel Utilities

Control Panel contains utilities for working with a system's setup and configuration. You can organize the Control Panel in different ways according to the view you're using. A view is simply a way of organizing and presenting options. The key utilities you'll want to use include:

Add Hardware   Starts the Add Hardware Wizard, which you can use to install and troubleshoot hardware.

Add Or Remove Programs   Used to install programs and to safely uninstall programs. Also used to modify Windows Server 2003 setup components. For example, if you didn't install an add-on component, such as Certificate Services, during installation of the OS, you can use this utility to add it later.

Date And Time   Used to view or set a system's date, time, and time zone. Rather than manually setting the time on individual computers in the domain, you can use the Windows Time Service to automatically synchronize time on the network.

Display   Used to configure backgrounds, screen savers, video display mode, and video settings. You can also use this utility to specify desktop icons and to control visual effects, such as the menu fade effect.

Folder Options   Used to set a wide variety of folder and file options, including the type of desktop used, the folder views used, whether offline files are used, and whether you need to single-click or double-click to open items.

Licensing   On a workstation you use this utility to manage licenses on a local system. On a server it also allows you to change the client-licensing mode of installed products, such as Windows Server 2003 or Microsoft SQL Server.

Network Connections   Used to view network identity information, to add network components, and to establish network connections. You can also use this utility to change a system's computer name and domain. See Chapter 7, "Core Active Directory Administration," and Chapter 16, "Managing TCP/IP Networking," for details.

Printers And Faxes   Provides quick access to the Printers And Faxes folder, which you can use to manage print devices on a system. See Chapter 17, "Administering Network Printers and Print Services," for more information on managing network printers.

Scheduled Tasks   Allows you to view and add scheduled tasks. You can schedule tasks on a one-time or recurring basis to handle common administrative jobs. To learn more about scheduled tasks, see Chapter 4, "Automating Administrative Tasks, Policies, and Procedures."

System   Used to display and manage system properties, including properties for startup/shutdown, environment, hardware profiles, and user profiles. This utility is explored in Chapter 2, "Managing Servers Running Microsoft Windows Server 2003."

Using Graphical Administrative Tools

Windows Server 2003 provides several types of tools for system administration. The graphical user interface (GUI)-based tools are the ones you'll use the most. Usually you can use graphical administrative tools to manage the system to which you're currently logged on, as well as systems throughout Windows Server 2003 domains. For example, in the Component Services console you specify the computer you want to work with by right-clicking the Event Viewer entry in the left panel and then choosing Connect To Another Computer. This opens the Select Computer dialog box shown in Figure 1-2. You can then choose Another Computer and type the name of the computer, as shown. You can access the graphical administrative tools by selecting them on the Administrative Tools submenu or by double clicking Administrative Tools in the Control Panel.

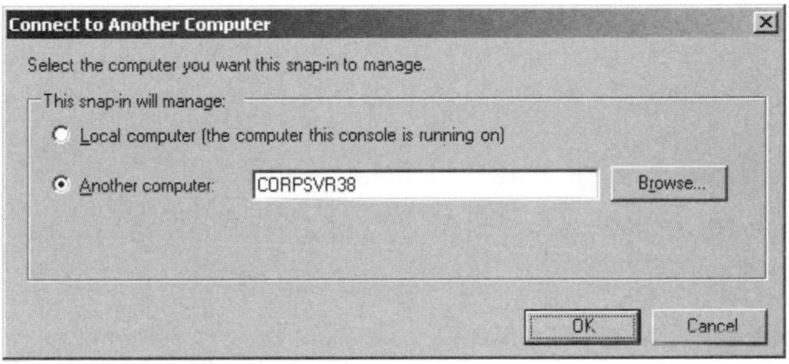

Figure 1-2   Connecting to another computer allows you to manage remote resources.

Tools and Configuration

Which administrative tools are available on your system depends on its configuration. When you add services, the tools needed to manage those services are installed on the server. These same tools might not be available in Windows XP Professional or on another server. In this case, you might want to install the administration tools on the workstation you're using. To install Windows Server 2003 Administration Tools, complete the following steps:

1. Log on to the workstation using an account with administrator privileges.

2. Insert the Windows Server 2003 CD-ROM into the CD-ROM drive.

3. When the Autorun screen appears, click Perform Additional Tasks, and then click Browse This CD. This starts Windows Explorer.

4. Double-click I386 and then double-click Adminpak.msi. The complete set of Windows Server 2003 management tools are installed on your workstation or server.

Real World   The Windows 2000 administration tools are incompatible with Windows XP Professional and Windows Server 2003. If you upgraded to Windows XP Professional from Windows 2000 Professional, you'll find that many of the

Windows 2000 administration tools won't work and you'll encounter errors frequently. You should uninstall these tools and instead install the Windows Server 2003 Administration Tools Pack (Adminpak.msi) on the Windows XP Professional systems that administrators use. The Windows Server 2003 administration tools are compatible with both Windows 2000 and Windows Server 2003.

Using Command-Line Utilities

Many command-line utilities are included with Windows Server 2003. Most of the utilities you'll work with as an administrator rely on Transmission Control Protocol/Internet Protocol (TCP/IP). Because of this, you should install TCP/IP networking before you experiment with these tools.

Utilities to Know

As an administrator, you should familiarize yourself with the following command-line utilities:

ARP   Displays and manages the IP-to-Physical address mappings used by Windows Server 2003 to send data on the TCP/ IP network.

AT   Schedules programs to run automatically.

DNSCMD   Displays and manages the configuration of DNS services.

FTP   Starts the built-in FTP client.

HOSTNAME   Displays the computer name of the local system.

IPCONFIG   Displays the TCP/IP properties for network adapters installed on the system. You can also use it to renew and release DHCP information.

NBTSTAT   Displays statistics and current connections for NetBIOS over TCP/IP.

NET   Displays a family of useful networking commands.

NETSH   Displays and manages the network configuration of local and remote computers.

NETSTAT   Displays current TCP/IP connections and protocol statistics.

NSLOOKUP   Checks the status of a host or IP address when used with DNS.

PATHPING   Traces network paths and displays packet loss information.

PING   Tests the connection to a remote host.

ROUTE   Manages the routing tables on the system.

TRACERT   During testing, determines the network path taken to a remote host.

To learn how to use these command-line tools, type the name at a command prompt followed by /?. Windows Server 2003 then provides an overview of how the command is used (in most cases).

Using NET Tools

You can more easily manage most of the tasks performed with the NET commands by using graphical administrative tools and Control Panel utilities. However, some of the NET tools are very useful for performing tasks quickly or for obtaining information, especially during telnet sessions to remote systems. These commands include:

NET SEND   Sends messages to users logged in to a particular system.

NET START   Starts a service on the system.

NET STOP   Stops a service on the system.

NET TIME   Displays the current system time or synchronizes the system time with another computer.

NET USE   Connects and disconnects from a shared resource.

NET VIEW   Displays a list of network resources available to the system.

To learn how to use any of the NET command-line tools, type **NET HELP** followed by the command name, such as **NET HELP SEND**. Windows Server 2003 then provides an overview of how the command is used.

Introducing Security and Maintenance Enhancements

Beginning with Service Pack 1, Microsoft introduced many system security and maintenance enhancements to Windows Server 2003. Two specific changes have a major impact on how Windows Server 2003 is installed:

Post-Setup Security Update   Designed to safeguard the server from malicious users and infection between the time the computer is installed and the most current security updates are applied through Windows Update. On a new installation of Windows Server 2003 with Service Pack 1 or later included, Post-Setup Security Update typically starts the first time an administrator logs on and blocks all inbound traffic to the server until updates are made or declined. After the initial log on the tool typically isn't displayed or run again.

Security Configuration Wizard   Designed to reduce the attack surface of a server. This wizard can be used to guide you through the process of creating security policies based on the roles performed by a specific server. Similarly configured servers can use the same security policy, and this policy can be edited or undone (rolled back) at any time.

Unlike Post-Setup Security Update, the Security Configuration Wizard is not installed by default. To install the Security Configuration Wizard, follow these steps:

1. In Control Panel, double-click Add Or Remove Programs.

2. Start the Windows Component Wizard by clicking Add/Remove Windows Components.

3. On the Windows Components page, select Security Configuration Wizard and then click Next.

4. When prompted, insert the Windows Server 2003 with SP1 CD-ROM into the CD-ROM drive and then click OK.

5. Click Finish. Close Add Or Remove Programs.

After it's installed, you can run the Security Configuration Wizard from the Administrative Tools menu. Click Start, Programs or All Programs, Administrative Tools and then select Security Configuration Wizard. Files and other resources used by the wizard are stored under %WinDir%\Security. The wizard has a command-line counterpart which can be started by typing **scwcmd** at a command prompt.

Similar to desktops running Windows XP Professional Service Pack 2 or later, key additional features for servers running Windows Server 2003 Service Pack 1 or later include:

Windows Firewall   A software-based firewall designed to help protect a server against network-based attacks and other security threats from remote systems. Windows Firewall requires the Windows Firewall/Internet Connection Sharing (ICS) service to be enabled and running. In a typical new installation of Windows Server 2003 with SP1, this service is disabled. If you want to use Windows Firewall, you can configure the service and start the firewall by completing the following steps:

1. Open Windows Firewall in Control Panel.

2. Click Yes when prompted to start the Windows Firewall/Internet Connection Sharing (ICS) service.

3. Select On and then click OK.

Data Execution Protection   A set of hardware and software technologies designed to help protect against malicious code. To better safeguard computers from memory-based vulnerabilities such as buffer overruns that allow too much data to be copied into areas of a computer's memory, the core components of the operating system were recompiled for Service Pack 1. Core code was also updated to support hardware-enforced execution protection (referred to as a no execute or NX feature). Execution protection tells the CPU to mark all memory locations in an application as nonexecutable unless the location explicitly contains executable code. This prevents malicious code such as a virus from inserting itself into most areas of the memory because only specific areas of memory are marked as having executable code. Typically Data Execution Protection is enabled if supported, and you can check the status of Data Execution Protection by completing the following steps:

1. Open System in Control Panel.

2. On the Advanced tab of the System dialog box, click Settings.

3. Select the Data Execution Prevention tab in the Performance Options dialog box. See Chapter 2 for more information.

Secure Browsing   A set of features to enhance Internet Explorer security and lock down the local machine. The key features include Browser Information Bar, which is displayed in Internet Explorer just below the address bar whenever Information Bar messages are displayed; Add-on Manager, which allows you to view and manage currently installed add-ons for Internet Explorer; and Pop-up Blocker, which allows you to block many types of pop-up windows. Chapter 15 of *Microsoft Windows XP Professional Administrator's Pocket Consultant 2nd Edition* describes these features in detail.

RPC Interface Restriction   A set of changes to the Remote Procedure Call (RPC) service and the Distributed Component Object Model (DCOM) to help safeguard server systems against some types of remote attacks. The changes affect the interaction of programs across networks and also ensure that both RPC and DCOM work with the Windows Firewall.

Introducing Release 2 Enhancements

Windows Server 2003 R2 is an update release of the Windows Server 2003 operating system that is built on top of Windows Server 2003 SP1. After you install Windows Server 2003 R2, you can install additional features for manageability and reliability like other Windows components using Add Or Remove Programs in Control Panel. To install additional features, complete the following steps:

1. In Control Panel, double-click Add Or Remove Programs.

2. Click Add/Remove Windows Components.

3. On the Windows Components page, select components to install. Click Next.

4. When prompted, insert the Windows Server 2003 R2 CD-ROM into the CD-ROM drive and then click OK.

5. Click Finish. Close Add Or Remove Programs.

Windows Server 2003 R2 features include the following:

File Server Resource Manager   Provides an improved disk quota management system that allows you to manage quotas for individual folders, sets of folders, and volumes. Quotas can be set per folder and per user, and there's an AutoQuota feature. You can also create storage reports. See Chapter 14 for details.

DFS Management   Provides improved management and functionality for the DFS. DFS replication enhancements improve handling of large files and large numbers of files. With Enterprise Edition and Datacenter Edition, compression features are included.

Print Management   Provides a central management interface for all Windows 2000 or later print servers as well as the related printers and print queues. Printer drives, forms, and ports can also be centrally managed, and there's an automatic detection feature that can add network printers to a local print server automatically. See Chapter 17 for details.

File Server Management   Provides an integrated interface for File Server Resource Manager, the DFS Management console, and Storage Manager for storage area networks (SANs). Also includes extensions for shared folder, disk, and volume management. See Chapters 11 to 15 for details.

Storage Manager for SANs   Provides a central management interface for SAN devices. You can view storage subsystems, create and manage logical unit numbers (LUNs), and manage Internet SCSI (iSCSI) target devices. The SAN device must support Visual Disk Services in Windows Server 2003.

Other Windows Server 2003 Resources

Before we examine administration tools, let's look at other resources that make Windows Server 2003 administration easier. One of the system administrator's greatest resources is the Windows Server 2003 distribution disk. It contains all the system information you'll need whenever you make changes to a Windows Server 2003 system. Keep the disk handy whenever you modify a system's configuration. You'll probably need it.

To avoid having to access a Windows Server 2003 distribution disk whenever you make system changes, you might want to copy the \I386 directory to a network drive. When you're prompted to insert the CD-ROM and specify the source directory, you simply point to the directory on the network drive. This technique is convenient and saves time. Other resources you might want to use are examined in the sections that follow.

Windows Server 2003 Support Tools

While you're working with the distribution CD-ROM, you might want to install the Windows Server 2003 Support Tools. The support tools are a collection of utilities for handling everything from system diagnostics to network monitoring.

Installing the Support Tools   To install the support tools:

1. Insert the Windows Server 2003 CD-ROM into the CD-ROM drive.

2. When the Autorun screen appears, click Perform Additional Tasks, and then click Browse This CD. This starts Windows Explorer.

3. In Windows Explorer, double-click Support and then double-click Tools.

   Note   Throughout this book I refer to double-clicking, which is the most common technique used for accessing folders and running programs. With a double-click, the first click selects the item and the second click opens and runs the item. In Windows Server 2003 you can also configure single-click open/run. Here, moving the mouse over the item selects it; a click opens and runs it. You can change the mouse click options with the Folder Options utility in the Control Panel. To do this, select the General Tab, and then choose Single-Click To Open An Item or Double-Click To Open An Item, as appropriate.

4. Double-click Suptools.msi. This starts the Windows Support Tools Setup Wizard. Click Next.

5. Read the End User License Agreement and then, if you agree and want to continue, click I Agree and then click Next.

6. Enter your user information, and then click Next.

7. Select the destination directory for the support tools. The default location is %ProgramFiles%\Support Tools. If you don't want to use the default location, type a new directory path or click Browse to search for a location. The tools use about 23 MB of disk space.

8. Click Install Now. Click Finish.

Note   %ProgramFiles% refers to the ProgramFiles environment variable. The Windows operating system has many environment variables, which are used to refer to user-specific and system-specific values. Often, I'll refer to environment variables using this syntax: %VariableName%.

Using the Support Tools   After installation you can access the support tools through the Tools Management Console shown in Figure 1-3. To start the console, click Start, click Programs or All Programs as appropriate, click Windows Support Tools, and then select Support Tools Help.

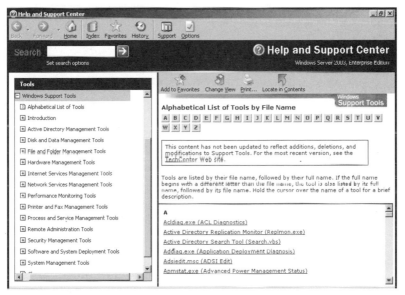

Figure 1-3   Use support tools to perform such tasks as system diagnostics and network monitoring.

As the figure shows, the tools are organized by file name, tool name, and category. Clicking a tool name accesses a help page that displays the online help documentation for the tool and that you can also use to run the tool.

Chapter 2
Managing Servers Running Microsoft Windows Server 2003

Servers are the heart of any Microsoft Windows network. One of your primary responsibilities as an administrator is to manage these resources. Your key tool is the Computer Management console, which provides a single integrated interface for handling such core system administration tasks as:

- Managing user sessions and connections to servers

- Managing file, directory, and share usage

- Setting administrative alerts

- Managing applications and network services

- Configuring hardware devices

- Viewing and configuring disk drives and removable storage devices

Although the Computer Management console is great for remote management of network resources, you also need a tool that gives you fine control over system environment settings and properties. This is where the System utility comes into the picture. You'll use this utility to:

- Configure application performance, virtual memory, and registry settings

- Manage system and user environment variables

- Set system startup and recovery options

- Manage hardware and user profiles

Managing Networked Systems

The Computer Management console is designed to handle core system administration tasks on local and remote systems. You'll spend a lot of time working with this tool, and you should get to know every nook and cranny. Access the Computer Management console with either of the following techniques:

- Choose Start, then Programs or All Programs as appropriate, then Administrative Tools, and finally Computer Management.

- Select Computer Management from the Administrative Tools folder.

As Figure 2-1 shows, the main window has a two-pane view that's similar to Windows Explorer. You use the console tree in the left pane for navigation and tool selection. The right pane is the details pane. Tools are divided into three broad categories:

System Tools   Provides access to general-purpose tools for managing systems and viewing system information

Storage   Displays information on removable and logical drives and provides access to drive management tools

Services And Applications   Lets you view and manage the properties of services and applications installed on the server

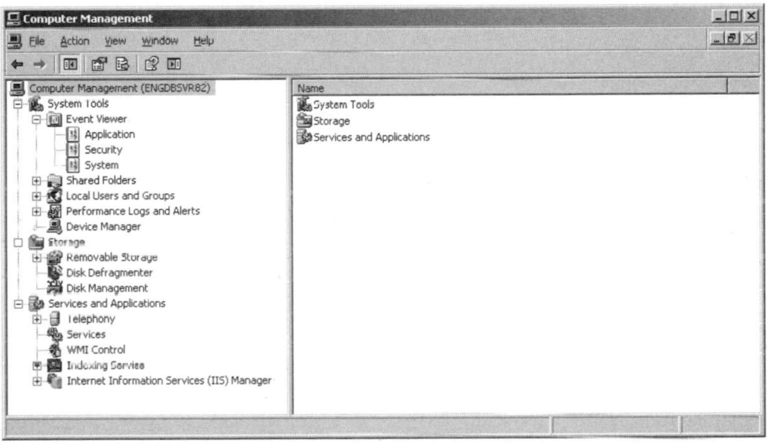

Figure 2-1   Use the Computer Management console to manage network computers and resources.

Tip   Management consoles such as Computer Management are created using the Microsoft Management Console (MMC) framework. MMC 3.0 is included with Windows Server 2003 R2 and Windows Server 2003 SP2. MMC 3.0 offers several enhancements: a revised Add/Remove Snap-in dialog box that allows easier management of snap-ins; improved error handling, which improves error reporting in consoles; and an Action pane that lists actions that can be performed based on the currently selected item or results. The Action pane is similar to the shortcut menu that is displayed when you right-click an item. To display or close the Action pane, you need to click the Show/Hide Action Pane button on the console toolbar.

Real World   The Action pane is meant to reduce confusion, because sometimes you might not see a shortcut menu when you right-click. Whether the shortcut menu appears when you right-click a menu item is controlled by the Enable Dragging And Dropping menu option. If you don't see a shortcut menu when you right-click an item, Enable Dragging And Dropping has been disabled. To enable shortcut menus, right-click Start, choose Properties, and then click Customize. If you are using the Simple Start Menu, click the Advanced tab, and then, in the Start Menu Items box, select Enable Dragging And Dropping. If you are using the Classic Start Menu, click Enable Dragging And Dropping in the Advanced Start Menu Options list.

The tools available through the console tree provide the core functionality for the Computer Management console. When Computer Management is selected in the console tree, you can easily access three important tasks:

- Connect to other computers
- View and change system properties
- Export information lists

In the following sections we'll examine these tasks, and then we'll take a detailed look at working with tools in the Computer Management console.

Connecting to Other Computers

The Computer Management console is designed to be used with local and remote systems. You can select a computer to manage by completing the following steps:

1. Right-click the Computer Management entry in the console tree and then select Connect To Another Computer on the shortcut menu. This opens the Select Computer dialog box.

2. Choose Another Computer and then type the fully qualified name of the computer you want to work with, such as **engsvr01.technology.microsoft.com**, where *engsvr01* is the computer name and *technology.microsoft.com* is the domain name. Or click Browse to search for the computer with which you want to work. Click OK.

Viewing and Changing System Properties

You can use the Computer Management console to view the system properties of the local or remote system to which you are currently connected. Essentially, this gives you access to the General, Computer Name, and Advanced tabs of the System utility for that computer. This means you can connect to a computer and access its properties to determine its operating system, service pack, processor type, total system random access memory (RAM), computer name, and more.

You view or change system properties by completing the following steps:

1. In the Computer Management console, connect to the computer with which you want to work and then right-click the Computer Management entry.

2. Choose Properties. This opens the dialog box shown in Figure 2-2.

Figure 2-2   Use the Computer Management Properties dialog box to view system properties on the computer to which you are currently connected.

3. Click the General, Computer Name, or Advanced tab as appropriate. In the Advanced tab you can view and configure settings for processor scheduling, memory usage, virtual memory, environment variables, startup, and recovery.

Note   The Advanced tab doesn't have options for viewing User Profile or Error Reporting settings. You can change these settings only by using the System utility. You can access the System utility by selecting System from the Control Panel menu. In addition, you must have appropriate permissions on a remote system to manage its settings.

Exporting Information Lists

The ability to export information lists is one of my favorite features of the Computer Management console, and if you maintain system information records or regularly work with Windows scripting, it'll probably be one of yours, too. The Export List feature allows you to save textual information displayed in the right pane to a tab-delimited or comma-delimited text file. You could, for example, use this feature to save detailed information on all the services running on the system by completing the following steps:

1. In the Computer Management console, click the plus sign (+) next to the Services And Applications node. This expands the node to display its contents.

2. Select and right-click Services, and then, from the shortcut menu, select Export List. This opens the Export List dialog box.

3. Use the Save In selection list to choose the save location and then enter a name for the export file in the File Name text box.

4. Use the Save As Type selection list to set the formatting of the export file. You can separate columns of information with tabs or commas and save as ASCII text or Unicode text. In most cases, you'll want to use tab-delimited ASCII text.

5. Click Save to complete the export process.

You can use a similar procedure to export lists of other information displayed in the Computer Management console.

Using Computer Management System Tools

The Computer Management system tools are designed to manage systems and view system information. The available system tools are the following:

Event Viewer   View the event logs on the selected computer. Event logs are covered in "Event Logging and Viewing" in Chapter 3, "Monitoring Processes, Services, and Events."

Shared Folders   Manage the properties of shared folders, user sessions, and open files. Managing user sessions, open files, and network shares is covered in Chapter 14, "Data Sharing, Security, and Auditing."

Local Users And Groups   Manage local users and local user groups on the currently selected computer. Working with users and groups is covered in Chapters 6 to 10, along with other types of accounts that you can manage in Active Directory directory service.

> **Note**   Local users and local user groups aren't a part of Active Directory and are managed instead through the Local Users And Groups view. Domain controllers don't have entries in the Local Users And Groups view.

Performance Logs And Alerts   Monitor system performance and create logs based on performance parameters. You can also use this tool to notify or alert users of performance conditions. For more information on monitoring systems, see Chapter 3.

Device Manager   Use as a central location for checking the status of any device installed on a computer and for updating the associated device drivers. You can also use it to troubleshoot device problems. Managing devices is covered in the section entitled "Managing Hardware Devices and Drivers," later in this chapter.

Using Computer Management Storage Tools

The Computer Management storage tools display drive information and provide access to drive management tools. These are the storage tools available:

Removable Storage   Manages removable media devices and tape libraries. Tracks work queues and operator requests related to removable media devices.

Disk Defragmenter   Corrects drive fragmentation problems by locating and combining fragmented files.

Disk Management   Manages hard disks, disk partitions, volume sets, and redundant array of independent disks (RAID) arrays. Replaces the Disk Administrator utility in Windows NT 4.0.

Working with files, drives, and storage devices is the subject of Chapters 11 to 15.

Working with Services and Applications

You use the Computer Management services and applications tools to manage services and applications installed on the server. Any application or service-related task that can be performed in a separate tool can be performed through the Services And Applications node as well. For example, if the currently selected system has Dynamic Host Configuration Protocol (DHCP) installed, you can manage DHCP through the Server Applications And Services node. You could also use the DHCP tool in the Administrative Tools folder. You can perform the same tasks either way.

This technology is possible because the DHCP tool is an MMC snap-in. When you access the DHCP tool in the Administrative Tools folder, the snap-in is displayed in a separate console. When you access the DHCP tool through the Server Applications And Services node, the snap-in is displayed within the Computer Management console. Working with services and applications is discussed in Chapter 3 and elsewhere in this book.

Managing System Environments, Profiles, and Properties

You use the System utility to manage system environments, profiles, and properties. To access the System utility, select or double-click System in the Control Panel. This displays the System Properties dialog box. Whether you must select or double-click System depends on whether Control Panel is displayed as a menu or in a separate window.

As shown in Figure 2-3, the System Properties dialog box is divided into six tabs. Each of these tabs is discussed in the sections that follow. When working with remote systems, keep in mind that General, Computer Name, and Advanced tab details are accessible in Computer Management, as discussed in the section entitled "Viewing and Changing System Properties," earlier in this chapter.

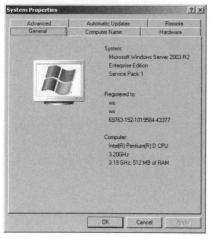

Figure 2-3   Use the System utility to manage system environment variables, profiles, and properties.

The General Tab

General system information is available for any server running Windows Server 2003 through the System utility's General tab, which is shown in Figure 2-3. To access the General tab, start the System utility by selecting or double-clicking the System icon in the Control Panel.

The information provided in the General tab includes: operating system version and service pack, registered owner, Windows serial number, computer type, amount of RAM installed on the computer, processor type, and total system RAM.

The Computer Name Tab

You can display and modify the computer's network identification with the System utility's Computer Name tab, shown in Figure 2-4. As the figure shows, the tab displays the full computer name of the system and its domain membership. The full computer name is essentially the Domain Name System (DNS) name of the computer, which also identifies the computer's place within the Active Directory hierarchy.

To access the Network Identification tab, start the System utility by selecting or double-clicking the System icon in the Control Panel; then click the Computer Name tab. You can now click Change to change the system name and domain associated with the computer.

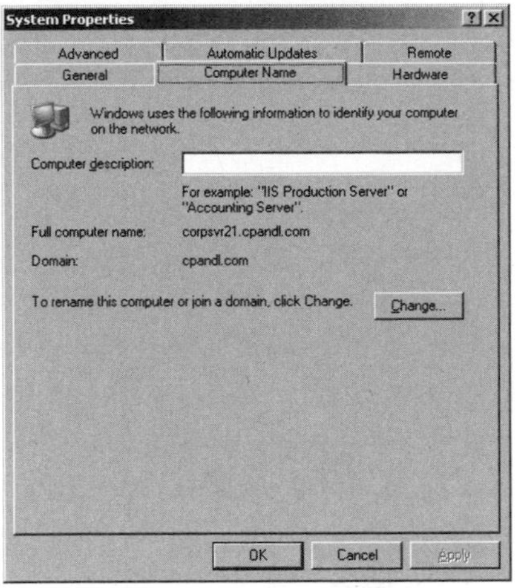

Figure 2-4   Use the Computer Name tab to display and configure system identification. Notice that you can't change the identification or access information for domain controllers.

The Hardware Tab

Servers running Windows Server 2003 can use multiple hardware profiles. Hardware profiles are most useful for mobile servers, such as those configured on laptops. Using hardware profiles, you can configure one profile for when the computer is connected to the network (*docked*) and one profile for when the computer is mobile (*undocked*).

Configuring the Way Hardware Profiles Are Used

To configure hardware profiles, click the System utility's Hardware tab and then click the Hardware Profiles button. This opens the dialog box shown in Figure 2-5. As with systems with multiple operating systems, Windows Server 2003 allows you to configure the way hardware profiles are used, as follows:

■ Set a default profile by changing the profile's position in the Available Hardware Profiles list. The top profile is the default profile.

■ Determine how long the system displays the startup hardware profile menu by setting a value using the field Select The First Profile Listed If I Don't Select A Profile In. The default value is 30 seconds.

■ Have the system wait indefinitely for user input by selecting Wait Until I Select A Hardware Profile.

Figure 2-5   You can configure multiple hardware profiles for any Windows Server 2003 system.

Configuring for Docked and Undocked Profiles

To configure a computer for docked and undocked profiles, complete the following steps:

1. In the Available Hardware Profiles list, select the default profile, and then click Copy.

2. In the Copy Profile dialog box, type a name for the Docked profile in the To text box and then click OK.

3. Select the new profile, and then click the Properties button.

4. Select the This Is A Portable Computer check box, and then choose The Computer Is Docked.

5. Select the Always Include This Profile As An Option When Windows Starts check box, and then click OK.

6. Select the default profile in the Available Hardware Profiles list, and then click Copy.

7. In the Copy Profile dialog box, type a name for the Undocked profile in the To text box and then click OK.

8. Select the new profile, and then click the Properties button.

9. Select the This Is A Portable Computer check box, and then choose The Computer Is Undocked.

10. Select the Always Include This Profile As An Option When Windows Starts check box, and then click OK.

11. Set the default hardware profile as appropriate for the computer's current state as either docked or undocked. Click OK.

When the system is booted, the hardware profiles are displayed, and you can select the appropriate profile.

The Advanced Tab

The System utility's Advanced tab, shown in Figure 2-6, controls many of the key features of the Windows operating system, including application performance, virtual memory usage, user profile, environment variables, and startup and recovery. To access the Advanced tab, start the System utility by selecting or double-clicking the System icon in the Control Panel; then click the Advanced tab.

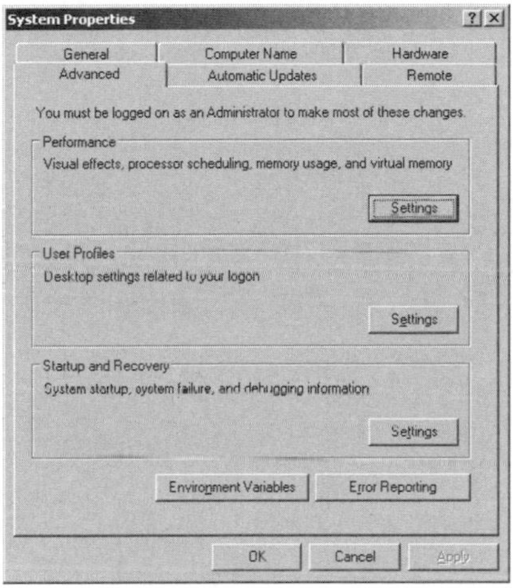

Figure 2-6   The Advanced tab lets you configure advanced options, including performance options, environment variables, and startup and recovery.

Setting Windows Performance

Many graphics enhancements have been added to the Windows Server 2003 interface. These enhancements include many visual effects for menus, toolbars, windows, and the taskbar. To ensure that the server performs at its best level, these options are turned off by default in an initial installation. This reduces the amount of work the server must do when administrators log on locally to perform tasks, and you usually shouldn't change this default setting. However, if you need to modify these options, you can do so by following these steps:

1. Click the Advanced tab in the System utility, and then click the Settings button in the Performance panel to display the Performance Options dialog box.

2. The Visual Effects tab should be selected by default. You have the following options for controlling visual effects:

Let Windows Choose What's Best For My Computer   Allows the operating system to choose the performance options based on the hardware configuration. On a server, this typically means that Windows selects only the Use Visual Styles On Windows And Buttons option and that all other options are cleared.

Adjust For Best Appearance   When you optimize Windows for best appearance, you enable all visual effects for all graphical interfaces. The menus and taskbar use transitions and shadows. Screen fonts have smooth edges. List boxes have smooth scrolling. Folders use Web views and more. On a server, this setting unnecessarily uses a lot of memory and system resources, and you should rarely use it.

Adjust For Best Performance   When you optimize Windows for best performance, you turn off the resource-intensive visual effects, such as slide transitions and smooth edges for fonts, while maintaining a basic set of visual effects. In some cases this completely turns off all visual effects.

Custom   You can customize the visual effects as well. To do this, select or clear the visual effects options in the Performance Options dialog box. If you clear all options, Windows doesn't use visual effects.

3. When you're finished changing visual effects, click OK and then click OK again.

Setting Application Performance

Application performance is related to the Processor Scheduling and Memory Usage options that you set for the Windows Server 2003 system. Processor Scheduling determines the responsiveness of the current active application (as opposed to background applications that might be running on the system). Memory Usage determines whether physical memory is optimized for applications or the system cache.

You control application performance by completing the following steps:

1. Access the Advanced tab in the System utility, and then display the Performance Options dialog box by clicking the Settings button in the Performance panel. Click the Advanced tab to modify the performance settings.

2. The Processor Scheduling panel has two options:

    Programs   To give the active application the best response time and the greatest share of available resources, select Applications. Generally, you'll want to use this option for Application, Web, and Streaming Media servers.

    Background Services   To give background applications a better response time than the active application, select Background Services. Generally, you'll want to use this option for Active Directory, File, Print, and Network and Communications servers.

3. The Memory Usage panel has two options:

Programs   Choose this option to optimize physical memory usage for applications. Generally, you'll want to use this option for Application, Web, and Streaming Media servers.

System Cache   Choose this option to optimize physical memory usage for the system cache. Generally, you'll want to use this option for Active Directory, File, Print, and Network and Communications servers.

4. Click OK.

Configuring Virtual Memory

Virtual memory allows you to use disk space to extend the amount of available RAM on a system. This feature of Intel 386 and later processors writes RAM to disks using a process called *paging*. With paging, a set amount of RAM, such as 32 megabytes (MB), is written to the disk as a paging file, where it can be accessed when needed.

An initial paging file is created automatically for the drive containing the operating system. By default, other drives don't have paging files, and you must create these paging files manually if you want them. When you create a paging file, you set an initial size and a maximum size. Paging files are written to the volume as a file called Pagefile.sys.

> **Best Practices**   Microsoft recommends that you create a paging file for each physical disk on the system. On most systems, multiple paging files can improve the performance of virtual memory. Thus, instead of a single large paging file, it's better to have several small ones. Keep in mind that removable drives don't need paging files.

You can configure virtual memory by completing the following steps:

1. Start the System utility, and then click the Advanced tab.

2. Click Setting in the Performance panel to display the Performance Options dialog box, and then click the Advanced tab. Then click Change to display the Virtual Memory dialog box shown in Figure 2-7.

This dialog box has three key areas:

Drive [Volume Label]   Shows how virtual memory is currently configured on the system. Each volume is listed with its associated paging file (if any). The paging file range shows the initial and maximum size values set for the paging file.

Paging File Size For Selected Drive   Provides information on the currently selected drive and allows you to set its paging file size. Space Available tells you how much space is available on the drive.

Total Paging File Size For All Drives   Provides a recommended size for virtual RAM on the system and tells you the amount currently allocated. If this is the first time you're configuring virtual RAM, you'll note that the recommended amount has already been given to the system drive (in most instances).

Best Practices   Although Windows Server 2003 can expand paging files incrementally as needed, this can result in fragmented files, which slows system performance. For optimal system performance, set the initial size and maximum size to the same value. This ensures that the paging file is consistent and can be written to a single contiguous file (if possible, given the amount of space on the volume). In most cases I recommend setting the total paging file size so that it's twice the physical RAM size on the system. For instance, on a computer with 512 MB of RAM, you would ensure that the Total Paging File Size For All Drives setting is at least 1024 MB. However, on servers with 2 GB or more of RAM, it's best to follow the hardware manufacturer's guidelines for paging file sizes.

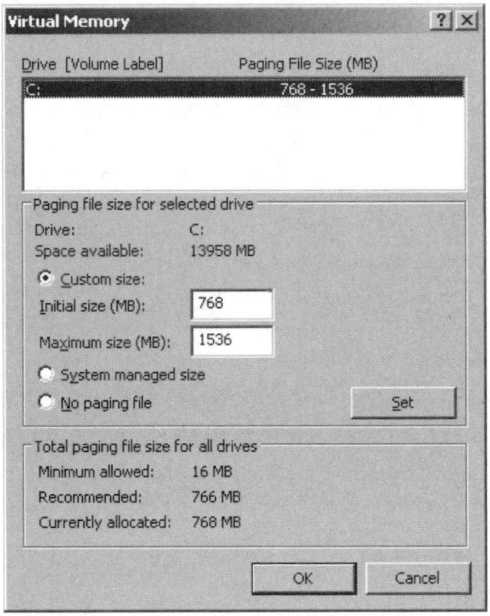

Figure 2-7   Virtual memory extends the amount of RAM on a system.

3. In the Drive list box, select the volume with which you want to work.

4. Use the Paging File Size For Selected Drive area to configure the paging file for the drive. Select Custom Size. Then enter an initial size and a maximum size and click Set to save the changes.

5. Repeat Steps 3 and 4 for each volume you want to configure.

Note   The paging file is also used for debugging purposes when a STOP error occurs on the system. If the paging file on the system drive is smaller than the minimum amount required to write the debugging information to the paging file, this feature will be disabled. If you want to use debugging, you should set the minimum size to the same figure as the amount of RAM on the system. For example, a system with 256 MB of RAM would need a paging file of 256 MB on the system drive.

6. On the system volume, the initial size must be as large as the current physical RAM. If it isn't, Windows won't be able to write STOP information to the system drive when fatal errors occur. Click Set to save the changes.

7. Repeat Steps 3 and 4 for each volume you want to configure.

8. Click OK, and, if prompted to overwrite an existing Pagefile.sys file, click Yes.

9. Close the System utility.

Note   If you updated the settings for the paging file that's currently in use, you'll see a prompt explaining that you need to restart the server for the changes to take effect. Click OK. When you close the System utility, you'll see a prompt telling you that you need to restart the system for the changes to take effect. On a server, you should schedule this reboot outside normal business hours.

Configuring Data Execution Prevention

Data Execution Prevention (DEP) is a memory protection technology enabled with Service Pack 1 or later. DEP tells the computer's processor to mark all memory locations in an application as nonexecutable unless the location explicitly contains executable code. If code is executed from a memory page marked as nonexecutable, the processor can raise an exception and prevent it from executing. This prevents malicious code, such as a virus, from inserting itself into most areas of memory because only specific areas of memory are marked as having executable code.

Note   32-bit versions of Windows support DEP as implemented by those processors that provide the no-execute page-protection (NX) processor feature. Such processors support the related instructions and must be running in Physical Address Extension (PAE) mode. 64-bit versions of Windows also support the NX processor feature.

Tip   As part of system startup, a Noexecute flag is added to the Boot.ini entry. When you change the DEP settings in the System utility, you are manually switching the type of DEP used between noexecute=optin and noexecute=optout. Two additional options are provided through noexecute=alwayson or noexecute=alwaysoff. These settings turn DEP on or off for all processes systemwide respectively, and they're more typically used with Windows XP SP2 or later than with Windows Server 2003.

You can determine whether a computer supports DEP by using the System utility. If a computer supports DEP, you can also configure it by completing the following steps:

1. Click the Advanced tab in the System utility, and then on the Performance panel click Settings to display the Performance Options dialog box.

2. The Performance Options dialog box has several tabs. Click the Data Execution Prevention tab. The text at the bottom of this tab specifies whether the computer supports execution protection.

3. If a computer supports execution protection and is configured appropriately, you can configure DEP by using the following options:

Turn On DEP For Essential Windows Programs And Services Only   Enables DEP for limited system binaries as well as programs that specifically opt-in. Applications and other programs running on the server are not configured to use DEP. (Same as using /noexecute=optin in Boot.ini.)

Turn On DEP For All Programs And Services Except Those I Select   Enables DEP for all programs and services running on the server. You can configure specific exceptions as necessary using the Add or Remove buttons. Click Add to specify the executable for a program or service that should run without execution protection. Selected an excepted program or service and then click Remove to remove it from the exception list. (Same as using /noexecute=optout in Boot.ini.)

4. Click OK.

Caution   If you set noexecute=alwaysoff in Boot.ini, DEP options will be dimmed in the Performance Options dialog box. This appearance is the same as on systems that do not support DEP.

Real World   To be compatible with this feature, applications must be able to explicitly mark memory with Execute permission. Applications that can't do this won't be compatible with the NX processor feature. If you're experiencing memory-related problems running applications, you should determine the applications that are having problems and configure them as exceptions rather than completely disabling execution protection. In this way, you still get the benefits of memory protection and can selectively disable memory protection for programs that aren't running properly with the NX processor feature.

Execution protection is applied to both user-mode and kernel-mode programs. A user-mode execution protection exception results in a STATUS_ACCESS_VIOLATION exception. In most processes, this exception will be an unhandled exception and will result in termination of the process. This is the desired behavior because most programs violating these rules will be malicious in nature, such as a virus or worm.

Unlike applications, execution protection for kernel-mode device drivers can't be selectively disabled or enabled. Furthermore, on compliant 32-bit systems, execution protection is applied by default to the memory stack. On compliant 64-bit systems, execution protection is applied by default to the memory stack, the paged pool, and the session pool. A kernel-mode execution protection access violation for a device driver results in an ATTEMPTED_EXECUTE_OF_NOEXECUTE_MEMORY exception.)

Configuring System and User Environment Variables

Windows tracks important strings, such as a path where files are located or the logon domain controller host name, using environment variables. Environment variables defined for use by Windows, called system environment variables, are the same no matter who is logged in to a particular computer. Environment variables defined for use by users or programs, called user environment variables, are different for each user of a particular computer.

You configure system and user environment variables by means of the Environment Variables dialog box, shown in Figure 2-8. To access this dialog box, start the System utility, click the Advanced tab, and then click Environment Variables.

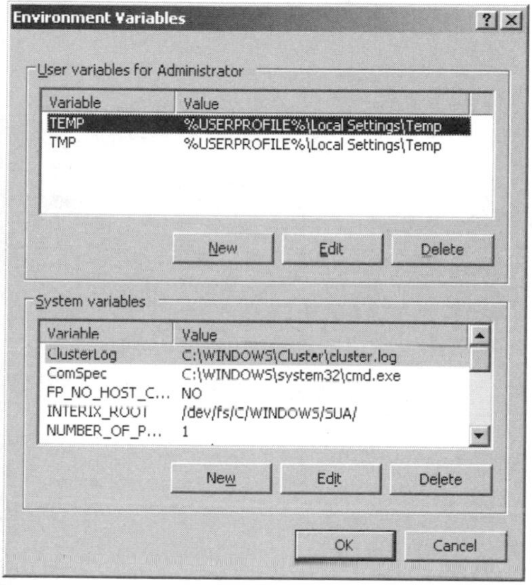

Figure 2-8   The Environment Variables dialog box lets you configure system and user environment variables.

Creating an Environment Variable

You can create environment variables by completing the following steps:

1. Click the New button under User Variables or System Variables, whichever is appropriate for the type of environment variable you want to create. This opens the New User Variable dialog box or the New System Variable dialog box, respectively.

2. In the Variable Name text box, type the variable name. Then, in the Variable Value text box, type the variable value. Click OK.

Editing an Environment Variable

You can edit an existing environment variable by completing the following steps:

1. Select the variable in the User Variables or System Variables list box.

2. Click the Edit button under User Variables or System Variables, whichever is appropriate for the type of environment variable you're modifying. This opens the Edit User Variable dialog box or the Edit System Variable dialog box, respectively.

3. Type a new value in the Variable Value text box. Click OK.

Deleting an Environment Variable

You can delete an environment variable by selecting the variable and then clicking the Delete button.

Note When you create or modify system environment variables, the changes take effect when you restart the computer. When you create or modify user environment variables, the changes take effect the next time the user logs on to the system.

Configuring System Startup and Recovery

You configure system startup and recovery properties by means of the Startup And Recovery dialog box, shown in Figure 2-9. To access this dialog box, start the System utility, click the Advanced tab, and then click Settings on the Startup And Recovery panel.

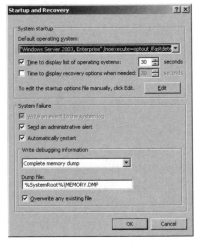

Figure 2-9   The Startup And Recovery dialog box lets you configure system startup and recovery procedures.

Setting Startup Options

The System Startup panel of the Startup And Recovery dialog box controls system startup. Some of the parameters and options are used to set related Boot Loader and Operating System entries in Boot.ini. Systems with multiple startup configurations, multiple operating system versions, or both will have multiple operating system entries in Boot.ini. During startup of the operating system, Windows uses Boot.ini to identify the boot device and boot flags. Various system startup flags are set through the operating system entries in Boot.ini, including NOEXECUTE flags for Data Execution Prevention (DEP) and FASTDETECT for faster operating system detection.

On a computer with multiple operating system entries in Boot.ini, to set the default operating system, select one of the operating systems listed in the Default Operating System field. These options are obtained from the operating system section of the system's Boot.ini file.

At startup of a computer with multiple operating system entries in Boot.ini, Windows Server 2003 displays the startup configuration menu for 30 seconds by default. You can modify this by taking either of the following actions:

- Boot immediately to the default operating system by clearing the Time To Display List Of Operating Systems check box.

- Display the available options for a specific amount of time by selecting the Time To Display List Of Operating Systems check box and then setting a time delay in seconds.

Generally, on most systems you'll want to use a value of 3–5 seconds. This is long enough to enable you to make a selection, yet short enough to expedite the system startup process.

When the system is in a recovery mode and booting, a list of recovery options might be displayed. As with the standard startup options, you can configure recovery startup options in one of two ways. You can set the computer to boot immediately using the default recovery option by clearing the Time To Display Recovery Options When Needed check box, or you can display the available options for a specific amount of time by selecting Time To Display Recovery Options When Needed and then setting a time delay in seconds.

Setting Recovery Options

The System Failure and Write Debugging Information areas of the Startup And Recovery dialog box control system recovery. Recovery options allow administrators to control precisely what happens when the system encounters a fatal system error (also known as a STOP error). The available options for the System Failure area are the following:

Write An Event To The System Log   Logs the error in the system log, which allows administrators to review the error later using the Event Viewer

Send An Administrative Alert Sends an alert to the recipients specified in the Alert dialog box

Automatically Restart Check this option to have the system attempt to reboot when a fatal system error occurs

> **Note** Configuring automatic restarts isn't always a good thing. Sometimes you might want the system to halt rather than reboot, which should ensure that the system gets proper attention. Otherwise, you can only know that the system rebooted when you view the system logs or if you happen to be in front of the system's monitor when it reboots.

The Write Debugging Information selection menu allows you to choose the type of debugging information that you want to write to a dump file. You can in turn use the dump file to diagnose system failures. The options are as follows:

None Use None if you don't want to write debugging information.

Small Memory Dump Use this option to dump the physical memory segment in which the error occurred. This dump is 64 KB in size.

Kernel Memory Dump Use this option to dump the physical memory area being used by the Windows kernel. The dump file size depends on the size of the Windows kernel.

Complete Memory Dump Use this option to dump all physical memory being used at the time of the failure. The maximum dump file size is the same as the total physical memory size.

If you elect to write a dump file, you must also set a location for the dump file. The default dump locations are %SystemRoot%\Minidump for small memory dumps and %SystemRoot%\Memory.dmp for all other memory dumps. You'll usually want to select Overwrite Any Existing File as well. This option ensures that any existing dump files are overwritten if a new STOP error occurs.

> **Note** You can create the dump file only if the system is properly configured. The system drive must have a sufficiently large memory-paging file (as set for virtual memory with the Advanced tab), and the drive where the dump file is written must have sufficient free space as well. For example, my server has 512 MB of RAM and requires a paging file on the system drive of the same size—512 MB. Since the same drive is used for the dump file, the drive must have at least 1 gigabyte (GB) of free space to create a complete dump of debugging information correctly (that's 512 MB for the paging file and 512 MB for the dump file).

Enabling and Disabling Error Reporting

Windows Server 2003 features built-in system and program error reporting. Error reporting sends information about errors to Microsoft or to a corporate file share that administrators can monitor. Error reporting is enabled by default for all Windows Server 2003 installations, and you can configure it to monitor the following specific areas:

Windows Operating System   Reports critical operating system errors that cause a blue screen crash. The error report contains all the information that's displayed on the blue screen.

Unplanned Machine Shutdowns   Reports when the server is shut down and the shutdown reason is listed as unplanned. Selecting this option helps you keep track of unplanned reasons for server shutdowns, which is essential to maintaining good uptime and service records.

Programs   Reports illegal program operations and internal program errors that cause a program to stop working. With program errors, you can specify which programs should be monitored for errors and which shouldn't. If you elect to report program errors, you can enable Force Queue Mode For Program Errors. In Queue mode, the last 10 errors are displayed the next time an administrator logs on and the administrator is able to choose which errors are reported. Without selecting this option, only the last error that occurs is reported, which might be misleading.

How an error is reported depends on where the error originated. When a component or program error occurs, a dialog box appears asking if you want to report the problem. If you choose to report the problem, the error report is sent over the Internet to Microsoft and a Thank You dialog box is displayed with additional information that might be helpful in resolving the problem. When an operating system error occurs, the system doesn't generate the error report until the next time you successfully boot and log on to the system.

You can enable and configure error reporting by completing the following steps:

1. Start the System utility. Click the Advanced tab and then click the Error Reporting button.

2. Select Enable Error Reporting and then select the check boxes for the areas you want to monitor.

   Tip   By default, all program errors are reported, regardless of who the manufacturer is. If you chose to report program errors, you can change the default configuration. To do this, select Programs, click Choose Programs in the Error Reporting dialog box, and then select All Programs In This List. You can now select programs to add to the reporting list and you can disable reporting for Programs From Microsoft and Windows Components. You can also add programs to the Do Not Report Errors list.

3. Click OK.

You can disable error reporting by completing these steps:

1. Start the System utility. Click the Advanced tab, and then click the Error Reporting button.

2. Select Disable Error Reporting, and then click OK.

Another way to configure Error Reporting is to do so through Group Policy. Because Group Policy is discussed in detail in Chapter 4, "Automating Administrative Tasks, Policies, and Procedures," and in other chapters, I won't go into depth on how Group Policy works. I will tell you, however, which policies you'll want to look at to help better manage Error Reporting for the enterprise. These policies are located in Computer Configuration\Administrative Templates\System\Error Reporting and in Computer Configuration\Administrative Templates\System\Error Reporting\Advanced Error Reporting Settings.

> **Tip** Error reporting can be distracting, but the information helps ensure that Microsoft resolves problems. To remove potential distraction, yet still help improve Windows for the future, you might want to disable Display Error Notification and enable Report Errors. When you do this, errors are automatically reported without notifying users that an error occurred.

The two most useful error reporting policies are:

Display Error Notification   Determines whether users are notified when errors occur. If not configured, users can specify error notification preferences using the System utility. If disabled, users aren't notified when an error occurs (but this doesn't prevent error reporting). If enabled, users are notified when an error occurs and given the opportunity to report the error.

Report Errors   Determines whether errors are reported and provides the opportunity to precisely control error reporting. If not configured, users can specify error reporting preferences using the System utility. If disabled, users won't be able to report errors but might still be notified when errors occur. If enabled, errors might be reported to Microsoft over the Internet or to a corporate file share that administrators can monitor. You can also specify whether More Information links are available, whether associated files and machine data is collected, and whether application errors are queued.

> **Real World**   Storing error reports on a file share can be helpful in resolving problems. Users might not tell you they're having problems. They might assume that a crashing program or other problems that they see are normal behavior. To be proactive in your support, you might want to store error reports on a corporate file share. If you want to do this, create a network share and then specify the share using the Universal Naming Convention (UNC) notation, such as \\Gamma\ErrorReports, where *Gamma* is the server name and *ErrorReports* is the network share.

Tip   If you display errors and report them, you might want to customize the error reporting text with your company name. To do this, type your company name in the Replace Instances Of The Word "Microsoft" With field of the Report Errors Properties dialog box. Now your company name appears in text instead of Microsoft.

The Automatic Updates Tab

The Automatic Update tab of the System utility controls the Automatic Updates configuration on the server. This feature is discussed in the section entitled "Understanding and Using Automatic Updates" in Chapter 5, "Working with Support Services and Remote Desktop."

The Remote Tab

The Remote tab of the System utility controls Remote Assistance invitations and Remote Desktop connections. These options are discussed in the section entitled "Managing Remote Access to Servers" in Chapter 5.

Managing Hardware Devices and Drivers

Windows Server 2003 provides four key tools for managing hardware devices and drivers. These tools are:

- Device Manager
- Add Hardware Wizard
- Hardware Update Wizard
- Hardware Troubleshooter

You'll use these tools whenever you install, uninstall, or troubleshoot hardware devices and drivers. Before you work with device drivers, you should know the basics of signed and unsigned device drivers as well as the system settings that might prevent the use of unsigned drivers.

Working with Signed and Unsigned Device Drivers

Microsoft recommends that you use signed device drivers whenever possible. Signed device drivers have a digital signature that authenticates them as having passed rigorous testing by the Windows Hardware Quality Labs. The digital signature also means the device driver hasn't been tampered with.

Now, there are situations when you might have to use an unsigned device driver. For example, you might find that a device installed on a server doesn't have a signed device driver. Your first response should be to check the manufacturer's Web site to see if a signed driver is available. A signed driver might be available but not distributed with the device or on the Windows Server 2003 distribution disks. However, if one isn't available, you might find that you have to use an unsigned driver. You have several options:

- Install an unsigned driver; a driver that worked with Windows 2000 might work in this instance. However, the system might become unstable. The system might crash, lose data, or even fail to restart.

- Stop using the device or use a different device with supported drivers. Cost might be a factor in your decision, but it shouldn't be the only factor you consider. An unstable system costs time and money as well.

By default, Windows Server 2003 warns you if you try to install an unsigned device driver. If you don't want to see this prompt, you can change the configuration so that this warning isn't displayed. You can also specify that unsigned drivers should never be installed. One way to configure device driver settings is to use the System utility in the Control Panel:

1. Start the System utility. Click the Hardware tab and then click Driver Signing.

2. Choose the action you want Windows to take when someone tries to install an unsigned device driver. The options are:

   Ignore   Install the software anyway and don't ask for my approval.

   Warn   Prompt me each time to choose an action.

   Block   Never install unsigned driver software.

3. If the settings are only for the current user, clear the Make This Action The System Default check box. Otherwise, select this check box to make these settings the default for all users.

4. Click OK twice.

If you want to assign device driver settings for the enterprise, you can do this through Group Policy. In this case, Group Policy specifies the least secure setting that is allowed, and, if Group Policy is set to Block, unsigned device drivers can't be installed without overriding Group Policy.

The Code Signing For Device Drivers policy controls device driver signing settings. This policy is located in User Configuration\Administrative Templates\System. If enabled, you can specify the action to take: Ignore, Warn, or Block.

Note   If you're trying to install a device and find that you can't install an unsigned driver, you should first check the System utility settings for driver signing. If you find that the settings are set to block and you can't change the setting, Code Signing For Device Drivers has been enabled and set to Block in Group Policy. You will need to override Group Policy in order to install the unsigned device driver.

Viewing and Managing Hardware Devices

You can view a detailed list of all the hardware devices installed on a system by completing the following steps:

1. Choose Start, Programs or All Programs as appropriate, Administrative Tools, and then Computer Management.

2. In the console tree, select Device Manager under System Tools. You should now see a complete list of devices installed on the system. By default, this list is organized by device type.

3. Click the plus sign (+) next to a device type to see a list of the specific instances of that device type.

4. If you right-click the device entry, you can manage the device using the shortcut menu. The options available depend on the type of device, but they include:

   Disable   Disables the device but doesn't uninstall it

   Enable   Enables a device if it's disabled

   Properties   Displays the Properties dialog box for the device

   Uninstall   Uninstalls the device and its drivers

   Update Driver   Updates the driver file

Tip   The device list shows warning symbols if there are problems with a device. A yellow warning symbol with an exclamation point indicates a problem with a device. A red X indicates a device that's improperly installed or that has been disabled by the user or administrator for some reason.

You can use the options on the View menu in the Computer Management console to change the defaults for what types of devices are displayed and how the devices are listed. The options are as follows:

Devices By Type   Displays devices by the type of device installed, such as Disk Drive or Printer. The connection name is listed below the type. This is the default view.

Devices By Connection   Displays devices by connection type, such as System Board or Logical Disk Manager.

Resources By Type   Displays the status of allocated resources by type of device using the resource. Resource types are direct memory access (DMA) channels, input/ output (I/O) ports, interrupt request (IRQ), and memory addresses.

Resources By Connection   Displays the status of all allocated resources by connection type rather than device type.

Show Hidden Devices   Displays non-Plug and Play devices as well as devices that
have been physically removed from the computer but haven't had their drivers
uninstalled.

Configuring Device Drivers

Device drivers are required for devices such as sound cards and display adapters to
work properly. Windows Server 2003 provides comprehensive management tools for
maintaining and updating device drivers. These tools allow you to track driver information, install and update driver versions, roll back to a previously installed driver,
and uninstall device drivers.

Tracking Driver Information

Each driver being used on a system has a driver file associated with it. You can view the
location of the driver file and related details by completing the following steps:

1. In Computer Management, select Device Manager under System Tools. You
    should now see a complete list of devices installed on the system identified
    either by type or by connection. By default, this list is organized by device type,
    but you can also list devices by connection using View menu options.

2. Right-click the device you want to manage and then choose Properties from the
    shortcut menu. This opens the Properties dialog box for the device. Click the
    Driver tab.

3. Display the Driver File Details dialog box by clicking Driver Details. The informa-
    tion displayed includes:

    Driver Files   Displays a list of file locations where the driver exists within
       %SystemRoot%

    Provider   The creator of the driver

    File Version   The version of the file

    Digital Signer   Indicates whether the driver is signed and by whom

Installing and Updating Drivers

To keep devices operating smoothly, it's essential that you keep their device drivers
current. You can install and update drivers using the Hardware Update Wizard. By
default, this wizard can search for updated device drivers in the following locations:

- On the local computer

- On a hardware installation CD

- On the Windows Update site or your organization's Windows Update server

In Group Policy, several policies control the search possibilities:

Turn Off Access To All Windows Update Features under Computer Configuration \Administrative Templates\System\Internet Communication Management \Internet Communication Settings   If this policy setting is enabled, all Windows Update features are blocked and not available to users. Users will also be unable to access the Windows Update Web site.

Turn Off Windows Update Device Driver Searching under Computer Configuration\Administrative Templates\System\Internet Communication Management\Internet Communication Settings   By default, Windows Update searching is optional when installing a device. If you enable this setting, Windows Update will not be searched when a new device is installed. If you disable this setting, Windows Update will always be searched when a new device is installed, if no local drivers are present.

Turn Off Windows Update Device Driver Search Prompt under Computer Configuration\Administrative Templates\System   If you disable or do not configure Turn Off Windows Update Device Driver Searching, this policy setting affects whether a search prompt is displayed for Windows Update of device drivers. If this policy setting is enabled, administrators aren't prompted to search Windows Update and the search will or will not take place automatically based on the Turn Off Windows Update Device Driver Searching setting. Otherwise, administrators will be prompted before Windows Update is searched.

You can install and update device drivers by completing the following steps:

1. In the Computer Management console, select Device Manager. You should now see a complete list of devices installed on the system. By default, this list is organized by device type.

2. Right-click the device you want to manage, and then select Update Driver from the shortcut menu. This starts the Hardware Update Wizard.

   > **Tip**   Updated drivers can add functionality to a device, improve performance, and resolve device problems. However, you should rarely install the latest drivers on a user's computer without first testing them in a test environment. Test first, then install.

3. If the Group Policy configuration allows administrators to be prompted to determine whether Windows Update should be searched for the new driver, the first wizard page has the options shown in Figure 2-10.

   These options are used as follows:

   Yes, This Time Only   Windows Update will be searched for this driver install only.

   Yes, Now And Every Time I Connect A Device   Windows Update will be searched automatically for driver updates. This setting applies to the installation of this driver and every time Driver Update is run.

No, Not This Time   Windows Update will not be searched for this install only.

Figure 2-10   If allowed by Group Policy, administrators are prompted to determine whether Windows Update should be searched.

4. Click Next after you make a selection. On the next page, you can specify whether you want to install the drivers automatically or manually by selecting the driver from a list or specific location.

5. If you choose to install the driver automatically, Windows Server 2003 looks for a more recent version of the device driver and, if found, installs the driver. If a more recent version of the driver is not found, Windows XP keeps the current driver. In either case, click Finish to complete the process and then skip the remaining steps.

6. If you choose to install the driver manually, you'll have the opportunity to select one of the following options:

   Search For The Best Driver In These Locations   If you search for drivers, the wizard checks for drivers on the driver database on the system and any of the optional locations you specify, such as a floppy disk or a CD-ROM. Any matching drivers found are displayed, and you can select a driver.

   Don't Search. I Will Choose The Driver To Install   If you decide to install drivers yourself, the next wizard page shows a list of compatible hardware and a recommended list of drivers for this hardware, as shown in Figure 2-11. If a correct driver is listed, all you need to do is to select it. If a correct driver isn't listed, clear the Show Compatible Hardware check box. You can now view a list of manufacturers to find the manufacturer of the device. Once you find the manufacturer, select the appropriate device driver in the right pane.

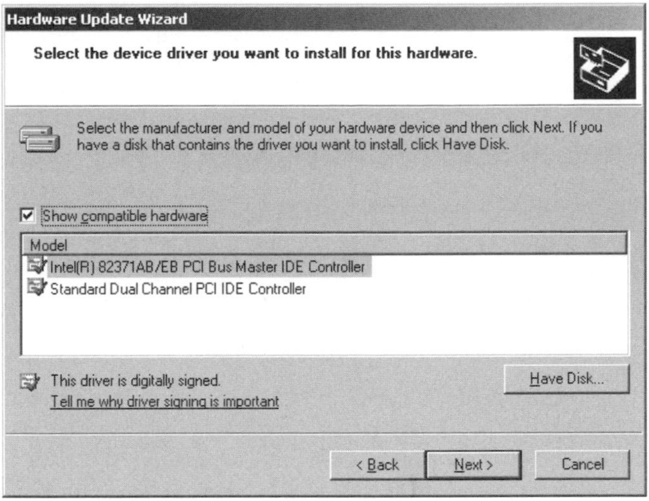

Figure 2-11   Select the appropriate device driver for the device you're adding.

> **Note**   If the manufacturer or device you want to use isn't listed, insert your device driver disk into the floppy drive or CD-ROM drive, and then click Have Disk. Follow the prompts. Afterward, select the appropriate device.

7. After selecting a device driver through a search or a manual selection, continue through the installation process by clicking Next. Click Finish when the driver installation is completed. Keep in mind that in some cases you'll need to reboot the system to activate the newly installed or updated device driver.

Rolling Back Drivers

Sometimes you'll find that a device driver that you've installed causes device failure or other critical problems on a system. Don't worry; you can recover the system to the previously installed device driver. To do this, follow these steps:

1. In Computer Management, select Device Manager. You should now see a complete list of devices installed on the system. By default, this list is organized by device type.

2. Right-click the device you want to manage and then choose Properties from the shortcut menu. This opens the Properties dialog box for the device.

3. Click the Driver tab and then click Roll Back Driver. When prompted to confirm the action, click Yes. Click OK.

> **Note**   If the driver file hasn't been updated, a backup driver file won't be available. Instead of being able to roll back the driver, you'll see a prompt telling you that no driver files have been backed up for this device. If you're having problems with the device, click Yes to start the Troubleshooter. Otherwise, click No to quit.

Removing Device Drivers for Removed Devices

Usually, when you remove a device from a system, Windows Server 2003 detects the change and removes the drivers for that device automatically. Sometimes, however, when you remove a device, Windows Server 2003 doesn't detect the change and you must remove the drivers manually. You can remove device drivers manually by completing the following steps:

1. In Computer Management, select Device Manager.

2. Right-click the device you want to remove and then select Uninstall.

3. When prompted to confirm the action, click OK.

Uninstalling Device Drivers

Uninstalling a device driver uninstalls the related device. Sometimes when a device isn't working properly you can completely uninstall the device, restart the system, and then reinstall the device driver to restore normal operations. You can uninstall and then reinstall a device by completing the following steps:

1. In Computer Management, select Device Manager. You should now see a complete list of devices installed on the system. By default, this list is organized by device type.

2. Right-click the device you want to manage and then choose Uninstall from the shortcut menu.

3. When prompted to confirm the action, click OK.

4. Reboot the system. Windows should detect the presence of the device and then automatically reinstall the necessary device driver. If the device isn't automatically reinstalled, reinstall it manually as discussed in the section entitled "Adding New Hardware," later in this chapter.

Note   To prevent a device from being reinstalled automatically, disable the device instead of uninstalling it. You disable a device by right-clicking it in Device Manager and then selecting Disable.

Managing Hardware

Windows Plug and Play technology does a good job of detecting and automatically configuring new hardware. However, if the hardware doesn't support Plug and Play or isn't automatically detected, you'll need to enter information about the new hardware into the Windows Server 2003 system. You do this by installing the hardware device and its related drivers on the system using the Add New Hardware Wizard. You can also use this wizard to troubleshoot problems with existing hardware.

Adding New Hardware

You can install new hardware using the Add Hardware Wizard by completing the following steps:

1. From Control Panel, select or double-click Add Hardware as appropriate. This starts the Add Hardware Wizard. Click Next.

2. At this point you have two options:

   ❑ If you've already connected the new hardware, select Yes, I Have Already Connected The Hardware and click Next to continue. The Add Hardware Wizard screen shown in Figure 2-12 should be displayed. Go on to Step 3.

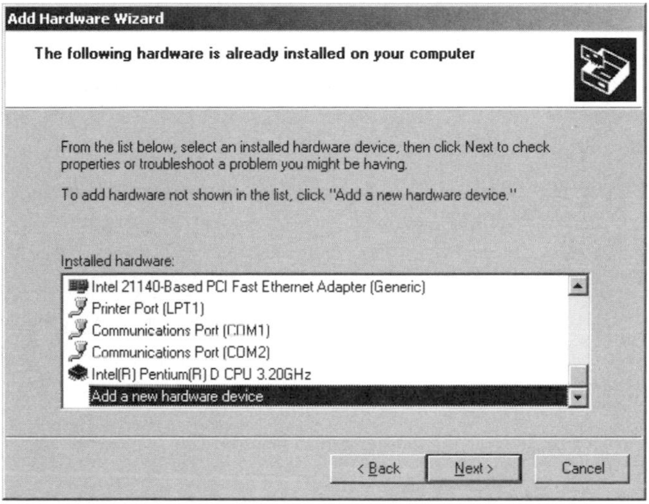

Figure 2-12   Use the Add Hardware Wizard to install, uninstall, or troubleshoot hardware devices.

   ❑ If you haven't connected the hardware, click No, I Have Not Added The Hardware Yet and then click Next. The only option you have now is to click Finish. You'll need to connect the hardware (which might require shutting down the computer) and then restart the Add Hardware Wizard. Skip the remaining steps.

3. To add new hardware, select Add A New Hardware Device from the Installed Hardware list box and then click Next. This option is located at the very bottom of the Installed Hardware list. On the What Do You Want The Wizard To Do? page, determine whether the wizard should search for new hardware or whether you want to select the hardware from a list.

   ❑ If you choose the search option, the wizard searches for and automatically detects new hardware. The process takes a few minutes to go through all the device types and options. When the search is completed, any new devices found are displayed, and you can select a device.

❑ If you choose the manual option or if no new devices are found in the automatic search, you'll have to select the hardware type yourself. Select the type of hardware, such as Modem or Network Adapter, and then click Next. Scroll through the list of manufacturers to find the device's manufacturer, and then choose the appropriate device in the Models pane.

4. After you complete the selection and installation process, click Next and then click Finish. The new hardware should now be available.

Enabling and Disabling Hardware

When a device isn't working properly, sometimes you'll want to uninstall or disable it. Uninstalling a device removes the driver association for the device so that it temporarily appears that the device has been removed from the system. The next time you restart the system, Windows Server 2003 might try to reinstall the device. Typically, Windows Server 2003 reinstalls Plug and Play devices automatically, but not non-Plug and Play devices.

Disabling a device turns it off and prevents Windows Server 2003 from using it. Because a disabled device doesn't use system resources, you can be sure that it isn't causing a conflict on the system. You can uninstall or disable a device by completing the following steps:

1. In Computer Management, select Device Manager. You should now see a complete list of devices installed on the system. By default, this list is organized by device type.

2. Right-click the connection for the device you want to manage and then select one of the following options:

   Enable   To enable the device

   Uninstall   To uninstall the device

   Disable   To disable the device

3. If prompted to confirm the action, click Yes or OK as appropriate.

Troubleshooting Hardware

You can use the Add Hardware Wizard to troubleshoot hardware problems as well. The basic steps are as follows:

1. From Control Panel, select or double-click Add Hardware as appropriate. This starts the Add Hardware Wizard. Click Next.

2. At this point, you have two options:

   ❑ If you've already connected the hardware that you want to examine, select Yes, I Have Already Connected the Hardware and click Next to display the Installed Hardware list box. Go on to Step 3.

❑   If you haven't connected the hardware, click No, I Have Not Added the Hardware Yet and then click Next. The only option you have now is to click Finish. You'll need to connect the hardware (which might require shutting down the computer) and then restart the Add Hardware Wizard. Skip the remaining steps.

3. From the Devices list, select the hardware device that you want to troubleshoot, and then click Next. The final wizard page provides a device status. When you click Finish, the wizard does one of two things:

❑   If an error code is shown with the device status, the wizard accesses the error code in the online help documentation—if it's available and installed. The help documentation should include a proposed technique to resolve the issue.

❑   The wizard starts the Hardware Troubleshooter, which attempts to solve the hardware problem using your responses to the questions it asks. Follow the advice of the Hardware Troubleshooter to resolve the hardware problem.

You can also access the Hardware Troubleshooter directly. To do that, complete the following steps:

1. In the Computer Management console, select Device Manager.

2. Right-click the device you want to troubleshoot and then select Properties.

3. On the General tab, click Troubleshoot.

Managing Dynamic-Link Libraries

As an administrator, you might be asked to install or uninstall dynamic-link libraries (DLLs), particularly if you work with IT (information technology) development teams. The utility you use to work with DLLs is Regsvr32. This utility is run at the command line.

After you start a command window, you install or register a DLL by typing **regsvr32 name.dll**, for example:

```
regsvr32 mylibs.dll
```

If necessary, you can uninstall or unregister a DLL by typing **regsvr32 /u name.dll**, for example:

```
regsvr32 /u mylibs.dll
```

Note   Windows File Protection prevents replacement of protected system files. You'll be able to replace only DLLs installed by the Windows Server 2003 operating system as part of a hot fix, service pack update, Windows update, or Windows upgrade. Windows File Protection is an important part of the Windows Server 2003 security architecture.

Chapter 3
Monitoring Processes, Services, and Events

As an administrator, it's your job to keep an eye on the network systems. The status of system resources and usage can change dramatically over time. Services might stop running. File systems might run out of space. Applications might throw exceptions, which in turn can cause system problems. Unauthorized users might try to break into the system. The techniques discussed in this chapter will help you find and resolve these and other system problems.

Managing Applications, Processes, and Performance

Any time you start an application or type a command on the command line, Microsoft Windows Server 2003 starts one or more processes to handle the related program. Generally, processes that you start in this manner are called *interactive processes*. That is, you start the processes *interactively* with the keyboard or mouse. If the application or program is active and selected, the related interactive process has control over the keyboard and mouse until you switch control by terminating the program or selecting a different one. When a process has control, it's said to be running *in the foreground*.

Processes can also run *in the background*. With processes started by users, this means that programs that aren't currently active can continue to operate—only they generally aren't given the same priority as the active process. You can also configure background processes to run independently of the user logon session; the operating system usually starts such processes. An example of this type of background process is a batch file started with an AT command. The AT command tells the system to run the file at a specified time, and, if permissions are configured correctly, the AT command can do so whether or not a user is logged on to the system.

Task Manager

The key tool you'll use to manage system processes and applications is Task Manager. You can access Task Manager using any of the following techniques:

- Press Ctrl+Shift+Esc.

- Press Ctrl+Alt+Del and then click Task Manager.

- Type **taskmgr** into the Run utility or a command prompt.

- Right-click the taskbar and select Task Manager from the shortcut menu.

Techniques you'll use to work with Task Manager are covered in the following sections.

Administering Applications

The Applications tab of Task Manager is shown in Figure 3-1. This tab shows the status of the programs that are currently running on the system. You can use the buttons on the bottom of this tab as follows:

- Stop an application by selecting the application and then clicking End Task.

- Switch to an application and make it active by selecting the application and then clicking Switch To.

- Start a new program by selecting New Task, and then enter a command to run the application. New Task functions like the Start menu's Run utility.

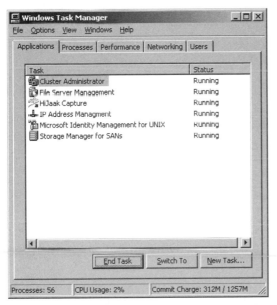

Figure 3-1   The Applications tab of the Windows Task Manager shows the status of programs currently running on the system.

Tip   The Status column tells you if the application is running normally or if the application has gone off into the ozone. A status of Not Responding is an indicator that an application might be frozen, and you might want to end its related task. However, some applications might not respond to the operating system during certain process-intensive tasks. Because of this, you should be certain the application is really frozen before you end its related task.

Right-clicking a Listing

Right-clicking an application's listing in the Windows Task Manager displays a short-cut menu that allows you to:

- Switch to the application and make it active.

- Bring the application to the front of the display.

- Minimize and maximize the application.

- Tile or cascade the application.

- End the application.

- Go to the related process in the Processes tab.

Note   The Go To Process is very helpful when you're trying to find the primary process for a particular application. Selecting this option highlights the related process in the Processes tab.

Administering Processes

The Task Manager Processes tab is shown in Figure 3-2. This tab provides detailed information about the processes that are running. By default, the Processes tab shows only processes run by the operating system, local services, network services, and the interactive user. The interactive user is the user account logged on to the local console. To see processes run by remote users, such as those connecting using a remote desktop connection, you'll need to select Show Processes From All Users.

The fields of the Processes tab provide lots of information about running processes. You can use this information to determine which processes are hogging system resources, such as CPU time and memory. The fields displayed by default are:

Image Name   The name of the process or executable running the process

User Name   The name of the user or system service running the process

CPU   The percentage of CPU utilization for the process

Mem Usage   The amount of memory the process is currently using

If you click View and choose Select Columns, you'll see a dialog box that will let you add columns to the Processes view. When you're trying to troubleshoot system problems using process information, you might want to add these columns to the view:

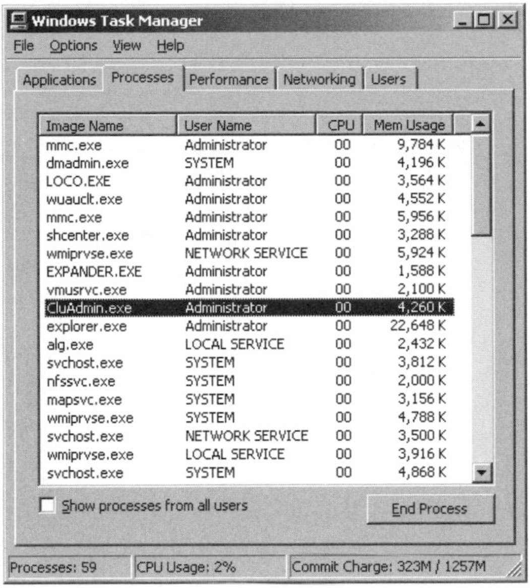

Figure 3-2   The Processes tab provides detailed information on running processes.

Base Priority   Priority determines how much of the system resources are allocated to a process. To set the priority of a process, right-click the process, choose Set Priority, and then select the new priority. Priorities are Low, Below Normal, Normal, Above Normal, High, and Real-Time. Most processes have a normal priority by default. The highest priority is given to real-time processes.

CPU Time   The total amount of CPU cycle time used by the process since it was started. To quickly see the processes that are using the most CPU time, display this column and then click the column header to sort process entries by CPU Time.

Handle Count   The total number of file handles maintained by the process. Use the handle count to gauge how dependent the process is on the file system. Some processes, such as those used by Microsoft Internet Information Services (IIS), have thousands of open file handles. Each file handle requires system memory to maintain.

I/O Reads, I/O Writes   The total number of disk input/output (I/O) reads or writes since the process was started. Together, the number of I/O reads and writes tell you how much disk I/O activity there is. If the number of I/O reads and writes is growing disproportional to actual activity on the server, the process might not be caching files or file caching might not be properly configured. Ideally, file caching will reduce the need for I/O read and writes.

Page Faults   A page fault occurs when a process requests a page in memory and the system can't find it at the requested location. If the requested page is elsewhere in memory, the fault is called a *soft page fault*. If the requested page must be retrieved from disk, the fault is called a *hard page fault*. Most processors can handle large numbers of soft faults. Hard faults, however, can cause significant delays.

Paged Pool, Non-paged Pool   The *paged pool* is an area of system memory for objects that can be written to disk when they aren't used. The *non-paged pool* is an area of system memory for objects that can't be written to disk. You should note processes that require a high amount of nonpaged pool memory. If there isn't enough free memory on the server, these processes might be the reason for a high level of page faults.

Peak Memory Usage   The highest amount of memory used by the process. The change or delta between current memory usage and peak memory usage is important to note as well. Applications, such as Microsoft SQL Server, that have a high delta between base memory usage and peak memory usage might need to be allocated more memory on startup so that they perform better.

Thread Count   The current number of threads that the process is using. Most server applications are multithreaded. Multithreading allows concurrent execution of process requests. Some applications can dynamically control the number of concurrently executing threads to improve application performance. Too many threads, however, can actually reduce performance because the operating system has to switch thread contexts too frequently.

If you examine processes running in Task Manager, you'll note a process called System Idle Process. You can't set the priority of this process. Unlike other processes that track resource usage, System Idle Process tracks the amount of system resources that aren't used. Thus, a 99 in the CPU column for the System Idle Process means 99 percent of the system resources currently aren't being used.

As you examine processes, keep in mind that a single application might start multiple processes. Generally, these processes are dependent on a central process and from this main process a process tree containing dependent processes is formed. You can find the main process for an application by right-clicking the application in the Applications tab and selecting Go To Process. When you terminate processes, you'll usually want to target the main application process or the application itself rather than dependent processes. This ensures that the application is stopped cleanly.

To stop the main application process and dependent processes, you have several choices. You can:

- Select the application in the Applications tab, and then click End Task.

- Right-click the main application process in the Processes tab, and then select End Process.

- Select the main or a dependent process in the Processes tab, and then select End Process Tree.

Viewing and Managing System Performance

The Task Manager Performance tab provides an overview of CPU and memory usage. As shown in Figure 3-3, the tab displays graphs as well as statistics. This information gives you a quick check on system resource usage. For more detailed information, use Performance Monitor, which will be explained later in this chapter.

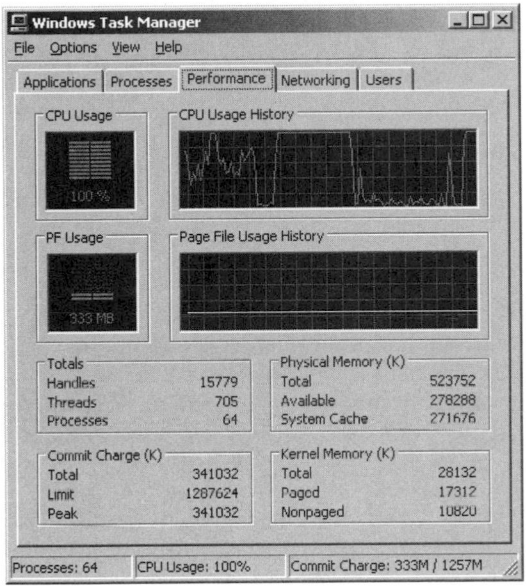

Figure 3-3   The Performance tab provides a quick check on system resource usage.

Graphs on the Performance Tab

The graphs on the Performance tab provide the following information:

CPU Usage   The percentage of processor resources currently being used.

CPU Usage History   A history graph of CPU usage plotted over time. The update speed determines how often the graph is updated.

PF Usage   The amount of the paging file (or virtual memory) currently being used by the system.

Page File Usage History   A history graph of paging file usage plotted over time.

> **Tip**   To view a close-up of the CPU graphs, double-click within the Performance tab. Double-clicking again returns you to normal viewing mode. If CPU usage is consistently high, even under average usage conditions, you might want to perform more detailed performance monitoring to determine the cause of the problem. Memory is often a source of performance problems, and you should rule it out before upgrading or adding CPUs. For more details, see the section entitled "Tuning System Performance," later in this chapter.

Customizing and Updating the Graph Display

To customize or update the graph display, use the following options on the View menu:

Update Speed   Allows you to change the speed of graph updating as well as to pause the graph. Updates occur once every four seconds for Low, once every two seconds for Normal, and twice per second for High.

CPU History   On multiprocessor systems, allows you to specify how CPU graphs are displayed. You can, for example, display one CPU in each graph or multiple CPUs in each graph.

Show Kernel Times   Allows you to display the amount of CPU time used by the operating system kernel. Usage by the kernel is shown in red plotting (as opposed to green plotting, which is used otherwise).

Beneath the graphs, you'll find several lists of statistics. These statistics provide the following information:

Totals   Provides information on CPU usage. *Processes* shows the number of processes in use; processes are running instances of applications or executable files. *Threads* shows the number of threads in use; threads are the basic units of execution within processes. *Handles* shows the number of I/O handles in use; I/O handles act as tokens that let programs access resources. I/O throughput and disk performance have more of an impact on a system than does a consistently high number of I/O handles.

Physical Memory   Provides information on the total RAM on the system. *Total* shows the amount of physical RAM. *Available* shows the RAM not currently being used and available for use. *System Cache* shows the amount of memory used for system caching. If the server has very little physical memory available, you might need to add memory to the system. In general, you want the available memory to be no less than 5 percent of the total physical memory on the server.

Commit Charge   Provides information on the total memory used by the operating system. *Total* lists all physical and virtual memory currently in use. *Limit* lists the total physical and virtual memory available. *Peak* lists the maximum memory used by the system since bootup. If the difference between the total memory used and the peak memory used is consistently large, you might want to add physical memory to the system to improve performance. If the peak memory usage is within 10 percent of the Limit value, you might want to add physical memory or increase the amount of virtual memory, or both.

Kernel Memory   Provides information on the memory used by the operating system kernel. Critical portions of kernel memory must operate in RAM and can't be paged to virtual memory. This type of kernel memory is listed as *Nonpaged*. The rest of kernel memory can be paged to virtual memory and is listed as *Paged*. The total amount of memory used by the kernel is listed under *Total*.

Viewing and Managing Networking Performance

The Task Manager Networking tab provides an overview of the network adapters a system is using. You can use the information provided to quickly determine the percent utilization, link speed, and operational status usage of each network adapter configured on a system.

If a system has one network adapter, a summary graph details the network traffic on this adapter over time. If a system has multiple network adapters, the graph displays a composite index of all network connections, which represents all network traffic. By default, the graph displays only the network traffic total byte count. You can change this by clicking View, choosing Network History, and then enabling Bytes Sent, Bytes Received, or both. Bytes Sent are shown in red, Bytes Received in yellow, Bytes Total in green.

The fields of the Networking tab provide lots of information about network traffic to and from the server. You can use this information to determine how much external traffic a server is experiencing at any time. The fields displayed by default are:

Adapter Name   Name of the network adapter in the Network Connections folder.

Network Utilization   Percentage of network usage based on the connection speed for the interface. For example, an adapter with a link speed of 100 megabits per second (Mbps) and current traffic of 10 Mbps would have a 10 percent utilization.

Link Speed   Interface connection speed as determined by the initial connection speed.

State   Operational status of network adapters.

> **Real World**   Any time you see usage consistently approaching or over 50 percent of total capacity, you'll want to start monitoring the server more closely and might also want to consider adding network adapters. Plan any upgrade carefully; there is a lot more planning required than you might think. Consider the implications not only for that server but also for the network as a whole. You might also have connectivity problems if you exceed the allotted bandwidth of your service provider—and it can often take months to obtain additional bandwidth for external connections.

If you click View and choose Select Columns, you'll see a dialog box that will let you add columns to the Processes view. When you're trying to troubleshoot networking problems, you might want to add the following columns to the view:

Bytes Sent Throughput   Percentage of current connection bandwidth used by traffic sent from the system

Bytes Received Throughput   Percentage of current connection bandwidth used by traffic received by the system

Bytes Throughput   Percentage of current connection bandwidth used for all traffic

Bytes Sent   Cumulative total bytes sent on the connection to date

Bytes Received   Cumulative total bytes received on the connection to date

Bytes Total   Cumulative total bytes on the connection to date

Viewing and Managing Remote User Sessions

Remote users can connect to systems using Terminal Services or Remote Desktop. Terminal Services allow remote terminal connections to systems. Remote Desktop allows you to administer systems remotely as if you were sitting at the keyboard.

Remote Desktop connections are automatically enabled on Windows Server 2003 installations. One way to view and manage remote desktop connections is to use Task Manager. To do this, start Task Manager, and then click the Users tab. The Users tab shows interactive user sessions for both local and remote users.

Each user connection is listed with the user account name, session ID, status, originating client computer, and session type. A user logged on to the local system is listed with Console as the session type. Other users have a session type that indicates the connection type and protocol, such as RDP-TCP for a connection using the Remote Desktop Protocol (RDP) with Transmission Control Protocol (TCP) as the transport protocol. If you right-click user sessions, you have the following options:

Connect   Connects the user session if it's inactive.

Disconnect   Disconnects the user session, halting all user-started applications without saving application data.

Log Off   Logs the user off, using the normal logoff process. Application data and system state information are saved as during a normal log off.

Remote Control   Sets the hot keys used to end remote control sessions. The default hot keys are Ctrl+*.

Send Message   Sends a console message to users logged on to remote systems.

Managing System Services

Services provide key functions to workstations and servers. To manage system services, you'll use the Services entry in the Computer Management console. You can start Computer Management and access the Services entry by completing the following steps:

1. Choose Start, then choose Programs or All Programs as appropriate, then Administrative Tools, and finally Computer Management. Or select Computer Management in the Administrative Tools folder.

2. Right-click the Computer Management entry in the console tree and select Connect To Another Computer on the shortcut menu. You can now choose the system on which you want to manage services.

3. Expand the Services And Applications node by clicking the plus sign (+) next to it, and then choose Services.

Note   Windows Server 2003 provides several other ways to access services. For example, you can also use the Services entry in the Component Services utility.

Figure 3-4 shows the Services view in the Computer Management console. The key fields of this dialog box are used as follows:

Name   The name of the service. Only services installed on the system are listed here. Double-click an entry to configure its startup options. If a service you need isn't listed, you can install it by using the Network Connection Properties dialog box or the Windows Optional Networking Components Wizard. See Chapter 16, "Managing TCP/ IP Networking," for details.

Description   A short description of the service and its purpose.

Status   Whether the status of the service is started, paused, or stopped. (Stopped is indicated by a blank entry.)

Startup Type   The startup setting for the service. Automatic services are started at bootup. Users or other services start manual services. Disabled services are turned off and can't be started while they remain disabled.

Log On As   The account the service logs on as. The default in most cases is the local system account.

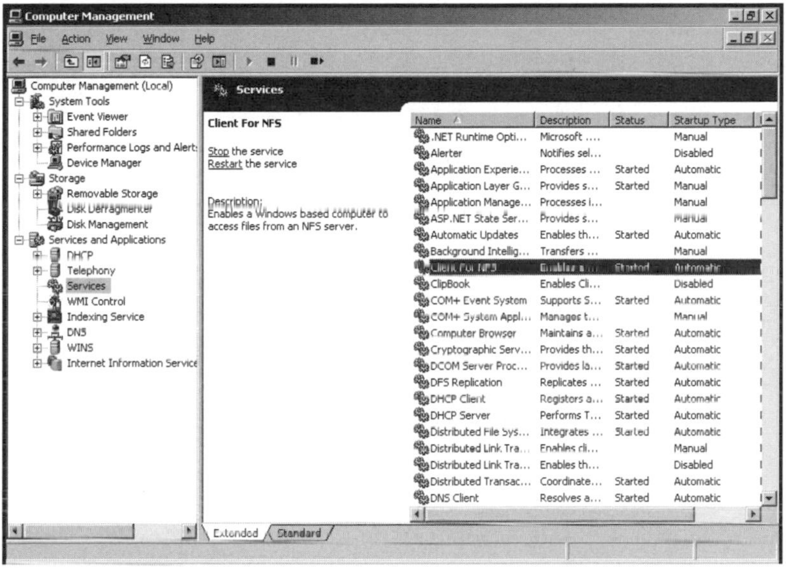

Figure 3-4   Use the Services view to manage services on workstations and servers.

The Services area has two views: extended and standard. To change the view, click the tabs at the bottom of the Services area. In extended view, quick links are provided for managing services. Click Start to start a stopped service. Click Restart to stop and then start a service—essentially resetting that service. If you select a service in extended view, a service description is shown, which details the service's purpose.

Note   Both the operating system and a user can disable Services. Generally, Windows Server 2003 disables services if there is a possible conflict with another service.

Starting, Stopping, and Pausing Services

As an administrator, you'll often have to start, stop, or pause Windows Server 2003 services. To start, stop, or pause a service, complete the following steps:

1. Start Computer Management and connect to the computer on which you want to manage services.

2. Expand the Services And Applications node by clicking the plus sign (+) next to it, and then choose Services.

3. Right-click the service you want to manipulate, and then select Start, Stop, or Pause as appropriate. You can also choose Restart to have Windows stop and then start the service after a brief pause. Additionally, if you pause a service, you can use the Resume option to resume normal operation.

Note   When services that are set to start automatically fail, the status is listed as blank and you'll usually receive notification in a pop-up dialog box. Service failures can also be logged to the system's event logs. In Windows Server 2003, you can configure actions to handle service failure automatically. For example, you could have Windows Server 2003 attempt to restart the service for you. For details, see the section entitled "Configuring Service Recovery," later in this chapter.

Configuring Service Startup

You can set Windows Server 2003 services to start manually or automatically. You can also turn them off permanently by disabling them. You configure service startup by completing the following steps:

1. In the Computer Management console, connect to the computer whose services you want to manage.

2. Expand the Services And Applications node by clicking the plus sign (+) next to it, and then choose Services.

3. Right-click the service you want to configure, and then choose Properties.

4. In the General tab, use the Startup Type drop-down list box to choose a startup option, as shown in Figure 3-5. Select Automatic to start services at bootup. Select Manual to allow the services to be started manually. Select Disabled to turn off the service. Click OK.

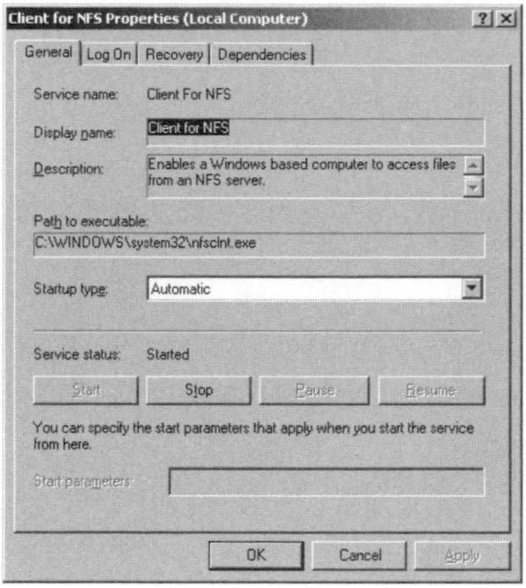

Figure 3-5   Use the General tab's Startup Type drop-down list box to configure service startup options.

Real World   When a server has multiple hardware profiles, you can enable or disable services for a particular profile. Before you disable services permanently, you might want to create a separate hardware profile for testing the server with these services disabled. In this way, you can use the original profile to quickly resume operations using the original service status. The profile doesn't save other service configuration options, however. To enable or disable a service by profile, use the Log On tab of the Service Properties dialog box. Select the profile that you want to work with under Hardware Profile, and then click Enable or Disable as appropriate.

Configuring Service Logon

You can configure Windows Server 2003 services to log on as a system account or as a specific user. To do either of these, complete the following steps:

1. In the Computer Management console, connect to the computer whose services you want to manage.

2. Expand the Services And Applications node by clicking the plus sign (+) next to it, and then choose Services.

3. Right-click the service you want to configure, and then choose Properties.

4. Select the Log On tab, as shown in Figure 3-6.

5. Select Local System Account if the service should log on using the system account (which is the default for most services). If the service provides a user interface that can be manipulated, select Allow Service To Interact With Desktop to allow users to control the service's interface.

6. Select This Account if the service should log on using a specific user account. Be sure to type an account name and password in the text boxes provided. Use the Browse button to search for a user account, if necessary. Click OK.

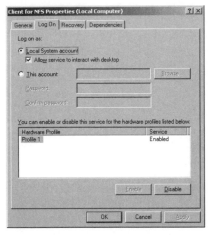

Figure 3-6   Use the Log On tab to configure the service logon account.

Security   As an administrator, you should keep track of any accounts that are used with services. These accounts can be the source of huge security problems if they're not configured properly. Service accounts should have the strictest security settings and as few permissions as possible while allowing the service to perform necessary functions. Typically, accounts used with services don't need many of the permissions you would assign to a normal user account. For example, most service accounts don't need the right to log on locally. Every administrator should know what service accounts are used (so they can better track use of these accounts), and the accounts should be treated as if they were administrator accounts. This means: secure passwords, careful monitoring of account usage, careful application of account permissions and privileges, and so on.

Configuring Service Recovery

You can configure Windows Server 2003 services to take specific actions when a service fails. For example, you could attempt to restart the service or run an application. To configure recovery options for a service, complete the following steps:

1. In the Computer Management console, connect to the computer whose services you want to manage.

2. Expand the Services And Applications node by clicking the plus sign (+) next to it, and then choose Services.

3. Right-click the service you want to configure, and then choose Properties.

4. Click the Recovery tab, as shown in Figure 3-7.

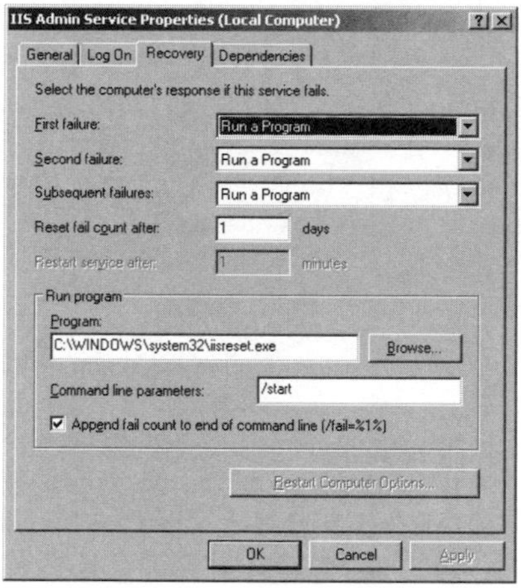

Figure 3-7 Use the Recovery tab to specify actions that should be taken in case of service failure.

Note Windows Server 2003 automatically configures recovery for some critical system services during installation. In Figure 3-7, you see that the IIS Admin service is set to run a program called lisreset.exe if the service fails. This program is an application that corrects service problems and safely manages dependent IIS services while working to restart the service. lisreset.exe requires the command line parameter/start as well.

5. You can now configure recovery options for the first, second, and subsequent recovery attempts. The available options are:

Take No Action The operating system won't attempt recovery for this failure but might still attempt recovery of previous or subsequent failures.

Restart the Service Stops and then starts the service after a brief pause.

Run a Program Allows you to run a program or a script in case of failure. The script can be a batch program or a Windows script. If you select this option, set the full file path to the program you want to run and then set any necessary command line parameters to pass in to the program when it starts.

Restart the Computer Shuts down and then restarts the computer. Before you choose this option, double-check Startup and Recovery options as well as Hardware Profile options, as discussed in the sections entitled "Configuring System Startup and Recovery" and "Configuring the Way Hardware Profiles Are Used," respectively, in Chapter 2, "Managing Servers Running Microsoft Windows Server 2003." You want the system to select defaults quickly and automatically.

Best Practices   When you configure recovery options for critical services, you might want to try to restart the service on the first and second attempts and then reboot the server on the third attempt.

6. Configure other options based on your previously selected recovery options. If you elected to run a program as a recovery option, you'll need to set options in the Run Program panel. If you elected to restart the service, you'll need to specify the restart delay. After stopping the service, Windows Server 2003 waits for the specified delay before trying to start the service. In most cases, a delay of 1–2 minutes should be sufficient. Click OK.

Disabling Unnecessary Services

As an administrator, it's your job to ensure server and network security, and unnecessary services are a potential source of security problems. For example, in many organizations that I've reviewed for security problems, I've found servers running Worldwide Web Publishing Service, Simple Mail Transfer Protocol (SMTP), and File Transfer Protocol (FTP) Publishing Service when these services weren't needed. Unfortunately, these services can make it possible for anonymous users to access servers and can also open the server to attack if not properly configured.

If you find services that aren't needed, you have several options. In the case of IIS Admin services, Domain Name System (DNS), and other services that are installed as separate Windows components, you could use the Add/Remove Programs utility in Control Panel to remove the unnecessary component and its related services. Or, you could simply disable the services that aren't being used. Typically, you'll want to start by disabling services rather than uninstalling components. This way, if you disable a service and another administrator or a user says they can't perform task X anymore, you can restore the related service, if necessary.

To disable a service, follow these steps:

1. In Computer Management, right-click the service you want to disable, and then choose Properties.

2. In the General tab, select Disabled as the option for the Startup Type drop-down list box.

Disabling a service doesn't stop a running service. It only prevents it from being started the next time the computer is booted, meaning the security risk still exists. To address this, click Stop in the Properties dialog box in the General tab, and then click OK.

Event Logging and Viewing

Event logs provide historical information that can help you track down system and security problems. The Event Log service controls whether events are tracked on Windows Server 2003 systems. When this service is started, you can track user actions and system resource usage events with the following event logs:

Application   Records events logged by applications, such as the failure of Microsoft SQL Server to access a database. Default location is %SystemRoot%\System32\Config\AppEvent.Evt.

DFS Replication   Records Distributed File System (DFS) replication activities. Default location is %SystemRoot%\System32\Donfig\Dfsr.Evt.

Directory Service   Records events logged by Active Directory directory service and its related services. Default location is %SystemRoot%\System32\Config\NTDS.Evt.

DNS Server   Records DNS queries, responses, and other DNS activities. Default location is %SystemRoot%\System32\Config\DNSEvent.Evt.

File Replication Service   Records file replication activities on the system. Default location is %SystemRoot%\System32\Config\NtFrs.Evt.

Forwarded Events   When event forwarding is configured, records forwarded events from other servers. Default location is %SystemRoot%\System32\Config\FwdEvents.Evt.

Hardware Events   When hardware subsystem event reporting is configured, records hardware events reported to the operating system. Default location is %SystemRoot%\System32\Config\HwrEvents.Evt.

Security Log   Records events you've set for auditing with local or global group policies. Default location is: %SystemRoot%\System32\Config\SecEvent.Evt.

> **Note**   Any user who needs access to the security log must be granted the user right to Manage Auditing and the Security Log. By default, members of the administrators group have this user right. To learn how to assign user rights, see the section entitled "Configuring User Rights Policies" in Chapter 9, "Creating User and Group Accounts."

System Log   Records events logged by the operating system or its components, such as the failure of a service to start at bootup. Default location is: %SystemRoot%\System32\Config\SysEvent.Evt.

> **Security**   As administrators, we tend to monitor the application and system logs the most—but don't forget about the security log. The security log is one of the most important logs, and you should monitor it closely. If the security log on a server doesn't contain events, the likeliest reason is that local auditing hasn't been configured or that domain-wide auditing is configured, in which case you should monitor the security logs on domain controllers rather than on member servers. Note also that any user who needs access to the security log must be granted the user right to Manage Auditing and the Security Log. By default, members of the Administrators group have this user right. To learn how to assign user rights, see the section entitled "Configuring User Rights Policies" in Chapter 9.

Accessing and Using the Event Logs

You access the event logs by completing the following steps:

1. In the Computer Management console, connect to the computer whose event logs you want to view or manage.

2. Expand the System Tools node by clicking the plus sign (+) next to it, and then double-click Event Viewer. You should now see a list of logs, as shown in Figure 3-8.

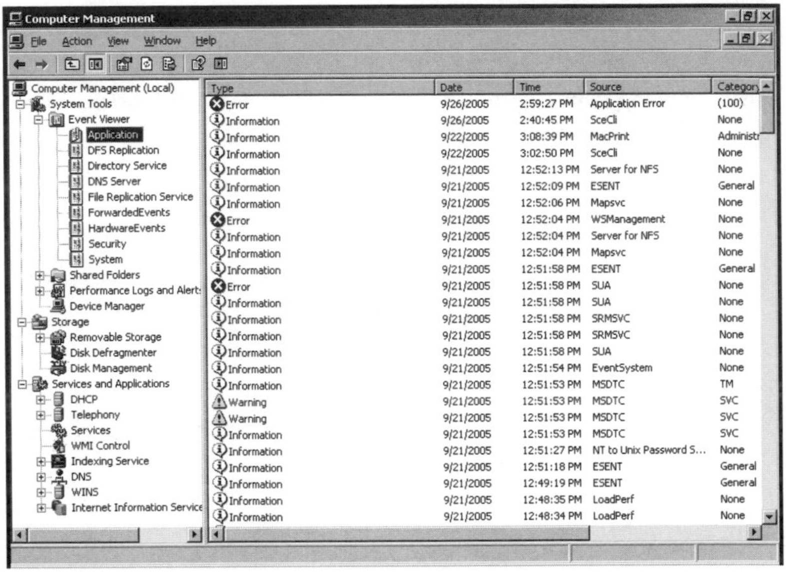

Figure 3-8   Event Viewer displays events for the selected log.

3. Select the log you want to view.

Entries in the main panel of Event Viewer provide a quick overview of when, where, and how an event occurred. To obtain detailed information on an event, double-click its entry. The event type precedes the date and time of the event. Event types include:

Information   An informational event, which is generally related to a successful action.

Success Audit   An event related to the successful execution of an action.

Failure Audit   An event related to the failed execution of an action.

Warning   A warning. Details for warnings are often useful in preventing future system problems.

Error   An error, such as the failure of a service to start.

> **Note**   Warnings and errors are the two types of events that you'll want to examine closely. Whenever these types of events occur and you're unsure of the cause, double-click the entry to view the detailed event description.

In addition to type, date, and time, the summary and detailed event entries provide the following information:

Source   The application, service, or component that logged the event

Category   The category of the event, which is sometimes used to further describe the related action

Event   An identifier for the specific event

User   The user account that was logged on when the event occurred

Computer   The name of the computer where the event occurred

Description   In the detailed entries, a text description of the event

Data   In the detailed entries, any data or error code output by the event

Setting Event Log Options

Log options allow you to control the size of the event logs as well as how logging is handled. By default, event logs are set with a maximum file size of 512 Kilobytes (KB). Then, when a log reaches this limit, events are overwritten to prevent the log from exceeding the maximum file size.

To set the log options, complete the following steps:

1. In the Computer Management console, double-click the Event Viewer entry. You should now see a list of event logs.

2. Right-click the event log whose properties you want to set and select Properties from the shortcut menu. This opens the dialog box shown in Figure 3-9.

3. Type a maximum size in the Maximum Log Size text box. Make sure that the drive containing the operating system has enough free space for the maximum log size you select. Log files are stored in the %SystemRoot%\system32\config directory by default.

> **Note**   Throughout this book you'll see references to %SystemRoot%. This is an environment variable that Windows Server 2003 uses to designate the base directory for the Windows Server 2003 operating system, such as C:\WINDOWS. For more information on environment variables, see the section entitled "Configuring the User's Environment Settings" in Chapter 10, "Managing Existing User and Group Accounts."

4. Select an event log-wrapping mode. The options available are:

   Overwrite Events As Needed   Events in the log are overwritten when the maximum file size is reached. Generally, this is the best option on a low priority system.

   Overwrite Events Older Than . . . Days   When the maximum file size is reached, events in the log are overwritten only if they are older than the setting you select. If the maximum size is reached and the events can't be overwritten, the system generates error messages telling you the event log is full.

Do Not Overwrite Events (Clear Log Manually)   When the maximum file size is reached, the system generates error messages telling you the event log is full.

5. Click OK when you're finished.

Note   On critical systems where security and event logging is very important, you might want to use Overwrite Events Older Than . . . Days or Do Not Overwrite Events (Clear Log Manually). When you use these methods, you should archive and clear the log file periodically to prevent the system from generating error messages.

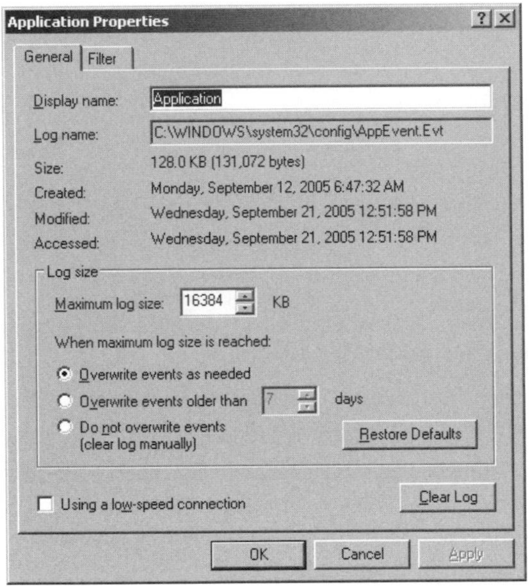

Figure 3-9   You should configure log settings according to the level of auditing on the system.

Clearing Event Logs

When an event log is full, you need to clear it. To do that, complete the following steps:

1. In the Computer Management console, double-click the Event Viewer entry. You should now see a list of event logs.

2. Right-click the event log whose properties you want to set and select Clear All Events from the shortcut menu.

3. Choose Yes to save the log before clearing it. Choose No to continue without saving the log file.

4. When prompted to confirm that you want to clear the log, click Yes.

Archiving Event Logs

On key systems such as domain controllers and application servers, you'll want to keep several months' worth of logs. However, it usually isn't practical to set the maximum log size to accommodate this. Instead, you should periodically archive the event logs.

Archive Log Formats

Logs can be archived in three formats:

- Event log format for access in Event Viewer

- Tab-delimited text format, for access in text editors or word processors or import into spreadsheets and databases

- Comma-delimited text format, for import into spreadsheets or databases

When you export log files to a comma-delimited file, a comma separates each field in the event entry. The event entries look like this:

```
12/11/02,9:43:24 PM,DNS,Information,None,2,N/A,ZETA,The DNS server has
started.12/11/02,9:40:04 PM,DNS,Error,None,4015,N/A,ZETA,The DNS server
has encountered a critical error from the Directory Service (DS). The data
is the error code.
```

The format for the entries is as follows:

```
Date,Time,Source,Type,Category,Event,User,Computer,Description
```

Creating Log Archives

To create a log archive, complete the following steps:

1. In the Computer Management console, double-click the Event Viewer entry. You should now see a list of event logs.

2. Right-click the event log you want to archive and select Save Log File As from the shortcut menu.

3. In the Save As dialog box, select a directory and a log file name.

4. In the Save As Type dialog box, Event Log (*.evt) will be the default file type. Select a log format as appropriate and then choose Save.

Note If you plan to archive logs regularly, you might want to create an archive directory. This way you can easily locate the log archives. You should also name the log file so that you can easily determine the log file type and the period of the archive. For example, if you're archiving the system log file for January 2003, you might want to use the file name System Log January 2003.

Tip The best format to use for archiving is the .evt format. Use this format if you plan to review old logs in the Event Viewer. However, if you plan to review logs in other applications, you might need to save the logs in a tab-delimited or comma-delimited format. With the tab-delimited or comma-delimited format, it's sometimes necessary to edit the log file in a text editor in order for the log to be properly interpreted. If you have saved the log in the .evt format, you can always save another copy as tab-delimited or comma-delimited format later by doing another Save As after opening the archive in the Event Viewer.

Viewing Log Archives

You can view log archives in text format in any text editor or word processor. You should view log archives in the event log format in Event Viewer. You can view log archives in Event Viewer by completing the following steps:

1. In the Computer Management console, right-click the Event Viewer entry. On the shortcut menu, select Open Log File. You should now see the Open dialog box shown in Figure 3-10.

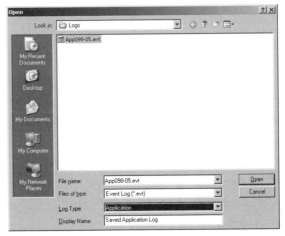

Figure 3-10   Use the Open dialog box to open the saved event log in a new view.

2. Use the Open dialog box to select a directory and a log file name. If the log isn't saved in Event Viewer format, select All Files from the Files Of Type selection menu.

3. Use Log Type to specify the type of log as Application, Directory Service, and so on.

4. Click Open. The archived log is displayed as a separate view in Event Viewer. Select this view to display the saved events in the log.

Monitoring Server Performance and Activity

Monitoring a server isn't something you should do haphazardly. You need to have a clear plan—a set of goals that you hope to achieve. Let's take a look at the reasons you might want to monitor a server and at the tools you can use to do this.

Why Monitor Your Server?

Troubleshooting server performance problems is a key reason for monitoring. For example, users might be having problems connecting to the server and you might want to monitor the server to troubleshoot these problems. Here, your goal would be to track down the problem using the available monitoring resources and then to resolve it.

Another common reason for wanting to monitor a server is to improve server performance. You do this by improving disk I/O, reducing CPU usage, and cutting down on the network traffic load on the server. Unfortunately, there are often tradeoffs to be made when it comes to resource usage. For example, as the number of users accessing a server grows, you might not be able to reduce the network traffic load, but you might be able to improve server performance through load balancing or by distributing key data files on separate drives.

Getting Ready to Monitor

Before you start monitoring a server, you might want to establish baseline performance metrics for your server. To do this, you measure server performance at various times and under different load conditions. You can then compare the baseline performance with subsequent performance to determine how the server is performing. Performance metrics that are well above the baseline measurements might indicate areas where the server needs to be optimized or reconfigured.

After you establish the baseline metrics, you should formulate a monitoring plan. A comprehensive monitoring plan includes the following steps:

1. Determining which server events should be monitored to help you accomplish your goal

2. Setting filters to reduce the amount of information collected

3. Configuring monitors and alerts to watch the events

4. Logging the event data so that it can be analyzed

5. Analyzing the event data in System Monitor, which is included in the Performance console

These procedures are examined later in this chapter. Although you should usually develop a monitoring plan, sometimes you might not want to go through all these steps to monitor your server. For example, you might want to monitor and analyze activity as it happens rather than log and analyze the data later.

Using System Monitor

The Performance console includes the System Monitor snap-in. System Monitor graphically displays statistics for the set of performance parameters you've selected for display. These performance parameters are referred to as counters. You can also update the available counters when you install services and add-ons on the server. For example, when you configure DNS on a server, System Monitor is updated with a set of objects and counters for tracking DNS performance. System Monitor creates a graph depicting the various counters you're tracking.

The update interval for this graph is completely configurable but, by default, is set to one second. As you'll see when you work with System Monitor, the tracking information is most valuable when you record the information in a log file and when you configure alerts to send messages when certain events occur or when certain thresholds are reached, such as when the CPU processor time reaches 99 percent. The sections that follow examine key techniques you'll use to work with performance monitor.

Choosing Counters to Monitor

The System Monitor displays information only for counters you're tracking. Dozens of counters are available, and as you add services, you'll find there are even more. These counters are organized into groupings called performance objects. For example, all CPU-related counters are associated with the Processor object.

To select which counters you want to monitor, complete the following steps:

1. Select the Performance option on the Administrative Tools menu. This displays the Performance console.

2. Select the System Monitor entry in the left pane, as shown in Figure 3-11.

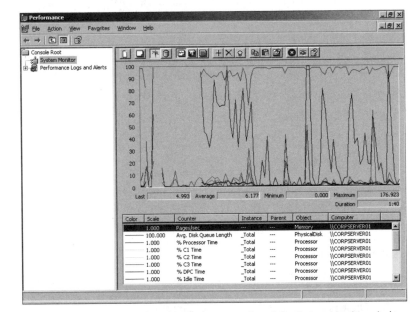

Figure 3-11   Counters are listed in the lower portion of the System Monitor window.

3. System Monitor has several viewing modes. Make sure you're in View Current Activity and View Graph display mode by clicking the View Current Activity and View Graph buttons on the Performance Monitor toolbar.

4. To add counters, click the Add (+) button on the System Monitor toolbar or press Ctl+L. This displays the Add Counters dialog box shown in Figure 3-12. The key fields are:

Use Local Computer Counters   Configure performance options for the local computer.

Select Counters From Computer   Enter the Universal Naming Convention (UNC) name of the server you want to work with, such as \\ZETA. Or, use the selection list to select the server from a list of computers you have access to over the network.

Performance Object   Select the type of object you want to work with, such as Processor.

> **Tip**   The easiest way to learn what you can track is to explore the objects and counters available in the Add Counters dialog box. Select an object in the Performance Object field, click the Explain button, and then scroll through the list of counters for this object.

All Counters   Select all counters for the current object.

Select Counters From List   Select one or more counters for the current object. For example, you could select % Processor Time and % User Time.

All Instances   Select all counter instances for monitoring.

Select Instances From List   Select one or more counter instances to monitor.

> **Best Practices**   Don't try to chart too many counters or counter instances at once. You'll make the display difficult to read and you'll use system resources—namely CPU time and memory—that might affect server responsiveness.

5. When you've selected all the necessary options, click Add to add the counters to the chart. Then repeat this process, as necessary, to add other performance parameters.

6. Click Done when you're finished adding counters.

7. You can delete counters later by clicking their entry in the lower portion of the Performance window and then clicking Delete displays.

Figure 3-12   Select counters you want to monitor.

Using Performance Logs

You can use performance logs to track the performance of a server, and you can replay them later. As you set out to work with logs, keep in mind that parameters that you track in log files are recorded separately from parameters that you chart in the Performance window. You can configure log files to update counter data automatically or manually. With automatic logging, a snapshot of key parameters is recorded at specific time intervals, such as every 10 seconds. With manual logging, you determine when snapshots are made. Two types of performance logs are available:

Counter logs   Record performance data on the selected counters when a predetermined update interval has elapsed

Trace logs   Record performance data whenever their related events occur

Creating and Managing Performance Logging

To create and manage performance logging, complete the following steps:

1. Access the Performance console by selecting the Performance option on the Administrative Tools menu.

2. Expand the Performance Logs And Alerts node and then select either Counter Logs or Trace Logs.

3. As shown in Figure 3-13, you should see a list of current logs (if any) in the right pane. A green log symbol next to the log name indicates logging is active. A red log symbol indicates logging is stopped.

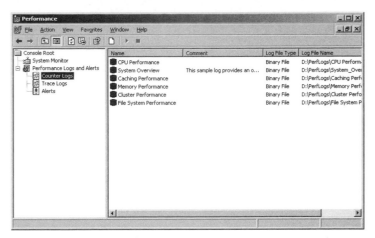

Figure 3-13   Current performance logs are listed with summary information.

4. You can create a new log by right-clicking in the right pane and selecting New Log Settings from the shortcut menu. A New Log Settings box appears, asking you to give a name to the new log settings. Type a descriptive name here before continuing.

5. To manage an existing log, right-click its entry in the right pane, and then select one of the following options:

Delete   To delete the log

Properties   To display the log properties dialog box

Start   To activate logging

Stop   To halt logging

Save Settings As   Saves the log configuration as a Web page that can be viewed in a browser, such as Internet Explorer, and imported into a new counter log using New Log Settings From

Real World   The Hypertext Markup Language (HTML) page created using Save Settings As has an embedded System Monitor that you can use to view the performance data you've configured. If you save the settings to a folder published under IIS, you'll be able to easily remotely view performance data. All you need to do is type the appropriate Uniform Resource Locator (URL) in the Web browser's Address text box

Creating Counter Logs

Counter logs record performance data on the selected counters at a specific sample interval. For example, you could sample performance data for the CPU every 15 minutes. To create a counter log, complete the following steps:

1. Right-click Counter Logs in the left pane of the Performance console, and then choose New Log Settings.

2. In the New Log Settings dialog box, type a name for the log, such as **System Performance** Monitor or **Processor Status Monitor**. Then click OK.

3. To add all counters for specific performance objects, click Add Objects, and then use the Add Object dialog box to select the objects you want to add. All counters for these objects will be logged.

4. To add specific counters for objects, click Add Counters, and then use the Select Counters dialog box to select the counters you want to add.

5. In the Sample Data Every... text box, type in a sample interval and select a time unit in seconds, minutes, hours, or days. The sample interval specifies when new data is collected. For example, if you sample every 15 minutes, the log is updated every 15 minutes.

   Best Practices   Log files can grow in size very quickly. If you plan to log data for an extended period, be sure to place the log file on a drive with lots of free space. Remember, the more frequently you update the log file, the higher the drive space and CPU resource usage on the system.

6. In the Run As text box, type the name of the account under which the counter log will run, and then click Set Password. After you type the password for the account and then confirm the password, click OK to close the Set Password dialog box. To run the log under the default system account, type **<Default>**.

7. Click the Log Files tab as shown in Figure 3-14. By default, counter logs are saved as sequentially numbered binary files in the %SystemDrive%\PerfLogs directory.

   If desired, change the log file defaults using the following options:

   Log File Type   Changes the default log type. Text File (Comma Delimited) creates a log file with comma-separated entries. Text File (Tab Delimited) creates a log file with tab-separated entries. Binary File creates a binary file that Performance Monitor can read. Binary Circular File creates a binary file that overwrites old data with new data when the file reaches a specified size limit. SQL Database writes the performance data to a SQL Database.

   End File Names With   Sets an automatic suffix for each new file created when you run the counter log. Logs can have a numeric suffix or a suffix in a specific date format.

   Start Numbering At   Sets the first serial number for a log that uses an automatic numeric suffix.

   Comment   Sets an optional description of the log, which is displayed in the Comment column.

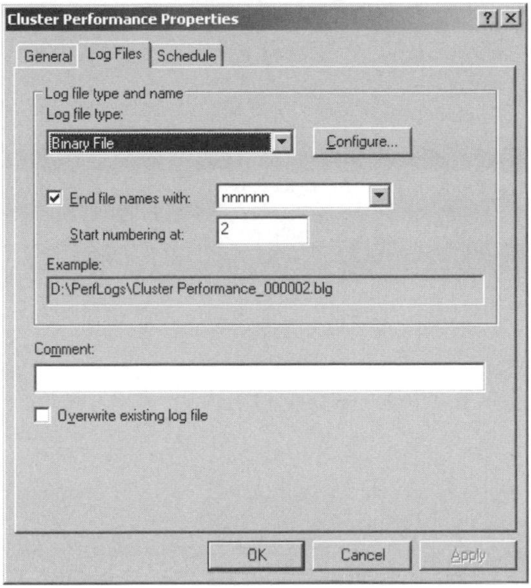

Figure 3-14   You can use the Log Files tab to configure the log file format and usage.

Tip   If you plan to use Performance Monitor to analyze or view the log, use one of the binary file formats.

8. After you set the log file type, click Configure to configure the log file location. If you selected SQL Database as the file type, use the Configure SQL Logs dialog box to select a previously configured system data source name (DSN). The DSN is used to establish a connection to a SQL-compliant database. If you selected another file type, you'll be able to set the log file name and folder location. With either selection you have the option of limiting the log file size to a specific value.

9. Click the Schedule tab, shown in Figure 3-15, and then specify when logging should start and stop.

10. You can configure the logging to start manually or automatically at a specific date. Select the appropriate option and then specify a start date if necessary.

11. You can configure the log file to stop manually after a specified period of time, such as seven days, at a specific date and time, or when the log file is full (if you've set a specific file size limit). When a log file closes, you can start a new log file or run a command automatically as well.

12. Click OK when you've finished setting the logging schedule. The log is then created, and you can manage it as explained in the section entitled "Creating and Managing Performance Logging," earlier in this chapter.

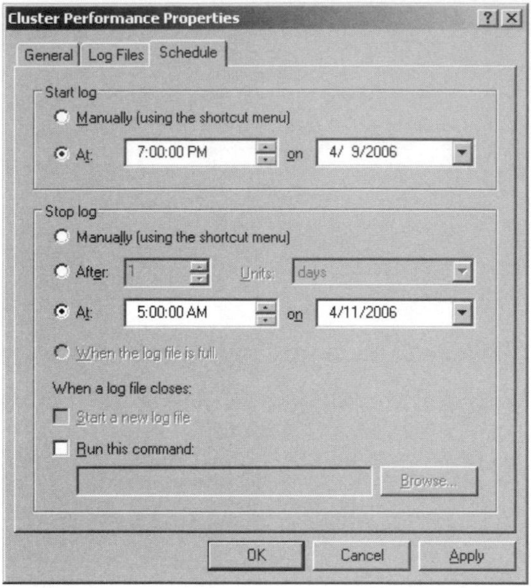

Figure 3-15   Use the Schedule tab to specify when logging starts and stops.

Creating Trace Logs

Trace logs record performance data whenever events related to their source providers occur. A source provider is an application or operating system service that has traceable events.

To create a trace log, complete the following steps:

1. Right-click Trace Logs in the left pane of the Performance console, and then choose New Log Settings.

2. In the New Log Settings dialog box, type a name for the log, such as Logon Trace or Disk I/O Trace. Then click OK. This opens the dialog box shown in Figure 3-16.

3. If you want to trace operating system events, select the Events Logged By System Provider option button. As shown in Figure 3-16, you can now select system events to trace.

   Collecting page faults and file details events puts a heavy load on the server and causes the log file to grow rapidly. Because of this, you should collect page faults and file details only for a limited time.

4. If you want to trace another provider, select the Nonsystem Providers option button and then click Add. This displays the Add Nonsystem Providers dialog box, which you'll use to select the provider to trace.

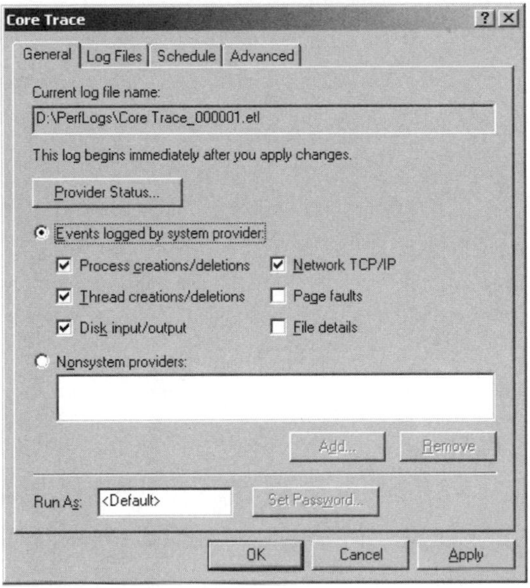

Figure 3-16   Use the General tab to select the provider to use in the trace.

5. In the Run As text box, type the name of the account under which the counter log will run, and then click Set Password. After you type the password for the account and then confirm the password, click OK to close the Set Password dialog box. To run the log under the default system account, type **<Default>**.

6. When you're finished selecting providers and events to trace, click the Log Files tab. You can now configure the trace file as explained in Steps 7 and 8 of the section of this chapter entitled "Creating Counter Logs." The only change is that the log file types are different. With trace logs, you have two log types:

Sequential Trace File. Writes events to the trace log sequentially up to the maximum file size (if any)

Circular Trace File. Overwrites old data with new data when the file reaches a specified size limit

7. Click the Schedule tab, and then specify when tracing starts and stops.

8. You can configure the logging to start manually or automatically at a specific date. Select the appropriate option, and then specify a start date, if necessary.

9. You can configure the log file to stop manually, after a specified period of time (such as seven days), at a specific date and time, or when the log file is full (if you've set a specific file size limit). When a log file closes, you can start a new log file or run a command automatically as well.

10. When you've finished setting the logging schedule, click OK. The log is then created and you can manage it as explained in the section entitled "Creating and Managing Performance Logging," later in this chapter.

Viewing and Replaying Performance Logs

When you're troubleshooting problems, you'll often want to log performance data over an extended period of time and then replay the data to analyze the results. To do this, complete the following steps:

1. Configure automatic logging as described in the section entitled "Using Performance Logs," earlier in this chapter.

2. In the Performance console, select the System Monitor entry on the left pane and then right-click the System Monitor details pane. Finally, select Properties from the shortcut menu. This displays the System Monitor Properties dialog box.

3. Click the Source tab. Under Data Source, click Log Files and then click Add to open the Select Log File dialog box. You can now select the log file you want to analyze.

4. Specify the time window that you want to analyze. Click Time Range, and then drag the Total Range bar to specify the appropriate starting and ending times. Drag the left edge to the right to move up the start time. Drag the right edge to the left to move down the end time.

5. Click the Data tab. You can now select counters to view. Click the Add button. This displays the Add Counter dialog box, which you can use to select the counters that you want to analyze.

   Only counters that you selected for logging are available. If you don't see a counter that you want to work with, you'll need to modify the log properties, restart the logging process, and then check the logs at a later date.

6. Click OK. Then, in System Monitor, use the View Graph, View Histogram, and View Report buttons on the toolbar to display information based on the counters selected.

Configuring Alerts for Performance Counters

You can configure alerts to notify you when certain events occur or when certain performance thresholds are reached. You can send these alerts as network messages and as events that are logged in the application event log. You can also configure alerts to start applications and performance logs.

To add alerts in the Performance console, complete the following steps:

1. Right-click Alerts in the left pane of the Performance console, and then choose New Alert Settings.

2. In the New Alert Settings dialog box, type a name for the alert, such as **Processor Alert** or **Disk I/O Alert**. Then click OK. This opens the dialog box shown in Figure 3-17.

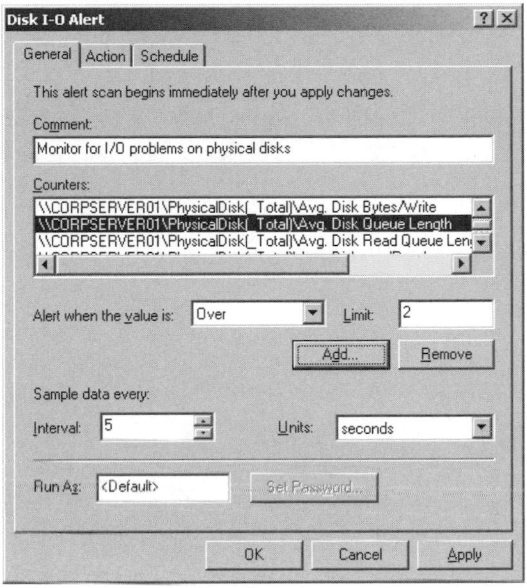

Figure 3-17   Use the Disk I-O Alert dialog box to configure counters that trigger alerts.

3. In the General tab, type an optional description of the alert. Then click Add to display the Add Counters dialog box. This dialog box is identical to the Add Counters dialog box shown previously in Figure 3-12.

4. Use the Add Counters dialog box to add counters that trigger the alert. Click Close when you're finished.

5. In the Counters panel, select the first counter and then use the Alert When Value Is ... text box to set the occasion when an alert for this counter is triggered. Alerts can be triggered when the counter is over or under a specific value. Select Over or Under, and then set the trigger value. The unit of measurement is whatever makes sense for the currently selected counter(s). For example, to alert if processor time is over 95 percent, you would select Over and then type **95**. Repeat this process to configure other counters you've selected.

6. In the Sample Data Every ... text box, type in a sample interval and select a time unit in seconds, minutes, hours, or days. The sample interval specifies when new data is collected. For example, if you sample every 10 minutes, the log is updated every 10 minutes.

    Caution   Don't sample too frequently. You'll use system resources and might cause the server to seem unresponsive to user requests.

7. In the Run As text box, type the name of the account under which the counter log will run, and then click Set Password. After you type the password for the account and then confirm the password, click OK to close the Set Password dialog box. To run alert logging under the default system account, type **<Default>**.

8. Click the Action tab, shown in Figure 3-18. You can now specify any of the following actions to happen when an alert is triggered:

Log An Entry In The Application Event Log   Creates log entries for alerts

Send A Network Message To   Sends a network message to the computer specified

Start Performance Data Log   Sets a counter log to start when an alert occurs

Run This Program   Sets the complete file path of a program or batch file script to run when the alert occurs

> **Note**   Alerts can be configured to run executable programs with the .exe extension and batch files with the .bat or .cmd extension when an alert is triggered. Be sure to type the full path to the program or batch file you want to run. The Run This Program text box will accept only valid file paths. If you enter an invalid file path, you'll see a warning specifying this when you click OK or try to access another tab. To pass arguments to an executable or batch file application, use the options of the Command Line Arguments panel. Normally, arguments are passed as individual strings. However, if you select Single Argument String, the arguments are passed in a comma-separated list within a single string. The Example Command Line Arguments list at the bottom of the tab shows how the arguments would be passed.

9. Click the Schedule tab, and then specify when alerting starts and stops. For example, you could configure the alerts to start on a Friday evening and stop on Monday morning. Then each time an alert occurs during this period, the specified action(s) are executed.

10. You can configure alerts to start manually or automatically at a specific date. Select the appropriate option, and then specify a start date, if necessary.

11. You can configure alerts to stop manually or automatically after a specified period of time, such as seven days, or at a specific date and time.

12. When you've finished setting the alert schedule, click OK. The alert is then created, and you can manage it in much the same way that you manage counter and trace logs.

> **Real World**   Figure 3-18 shows the Run This Program text box with the path to a Windows script with the .vbs extension as the action to take. If the .vbs script exists in the location specified, this will be accepted as a valid entry. However, when the alert is triggered, the Windows script won't run and an error will be entered in the Application event log. To run a Windows script as an action, you must follow the steps outlined in the following section, "Running Scripts as Actions."

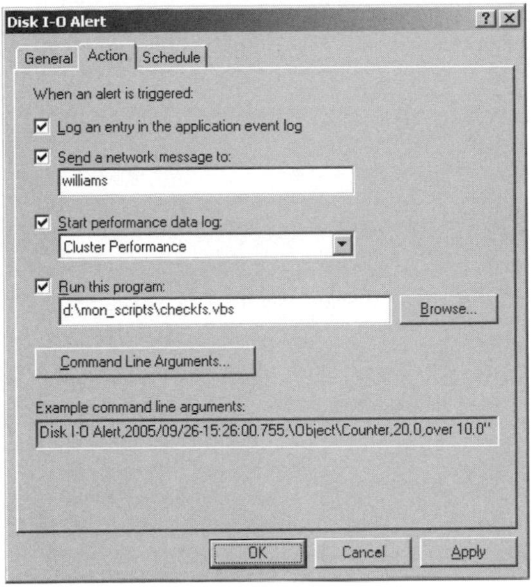

Figure 3-18   Set actions that are executed when the alert occurs.

Running Scripts as Actions

Performance Logs And Alerts is the service responsible for handling alerts. To run batch scripts or any programs that launch command prompts or perform other actions that require access to the desktop, you'll need to configure the service so that it can interact with the desktop. To do this, complete the following steps:

1. Click Start, choose Administrative Tools, and then click Services.

2. Right-click Performance Logs And Alerts, and then select Properties.

3. In the Log On tab, select the Local System Account and Allow Service To Interact With Desktop check boxes.

4. In the General tab, click Start, and then click OK.

This allows the Performance Logs And Alerts service to execute batch (.bat, .cmd) and script (.js, .vbs, .wsf) files interactively. However, you can't enter the name of a Windows script directly in the Run This Program text box. Instead, you must enter the path to the Windows Script engine that you want to run when the action is triggered, such as C:\WINDOWS\system32\Cscript.exe, and then set Command Line Arguments that point to the script you want to execute. To do this, follow these steps:

1. Set up the alert. For the alert action, select Run This Program. Click Browse. Use the Select File To Run dialog box to find the full path to the Windows Script engine you want to use, such as C:\WINDOWS\system32\Cscript.exe. Click Open.

2. In the Action tab of the alert Properties dialog box, click Command Line Arguments. In the Command Line Arguments dialog box, select Single Argument String and Text Message. Clear all other arguments.

3. In the Text Message text box, type the full path to the script, such as c:\scripts\Test.vbs.

4. Click OK twice.

5. Click the Schedule tab, and then specify when alerting starts and stops. For example, you could configure the alerts to start on a Friday evening and stop on Monday morning. Then, each time an alert occurs during this period, the specified action(s) are executed.

6. You can configure alerts to start manually or automatically at a specific date. Select the appropriate option, and then specify a start date, if necessary.

7. You can configure alerts to stop manually, after a specified period of time, such as seven days, or at a specific date and time.

8. When you've finished setting the alert schedule, click OK. The alert is then created, and you can manage it like a counter or trace log.

Tuning System Performance

Now that you know how to monitor your system, let's look at how you can tune the operating system and hardware performance. I'll examine the following areas:

- Memory usage and caching
- Processor utilization
- Disk I/O
- Network bandwidth and connectivity

Monitoring and Tuning Memory Usage

Memory is often the source of performance problems, and you should always rule out memory problems before examining other areas of the system. Systems use both physical and virtual memory. To rule out memory problems with a system, you should configure application performance, memory usage, and data throughput settings, and then monitor the server's memory usage to check for problems.

Setting Application Performance and Memory Usage

Application performance and memory usage settings determine how system resources are allocated. In most cases, you want to give the operating system and background applications the lion's share of resources. This is especially true for Active Directory, file, print, and network and communications servers. On the other hand, for application, database, and streaming media servers, you'll want to give the programs the server is running the most resources.

To check these settings, follow these steps:

1. Start the System utility from the Control Panel.

2. Click the Advanced tab in the System utility, and then display the Performance Options dialog box by clicking Settings on the Performance panel. Click the Advanced tab.

3. The Processor Scheduling panel controls allocation of CPU time. To give more CPU time to the operating system and background services, select Background Services. Otherwise, select Programs.

4. The Memory Usage panel controls allocation of memory. To give more memory to the operating system and background services, select System Cache. Otherwise, select Programs. Click OK.

Setting Data Throughput

Data throughput settings control how well a server responds to user requests, file handles, and client connections. You can optimize data throughput settings in one of four ways:

Minimize Memory Used   Optimizes the server to serve a small number of users. This means very little system memory is reserved for user requests, file handles, and client connections. This allows the server to reserve memory for other purposes but doesn't necessarily reduce the size of the system cache or reserved memory. (You'll experience poor responsiveness and performance if there are a lot of user requests, file handles, and client connections.)

Balance   Optimizes the server for mixed usage environments where the server has multiple roles that include file and printer sharing as well as other tasks. This results in average responsiveness to requests, file handles, and client connections.

Maximize Data Throughput For File Sharing   Optimizes the server to handle file and print services. This means the server will dedicate as many resources as possible to handling user requests, file handles, and client connections, which improves responsiveness and can also improve performance for user, file, and client actions.

Maximize Data Throughput For Network Applications   Optimizes the server memory for distributed applications that manage their own memory cache, such as SQL Server and IIS. This reduces the size of the system cache and allows more memory to be allocated to applications.

To configure data throughput, complete the following steps:

1. Access Network Connections in Control Panel

2. Right-click Local Area Connection, and then select Properties. This displays the Properties dialog box. Servers with multiple network interface cards will have multiple network connections shown in Network Connections. You should optimize each of these connections appropriately.

3. Select File And Printer Sharing For Microsoft Networks, and then click Properties.

4. In the Server Optimization tab, select the setting. Click OK.

5. You'll need to reboot the server for these changes to take effect.

Checking Memory, Caching, and Virtual Memory Usage

Now that you've optimized the system, you can determine how the system is using memory and check for problems. Table 3-1 provides an overview of counters that you'll want to track to uncover memory, caching, and virtual memory (paging) bottlenecks. The table is organized by issue category.

Table 3-1   Uncovering Memory-Related Bottlenecks

Issue	Counters to Track	Details
Physical and virtual memory usage	Memory\Available Kbytes Memory\Committed Bytes	Memory\Available Kbytes is the amount of physical memory available to processes running on the server. Memory\Committed Bytes is the amount of committed virtual memory. If the server has very little available memory, you might need to add memory to the system. In general, you want the available memory to be no less than 5 percent of the total physical memory on the server. If the server has a high ratio of committed bytes to total physical memory on the system, you might need to add memory as well. In general, you want the committed bytes value to be no more than 75 percent of the total physical memory.
Memory page faults	Memory\PageFaults /sec Memory\Pages Input/sec Memory\PageReads /sec	A page fault occurs when a process requests a page in memory and the system can't find it at the requested location. If the requested page is elsewhere in memory, the fault is called a *soft page fault*. If the requested page must be retrieved from disk, the fault is called a *hard page fault*. Most processors can handle large numbers of soft faults. Hard faults, however, can cause significant delays. Page Faults/sec is the overall rate at which the processor handles all types of page faults. Pages Input/sec is the total number of pages read from disk to resolve hard page faults. Page Reads/sec is the total disk reads needed to resolve hard page faults. Pages Input/sec will be greater than or equal to Page Reads/sec and can give you a good idea of your hard page fault rate. If there are a high number of hard page faults, you may need to increase the amount of memory or reduce the cache size on the server.

Table 3-1   Uncovering Memory-Related Bottlenecks

Issue	Counters to Track	Details
Memorypaging	Memory\PoolPaged Bytes, Memory \PoolNonpaged Bytes	These counters track the number of bytes in the page and nonpaged pool. The paged pool is an area of system memory for objects that can be written to disk when they aren't used. The nonpaged pool is an area of system memory for objects that can't be written to disk. If the size of the page pool is large relative to the total amount of physical memory on the system, you might need to add memory to the system. If the size of the nonpaged pool is large relative to the total amount of virtual memory allocated to the server, you might want to increase the virtual memory size.

Monitoring and Tuning Processor Usage

The CPU does the actual processing of information on your server. As you examine a server's performance, you should focus on the CPU after memory bottlenecks have been eliminated. If the server's processors are the performance bottleneck, adding memory, drives, or network connections won't overcome the problem. Instead, you might need to upgrade the processors to faster clock speeds or add processors to increase the server's upper capacity. You could also move processor-intensive applications, such as SQL Server, to another server.

Before you make a decision to upgrade CPUs or add CPUs, you should rule out problems with memory and caching. If signs still point to a processor problem, you should monitor the performance counters discussed in Table 3-2. Be sure to monitor these counters for each CPU installed on the server.

Table 3-2   Uncovering Processor-Related Bottlenecks

Issue	Counters to Track	Details
Threadqueuing	System\Processor Queue Length	This counter displays the number of threads waiting to be executed. These threads are queued in an area shared by all processors on the system. If this counter has a sustained value of two or more threads, you'll need to upgrade or add processors.
CPU usage	Processor \%Processor Time	This counter displays the percentage of time the selected CPU is executing a nonidle thread. You should track this counter separately for all processor instances on the server. If the % Processor Time values are high while the network interface and disk I/O throughput rates are relatively low, you'll need to upgrade or add processors.

Monitoring and Tuning Disk I/O

With today's high-speed disks, the disk throughput rate is rarely the cause of a bottleneck. That said, however, accessing memory is much faster than accessing disks. So, if the server has to do a lot of disk reads and writes, the server's overall performance can be degraded. To reduce the amount of disk I/O, you want the server to manage memory very efficiently and page to disk only when necessary. You can monitor and tune memory usage as discussed in the section entitled "Monitoring and Tuning Memory Usage," earlier in this chapter.

Beyond the memory tuning discussion, you can monitor some counters to gauge disk I/O activity. Specifically, you should monitor the counters discussed in Table 3-3.

Table 3-3   Uncovering Drive-Related Bottlenecks

Issue	Counters to Track	Details
Overall drive performance	PhysicalDisk\% Disk Time in conjunction with Processor\% Processor Time and Network Interface Connection\Bytes Total/sec	If the % Disk Time value is high and the processor and network connection values aren't high, the system's hard disk drives might be creating a bottleneck. Be sure to monitor % Disk Time for all hard disk drives on the server.
Disk I/O	PhysicalDisk\Disk Writes/ sec, Physical Disk\Disk Reads/sec, Physical Disk\Avg. DiskWrite Queue Length, Physical Disk\Avg. DiskRead Queue Length, Physical Disk\CurrentDisk Queue Length	The number of writes and reads per second tell you how much disk I/O activity there is. The write and read queue lengths tell you how many write or read requests are waiting to be processed. In general, you want there to be very few waiting requests. Keep in mind that the request delays are proportional to the length of the queues minus the number of drives in a redundant array of independent disks (RAID) set.

Monitoring and Tuning Network Bandwidth and Connectivity

No other factor counts for more in the way a user perceives your server's performance than the network that connects your server to the user's computer. The delay, or latency, between when a request is made and the time it's received can make all the difference. If there's a high degree of latency, it doesn't matter if you have the fastest server on the planet. The user experiences a delay and perceives that your servers are slow.

Generally speaking, the latency the user experiences is beyond your control. It's a function of the type of connection the user has and the route the request takes to your server. The total capacity of your server to handle requests and the amount of bandwidth available to your servers are factors under your control, however. Network bandwidth availability is a function of your organization's network infrastructure. Network capacity is a function of the network cards and interfaces configured on the servers.

The capacity of your network card can be a limiting factor in some instances. Most servers use 10/100 network cards, which can be configured in many ways. Someone might have configured a card for 10 Mbps, or the card might be configured for half duplex instead of full duplex. If you suspect a capacity problem with a network card, you should always check the configuration.

To determine the throughput and current activity on a server's network cards, you can check the following counters:

- Network\Bytes Received/sec
- Network\Bytes Sent/sec
- Network\Bytes Total/sec
- Network Current Bandwidth

If the total bytes per second value is more than 50 percent of the total capacity under average load conditions, your server might have problems under peak load conditions. You might want to ensure that operations that take a lot of network bandwidth, such as network backups, are performed on a separate interface card. Keep in mind that you should compare these values in conjunction with PhysicalDisk\% Disk Time and Processor\% Processor Time. If the disk time and processor time values are low but the network values are very high, there might be a capacity problem. Solve the problem by optimizing the network card settings or by adding a network card. Remember, planning is everything—it isn't always as simple as inserting a card and plugging it into the network.

Chapter 4
Automating Administrative Tasks, Policies, and Procedures

Performing routine tasks day after day, running around policing systems, and walking users through the basics aren't efficient uses of your time. You'd be much more effective if you could automate these chores and focus on more important issues. Well, increasing productivity and allowing you to focus less on mundane matters and more on important ones is what automation is all about.

Microsoft Windows Server 2003 provides many resources that help you automate administrative tasks, policies, and procedures. This chapter concentrates on four areas:

- Group policy management
- User and computer script management
- Security templates
- Scheduling tasks

Group Policy Management

Group policies simplify administration by giving administrators central control over privileges, permissions, and capabilities of both users and computers. Through group policies you can:

- Create centrally managed directories for special folders, such as My Documents. This is covered in the section of this chapter entitled "Centrally Managing Special Folders."

- Control access to Windows components, system resources, network resources, Control Panel utilities, the desktop, and the Start menu. This is covered in the section of this chapter entitled "Using Administrative Templates to Set Policies."

- Define user and computer scripts to run at specified times. This is covered in the section of this chapter entitled "User and Computer Script Management."

- Configure policies for account lockout and passwords, auditing, user rights assignment, and security. This is covered in Chapters 6 to 10.

The sections that follow explain how you can work with group policies. The focus is on understanding and applying group policies.

Understanding Group Policies

You can think of a group policy as a set of rules that helps you manage users and computers. You can apply group policies to multiple domains, to individual domains, to subgroups within a domain, or to individual systems. Policies that apply to individual systems are referred to as *local group policies* and are stored on the local system only. Other group policies are linked as objects in the Active Directory directory service.

To understand group policies, you need to know a bit about the structure of Active Directory. In Active Directory, logical groupings of domains are called *sites* and subgroups within a domain are called *organizational units* (OUs). Thus, your network could have sites called NewYorkMain, CaliforniaMain, and WashingtonMain. Within the WashingtonMain site, you could have domains called SeattleEast, SeattleWest, SeattleNorth, and SeattleSouth. Within the SeattleEast domain, you could have organizational units called Information Services (IS), Engineering, and Sales.

Group policies apply only to systems running Windows 2000, Windows XP Professional, and Windows Server 2003. You set policies for Windows NT 4.0 systems with the System Policy Editor (Poledit.exe). For Windows 95 and Windows 98, you need to use the System Policy Editor provided with Windows 95 or Windows 98, respectively, and then copy the policy file to the Sysvol share on a domain controller.

Group Policy settings are stored in a Group Policy Object (GPO). One way to think of a GPO is as a container for the policies you apply and their settings. You can apply multiple GPOs to a single site, domain, or organizational unit. Because policy is described using objects, many object-oriented concepts apply. If you know a bit about object-oriented programming, you might expect the concepts of parent-child relationships and inheritance to apply to GPOs—and you'd be right.

Through inheritance, a policy applied to a parent container is inherited by a child container. Essentially, this means that a policy setting applied to a parent object is passed down to a child object. For example, if you apply a policy setting in a domain, the setting is inherited by organizational units within the domain. In this case, the

GPO for the domain is the parent object and the GPOs for the organizational units are the child objects.

The order of inheritance is as follows:

Site –> Domain –> Organizational Unit

This means that the group policy settings for a site are passed down to the domains within that site and the settings for a domain are passed down to the organizational units within that domain.

As you might expect, you can override inheritance. To do this, you specifically assign a policy setting for a child container that contradicts the policy setting for the parent. As long as overriding of the policy is allowed (that is, overriding isn't blocked), the child's policy setting will be applied appropriately. To learn more about overriding and blocking GPOs, see the section entitled "Blocking, Overriding, and Disabling Policies," later in this chapter.

In What Order Are Multiple Policies Applied?

When multiple policies are in place, policies are applied in the following order:

1. Windows NT 4.0 policies (Ntconfig.pol)

2. Local group policies

3. Site group policies

4. Domain group policies

5. Organizational unit group policies

6. Child organizational unit group policies

If there are conflicts among the policy settings, the policy settings applied later have precedence and overwrite previously set policy settings. For example, organizational unit policies have precedence over domain group policies. As you might expect, there are exceptions to the precedence rule. These exceptions are discussed in the section entitled "Blocking, Overriding, and Disabling Policies," later in this chapter.

When Are Group Policies Applied?

As you'll discover when you start working with group policies, policy settings are divided into two broad categories:

■ Those that apply to computers

■ Those that apply to users

Although computer policies are normally applied during system startup, user policies are normally applied during logon. The exact sequence of events is often important in troubleshooting system behavior. The events that take place during startup and logon are as follows:

1. The network starts and then Windows Server 2003 applies computer policies. By default, the computer policies are applied one at a time in the previously specified order. No user interface is displayed while computer policies are being processed.

2. Windows Server 2003 runs startup scripts. By default, startup scripts are executed one at a time, with each completing or timing out before the next one starts. Script execution isn't displayed to the user unless specified.

3. A user presses Ctrl+Alt+Del to log on. After the user is validated, Windows Server 2003 loads the user profile.

4. Windows Server 2003 applies user policies. By default, the policies are applied one at a time in the previously specified order. The user interface is displayed while user policies are being processed.

5. Windows Server 2003 runs logon scripts. Group policy logon scripts are executed simultaneously by default. Script execution isn't displayed to the user unless specified. Scripts in the Netlogon share are run last in a normal command-shell window as in Windows NT 4.0.

6. Windows Server 2003 displays the start shell interface configured in Group Policy.

By default, Group Policy is refreshed only when a user logs off or a computer is restarted. You can change this behavior by setting a Group Policy refresh interval, as discussed in the section of this chapter entitled "Refreshing Group Policy." To do this, open a command prompt and type **gpupdate**.

> **Real World**   Some user settings, such as Folder Redirection, can't be updated when a user is logged on. The user must log off and then log back on for these settings to be applied. You can type **gpupdate /logoff** at the command line to log the user off automatically after the refresh. Similarly, some computer settings can be updated only at startup. The computer must be restarted for these settings to be applied. You can enter **gpupdate /boot** at the command line to restart the computer after the refresh.

Group Policy Requirements and Version Compatibility

Group policies were introduced with Windows 2000 and apply only to systems running Windows 2000, Windows XP Professional, and Windows Server 2003. As you might expect, each new version of the Windows operating system has brought with it changes to Group Policy. Sometimes these changes have made older policies obsolete on newer versions of Windows. In this case, the policy works only on a specific version of the Windows operating system, such as only on Windows 2000.

Generally speaking, however, most policies are forward-compatible. This means that policies introduced in Windows 2000 can, in most cases, be used on Windows 2000, Windows XP Professional, and Windows Server 2003. It also means that Windows XP Professional policies usually aren't applicable to Windows 2000 and that policies introduced in Windows Server 2003 aren't applicable to Windows 2000 or Windows XP Professional.

If a policy isn't applicable to a particular version of the Windows operating system, you can't enforce the policy on computers running those versions of the Windows operating system.

How will you know if a policy is supported on a particular version of Windows? Easy. The properties dialog box for each policy has a Supported On field in the Setting tab. This text-only field lists the policy's compatibility with various versions of the Windows operating system. If you select the policy with the Extended display in the Group Policy Object Editor (GPOE), you'll also see a Requirements entry that lists compatibility.

You can also install new policies when you add a service pack, install Windows applications, or add Windows components. This means that you'll see a wide range of compatibility entries.

Managing Local Group Policies

Each computer running Windows Server 2003 has one local group policy. The quickest way to access local policy on a local computer is to type the following command at a command prompt:

```
gpedit.msc /gpcomputer: "%computername%"
```

This command starts the Group Policy Editor in a Microsoft Management Console (MMC) with its target set to the local computer. Here, *%ComputerName%* is an environment variable that sets the name of the local computer and must be enclosed in double quotation marks as shown. To access local policy on a remote computer, type the following command at a command prompt:

```
gpedit.msc /gpcomputer: "RemoteComputer"
```

where *RemoteComputer* is the host name or fully qualified domain name (FQDN) of the remote computer. Again, the double quotation marks are required as shown in the following example:

```
gpedit.msc /gpcomputer: "corpsvr82"
```

You can also manage local policies on a computer by completing the following steps:

1. Open the Run dialog box by clicking Start and then choosing Run.

2. Type **mmc** in the Open field and then click OK. This opens the MMC.

3. In MMC, choose File, and then choose Add/Remove Snap-In. This opens the Add/ Remove Snap-In dialog box.

4. In the Standalone tab, click Add.

5. In the Add Standalone Snap-In dialog box, select Group Policy Object Editor, and then click Add. This starts the Select Group Policy Object Wizard.

6. Under Group Policy Object, Local Computer should be selected by default. If you want to edit the local policy on your computer, simply click Finish. To find the local policy on another computer, click Browse. After you find the policy you want to work with, click OK and then click Finish.

7. Click Close and then click OK. You can now manage the local policy on the selected computer. For details, see the section entitled "Working with Group Policies," later in this chapter.

Local group policies are stored in the %SystemRoot%\System32\GroupPolicy folder on each Windows Server 2003 computer. In this folder you'll find the following subfolders:

Adm   Stores administrative template files currently being used. These files end with the .adm file extension. The Adm folder is only on domain controllers.

Machine   Stores computer scripts in the Script folder and registry-based policy information for HKEY_LOCAL_MACHINE (HKLM) in the Registry.pol file.

User   Stores user scripts in the Script folder and registry-based policy information for HKEY_CURRENT_USER (HKCU) in the Registry.pol file.

> **Caution**   You shouldn't edit these folders and files directly. Instead, you should use the appropriate features of one of the Group Policy management tools. By default, these files and folders are hidden. If you want to view hidden files and folders in Windows Explorer, select Folder Options from the Tools menu, click the View tab, choose Show Hidden Files And Folders, clear Hide Protected Operating System Files, and then click OK.

Managing Site, Domain, and Organizational Unit Policies

Each site, domain, and organizational unit can have one or more group policies. Group policies listed higher in the group policy list have a higher precedence than policies listed lower in the list. As stated earlier, group policies set at this level are associated with Active Directory. This ensures that site policies are applied appropriately throughout the related domains and organizational units.

Understanding Group Policy Management and the Default Policies

When you want to work with Active Directory-based group policy, you'll find there are two available tools:

Group Policy Object Editor (GPOE)   A standard editor for working with and managing Group Policy that's included with a standard installation of Windows Server 2003.

Group Policy Management Console (GPMC)   An extended management interface for Group Policy that's available as a free download from the Microsoft Download Center (*http://www.microsoft.com/downloads*).

Note   In this book, I focus primarily on GPOE because it's the standard management tool. If you want to use GPMC, you install it on the machines from which you will manage your organization's policy settings and then use it as the primary management tool on those machines. Keep in mind that if you were to log on locally to a server or to another computer on which GPMC hasn't been installed, you will see GPOE instead of GPMC.

Regardless of whether you are working with the GPOE or the GPMC, you'll find that each domain in your organization has two default GPOs:

Default Domain Controllers Policy GPO   A default GPO created for and linked to the Domain Controllers organizational unit. This GPO is applicable to all domain controllers in a domain (as long as they aren't moved from this organizational unit) and is used to manage security settings for domain controllers in a domain.

Default Domain Policy GPO   A default GPO created for and linked to the domain itself within Active Directory. This GPO is used to establish baselines for a wide variety of policy settings that apply to all users and computers in a domain.

The default GPOs are essential to the proper operation and processing of Group Policy. By default, the Default Domain Controllers Policy GPO has the highest precedence among GPOs linked to the Domain Controllers organizational unit, and the Default Domain Policy GPO has the highest precedence among GPOs linked to the domain.

Although the Default Domain Policy GPO includes a complete policy set, it isn't meant for general management of Group Policy. As a best practice, you should edit the Default Domain Policy GPO (or the highest precedence GPO linked to the domain) only to manage the default Account Policies settings and, in particular, three specific areas of Account Policies: Password Policy, Account Lockout Policy, and Kerberos Policy. You should manage four other specific policies using the highest precedence GPO linked to the domain level as well. These policies (located in Group Policy under Computer Configuration\Windows Settings\Security Settings\Local Policies\Security Options) are Accounts: Rename Administrator Account, Accounts: Rename Guest Account, Network Security: Force Logoff When Logon Hours Expire, and Network Access: Allow Anonymous SID/Name Translation.

To manage other areas of policy, you should create a new GPO and link it to the domain or an appropriate organizational unit within the domain. Why? You can configure some policy settings only at the domain level. Although configuring them in the Default Domain Policy GPO might seem to make the most sense, it's better to create a separate GPO for these customized settings. Also, if group policy becomes corrupted and stops working, you can use the DCGPOFIX command-line tool to restore the

Default Domain Policy GPO to its original state without having to worry about losing every customized setting you've applied to the GPO (only those that must be set at the domain level would be lost).

Real World   Typically, the Default Domain Policy GPO is the highest precedence GPO linked to the domain level. The link precedence order can be changed, and in this case, the previous discussion about account policies applies to the highest precedence GPO linked to the domain level.

Creating and Editing Site, Domain, and Organizational Unit Policies

You create and edit site, domain, and organizational unit policies by completing the following steps:

1. For sites, you start the Group Policy snap-in from the Active Directory Sites And Services console. Open the Active Directory Sites And Services console.

2. For domains and organizational units, you start the Group Policy snap-in from the Active Directory Users And Computers console. Open the Active Directory Users And Computers console.

3. In the appropriate console root, right-click the site, domain, or organizational unit on which you want to create or manage a group policy. Then select Properties on the shortcut menu. This opens a Properties dialog box. Keep the following in mind:

   ❑ If you right-click the domain node in Active Directory Users And Computers, you'll have access to the Default Domain Policy GPO.

   ❑ If you right-click the Domain Controllers organizational unit in Active Directory Users And Computers, you'll have access to the Default Domain Controllers Policy GPO.

   ❑ In the Properties dialog box, click the Group Policy tab. As Figure 4-1 shows, existing policies are listed in the Group Policy Object Links list.

4. To create a new policy, click New. You can now configure the policy as explained in the section entitled "Working with Group Policies," later in this chapter.

5. To edit an existing policy, select the policy and then click Edit. You can now edit the policy as explained in the section entitled "Working with Group Policies."

6. To change the priority of a policy, select the policy that you want to work with and then use the Up or Down button to change its position in the Group Policy Object Links list.

Site, domain, and organizational unit group policies are stored in the %SystemRoot% \Sysvol\Domain\Policies folder on domain controllers. In this folder, you'll find one subfolder for each policy you've defined on the domain controller. The policy folder names are the policy's Global Unique Identifier (GUID). The GUIDs can be found on the policy's Properties page in the General tab in the summary frame. Within these individual policy folders you'll find the following subfolders:

Adm   Stores administrative template files currently being used. These files end with the .adm file extension. The Adm folder is only on domain controllers.

Machine   Stores computer scripts in the Script folder and registry-based policy information for HKEY_LOCAL_MACHINE (HKLM) in the Registry.pol file.

User   Stores user scripts in the Script folder and registry-based policy information for HKEY_CURRENT_USER (HKCU) in the Registry.pol file.

> **Caution**   You shouldn't edit these folders and files directly. Instead, you should use the appropriate features of one of the Group Policy management tools.

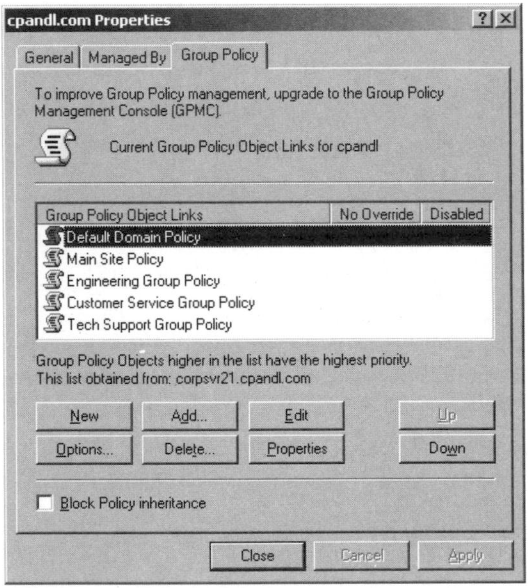

Figure 4-1   Use the Group Policy tab to create and edit policies.

Blocking, Overriding, and Disabling Policies

You can block policy inheritance at the site, domain, and OU level. This means that you could block policies that would otherwise be applied. At the site and domain level, you can also enforce policies that would otherwise be contradicted or blocked. This gives top-level administrators the ability to enforce policies and prevent them from being blocked. Another available option is to disable policies. You can disable a policy partially or entirely without deleting its definition.

You configure these policy options by completing the following steps:

1. Access the Group Policy tab for the site, domain, or OU you want to work with, as specified in Steps 1–4 of the section entitled "Creating and Editing Site, Domain, and Organizational Unit Policies," earlier in this chapter.

2. Select Block Policy Inheritance to prevent the inheritance of higher-level policies (unless those policies have the No Override option set).

3. Use the No Override option to prevent lower-level policies from blocking the policy settings. Select or clear the No Override option by double-clicking in the appropriate column to the right of the group policy entry. A check mark indicates that the option is selected.

4. Use the Disabled option to prevent the policy from being used. Select or clear the Disabled option by double-clicking in the appropriate column to the right of the group policy entry. A check mark indicates that the option is selected.

Disabling an Unused Part of Group Policy

Another way to disable a policy is to disable an unused part of the GPO. When you do this, you block the Computer Configuration or User Configuration settings, or both, and don't allow them to be applied. By disabling part of a policy that isn't used, the application of GPOs and security will be faster.

You can enable or disable configuration settings in Group Policy by following these steps:

1. Access the Group Policy tab for the site, domain, or organizational unit you want to work with as specified in Steps 1–4 in the section entitled "Creating and Editing Site, Domain, and Organizational Unit Policies," earlier in this chapter.

2. Click Properties in the Global Policy tab, and then select or clear Disable Computer Configuration Settings and Disable User Configuration Settings.

> **Caution**   Any settings of the blocked node aren't applied and are essentially lost. To get these settings back, you'll have to clear the Disable ... Settings options.

Applying an Existing Policy to a New Location

Any group policy that you've created can be associated with another computer, organizational unit, domain, or site. By associating the policy with another object, you can use the policy settings without having to recreate them.

You apply an existing policy to a new location by completing the following steps:

1. Access the Group Policy tab for the site, domain, or organizational unit with which you want to work.

2. In the Group Policy tab, click Add. As shown in Figure 4-2, this opens the Add A Group Policy Object Link dialog box.

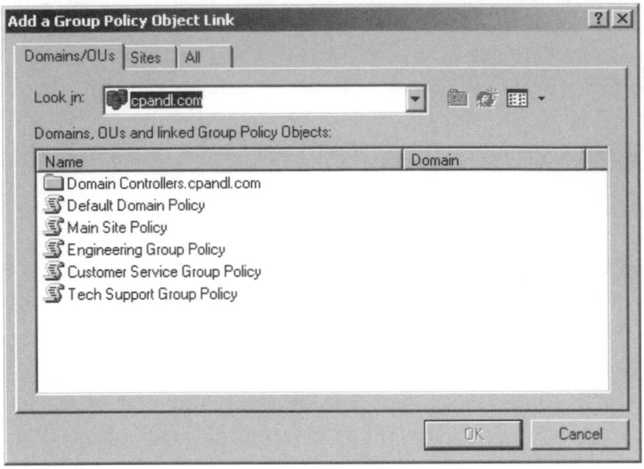

Figure 4-2   Use the Add A Group Policy Object Link dialog box to link existing policies to new locations without having to recreate the policy definition.

3. Use the tabs and fields provided to find the group policy you want to apply to the current location. When you find the policy, click OK.

4. Active Directory creates a link between the GPO and the site, domain, or organizational unit container you're working with. Now, when you edit the policy in any location, you edit the master copy of the object and the changes are reflected globally.

Deleting a Group Policy

You can disable or delete group policies that you don't use. To disable a policy, double-click in the Disabled column to the right of the group policy entry. A check mark indicates that the option is selected. To delete a policy, follow these steps:

1. Access the Group Policy tab for the site, domain, or organizational unit you want to work with, as specified in Steps 1–4 in the section entitled "Creating and Editing Site, Domain, and Organizational Unit Policies," earlier in this chapter.

2. Select the policy you want to delete and then click Delete.

3. If the policy is linked, you have the option of deleting the link without affecting other containers that use the policy. To do this, in the Delete dialog box, select the Remove The Link From The List check box.

4. If the policy is linked, you can also delete the link and the related policy object, which permanently deletes the policy. To do this, select the Remove The Link And Delete The Group Policy Object Permanently check box.

Refreshing Group Policy

When you make changes to a group policy, those changes are immediate. However, they aren't propagated automatically. Client computers request policy when:

- The computer starts
- A user logs on
- An application or user requests a refresh
- A refresh interval is set for group policy and the interval has elapsed

As you learned previously in this chapter, you can request that a policy be refreshed on a local computer using the Gpupdate command-line utility. Simply type **gpupdate** at the command prompt. You can also refresh a policy by setting a specific refresh interval, which thereby periodically forces a refresh. Either way, however, the refresh is only a background refresh and some policies might not be updated. The only way to ensure that all user policies are updated is to have the user log off. The only way to ensure that all computer policies are updated is to restart the computer.

To set a refresh interval in a group policy, follow these steps:

1. Access the GPO for the site, domain, or organizational unit you want to work with, as specified in the section entitled "Creating and Editing Site, Domain, and Organizational Unit Policies," earlier in this chapter.

2. Access the Group Policy node by expanding Computer Configuration \Administrative Templates\System and then selecting Group Policy.

3. In the details pane, double-click Group Policy Refresh Interval For Computers. This policy controls the background refresh rate for computer policies.

4. In the Setting tab, select Enabled. You can now set the refresh interval for computer policies using the options provided. With the default settings, group policy is updated every 90 minutes with a random offset of 0 to 30 minutes. The offset makes it less likely that multiple computers will request updates at the same time. Click OK.

5. Access User Configuration\Administrative Templates\System\Group Policy.

6. In the details pane, double-click Group Policy Refresh Interval For Users. This policy controls the background refresh rate for computer policies.

7. In the Setting tab, select Enabled. You can now set the refresh interval for user policies using the options provided. Click OK when finished.

8. When applying a refresh, network traffic is generated. During the update, the local computer might be less responsive than normal, which might affect the user's work.

Note   The refresh interval for computers doesn't apply to domain controllers. If you want domain controllers to regularly refresh a policy, access Computer

Configuration\Administrative Templates\System\Group Policy and then double-click Group Policy Refresh Interval For Domain Controllers. You can now set the refresh interval.

Real World   You want to ensure that updates don't occur too frequently yet are timely enough to meet expectations or requirements. The more often a policy is refreshed, the more traffic that's generated over the network. In a large installation, you typically want to set a longer refresh rate than the default to reduce network traffic, particularly if the policy affects hundreds of users or computers. In any installation where users complain about their computers periodically getting sluggish, you might want to increase the policy refresh interval as well. Consider that a once a day or once a week update might be all that it takes to keep policies current enough to meet your organization's needs.

Working with Group Policies

After you've selected a policy for editing or created a new policy, you use the GPOE to work with group policies. Techniques for working with this console are examined in this section.

Getting to Know the Group Policy Object Editor

As Figure 4-3 shows, the GPOE has two main nodes:

Computer Configuration   Allows you to set policies that should be applied to computers, regardless of who logs on

User Configuration   Allows you to set policies that should be applied to users, regardless of which computer to which they log on

The exact configuration of Computer Configuration and User Configuration depends on the add-ons installed and which type of policy you're creating. Still, you'll usually find that both Computer Configuration and User Configuration have subnodes for:

Software Settings   Sets policies for software settings and software installation. When you install software, subnodes might be added to Software Settings.

Windows Settings   Sets policies for folder redirection, scripts, and security.

Administrative Templates   Sets policies for the operating system, Windows components, and programs. Administrative templates are configured through template files. You can add or remove template files whenever you need to.

Note   A complete discussion of all the available options is beyond the scope of this book. The sections that follow focus on using folder redirection and administrative templates. Scripts are discussed in the section of this chapter entitled "User and Computer Script Management." Security is covered in Chapters 6 to 10.

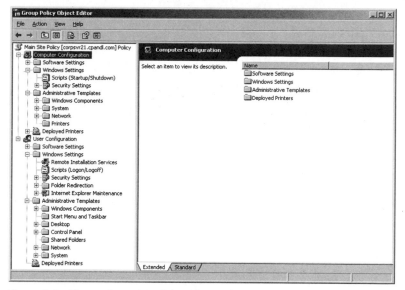

Figure 4-3   The configuration of the Group Policy Object Editor depends on the type of policy you're creating and the add-ons installed.

Centrally Managing Special Folders

You can centrally manage special folders used by Windows Server 2003 through folder redirection. You do this by redirecting special folders to a central network location instead of using multiple default locations on each computer. The special folders you can centrally manage are:

- Application Data
- Desktop
- Start Menu
- My Documents
- My Pictures

You have two options for redirection. You can redirect a special folder to the same network location for all users or you can designate locations based on user membership in security groups. In either case, you should make sure that the network location you plan to use is available as a network share. See Chapter 14, "Data Sharing, Security, and Auditing," for details on sharing data on the network.

Redirecting a Special Folder to a Single Location

You redirect a special folder to a single location by completing the following steps:

1. Access the GPO for the site, domain, or organizational unit you want to work with as specified in the section entitled "Creating and Editing Site, Domain, and Organizational Unit Policies," earlier in this chapter.

2. In the User Configuration node, you'll find Windows Settings. Expand this entry by double-clicking it, and then select Folder Redirection.

3. Right-click the special folder with which you want to work, such as Application Data, and then select Properties on the shortcut menu. This opens a properties dialog box similar to the one shown in Figure 4-4.

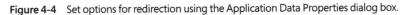

```
┌─────────────────────────────────────────────────────────┐
│ Application Data Properties                        ? X   │
├─────────────────────────────────────────────────────────┤
│  ┌ Target │ Settings ┐                                   │
│                                                          │
│   ┌──┐   You can specify the location of the Application │
│   │  │   Data folder.                                    │
│   └──┘                                                   │
│  Setting:  │Basic - Redirect everyone's folder to the  ▼│
│            the same location                             │
│  This folder will be redirected to the specified         │
│  location.                                               │
│                                                          │
│  ┌─ Target folder location ───────────────────────────┐  │
│  │ │Create a folder for each user under the root path ▼│ │
│  │                                                     │  │
│  │ Root Path:                                          │  │
│  │ │\\CORPSERVER03\UserData                          │ │  │
│  │                                                     │  │
│  │                                        Browse...    │  │
│  │                                                     │  │
│  │ For user Clair, this folder will be redirected to:  │  │
│  │ \\CORPSERVER03\UserData\Clair\Application Data      │  │
│  └─────────────────────────────────────────────────────┘│
│                                                          │
│               ┌──────┐   ┌────────┐   ┌────────┐         │
│               │  OK  │   │ Cancel │   │ Apply  │         │
│               └──────┘   └────────┘   └────────┘         │
└─────────────────────────────────────────────────────────┘
```

Figure 4-4   Set options for redirection using the Application Data Properties dialog box.

4. Because you're redirecting the folder to a single location, use the Setting selection list in the Target tab to choose Basic—Redirect Everyone's Folder To The Same Location.

5. Under Target Folder Location, you have several options. The exact options available depend on the folder you're working with and include the following:

   Redirect To The User's Home Directory   If you use this option, the folder is redirected to a subdirectory within the user's home directory. You set the location of the user's home directory with the %HomeDrive% and %HomePath% environment variables.

Create A Folder For Each User Under The Root Path   If you use this option, a folder is created for each user at the location you enter in the Root Path field. The folder name is the user account name as specified by %UserName%. Thus, if you entered the root path value \\Zeta\UserDocuments, the folder for WilliamS would be located at \\Zeta\UserDocuments\WilliamS.

Redirect To The Following Location   If you use this option, the folder is redirected to the exact location you enter in the Root Path field. Here, you typically want to use an environment variable to customize the folder location for each user. For example, you could use the root path value \\Zeta\UserData\%UserName%\docs.

Redirect To The Local Userprofile Location   If you use this option, the folder is redirected to a subdirectory within the user profile directory. You set the location of the user profile with the %UserProfile% variable.

6. Click the Settings tab, and then configure additional options using the following fields:

    Grant The User Exclusive Rights To ...   Gives users full rights to access their data in the special folder

    Move The Contents Of ... To The New Location   Moves the data in the special folders from the individual systems on the network to the central folder(s)

7. Click OK to complete the process.

Redirecting a Special Folder Based on Group Membership

You redirect a special folder based on group membership by completing the following steps:

1. Access the GPO for the site, domain, or organizational unit with which you want to work.

2. In the User Configuration node, you'll find Windows Settings. Expand this entry by double-clicking it, and then select Folder Redirection.

3. Right-click the special folder you want to work with, such as Application Data, and then select Properties on the shortcut menu.

4. In the Target tab, use the Setting selection list to choose Advanced–Specify Locations For Various User Groups. As shown in Figure 4-5, a Security Group Membership panel is added to the properties dialog box.

5. Click Add to display the Specify Group And Location dialog box. Or select an existing group entry and click Edit to modify its settings.

6. In the Security Group Membership field, type the name of the security group for which you want to configure redirection. Or click Browse to find a security group to add.

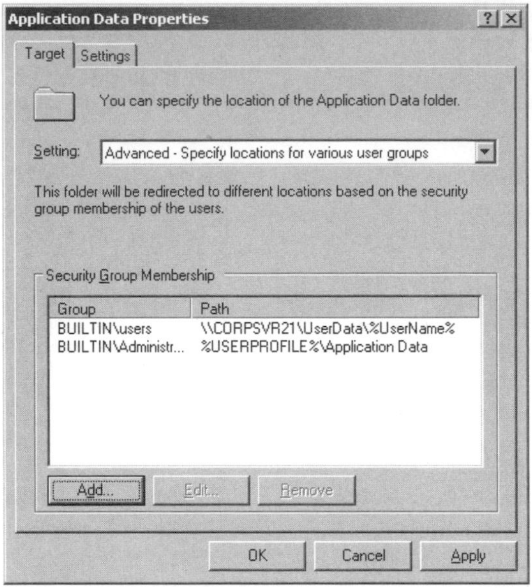

Figure 4-5   Configure advanced redirection using the Security Group Membership panel.

7. As with basic redirection, the options available depend on the folder you're working with and include the following:

Redirect To The User's Home Directory   If you use this option, the folder is redirected to a subdirectory within the user's home directory. You set the location of the user's home directory with the %HomeDrive% and %HomePath% environment variables.

Create A Folder For Each User Under The Root Path   If you use this option, a folder is created for each user at the location you enter in the Root Path field. The folder name is the user account name as specified by %UserName%. Thus, if you entered the root path value \\Zeta\UserDocuments, the folder for WilliamS would be located at \\Zeta\UserDocuments\WilliamS.

Redirect To The Following Location   If you use this option, the folder is redirected to the exact location you enter in the Root Path field. Here, you typically want to use an environment variable to customize the folder location for each user. For example, you could use the root path value \\Zeta \UserData\%UserName%\docs.

Redirect To The Local Userprofile Location   If you use this option, the folder is redirected to a subdirectory within the user profile directory. You set the location of the user profile with the %UserProfile% variable.

8. Click OK. Then repeat Steps 5–7 for other groups that you want to configure.

9. When you're done creating group entries, click the Settings tab and then configure additional options using the following fields:

Grant The User Exclusive Rights To ...   Gives users full rights to access their data in the special folder

Move The Contents Of ... To The New Location   Moves the data in the special folders from the individual systems on the network to the central folder(s)

10. Click OK to complete the process.

Removing Redirection

Sometimes you might want to remove redirection from a particular special folder. You remove redirection by completing the following steps:

1. Access the Folder Redirection subnode in the GPOE.

2. Right-click the special folder you want to work with, and then select Properties on the shortcut menu.

3. Click the Settings tab, and then make sure that an appropriate Policy Removal option is selected. Two options are available:

Leave The Folder In The New Location When Policy Is Removed   When you select this option, the folder and its contents remain at the redirected location and current users are still permitted to access the folder and its contents at this location.

Redirect The Folder Back To The Local Userprofile Location When Policy Is Removed   When you select this option, the folder and its contents are copied back to the original location. The contents aren't deleted from the previous location, however.

4. If you changed the Policy Removal option, click Apply. Then click the Target tab. Otherwise, just click the Target tab.

5. To remove all redirection definitions for the special folder, use the Setting selection list to choose Not Configured.

6. To remove redirection for a particular security group, select the security group in the Security Group Membership panel and then click Remove. Click OK.

Using Administrative Templates to Set Policies

Administrative templates provide easy access to registry-based policy settings that you might want to configure.

Viewing Administrative Templates and Policies

As Figure 4-6 shows, a default set of administrative templates is configured for users and computers in the GPOE. You can add or remove administrative templates as well. Any changes you make to policies available through the administrative templates are saved in the registry. Computer configurations are saved in HKEY_LOCAL_MACHINE (HKLM), and user configurations are saved in HKEY_CURRENT_USER (HKCU).

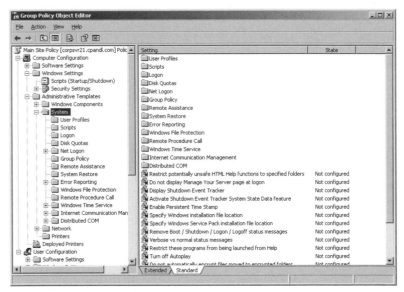

Figure 4-6 You set policies through administrative templates.

You can view the currently configured templates in the Administrative Templates node of the GPOE. This node contains policies that can be configured for local systems, organizational units, domains, and sites. Different sets of templates are found under Computer Configuration and User Configuration. You can manually add templates containing new policies in the GPOE when you install new Windows components.

You set the user interface for the Administrative Templates node in .adm files. These files are formatted as ASCII text, and you can edit them using a standard text editor. When you set policies through the Administrative Templates node, the policy settings are saved in Registry.pol files. Separate Registry.pol files are used for HKEY_LOCAL_MACHINE (HKLM) and HKEY_CURRENT_USER (HKCU).

The best way to get to know what administrative template policies are available is to browse the Administrative Templates nodes in the GPOE. As you browse the templates, you'll find that policies are in one of three states:

Not Configured   The policy isn't used and no settings for it are saved in the registry.

Enabled   The policy is actively being enforced and its settings are saved in the registry.

Disabled   The policy is turned off and isn't enforced unless overridden. This setting is saved in the registry.

Enabling, Disabling, and Configuring Policies

You can enable, disable, and configure policies by completing the following steps:

1. Access the GPO for the site, domain, or organizational unit with which you want to work.

2. Access the Administrative Templates folder in the Computer Configuration or User Configuration node, whichever is appropriate for the type of policy you want to set.

3. In the left pane, select the subfolder containing the policies with which you want to work. The related policies are then displayed in the right pane.

4. Double-click or right-click a policy and choose Properties to display its related Properties dialog box.

5. Click the Explain tab to see a description of the policy. The description is available only if one is defined in the related .adm file.

6. To set the policy's state, click the Setting tab and then use the following option buttons to change the policy's state:

   Not Configured   The policy isn't configured.

   Enabled   The policy is enabled.

   Disabled   The policy is disabled.

   > **Note**   Computer policies have precedence in Windows Server 2003. So, if there's a conflict between a computer policy setting and a user policy setting, the computer policy is the one that is enforced.

7. If you enabled the policy, set any additional parameters specified in the Setting tab, and then click Apply.

8. Use the Previous Policy and Next Policy buttons to manage other policies in the current folder. Then configure them in the same way.

9. Click OK when you're finished managing policies.

Adding or Removing Templates

You can add or remove template folders in the GPOE. To do this, complete the following steps:

1. Access the GPO for the site, domain, or organizational unit with which you want to work.

2. Right-click the Administrative Templates folder in the Computer Configuration or User Configuration node, whichever is appropriate for the type of template you want to add or remove. This displays the Add/Remove Templates dialog box shown in Figure 4-7.

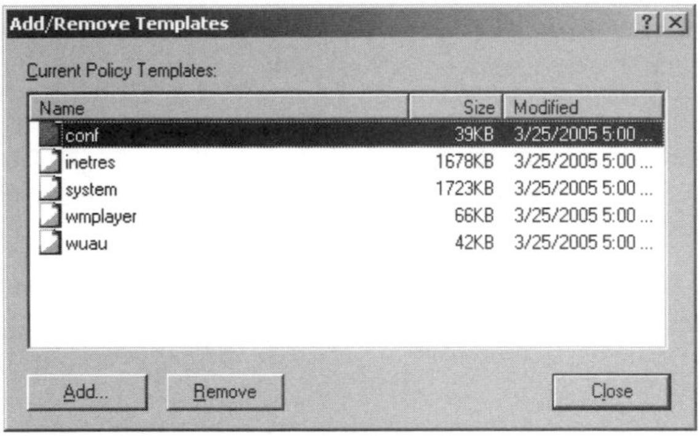

Figure 4-7   You can use the Add/Remove Templates dialog box to add more templates or remove existing ones.

3. To add new templates, click Add. Then, in the Policy Templates dialog box, click the template you want to add and click Open.

4. To remove an existing template, select the template to remove, and then click Remove.

5. When you're finished adding and removing templates, click Close.

User and Computer Script Management

With Windows Server 2003, you can configure four types of scripts:

Computer Startup   Executed during startup

Computer Shutdown   Executed prior to shutdown

User Logon   Executed when a user logs on

User Logoff   Executed when a user logs off

You can write scripts as command-shell batch scripts ending with the .bat or .cmd extension or as scripts that use the Windows Script Host (WSH). WSH is a feature of Windows Server 2003 that lets you use scripts written in a scripting language, such as VBScript, without the need to insert the script into a Web page. To provide a multipurpose scripting environment, WSH relies on scripting engines. A scripting engine is the component that defines the core syntax and structure of a particular scripting language. Windows Server 2003 ships with scripting engines for VBScript and JScript. Other scripting engines are also available.

Assigning Computer Startup and Shutdown Scripts

Computer startup and shutdown scripts are assigned as part of a group policy. In this way, all computers that are members of the site, domain, or organizational unit, or all three, execute scripts automatically when they're booted or shut down.

Note   You can also assign computer startup scripts as scheduled tasks. You schedule tasks using the Scheduled Task Wizard. See the section entitled "Scheduling Tasks," later in this chapter, for details.

To assign a computer startup or shutdown script, follow these steps:

1. For easy management, copy the scripts you want to use to the Machine \Scripts\Startup or Machine\Scripts\Shutdown folder for the related policy. Policies are stored in the %SystemRoot%\Sysvol\Domain\Policies folder on domain controllers.

2. Access the GPO for the site, domain, or organizational unit with which you want to work.

3. In the Computer Configuration node, double-click the Windows Settings folder. Then click Scripts.

4. To work with startup scripts, right-click Startup and then select Properties. Or right-click Shutdown and then select Properties to work with shutdown scripts. This opens a dialog box similar to the one shown in Figure 4-8.

5. Click Show Files. If you copied the computer script to the correct location in the policies folder, you should see the script.

6. Click Add to assign a script. This opens the Add A Script dialog box. In the Script Name field, type the name of the script you copied to the Machine\Scripts\Startup or the Machine\Scripts\Shutdown folder for the related policy. In the Script Parameters field, enter any command-line arguments to pass to the command-line script or parameters to pass to the scripting host for a WSH script. Repeat this step to add other scripts.

7. During startup or shutdown, scripts are executed in the order in which they're listed in the properties dialog box. Use the Up or Down button to reposition scripts as necessary.

8. If you want to edit the script name or parameters later, select the script in the Script For list and then click Edit.

9. To delete a script, select the script in the Script For list, and then click Remove.

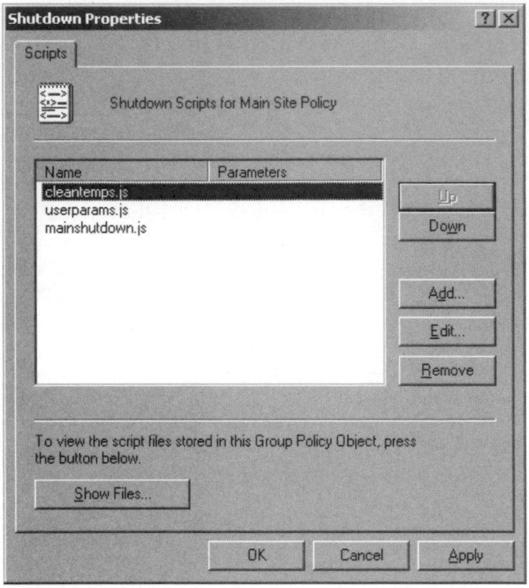

Figure 4-8   Add, edit, and remove computer scripts using the Shutdown Properties dialog box.

Assigning User Logon and Logoff Scripts

You can assign user scripts in one of three ways:

- You can assign logon and logoff scripts as part of a group policy. In this way, all users who are members of the site, domain, or organizational unit, or all three, execute scripts automatically when they log on or log off.

- You can also assign logon scripts individually through the Active Directory Users And Computers console. In this way, you can assign each user or group a separate logon script. For details, see the section entitled "Configuring the User's Environment Settings" in Chapter 10, "Managing Existing User and Group Accounts."

- You can also assign individual logon scripts as scheduled tasks. You schedule tasks using the Scheduled Task Wizard. See the section entitled "Scheduling Tasks," later in this chapter, for details.

To assign a group policy user script, complete the following steps:

1. For easy management, copy the scripts you want to use to the User\Scripts \Logon or the User\Scripts\Logoff folder for the related policy. Policies are stored in the %SystemRoot%\Sysvol\Domain\Policies folder on domain controllers.

2. Access the GPO for the site, domain, or organizational unit with which you want to work.

3. Double-click the Windows Settings folder in the User Configuration node. Then click Scripts.

4. To work with logon scripts, right-click Logon and then select Properties. Or right-click Logoff and then select Properties to work with logoff scripts. This opens a dialog box similar to the one shown in Figure 4-9.

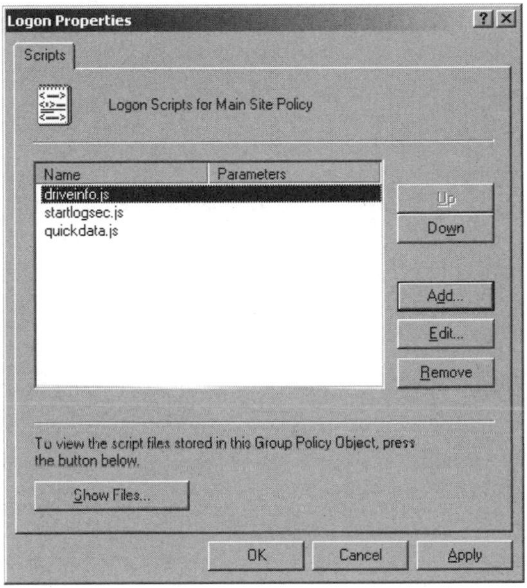

Figure 4-9   Add, edit, and remove user scripts using the Logon Properties dialog box.

5. Click Show Files. If you copied the user script to the correct location in the policies folder, you should see the script.

6. Click Add to assign a script. This opens the Add A Script dialog box. In the Script Name field, type the name of the script you copied to the User\Scripts\Logon or the User\Scripts\Logoff folder for the related policy. In the Script Parameter field, enter any command-line arguments to pass to the command-line script or parameters to pass to the scripting host for a WSH script. Repeat this step to add other scripts.

7. During logon or logoff, scripts are executed in the order in which they're listed in the Properties dialog box. Use the Up or Down button to reposition scripts as necessary.

8. If you want to edit the script name or parameters later, select the script in the Script For list and then click Edit.

9. To delete a script, select the script in the Script For list, and then click Remove.

Applying Security Policy Through Templates

Sound security practices and settings are essential to successful systems administration. One way to set security policy is to use security templates.

Understanding Security Policies and Administration Tools

Security templates provide a centralized way of managing security-related settings for workstations and servers. You use security templates to apply customized sets of group policy definitions that are security-related. These policy definitions generally affect:

Account policies   Settings control security for passwords, account lockout, and Kerberos.

Local policies   Settings control security for auditing, user rights assignment, and other security options.

Event log policies   Settings control security for event logging.

Restricted groups policies   Settings control security for local group membership administration.

System services policies   Settings control security and startup mode for local services.

File system policies   Settings control security for the local file system.

Registry policies   Settings control the values of security-related registry keys.

Security templates are available in all Windows Server 2003 installations and can be imported into any group policy. Templates are stored in the %SystemRoot%\Security \Templates directory and you can access them using the Security Templates snap-in, shown in Figure 4-10.

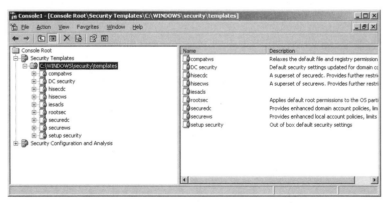

Figure 4-10   Use the Security Templates snap-in to view and create security templates.

You can also use the snap-in to create new templates. The standard templates distributed with Windows Server 2003 include:

DC security   Contains the default security settings for domain controllers

setup security   Contains the default security settings for member servers

securedc   Contains moderate security settings for domain controllers

securews   Contains moderate security settings for workstations

hisecdc   Contains very stringent security settings for domain controllers

hisecws   Contains very stringent security settings for workstations

> **Tip**   After you select the template that you want to use, you should go through each setting that the template will apply and evaluate how the setting will affect your environment. If a setting doesn't make sense, you should modify or delete it as appropriate.

You don't use the Security Templates snap-in to apply templates. You apply templates using the Security Configuration And Analysis snap-in. You can also use Security Configuration And Analysis to compare the settings in a template to the existing settings on a computer. The results of the analysis will highlight areas where the current settings don't match those in the template. This is useful to determine if security settings have changed over time.

You can access the security snap-ins by completing the following steps:

1. Open the Run dialog box by clicking Start and then selecting Run.

2. Type **mmc** in the Open field and then click OK. This opens the MMC.

3. In MMC, click File, and then click Add/Remove Snap-In. This opens the Add/Remove Snap-In dialog box.

4. In the Standalone tab, click Add.

5. In the Add Standalone Snap-In dialog box, click Security Templates, and then click Add.

6. Click Security Configuration And Analysis, and then click Add.

7. Close the Add Standalone Snap-In dialog box by clicking Close, and then click OK.

Applying Security Templates

As stated previously, you use the Security Templates snap-in to view existing templates or to create new templates. Once you've created a template or determined that you want to use an existing template, you can then configure and analyze the template by completing the following steps:

1. Access the Security Configuration And Analysis snap-in.

2. Right-click the Security Configuration And Analysis node and then select Open Database. This displays the Open Database dialog box.

3. Type a new database name in the File Name field and then click Open.

4. The Import Template dialog box is displayed. Select the security template that you want to use, and then click Open.

5. Right-click the Security Configuration And Analysis node, and then choose Analyze Computer Now. When prompted to set the error log path, type a new path or click OK to use the default path.

6. Wait for the snap-in to complete the analysis of the template. Afterward, review the findings and update the template as necessary. You can view the error log by right-clicking the Security Configuration And Analysis node and choosing View Log file.

7. When you're ready to apply the template, right-click the Security Configuration And Analysis node and choose Configure Computer Now. When prompted to set the error log path, click OK. The default path should be fine.

8. View the configuration error log by right-clicking the Security Configuration And Analysis node and choosing View Log File. Note any problems and take action as necessary.

Scheduling Tasks

When you manage systems, you'll often want to perform tasks such as updates or maintenance during nonbusiness hours. This way, you don't affect productivity and workflow. But who wants to come in at 3:00 on a Monday morning? Fortunately, using the Task Scheduler service, you can schedule one-time or recurring tasks to run automatically at any hour of the day or night.

You automate tasks by running command-shell scripts, WSH scripts, or applications that execute the necessary commands for you. For example, if you wanted to back up the system drive every weekday at midnight, you could create a script that runs backups for you and records progress and success/failure results in a log file.

Utilities for Scheduling Tasks

In Windows Server 2003, you can schedule tasks on local and remote systems using the Scheduled Task Wizard, the command-line AT utility, or the command-line SCHTASK utility. Each utility has its advantages and disadvantages.

Scheduled Task Wizard provides a point-and-click interface to task assignment. This makes it easy to configure tasks quickly without having to worry about syntax issues. The disadvantage is that you don't have a central location that you can use to check for scheduled tasks throughout the enterprise and you have to access the wizard separately on each individual system that you want to configure.

The command-line AT scheduler, on the other hand, doesn't have a friendly point-and-click interface. This means you'll have to learn the necessary command syntax and type in commands. The advantage to AT is that you can designate a single server as a task scheduler and you can view and set tasks throughout the enterprise on this single server.

SCHTASKS is a command-line utility that is just as versatile as the Scheduled Task Wizard. You can use the utility to configure tasks to run on a specific schedule, set run permissions, and configure startup, log on, and idle processor commands. Like AT, SCHTASKS allows you to schedule tasks to run anywhere on the network. More important, you can use SCHTASKS to view status information for any scheduled tasks that are configured on a system, including those created using AT, SCHTASKS itself, and the Scheduled Task Wizard.

The following sections discuss how to use the Scheduled Task Wizard. A complete discussion of AT and SCHTASKS is beyond the scope of this book. However, if you want to use SCHTASKS to examine scheduled tasks configured on any system on the network, simply type the following command at a command prompt:

schtasks /query /s SystemName

where *SystemName* is the name of the system that you want to examine, such as

schtasks /query /s corpserver01

Preparing to Schedule Tasks

The Windows Server 2003 service that controls task scheduling is the Task Scheduler service. Task Scheduler logs on as the LocalSystem account by default. This account usually doesn't have adequate permissions to perform administrative tasks. Because of this, when you use the AT scheduler, you should configure Task Scheduler to use a specific user account that has adequate user privileges and access rights to run the tasks you want to schedule.

You should also make sure that the Task Scheduler service is configured to start automatically on all the systems on which you want to schedule tasks. Set the Task Scheduler startup and logon account as specified in the sections entitled "Configuring Service Startup" and "Configuring Service Logon" in Chapter 3, "Monitoring Processes, Services, and Events."

A script should configure whatever user settings are necessary. This ensures that everything the script does is under its control and that domain user settings, such as drive mappings, are available as needed.

Scheduling Tasks with the Scheduled Task Wizard

You can use the Scheduled Task Wizard to schedule tasks on the local or remote system to which you're currently connected. You access the Scheduled Task Wizard and currently scheduled tasks through the Scheduled Tasks folder.

Accessing the Scheduled Tasks Folder

You can access the Scheduled Tasks folder on a local system with either of the following techniques:

- Start Control Panel and then click Scheduled Tasks.

- Start Windows Explorer, click My Computer, then Control Panel, and then Scheduled Tasks.

You can access the Scheduled Tasks folder on a remote system by completing the following steps:

1. Start Windows Explorer, and then use the My Network Places node to navigate to the computer with which you want to work.

2. Select the computer's icon and then double-click Scheduled Tasks.

3. To create scheduled tasks on remote computers, right-click in the details pane to display a shortcut menu. Point to New and then select Scheduled Task. You then configure the scheduled task using a properties dialog box rather than the Scheduled Task Wizard.

Viewing and Managing Existing Tasks

Entries in the Scheduled Tasks folder show currently scheduled tasks. You can work with entries in the Scheduled Tasks folder using any of the following techniques:

- Double-click Add Scheduled Task to start the Scheduled Task Wizard. This option is not available on a remote system. However, you could create the task locally using the wizard and then copy the scheduled task to the Scheduled Tasks folder on the remote system.

- Double-click an existing task entry to view or change its properties. You can set advanced options through the Settings tab.

- Select a task entry and click the Delete button on the toolbar to delete the task.

Creating Tasks with the Scheduled Task Wizard

To schedule a task with the Scheduled Task Wizard, follow these steps:

1. Start the Scheduled Task Wizard by double-clicking Add Scheduled Task in the Scheduled Tasks folder. Read the Welcome dialog box and then click Next.

2. Using the page shown in Figure 4-11, select a program to schedule. The page shows key applications registered on the system, such as Disk Cleanup and

Synchronize. The page doesn't show available scripts, however. If the program or script you want to use isn't listed, click Browse to open the Select Program To Schedule dialog box. In the dialog box, select the program or script you want to run and then click Next.

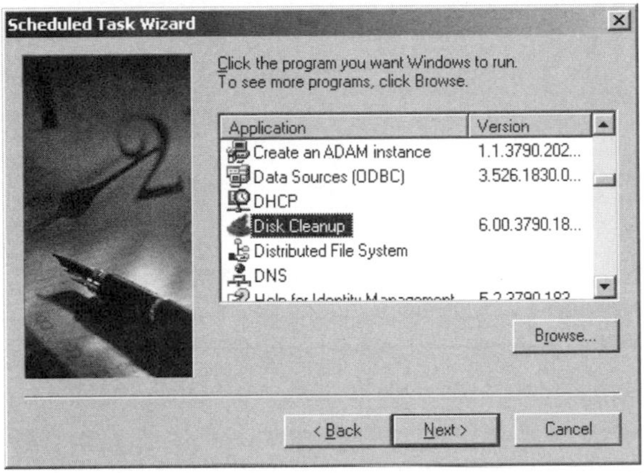

Figure 4-11   Use the Scheduled Task Wizard to select a program to run. Click Browse to find scripts and other applications.

3. Type a name for the task. The name should be short but descriptive so you can quickly determine what the task does.

4. Select a run schedule for the task. Tasks can be scheduled to run periodically (daily, weekly, or monthly), or when a specific event occurs, such as when the computer starts or when the task's user logs on.

5. Click Next and then select a date and time to run the scheduled task. The next dialog box you see depends on when the task is scheduled to run.

6. After you've configured a start date and time, click Next to continue. Then type a user name and password that can be used when running the scheduled task This user name must have appropriate permissions and privileges to run the scheduled task.

7. The final wizard page provides a summary of the task you're scheduling. Click Finish to complete the scheduling process. If an error occurs when you create the task, you'll see an error prompt. Click OK. The task should still be created. Afterward, in the Scheduled Tasks folder, double-click the task to correct the problem in the related Properties dialog box.

Chapter 5
Working with Support Services and Remote Desktop

Many major enhancements to Microsoft Windows Server 2003 have to do with support services and remote desktop connectivity through terminal services. This chapter focuses on the key enhancements, including automatic updates, error reporting, help and support, remote desktop, and time services.

Introducing Support Services

Windows Server 2003 features built-in support services at several levels. If you access the Services node in Computer Management, you'll find a bundle of services dedicated to system support, including:

Automatic Updates   Responsible for performing automatic updates to the Windows Server 2003 operating system. Although this service typically is enabled, the Automatic Updates tab of the System properties dialog box controls how the service works. On servers, the default setting in the System utility is for manual updates only.

Error Reporting Service   Provides automated error collection, tracking, and reporting. When an application or component error occurs and the service is running, automated error information is generated and can be reported to Microsoft. Error reporting is discussed in the section entitled "Enabling and Disabling Error Reporting" in Chapter 2, "Managing Servers Running Microsoft Windows Server 2003."

Help And Support   Provides the application framework for automatic system monitoring. This is the heart of the help and support facility built into Windows Server 2003.

Terminal Services   Enables users to remotely connect to the computer and handles the display of the desktop and application to those remote users. This one service provides the necessary background framework for Remote Desktop, Remote Assistance, Fast User Switching, and Terminal Server.

> **Caution**   Don't disable Terminal Services to prevent remote access. Instead, clear the Allow Remote Assistance and Allow Remote Desktop check boxes in the Remote tab of the System Properties dialog box.

Volume Shadow Copy   Creates and manages volume shadow copies for backups and redundancy. A shadow copy is a point-in-time copy of files on a network share. Although this feature is disabled by default, you can use the Disk Management tool to configure shadow copies and allow for file recovery from accidental deletion or overwriting and for version checking. See Chapter 14, "Data Sharing, Security, and Auditing," for details.

Windows Time   Synchronizes the system time with world time to ensure that the system time is accurate. You can configure computers to synchronize with a specific time server.

These support services provide the foundation for many of the enhanced features in Windows Server 2003. If they aren't running or aren't correctly configured, you might have problems using certain support features and, in some cases, Windows Server 2003 might not operate properly.

Many other services provide support features. However, you need these additional support services only in specific scenarios and they usually aren't configured to start automatically. For example, on all versions of Windows Server 2003 (except Windows Server 2003, Web Edition) the application framework services are disabled or set to manual startup. If you're using a different version of Windows Server 2003 to provide application services that take advantage of the Windows Server 2003 framework, you might need to reconfigure these services.

Working with the Automated Help System

The automated help system built into Windows Server 2003 is fairly complex. The system is designed to automatically monitor system health, to perform preventative maintenance, and to report problems so they can be resolved. The help system has three key components:

- A Help and Support Center with integrated help facilities
- An application framework
- A monitor that gathers and logs state information

Using the Help and Support Center

The Help and Support Center is where you go to find system documentation and support services. You can start the Help and Support Center by clicking Start and then choosing Help And Support.

As you can see from Figure 5-1, the Help and Support Center is very different from the Help facilities built into previous versions of Windows. The Help And Support Center home page features links to online help documentation, support services, and important issues. The Help and Support Center is designed so that it seamlessly integrates locally stored content as well as content made available through remote sites. Overall, the documentation is much more task-focused and solution-focused than previous versions.

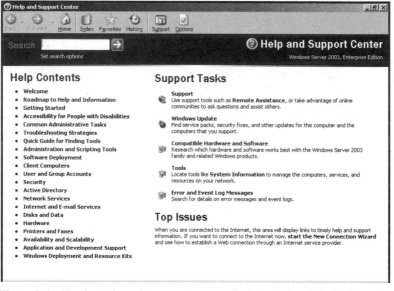

Figure 5-1   Use the Help and Support Center to find detailed technical information and to get support when you need it.

In the Support Tasks area of the Help And Support Center home page, you'll find a link labeled Support. Click this link or the Support button on the toolbar to access the integrated support utilities, including:

Get Remote Assistance   Allows users to get live help from a technician. By clicking the link and sending a remote control invitation through e-mail, a user can get immediate help.

Get Help From Microsoft   Provides a list of online resources that you can use to contact Microsoft's Technical Support staff, to access support communities, and to get follow-up information, such as the status of a previously submitted support request.

Visit The Windows Server Community   Allows users to access a help forum on the Web where they might be able to find answers to their questions.

The Get Remote Assistance and Get Help From Microsoft options use the Remote Assistance feature. Remote assistance is made possible through the Remote Desktop Help Session Manager service. If you're the technician receiving the remote control request, you see a control panel that allows you to view the user's desktop and to send chat messages to the user. You also have the option of taking control of the user's system, sending a file to the user's system, or exiting the session. If you take control of the user's system, you can configure the computer just as if you were sitting at the keyboard, and the user will see these changes as well.

Introducing the Application Framework

The Help And Support Center and the entire Windows Server 2003 help system are built on top of the application framework provided by the Windows service called Help and Support. As a Windows Server 2003 administrator, you don't really need to understand the intricacies of the application framework. You should, however, know where the necessary files are stored so you can check them if you need to.

With this in mind, it's important to note that the Help and Support service runs under the Svchost.exe process with the flags –K NETSVCS. When run in this mode, the Svchost.exe process acts as a listener that monitors the health and well-being of the system on which it's running. The listener also periodically performs checkpoint operations that write system configuration information to subdirectories of the %SystemRoot% directory. These files contain logs and checkpoint data as well as temporary workspace for processing help system transactions.

After a checkpoint has been finalized, it's written to a database file in the %System-Root%\PCHEALT\HELPCTR\Database directory. This file is called Hcdata.edb. The database contains other types of help system information as well.

> **Note**   Throughout this book you'll see references to %SystemRoot%. This is an environment variable used by Windows Server 2003 to designate the base directory for the Windows Server 2003 operating system, such as C:\WINDOWS. For more information on environment variables, see the section entitled "Configuring the User's Environment Settings" in Chapter 10, "Managing Existing User and Group Accounts."

Monitoring System Health

Status, a health monitor, is another key part of the Windows Server 2003 help system. Its goal is to collect system state information that can be used to identify current or potential system problems, such as an abnormal boot or a drive low on free space. The operating system can then process the information and make it available through the Help and Support Center.

To gather system information, Status relies on the Help and Support service. If you examine this service, you'll find that it runs an executable called Svchost.exe, which in turn uses Wmiprvse.exe to gather system information. The information gathered by the Windows Management Instrumentation (WMI) provider service (WMIPRVSE) is obtained and displayed in the Help and Support Center using separate executables. The Help and Support Center runs under the Helpctr.exe executable, which provides the primary interface, and uses Helphost.exe and Helpsvc.exe to provide essential host listener and support services.

Viewing PC Health Statistics

You can view the information gathered by Status by completing the following steps:

1. Click Start and then choose Help And Support.

2. Click the Support button on the toolbar to access the Support area and then click My Computer Information. This link is listed under the See Also heading.

3. In the right pane, click View The Status Of My System Hardware And Software.

4. As shown in Figure 5-2, you'll see a summary of the system state. If there are any current or potential problems, these problems will be identified and, if available, there will be a link to a help document that you can use to resolve the problem.

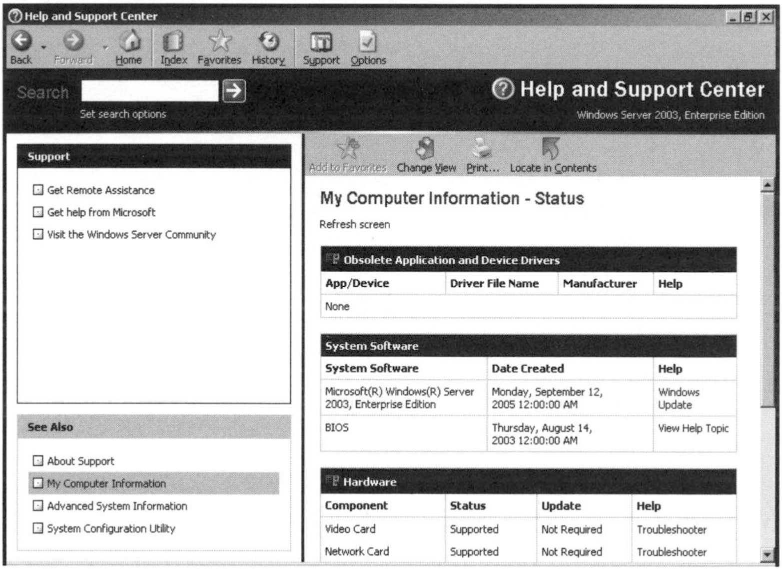

Figure 5-2 Periodically monitor system health to ensure that there aren't current or potential problems on the system.

Note   Interestingly enough, system state information is gathered using the WMI service. WMI provides a set of interfaces that implement object classes for accessing the operating system and its components and representing their state values. One of these object classes is Win32_Computer, which has a property called Bootup-State. The bootup state indicates how the system was started. If the computer was started normally, the bootup state is set to "Normal boot." If the computer was started in Safe Mode, the bootup state is set to "Fail-safe boot." This property value and other property values gathered through WMI are reflected in the Help and Support Center under My Computer Information and Advanced System Information.

Troubleshooting Problems with PC Health Monitoring

The Help and Support service must be running for Status to gather information. If the health statistics aren't accessible or aren't being updated, you should ensure that the service is running and that it's configured properly. You can access Services through Computer Management or through the Services utility.

After you access Services, ensure that the Help and Support service is running. If it isn't, right-click the service and then select Start. The service should be configured to start up automatically. If it isn't, double-click the service, select Automatic as the Startup Type, and then click OK.

Another reason you might be experiencing problems obtaining system health information is if the system drive (the drive containing the Windows operating system) has no available space. The Help and Support service collects system health information and stores it in the data collection directory (%SystemRoot%\Pchealth\Helpctr\Datacoll). System state information collected by Status is stored in files formatted in Extensible Markup Language (XML), a markup language for structuring information. These files must be written properly so that the help subsystem can process them. If the system drive is out of free space, you'll need to free some space so that system health information can be written to the drive.

Understanding and Using Automatic Updates

Automatic Updates help you keep the Windows Server 2003 operating system up to date. It compares the programs, operating system components, and drivers installed on a system to a master list of items available at the Microsoft Web site and determines whether there are updates that should be installed.

An Overview of Automatic Updates

You configure Automatic Updates using the System utility. When you enable Automatic Updates, an update icon appears in the system tray when there are updates to download or install. The background process running the update process is the Automatic Updates service. This service is responsible for periodically checking for compatible updates for a system. When an automatic update is available, you'll see a bubble over the update icon announcing the update's availability.

The updates installed through the Automatic Updates service appear on the Change Or Remove Programs page of the Add Or Remove Programs dialog box when you select the Show Updates check box. You can remove an automatic update the same way that you uninstall any other program. For details, see the section entitled "Removing Automatic Updates to Recover from Problems," later in this chapter.

When you open the System Properties dialog box, you'll find that you can configure Automatic Updates in several ways. You can set the update configuration to any of the following options:

Automatic Updates are automatically downloaded and installed according to a schedule that you specify. When updates have been downloaded, the operating system notifies you so you can review the updates that are scheduled to be installed. You can install the updates then or wait for the scheduled installation time.

Download only The operating system retrieves all updates as they become available and then prompts you when they're ready to be installed. You can then accept or reject the update. Accepted updates are installed. Rejected updates aren't installed but remain on the system, where they can be installed later.

Notify only The operating system notifies you before retrieving any updates. If you elect to download the update, you still have the opportunity to accept or reject it. Accepted updates are installed. Rejected updates aren't installed but remain on the system, where you can install them later.

Manual All automatic download and notification options are disabled and you must manually apply updates by visiting the Windows Update Web site.

Configuring Automatic Updates

If you want to use Automatic Updates on a system, complete the following steps:

1. From the Control Panel, select or double-click System, and then click the Automatic Updates tab of the System Properties dialog box, as shown in Figure 5-3.

2. To disable automatic updates, select Turn Off Automatic Updates. This option turns off Automatic Updates completely, requiring manual installation of updates.

Security To ensure the integrity of critical production systems, you might want to disable automatic updates. Before applying updates to operational servers, you should test the updates on nonproduction (development or test) servers. The test period should usually last one to two weeks, or longer, to ensure that problems don't crop up when you least expect them. After you finish testing the updates, you can manually apply them to your production systems.

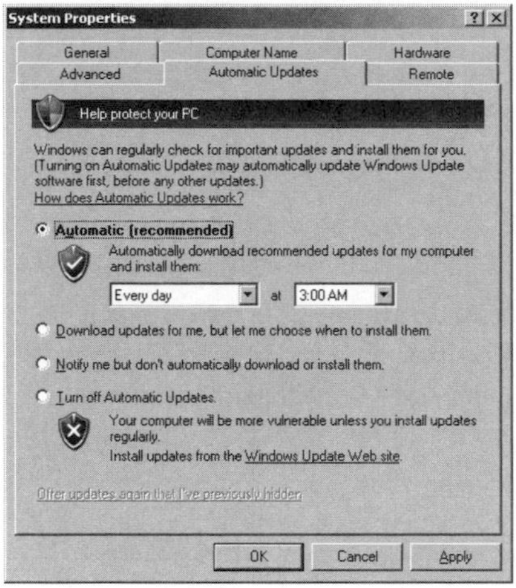

Figure 5-3   Configure Automatic Updates differently for different needs. Choose the option that makes the best sense for your environment.

3. To enable automatic updates, choose one of the following update options:

   Automatic   This option is good when you don't want the installation of updates to interfere with business operations. The update schedule is either Every Day at a specific hour, such as 3:00 a.m., or on a specific day of the week and hour, such as Every Sunday at 5:00 a.m. If you're logged on to the system as an administrator, you'll be notified of pending installations and have the opportunity to postpone the installation. If a restart is required as a result of an update and you're logged on as an administrator, you'll have the opportunity to postpone the restart. Other users don't have this option. Local users and terminal services users will be notified, however, of a pending restart. Other users, such as those accessing an application or file on the system, won't be notified.

   Download Updates For Me, But Let Me Choose When To Install Them   This is the best option to use when you want to be sure updates are downloaded, but it doesn't ensure that updates will be installed.

   Notify Me But Don't Automatically Download Or Install Them   This option allows you to control whether downloads occur at all. Use this option when you need more control over the application of updates.

   Sometimes installing updates might make a system less responsive and might require a system restart. Because of this, you might want to manually install updates or schedule installation of updates for nonbusiness or nonpeak usage hours. In this way, there should be less impact on users and business operations. It won't prevent data loss, however, if active users are working with resources on the system. Click OK.

Another way to configure Automatic Updates is through Group Policy. The most useful policies for Automatic Updates are:

Windows Automatic Updates   Whenever a user connects to the Internet, Windows searches for updates that are available for the computer. If you don't want the operating system to search for updates, enable this policy. Windows will then be prohibited from searching for updates. This policy is located in User Configuration\Administrative Templates\System.

Turn Off Automatic Update Of ADM Files   Group Policy can be modified by the automatic updates process. Typically, this means that new policies are installed and made available the next time you open the Group Policy Object Editor. If you don't want Group Policy to be updated through the automatic updates process, enable this policy. This policy is located in User Configuration\Administrative Templates\System\Group Policy, and its settings are ignored if the policy Always Use Local ADM Files For The Group Policy Object Editor is enabled.

Remove Access To Use All Windows Update Features   Prohibits access to all Windows Update features. If enabled, all Automatic Updates features are removed and can't be configured. This includes the Automatic Updates tab in the System utility, the Windows Update link on the Start Menu and on the Tools menu in Internet Explorer, and driver updates from the Windows Update Web site in the Device Manager. This policy is located in User Configuration\Administrative Templates\Windows Components\Windows Update.

Configure Automatic Updates   Configures automatic updates settings for a domain, site, organizational unit, or local computer through Group Policy. If enabled, you set the options much as you do in the Automatic Updates tab of the System utility. If disabled, automatic updates must be manually installed. This policy is located in Computer Configuration\Administrative Templates\Windows Components\Windows Update.

Specify Intranet Microsoft Update Service Location   Designates an internal Web server rather than the Windows Update Web site as the location from which to check for and download updates. This policy is located in Computer Configuration\Administrative Templates\Windows Components\Windows Update and is discussed in the next section.

Configuring Update Servers

On networks with hundreds or thousands of computers, the Automatic Updates process could use a considerable amount of network bandwidth, and having all the computers check for updates and install them over the Internet won't make sense. Instead, you'll want to consider enabling this policy, which tells individual computers to check a designated internal server for updates.

The designated update server must run Windows Server Update Services (WSUS), be configured as a Web server running Microsoft Internet Information Services (IIS), and be able to handle the additional workload, which might be considerable on a large network during peak usage times. Additionally, the update server must have access to the external network on port 80. The use of a firewall or proxy server on this port shouldn't present any problems.

The update process also tracks configuration and statistics information for each computer. This information is necessary for the update process to work properly and can be stored on a separate statistics server (an internal server running IIS) or on the update server itself.

To specify an internal update server, follow these steps:

1. Configure the necessary server(s) as previously discussed.

2. In Group Policy for the appropriate domain, site, or organizational unit Group Policy Object, access Computer Configuration\Administrative Templates \Windows Components\Windows Update, and then double-click Specify Intranet Microsoft Update Service Location.

3. Select Enabled.

4. Type the Uniform Resource Locator (URL) of the update server in the Set The Intranet Update Service For Detecting Updates text box. In most cases, this is http://*servername*, such as **http://CorpUpdateServer01**. For example, see Figure 5-4.

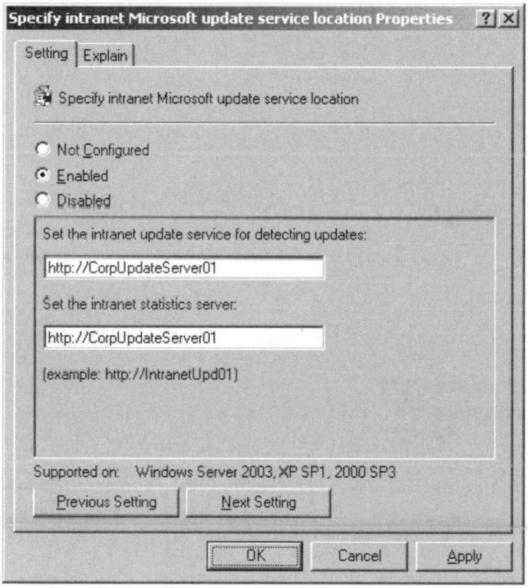

Figure 5-4   Use intranet update servers to centralize the update process and reduce external network traffic.

5. Type the URL of the statistics server in the Set The Intranet Statistics Server text box. This doesn't have to be a separate server; you can specify the update server in this text box.

> **Note**   If you want a single server to handle both updates and statistics, you enter the same URL in both fields. Otherwise, if you want a different server for updates and statistics, you would enter the URL for each server in the appropriate field.

6. Click OK. After the applicable Group Policy Object is refreshed, systems running Windows 2000 Service Pack 3 or later, Windows XP Service Pack 1 or later, and Windows Server 2003 will look to the update server for updates. You'll want to monitor the update and statistics server(s) closely for several days or weeks to ensure that everything is working properly. Directories and files will be created on the update and statistics server(s).

Downloading and Installing Automatic Updates

When Automatic Updates are enabled and an automatic update is available, you'll see a bubble over the update icon announcing the update's availability. Click the Auto-Update icon to open the Updates window. From that window, click Install/Download if you've chosen to autodownload or if you've chosen to be notified before the download. This starts the Automatic Updates process. You can also click Remind Me Later to postpone the update.

If you want to see more information about the update or be able to selectively enable or disable update components, click Details. You then see descriptive information on each update. To disable an update for a specific component, clear the related check box. When you're ready to proceed, click Install.

> **Caution**   Some updates require you to reboot the computer. Rather than bring down a production server, you might want to schedule the install and reboot for a specific date and time.

Removing Automatic Updates to Recover from Problems

If an automatic update caused a problem on a system, don't worry. You can remove the automatic update in the same way that you uninstall any other program. Simply follow these steps:

1. From the Control Panel menu, select Add Or Remove Programs. The Add Or Remove Programs dialog box is displayed with the Change Or Remove Programs option selected.

2. Select the automatic update that you want to remove and then click Change/Remove. Repeat this step to remove other updates as desired.

3. Click Close. If the system needs to be restarted, you'll see a restart prompt.

Managing Remote Access to Servers

Windows Server 2003 has several remote connectivity features. With Remote Assistance, users can send invitations to support technicians, allowing them to service a computer remotely. With Remote Desktop, users can connect remotely to a computer and access its resources. In this section, you learn how to configure Remote Assistance and Remote Desktop. By default, neither of the remote connectivity features is enabled. You must manually enable the remote assistance and remote desktop features.

Configuring Remote Assistance

Remote Assistance is a useful feature for help desks to take advantage of. Not only can administrators allow higher-level support personnel to view the server's desktop, but also administrators can allow the support personnel to take control of the desktop and solve problems. This feature could be used to walk junior administrators through a complex process or even to manage system configuration while another administrator watches the progress of the changes. The key to Remote Assistance is in the access levels that you grant.

By default, Remote Assistance is configured to allow support personnel to view and remotely control desktop computers running Windows XP Professional. Anyone logged on to a Windows Server 2003 system can send assistance invitations to internal and external resources, and this might present a security concern for organizations. To reduce potential security problems, you might want to allow support staff to view but not control desktop computers.

> **Security**   If you're using Remote Assistance on a computer also running Windows Firewall, it's important to point out that no additional configuration is necessary to bypass the firewall. Remote Assistance will temporarily and automatically open firewall ports during an assistance session. Other types of firewalls that might be between the source and destination computers in an assistance session are another matter entirely, and you'll typically need to open TCP Port 135. See the Microsoft Knowledge Base Article 301527 for troubleshooting details (*http://support .microsoft.com/default.aspx?scid=kb;en-us;301527*).

To configure Remote Assistance, follow these steps:

1. From the Control Panel menu, select System and then click the Remote tab.

2. To disable Remote Assistance, clear the Turn On Remote Assistance And Allow Invitations To Be Sent From This Computer check box and then click OK. Skip the remaining steps.

3. To enable Remote Assistance, select the Turn On Remote Assistance And Allow Invitations To Be Sent From This Computer check box. Afterward, click Advanced. This displays the Remote Assistance Settings dialog box shown in Figure 5-5.

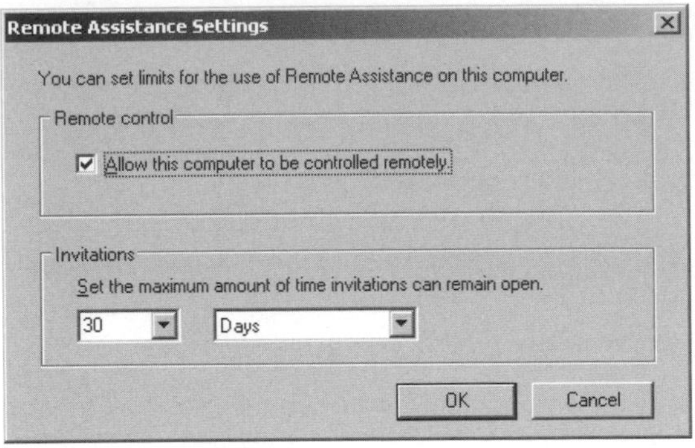

Figure 5-5   Use the Remote Assistance Settings dialog box to set limits for remote assistance.

4. The Allow This Computer To Be Controlled Remotely option sets limits for Remote Assistance. When selected, this setting allows assistants to view and control the computer. To provide view-only access to the computer, clear this check box.

5. The Invitations options control the maximum time window for invitations. You can set a value in minutes, hours, or days, up to a maximum of 30 days. If you set a maximum limit value of 10 days, for example, you can create an invitation with a time limit up to, but not more than, 10 days. The default maximum expiration limit is 30 days.

Real World   Another key aspect of Remote Assistance that you can control is the time limit for invitations. The default maximum time limit is 30 days. Although the intent is to give support personnel a time window in which to respond to requests, it also means that they could use an invitation to access a computer over a period of 30 days. For instance, suppose you send an invitation with a 30-day time limit to a support person who resolves the problem the first day. That person would then still have access to the computer for another 29 days, which wouldn't be desirable for security reasons. To reduce the risk to your systems, you'll usually want to reduce the default maximum time limit considerably—say, to 1 hour. If the problem isn't solved in the allotted time period, you can issue another invitation.

6. Click OK twice when you're finished configuring Remote Assistance options.

Configuring Remote Desktop Access

Unlike Remote Assistance, which provides a view of the current user's desktop, Remote Desktop provides several levels of access:

1. If you're currently logged on to the desktop locally and you then try to log on remotely, the local desktop locks automatically and you can access all the currently running applications as if you were sitting at the keyboard working locally. This feature is useful if you want to work from home or an alternate location.

2. If you're included on the computer's remote access list and not logged on otherwise, you can initiate a new Windows session from a remote location. The Windows session will behave as if you were sitting at the keyboard working locally and can be used when other users are also logged on to the computer. In this way, multiple users could access the same computer simultaneously.

Remote Desktop isn't enabled by default. You must specifically enable it, thereby allowing remote access to the computer. When it's enabled, any members of the Administrators group can connect to the computer by default. You must place other users specifically on a remote access list to permit them to gain access to the computer.

Security   If you're configuring Remote Desktop on a computer also running Windows Firewall, you must specify Remote Desktop as an access exception as discussed in Chapter 14. Other types of firewalls that might be between the source and destination computers in a Remote Desktop session are another matter entirely, and you'll typically need to open TCP Port 3389. See the Microsoft Knowledge Base article 875357 for troubleshooting details (*http://support.microsoft.com/default .aspx?scid=kb;en-us;875357*).

To configure Remote Desktop, follow these steps:

1. Access the System Properties dialog box from Control Panel and then click the Remote tab.

2. To disable Remote Desktop access, clear the Enable Remote Desktop On This Computer check box and then click OK. Skip the remaining steps.

3. To enable remote desktop access, select the Enable Remote Desktop On This Computer check box. Afterward, click Select Remote Users.

4. To grant Remote Desktop access to a user, click Add. This opens the Select Users Or Groups dialog box. In the Select Users Or Groups dialog box, type the name of a user you want to use in the Name text box and then click Check Names. If matches are found, select the account you want to use and then click OK. If no matches are found, update the name you entered and try searching again. Repeat this step as necessary and then click OK when finished.

Tip   By default, the scope of the Select Users Or Groups dialog box is set to Users to prevent novice administrators from accidentally granting remote access to large numbers of users. If you're an experienced administrator and are sure you want to grant all members of an entire group remote access privileges, click Object Types, select Groups, and then click OK. You'll then be able to specify users or groups in the Select Users Or Groups dialog box.

5. To revoke remote access permissions for a user account, select the account and then click Remove.

6. Click OK twice when you're finished.

Making Remote Desktop Connections

As an administrator, you can make Remote Desktop connections to Windows servers and workstations. With Windows 2000 Server, you enable Remote Desktop connections by installing Terminal Services and then configuring Terminal Services in Remote Access mode. With Windows XP, Remote Desktop connections are enabled by default and all administrators are granted access automatically. With Windows Server 2003, Remote Desktop is installed automatically but not enabled until you specifically do so.

One way to make a Remote Desktop connection to a server or workstation is to follow these steps:

1. Choose Start, All Programs, Accessories, Communications, and then Remote Desktop Connection. This displays the Remote Desktop Connection dialog box.

2. In the Computer text box, type the name of the computer to which you want to connect. If you don't know the name of the computer, use the drop-down list provided to choose an available computer or select Browse For More from the drop-down list to display a list of domains and computers in those domains.

3. By default, Windows Server 2003 uses your current user name, domain, and password to log on to the remote computer. If you want to use different account information, click Options and then enter values in the related User Name, Password, and Domain text boxes.

4. Click Connect. Enter your account password if prompted, and then click OK. If the connection is successful, you'll see the Remote Desktop window on the selected computer and you'll be able to work with resources on the computer. In the case of a failed connection, check the information you provided and then try to connect again.

Note   Clicking Options in the Remote Desktop Connection dialog box displays additional options for creating and saving connections. These advanced options allow you to change display size for the remote desktop; manage connections to local resources, such as printers, serial ports, and disk drives; run programs automatically on connection; and enable or disable local caching and data compression.

Although Remote Desktop Connection is easy to use, it isn't the best tool to use if you routinely connect to computers remotely. Instead, you'll want to use the Remote Desktops console, which is available on a computer when you install the Windows Server 2003 administrative tools. With Remote Desktops you can configure connections for multiple systems and afterward you can easily switch between connections.

You'll find Remote Desktops as an option on the Administrative Tools menu. Figure 5-6 shows the console with connections configured for CorpServer01, CorpServer02, CorpServer03, and CorpServer04. These connections were added by right-clicking the Remote Desktops node in the console, selecting Add New Connection, and then entering the server name (or Internet Protocol [IP] address) and the necessary logon information. The requirements are the same as for the Remote Desktop Connection utility.

After you define a connection, you can connect to the server and display the remote desktop simply by clicking the connection entry. If, for some reason, the connection fails, you can force Windows to try to connect again by right-clicking the connection and selecting Connect.

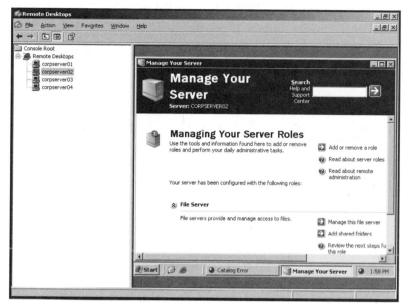

Figure 5-6   If you routinely connect to remote systems, Remote Desktops should be your tool of choice. You can configure persistent connection information and then establish connection simply by clicking on a server.

Configuring Windows Time

System time has had an increasingly important role as the Windows operating system has matured, particularly with regard to Kerberos security, which is the default Windows Server 2003 authentication mechanism. With Kerberos security, the network depends on system clocks being in close synchronization. If the clocks on different systems aren't closely synchronized, authentication tickets can become invalid before they reach a destination host.

Keeping the system in sync with the actual time isn't easy. System clocks can lose time. Users can accidentally set the system clock to the wrong time. Other things can go wrong as well. To help resolve problems with system time and time synchronization, Windows systems can use the Windows Time service to set a consistent network time based on the time at an Internet time server. Time services allow precise synchronization with world time.

Workstations and servers are configured to synchronize with a time server automatically. This time server is referred to as the *authoritative time server*. The way Windows

Time works depends on whether the system is part of a workgroup or a domain. Although you can use the registry to control Windows Time on an individual computer, Group Policy offers the easiest way to manage Windows Time throughout the enterprise. Group Policy settings that control Windows Time are under Computer Configuration\Administrative Templates\System\Windows Time Service\Global Configuration Settings. Global Configuration Settings have precedence over registry settings. If you change Registry values for time services, you can apply them by typing the following command at the command prompt:

```
w32tm /config /update
```

For computers in a workgroup, you can enable Internet time using the Date And Time utility in Control Panel. In Active Directory domains, a domain controller is chosen automatically as the reliable time source for the domain and other computers in the domain synchronize time with this server. Should this server be unavailable to provide time services, another domain controller takes over. You can't, however, change the Windows Time configuration. If you want to manage Windows Time in a different way, you must first enable and configure Internet Time through Group Policy. The related policies are found under Computer Configuration\Administrative Templates\System \Windows Time Service\Time Providers. You can also configure global time service options using Global Configuration Settings under Computer Configuration \Administrative Templates\System\Windows Time Service.

Chapter 6
Using Active Directory

Active Directory directory service is an extensible and scalable directory service that enables you to manage network resources efficiently. As an administrator, you'll need to be very familiar with how Active Directory technology works, and that's exactly what this chapter is about. If you haven't worked with Active Directory technology before, one thing you'll note immediately is that the technology is fairly advanced and has many features. To help manage this complex technology, I'll start with an overview of Active Directory and then explore its components.

Introducing Active Directory

Active Directory is the heart of Microsoft Windows Server 2003. Just about every administrative task you'll perform will affect Active Directory in some way. Active Directory technology is based on standard Internet protocols and has a design that helps you clearly define your network's structure.

Active Directory and DNS

Active Directory uses the Domain Name System (DNS). DNS is a standard Internet service that organizes groups of computers into domains. Unlike Windows NT 4 domains, which have a flat structure, DNS domains are organized into a hierarchical structure. The DNS domain hierarchy is defined on an Internet-wide basis, and the different levels within the hierarchy identify computers, organizational domains, and top-level domains. DNS is also used to map host names, such as zeta.microsoft.com, to numeric Transmission Control Protocol/Internet Protocol (TCP/IP) addresses, such as 192.168.19.2. Through DNS, an Active Directory domain hierarchy can also be defined on an Internet-wide basis or the domain hierarchy can be separate and private.

When you refer to computer resources in this type of domain, you use the fully qualified domain name (FQDN), such as zeta.microsoft.com. Here, *zeta* represents the name of an individual computer, *microsoft* represents the organizational domain, and *com* is the top-level domain (TLD). TLDs are at the base of the DNS hierarchy and are organized geographically, by using two-letter country codes, such as *CA* for Canada; by organization type, such as *com* for commercial organizations; and by function, such as *mil* for U.S. military installations.

Normal domains, such as microsoft.com, are also referred to as *parent domains*. They have this name because they're the parents of an organizational structure. Parent domains can be divided into subdomains, which can be used for different offices, divisions, or geographic locations. For example, the FQDN for a computer at Microsoft's Seattle office could be designated as jacob.seattle.microsoft.com. Here, *jacob* is the computer name, *seattle* is the subdomain, and *microsoft.com* is the parent domain. Another term for a subdomain is a *child domain*.

As you can see, DNS is an integral part of Active Directory technology—so much so, in fact, that you must configure DNS on the network before you can install Active Directory. Working with DNS is covered in Chapter 20, "Optimizing DNS." You can install Active Directory by running the Active Directory Installation Wizard (click Start, click Run, type **dcpromo** in the Open field, and then click OK). If DNS isn't installed already, you will be prompted to install DNS. If there isn't an existing domain, the wizard helps you create a domain and configure Active Directory in a new domain. The wizard can also help you add child domains to existing domain structures.

> **Note**   In the rest of this chapter, I'll often use the terms *directory* and *domains* to refer to Active Directory and Active Directory domains, respectively, except when I need to distinguish Active Directory structures from DNS or Windows NT structures.

Getting Started with Active Directory

Active Directory provides both logical and physical structures for network components. Logical structures are:

Organizational units   A subgroup of domains that often mirrors the organization's business or functional structure

Domains   A group of computers that share a common directory database

Domain trees   One or more domains that share a contiguous namespace

Domain forests   One or more domain trees that share common directory information

Physical structures are:

Subnets   A network group with a specific Internet Protocol (IP) address range and network mask

Sites   One or more subnets; they're used to configure directory access and replication.

Working with Domain Structures

Logical structures help you organize directory objects and manage network accounts and shared resources. Logical structures include domain forests, domain trees, domains, and organizational units. Sites and subnets, on the other hand, are physical structures that help you map the physical network structure. Physical structures serve to facilitate network communication and to set physical boundaries around network resources.

Understanding Domains

An Active Directory domain is simply a group of computers that share a common directory database. Active Directory domain names must be unique. For example, you can't have two microsoft.com domains, but you could have a microsoft.com parent domain with seattle.microsoft.com and ny.microsoft.com child domains. If the domain is part of a private network, the name assigned to a new domain must not conflict with any existing domain name on the private network. If the domain is part of the global Internet, the name assigned to a new domain must not conflict with any existing domain name throughout the Internet. To ensure uniqueness on the Internet, you must register the parent domain name before using it. You can register a domain through any designated registrar. A current list of designated registrars can be found at InterNIC (*http://www.internic.net*).

Each domain has its own security policies and trust relationships with other domains. Domains can also span more than one physical location, which means a domain could consist of multiple sites and those sites could have multiple subnets, as shown in Figure 6-1. Within a domain's directory database, you'll find objects defining accounts for users, groups, and computers as well as shared resources, such as printers and folders.

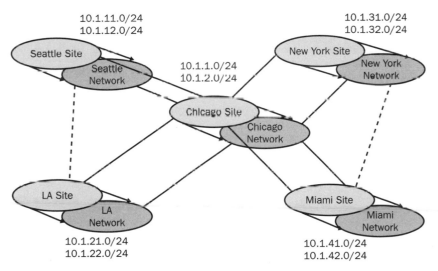

Figure 6-1   Network diagram for a wide area network (WAN) with multiple sites and subnets.

Note   User and group accounts are discussed in Chapter 8, "Understanding User and Group Accounts." Computer accounts and the various types of computers used in Windows Server 2003 domains are discussed in the section entitled "Working with Active Directory Domains," later in this chapter.

Domain functions are limited and controlled by the domain functional level. Four domain functional levels are available:

Windows 2000 mixed   Supports domain controllers running Windows NT 4.0, Windows 2000, and Windows Server 2003

Windows 2000 native   Supports domain controllers running Windows 2000 and Windows Server 2003

Windows Server 2003 interim   Supports domain controllers running Windows NT 4.0 and Windows Server 2003

Windows Server 2003   Supports domain controllers running Windows Server 2003

For a further discussion of domain functional levels, see the section entitled "Using Windows NT and Windows 2000 Domains with Active Directory," later in this chapter.

Understanding Domain Forests and Domain Trees

Each Active Directory domain has a DNS domain name, such as microsoft.com. When one or more domains share the same directory data, they're referred to as a *forest*. The domain names within this forest can be discontiguous or contiguous in the DNS naming hierarchy.

When domains have a contiguous naming structure, they're said to be in the same *domain tree*. An example of a domain tree is shown in Figure 6-2. In this example, the root domain msnbc.com has two child domains—seattle.msnbc.com and ny.msnbc.com. These domains in turn have subdomains. All the domains are part of the same tree because they have the same root domain.

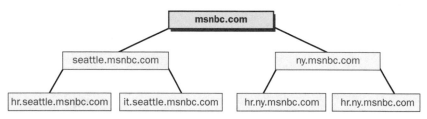

Figure 6-2   Domains in the same tree share a contiguous naming structure.

If the domains in a forest have discontiguous DNS names, they form separate domain trees within the forest. As shown in Figure 6-3, a domain forest can have one or more domain trees. In this example, the msnbc.com and microsoft.com domains form the roots of separate domain trees in the same forest.

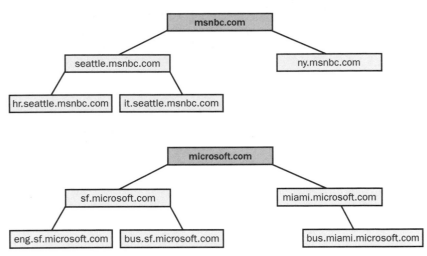

Figure 6-3   Multiple trees in a forest have discontiguous naming structures.

You access domain structures in Active Directory Domains And Trusts, which is shown in Figure 6-4. Active Directory Domains And Trusts is a snap-in for the Microsoft Management Console (MMC), and you can also access it on the Administrative Tools menu. You'll find separate entries for each root domain. In the figure, the active domain is *adatum.com*.

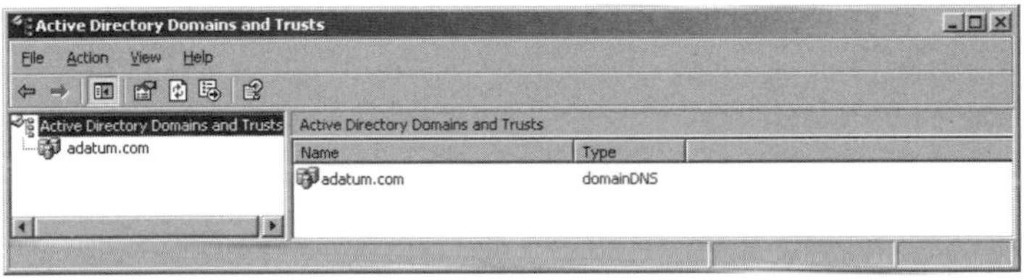

Figure 6-4   Use Active Directory Domains And Trusts to work with domains, domain trees, and domain forests.

Forest functions are limited and controlled by the forest functional level. Three forest functional levels are available:

Windows 2000   Supports domain controllers running Windows NT 4.0, Windows 2000, and Windows Server 2003

Windows Server 2003 interim   Supports domain controllers running Windows NT 4.0 and Windows Server 2003

Windows Server 2003   Supports domain controllers running Windows Server 2003

The Windows Server 2003 forest functional level offers the most current Active Directory features. When all domains within a forest are operating in this mode, you'll get improvements for global catalog replication and improved replication efficiency for Active Directory data, and because link values are replicated, you might see improved intersite replication as well. You'll be able to deactivate schema class objects and attributes, use dynamic auxiliary classes, rename domains, and create one-way, two-way, and transitive forest trusts.

Understanding Organizational Units

Organizational units are subgroups within domains that often mirror an organization's functional or business structure. You can also think of organizational units as logical containers into which you can place accounts, shared resources, and other organizational units. For example, you could create organizational units named HumanResources, IT, Engineering, and Marketing for the microsoft.com domain. You could later expand this scheme to include child units. Child organizational units for Marketing could include OnlineSales, ChannelSales, and PrintSales.

Objects placed in an organizational unit can only come from the parent domain. For example, organizational units associated with seattle.microsoft.com can contain objects for this domain only. You can't add objects from ny.microsoft.com to these containers, but you could create separate organizational units to mirror the business structure of seattle.microsoft.com.

Organizational units are very helpful in organizing the objects around the organization's business or functional structure. Still, this isn't the only reason to use organizational units. Other reasons to use organizational units are as follows:

- Organizational units allow you to assign a group policy to a small set of resources in a domain without applying this policy to the entire domain. This helps you set and manage group policies at the appropriate level in the enterprise.

- Organizational units create smaller, more manageable views of directory objects in a domain. This helps you manage resources more efficiently.

- Organizational units allow you to delegate authority and to easily control administrative access to domain resources. This helps you control the scope of administrator privileges in the domain. You could grant user A administrative authority for one organizational unit and not for others. Meanwhile, you could grant user B administrative authority for all organizational units in the domain.

Organizational units are represented as folders in Active Directory Users And Computers, as shown in Figure 6-5. This utility is a snap-in for the MMC, and you can also access it on the Administrative Tools menu.

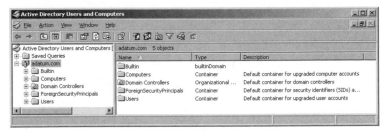

Figure 6-5   Use Active Directory Users And Computers to manage users, groups, computers, and organizational units.

Understanding Sites and Subnets

A site is a group of computers in one or more IP subnets. You use sites to map your network's physical structure. Site mappings are independent from logical domain structures, so there's no necessary relationship between a network's physical structure and its logical domain structure. With Active Directory, you can create multiple sites within a single domain or create a single site that serves multiple domains. There's also no connection between the IP address ranges used by a site and the domain namespace.

You can think of a subnet as a group of network addresses. Unlike sites, which can have multiple IP address ranges, subnets have a specific IP address range and network mask. Subnet names are shown in the form *network/bits-masked*, such as 192.168.19.0/24. Here, the network address 192.168.19.9 and network mask 255.255.255.0 are combined to create the subnet name 192.168.19.0/24.

Note   Don't worry, you don't need to know how to create a subnet name. In most cases, you enter the network address and the network mask and then Windows Server 2003 generates the subnet name for you.

Computers are assigned to sites based on their location in a subnet or a set of subnets. If computers in subnets can communicate efficiently with one another over the network, they're said to be *well connected*. Ideally, sites consist of subnets and computers that are all well connected. If the subnets and computers aren't well connected, you might need to set up multiple sites. Being well connected gives sites several advantages:

- When clients log on to a domain, the authentication process first searches for domain controllers that are in the same site as the client. This means local domain controllers are used first, if possible, which localizes network traffic and can speed up the authentication process.

- Directory information is replicated more frequently within sites than between sites. This reduces the network traffic load caused by replication while ensuring that local domain controllers get up-to-date information quickly. You can also customize how directory information is replicated using site links. For example, you could designate a bridgehead server to handle replication between sites. This places the bulk of the intersite replication burden on a specific server rather than on any available server in a site.

You access sites and subnets through Active Directory Sites And Services, as shown in Figure 6-6. Since this is a snap-in for the MMC, you can add it to any updateable console. You can access Active Directory Sites And Services on the Administrative Tools menu as well.

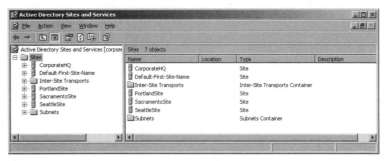

Figure 6-6   Use Active Directory Sites and Services to manage sites and subnets.

Working with Active Directory Domains

Although both Active Directory and DNS must be configured on a Windows Server 2003 network, Active Directory domains and DNS domains have different purposes. Active Directory domains help you manage accounts, resources, and security. DNS domains establish a domain hierarchy that's primarily used for name resolution. Windows Server 2003 uses DNS to map host names, such as zeta.microsoft.com, to numeric TCP/IP addresses, such as 172.16.18.8. To learn more about DNS and DNS domains, see Chapter 20.

Active Directory is designed to work with systems running Windows Server 2003 as well as systems running Windows 95, Windows 98, Windows NT, Windows XP, and Windows 2000. If the necessary client software is installed, Windows 95, Windows 98, Windows XP, and Windows 2000 systems access the network as Active Directory clients. Windows NT systems (and Windows 95 or Windows 98 systems not upgraded with Active Directory client software) access the network as if they were in a Windows NT domain, provided Active Directory's domain functional level allows this and a Windows NT domain is configured.

Using Windows 2000 and Later Computers with Active Directory

Computers running Windows 2000, Windows XP Professional, and Windows Vista can make full use of Active Directory. These computers access the network as Active Directory clients and have full use of Active Directory features. As clients, these systems can use transitive trust relationships that exist within the domain tree or forest. A transitive trust is one that isn't established explicitly. Rather, the trust is established automatically based on the forest structure and permissions set in the forest. These relationships allow authorized users to access resources in any domain in the forest.

Systems running Windows Server 2003 provide services to other systems and can act as domain controllers or member servers. A domain controller is distinguished from a member server because it runs Active Directory. You promote member servers to domain controllers by installing Active Directory. You demote domain controllers to member servers by uninstalling Active Directory. You handle both processes through the Active Directory Installation Wizard.

Domains can have one or more domain controllers. When there are multiple domain controllers, the controllers automatically replicate directory data with one another using a multimaster replication model. This model allows any domain controller to process directory changes and then replicate those changes to other domain controllers.

Because of the multimaster domain structure, all domain controllers have equal responsibility by default. You can, however, give some domain controllers precedence over others for certain tasks, such as specifying a bridgehead server that has priority in replicating directory information to other sites. In addition, some tasks are best performed by a single server. A server that handles this type of task is called an *operations master*. There are five operations master roles, and you can assign each to a different domain controller. For more information, see the section entitled "Understanding Operations Master Roles," later in this chapter.

All Windows 2000, Windows XP Professional, Windows Vista, and Windows Server 2003 computers that join a domain have computer accounts. Like other resources, computer accounts are stored in Active Directory as objects. You use computer accounts to control access to the network and its resources. A computer accesses a domain using its account, which is authenticated before the computer can access the network.

Real World   Windows Server 2003 uses Active Directory's global catalog to authenticate both computer and user logons. If the global catalog is unavailable, only members of the Domain Admins group can log on to the domain. The reason for this is that the universal group membership information is stored in the global catalog and this information is required for authentication. In Windows Server 2003, you have the option of caching universal group membership locally, which solves this problem. For more information, see the section entitled "Understanding the Directory Structure," later in this chapter.

Using Windows 95 and Windows 98 with Active Directory

Systems running Windows 95 and Windows 98 can work with Active Directory in two ways. They can access the network as part of a Windows NT domain, or they can access the network as part of an Active Directory domain. Both techniques depend on a specific network configuration.

Accessing the Network Through a Windows NT Domain

When Windows 95 and Windows 98 systems are used on the network but Active Directory clients aren't installed, these systems can access the network as part of an existing Windows NT domain. Keep the following in mind:

- When Active Directory is in mixed-mode operations, a primary domain controller (PDC) emulator or backup domain controller (BDC) must be available to authenticate logons.

- When Active Directory is in native-mode operations, a BDC must be available to authenticate logons.

- When acting as part of a Windows NT domain, Windows 95 and Windows 98 systems can access only resources available through Windows NT one-way trusts, which must be explicitly established by administrators. This remains true whether the system is using a Windows Server 2003 domain controller or a Windows NT BDC.

Accessing the Network as an Active Directory Client

When using native-mode operations, Windows 95 and Windows 98 systems can access the network as part of an Active Directory domain. To allow a system to access the network as part of an Active Directory domain, you must install Active Directory client software on the system. With the client software, these systems have full use of Active Directory features and can use transitive trust relationships that exist within the domain tree or forest. Transitive trust relationships allow authorized users to access resources in any domain in the domain tree or forest automatically.

> **Tip** Transitive trusts are automatically configured during installation of a domain controller, and you might not need to configure explicit trust relationships. Still, Windows Server 2003 does support explicit trust relationships, and you can establish these relationships if necessary. The main reasons to establish an explicit trust are to enable user authentication in another domain or to simplify the trust path in a complex domain forest.

Installing Active Directory Clients

You install Active Directory client on a Windows 95 or Windows 98 system by completing the following steps:

1. Log on to the Windows 95 or Windows 98 system you want to configure as a client. Then insert the Windows 2000 Server or Windows Server 2003 distribution CD-ROM into the CD-ROM drive.

2. Open the Run dialog box by clicking Start and then clicking Run.

3. Type **E:\Clients\Win9X\Dsclient.exe**, where E is the drive letter of the CD-ROM drive, and click OK. Or, click Browse to search the distribution CD-ROM. In the Clients folder you'll find a subfolder called Win9X. This folder should contain the client executable. Select the client executable, click Open, and then click OK.

4. Running the client executable transfers a few essential files to the client and then starts the Directory Service Client Setup Wizard. Read the welcome page, and then click Next.

5. Install the client software by clicking Next. The wizard detects the system configuration and then installs the necessary client files on the system.

6. Click Finish to complete the operation and restart the system.

7. Click Start, choose Settings, and then choose Control Panel. In the Control Panel, double-click Network.

8. In the Configuration tab, select the Ethernet adapter card entry and then click Properties. Make sure that the TCP/IP settings are configured properly to access the Active Directory domain. Configuring TCP/IP settings is discussed in Chapter 16, "Managing TCP/IP Networking."

9. In the Identification tab, check the computer name and workgroup information provided. The computer name and workgroup should be set as explained in Chapter 16.

10. If you changed settings, you'll probably need to restart the computer. After the computer restarts, log on to the system using an account with access permissions in the Active Directory domain. You should be able to access resources in the domain.

Note   Windows 95 and Windows 98 systems running as clients don't have computer accounts and aren't displayed in Network Neighborhood. You can, however, view session information for Windows 95 and Windows 98 running as Active Directory clients. Start Computer Management, double-click System Tools, double-click Shared Folders, and then select Sessions. Current user and computer sessions are displayed in the details pane. For more information on shared resources, see Chapter 14, "Data Sharing, Security, and Auditing."

Using Windows NT and Windows 2000 Domains with Active Directory

All Windows NT and Windows 2000 computers must have computer accounts before they can join a domain. To support Windows NT and Windows 2000 domains, Active Directory has the following domain functional levels:

Windows 2000 mixed mode   When operating in Windows 2000 mixed mode, the directory can support Windows Server 2003, Windows 2000, and Windows NT domains. Although being able to work with Windows NT, Windows 2000, and Windows Server 2003 is an advantage, domains operating in this mode can't use many of the latest Active Directory features, including universal groups, group nesting, group type conversion, easy domain controller renaming, update logon timestamps, and Kerberos key distribution center (KDC) key version numbers.

Windows 2000 native mode   When operating in Windows 2000 native mode, the directory supports Windows Server 2003 and Windows 2000 domains only.

Windows NT domains are no longer supported. Domains operating in this mode aren't able to use easy domain controller renaming, update logon timestamps, and Kerberos KDC key version numbers.

Windows Server 2003 interim mode   When operating in interim mode, the directory supports Windows Server 2003 and Windows NT domains only. Windows 2000 domains aren't supported. This mode allows the upgrade from a Windows NT domain directly to a Windows Server 2003 domain without having to upgrade through Windows 2000. It's similar to the Windows 2000 mixed-mode domain, but it supports only servers running Windows NT and Windows Server 2003.

Windows Server 2003 mode   When operating in Windows Server 2003 mode, the directory supports only Windows Server 2003 domains. Windows NT and Windows 2000 domains are no longer supported. The good news, however, is that a domain operating in Windows Server 2003 mode can use all the latest Active Directory features, including universal groups, group nesting, group type conversion, easy domain controller renaming, update logon timestamps, and Kerberos KDC key version numbers.

Using Windows 2000 Mixed Mode Operations

You set the domain functional level when you install Active Directory on the first Windows Server 2003 domain controller in a domain. If your domain uses Windows NT 4.0 Server, Windows 2000 Server, and Windows Server 2003, you'll want to use mixed-mode operations (at least initially).

In mixed-mode operations, systems that are configured to use Windows NT domains access the network as if they were part of a Windows NT domain. These systems can include Windows 95 and Windows 98 systems that aren't running the Active Directory client, Windows NT workstations, and Windows NT servers. Although the role of Windows NT workstations doesn't change, Windows NT servers have a slightly different role. Here, Windows NT servers can act as BDCs or member servers only. The Windows NT domain no longer has a PDC. Instead, the Windows NT domain has a Windows Server 2003 domain controller that acts as a PDC to replicate read-only copies of Active Directory and to synchronize security changes to any remaining Windows NT BDCs.

The Windows Server 2003 domain controller acting as a PDC is automatically configured as a PDC emulator operations master. You can assign this role to another Windows Server 2003 domain controller at any time. A controller acting as a PDC emulator supports two authentication protocols:

Kerberos   Kerberos is a standard Internet protocol for authenticating users and systems and the primary authentication mechanism for Windows Server 2003.

NTLM   NT LAN Manager (NTLM) is the primary Windows NT authentication protocol. It's used to authenticate computers in a Windows NT domain.

Note Windows Server 2003 also supports Secure Socket Layer/Transport Layer Security (SSL/TLS) authentication. This authentication mechanism is used with secure Web servers.

Using Windows 2000 Native Mode Operations

After upgrading the PDC, BDCs, and other Windows NT systems, and if you still have Windows 2000 domain resources, you can change to the Windows 2000 native mode operations and then use only Windows 2000 and Windows Server 2003 resources in the domain. Once you set the Windows 2000 native mode operations, however, you can't go back to mixed mode. Because of this, you should use native mode operations only when you're certain that you don't need the old Windows NT domain structure or Windows NT BDCs.

When you change to Windows 2000 native mode, you'll notice the following:

- NTLM authentication is no longer supported.
- The PDC emulator can no longer synchronize data with any existing Windows NT BDCs.
- You can't add any Windows NT domain controllers to the domain.

In Windows Server 2003, you switch from Windows 2000 mixed mode to Windows 2000 native mode operations by raising the domain functional level.

Using Windows Server 2003 Interim Mode Operations

If you're upgrading from a Windows NT domain structure to Windows Server 2003, you don't have to use mixed-mode operations. You can use the Windows Server 2003 interim mode instead. Interim mode is an option only for the first Windows NT domain controller upgraded to Windows Server 2003. Here, you upgrade the Windows NT 4.0 PDC first and, when prompted during upgrade, you should set the forest functional level to Windows Server 2003 interim mode. This level has all the features of the Windows 2000 forest functional level.

When your domain is operating in Windows Server 2003 interim mode, the domain functions very similarly to Windows 2000 mixed-mode operations. The exception to this is that Windows 2000 domain controllers aren't supported.

After you upgrade the PDC, you can upgrade the remaining BDCs. Microsoft recommends having a backup BDC offline that you can go back to just in case anything goes wrong. When you're sure everything is working, you might want to consider raising the domain and forest level functions so that your organization can take advantage of the latest Active Directory enhancements.

Using Windows Server 2003 Mode Operations

After you've upgraded the Windows NT structures in your organization, you can look to upgrading to Windows Server 2003 domain structures. You do this by upgrading Windows 2000 domain controllers to Windows Server 2003 domain controllers and then, if desired, you can change the functional level to support only Windows Server 2003 domain structures.

Before being allowed to update Windows 2000 domain controllers, you'll be prompted to prepare the domain for Windows Server 2003 before continuing. To do this, you'll need to update the domain forest and the domain schema so that it's compatible with Windows Server 2003 domains. A tool, called Adprep.exe, is provided to automatically perform the update for you. All you need to do is run the tool on the schema operations master and then on the infrastructure operations master for each domain in the forest. As always, you should test out any procedure in the lab before performing it in an operational environment.

The steps you follow to perform the upgrade are as follows:

1. Check upgrade compatibility on the schema operations master and the infrastructure operations master for each domain in the forest. After inserting the Windows Server 2003 CD-ROM into the CD-ROM drive, click Start and then select Run. Type **E:\i386\winnt32.exe / checkupgradeonly**, where E is the drive letter for the CD-ROM drive, in the Open field of the Run dialog box, and then click OK. This starts the Microsoft Windows Upgrade Advisor. Select No, Skip This Step and then click Next. The Microsoft Windows Upgrade Advisor searches the hardware for any incompatibilities. You should note and correct any incompatibilities found before continuing.

2. You should upgrade all Windows 2000 domain controllers in the forest to Service Pack 2 or later before continuing. Access the Control Panel and then double-click System to check the current service pack. You'll find the service pack listed in the General tab.

3. Log on to the schema operations master for the first domain you want to upgrade in the forest, and then insert the Windows Server 2003 CD-ROM into the CD-ROM drive. Click Start and then select Run. In the Open field of the Run dialog box, type **E:\i386\adprep.exe /forestprep**, where E is the drive letter for the CD-ROM drive, and then click OK. This starts a command prompt window. Read the directions carefully before continuing. Type **C** to continue or press any other letter to quit.

    > **Note**   To determine which server is the current schema operations master for the domain, start a command prompt and type **dsquery server -hasfsmo schema**. A directory service path string is returned containing the name of the server, such as: "CN=CORPSERVER01,CN=Servers, CN=Default-First-Site-Name,CN=Sites,CN=Configuration,DC=microsoft, DC=com." This string tells you that the schema operations master is COPRSERVER01 in the microsoft.com domain.

4. Log on to the infrastructure operations master for the first domain you want to upgrade in the forest and then insert the Windows Server 2003 CD-ROM into the CD-ROM drive. Click Start and then select Run. In the Open field of the Run dialog box, type **E:\i386\adprep.exe /domainprep**, where E is the drive letter

for the CD-ROM drive, and then click OK. This starts a command prompt window. Read the directions carefully before continuing. Type **C** to continue or press any other letter to quit.

> **Note**   To determine which server is the current infrastructure operations master for the domain, start a command prompt and type **dsquery server -hasfsmo infr**.

5. Repeat Steps 3 and 4 for other domains in the forest as necessary.

After upgrading all Windows NT and Windows 2000 domain controllers and member servers, you can raise the domain and forest level functionality to take advantage of the latest Active Directory features. If you do this, however, you can use only Windows Server 2003 resources in the domain. After you set the Windows Server 2003 domain or forest functional level, however, you can't go back to any other mode. Because of this, you should use Windows Server 2003 mode only when you're certain that you don't need old Windows NT domain structures, Windows NT BDCs, or Windows 2000 domain structures.

Raising Domain and Forest Functionality

Domains operating in Windows Server 2003 functional level can use all the latest enhancements for Active Directory domains, including universal groups, group nesting, group type conversion, update logon timestamps, and Kerberos KDC key version numbers. In this mode, administrators will also be able to:

- Rename domain controllers without having to demote them first
- Rename domains running on Windows Server 2003 domain controllers
- Create extended two-way trusts between two forests
- Restructure domains in the domain hierarchy by renaming them and putting them at different levels
- Take advantage of replication enhancements for individual group members and global catalogs

Domain forests operating in Windows Server 2003 functional level can use all the latest enhancements for Active Directory forests, which means improved global catalog replication and intrasite and intersite replication efficiency, as well as the ability to establish one-way, two-way, and transitive forest trusts.

> **Real World**   The domain and forest upgrade process can generate a lot of network traffic as information is being replicated around the network. Sometimes it can take 15 minutes or longer for the entire upgrade process to complete. During this time, you might experience delayed responsiveness when communicating with servers and higher latency on the network. Because of this, you might want to schedule the upgrade outside of normal business hours. It's also a good idea to thoroughly test compatibility with existing applications (especially legacy applications) before performing this operation.

You can raise the domain level functionality by completing the following steps:

1. Click Start, choose All Programs, Administrative Tools, and then select Active Directory Domains And Trusts.

2. Right-click the domain you want to work with in the console tree and then select Raise Domain Functional Level.

3. The current domain name and functional level is displayed in the Raise Domain Functional Level dialog box.

4. To change the domain functionality, select the new domain functional level using the selection list provided and then click Raise. However, you can't reverse this action. Consider the implications carefully before you do this.

5. When you click OK, the new domain functional level will be replicated to each domain controller in the domain. This operation can take some time in a large organization.

You can raise the forest level functionality by completing the following steps:

1. Click Start, choose All Programs, Administrative Tools, and then select Active Directory Domains And Trusts.

2. Right-click the Active Directory Domains And Trusts node in the console tree and then select Raise Forest Functional Level.

3. The current forest name and functional level is displayed in the Raise Forest Functional Level dialog box.

4. To change the forest functionality, select the new forest functional level using the selection list provided and then click Raise. However, you can't reverse this action. Consider the implications carefully before you do this.

5. When you click OK, the new forest functional level will be replicated to each domain controller in each domain in the forest. This operation can take some time in a large organization.

Understanding the Directory Structure

Active Directory has many components and is built on many technologies. Directory data is made available to users and computers through data stores and global catalogs. Although most Active Directory tasks affect the data store, global catalogs are equally important. This is because they're used during logon and for information searches. In fact, if the global catalog is unavailable, normal users can't log on to the domain. The only way to change this behavior is to cache universal group membership locally. As you might expect, there are advantages and disadvantages to caching universal group membership, which I'll discuss in a moment.

You access and distribute Active Directory data using directory access protocols and replication. Directory access protocols allow clients to communicate with computers running

Active Directory. Replication is necessary to ensure that updates to data are distributed to domain controllers. Although multimaster replication is the primary technique that you use to distribute updates, some data changes can be handled only by individual domain controllers called *operations masters*. A new feature of Windows Server 2003 called *application directory partitions* also changes the way multimaster replication works.

With application directory partitions, enterprise administrators (those belonging to the Enterprise Admins group) can create replication partitions in the domain forest. These partitions are logical structures used to control replication of data within a domain forest. For example, you could create a partition to strictly control the replication of DNS information within a domain. This would prevent other systems in the domain from replicating DNS information.

Application directory partitions can appear as a child of a domain, a child of another application partition, or a new tree in the domain forest. Replicas of the application directory partition can be made available on any Active Directory domain controller running Windows Server 2003, including global catalogs. Although application directory partitions are useful in large domains and forests, they add overhead in terms of planning, administration, and maintenance.

Exploring the Data Store

The data store contains information about objects such as accounts, shared resources, organizational units, and group policies. Another name for the data store is the directory, which refers to Active Directory itself.

Domain controllers store the directory in a file called Ntds.dit. This file's location is set when Active Directory is installed, and it must be on an NTFS file system drive formatted for use with Windows Server 2003. You can also save directory data separately from the main data store. This is true for group policies, scripts, and other types of public information that's stored on the shared system volume (Sysvol).

Because the data store is a container for objects, the term *publish* is used when you share directory information. For example, you publish information about a printer by sharing the printer over the network. Similarly, you publish information about a folder by sharing the folder over the network.

Domain controllers replicate most changes to the data store in multimaster fashion. As an administrator for a small or medium-sized organization, you'll rarely need to manage replication of the data store. Replication is handled automatically, after all, but you can customize it to meet the needs of large organizations or organizations with special requirements.

Not all directory data is replicated. Instead, only public information that falls into one of these three categories is replicated:

Domain data   Contains information about objects within a domain. This includes objects for accounts, shared resources, organizational units, and group policies.

Configuration data   Describes the directory's topology. This includes a list of all domains, domain trees, and forests, as well as the locations of the domain controllers and global catalog servers.

Schema data   Describes all objects and data types that can be stored in the directory. The default schema provided with Windows Server 2003 describes account objects, shared resource objects, and more. You can extend the default schema by defining new objects and attributes or by adding attributes to existing objects.

Exploring Global Catalogs

When universal group membership isn't cached locally, global catalogs enable network logon by providing universal group membership information when a logon process is initiated. Global catalogs also enable directory searches throughout all the domains in a forest. A domain controller designated as a global catalog stores a full replica of all objects in the directory for its host domain and a partial replica for all other domains in the domain forest.

> **Note**   Partial replicas are used because only certain object properties are needed for logon and search operations. Partial replication also means that less information needs to be circulated on the network, which reduces the amount of network traffic.

By default, the first domain controller installed on a domain is designated as the global catalog. So, if there's only one domain controller in the domain, the domain controller and the global catalog are the same server. Otherwise, the global catalog is on the domain controller that you've configured as such. You can also add global catalogs to a domain to help improve response time for logon and search requests. The recommended technique is to have one global catalog per site within a domain.

Domain controllers hosting the global catalog should be well connected to domain controllers acting as infrastructure masters. Infrastructure master is one of the five operations master roles that you can assign to a domain controller. In a domain the infrastructure master is responsible for updating object references. The infrastructure master does this by comparing its data with that of a global catalog. If the infrastructure master finds outdated data, it requests the updated data from a global catalog. The infrastructure master then replicates the changes to the other domain controllers in the domain. For more information on operations master roles, see the section entitled "Understanding Operations Master Roles," later in this chapter.

When there's only one domain controller is in a domain, you can assign the infrastructure master role and the global catalog to the same domain controller. When two or more domain controllers are in the domain, however, the global catalog and the infrastructure master must be on separate domain controllers. If they aren't, the infrastructure master won't find data that's out of date and, as a result, will never replicate changes. The only exception is when all domain controllers in the domain host the global catalog. In this case, it doesn't matter which domain controller serves as the infrastructure master.

One of the key reasons to configure additional global catalogs in a domain is to ensure that a catalog is available to service logon and directory search requests. Again, if the domain has only one global catalog and the catalog isn't available and there's no local caching of universal group membership, normal users can't log on and you can't search the directory. In this scenario, the only users who can log on to the domain when the global catalog is unavailable are members of the Domain Admins group.

Searches in the global catalog are very efficient. The catalog contains information about objects in all domains in the forest. This allows directory search requests to be resolved in a local domain rather than in a domain in another part of the network. Resolving queries locally reduces the network load and allows for quicker responses in most cases.

> **Tip**   If you notice slow logon or query response times, you might want to configure additional global catalogs. But more global catalogs usually mean more replication data being transferred over the network.

Universal Group Membership Caching

In a large organization, it might not be practical to have global catalogs at every office location. Not having global catalogs at every office location presents a problem, however, if a remote office loses connectivity with the main office or a designated branch office where global catalog servers reside: Normal users won't be able to log on; only domain admins will be able to log on. The reason for this is that logon requests must be routed over the network to a global catalog server at a different office and, when there's no connectivity, this isn't possible.

As you might expect, there are many ways to resolve this problem. You could make one of the domain controllers at the remote office a global catalog server by following the procedure discussed in the section entitled "Configuring Global Catalogs" in Chapter 7, "Core Active Directory Administration." The disadvantage is that the designated server or servers will have an additional burden placed on them and might require additional resources. You also have to more carefully manage the up time of the global catalog server.

Another way to resolve this problem is to cache universal group membership locally. Here, any domain controller can resolve logon requests locally without having to go through the global catalog server. This allows for faster logons and makes it much easier to manage server outages: Your domain isn't relying on a single server or a group of servers for logons. It also reduces replication traffic. Instead of replicating the entire global catalog periodically over the network, only the universal group membership information in the cache is refreshed. By default, a refresh occurs every eight hours on each domain controller that's caching membership locally.

Universal group membership is site-specific. Remember, a site is a physical directory structure consisting of one or more subnets with a specific IP address range and network mask. The domain controllers running Windows Server 2003 and the global catalog they're contacting must be in the same site. If you have multiple sites, you'll need to configure local caching in each site. Additionally, users in the site must be part of a Windows

Server 2003 domain running in Windows Server 2003 forest functional mode. To learn how to configure caching, see the section of Chapter 7 entitled "Configuring Universal Group Membership Caching."

Replication and Active Directory

The three types of information stored in the directory are domain data, schema data, and configuration data.

Domain data is replicated to all domain controllers within a particular domain. Schema and configuration data are replicated to all domains in the domain tree or forest. In addition, all objects in an individual domain, and a subset of object properties in the domain forest, are replicated to global catalogs.

This means that domain controllers store and replicate schema information for the domain tree or forest, configuration information for all domains in the domain tree or forest, and all directory objects and properties for their respective domains.

Domain controllers hosting a global catalog, however, store and replicate schema information for the forest, configuration information for all domains in the forest, a subset of the properties for all directory objects in the forest that's replicated between servers hosting global catalogs only, and all directory objects and properties for their respective domain.

To get a better understanding of replication, consider the following scenario, where you're installing a new network:

1. You start by installing the first domain controller in domain A. The server is the only domain controller and also hosts the global catalog. No replication occurs because other domain controllers are on the network.

2. You install a second domain controller in domain A. Because there are now two domain controllers, replication begins. To make sure that data is replicated properly, you assign one domain controller as the infrastructure master and the other as the global catalog. The infrastructure master watches for updates to the global catalog and requests updates to changed objects. The two domain controllers also replicate schema and configuration data.

3. You install a third domain controller in domain A. This server isn't a global catalog. The infrastructure master watches for updates to the global catalog, requests updates to changed objects, and then replicates those changes to the third domain controller. The three domain controllers also replicate schema and configuration data.

4. You install a new domain, domain B, and add domain controllers to it. The global catalog hosts in domain A and domain B begin replicating all schema and configuration data, as well as a subset of the domain data in each domain. Replication within domain A continues as previously described. Replication within domain B begins.

Active Directory and LDAP

The Lightweight Directory Access Protocol (LDAP) is a standard Internet communications protocol for TCP/IP networks. LDAP is designed specifically for accessing directory services with the least amount of overhead. LDAP also defines operations that can be used to query and modify directory information.

Active Directory clients use LDAP to communicate with computers running Active Directory whenever they log on to the network or search for shared resources. You can also use LDAP to manage Active Directory.

LDAP is an open standard that many other directory services can use. This makes interdirectory communications easier and provides a clearer migration path from other directory services to Active Directory. You can also use Active Directory Service Interface (ADSI) to enhance interoperability. ADSI supports the standard application programming interfaces (APIs) for LDAP that are specified in Internet standard Request For Comments (RFC) 1823. You can use ADSI with Windows Script Host to script objects in Active Directory.

Understanding Operations Master Roles

Operations master roles accomplish tasks that are impractical to perform in multimaster fashion. Five operations master roles are defined; you can assign them to one or more domain controllers. Although certain roles can be assigned only once in a domain forest, other roles must be defined once in each domain.

Every Active Directory forest must have the following roles:

Schema master   Controls updates and modifications to directory schema. To update directory schema, you must have access to the schema master. To determine which server is the current schema master for the domain, start a command prompt and type **dsquery server -hasfsmo schema**.

Domain naming master   Controls the addition or removal of domains in the forest. To add or remove domains, you must have access to the domain naming master. To determine which server is the current domain naming master for the domain, start a command prompt and type **dsquery server -hasfsmo name**.

These forest-wide roles must be unique in the forest. This means you can assign only one schema master and domain naming master in a forest.

Every Active Directory domain must have the following roles:

Relative ID master   Allocates relative IDs to domain controllers. Whenever you create a user, group, or computer object, domain controllers assign a unique security ID to the related object. The security ID consists of the domain's security ID prefix and a unique relative ID, which was allocated by the relative ID master. To determine which server is the current relative ID master for the domain, start a command prompt and type **dsquery server -hasfsmo rid**.

PDC emulator   When using mixed or interim mode operations, the PDC emulator acts as a Windows NT PDC. Its job is to authenticate Windows NT logons, process password changes, and replicate updates to the BDCs. To determine which server is the current PDC emulator master for the domain, start a command prompt and type **dsquery server -hasfsmo pdc**.

Infrastructure master   Updates object references by comparing its directory data with that of a global catalog. If the data is outdated, the infrastructure master requests the updated data from a global catalog and then replicates the changes to the other domain controllers in the domain. To determine which server is the current infrastructure operations master for the domain, start a command prompt and type **dsquery server -hasfsmo infr**.

These domain-wide roles must be unique in each domain. This means you can assign only one relative ID master, PDC emulator, and infrastructure master in each domain.

Operations master roles are usually assigned automatically, but you can reassign them. When you install a new network, the first domain controller in the first domain is assigned all the operations master roles. If you later create a new child domain or a root domain in a new tree, the first domain controller in the new domain is automatically assigned operations master roles as well. In a new domain forest, the domain controller is assigned all operations master roles. If the new domain is in the same forest, the assigned roles are relative ID master, PDC emulator, and infrastructure master. The schema master and domain naming master roles remain in the first domain in the forest.

When a domain has only one domain controller, that computer handles all the operations master roles. If you're working with a single site, the default operations master locations should be sufficient. As you add domain controllers and domains, however, you'll probably want to move the operations master roles to other domain controllers.

When a domain has two or more domain controllers, you should configure two domain controllers to handle operations master roles. Here, you would make one domain controller the operations master and the other the standby operations master. The standby operations master is then used if the primary fails. Be sure that the domain controllers are direct replication partners and are well connected.

As domain structure grows, you might want to split up operations master roles and place them on separate domain controllers to improve responsiveness. Pay particular attention to the current responsibilities of the domain controller you plan to use.

Best Practices   Two roles that shouldn't be separated are schema master and domain naming master. Always assign these roles to the same server. For the most efficient operations, you'll usually want the relative ID master and PDC emulator to be on the same server as well. But you can separate these roles if necessary. For example, on a large network where peak loads are causing performance problems, you would probably want to place the relative ID master and PDC emulator on separate domain controllers. Additionally, you usually shouldn't place the infrastructure master on a domain controller hosting a global catalog. See the section entitled "Exploring Global Catalogs," earlier in this chapter, for details.

Chapter 7

Core Active Directory Administration

Core Active Directory administration focuses on key tasks that you'll perform routinely with Active Directory directory service, such as creating computer accounts or joining computers to a domain. In this chapter, you'll learn about the tools you can use to manage Active Directory as well as about specific techniques for managing computers, domain controllers, and organizational units.

Tools for Managing Active Directory

Several sets of tools are available for managing Active Directory, including graphical administration tools, command-line tools, and support tools.

Active Directory Administration Tools

The Active Directory administration tools are provided as snap-ins to the Microsoft Management Console (MMC). The key tools you'll use to manage Active Directory are:

Active Directory Users And Computers Used to manage users, groups, computers, and organizational units

Active Directory Domains And Trusts Used to work with domains, domain trees, and domain forests

Active Directory Sites And Services Used to manage sites and subnets

Active Directory Schema Used to view and work with the definitions of object classes and their attributes

Group Policy Object Editor/Group Policy Management Console Used to manage group policy settings

Resultant Set Of Policy   Used to view current policy for a user on a system and to plan policy changes

> **Security**   Windows Firewall can affect remote administration with some MMC tools. If Windows Firewall is enabled on a remote computer and you receive an error message stating that you don't have appropriate rights, the network path isn't found, or access is denied, you might need to configure an exception on the remote computer for incoming Transmission Control Protocol (TCP) port 445. You can resolve this problem by enabling the Windows Firewall: Allow Remote Administration Exception policy setting within Computer Configuration\Administrative Templates\Network\Network Connections\Windows Firewall\Domain Profile. Alternatively, type the following at a command prompt on the remote computer: **netsh firewall set portopening tcp 445 smb enable**. See Microsoft Knowledge Base Article 840634 for more details (*http://support.microsoft.com/default.aspx?scid=kb; en-us;840634*).

If you're running Microsoft Windows Server 2003, you can add the related snap-ins to any updateable console or access the tools directly on the Administrative Tools menu. If you're using another computer with access to a Windows Server 2003 domain, the tools won't be available until you install them. One technique for installing these tools is covered in the section entitled "Tools and Configuration" in Chapter 1, "Overview of Microsoft Windows Server 2003 System Administration," but you could also create a software installation package for the tools that would be distributed and installable through Active Directory.

For Windows Server 2003, these tools have been enhanced to allow you to perform tasks that you couldn't perform with the original Windows 2000 toolset. You can now perform the following actions:

Select multiple resources individually   Hold down the Ctrl key and then click the left mouse button on each object you want to select.

Select a series of resources at once   Hold down the Shift key, select the first object, and then click the last object.

Drag resources to new locations   Select the objects you want to move and press and hold down the left mouse button while moving the mouse.

Edit and set properties of multiple resources   Select the objects you want to work with, right-click, and then select the operation, such as Add To Group, Disable Account, or Properties.

With Windows Server 2003 R2, the Active Directory Management console is available. This console, shown in Figure 7-1, includes the following snap-ins: Domain Name System (DNS), Active Directory Sites And Services, Active Directory Domains And Trusts, and Active Directory Users And Computers.

Tip   You might prefer to use Active Directory Management rather than the individual consoles. If so, when I say to start one of the other consoles, you would start this console instead. To work with a particular snap-in, you simply expand the related node in Active Directory Management.

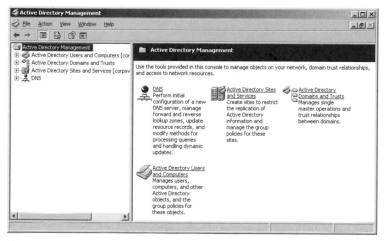

Figure 7-1   Active Directory Management provides easy access to key directory management tools.

Another Active Directory administration tool you might want to use is the Active Directory Schema snap-in. You use Active Directory Schema to manage and modify the directory schema, such as might be necessary if you want to create custom attributes for user accounts. If you have loaded the AdminPak (as discussed in the section of Chapter 1 entitled "Tools and Configuration"), you can add the Active Directory Schema snap-in to an MMC by completing the following steps:

1. Open the Run dialog box by clicking Start and then selecting Run.

2. Type **mmc** in the Open text box and then click OK. This opens the MMC.

3. In MMC, select File, and then select Add/Remove Snap-In. This opens the Add/Remove Snap-In dialog box.

4. In the Standalone tab, click Add.

5. In the Add Standalone Snap-In dialog box, select Active Directory Schema and then click Add.

6. Click Close and then click OK.

7. Right-click Active Directory Schema in the console tree and then select Change Domain Controller. This displays the Change Domain Controller dialog box.

8. In the Change Domain Controller dialog box, the information for the current domain controller (the one that you're logged in to in the default domain) should be provided automatically. Click OK, or enter the necessary information to access a different domain controller in another domain and then click OK. You can now view and manage the Active Directory schema for the domain.

Active Directory Command-Line Tools

Several tools are provided to let you manage Active Directory from the command line. You can use:

ADPREP   Prepares a Windows 2000 forest or domain for installation of Windows 2003 domain controllers (DCs). Use **adprep /forestprep** and **adprep /domainprep** to prepare a forest or a domain, respectively.

> **Security**   For Windows Server 2003 SP1 or later, a domain's group policy isn't automatically updated. You must use the command **adprep /domainprep /gpprep** to prepare Group Policy for the domain. This modifies the access control entries for all Group Policy Object (GPO) folders in the SYSVOL directory to grant read access to all enterprise domain controllers, which is required to support Resultant Set of Policy for site-based policy. Because this security change causes the NT File Replication Service (NTFRS) to resend all GPOs to all DCs, you should only use **adprep /domainprep /gpprep** after careful planning.

DSADD   Adds computers, contacts, groups, organizational units, and users to Active Directory. Type **dsadd** objectname **/?** at the command line to display help information on using the command, such as **dsadd computer /?**.

DSGET   Displays properties of computers, contacts, groups, organizational units, users, sites, subnets, and servers registered in Active Directory. Type **dsget** objectname **/?** at the command line to display help information on using the command, such as **dsget subnet /?**.

DSMOD   Modifies properties of computers, contacts, groups, organizational units, users, and servers that already exist in Active Directory. Type **dsmod** objectname **/?** at the command line to display help information on using the command, such as **dsmod server /?**.

DSMOVE   Moves a single object to a new location within a single domain or renames the object without moving it. Type **dsmove /?** at the command line to display help information on using the command.

DSQUERY   Finds computers, contacts, groups, organizational units, users, sites, subnets, and servers in Active Directory using search criteria. Type **dsquery /?** at the command line to display help information on using the command.

DSRM   Removes objects from Active Directory. Type **dsrm /?** at the command line to display help information on using the command.

NTDSUTIL   Allows the user to view site, domain, and server information, manage operations masters, and perform database maintenance of Active Directory. Type **ntdsutil /?** at the command line to display help information on using the command.

Active Directory Support Tools

Many Active Directory tools are provided in the support toolkit. A list of some of the most useful support tools you can use to configure, manage, and troubleshoot Active Directory is shown in Table 7-1.

Table 7-1   Quick Reference for Active Directory Support Tools

Support Tool	Executable Name	Description
Active Directory Service Interface Edit	ADSIEDIT.msc	Accesses and edits the Active Directory Services Interface for domain, schema, and configuration containers
Active Directory Administration Tool	Ldp.exe	Performs Lightweight Directory Access Protocol (LDAP) operations on Active Directory
Active Directory Replication Monitor	Replmon.exe	Manages and monitors replication using a graphical user interface (GUI)
Directory Services Access Control Lists Utility	Dsacls.exe	Manages access control lists for objects in Active Directory
Distributed File System Utility	Dfsutil.exe	Manages the Distributed File System (DFS) and displays DFS information
DNS Server Troubleshooting Tool	Dnscmd.exe	Manages properties of DNS servers, zones, and resource records
Move Tree	Movetree.exe	Moves objects from one domain to another
Replication Diagnostics Tool	Repadmin.exe	Manages and monitors replication using the command line
Security Descriptor Check Utility	Sdcheck.exe	Checks access control list propagation, replication, and inheritance
Security ID Checker	Sidwalker.exe	Sets access control lists on objects previously owned by moved, deleted, or orphaned accounts
Windows Domain Manager	Netdom.exe	Allows domain and trust relationships management from the command line

Using the Active Directory Users And Computers Tool

Active Directory Users And Computers is the primary administration tool you'll use to manage Active Directory. You use this utility to handle all user, group, and computer-related tasks and to manage organizational units.

Starting Active Directory Users And Computers

You can start Active Directory Users And Computers by selecting its related option on the Administrative Tools menu. You can also add Active Directory Users And Computers as a snap-in to any console that can be updated. To do that, follow these steps:

1. In MMC, select File, and then select Add/Remove Snap-In. This opens the Add/Remove Snap-In dialog box.

2. In the Standalone tab, click Add.

3. In the Add Snap-In dialog box, select Active Directory Users And Computers, and then click Add. Click Close and then click OK.

Getting Started with Active Directory Users And Computers

By default, Active Directory Users And Computers works with the domain to which your computer is currently connected. You can access computer and user objects in this domain through the console tree, as shown in Figure 7-2. However, if you can't find a domain controller or if the domain you want to work with isn't shown, you might need to connect to a domain controller in the current domain or a domain controller in a different domain. Other high-level tasks you might want to perform with Active Directory Users And Computers are viewing advanced options or searching for objects.

When you access a domain in Active Directory Users And Computers, you'll note that a standard set of folders is available. These folders are:

Saved Queries   Contains saved search criteria so that you can quickly perform previously run Active Directory searches.

Builtin   The list of built-in user accounts.

Computers   The default container for computer accounts.

Domain Controllers   The default container for domain controllers.

ForeignSecurityPrincipals   Contains information on objects from a trusted external domain. Normally, these objects are created when an object from an external domain is added to a group in the current domain.

Users   The default container for users.

Active Directory Users And Computers has advanced options that aren't displayed by default. To access these options, select View and then select Advanced Features. You now see the following additional folders:

LostAndFound   Contains objects that have been orphaned. You can delete or recover them.

NTDS Quotas   Contains directory service quota data.

Program Data   Contains stored Active Directory data for Microsoft applications.

System   Contains built-in system settings.

You can also add folders for organizational units. In Figure 7-2, four administrator-created organizational units are in the cpandl.com domain: Customer Support, Engineering, Marketing, and Sales.

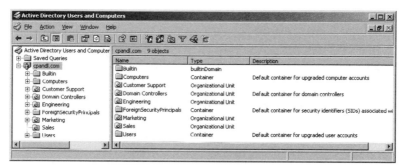

Figure 7-2   When you're working with Active Directory Users And Computers, you can access computer and user objects through the console tree.

Connecting to a Domain Controller

Connecting to a domain controller serves several purposes. If you start Active Directory Users And Computers and no objects are available, you can connect to a domain controller to access user, group, and computer objects in the current domain. You might also want to connect to a domain controller when you suspect replication isn't working properly and want to inspect the objects on a specific controller. After you're connected, you'd look for discrepancies in recently updated objects.

To connect to a domain controller, complete the following steps:

1. In the console tree, right-click Active Directory Users And Computers. Then select Connect To Domain Controller.

2. You'll see the current domain and domain controller you're working with in the Connect To Domain Controller dialog box shown in Figure 7-3.

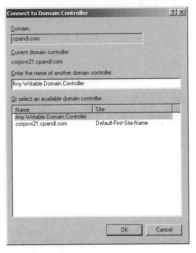

Figure 7-3   Select a new domain controller to work with using the Connect To Domain Controller dialog box.

3. The Or Select An Available Domain Controller list box lists the available controllers in the domain. The default selection is Any Writable Domain Controller. If you select this option, you'll connect to the domain controller that responds to your request first. Otherwise, choose a specific domain controller to connect to. Click OK.

Connecting to a Domain

In Active Directory Users And Computers, you can work with any domain in the forest, provided you have the proper access permissions. You connect to a domain by completing the following steps:

1. In the console tree, right-click Active Directory Users And Computers. Then select Connect To Domain.

2. The Connect To Domain dialog box displays the current (or default) domain. Type a new domain name and then click OK. Or click Browse, select a domain in the Browse For Domain dialog box, and then click OK twice.

Searching for Accounts and Shared Resources

Active Directory Users And Computers has a built-in search feature that allows you to find accounts, shared resources, and other directory objects. You can easily search the current domain, a specific domain, or the entire directory.

You search for directory objects by completing the following steps:

1. In the console tree, right-click the current domain or a specific container that you want to search. Then select Find. This opens a Find dialog box similar to the one shown in Figure 7-4.

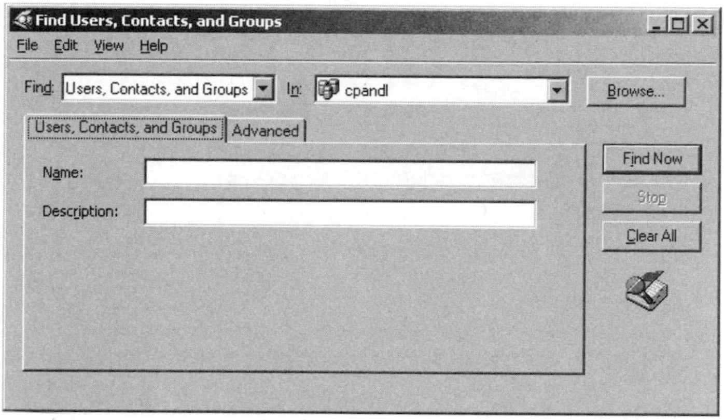

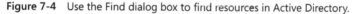

Figure 7-4   Use the Find dialog box to find resources in Active Directory.

2. Use the Find selection list to choose the type of search. The options include:

   Users, Contacts, And Groups   Search for user and group accounts, as well as contacts listed in the directory service

   Computers   Search for computer accounts by type, name, and owner

   Printers   Search for printers by name, model, and features

   Shared Folders   Search for shared folders by name or keyword

   Organizational Units   Search for organizational units by name

   Custom Search   Perform an advanced search or LDAP query

   Common Queries   Search quickly for account names, account descriptions, disabled accounts, nonexpiring passwords, and days since last logon

3. Use the In selection list to choose the location to search. If you right-clicked a container, such as Computers, this container is selected by default. To search all objects in the directory, select Entire Directory.

4. Type your search parameters and then click Find Now. As shown in Figure 7-5, any matching entries are displayed in the Find view. Double-click an object to view or modify its property settings. Right-click the object to display a shortcut menu that you can use to manage the object.

Figure 7-5 Matching objects are displayed in the Find view, and you can manage them by right-clicking their entries.

Note The search type determines which fields and tabs are available in the Find dialog box. In most cases, you'll simply want to type the name of the object you're looking for in the Name field. But other search options are available. For example, with printers, you can search for a color printer, a printer that can print on both sides of the paper, a printer that can staple, and more.

Managing Computer Accounts

Computer accounts are stored in Active Directory as objects. You use them to control access to the network and its resources. You can add computer accounts to any container displayed in Active Directory Users And Computers. The best containers to use are Computers, Domain Controllers, and any organizational units that you've created.

Note Microsoft Windows 95 and Microsoft Windows 98 computers access the network as Active Directory clients but don't have computer accounts. To learn more about accessing Active Directory domains, see the section entitled "Working with Active Directory Domains" in Chapter 6, "Using Active Directory."

Creating Computer Accounts on a Workstation or Server

The easiest way to create a computer account is to log on to the computer you want to configure and join a domain, as described in the section entitled "Joining a Computer to a Domain or Workgroup," later in this chapter. When you do this, the necessary computer account is created automatically and placed in the Computers folder or the

Domain Controllers folder, as appropriate. You can also create computer accounts in Active Directory Users And Computers before you try to install the computer.

Creating Computer Accounts in Active Directory Users And Computers

Using Active Directory Users And Computers, you can create computer accounts by following these steps:

1. In the Active Directory Users And Computers console tree, right-click the container into which you want to place the computer account.

2. Select New and then select Computer. This starts the New Object - Computer wizard shown in Figure 7-6. Type the client computer name.

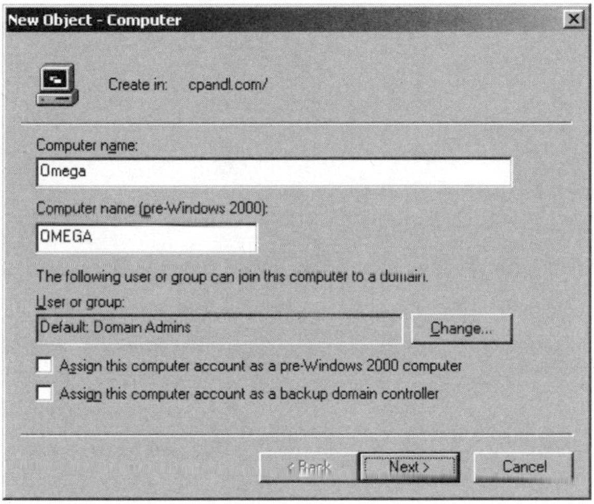

Figure 7-6   Create new computer accounts using the New Object - Computer wizard.

3. By default, only members of Domain Admins can join computers to the domain. To allow a different user or group to join the computer to the domain, click Change. Then use the Select User Or Group dialog box to select a user or group account.

   Note   You can select any existing user or group account. This allows you to delegate the authority to join this computer account to the domain.

4. If Windows NT systems can use this account, select Assign This Computer Account As A Pre-Windows 2000 Computer.

5. Click Next twice and then click Finish.

Viewing and Editing Computer Account Properties

You can view and edit computer account properties by completing the following steps:

1. Open Active Directory Users And Computers. In the console tree, expand the domain node.

2. Select the container or organizational unit in which the computer account is located.

3. Right-click the account you want to work with, and then select Properties. This displays a Properties dialog box that allows you to view and edit settings.

Deleting, Disabling, and Enabling Computer Accounts

If you no longer need a computer account, you can delete it permanently from Active Directory. Or, you can temporarily disable the account and later enable it to be used again.

To delete, disable, or enable computer accounts, complete the following steps:

1. Open Active Directory Users And Computers.

2. In the console tree, select the container in which the computer account is located. Then right-click the computer.

3. Select Delete to delete the account permanently and then confirm the deletion by clicking Yes.

4. Select Disable Account to temporarily disable the account, and then confirm the action by clicking Yes. A red circle with an X should indicate that the account is disabled.

5. Select Enable Account to enable the account so that it can be used again.

Tip If an account is currently in use, you might not be able to disable it. Try shutting down the computer or disconnecting the computer session in the Sessions folder of Computer Management.

Resetting Locked Computer Accounts

Computer accounts have passwords, just like user accounts. Unlike user accounts, however, computer account passwords are managed and maintained automatically. To perform this automated management, computers in the domain store a computer account password, which by default is changed every 30 days, and a secure channel password for establishing secure communications with domain controllers. The secure channel password is also updated by default every 30 days, and both passwords must be synchronized. If the secure channel password and the computer account password get out of sync, the computer won't be allowed to log on to the domain and a domain authentication error message will be logged for the Netlogon service with an event ID of 3210 or 5722.

If this happens, you'll need to reset the computer account password. One way to do this is to right-click the computer account in Active Directory Users And Computers and select Reset Account. You then need to remove the computer from the domain (by making the computer a member of a workgroup or another domain) and then rejoin the computer to the domain. The Windows Support Tools, discussed in Chapter 1, include the NETDOM command-line utility. This utility can be used to reset a computer's password. See Microsoft Knowledge Base Article 325850 for more details (*http://support.microsoft.com/default.aspx?scid=kb;en-us;325850*).

For a member server, you can reset the computer account password by completing the following steps:

1. Log on locally to the computer.

2. At a command prompt, type **netdom resetpwd /s:ServerName /ud:domain\UserName /pd:*** where ServerName is the name of the domain controller to use to set the password, domain\UserName specifies an administrator account with the authority to change the password, and * tells NETDOM to prompt you for the account password before continuing.

3. Type your password when prompted. NETDOM will then change the computer account password locally and on the domain controller. The domain controller will then distribute the password change to other domain controllers in the domain.

4. Restart the computer.

For domain controllers, you must perform additional steps. After you log on locally, you must stop the Kerberos Key Distribution Center service and set its startup type to Manual. After you restart the computer and verify that the password has been successfully reset, you can restart the Kerberos Key Distribution Center service and set its startup type back to Automatic.

Moving Computer Accounts

Computer accounts are normally placed in the Computers, Domain Controllers, or customized organizational unit containers. You can move an account to a different container by selecting the computer account in Active Directory Users And Computers, pressing and holding down the left mouse button while moving the mouse, and then releasing the mouse button when you've dragged the account to the new location.

The following steps describe another technique you can use to move computer accounts:

1. Open Active Directory Users And Computers.

2. In the console tree, select the container in which the computer account is located.

3. Right-click the computer account you want to move, and then select Move. This displays the Move dialog box shown in Figure 7-7.

Figure 7-7   Move computer accounts to different containers using the Move dialog box.

4. In the Move dialog box, expand the domain node and then select the container to which you want to move the computer. Click OK.

Managing Computers

As the name indicates, you use Computer Management to manage computers. When you're working with Active Directory Users And Computers, you can open Computer Management and connect to a specific computer directly by right-clicking the computer entry and selecting Manage on the shortcut menu. This launches Computer Management and automatically connects to the selected computer.

Joining a Computer to a Domain or Workgroup

Joining a computer to a domain or workgroup allows a Windows NT, Windows 2000, Microsoft Windows XP, or Windows Server 2003 computer to log on and access the network. Windows 95 and Windows 98 computers don't need computer accounts and don't join the network using this technique. With Windows 95 and Windows 98, you must configure the computer as an Active Directory client. For details, see the section of Chapter 6 entitled "Installing Active Directory Clients."

Before you get started, make sure that networking components are properly installed on the computer. These should have been installed during the setup of the operating system. You might also want to refer to Chapter 16, "Managing TCP/IP Networking," for details on configuring Transmission Control Protocol/Internet Protocol (TCP/IP) connections. TCP/IP settings must be correct and permit communications between the computer you're configuring and a controller in the domain. If Dynamic Host Configuration Protocol (DHCP), Windows Internet Name Service (WINS), and DNS are properly installed on the network, workstations don't need to be assigned a static IP address or have a special configuration. The only requirements are a computer name and a domain name, which you can specify when joining the domain.

Real World   Windows Server 2003 automatically grants the Add Workstations To The Domain user right to the implicit group Authenticated Users. This means that any user who logs on to the domain as a User and is authenticated can add workstations to the domain without needing administration privileges. However, as a security precaution, the number of workstations any such user can add to the domain is limited to 10. If an authenticated user exceeds this limit, an error message is displayed. For Windows NT workstations, this message states The Machine Account For This Computer Either Does Not Exist Or Is Unavailable. For Windows 2000 and Windows XP workstations, this message states Your Computer Could Not Be Joined To The Domain; You Have Exceeded The Maximum Number Of Computer Accounts You Are Allowed To Create In This Domain. Although you can use the Ldp.exe tool from the Windows Server 2003 Support Tools to override the default limit on the number of computers an authenticated user can join to a domain (as set by the ms-DS-MachineAccountQuota attribute), this isn't a good security practice. A better technique, and a more appropriate technique where security is a concern, is to precreate the necessary computer account in a specific organizational unit (OU) or to grant the user the advanced security privilege Create Computer Objects in a specific OU.

During installation of the operating system, a network connection was probably configured for the computer. Or you might have previously joined the computer to a domain or workgroup. If so, you can join the computer to a new domain or workgroup by completing the following steps (which are nearly identical for configuring Windows 2000 Professional, Windows 2000 Server, Windows XP Professional, and Windows Server 2003):

1. Log on to the workstation or server you want to configure.

2. Access Control Panel and then double-click System. In the System Properties dialog box, click the Computer Name tab as shown in Figure 7-8.

3. Click Change.

4. To rename the computer, type a new name in the Computer Name field, such as **Zeta.**

5. To join a new domain, in the Member Of panel select Domain and then type the local part of the domain name, such as **SEATTLE** for the domain *seattle.microsoft.com.*

6. To join a new workgroup, in the Member Of panel select Workgroup and then type the workgroup name, such as TestDevGroup.

7. If you made changes, click OK. When prompted, type the name and password of a user account with administrator permission to make these changes. Click OK again.

8. The changes are made and a new computer account is created, as necessary. If the changes are successful, you'll see a confirmation dialog box to this effect. Click OK to reboot the computer.

9. If the changes are unsuccessful, you'll see either a message informing you that they're unsuccessful or a message telling you that the account credentials already exist. This problem can occur when you're changing the name of a computer that's already connected to a domain and when the computer has active sessions in that domain. Close applications that might be connecting to the domain, such as Windows Explorer accessing a shared folder over the network. Then repeat this process.

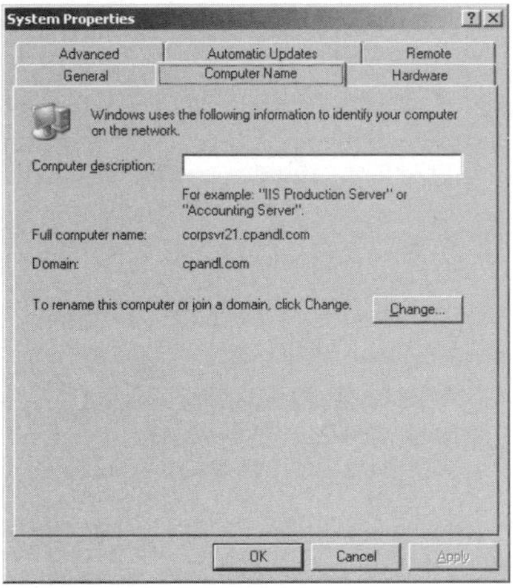

Figure 7-8   Use the Computer Name tab to change properties or reconfigure the network ID.

Tip   If you have problems joining a domain, ensure that the computer you're configuring has the proper networking configuration. The computer must have Networking Services installed and the TCP/IP properties must have the correct DNS server settings.

Managing Domain Controllers, Roles, and Catalogs

Domain controllers perform many important tasks in Active Directory domains. Many of these tasks were discussed in Chapter 6.

Installing and Demoting Domain Controllers

You install a domain controller by configuring Active Directory on a member server. Later, if you don't want the server to handle controller tasks, you can demote the server. It will then act as a member server again. You install or demote servers following a similar procedure, but before you do, you should consider the impact on the network and read the section of Chapter 6 entitled "Understanding the Directory Structure."

As that section explains, when you install a domain controller you might need to transfer operations master roles and reconfigure the global catalog structure. Also, before you can install Active Directory, DNS must be working on the network and you must convert the Active Directory data drive to NTFS file system 5.0 or later. Converting drive formats is covered in the section entitled "Converting a Volume to NTFS" in Chapter 11, "Managing File Systems and Drives." Similarly, before you demote a domain controller, you should shift any key responsibilities to other domain controllers. This means moving the global catalog off the server and transferring any operations master roles, if necessary. You must also remove any application directory partitions that are on the server.

> **Real World**   It's important to point out that in Windows Server 2003, it's no longer necessary to demote a domain controller to rename it. You can rename a domain controller at any time. The only problem is that the server is unavailable to users during the renaming process and you might need to force a directory refresh to reestablish proper communications with the server. You can't, however, move a domain controller to a different domain. You must demote the domain controller, update the domain settings for the server and its computer account, and then promote the server to be a domain controller once more.

To install or demote a domain controller, complete the following steps:

1. Log on to the server you want to reconfigure.

2. Click Start and then select Run.

3. Type **dcpromo** and then click OK This starts the Active Directory Installation Wizard.

4. If the computer is currently a member server, the wizard takes you through the steps needed to install Active Directory. You'll need to specify whether this is a domain controller for a new domain or an additional domain controller for an existing domain.

5. If the computer is currently a domain controller, the Active Directory Installation Wizard takes you through the process of demoting the domain controller. After it's demoted, the computer acts as a member server.

> **Caution**   Demoting the server using DCPROMO gracefully transfers any roles held by the server. Microsoft Knowledge Base article 332199 describes how to

force demotion using **dcpromo /forceremoval.** However, if you use **dcpromo /forceremoval,** the FSMO roles of the demoted server are left in an invalid state until they are reassigned by an administrator. If you force demote a domain controller and the demotion fails or you are unable to demote a server, the domain data may be in an inconsistent state. See Microsoft Knowledge Base article 216498 for details on how to resolve this issue (*http://support.microsoft.com/default.aspx?scid=kb;en-us; 216498*).

Real World An alternative technique for installing domain controllers is to do so from backup media. This option is new for Windows Server 2003. To install a domain controller from backup media, you create a backup of the System State data of a domain controller and restore it on a different server running Windows Server 2003. When you create a domain controller from backup media, you eliminate the need to replicate the entire directory database over the network to the new domain controller. This can really save the day when you have bandwidth limitations or the directory database has thousands of entries.

Viewing and Transferring Domain-Wide Roles

You can use Active Directory Users And Computers to view or change the location of domain-wide operations master roles. At the domain level, you can work with roles for relative ID (RID) masters, primary domain controller (PDC) emulator masters, and infrastructure masters.

Note Operations master roles are discussed in the section of Chapter 6 entitled "Understanding Operations Master Roles." You use Active Directory Domains And Trusts to set the domain naming master role and Active Directory Schema to change the schema master role. The fastest way to determine the current FSMO for all roles is to type **netdom query fsmo** at a command prompt.

You can view the current operations master roles by following these steps:

1. Open Active Directory Users And Computers.

2. In the console tree, right-click Active Directory Users And Computers. On the shortcut menu, point to All Tasks, then select Operations Masters. This opens the Operations Masters dialog box shown in Figure 7-9.

3. The Operations Masters dialog box has three tabs. The RID tab shows the location of the current RID master. The PDC tab shows the location of the current PDC emulator master. The Infrastructure tab shows the location of the current infrastructure master.

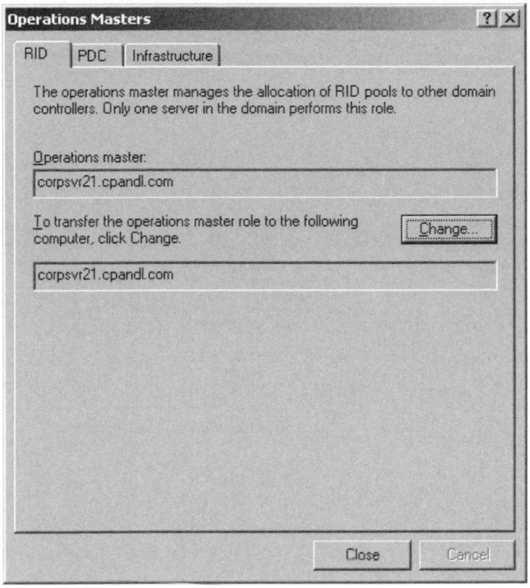

Figure 7-9   Use the Operations Masters dialog box to transfer operations masters to new locations or to simply view their current locations.

You can transfer the current operations master roles by following these steps:

1. Start Active Directory Users And Computers. In the console tree, right-click Active Directory Users And Computers and select Connect To Domain Controller.

2. In the Connect To Domain Controller dialog box, enter the name of the domain controller to which you want to transfer an operations master role or select this domain controller in the Available Domain Controller list, and then click OK.

3. In the console tree, right-click Active Directory Users And Computers and select Operations Masters.

4. In the Operations Masters dialog box, select the RID, PDC, or Infrastructure tab as appropriate for the type of role you want to transfer.

5. Click Change to transfer the role to the previously selected domain controller. Click OK.

Viewing and Transferring the Domain Naming Master Role

You can use Active Directory Domains And Trusts to view or change the location of the domain-naming master in the domain forest. In Active Directory Domains And Trusts, the root level of the control tree shows the currently selected domain.

Tip   If you need to connect to a different domain, connect to a domain controller following steps similar to those described in the section entitled "Connecting to a Domain Controller," earlier in this chapter. The only difference is that you right-click Active Directory Domains And Trusts in the console tree.

You transfer the domain naming master role by following these steps:

1. Start Active Directory Domains And Trusts. In the console tree, right-click Active Directory Domains And Trusts and select Connect To Domain Controller.

2. In the Connect To Domain Controller dialog box, enter the name of the domain controller to which you want to transfer the domain naming master role or select this domain controller in the Available Domain Controller list, and then click OK.

3. In the console tree, right-click Active Directory Domains And Trusts. Then select Operations Master. This opens the Change Operations Master dialog box.

4. The Domain Naming Operations Master field displays the current domain-naming master. Click Change to transfer this role to the previously selected domain controller. Click Close.

Viewing and Transferring Schema Master Roles

You use Active Directory Schema to view or change the schema master's location. This utility is provided in the Windows Server 2003 Adminpak. After you install the Adminpak from the I386 directory of the Windows Server 2003 CD-ROM, type **regsvr32 schmmgmt.dll** at a command prompt to register Active Directory Schema. You can then transfer the schema master role by completing the following steps:

1. Add the Active Directory Schema snap-in to an MMC.

2. In the console tree, right-click Active Directory Schema. Then select Change Domain Controller.

3. Select Any Domain Controller to let Active Directory select the new schema master. Or select Specify Name and type the name of the new schema master, such as **zeta.seattle.domain.com**. Click OK.

4. In the console tree, right-click Active Directory Schema and then select Operations Master.

5. Click Change in the Change Schema Master dialog box.

6. Click OK. Click Close.

Transferring Roles Using the Command Line

Another way to transfer roles is to use NETDOM to list current FSMO role holders and Ntdsutil.exe to transfer roles. Ntdsutil is a command-line tool for managing Active Directory. Follow these steps to transfer roles at the command line:

1. Get a list of the current FSMO role holders by typing **netdom query fsmo** at a command prompt.

2. It is recommended that you log on to the console of the server you want to assign as the new operations master. You can log on to the console locally or use Remote Desktop.

3. Click Start, select Run, type **cmd** in the Open field, and then click OK.

4. At the command prompt, type **ntdsutil**. This starts the Directory Services Management Tool.

5. At the ntdsutil prompt, type **roles**. This puts the utility in Operations Master Maintenance mode.

6. At the fsmo maintenance prompt, type **connections** and then at the server connections prompt, type **connect to server** followed by the fully qualified domain name of the domain controller to which you want to assign the FSMO role, such as:

   ```
   connect to server engdc01.technology.adatum.com
   ```

7. After you've established a successful connection, type **quit** to exit the server connections prompt, and then at the fsmo maintenance prompt, type **transfer** and then type the identifier for the role to transfer. The identifiers are:

   pdc   For the PDC emulator role

   rid master   For the RID master role

   infrastructure master   For the infrastructure master role

   schema master   For the schema master role

   domain naming master   For the domain naming master role

8. Type **quit** at the fsmo maintenance prompt and type **quit** at the ntdsutil prompt.

Seizing Roles Using the Command Line

Occasionally, you might find yourself in a situation where you can't gracefully transfer server roles. For example, a domain controller acting as the RID master might have a drive failure that takes down the entire server. If you're unable to get the server back online, you might need to seize the RID master role and assign this role to another domain controller.

> **Caution**   Seizing a server role is a drastic procedure that you should perform only as a last resort. Seize a server role only if the domain controller managing the current role is permanently out of service. The only way to bring the original server master back online is to format the boot disk and reinstall Windows Server 2003. After seizing the FSMO role of a domain controller no longer present in the domain, you must remove the related data from Active Directory. See Microsoft

Knowledge Base article 216498 for more details (*http://support.microsoft.com /default.aspx?scid=kb;en-us;216498*).

Follow these steps to seize a server role:

1. Get a list of the current FSMO role holders by typing **netdom query fsmo** at a command prompt.

2. Ensure that the current domain controller with the role you want to seize is permanently offline. If the server can be brought back online, don't perform this procedure unless you intend to completely reinstall this server.

3. It is recommended that you log on to the console of the server you want to assign as the new operations master. You can log on to the console locally or use Remote Desktop.

4. Open a command prompt window.

5. At the command prompt, type **ntdsutil**. This starts the Directory Services Management Tool.

6. At the ntdsutil prompt, type **roles**. This puts the utility in Operations Master Maintenance mode.

7. At the fsmo maintenance prompt, type **connections** and then, at the server connections prompt, type **connect to server** followed by the fully qualified domain name of the domain controller to which you want to assign the FSMO role, such as:

   `connect to server engdc01.technology.adatum.com`

8. After you've established a successful connection, type **quit** to exit the server connections prompt and then, at the fsmo maintenance prompt, type **seize** and then type the identifier for the role to seize. The identifiers are:

   pdc   For the PDC emulator role

   rid master   For the RID master role

   infrastructure master   For the infrastructure master role

   schema master   For the schema master role

   domain naming master   For the domain naming master role

9. Type **quit** at the fsmo maintenance prompt and type **quit** at the ntdsutil prompt.

Configuring Global Catalogs

Global catalogs have an important role on the network. This role is discussed in the section of Chapter 6 entitled "Understanding the Directory Structure." You configure additional global catalogs by enabling domain controllers to host the global catalog. In addition, if you have two or more global catalogs within a site, you might want a domain controller to stop hosting the global catalog. You do this by disabling the global catalog on the domain controller.

You enable or disable a global catalog by completing the following steps:

1. Start Active Directory Sites And Services.

2. In the console tree, expand the site you want to work with.

3. Expand the Servers folder for the site, and then select the server you want to configure to host the global catalog.

4. In the details pane, right-click NTDS Settings and then select Properties.

5. To enable the server to host the global catalog, select the Global Catalog check box in the General tab. An example is shown in Figure 7-10.

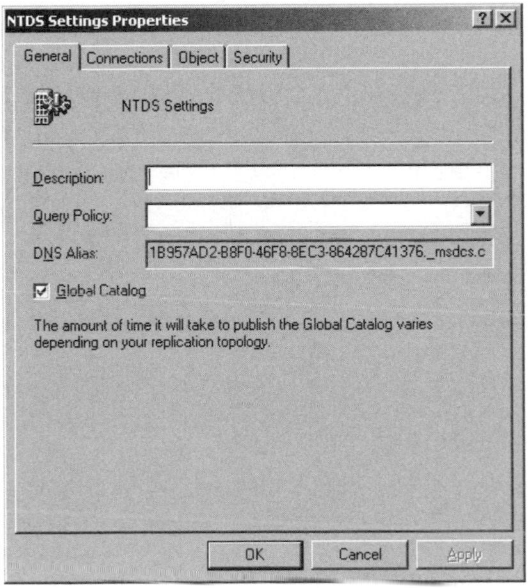

Figure 7-10   Enable and disable global catalogs through a server's NTDS settings.

6. To disable the global catalog, clear the Global Catalog check box in the General tab.

Caution   Don't enable or disable global catalogs without proper planning and analysis of network impact. In a large enterprise environment, designating a domain controller as a global catalog can cause data related to thousands of Active Directory objects to be replicated across the network.

Configuring Universal Group Membership Caching

Universal membership caching eliminates the dependency on the availability of a global catalog server during logons. When this feature is enabled on a domain operating in Windows Server 2003 operations mode, any domain controller can resolve logon requests locally without having to go through the global catalog server. As discussed in the section of Chapter 6 entitled "Universal Group Membership Caching," this has advantages and disadvantages.

You can enable or disable universal group membership caching by completing the following steps:

1. Open Active Directory Sites And Services.

2. In the left pane, expand and then select the site with which you want to work.

3. In the details pane, right-click NTDS Site Settings and then select Properties.

4. To enable universal group membership caching, select the Enable Universal Group Membership Caching check box in the Site Settings tab. Afterward, use the Refresh Cache From list to specify a site from which to cache universal group memberships. The selected site must have a working global catalog server.

5. To disable universal group membership caching, clear the Enable Universal Group Membership Caching check box in the Site Settings tab.

6. Click OK.

Managing Organizational Units

As discussed in Chapter 6, organizational units help you organize objects, set Group Policy with a limited scope, and more. In this section you'll learn how to create and manage OUs.

Creating Organizational Units

You usually create OUs to mirror your organization's business or functional structure. You may also want to create units for administrative reasons, such as if you want to delegate rights to users or administrators. You can create OUs as subgroups of a domain or as child units within an existing OUs.

To create an OU, follow these steps:

1. Open Active Directory Users And Computers.

2. Right-click the domain node or existing organizational unit folder in which you want to add the OU. On the shortcut menu, select New, and then select Organizational Unit.

3. Type the name of the OU. Click OK.

4. You can now move accounts and shared resources to the OU. See the section entitled "Moving Computer Accounts," earlier in this chapter, for an example.

Viewing and Editing Organizational Unit Properties

You can view and edit organizational unit properties by completing the following steps:

1. Open Active Directory Users And Computers.

2. Right-click the OU with which you want to work, and then select Properties. This displays a properties dialog box that lets you view and edit settings.

Renaming and Deleting Organizational Units

You can rename or delete an organizational unit by completing the following steps:

1. In Active Directory Users And Computers, right-click the OU folder with which you want to work.

2. To delete the unit, select Delete. Then confirm the action by clicking Yes.

3. To rename the unit, select Rename. Type a new name for the OU and then press Enter.

Moving Organizational Units

You can move organizational units to different locations within a domain by selecting the OU in Active Directory Users And Computers, pressing down and holding the left mouse button while moving the mouse, and then releasing the mouse button when you've dragged the account to the new location.

The following steps comprise another technique you can use to move OUs:

1. In Active Directory Users And Computers, right-click the OU folder you want to move. Then select Move.

2. In the Move dialog box, expand the domain and then select the container to which you want to move the OU. Click OK.

Understanding User and Group Accounts

Managing accounts is one of your primary tasks as a Microsoft Windows Server 2003 administrator. Chapter 7, "Core Active Directory Administration," discussed computer accounts. This chapter examines user and group accounts. You use user accounts to enable individual users to log on to the network and access network resources. You use group accounts to manage resources for multiple users. The permissions and privileges you assign to user and group accounts determine which actions users can perform, as well as which computer systems and resources they can access.

Although you might be tempted to give users wide access, you need to balance the user's need for job-related resources with your need to protect sensitive resources or privileged information. For example, you wouldn't want everyone in the company to have access to payroll data. Consequently, you'd make sure that only those who need that information have access to it.

The Windows Server 2003 Security Model

You control access to network resources with the components of the Windows Server 2003 security model. The key components you need to know about are the ones used for authentication and access controls.

Authentication Protocols

Windows Server 2003 authentication is implemented as a two-part process. That process consists of interactive logon and network authentication. When a user logs on to a computer using a domain account, the interactive logon process authenticates the user's logon, which confirms the user's identity to the local computer and grants access to Active Directory directory service. Afterward, whenever the user attempts to access network resources, network authentication is used to determine whether the user has permission to do so.

Windows Server 2003 supports many network authentication protocols. The key protocols are:

Kerberos v5   A standard Internet protocol for authenticating users and systems. It's the primary authentication mechanism for Windows Server 2003.

NT LAN Manager (NTLM)   The primary Microsoft Windows NT authentication protocol. It's used to authenticate computers in a Windows NT domain.

> **Note**   Windows Server 2003 web and application services support authentication using Anonymous Authentication, Basic Authentication, Integrated Windows Authentication, Digest Authentication, and .NET Passport Authentication. With Microsoft Internet Information Services (IIS) 6.0, Passport authentication enables you to use Active Directory information to authenticate Internet, intranet, and extranet users. For details, see Chapter 7, "Enhancing Web Server Security," of the *Microsoft IIS 6.0 Administrator's Pocket Consultant* (Microsoft Press, 2003).

A key feature of the Windows Server 2003 authentication model is that it supports Single Sign-On. Single Sign-On works in the following way:

1. A user logs on to the domain by using a logon name and password or by inserting a smart card into a card reader.

2. The interactive logon process authenticates the user's access. With a local account, the credentials are authenticated locally and the user is granted access to the local computer. With a domain account, the credentials are authenticated in Active Directory and the user has access to local and network resources.

3. Now the user can authenticate to any computer in the domain through the network authentication process. With domain accounts, the network authentication process typically is automatic (through Single Sign-On). With local accounts, on the other hand, users must provide a user name and password every time they access a network resource.

Windows Server 2003 R2 features Active Directory Federation Services (ADFS), which extends Single Sign-On to trusted resources on the Internet. Using ADFS, organizations can extend their existing Active Directory infrastructure to provide access to trusted Internet resources, which can include third parties as well as geographically separated units of the same organizations. After you configure federated servers, users at the organization can sign on once to the organization's network and are then automatically logged on to trusted Web applications hosted by partners on the Internet. Federated Web Single Sign-On uses Federated Authorization for seamless access. In addition to user identity and account information, security tokens used in Federated Authorization include authorization claims that detail user authorization and specific application entitlement.

Access Controls

Active Directory is object-based. Users, computers, groups, shared resources, and many other entities are all defined as objects. Access controls are applied to these objects with security descriptors. Security descriptors do the following:

- List the users and groups that are granted access to objects
- Specify permissions the users and groups have been assigned
- Track events that should be audited for objects
- Define ownership of objects

Individual entries in the security descriptor are referred to as *access control entries* (ACEs). Active Directory objects can inherit ACEs from their parent objects. This means that permissions for a parent object can be applied to a child object. For example, all members of the Domain Admins group inherit permissions granted to this group.

When working with ACEs, keep the following points in mind:

- ACEs are created with inheritance enabled by default.
- Inheritance takes place immediately after the ACE is written.
- All ACEs contain information specifying whether the permission is inherited or explicitly assigned to the related object.

Differences Between User and Group Accounts

Windows Server 2003 provides user accounts and group accounts (of which users can be a member). User accounts are designed for individuals. Group accounts are designed to make the administration of multiple users easier. Although you can log on with user accounts, you can't log on with a group account. Group accounts are usually referred to simply as groups.

Real World   Windows Server 2003 supports the InetOrgPerson object. Essentially, this object is the same as a user object and you could use it as such. However, the real purpose for the InetOrgPerson object is to allow for compatibility and transition from third-party X.500 and Lightweight Directory Access Protocol (LDAP) directory services that use this object to represent users. If you are migrating from a third-party directory service and end up with many InetOrgPerson objects, don't worry. These objects can be used as security principals just like user accounts. The InetOrgPerson object is fully enabled only when working in Windows Server 2003 operations mode. In this mode, you can set passwords for InetOrgPerson objects and you can change the object class if desired. When you change the object class, the InetOrgPerson object is converted to a user object and from then on is listed as the User type in Active Directory Users And Computers.

User Accounts

In Windows Server 2003, two types of user accounts are defined:

Domain user accounts   User accounts defined in Active Directory are called *domain user accounts*. Through Single Sign-On, domain user accounts can access resources throughout the domain. You create domain user accounts in Active Directory Users And Computers.

Local user accounts   User accounts defined on a local computer are called *local user accounts*. Local user accounts have access to the local computer only, and they must authenticate themselves before they can access network resources. You create local user accounts with the Local Users And Groups utility.

> **Note**   In a domain, only member servers and workstations have local user and group accounts. On the initial domain controller for a domain, these accounts are moved from the local Security Account Manager (SAM) database to Active Directory and then become domain accounts.

Logon Names, Passwords, and Public Certificates

All user accounts are identified with a logon name. In Windows Server 2003, this logon name has two parts:

User name   The text label for the account

User domain or workgroup   The workgroup or domain where the user account exists

For the user wrstanek, whose account is created in the microsoft.com domain, the full logon name for Windows Server 2003 is wrstanek@microsoft.com. The pre-Windows 2000 logon name is MICROSOFT\wrstanek.

When working with Active Directory, you might also need to specify the *fully qualified domain name* (FQDN) for a user. The FQDN for a user is the combination of the Domain Name System (DNS) domain name, the container or organizational unit that contains the user, and the user name. For the user microsoft.com\users\wrstanek, *microsoft.com* is the DNS domain name, *users* is the container or organizational unit location, and *wrstanek* is the user name.

User accounts can also have passwords and public certificates associated with them. Passwords are authentication strings for an account. Public certificates combine a public and private key to identify a user. You log on with a password interactively. You log on with a public certificate using a smart card and a smart card reader.

Security Identifiers and User Accounts

Although Windows Server 2003 displays user names to describe privileges and permissions, the key identifiers for accounts are *security identifiers* (SIDs). SIDs are unique identifiers that are generated when you create accounts. Each account's SID consists of the domain's security ID prefix and a unique relative ID, which is allocated by the relative ID master.

Windows Server 2003 uses these identifiers to track accounts independently from user names. SIDs serve many purposes. The two most important ones are to allow you to change user names easily and to allow you to delete accounts without worrying that someone might gain access to resources simply by recreating an account with the same name.

When you change a user name, you tell Windows Server 2003 to map a particular SID to a new name. When you delete an account, you tell Windows Server 2003 that a particular SID is no longer valid. Afterward, even if you create an account with the same user name, the new account won't have the same privileges and permissions as the previous one. That's because the new account will have a new SID.

Group Accounts

In addition to user accounts, Windows Server 2003 provides groups. Generally speaking, you use groups to grant permissions to similar types of users and to simplify account administration. If a user is a member of a group that can access a resource, that particular user can access the same resource. Thus, you can give a user access to various work-related resources just by making the user a member of the correct group. Note that although you can log on to a computer with a user account, you can't log on to a computer with a group account.

Because different Active Directory domains might have groups with the same name, groups are often referred to by *domain\groupname*, such as work\gmarketing for the gmarketing group in the work domain. When you work with Active Directory, you might also need to specify the FQDN for a group. The FQDN for a group is the concatenation of the DNS domain name, the container or organizational unit location, and the group name. For the group microsoft.com\users\gmarketing, *microsoft.com* is the DNS domain name, *users* is the container or organizational unit location, and *gmarketing* is the group name.

> **Real World**   Employees in a marketing department probably need access to all marketing-related resources. Instead of granting access to these resources individually, you could make the users members of a marketing group. That way they automatically obtain the group's privileges. Later, if a user moves to a different department, you simply remove the user from the group, thus revoking all access permissions. Compared to having to revoke access for each individual resource, this technique is pretty easy—so, you'll want to use groups whenever possible.

Group Types

In Windows Server 2003, there are three types of groups:

Local groups   Groups that are defined on a local computer. Local groups are used on the local computer only. You create local groups with the Local Users And Groups utility.

Security groups   Groups that can have security descriptors associated with them. You define security groups in domains using Active Directory Users And Computers.

Distribution groups   Groups that are used as e-mail distribution lists. They can't have security descriptors associated with them. You define distribution groups in domains using Active Directory Users And Computers.

Note   Most general discussions about groups focus on local groups and security groups rather than distribution groups. Distribution groups are only for email distribution and are not for assigning or managing access.

Group Scope

In Active Directory, groups can have different scopes—domain local, built-in local, global, and universal. That is, the groups have different areas in which they're valid.

Domain local groups   Groups primarily used to assign access permissions to resources within a single domain. Domain local groups can include members from any domain in the forest and from trusted domains in other forests. Typically, global and universal groups are members of domain local groups.

Built-in local groups   Groups with a special group scope that have domain local permissions and, for simplicity, are often included in the term domain local groups. The difference between built-in local groups and other groups is that you can't create or delete built-in local groups. You can only modify built-in local groups. References to domain local groups apply to built-in local groups unless otherwise noted.

Global groups   Groups that are used primarily to define sets of users or computers in the same domain that share a similar role, function, or job. Members of global groups can include only accounts and groups from the domain in which they're defined.

Universal groups   Groups that are used primarily to define sets of users or computers that should have wide permissions throughout a domain or forest. Members of universal groups include accounts, global groups, and other universal groups from any domain in the domain tree or forest. Security universal groups are available only when Active Directory is running in Windows 2000 native operations mode or in Windows Server 2003 operations mode. Distribution universal groups are available in any domain functional mode.

Best Practices   Universal groups are very useful in large enterprises where you have multiple domains. If you plan properly, you can use universal groups to simplify system administration. Members of universal groups shouldn't change frequently. Each time you change the members of a universal group, you need to replicate these changes to all the global catalogs in the domain tree or forest. To cut down on changes, assign other groups to the universal group rather than user accounts. For more information, see the section in this chapter entitled "When to Use Domain Local, Global, and Universal Groups."

When you work with groups, there are many things you can and can't do based on the group's scope. A quick summary of these items is shown in Table 8-1. For complete details on creating groups, see Chapter 9, "Creating User and Group Accounts."

Table 8-1   How Group Scope Affects Group Capabilities

Group Capability	Domain Local Scope	Global Scope	Universal Scope
Windows Server 2003/Windows 2000 Native Mode	Accounts, global groups, and universal groups from any domain; domain local groups from the same domain only	Accounts and global groups from the same domain only	Accounts from any domain, as well as global and universal groups from any domain
Windows 2000 Mixed Mode	Accounts and global groups from any domain	Only accounts from the same domain	Security universal groups can't be created in mixed-mode domains
Member Of	Can be put into other domain local groups and assigned permissions only in the same domain	Can be put into other groups and assigned permissions in any domain	Can be put into other groups and assigned permissions in any domain
Scope Conversion	Can be converted to universal scope, provided it doesn't have as its member another group having domain local scope	Can be converted to universal scope, provided it's not a member of any other group having global scope	Can't be converted to any other group scope

Security Identifiers and Group Accounts

As with user accounts, Windows Server 2003 uses unique SIDs to track group accounts. This means that you can't delete a group account, recreate it, and then expect all the permissions and privileges to remain the same. The new group will have a new SID, and all the permissions and privileges of the old group will be lost.

Windows Server 2003 creates a security token for each user logon. The security token specifies the user account ID and the SIDs of all the security groups to which the user belongs. The token's size grows as the user is added to additional security groups. This has several consequences:

- The security token must be passed to the user logon process before logon can be completed. Because of this, as the number of security group memberships grows, the logon process takes longer.

- To determine access permissions, the security token is sent to every computer that the user accesses. Because of this, the size of the security token has a direct impact on the network traffic load.

Note   Distribution group memberships aren't distributed with security tokens. Because of this, distribution group memberships don't affect the token size.

When to Use Domain Local, Global, and Universal Groups

Domain local, global, and universal groups provide a lot of options for configuring groups in the enterprise. Although these group scopes are designed to simplify administration, poor planning can make these group scopes your worst administration nightmare. Ideally, you'll use group scopes to help you create group hierarchies that are similar to your organization's structure and the responsibilities of particular groups of users. The best uses for domain local, global, and universal groups are as follows:

Domain local groups   Groups with domain local scope have the smallest extent. Use groups with domain local scope to help you manage access to resources, such as printers and shared folders.

Global groups   Use groups with global scope to help you manage user and computer accounts in a particular domain. Then you can grant access permissions to a resource by making the group with global scope a member of the group with domain local scope.

Universal groups   Groups with universal scope have the largest extent. Use groups with universal scope to consolidate groups that span domains. Normally, you do this by adding global groups as members. Now when you change membership of the global groups, the changes aren't replicated to all the global catalogs. This is because the membership of the universal group didn't change.

Tip   If your organization doesn't have two or more domains, you don't really need to use universal groups. Instead, build your group structure with domain local and global groups. Then, if you ever bring another domain into your domain tree or forest, you can easily extend the group hierarchy to accommodate the integration.

To put this in perspective, consider the following scenario. Say that you have branch offices in Seattle, Chicago, and New York. Each office has its own domain, which is a part of the same domain tree or forest. These domains are called Seattle, Chicago, and NY. You want to make it easy for any administrator (from any office) to manage network resources, so you create a group structure that is very similar at each location. Although the company has marketing, IT, and engineering departments, let's focus on the structure of the marketing department. At each office, members of the marketing department need access to a shared printer called MarketingPrinter and a shared data folder called MarketingData. You also want users to be able to share and print documents. For example, Bob in Seattle should be able to print documents so that Ralph in New York can pick them up on his local printer, and Bob should also be able to access the quarterly report on the shared folder at the New York office.

To configure the groups for the marketing departments at the three offices, you'd perform these steps:

1. Start by creating global groups for each marketing group. In the Seattle domain, create a group called GMarketing and add the members of the Seattle marketing department to it. In the Chicago domain, create a group called GMarketing and add the members of the Chicago marketing department to it. In the NY domain, create a group called GMarketing and add the members of the New York marketing department to it.

2. In each location, create domain local groups that grant access to the shared printers and shared folders. Call the printer group LocalMarketingPrinter. Call the New York shared folder group LocalMarketingData. The Seattle, Chicago, and NY domains should each have their own local groups.

3. Create a group with universal scope called UMarketing on the domain at any branch office. Add Seattle\GMarketing, Chicago\GMarketing, and NY\GMarketing to this group.

4. Add UMarketing to the LocalMarketingPrinter and LocalMarketingData groups at each office. Marketing users should now be able to share data and printers.

Default User Accounts and Groups

When you install Windows Server 2003, the operating system installs default users and groups. These accounts are designed to provide the basic setup necessary to grow your network. Three types of default accounts are provided:

Built-In   User and group accounts installed with the operating system, applications, and services

Predefined   User and group accounts installed with the operating system

Implicit   Special groups created implicitly when accessing network resources; also known as *special identities*

> **Note**   Although you can modify the default users and groups, you can't delete default users and groups created by the operating system. The reason you can't delete these accounts is that you wouldn't be able to recreate them. The SIDs of the old and new accounts wouldn't match, and the permissions and privileges of these accounts would be lost.

Built-In User Accounts

Built-in user accounts have special purposes in Windows Server 2003. All Windows Server 2003 systems have three built-in user accounts:

LocalSystem   LocalSystem is a pseudo-account for running system processes and handling system-level tasks. This account grants the logon right Log On As A Service. Most services run under the LocalSystem account. In some cases, these services have the privilege to interact with the desktop. Services that need alternative privileges or logon rights run under the LocalService or NetworkService accounts.

LocalService   LocalService is a pseudo-account for running services that need additional privileges and logon rights on a local system. Services that run under this account are granted the right to Log On As A Service and the privileges Change The System Time and Generate Security Audits by default. Services that run as LocalService include Alerter, Messenger, Remote Registry, Smart Card, Smart Card Helper, SSDP Discovery Service, TCP/IP NetBIOS Helper, Uninterruptible Power Supply, and WebClient.

NetworkService   NetworkService is a pseudo-account for running services that need additional privileges and logon rights on a local system and the network. As with LocalService, services that run under the NetworkService account are granted the right to Log On As A Service and the privileges Change The System Time and Generate Security Audits. Services that run as NetworkService include Distributed Transaction Coordinator, DNS Client, Performance Logs and Alerts, and Remote Procedure Call (RPC) Locator.

When you install add-ons or other applications on a server, other default accounts might be installed. You can usually delete these accounts.

When you install IIS, you might find several new accounts, including IUSR_*hostname* and IWAM_*hostname*, where *hostname* is the computer name. The IUSR_*hostname* account is the built-in account for anonymous access to IIS. IIS uses the IWAM_*hostname* account to start out-of-process applications. These accounts are defined in Active Directory when they're configured on a domain. However, they're defined as local users when they're configured on a stand-alone server or workstation. Another built-in account that you might see is TSInternetUser. Terminal Services uses this account.

Predefined User Accounts

Several predefined user accounts are installed with Windows Server 2003: Administrator, ASPNET, Guest, and Support. With member servers, predefined accounts are local to the individual system they're installed on.

Predefined accounts have counterparts in Active Directory. These accounts have domain-wide access and are completely separate from the local accounts on individual systems.

The Administrator Account

Administrator is a predefined account that provides complete access to files, directories, services, and other facilities. You can't delete or disable this account. In Active Directory, the Administrator account has domain-wide access and privileges. Otherwise, the Administrator account generally has access only to the local system. Although files and directories can be protected from the Administrator account temporarily, the Administrator account can take control of these resources at any time by changing the access permissions. See Chapter 13, "Managing Files and Folders."

> **Security**   To prevent unauthorized access to the system or domain, be sure to give the account an especially secure password. Also, because this is a known Windows account, you might want to rename the account as an extra security precaution. If you rename the original Administrator account, you might also want to create a dummy Administrator account. This dummy account should have no permissions, rights, or privileges, and you should disable it.

You usually won't need to change the basic settings for this account. However, you might need to change its advanced settings, such as membership in particular groups. By default, the Administrator account for a domain is a member of these groups: Administrators, Domain Admins, Domain Users, Enterprise Admins, Group Policy Creator Owners, and Schema Admins. You'll find more information on these groups in the next section.

> **Real World**   In a domain environment, you'll use the local Administrator account primarily to manage the system when you first install it. This allows you to set up the system without getting locked out. You probably won't use the account once the system has been installed. Instead, you'll probably want to make your administrators members of the Administrators group. This ensures that you can revoke administrator privileges without having to change the passwords for all the Administrator accounts.
>
> For a system that's part of a workgroup where each individual computer is managed separately, you'll typically rely on this account anytime you need to perform your system administration duties. Here, you probably won't want to set up individual accounts for each person who has administrative access to a system. Instead, you'll use a single Administrator account on each computer.

The ASPNET Account

The ASPNET account is used by the built-in .NET framework and is designed so that the account can run ASP.NET worker processes. The account is a member of the Domain Users Group and, as such, the account has all the same privileges as ordinary users in the domain.

The Guest Account

Guest is designed for users who need one-time or occasional access. Although guests have limited system privileges, you should be very careful about using this account. Whenever you use this account, you open the system to potential security problems. The risk is so great that the account is initially disabled when you install Windows Server 2003.

The Guest account is a member of Domain Guests and Guests by default. It is important to note that the Guest account—like all other named accounts—is also a member of the implicit group Everyone. The Everyone group typically has access to files and folders by default. The Everyone group also has a default set of user rights.

Security   If you decide to enable the Guest account, be sure to restrict its use and to change the password regularly. As with the Administrator account, you might want to rename the account as an added security precaution.

The Support Account

The Support account is used by the built-in Help And Support service. The account is a member of the HelpServicesGroup and Domain Users. The account has the right to log on as a batch job. This user rights assignment allows the Support account to execute batch updates.

Security   The Support account is denied the right to log on locally (other than as a batch job) and is also denied the right to log on to the computer over the network. These restrictions are important to ensure that system security isn't compromised.

Built-In and Predefined Groups

Built-in groups are installed with all Windows Server 2003 systems. Use built-in and predefined groups to grant a user the group's privileges and permissions. You do this by making the user a member of the group. For example, you give a user administrative access to the system by making a user a member of the local Administrators group. You give a user administrative access to the domain by making a user a member of the domain local Administrators group in Active Directory.

Implicit Groups and Special Identities

In Windows NT, implicit groups were assigned implicitly during logon and were based on how a user accessed a network resource. For example, if a user accessed a resource through interactive logon, the user was automatically a member of the implicit group called Interactive. In Windows 2000 and Windows Server 2003, the object-based approach to the directory structure changes the original rules for implicit groups.

Although you still can't view the membership of special identities, you can grant membership in implicit groups to users, groups, and computers.

To reflect the new role, implicit groups are also referred to as *special identities*. A special identity is a group whose membership can be set implicitly, such as during logon, or explicitly through security access permissions. As with other default groups, the availability of a specific implicit group depends on the current configuration. Use Table 8-2 to determine the availability of the various implicit groups. Implicit groups are discussed later in this chapter.

Table 8-2   Availability of Implicit Groups Based on the Type of Network Resource

Group Name	Active Directory Domain	Windows Server 2003 Member Server
Anonymous Logon	Yes	Yes
Authenticated Users	Yes	Yes
Batch	Yes	Yes
Creator Group	Yes	Yes
Creator Owner	Yes	Yes
Dialup	Yes	Yes
Enterprise Domain Controllers	Yes	No
Everyone	Yes	Yes
Interactive	Yes	Yes
Local Service	No	Yes
Network	Yes	Yes
Network Service	No	Yes
Proxy	Yes	No
Remote Interactive Logon	No	Yes
Restricted	Yes	No
Self	Yes	No
Service	Yes	Yes
System	Yes	Yes
Terminal Server User	Yes	Yes

Account Capabilities

When you set up a user account, you can grant the user specific capabilities. You generally assign these capabilities by making the user a member of one or more groups, thus giving the user the capabilities of these groups. You withdraw capabilities by removing group membership.

In Windows Server 2003, you can assign various types of capabilities to an account. These capabilities include:

Privileges   A type of user right that grants permissions to perform specific administrative tasks. You can assign privileges to both user and group accounts. An example of a privilege is the ability to shut down the system.

Logon rights   A type of user right that grants logon permissions. You can assign logon rights to both user and group accounts. An example of a logon right is the ability to log on locally.

Built-in capabilities   A type of user right that is assigned to groups and includes the group's automatic capabilities. Built-in capabilities are predefined and unchangeable, but they can be delegated to users with permission to manage objects, organizational units, or other containers. An example of a built-in capability is the ability to create, delete, and manage user accounts. This capability is assigned to administrators and account operators. Thus, if a user is a member of the Administrators group, the user can create, delete, and manage user accounts.

Access permissions   A type of user right that defines the operations that can be performed on network resources. You can assign access permissions to users, computers, and groups. An example of an access permission is the ability to create a file in a directory. Access permissions are discussed in Chapter 13.

As an administrator, you'll be dealing with account capabilities every day. To help track built-in capabilities, refer to the following sections. Keep in mind that although you can't change a group's built-in capabilities, you can change a group's default rights. For example, an administrator could revoke network access to a computer by removing a group's right to access the computer from the network.

Privileges

A privilege is a type of user right that grants permissions to perform a specific administrative task. You assign privileges through group policies, which can be applied to individual computers, organizational units, and domains. Although you can assign privileges to both users and groups, you'll usually want to assign privileges to groups. In this way, users are automatically assigned the appropriate privileges when they become members of a group. Assigning privileges to groups also makes it easier to manage user accounts.

Table 8-3 provides a brief summary of each of the privileges that you can assign to users and groups. To learn how to assign privileges, see Chapter 9.

Table 8-3   Windows Server 2003 Privileges for Users and Groups

Privilege	Description
Act As Part Of The Operating System	Allows a process to authenticate as any user and gain access to resources as any user. Processes that require this privilege should use the LocalSystem account, which already has this privilege.
Add Workstations To Domain	Allows users to add computers to the domain.
Adjust Memory Quotas For A Process	Allows users to adjust process-based memory usage quotas.
Back Up Files And Directories	Allows users to back up the system regardless of the permissions set on files and directories.
Bypass Traverse Checking	Allows users to pass through directories while navigating an object path regardless of permissions set on the directories. The privilege doesn't allow the user to list directory contents.
Change The System Time	Allows users to set the time for the system clock.
Create A Pagefile	Allows users to create and change paging file size for virtual memory.
Create A Token Object	Allows processes to create token objects that can be used to gain access to local resources. Processes that require this privilege should use the LocalSystem account, which already has this privilege.
Create Permanent Shared Objects	Allows processes to create directory objects in the Windows 2000, Windows XP Professional, or Windows Server 2003 object manager. Most components already have this privilege, and it's not necessary to specifically assign it.
Debug Programs	Allows users to perform debugging.
Enable User And Computer Accounts To Be Trusted For Delegation	Allows users and computers to change or apply the trusted for delegation setting, provided they have write access to the object.
Force Shutdown Of A Remote System	Allows users to shut down a computer from a remote location on the network.
Generate Security Audits	Allows processes to make security log entries for auditing object access.
Impersonate A Client After Authentication	Allows Web applications to act as clients during processing of requests. Services and users can also act as clients.
Increase Scheduling Priority	Allows processes to increase the scheduling priority assigned to another process, provided they have write access to the process.

Table 8-3   Windows Server 2003 Privileges for Users and Groups

Privilege	Description
Load And Unload Device Drivers	Allows users to install and uninstall Plug and Play device drivers. This doesn't affect device drivers that aren't Plug and Play, which can only be installed by administrators.
Lock Pages In Memory	Allows processes to keep data in physical memory, preventing the system from paging data to virtual memory on disk.
Manage Auditing And Security Log	Allows users to specify auditing options and access the security log. You must turn on auditing in the group policy first.
Modify Firmware Environment Values	Allows users and processes to modify system environment variables.
Perform Volume Maintenance Tasks	Allows administration of removable storage, disk defragmenter, and disk management.
Profile A Single Process	Allows users to monitor the performance of nonsystem processes.
Profile System Performance	Allows users to monitor the performance of system processes.
Remove Computer From Docking Station	Allows undocking a laptop and removing it from the network.
Replace A Process Level Token	Allows processes to replace the default token for subprocesses.
Restore Files And Directories	Allows users to restore backed-up files and directories, regardless of the permissions set on files and directories.
Shut Down The System	Allows users to shut down the local computer.
Synchronize Directory Service Data	Allows users to synchronize directory service data on domain controllers.
Take Ownership Of Files Or Other Objects	Allows users to take ownership of files and any other Active Directory objects.

Logon Rights

A *logon right* is a type of user right that grants logon permissions. You can assign logon rights to both user and group accounts. As with privileges, you assign logon rights through group policies, and you'll usually want to assign logon rights to groups rather than to individual users.

Table 8-4 provides a brief summary of each of the logon rights that you can assign to users and groups. To learn how to assign logon rights, see Chapter 9.

Table 8-4   Windows Server 2003 Logon Rights for Users and Groups

Logon Right	Description
Access This Computer From The Network	Grants remote access to the computer.
Allow Logon Locally	Grants permission to log on at the computer's keyboard. On servers, this right is restricted by default and only members of these groups can log on locally: Administrators, Account Operators, Backup Operators, Print Operators, and Server Operators.
Allow Logon Through Terminal Services	Grants access through Terminal Services; necessary for remote assistance and remote desktop.
Deny Access To This Computer From The Network	Denies remote access to the computer through network services.
Deny Logon As Batch Job	Denies the right to log on through a batch job or script.
Deny Logon As Service	Denies the right to log on as a service.
Deny Logon Locally	Denies the right to log on to the computer's keyboard.
Deny Logon Through Terminal Services	Denies the right to log on through Terminal Services.
Log On As A Batch Job	Grants permission to log on as a batch job or script.
Log On As A Service	Grants permission to log on as a service. LocalSystem account has this right. A service that runs under a separate account should be assigned this right.

Built-In Capabilities for Groups in Active Directory

The built-in capabilities for groups in Active Directory are fairly extensive. The tables that follow summarize the most common capabilities that are assigned by default. Table 8-5 shows the default user rights for groups in Active Directory domains. This includes both privileges and logon rights. Note that any action that's available to the Everyone group is available to all groups, including the Guests group. This means that although the Guests group doesn't have explicit permission to access the computer from the network, a member of the Guests group can still access the system because the Everyone group has this right.

Table 8-5   Default User Rights for Groups in Active Directory

User Right	Groups Assigned
Access This Computer From The Network	Everyone, Administrators, Authenticated Users, Enterprise Domain Controllers, IWAM_host, IUSR_host, Pre-Windows 2000 Compatible Access
Add Workstations To Domain	Authenticated Users
Adjust Memory Quotas For A Process	Administrators, IWAM_host, Local Service, Network Service
Allow Logon Locally	Account Operators, Administrators, Backup Operators, IUSR_host, Print Operators, Server Operators
Back Up Files And Directories	Administrators, Server Operators, Backup Operators
Bypass Traverse Checking	Everyone, Authenticated Users, Administrators, Pre-Windows 2000 Compatible Access
Change The System Time	Administrators, Server Operators
Create A Pagefile	Administrators
Debug Programs	Administrators
Deny Access To This Computer From The Network	Support
Deny Logon Locally	Support
Enable Computer And User Accounts To Be Trusted For Delegation	Administrators
Force Shutdown From A Remote System	Administrators, Server Operators
Generate Security Audits	Local Service, Network Service
Increase Quotas	Administrators
Increase Scheduling Priority	Administrators
Load And Unload Device Drivers	Administrators, Print Operators
Log On As Batch Job	Administrator, IUSR_host, IWAM_host, Support, Local Service, IIS_WPG
Log On As A Service	Network Service
Manage Auditing And Security Log	Administrators
Modify Firmware Environment Variables	Administrators
Profile Single Process	Administrators
Profile System Performance	Administrators

Table 8-5   Default User Rights for Groups in Active Directory

User Right	Groups Assigned
Remove Computer From Docking Station	Administrators
Replace A Process Level Token	IWAM_host, Local Service, Network Service
Restore Files And Directories	Administrators, Backup Operators, Server Operators
Shut Down The System	Account Operators, Administrators, Backup Operators, Print Operators, Server Operators
Take Ownership Of Files Or Other Objects	Administrators

Table 8-6 shows the default user rights for local groups on member servers. Again, this includes both privileges and logon rights. Note that on these systems, Power Users have privileges that normal users don't.

Table 8-6   Default User Rights for Workgroups and Member Servers

User Right	Groups Assigned
Adjust Memory Quotas For A Process	Administrators, Local Service, Network Service, IWAM_host
Allow Logon Through Terminal Services	Administrators, Remote Desktop Users
Back Up Files And Directories	Administrators, Backup Operators
Bypass Traverse Checking	Everyone, Administrators, Users, Power Users, Backup Operators
Change The System Time	Administrators, Power Users
Create A Pagefile	Administrators
Debug Programs	Administrators
Deny Access To The Computer From The Network	Support
Deny Logon Locally	Support
Deny Logon Through Terminal Services	ASPNET
Force Shutdown From A Remote System	Administrators
Generate Security Audits	Local Service, Network Service
Impersonate A Client After Authentication	Administrators, ASPNET, IIS_WPG, Service
Increase Scheduling Priority	Administrators
Load And Unload Device Drivers	Administrators
Log On As A Batch Job	ASPNET, IIS_WPG, IUSR_host, IWAM_host, Local Service

Table 8-6   Default User Rights for Workgroups and Member Servers

User Right	Groups Assigned
Log On As Service	ASPNET, Network Service
Log On Locally	IUSR_host, Administrators, Users, Power Users, Backup Operators
Manage Auditing And Security Log	Administrators
Modify Firmware Environment Variables	Administrators
Perform Volume Maintenance Tasks	Administrators
Profile Single Process	Administrators, Power Users
Profile System Performance	Administrators
Remove Computer From Docking Station	Administrators, Power Users
Replace A Process Level Token	Local Service, Network Service, IWAM_host
Restore Files And Directories	Administrators, Backup Operators
Shut Down The System	Administrators, Backup Operators, Power Users
Take Ownership Of Files Or Other Objects	Administrators

Table 8-7 summarizes capabilities that you can delegate to other users and groups. As you study the table, note that restricted accounts include the Administrator user account, the user accounts of administrators, and the group accounts for Administrators, Server Operators, Account Operators, Backup Operators, and Print Operators. Because these accounts are restricted, Account Operators can't create or modify them.

Table 8-7   Other Capabilities for Built-In and Local Groups

Task	Description	Group Normally Assigned
Assign User Rights	Allows user to assign user rights to other users	Administrators
Create, Delete, And Manage User Accounts	Allows user to administer domain user accounts	Administrators, Account Operators
Modify The Membership Of A Group	Allows user to add and remove users from domain groups	Administrators, Account Operators
Create And Delete Groups	Allows user to create new group and delete existing groups	Administrators, Account Operators
Reset Passwords On User Accounts	Allows user to reset passwords on user accounts	Administrators, Account Operators

Table 8-7   Other Capabilities for Built-In and Local Groups

Task	Description	Group Normally Assigned
Read All User Information	Allows user to view user account information	Administrators, Server Operators, Account Operators
Manage Group Policy Links	Allows user to apply existing group policies to sites, domains, and organizational units for which they have write access to the related objects	Administrators
Manage Printers	Allows user to modify printer settings and manage print queues	Administrators, Server Operators, Printer Operators
Create And Delete Printers	Allows user to create and delete printers	Administrators, Server Operators, Printer Operators

Using Default Group Accounts

The default group accounts are designed to be versatile. By assigning users to the correct groups, you can make managing your Windows Server 2003 workgroup or domain a lot easier. Unfortunately, with so many groups, understanding the purpose of each isn't easy. To help, let's take a closer look at groups used by administrators and groups that are implicitly created.

Groups Used by Administrators

An administrator is someone who has wide access to network resources. Administrators can create accounts, modify user rights, install printers, manage shared resources, and more. The main administrator groups are Administrators, Domain Admins, and Enterprise Admins, as compared in Table 8-8.

Tip   The local group Administrator and the global groups Domain Admins and Enterprise Admins are members of the Administrators group. The Administrator user membership is used to access the local computer. The Domain Admins membership allows other administrators to access the system from elsewhere in the domain. The Enterprise Admins membership allows other administrators to access the system from other domains in the current domain tree or forest. To prevent enterprise-wide access to a domain, you can remove Enterprise Admins from this group.

Table 8-8 Administrator Groups Overview

Administrator Group Type	Network Environment	Group Scope	Membership	Account Administration
Administrators	Active Directory domains	Domain Local	Administrator, Domain Admins, Enterprise Admins	Administrators
Administrators	Workgroups, computers not part of a domain	Local	Administrator	Administrators
Domain Admins	Active Directory domains	Global	Administrator	Administrators
Enterprise Admins	Active Directory domains	Global or Universal	Administrator	Administrators

Administrators is a local group that provides full administrative access to an individual computer or a single domain, depending on its location. Because this account has complete access, you should be very careful about adding users to this group. To make someone an administrator for a local computer or domain, all you need to do is make that person a member of this group. Only members of the Administrators group can modify this account.

Domain Admins is a global group designed to help you administer all the computers in a domain. This group has administrative control over all computers in a domain because it's a member of the Administrators group by default. To make someone an administrator for a domain, make that person a member of this group.

Tip In a Windows Server 2003 domain, the Administrator local user is a member of Domain Admins by default. This means that if someone logs on to a computer as the administrator and the computer is a member of the domain, the user will have complete access to all resources in the domain. To prevent this, you can remove the local Administrator account from the Domain Admins group.

Enterprise Admins is a global group designed to help you administer all the computers in a domain tree or forest. This group has administrative control over all computers in the enterprise because it's a member of the Administrators group by default. To make someone an administrator for the enterprise, make that person a member of this group.

Tip In a Windows Server 2003 domain, the Administrator local user is a member of Enterprise Admins by default. This means that if someone logs on to a computer as the administrator and the computer is a member of the domain, the user will have complete access to the domain tree or forest. To prevent this, you can remove the local Administrator account from the Enterprise Admins group.

Implicit Groups and Identities

Windows Server 2003 defines a set of special identities that you can use to assign permissions in certain situations. You usually assign permissions implicitly to special identities. However, you can assign permissions to special identities when you modify Active Directory objects. The special identities include:

The Anonymous Logon identity   Any user accessing the system through anonymous logon has the Anonymous Logon identity. This identity is used to allow anonymous access to resources, such as a Web page published on the corporate presence servers.

The Authenticated Users identity   Any user accessing the system through a logon process has the Authenticated Users identity. This identity is used to allow access to shared resources within the domain, such as files in a shared folder that should be accessible to all the workers in the organization.

The Batch identity   Any user or process accessing the system as a batch job (or through the batch queue) has the Batch identity. This identity is used to allow batch jobs to run scheduled tasks, such as a nightly cleanup job that deletes temporary files.

The Creator Group identity   Windows Server 2003 uses this group to automatically grant access permissions to users who are members of the same group(s) as the creator of a file or a directory.

The Creator Owner identity   The person who created the file or the directory is a member of this group. Windows Server 2003 uses this group to automatically grant access permissions to the creator of a file or directory.

The Dial-Up identity   Any user accessing the system through a dial-up connection has the Dial-Up identity. This identity is used to distinguish dial-up users from other types of authenticated users.

The Enterprise Domain Controllers identity   Domain controllers with enterprise-wide roles and responsibilities have the Enterprise Domain Controllers identity. This identity allows them to perform certain tasks in the enterprise using transitive trusts.

The Everyone identity   All interactive, network, dial-up, and authenticated users are members of the Everyone group. This group is used to give wide access to a system resource.

The Interactive identity   Any user logged on to the local system has the Interactive identity. This identity is used to allow only local users to access a resource.

The Network identity   Any user accessing the system through a network has the Network identity. This identity is used to allow only remote users to access a resource.

The Proxy identity   Users and computers accessing resources through a proxy have the Proxy identity. This identity is used when proxies are implemented on the network.

The Restricted identity   Users and computers with restricted capabilities have the Restricted identity. On a member server or workstation, a local user who is a member of the Users group (rather than the Power Users group) has this identity.

The Self identity   The Self identity refers to the object itself and allows the object to modify itself.

The Service identity   Any service accessing the system has the Service identity. This identity grants access to processes being run by Windows Server 2003 services.

The System identity   The Windows Server 2003 operating system itself has the System identity. This identity is used when the operating system needs to perform a system-level function.

The Terminal Server User identity   Any user accessing the system through Terminal Services has the Terminal Server User identity. This identity allows terminal server users to access terminal server applications and to perform other necessary tasks with Terminal Services.

Chapter 9

Creating User and Group Accounts

A key part of your job as an administrator is to create accounts, and this chapter will show you how to do so. User and group accounts allow Microsoft Windows Server 2003 to track and manage information about users, including permissions and privileges. When you create user accounts, the primary account administration tools you use are:

■ Active Directory Users And Computers, which is designed to administer accounts throughout an Active Directory directory service domain

■ Local Users And Groups, which is designed to administer accounts on a local computer

Creating domain accounts, as well as local users and groups, is covered in this chapter.

User Account Setup and Organization

The most important aspects of account creation are account setup and organization. Without the appropriate guidelines and policies, you might quickly find that you need to rework all your user accounts. So, before you create accounts, determine the policies you'll use for setup and organization.

Account Naming Policies

A key policy you'll need to set is the naming scheme for accounts. User accounts have display names and logon names. The *display name* (or full name) is the name displayed to users and the name referenced in user sessions. The *logon name* is the name used to log on to the domain. Logon names were discussed briefly in the section entitled "Logon Names, Passwords, and Public Certificates" in Chapter 8, "Understanding User and Group Accounts."

Rules for Display Names

For domain accounts, the display name is normally the concatenation of the user's first name, middle initial, and last name, but you can set it to any string value. The display names must follow these rules:

- Local display names must be unique on an individual computer.

- Display names must be unique throughout a domain.

- Display names must be no more than 64 characters long.

- Display names can contain alphanumeric characters and special characters.

Rules for Logon Names

Logon names must follow these rules:

- Local logon names must be unique on an individual computer, and global logon names must be unique throughout a domain.

- Logon names can be up to 256 characters. However, it isn't practical to use logon names that are longer than 64 characters.

- A pre-Windows 2000 logon name is given to all accounts, which by default is set to the first 20 characters of the Windows logon name. The pre-Windows 2000 logon name must be unique throughout a domain.

- Users logging on to the domain with Windows 2000 or later can use their standard logon name or their pre-Windows 2000 logon name, regardless of the domain operations mode.

- Logon names can't contain certain characters. Invalid characters are:

  " / \ [ ] ; | = , + * ? < >

- Logon names can contain all other special characters, including spaces, periods, dashes, and underscores. But, it's generally not a good idea to use spaces in account names.

Note   Although Windows Server 2003 stores user names in the case that you enter, user names aren't case sensitive. For example, you can access the Administrator account with the user name Administrator, administrator, or ADMINISTRATOR. Thus, user names are case aware but not case sensitive.

Naming Schemes

You'll find that most small organizations tend to assign logon names that use the user's first or last name. But you can have more than one Tom, Dick, or Jane in an organization of any size. So, rather than having to rework your logon naming scheme when you run into problems, select a good naming scheme now and make sure other administrators use it. For naming accounts, you should use a consistent procedure that allows your user base to grow, limits the possibility of name conflicts, and ensures that your accounts have secure names that aren't easily exploited. If you follow these guidelines, the types of naming schemes you might want to use include:

- User's first name and last initial

- User's first initial and last name

- User's first initial, middle initial, and last name

- User's first initial, middle initial, and first five characters of the last name

- User's first name and last name

Security   In tight security environments, you can assign a numeric code for the logon name. This numeric code should be at least 20 characters long. Combine this strict naming method with smart cards and smart card readers to allow users to quickly log on to the domain without having to type in all those characters. Don't worry, users can still have a display name that humans can read.

Password and Account Policies

Domain accounts use passwords or private keys from certificates to authenticate access to network resources. This section focuses on passwords.

Using Secure Passwords

A password is a case-sensitive string that can contain in excess of 127 characters with Active Directory and up to 14 characters with Windows NT Security Manager. Valid characters for passwords are letters, numbers, and symbols. When you set a password for an account, Windows Server 2003 stores the password in an encrypted format in the account database.

But simply having a password isn't enough. The key to preventing unauthorized access to network resources is to use secure passwords. The difference between an average password and a secure password is that secure passwords are difficult to guess and crack. You make passwords difficult to guess and crack by using combinations of all the available character types—including lowercase letters, uppercase letters, numbers, and symbols. For example, instead of using happydays for a password, you would use haPPy2Days&, Ha**y!dayS, or even h*PPY%d*ys.

You might also want to use password phrases. With a password phrase, you use multiple words and punctuation, like a sentence, as the password. For example, you might use the password phrase: This problem is 99 times ten! A password phrase that includes punctuation and numbers meets all complexity requirements and is incredibly difficult to crack.

Unfortunately, no matter how secure you initially make a user's password, eventually the user usually chooses the password. Because of this, you'll want to set account policies that define a secure password for your systems. Account policies are a subset of the policies configurable as a group policy.

Setting Account Policies

As you know from previous discussions, you can apply group policies at various levels within the network structure. You manage local group policies in the manner discussed in the section entitled "Managing Local Group Policies" in Chapter 4, "Automating Administrative Tasks, Policies, and Procedures." You manage global group policies as explained in the section of Chapter 4 entitled "Managing Site, Domain, and Unit Policies."

Account policies should be configured in the highest precedence Group Policy Object (GPO) linked to a domain. By default, the highest precedence GPO linked to a domain is the Default Domain Policy GPO. Once you access the Default Domain Policy GPO or other appropriate GPO, you can set account policies by completing the following steps:

1. As shown in Figure 9-1, access the Account Policies node within Group Policy. To do so, expand Computer Configuration, then Windows Settings, and then Security Settings.

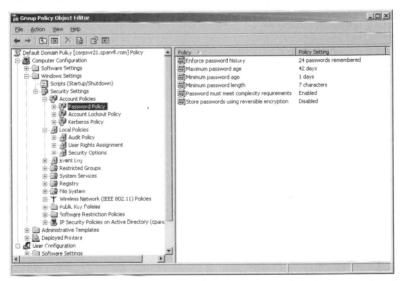

Figure 9-1 Use entries in the Account Policies node to set policies for passwords and general account use. The console tree shows the name of the computer or domain you're configuring. Be sure this is the appropriate network resource to configure.

2. You can now manage account policies through the Password Policy, Account Lockout Policy, and Kerberos Policy nodes.

Note Kerberos policies aren't used with local computers. Kerberos policies are only available with group policies that affect domains.

3. To configure a policy, double-click its entry or right-click it and select Properties. This opens a Properties dialog box for the policy.

4. For a local policy, the Properties dialog box is similar to the one shown in Figure 9-2. In domains, the effective policy for the computer is displayed but you can't change it. For stand-alone servers, you can change the local policy settings, however. Use the fields provided to configure the local policy. For a local policy, skip the remaining steps; those steps apply to global group policies.

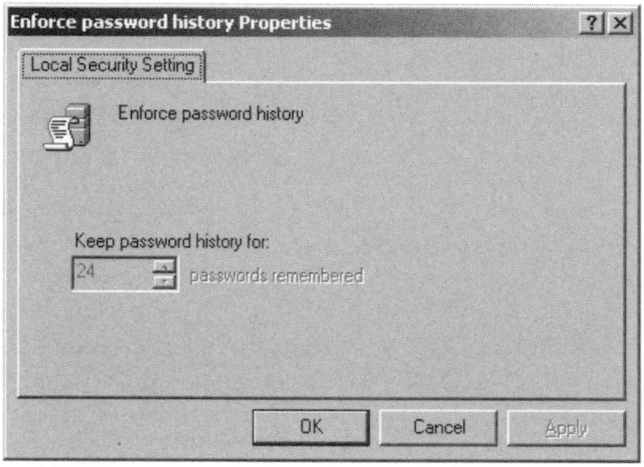

Figure 9-2 With local policies, you'll see the effective policy. For controllers and member servers, you must use the appropriate site, domain, or unit policy to change the settings.

Note Domain policies have precedence over local policies. The GPO with a link order of 1 in the domain will always have the highest precedence.

5. For a domain, the Properties dialog box is similar to the one shown in Figure 9-3.

6. All policies are either defined or not defined. That is, they are either configured for use or not configured for use. A policy that isn't defined in the current container could be inherited from another container.

7. Select or clear the Define This Policy Setting check box to determine whether a policy is defined.

Tip Policies can have additional fields for configuring the policy. Often these fields are option buttons labeled Enabled and Disabled. Enabled turns on the policy restriction. Disabled turns off the policy restriction. Some policies are negations, which means that by enabling them you are actually negating the item. For example, Disable Log On As A Service is the negation of the item Log On As A Service.

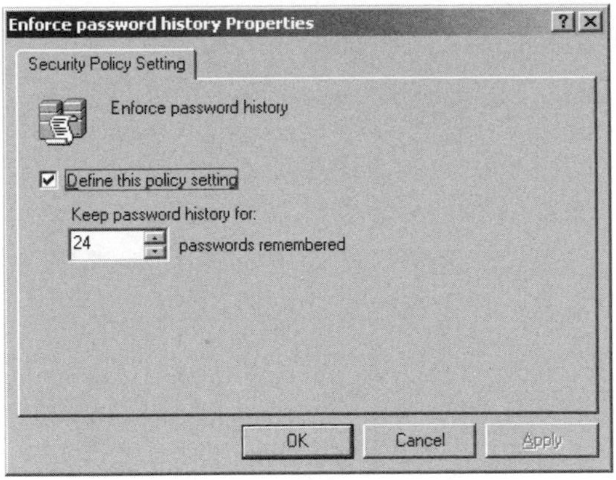

Figure 9-3   Define and configure global group policies using their Properties dialog box.

Specific procedures for working with account policies are discussed in the sections of this chapter entitled "Configuring Password Policies," "Configuring Account Lockout Policies," and "Configuring Kerberos Policies." This chapter's next section, "Viewing Effective Policies," teaches you more about viewing the effective policy on a local computer.

Viewing Effective Policies

When working with account policies and user rights assignment, you'll often want to view the effective policy on a system and see from where a particular policy setting originates. The effective policy is the policy being enforced, and, as discussed in the section of Chapter 4 entitled "Group Policy Management," the effective policy depends on the order in which you apply the policies.

To view the effective policy on a system and see from where it originates, complete the following steps.

1. Open the Run dialog box by clicking Start and then selecting Run.

2. Type **mmc** in the Open field and then click OK. This opens the Microsoft Management Console (MMC).

3. In MMC, select File, and then select Add/Remove Snap-In. This opens the Add/Remove Snap-In dialog box.

4. In the Standalone tab, click Add.

5. In the Add Standalone Snap-In dialog box, select Resultant Set Of Policy, and then click Add.

6. Close the Add Standalone Snap-In dialog box by clicking Close, and then click OK.

7. Right-click the Resultant Set Of Policy node and then select Generate RSoP Data. This starts the Resultant Set Of Policy Wizard. Click Next twice.

8. To view Computer Configuration policy settings for the local computer, select This Computer. Otherwise, select Another Computer and then type the name of the system to check. Click Browse if you want to use the Select Computer dialog box to find the system you want to use. Click Next.

9. To view User Configuration policy settings for the current user, select Current User. Otherwise, choose Select A Specific User and then select the account entry for a different user who's logged on to the system.

10. Click Next twice and then click Finish. Now when you access a policy node in the Resultant Set Of Policy console as shown in Figure 9-4, you'll see the effective setting, listed as the Computer Setting, and the source Group Policy Object (GPO).

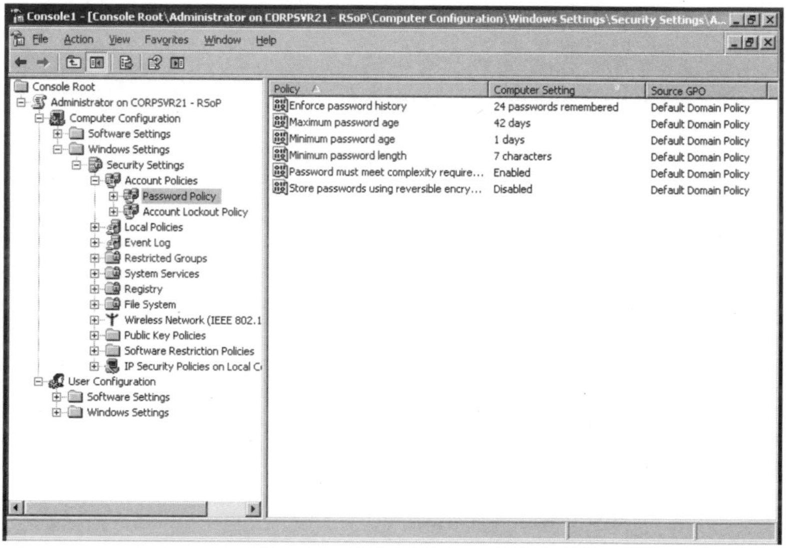

Figure 9-4   Resultant Set of Policy shows the effective setting as well as the source Group Policy Object.

Configuring Account Policies

As you learned in the previous section, there are three types of account policies: password policies, account lockout policies, and Kerberos policies. The sections that follow show you how to configure each one of these policies.

Configuring Password Policies

Password policies control security for passwords, and they are:

- Enforce Password History

- Maximum Password Age

- Minimum Password Age

- Minimum Password Length

- Passwords Must Meet Complexity Requirements

- Store Password Using Reversible Encryption For All Users In The Domain

The uses of these policies are discussed in the following sections.

Enforce Password History

Enforce Password History sets how frequently old passwords can be reused. You can use this policy to discourage users from changing among a set of common passwords. Windows Server 2003 can store up to 24 passwords for each user in the password history.

To disable this feature, set the size of the password history to zero. To enable this feature, set the size of the password history using the Passwords Remembered field. Windows Server 2003 then tracks old passwords using a password history that's unique for each user, and users aren't allowed to reuse any of the stored passwords.

> **Note**   To discourage users from bypassing Enforce Password History, you shouldn't allow them to change passwords immediately. This prevents users from changing their passwords several times to get back to their old passwords. You set the time required to keep a password with the Minimum Password Age policy, as discussed in the next section.

Maximum Password Age

Maximum Password Age determines how long users can keep a password before they have to change it. The aim is to force users to change their passwords periodically. When you use this feature, set a value that makes sense for your network. Generally, you use a shorter period when security is very important and a longer period when security is less important.

You can set the maximum password age to any value from 0 to 999. A value of zero specifies that passwords don't expire. Although you might be tempted to set no expiration date, users should change passwords regularly to ensure the network's security. Where security is a concern, good values are 30, 60, or 90 days. Where security is less important, good values are 120, 150, or 180 days.

> **Note**   Windows Server 2003 notifies users when they're getting close to the password expiration date. Any time the expiration date is less than 30 days away, users see a warning when they log on that they have to change their password within a specific number of days.

Minimum Password Age

Minimum Password Age determines how long users must keep a password before they can change it. You can use this field to prevent users from bypassing the password system by entering a new password and then changing it right back to the old one.

If the minimum password age is set to zero, users can change their passwords immediately. To prevent this, set a specific minimum age. Reasonable settings are from three to seven days. In this way you make sure that users are less inclined to switch back to an old password but are able to change their passwords in a reasonable amount of time if they want to. Keep in mind that a minimum password age could prevent a user from changing a compromised password. If a user can't change the password, then an administrator will have to do it for them.

Minimum Password Length

Minimum Password Length sets the minimum number of characters for a password. If you haven't changed the default setting, you'll want to do so immediately. The default in some cases is to allow empty passwords (passwords with zero characters), which is definitely not a good idea.

For security reasons you'll generally want passwords of at least eight characters. The reason for this is that long passwords are usually harder to crack than short ones. If you want greater security, set the minimum password length to 14 characters.

Passwords Must Meet Complexity Requirements

Beyond the basic password and account policies, Windows Server 2003 includes facilities for creating additional password controls. These facilities enforce the use of secure passwords that follow these guidelines:

- Passwords must be at least six characters long.

- Passwords can't contain the user name, such as *stevew*, or parts of the user's full name, such as *steve*.

- Passwords must use at least three of the four available character types: lowercase letters, uppercase letters, numbers, and symbols.

To enforce these rules, enable Passwords Must Meet Complexity Requirements. Passwords are then required to meet the security requirements listed previously.

Store Password Using Reversible Encryption For All Users In The Domain

Passwords in the password database are encrypted. This encryption normally can't be reversed. The only time you'd want to change this setting is if your organization uses applications that need to be able to read the password. If this is the case, you could enable Store Password Using Reversible Encryption For All Users In The Domain.

With this policy enabled, passwords might as well be stored as plain text. It presents the same security risks. With this in mind, a much better technique would be to enable the option on a per-user basis and then only as required to meet the user's actual needs.

Configuring Account Lockout Policies

Account lockout policies control how and when accounts are locked out of the domain or the local system. These policies are:

- Account Lockout Threshold
- Account Lockout Duration
- Reset Account Lockout Counter After

Account Lockout Threshold

Account Lockout Threshold sets the number of logon attempts that are allowed before an account is locked out. If you decide to use lockout controls, you should set this field to a value that balances the need to prevent account cracking against the needs of users who are having difficulty accessing their accounts.

The main reason users might not be able to access their accounts properly the first time is that they forgot their passwords. If this is the case, it might take them several attempts to log on properly. Workgroup users could also have problems accessing a remote system where their current passwords don't match the passwords that the remote system expects. If this happens, the remote system might record several bad logon attempts before the user ever gets a prompt to enter the correct password. The reason is that Windows Server 2003 might attempt to automatically log on to the remote system. In a domain environment, this normally doesn't happen because of the Single Log-On feature.

You can set the lockout threshold to any value from 0 to 999. The lockout threshold is set to zero by default, which means that accounts won't be locked out because of invalid logon attempts. Any other value sets a specific lockout threshold. Keep in mind that the higher the lockout value, the higher the risk that a hacker might be able to break into your system. A reasonable range of values for this threshold is between 7 and 15. This is high enough to rule out user error and low enough to deter hackers.

Account Lockout Duration

If someone violates the lockout controls, Account Lockout Duration sets the length of time the account is locked. You can set the lockout duration to a specific length of time using a value between 1 and 99,999 minutes or to an indefinite length of time by setting the lockout duration to zero.

The best security policy is to lock the account indefinitely. When you do, only an administrator can unlock the account. This prevents hackers from trying to access the system again and forces users who are locked out to seek help from an administrator, which is usually a good idea. By talking to the user, you can determine what the user is doing wrong and help the user avoid problems.

Tip When an account is locked out, access the Properties dialog box for the account in Active Directory Users And Computers. Then click the Account tab and clear the Account Is Locked Out check box. This unlocks the account.

Reset Account Lockout Counter After

Every time a logon attempt fails, Windows Server 2003 raises the value of a threshold that tracks the number of bad logon attempts. To balance potential lockouts due to valid security concerns against lockouts that could occur due to simple human error, there's another policy that determines how long to maintain information regarding bad logon attempts. This policy is called Reset Account Lockout Counter After, and it's used to reset the bad logon attempts counter to zero after a certain waiting period. The way the policy works is simple: if the waiting period for Reset Account Lockout Counter After has elapsed since the last bad logon attempt, the bad logon attempts counter is reset to zero. The bad logon attempts counter is also reset when a user logs on successfully.

If the Reset Account Lockout Counter After policy is enabled, you can set any value from 1 to 99,999 minutes. As with Account Lockout Threshold, you need to select a value that balances security needs against user access needs. A good value is from one to two hours. This waiting period should be long enough to force hackers to wait longer than they want to before trying to access the account again.

If the Reset Account Lockout Counter After policy isn't set or is disabled, the bad logon attempts counter is reset only when a user successfully logs on.

Note Bad logon attempts to a workstation against a password-protected screen saver don't increase the lockout threshold. Similarly, if you lock a server or workstation using Ctrl+Alt+Delete, bad logon attempts against the Unlock dialog box don't count.

Configuring Kerberos Policies

Kerberos v5 is the primary authentication mechanism used in an Active Directory domain. To verify the identification of users and network services, Kerberos uses tickets. Tickets contain encrypted data that confirm identity for the purposes of authentication and authorization.

You can control ticket duration, renewal, and enforcement with the following policies:

- Enforce User Logon Restrictions
- Maximum Lifetime For Service Ticket

- Maximum Lifetime For User Ticket
- Maximum Lifetime For User Ticket Renewal
- Maximum Tolerance For Computer Clock Synchronization

These policies are discussed in the sections that follow.

Security   Only administrators with an intimate understanding of Kerberos security should change these policies. If you change these policies to inefficient settings, you might cause serious problems on the network. The default Kerberos policy settings usually work just fine.

Enforce User Logon Restrictions

Enforce User Logon Restrictions ensures that any restrictions placed on a user account are enforced. For example, if the user's logon hours are restricted, this policy is what enforces the restriction. By default, the policy is enabled and you should disable it only in rare circumstances.

Maximum Lifetime

Maximum Lifetime For Service Ticket and Maximum Lifetime For User Ticket set the maximum duration for which a service or user ticket is valid. By default, service tickets have a maximum duration of 600 minutes and user tickets have a maximum duration of 10 hours.

You can change the duration of tickets. For service tickets, the valid range is from 0 to 99,999 minutes. For user tickets, the valid range is from 0 to 99,999 hours. A value of zero effectively turns off expiration. Any other value sets a specific ticket lifetime.

A user ticket that expires can be renewed, provided the renewal takes place within the time set for Maximum Lifetime For User Ticket Renewal. By default, the maximum renewal period is seven days. You can change the renewal period to any value from 0 to 99,999 days. A value of zero effectively turns off the maximum renewal period, and any other value sets a specific renewal period.

Maximum Tolerance

Maximum Tolerance For Computer Clock Synchronization is one of the few Kerberos policies that you might need to change. By default, computers in the domain must be synchronized within five minutes of one another. If they aren't, authentication fails.

If you have remote users who log on to the domain without synchronizing their clock to the network time server, you might need to adjust this value. You can set any value from 0 to 99,999. A value of zero says that there's no tolerance for a time difference, which means the remote user's system must be precisely time-synchronized or authentication will fail.

Configuring User Rights Policies

Chapter 8 covered built-in capabilities and user rights. Although you can't change built-in capabilities for accounts, you can administer user rights for accounts. Normally, you apply user rights to users by making them members of the appropriate group or groups. You can also apply rights directly, and you do this by managing the user rights for the user's account.

Security   Any user who's a member of a group that's assigned a certain right also has that right. For example, if the Backup Operators group has a right and *jsmith* is a member of this group, jsmith has this right as well. Keep in mind that changes that you make to user rights can have a far-reaching effect. Because of this, only experienced administrators should make changes to the user rights policy.

You assign user rights through the Local Policies node of Group Policy. As the name implies, local policies pertain to a local computer. However, you can configure local policies and then import them into Active Directory. You can also configure these local policies as part of an existing group policy for a site, domain, or organizational unit. When you do this, the local policies apply to computer accounts in the site, domain, or organizational unit.

To administer user rights policies, complete the following steps:

1. Access the group policy you want to work with, and then access the Local Policies node by working your way down the console tree. To do so, expand Computer Configuration, Windows Settings, Security Settings, and then Local Policies.

2. Select User Rights Assignment and you can now manage user rights. To configure a user rights assignment, double-click a user right or right-click it and select Properties. This opens a Properties dialog box.

3. You can now configure the user rights as described in Steps 1–4 of the section entitled "Configuring User Rights Locally," later in this chapter, or in Steps 1–6 of the following section.

Configuring User Rights Globally

For a site, domain, or organizational unit, you configure individual user rights by completing the following steps:

1. Open the Properties dialog box for the user right, which will be similar to the one shown in Figure 9-5. If the policy isn't defined, select Define These Policy Settings.

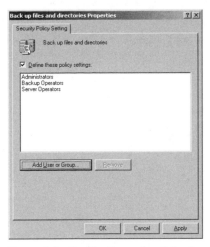

Figure 9-5 Use the Properties dialog box to define the user right and then apply the right to users and groups.

2. To apply the right to a user or group, click Add User Or Group. Then, in the Add User Or Group dialog box, click Browse. This opens the Select Users, Computers, Or Groups dialog box shown in Figure 9-6.

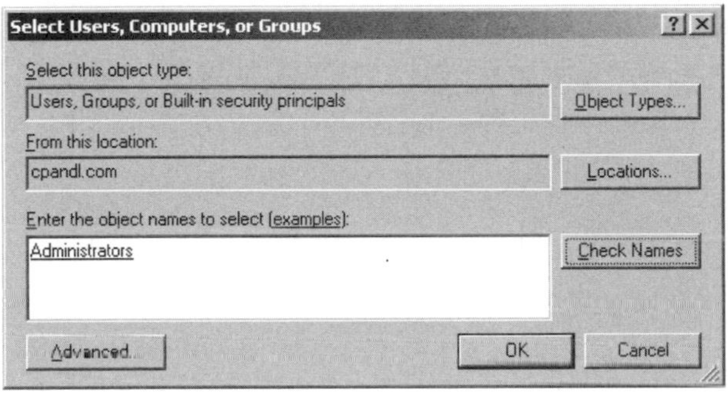

Figure 9-6 Use the Select Users, Computers, Or Groups dialog box to apply the user right to users and groups.

Security   Windows Firewall running on a domain controller might prevent you from using the Select Users, Computers, Or Groups dialog box. This can occur when you aren't logged on locally to the domain controller and are working remotely. You might need to configure an exception on the domain controller for incoming Transmission Control Protocol (TCP) port 445. You can do this by expanding Computer Configuration\Administrative Templates\Network \Network Connections\Windows Firewall\Domain Profile. In the details pane, double-click Windows Firewall: Allow Remote Administration Exception policy and then select Enabled. Alternatively, you can configure an exception by typing the following at a command prompt on the remote computer: **netsh firewall set portopening tcp 445 smb enable**. See Microsoft Knowledge Base Article 840634 (*http://support.microsoft.com/default.aspx?scid=kb;en-us ;840634*) for more details.

3. Type the name of the user or group you want to use in the field provided and then click Check Names. By default, the search is configured to find built-in security principals and user accounts. To add groups to the search, click Object Types in the list box, select Groups, and then click OK.

4. After you select the account names or groups to add, click OK. The Add User Or Group dialog box should now show the selected accounts. Click OK again.

5. The Properties dialog box is updated to reflect your selections. If you made a mistake, select a name and remove it by clicking Remove.

6. When you're finished granting the right to users and groups, click OK.

Configuring User Rights Locally

For local computers, you apply user rights by completing the following steps:

1. Open the Properties dialog box for the user right, which will be similar to the one shown in Figure 9-7.

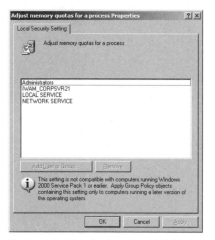

Figure 9-7   Use the Properties dialog box to define the user right and then apply the right to users and groups.

2. Remember that site, domain, and organizational unit policies have precedence over local policies.

3. The Properties dialog box shows current users and groups that have been given a user right. To remove the user right, select a user or group and click Remove.

4. You can apply the user right to additional users and groups by clicking Add User Or Group. This opens the Select Users, Computers, Or Groups dialog box shown previously in Figure 9-6. You can now add users and groups.

Adding a User Account

You need to create a user account for each user who wants to use your network resources. You create domain user accounts with Active Directory Users And Computers. You create local user accounts with Local Users And Groups.

Creating Domain User Accounts

Generally, there are two ways to create new domain accounts:

Create a completely new user account   Create a completely new account by right-clicking the container in which you want to place the user account, selecting New, and then selecting User. This opens the New Object - User wizard shown in Figure 9-8. When you create a new account, the default system settings are used.

Base the new account on an existing account   Right-click the user account you want to copy in Active Directory Users And Computers, and then select Copy. This starts the Copy Object - User wizard, which is essentially the same as the New Object - User wizard. However, when you create a copy of an account, the new account gets most of its environment settings from the existing account. For more information on copying accounts, see the section entitled "Copying Domain User Accounts" in Chapter 10, "Managing Existing User and Group Accounts."

When either the New Object - User wizard or the Copy Object - User wizard is started, you can create the account by completing the following steps:

1. As shown in Figure 9-8, the first wizard page lets you configure the user display name and logon name.

2. Type the user's first name, middle initial, and last name in the fields provided. These fields are used to create the full name, which is the user's display name.

3. Make changes to the Full Name field as necessary. For example, you might want to type the name in LastName FirstName MiddleInitial format or in FirstName MiddleInitial LastName format. The full name must be unique in the domain and must be 64 characters or less.

4. In User Logon Name, type the user's logon name. Then use the drop-down list to select the domain with which the account is to be associated. This sets the fully qualified logon name.

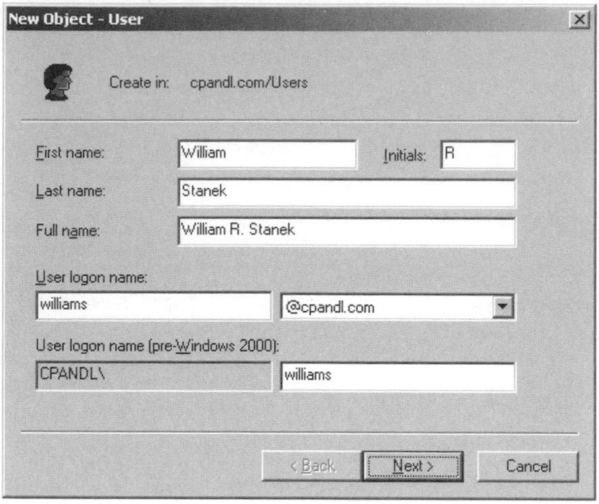

Figure 9-8 Configure the user display and logon names.

5. The first 20 characters of the logon name are used to set the pre-Windows 2000 logon name. This logon name must be unique in the domain. If necessary, change the pre-Windows 2000 logon name.

6. Click Next. Then configure the user's password using the wizard page shown in Figure 9-9. The options for this page are used as follows:

   Password The password for the account. This password should follow the conventions of your password policy.

   Confirm Password A field to ensure that you assign the account password correctly. Simply reenter the password to confirm it.

   User Must Change Password At Next Logon If selected, the user must change the password upon logon.

   User Cannot Change Password If checked, the user can't change the password.

   Password Never Expires If selected, the password for this account never expires. This setting overrides the domain account policy. Generally, it's not a good idea to set a password so it doesn't expire because this defeats the purpose of having passwords in the first place.

   Account Is Disabled If checked, the account is disabled and can't be used. Use this field to temporarily prevent anyone from using an account.

7. Click Next and then click Finish to create the account. If there are problems creating the account, you'll see a warning and you'll need to use the Back button to retype information in the user name and password pages, as necessary.

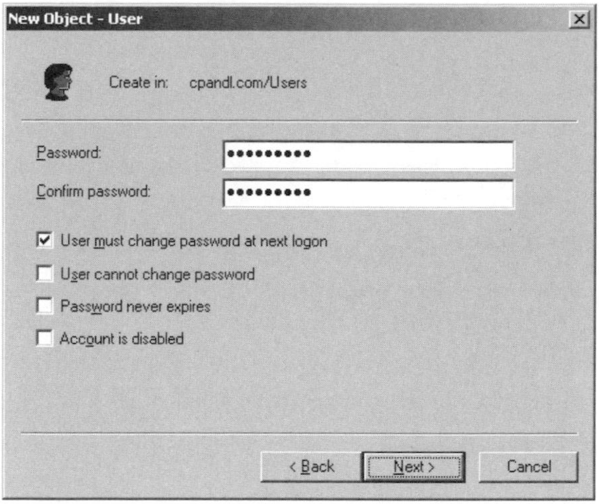

Figure 9-9   Use the New Object - User Wizard to configure the user's password.

After you create the account, you can set advanced properties for the account as discussed later in this chapter.

Creating Local User Accounts

You create local user accounts with Local Users And Groups. You can access this utility and create an account by completing the following steps:

1. Choose Start, All Programs, Administrative Tools, and then Computer Management. Or select Computer Management in the Administrative Tools folder.

2. Right-click the Computer Management entry in the console tree and select Connect To Another Computer on the shortcut menu. You can now choose the system whose local accounts you want to manage. Domain controllers don't have local users and groups.

3. Expand the System Tools node by clicking the plus sign (+) next to it, and then choose Local Users And Groups.

4. Right-click Users and then select New User. This opens the New User dialog box shown in Figure 9-10. You use each of the fields in the dialog box as follows:

   User Name   The logon name for the user account. This name should follow the conventions for the local user name policy

   Full Name   The full name of the user, such as William R. Stanek.

   Description   A description of the user. Normally, you'd type the user's job title, such as Webmaster. You could also type the user's job title and department.

Password The password for the account. This password should follow the conventions of your password policy.

Confirm Password A field to ensure that you assign the account password correctly. Simply reenter the password to confirm it.

User Must Change Password At Next Logon If selected, the user must change the password upon logon.

User Cannot Change Password If checked, the user can't change the password.

Password Never Expires If selected, the password for this account never expires. This setting overrides the local account policy.

Account Is Disabled If checked, the account is disabled and can't be used. Use this field to temporarily prevent anyone from using an account.

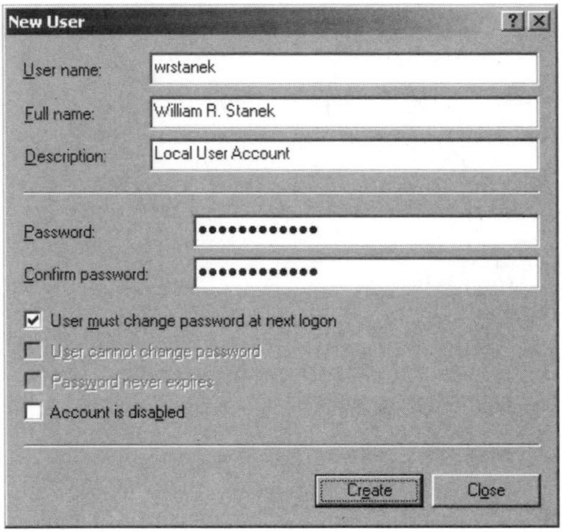

Figure 9-10 Configuring a local user account is different from configuring a domain user account.

5. Click Create when you're finished configuring the new account.

Adding a Group Account

You use group accounts to manage privileges for multiple users. You create global group accounts in Active Directory Users And Computers. You create local group accounts in Local Users And Groups.

As you set out to create group accounts, remember that you create group accounts for similar types of users. Following this, the types of groups you might want to create include the following:

Groups for departments within the organization Generally, users who work in the same department need access to similar resources. Because of this, you can create groups that are organized by department, such as Business Development, Sales, Marketing, or Engineering.

Groups for users of specific applications   Often users will need access to an application and resources related to the application. If you create application-specific groups, you can be sure that users get proper access to the necessary resources and application files.

Groups for roles within the organization   Groups could also be organized by the user's role within the organization. For example, executives probably need access to different resources than supervisors and general users. Thus, by creating groups based on roles within the organization, you can ensure that proper access is given to the users who need it.

Creating a Global Group

To create a global group, complete the following steps:

1. Start Active Directory Users And Computers. Right-click the container in which you want to place the user account. Afterward, select New, and then select Group. This opens the New Object - Group dialog box shown in Figure 9-11.

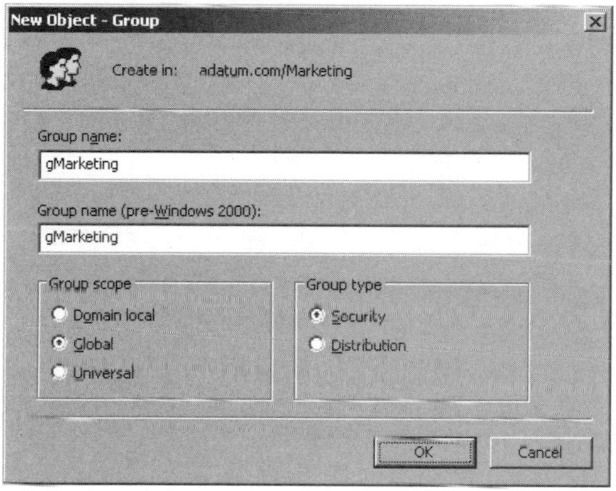

Figure 9-11   The New Object - Group dialog box allows you to add a new global group to the domain.

2. Type a name for the group. Global group account names follow the same naming rules as display names for user accounts. They aren't case sensitive and can be up to 64 characters long.

3. The first 20 characters of the group name are used to set the pre-Windows 2000 group name. This group name must be unique in the domain. If necessary, change the pre-Windows 2000 group name.

4. Select a group scope, either Domain Local, Global, or Universal.

    Universal groups are available only when Active Directory is running in Windows 2000 native operations mode or in Windows Server 2003 operations mode. For more information on operations modes, see the section entitled "Using Windows NT and Windows 2000 Domains with Active Directory" in Chapter 6, "Using Active Directory."

5. Select a group type, either Security or Distribution.

6. Click OK to create the group. After the account is created, you can add members and set additional properties, as discussed later in this chapter.

Creating a Local Group and Assigning Members

You create local groups with Local Users And Groups. You can access this utility and create a group by completing the following steps:

1. Choose Start, then Programs or All Programs as appropriate, then Administrative Tools, and then Computer Management. Or select Computer Management in the Administrative Tools folder.

2. Right-click the Computer Management entry in the console tree and select Connect To Another Computer on the shortcut menu. You can now choose the system whose local accounts you want to manage. Domain controllers don't have local users and groups.

3. Expand the System Tools node by clicking the plus sign (+) next to it and then choose Local Users And Groups.

4. Right-click Groups and then select New Group. This opens the New Group dialog box shown in Figure 9-12.

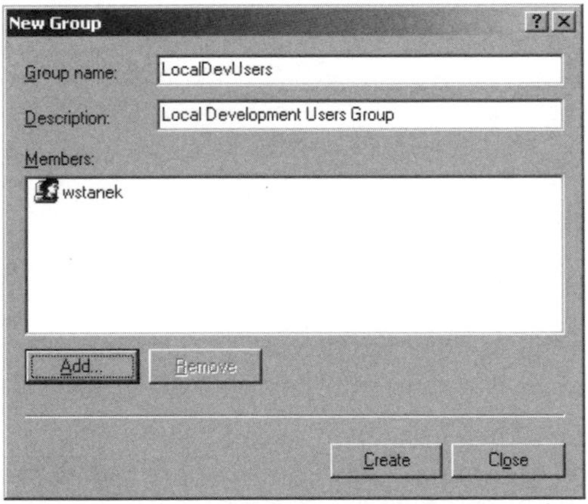

Figure 9-12   The New Group dialog box allows you to add a new local group to a computer.

5. After you type a name and description of the group, use the Add button to add names to the group. This opens the Select Users dialog box.

6. In the Select Users dialog box, type the name of a user you want to use in the Name field and then click Check Names. If matches are found, select the account you want to use and then click OK. If no matches are found, update the name you entered and try searching again. Repeat this step as necessary, and then click OK when you are finished.

7. The New Group dialog box is updated to reflect your selections. If you made a mistake, select a name and remove it by clicking Remove.

8. Click Create when you've finished adding or removing group members.

Handling Global Group Membership

To configure group membership, you use Active Directory Users And Computers. When working with groups, keep the following points in mind:

- All new domain users are members of the group Domain Users, and their primary group is specified as Domain Users.

- All new domain workstations and member servers are members of Domain Computers, and their primary group is Domain Computers.

- All new domain controllers are members of Domain Controllers and their primary group is Domain Controllers.

Active Directory Users And Computers gives you several ways to manage group membership. You can:

- Manage individual membership.

- Manage multiple memberships.

- Set primary group membership for individual users and computers.

Managing Individual Membership

You can add or remove group membership for any type of account by completing the following steps:

1. Double-click the user, computer, or group entry in Active Directory Users And Computers. This opens the account's Properties dialog box.

2. Click the Member Of tab.

3. To make the account a member of a group, click Add. This opens the Select Groups dialog box, which is the same as the Select Users Or Groups dialog box discussed in previous examples. You can now choose groups of which the currently selected account should be a member.

4. To remove the account from a group, select a group and then click Remove. Click OK.

If you're working exclusively with user accounts, you can add users to groups by following these steps:

1. Select the user accounts that you want to work with in Active Directory Users And Computers.

> **Tip**   To select multiple users individually, hold down the Ctrl key and then click the left mouse button on each user account that you want to select. To select a sequence of accounts, hold down the Shift key, select the first user account, and then click the last user account.

2. Right-click one of the selections, and then select Add To A Group. This opens the Select Groups dialog box. You can now choose groups of which the currently selected accounts should be members. Click OK.

Managing Multiple Memberships in a Group

Another way to manage group membership is to use a group's Properties dialog box to add or remove multiple accounts. To do this, follow these steps:

1. Double-click the group entry in Active Directory Users And Computers. This opens the group's Properties dialog box.

2. Click the Members tab.

3. To add accounts to the group, click Add. This opens the Select Users, Computers, Or Groups dialog box. You can now choose users, computers, and groups that should be members of this currently selected group.

4. To remove members from a group, select an account and then click Remove. Click OK.

Setting the Primary Group for Users and Computers

Users who access Windows Server 2003 through services for Macintosh use primary groups. When a Macintosh user creates files or directories on a system running Windows Server 2003, the primary group is assigned to these files or directories.

All user and computer accounts must have a primary group whether or not the accounts access Windows Server 2003 systems through Macintosh. This group must be a group with global or universal scope, such as the global group Domain Users or the global group Domain Computers.

To set the primary group, complete the following steps:

1. Double-click the user or computer entry in Active Directory Users And Computers. This opens the account's Properties dialog box.

2. Click the Member Of tab.

3. Select a group with global or universal scope in the Member Of list box.

4. Click Set Primary Group.

All users must be a member of at least one primary group. You can't revoke membership in a primary group without first assigning the user to another primary group. To do this, complete the following steps:

1. Select a different group with global or universal scope in the Member Of list box, and then click Set Primary Group.

2. In the Member Of list box, click the former primary group and then click Remove. The group membership is now revoked.

In the Member Of list box, click the former primary group and then click Remove. The group membership is now revoked.

Chapter 10

Managing Existing User and Group Accounts

In this chapter:

In a perfect world, you could create user and group accounts and never have to touch them again. Unfortunately, we live in the real world. After you create accounts, you'll spend a lot of time managing them. This chapter provides guidelines and tips to make that task easier.

Managing User Contact Information

Active Directory is a directory service. When you create user accounts, those accounts can have detailed contact information associated with them. The contact information is then available to anyone in the domain tree or forest, and they can use it as criteria to search for users and to create address book entries.

Setting Contact Information

You can set contact information for a user account by completing the following steps:

1. Double-click the user name in Active Directory Users And Computers. This opens the account's Properties dialog box.

2. Click the General tab, shown in Figure 10-1. Use the following fields to set general contact information:

   First Name, Initials, Last Name   Sets the user's full name.

Display Name   Sets the user's display name as seen in logon sessions and in Active Directory directory service.

Description   Sets a description of the user.

Office   Sets the user's office location.

Telephone Number   Sets the user's primary business telephone number. If the user has other business telephone numbers that you want to track, click Other and then use the Phone Number (Others) dialog box to enter additional phone numbers.

E-Mail   Sets the user's business e-mail address.

Web Page   Sets the Uniform Resource Locator (URL) of the user's home page, which can be either on the Internet or on the company intranet. If the user has other Web pages that you want to track, click Other and then use the Web Page Address (Others) dialog box to enter additional Web page addresses.

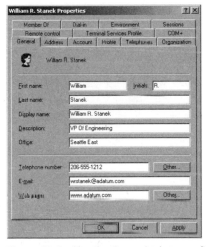

Figure 10-1   Use the General tab to configure general contact information for the user. This information can then be used in searches and address books.

Tip   The E-Mail and Web Page fields must be filled in if you want to use the Send Mail and Open Home Page features of Active Directory Users And Computers. For more information, see the section of this chapter entitled "Updating User and Group Accounts."

3. Click the Address tab. Use the fields provided to set the user's business or home address. You'll usually want to enter the user's business address. In this way, you can track the business locations and mailing addresses of users at various offices.

Note   You need to consider privacy issues before you enter users' home addresses. Discuss the matter with your Human Resources and Legal departments. You might also want to get user consent before releasing home addresses.

4. Click the Telephones tab. Type the primary telephone numbers that should be used to contact the user, such as home, pager, mobile, fax, and Internet Protocol (IP) phone.

5. You can configure other numbers for each type of telephone number. Click the associated Others button and then use the dialog box provided to enter additional phone numbers.

6. Click the Organization tab. As appropriate, type the user's title, department, and company.

7. To specify the user's manager, click Change and then select the user's manager in the Select User Or Contact dialog box. When you specify a manager, the user shows up as a direct report in the manager's account.

8. Click Apply or OK to apply the changes.

Searching for Users and Creating Address Book Entries

Active Directory makes it easy for you to find users in the directory and then create address book entries using the search results. Normally, these are tasks that you'll need to help users with. You do that by completing the following steps:

1. With the Classic Start Menu, click Start, point to Search, select For People, and then proceed to Step 2. With the Simple Start Menu, click Start, and then select Search. In the Search Results dialog box, click Other Search Options, click Printers, Computers, or People, and then click People In Your Address Book. This opens the Find People dialog box.

2. Click the Look In drop-down list, select Active Directory, and then type the name or email address of the user you want to search for.

3. Click Find Now to begin the search. If matches are found, the search results are displayed as shown in Figure 10-2. Otherwise, type new search parameters and search again.

4. You can view an account's properties by selecting a display name and then clicking Properties.

5. You can add contact information to an address book by selecting a display name and then clicking Add To Address Book.

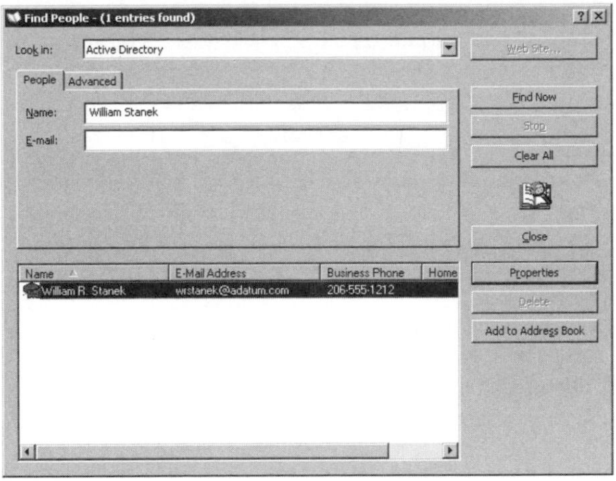

Figure 10-2   Search for users in Active Directory, and then use the results to create address book entries.

Configuring the User's Environment Settings

User accounts can also have profiles, logon scripts, and home directories associated with them. To configure these optional settings, double-click a display name in Active Directory Users And Computers and then click the Profile tab, as shown in Figure 10-3. In the Profile tab, you can set the following fields:

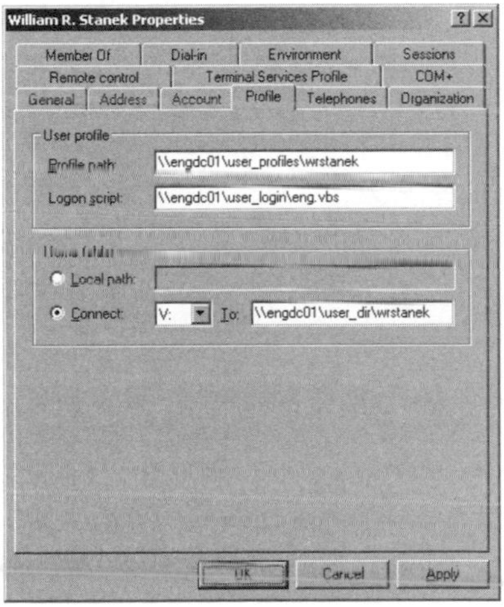

Figure 10-3   The Profile tab allows you to create a user profile. Profiles let you configure the network environment for a user.

Profile Path   The path to the user's profile. Profiles provide the environment settings for users. Each time a user logs on to a computer, that user's profile is used to determine desktop and control panel settings, the availability of menu options and applications, and more. Setting the profile path is covered later in this chapter in the section entitled "Managing User Profiles."

Logon Script   The path to the user's logon script. Logon scripts are batch files that run whenever a user logs on. You use logon scripts to set commands that should be executed each time a user logs on. Chapter 4, "Automating Administrative Tasks, Policies, and Procedures," discusses logon scripts in detail.

Home Folder   The directory the user should use for storing files. Here, you assign a specific directory for the user's files as a local path on the user's system or a connected network drive. If the directory is available to the network, the user can access the directory from any computer on the network, and this is a definite advantage.

System Environment Variables

System environment variables often come in handy when you're setting up the user's environment, especially when you work with logon scripts. You'll use environment variables to specify path information that can be dynamically assigned. The environment variables you'll use the most are the following:

%SystemRoot%   The base directory for the operating system, such as C:\WINNT. Use it with the Profile tab of the user's Properties dialog box and logon scripts.

%UserName%   The user account name, such as wrstanek. Use it with the Profile tab of the user's Properties dialog box and logon scripts.

%HomeDrive%   The drive letter of the user's home directory followed by a colon character, such as C:. Use it with logon scripts.

%HomePath%   The full path to the user's home directory on the respective home drive, such as \Users\Mkg\Georgej. Use it with logon scripts.

%Processor_Architecture%   The processor architecture of the user's computer, such as x86. Use it with logon scripts.

Figure 10-4 shows how you might use environment variables when creating user accounts. Note that by using the %UserName% variable, you allow the system to determine the full path information on a user-by-user basis. If you use this technique, you can use the same path information for multiple users and all the users will have unique settings.

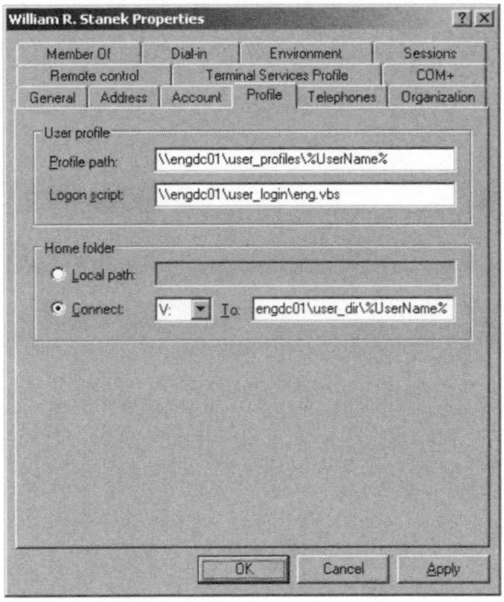

Figure 10-4   When you use the Profile tab, environment variables can save you typing, especially when you create an account based on another account.

Logon Scripts

Logon scripts set commands that should be executed each time a user logs on. You can use logon scripts to set the system time, network drive paths, network printers, and more. Although you can use logon scripts to execute onetime commands, you shouldn't use them to set environment variables. Any environment settings used by scripts aren't maintained for subsequent user processes. Also, you shouldn't use logon scripts to specify applications that should run at startup. You should set startup applications by placing the appropriate shortcuts in the user's Startup folder.

Normally, logon scripts contain Microsoft Windows commands. However, logon scripts can be:

- Windows Script Host files with the .vbs, .js, or other valid script extensions.
- Batch files with the .bat extension.
- Command files with the .cmd extension.
- Executable programs with the .exe extension.

One user or many users can use a single logon script, and, as the administrator, you control which users use which scripts. As the name implies, logon scripts are accessed when users log on to their accounts. You can specify a logon script by completing the following steps:

1. Access the user's Properties dialog box in Active Directory Users And Computers, and then click the Profile tab.

2. Type the path to the logon script in the Logon Script field. Be sure to set the full path to the logon script, such as \\Zeta\User_Logon\Eng.vbs.

Note   You can specify logon and logoff scripts using other techniques. For complete details, see the section of Chapter 4 entitled "User and Computer Script Management."

Creating logon scripts is easier than you might think, especially when you use the Windows command language. Just about any command you can type into a command prompt can be set to run in a logon script. The most common tasks you'll want logon scripts to handle are to set the default printers and network paths for users. You can set this information with the NET USE command. The following NET USE commands define a network printer and a network drive:

```
net use lpt1: \\zeta\techmain
net use G: \\gamma\corp\files
```

If these commands were in the user's logon script, the user would have a network printer on LPT1 and a network drive on G. You can create similar connections in a script. With VBScript, you need to initialize the variables and objects you plan to use and then call the appropriate methods of the Network object to add the connections. Consider the following example:

```
Option Explicit
Dim wNetwork, printerPath

Set wNetwork = WScript.CreateObject("WScript.Network")

printerPath = \\zeta\techmain
wNetwork.AddWindowsPrinterConnection printerPath
wNetwork.SetDefaultPrinter printerPath

wNetwork.MapNetworkDrive "G:", \\gamma\corpfiles

Set wNetwork = vbEmpty
Set printerPath = vbEmpty
```

Here, you use the AddWindowsPrinterConnection method to add a connection to the TechMain printer on CorpSvr02 and the SetDefaultPrinter method to set the printer as the default for the user. You then use the MapNetworkDrive method to define on network drive on G.

Assigning Home Directories

Windows Server 2003 lets you assign a home directory for each user account. Users can store and retrieve their personal files in this directory. Many applications use the home directory as the default for File Open and Save As operations, which helps users find their resources easily. The command prompt also uses the home directory as the initial current directory.

Home directories can be located on a user's local hard disk drive or on a shared network drive. On a local drive the directory is accessible only from a single workstation. On the other hand, shared network drives can be accessed from any computer on the network, which makes for a more versatile user environment.

Tip   Although users can share home directories, it's not a good idea. You'll usually want to provide each user with a unique home directory.

You don't need to create the user's home directory ahead of time. Active Directory Users And Computers automatically creates the directory for you. If there's a problem creating the directory, Active Directory Users And Computers will instruct you to create it manually.

To specify a local home directory, complete the following steps:

1. Access the user's Properties dialog box in Active Directory Users And Computers, and then click the Profile tab.

2. Select Local Path, and then type the path to the home directory in the associated text box. Here's an example: **C:\Home\%UserName%**.

To specify a network home directory, complete the following steps:

1. Access the user's Properties dialog box in Active Directory Users And Computers, and then click the Profile tab.

2. Select the Connect option in the Home Folder section, and then select a drive letter for the home directory. For consistency, you should use the same drive letter for all users. Also, be sure to select a drive letter that won't conflict with any currently configured physical or mapped drives. To avoid problems, you might want to use Z as the drive letter.

3. Type the complete path to the home directory using the Universal Naming Convention (UNC) notation, such as **\\Gamma\User_Dirs\%UserName%**. You include the server name in the drive path to ensure that the user can access the directory from any computer on the network.

Note   If you don't assign a home directory, Windows Server 2003 uses the default local home directory. On systems where the operating system is installed as an upgrade, this directory typically is \Users\Default. Otherwise, this directory is the root directory.

Setting Account Options and Restrictions

Windows Server 2003 gives you many ways to control user accounts and their access to the network. You can define logon hours, permitted workstations for logon, dial-in privileges, and more.

Managing Logon Hours

Windows Server 2003 lets you control when users can log on to the network. You do this by setting their valid logon hours. You can use logon hour restrictions to tighten security and prevent system cracking or malicious conduct after normal business hours.

During valid logon hours, users can work as they normally do. They can log on to the network and access network resources. During restricted logon hours, users can't work. They can't log on to the network or make connections to network resources. If users are logged on when their logon time expires, what follows depends on the account policy you've set for them. Generally, one of two things happens to the user:

Forcibly disconnected   You can set a policy that tells Windows Server 2003 to forcibly disconnect users when their logon hours expire. If this policy is set, remote users are disconnected from all network resources and logged off the system when their hours expire.

Not disconnected   Users aren't disconnected from the network when they enter the restricted hours. Instead, Windows Server 2003 simply doesn't allow them to make any new network connections.

Configuring Logon Hours

To configure the logon hours, follow these steps:

1. Access the user's Properties dialog box in Active Directory Users And Computers, and then click the Account tab.

2. Click Logon Hours. You can now set the valid and invalid logon hours using the Logon Hours dialog box shown in Figure 10-5. In this dialog box, each hour of the day or night is a field that you can turn on and off.

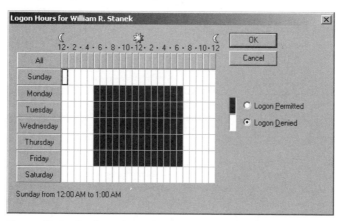

Figure 10-5   Configure logon hours for users using the fields provided.

❑ Hours that are allowed are filled in with a dark bar—you can think of these hours as being turned on.

❑ Hours that are disallowed are blank—you can think of these hours as being turned off.

3. To change the setting for an hour, click it. Then select either Logon Permitted or Logon Denied.

Logon Hours features are listed in Table 10-1.

Table 10-1   Logon Hours Features

Feature	Function
All	Allows you to select all the time periods
Day of week buttons	Allow you to select all the hours in a particular day
Hourly buttons	Allow you to select a particular hour for all the days of the week
Logon Permitted	Sets the allowed logon hours
Logon Denied	Sets the disallowed logon hours

Tip   When you set logon hours, you'll save yourself a lot of work in the long run if you give users a moderately restricted time window. For example, rather than explicit 9–5 hours, you might want to allow a few hours on either side of the normal work hours. This will let the early birds onto the system and allow the night owls to keep working until they finish for the day.

Enforcing Logon Hours

If you want to forcibly disconnect users when their logon hours expire, complete the following steps:

1. Access the group policy with which you want to work, as detailed in the section of Chapter 4 entitled "Managing Site, Domain, and Unit Policies."

2. Access the Security Options node by working your way down through the console tree. Expand Computer Configuration, Windows Settings, and then Security Settings. In Security Settings, expand Local Policies and then select Security Options.

3. Double-click Network Security: Force Logoff When Logon Hours Expire. This opens a Properties dialog box for the policy.

4. Select the Define This Policy Setting check box and then click Enabled. This turns on the policy restriction and enforces the logon hours. Click OK.

Setting Permitted Logon Workstations

Windows Server 2003 has a formal policy that allows users to log on to systems locally. This policy controls whether or not a user can sit at the computer's keyboard and log on. By default, on workstations you can use any valid user account, including the guest account, to log on locally.

As you might imagine, allowing users to log on to any workstation is a security risk. Unless you restrict workstation use, anyone who obtains a user name and password can use it to log on to any workstation in the domain. By defining a permitted workstation list, you close the opening in your domain and reduce the security risk. Now not only must hackers find a user name and password, but they must also find the permitted workstations for the account.

Note The permitted logon workstation restrictions affect only Windows NT, Windows 2000, and Windows XP computers in the domain. If any Windows 95 or Windows 98 computers are in the domain, they aren't subject to the restrictions, which means you need only a valid user name and password to log on to these systems.

For domain users, you define permitted logon workstations by completing the following steps:

1. Access the user's Properties dialog box in Active Directory Users And Computers and then click the Account tab.

2. Open the Logon Workstations dialog box by clicking Log On To.

3. Select The Following Computers, as shown in Figure 10-6.

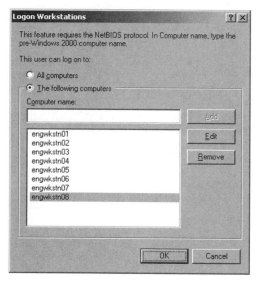

Figure 10-6 To restrict access to workstations, specify the permitted logon workstations.

4. Type the name of a permitted workstation and then click Add. Repeat this procedure to specify additional workstations.

5. If you make a mistake, select the erroneous entry and then click Edit or Remove, as appropriate.

Setting Dial-In and VPN Privileges

Windows Server 2003 lets you set remote access privileges for accounts using the Dial-In tab of the user's Properties dialog box. These settings control access for dial-in and virtual private network (VPN). As shown in Figure 10-7, remote access privileges are controlled through Remote Access Policy, by default. This is the preferred method of controlling remote access. You can explicitly grant or deny dial-in privileges by selecting Allow Access or Deny Access. In any event, before users can remotely access the network, you'll need to complete the following steps:

1. Install Remote Access Services using the Configure Your Server Wizard.

2. To enable remote access connections, access the Group Policy Object (GPO) for the site, domain, or organizational unit you want to work with, as specified in the section of Chapter 4 entitled "Creating and Editing Site, Domain, and Organizational Unit Policies." In the Group Policy Object Editor (GPOE), expand User Configuration, Administrative Templates, and then Network. Then select Network Connections. Afterward, configure the Network Connections policies as appropriate for the site, domain, or organizational unit.

3. Configure remote access using Routing And Remote Access. In Computer Management, expand Services And Applications, and then select Routing And Remote Access. Configure Routing And Remote Access as appropriate.

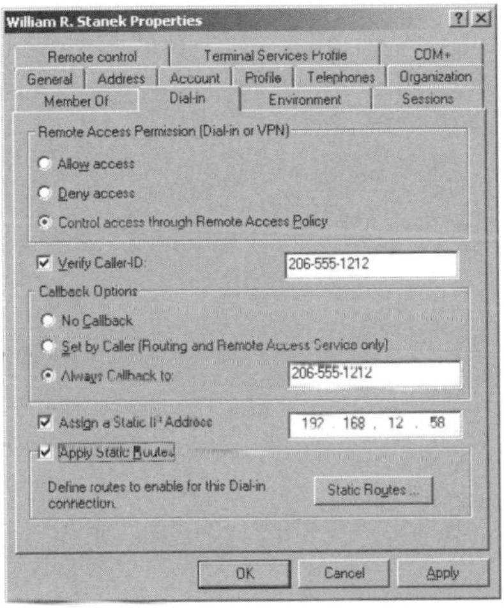

Figure 10-7   Dial-in privileges control remote access to the network.

After you grant a user permission to access the network remotely, configure additional dial-in parameters using the Dial-In tab of the user's Properties dialog box, shown in Figure 10-7, by completing the following steps:

1. If the user must dial in from a specific phone number, select Verify Caller-ID and then type the telephone number from which this user is required to log on. Your telephone system must support Caller ID for this feature to work.

2. Define callback parameters using the following options:

   No Callback   Allows the user to dial in directly and remain connected. The user pays the long-distance telephone charges, if applicable.

   Set By Caller   Allows the user to dial in directly, and then the server prompts the user for a callback number. Once the number is entered, the user is disconnected and the server dials the user back at the specified number to reestablish the connection. The company pays the long-distance telephone charges, if applicable.

   Always Callback To   Allows you to set a predefined callback number for security purposes. When a user dials in, the server calls back the preset number. The company pays the long-distance telephone charges, if applicable, and reduces the risk of an unauthorized person accessing the network.

   Note   You shouldn't assign callback for users who dial in through a switchboard. The switchboard might not allow the user to properly connect to the network. You also shouldn't use preset callback numbers with multilinked lines. The multilinked lines won't function properly.

3. If necessary, you can also assign static IP addresses and static routes for dial-in connections using Assign A Static IP Address and Apply Static Routes, respectively. For more information on IP addresses and routing, see Chapter 16, "Managing TCP/IP Networking."

Setting Account Security Options

The Account tab of the user's Properties dialog box has many options designed to help you maintain a secure network environment. Use these options to control how user accounts are used and what options are available. The options are:

User Must Change Password At Next Logon   Forces the user to change his or her password when the user logs on next.

User Cannot Change Password   Doesn't allow the user to change the account password.

Password Never Expires   Ensures that the account password never expires, which overrides the normal password expiration period.

   Caution   Selecting this option creates a security risk on the network. Although you might want to use Password Never Expires with administrator accounts, you usually shouldn't use this option with normal user accounts.

Store Password Using Reversible Encryption   Saves the password as encrypted clear text.

Account Is Disabled   Disables the accounts, which prevents the user from accessing the network and logging on.

Smart Card Is Required For Interactive Logon   Requires the user to log on to a workstation using a smart card. The user can't log on to the workstation by typing a logon name and password at the keyboard.

Account Is Trusted For Delegation   Specifies that the user account can request a Kerberos service ticket on behalf of a user and that it is trusted to use another user's authentication credentials on behalf of that user. If a service account is running under a user account rather than as a local system, you can set a user account to execute procedures on behalf of a different account, allowing the user to mimic a client to gain access to network resources.

Account Is Sensitive And Cannot Be Delegated   Specifies that the user's account credentials cannot be delegated using Kerberos. Use this for sensitive accounts that should be carefully controlled.

Use DES Encryption Types For This Account   Specifies that the user account will use Data Encryption Standard (DES) encryption.

Do Not Require Kerberos Preauthentication   Specifies that the user account doesn't need Kerberos preauthentication to access network resources. Preauthentication is a part of the Kerberos v5 security procedure. The option to log on without it is available in order to allow authentication from clients using a previous, or nonstandard, implementation of Kerberos.

Managing User Profiles

User profiles contain settings for the network environment, such as desktop configuration and menu options. Problems with a profile can sometimes prevent a user from logging on. For example, if the display size in the profile isn't available on the system being used, the user might not be able to log on properly. In fact, the user might get nothing but a blank screen. You could reboot the machine, go into Video Graphics Adapter (VGA) mode, and then reset the display manually, but solutions for profile problems aren't always this easy and you might need to update the profile itself.

Windows Server 2003 provides several ways to manage user profiles:

1. You can assign profile paths in Active Directory Users And Computers.

2. You can copy, delete, and change the type of an existing local profile with the System utility in the Control Panel.

3. You can set system policies that prevent users from manipulating certain aspects of their environment.

Local, Roaming, and Mandatory Profiles

In Windows Server 2003, every user has a profile. Profiles control startup features for the user's session, the types of programs and applications that are available, the desktop settings, and a lot more. Each computer that a user logs on to has a copy of the user's profile. Because this profile is stored on the computer's hard disk, users who access several computers will have a profile on each of them. Another computer on the network can't access a locally stored profile, called a local profile, and, as you might expect, this has some drawbacks. For example, if a user logs on to three different workstations, the user could have three very different profiles, one on each system. As a result, the user might get confused about what network resources are available on a given system.

To solve the problem of multiple profiles and reduce confusion, you might want to create a profile that other computers can access. This type of profile is called a *roaming profile*. With a roaming profile users can access the same profile no matter which computer they're using within the domain. Roaming profiles are server-based and can be stored only on a server running Windows 2000 or Windows Server 2003. When a user with a roaming profile logs on, the profile is downloaded, which creates a local copy on the user's computer. When the user logs off, changes to the profile are updated both on the local copy and on the server.

Real World   When your organization uses the Encrypting File System (EFS) to make file access more secure, the use of roaming profiles becomes extremely important for users who log on to multiple computers. The reason for this is that encryption certificates are stored in user profiles and the encryption certificate is needed to access and work with the user's encrypted files. If a user has encrypted files and doesn't have a roaming profile, that user won't be able to work with these encrypted files on another computer (unless they use credential roaming with digital identification management service.)

As an administrator, you can control user profiles or let users control their own profiles. One reason to control profiles yourself is to make sure that all users have a common network configuration, which can reduce the number of environment-related problems.

Profiles controlled by administrators are called *mandatory profiles*. Users who have a mandatory profile can make only transitory changes to their environment. Here, any changes that users make to the local environment aren't saved, and the next time they log on, they're back to the original profile. The idea is that if users can't permanently modify the network environment, they can't make changes that cause problems. A key drawback to mandatory profiles is that the user can log on only if the profile is accessible. If, for some reason, the server that stores the profile is inaccessible and a cached profile isn't accessible, the user normally won't be able to log on. If the server is inaccessible but a cached profile is accessible, the user receives a warning message and is logged on to the local system using the system's cached profile.

Note   Mandatory profiles are deleted when you restart a computer running Windows XP. Users may receive an unrestricted temporary profile when they log on to a computer running Windows XP. This can occur if no network connection to the domain or a domain controller is available and if a cached profile isn't available. See Microsoft Knowledge Base article 893243 for more details (*support.microsoft.com/default.aspx ?scid=kb;en-us;893243*).

Creating Local Profiles

In Windows 2000 or later, user profiles are maintained either in a default directory or in the location set by the Profile Path field in the user's Properties dialog box. The default location for profiles depends on the workstation configuration in the following way:

Windows Upgrade Installation   The user profile is located at %SystemRoot%\Profiles \%UserName%\Ntuser.dat, where %SystemRoot% is the root directory for the operating system, such as C:\Winnt, and %UserName% is the user name, such as wrstanek.

New Installation of Windows   The user profile is located at %SystemDrive%\Documents and Settings\%UserName%.%UserDomain%, such as F:\Documents and Settings \wrstanek.adatum\Ntuser.dat. If the user logs on to a domain controller, the profile might be located at %SystemDrive%\Documents and Settings\%UserName%, such as F:\Documents and Settings\wrstanek\Ntuser.dat.

If you don't change the default location, the user will have a local profile.

Creating Roaming Profiles

Roaming profiles are stored on servers running Windows 2000 or Windows Server 2003. When users log on to multiple computers and use EFS, they'll need a roaming profile to ensure that the certificates necessary to read and work with encrypted files are available on computers other than their primary work computers.

If you want a user to have a roaming profile, you must set a server-based location for the profile directory by completing the following steps:

1. Create a shared directory on a server running Windows Server 2003 and make sure that the group Everyone has at least Change and Read access.

2. Access the user's Properties dialog box in Active Directory Users And Computers, and then click the Profile tab. Type the path to the shared directory in the Profile Path field. The path should have the form \\server name\profile folder name \user name. An example is \\Zeta\User_Profiles\Georgej, where *Zeta* is the server name, *User_Profiles* is the shared directory, and *Georgej* is the user name.

3. The roaming profile is then stored in the Ntuser.dat file in the designated directory, such as \\Zeta\User_Profiles\Georgej\Ntuser.dat.

Note   You don't usually need to create the profile directory. The directory is created automatically when the user logs on and NTFS File System (NTFS) permissions are set so that only the user has access. You can select multiple user accounts for simultaneous editing by holding down the Shift or Ctrl key when clicking the user names. When you right-click one of the selected users and select Properties, you'll be able to edit properties for all the selected users. Be sure to use %UserName% in the profile path, such as \\Zeta\User_Profiles\%UserName%.

4. As an optional step, you can create a profile for the user or copy an existing profile to the user's profile folder. If you don't create an actual profile for the user, the next time the user logs on the user will use the default local profile. Any changes the user makes to this profile will be saved when the user logs off. Thus, the next time the user logs on, the user can have a personal profile.

Creating Mandatory Profiles

Mandatory profiles typically are stored on a server. If you want a user to have a server-stored mandatory profile, you define the profile as follows:

1. Follow Steps 1–3 in the previous section, "Creating Roaming Profiles."

2. Create a mandatory profile by renaming the Ntuser.dat file as %UserName% \Ntuser.man. The next time the user logs on, he or she will have a mandatory profile.

> **Note**   Ntuser.dat contains the registry settings for the user. When you change the extension for the file to Ntuser.man, you tell Windows Server 2003 to create a mandatory profile.

Using the System Utility to Manage Local Profiles

To manage local profiles, you'll need to log on to the user's computer. Afterward, you can use the System utility in the Control Panel to manage local profiles. To view current profile information, start the System utility, click the Advanced tab, and then, under User Profiles, click Settings.

As shown in Figure 10-8, the User Profiles dialog box displays various information about the profiles stored on the local system. You can use this information to help you manage profiles.

The fields have the following meanings:

Name   The local profile's name, which generally includes the name of the originating domain or computer and the user account name. For example, the name ADATUM\wrstanek tells you that the original profile is from the domain adatum and the user account is wrstanek.

> **Note**   If you delete an account but don't delete the associated profile, you might also see an entry that says Account Deleted or Account Unknown. Don't worry, the profile is still available for copying if you need it, or you can delete the profile here.

Size   The profile's size. Generally, the larger the profile, the more the user has customized the environment.

Type   The profile type, which is either local or roaming.

Status   The profile's current status, such as whether it's from a local cache.

Modified   The date when the profile was last modified.

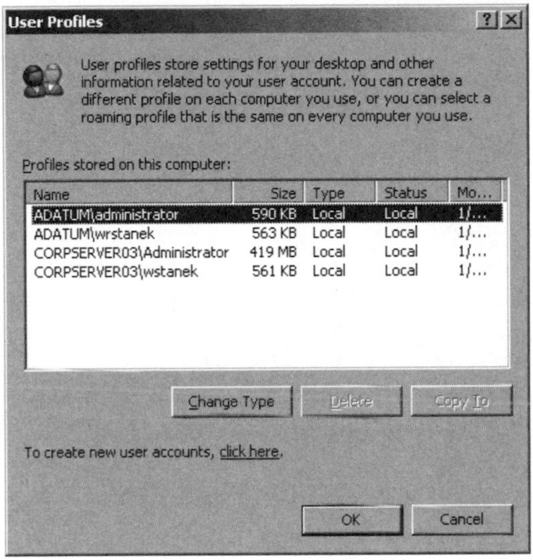

Figure 10-8   The User Profiles dialog box lets you manage existing local profiles.

Creating a Profile by Hand

Sometimes you might want to create the profile by hand. You do this by logging on to the user account, setting up the environment, and then logging off. As you might guess, creating accounts in this manner is time-consuming. A better way to handle account creation is to create a base user account. Here, you create the base user account, set up the account environment, and then use this account as the basis of other accounts.

Copying an Existing Profile to a New User Account

If you have a base user account or a user account that you want to use in a similar manner, you can copy an existing profile to the new user account. To do this, you'll use the System Control Panel utility and complete the following steps:

1. Start the System Control Panel utility, click the Advanced tab, and then under User Profiles, click Settings.

2. Select the existing profile you want to copy using the Profiles Stored On This Computer list (see Figure 10-8).

3. Copy the profile to the new user's account by clicking the Copy To button. Next, type the path to the new user's profile directory in the Copy Profile To field (see Figure 10-9). For example, if you were creating the profile for our user, georgej, you'd type **\\Zeta\User_Profiles\Georgej**.

4. Now you need to give the user permission to access the profile. Click the Change button in the Permitted To Use area, and then use the Select User Or Group dialog box to grant access to the new user account.

5. Close the Copy To dialog box by clicking OK. Windows Server 2003 then copies the profile to the next location.

> **Tip** If you know the name of the user or group you want to use, you can type it directly into the Name field. This will save you time.

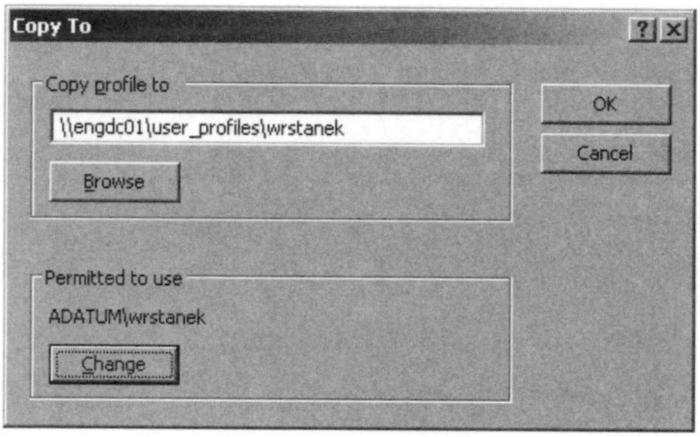

Figure 10-9 Use the Copy To dialog box to enter the location of the profile directory and to assign access permissions to the user.

Copying or Restoring a Profile

When you work with workgroups where each computer is managed separately, you'll often have to copy a user's local profile from one computer to another. Copying a profile allows users to maintain environment settings when they use different computers. Of course, in a Windows Server 2003 domain, you can use a roaming profile to create a single profile that can be accessed from anywhere within the domain. The problem is that sometimes you might need to copy an existing local profile over the top of a user's roaming profile (when the roaming profile is corrupt) or you might need to copy an existing local profile to a roaming profile in another domain.

You can copy an existing profile to a new location by doing the following:

1. Log on to the user's computer, and then start the System Control Panel utility, click the Advanced tab, and, under User Profiles, click Settings.

2. Select the existing profile you want to copy using the Profiles Stored On This Computer list box.

3. Copy the profile to the new location by clicking the Copy To button, and then type the path to the new profile directory in the Copy Profile To field. For example, if you're creating the profile for janew, you could type **\\Gamma\User_Profiles \anew.**

4. Now you need to give the user permission to access the profile. Click the Change button in the Permitted To Use area, and then use the Select User Or Group dialog box to grant access to the appropriate user account.

5. When you're finished, close the Copy To dialog box by clicking OK. Windows Server 2003 then copies the profile to the new location.

Deleting a Local Profile and Assigning a New One

Profiles are accessed when a user logs on to a computer. Windows Server 2003 uses local profiles for all users who don't have roaming profiles. Generally, local profiles are also used if the local profile has a more recent modification date than the user's roaming profile. Because of this, sometimes you might need to delete a user's local profile. For example, if a user's local profile becomes corrupt, you can delete the profile and assign a new one. Keep in mind that when you delete a local profile that isn't stored anywhere else on the domain, you can't recover the user's original environment settings.

To delete a user's local profile, complete the following steps:

1. Log on to the user's computer using an account with Administrator privileges.

2. Start the System utility, click the Advanced tab and then, under User Profiles, click Settings.

3. Select the profile you want to delete and then click Delete. When asked to confirm that you want to delete the profile, click Yes.

Note   You can't delete a profile that's in use. If the user is logged on to the local system (the computer from which you're deleting the profile), the user will need to log off. In some instances, Windows Server 2003 marks profiles as in use when they aren't. This is typically a result of an environment change for the user that hasn't been properly applied. To correct this, you might need to reboot the computer.

Now the next time the user logs on, Windows Server 2003 does one of two things. Either the operating system gives the user the default local profile for that system or it retrieves the user's roaming profile stored on another computer. To prevent the use of either of these profiles, you'll need to assign the user a new profile. To do this, you can:

■ Copy an existing profile to the user's profile directory. Copying profiles is covered in the next section.

■ Update the profile settings for the user in Active Directory Users And Computers. Setting the profile path is covered in this chapter in the section entitled "Configuring the User's Environment Settings."

Changing the Profile Type

With roaming profiles the System utility lets you change the profile type on the user's computer. To do this, select the profile and then click Change Type. The options in this dialog box allow you to:

Change a roaming profile to a local profile   If you want the user to always work with the local profile on this computer, set the profile for local use. Here, all changes to the profile are made locally and the original roaming profile is left untouched.

Change a local profile (that was defined originally as a roaming profile) to a roaming profile   The user will use the original roaming profile for the next logon. Afterward, Windows Server 2003 treats the profile like any other roaming profile, which means that any changes to the local profile are copied to the roaming profile.

Note   If these options aren't available, the user's original profile is defined locally.

Updating User and Group Accounts

Active Directory Users And Computers is the tool to use when you want to update a domain user or group account. If you want to update a local user or group account, you'll need to use Local Users And Groups.

When you work with Active Directory, you'll often want to get a list of accounts and then do something with those accounts. For example, you might want to list all the user accounts in the organization and then disable the accounts of users who have left the company. One way to perform this task is to follow these steps:

1. In Active Directory Users and Computers, right-click the domain name and then click Find.

2. From the Find selection list, select Custom Search. This updates the Find dialog box to display a Custom Search tab.

3. Using the In selection list, select the area you want to search. To search the enterprise, select Entire Directory.

4. In the Custom Search tab, click Field to display a shortcut menu, select User, and then select Logon Name (Pre-Windows 2000).

5. Using the Condition selection list, choose Present and then click Add. If prompted to confirm, click Yes.

   Tip   Be sure to select Logon Name (Pre-Windows 2000). Don't use Logon Name—user accounts aren't required to have a Windows Server 2003 logon name, but they're required to have a pre-Windows 2000 logon name.

6. Click Find Now. Active Directory Users and Computers gathers a list of all users in the designated area.

7. You can now work with the accounts one by one or several at a time. To select multiple resources not in sequence, hold down the Ctrl key and then click the left mouse button on each object you want to select. To select a series of resources at once, hold down the Shift key, select the first object, and then click the last object.

8. Right-click and then select an action from the shortcut menu that's displayed, such as Disable Account.

Tip   The actions you can perform on multiple accounts include: Add Member To Group (used to add the selected accounts to a designated group), Enable Account, Disable Account, Delete, and Move. Although Properties is listed as a possible action on the right-click shortcut menu, you can't edit the properties of multiple accounts in Windows 2000. This feature is only in Windows Server 2003.

Use this same procedure to get a list of computers, groups, or other Active Directory resources. With computers, use a custom search, click Field, choose Computer, and then select Computer Name (Pre-Windows 2000). With groups, use a custom search, click Field, choose Group, and then select Group Name (Pre-Windows 2000).

The sections that follow examine other techniques you can use to update (rename, copy, delete, and enable) accounts as well as to change and reset passwords. You'll also learn how to troubleshoot account logon problems.

Renaming User and Group Accounts

To rename an account, complete the following steps:

1. Access Active Directory Users And Computers or Local Users And Groups, whichever is appropriate for the type of account you're renaming.

2. Right-click the account name, and then choose Rename. Type the new account name when prompted

Security Identifiers

When you rename a user account, you give the account a new label. As discussed in Chapter 9, "Creating User and Group Accounts," user names are meant to make managing and using accounts easier. Behind the scenes, Windows Server 2003 uses security identifiers (SIDs) to identify, track, and handle accounts independently from user names. SIDs are unique identifiers that are generated when accounts are created.

Because SIDs are mapped to account names internally, you don't need to change the privileges or permissions on renamed accounts. Windows Server 2003 simply maps the SIDs to the new account names as necessary.

One common reason for changing the name of a user account is that the user gets married and decides to change her last name. For example, if Linda Martin (lindam) gets married, she might want her user name to be changed to Linda Randall (lindar). When you change the user name from lindam to lindar, all associated privileges and permissions will reflect the name change. Thus, if you view the permissions on a file that lindam had access to, lindar will now have access (and lindam will no longer be listed).

Changing Other Information

When you change lindam to lindar, the user properties and names of files associated with the account aren't changed. This means you should update the account information. The information you might need to change includes:

Display Name   Change the user account's Display Name in Active Directory Users And Computers.

User Profile Path   Change the Profile Path in Active Directory Users And Computers, and then rename the corresponding directory on disk.

Logon Script Name   If you use individual logon scripts for each user, change the Logon Script Name in Active Directory Users And Computers, and then rename the logon script on disk.

Home Directory   Change the home directory path in Active Directory Users And Computers, and then rename the corresponding directory on disk.

> **Note**   Changing directory and file information for an account when a user is logged on might cause problems. So you might want to update this information after hours or ask the user to log off for a few minutes and then log back on. You can usually write a simple Windows script that will perform the tasks for you quickly and automatically.

Copying Domain User Accounts

Creating domain user accounts from scratch every time can be tedious. Instead of starting anew each time, you might want to use an existing account as a starting point. To do this, follow these steps:

1. Right-click the account you want to copy in Active Directory Users And Computers, and then choose Copy. This opens the Copy Object – User dialog box.

2. Create the account as you would any other domain user account. Then update the properties of the account, as appropriate.

As you might expect, when you create a copy of an account, Active Directory Users And Computers doesn't retain all the information from the existing account. Instead, Active Directory Users And Computers tries to copy only the information you'll need and to discard the information that you'll need to update. The properties that are retained include

- City, state, ZIP code, and country values set in the Address tab
- Department and company set in the Organization tab
- Account options set using the Account Options fields in the Account tab

- Logon hours and permitted logon workstations
- Account expiration date
- Group account memberships
- Profile settings
- Dial-in privileges

Note   If you used environment variables to specify the profile settings in the original account, the environment variables are used for the copy of the account as well. For example, if the original account used the %UserName% variable, the copy of the account will also use this variable.

Deleting User and Group Accounts

Deleting an account permanently removes the account. Once you delete an account, you can't create an account with the same name to get the same permissions. That's because the SID for the new account won't match the SID for the old account.

Because deleting built-in accounts can have far-reaching effects on the domain, Windows Server 2003 doesn't let you delete built-in user accounts or group accounts. You could remove other types of accounts by selecting them and pressing the Delete key or by right-clicking and selecting Delete. When prompted, click OK and then click Yes.

With Active Directory Users And Computers, you can select multiple accounts by doing one of the following:

- Select multiple user names for editing by holding down the Ctrl key and clicking the left mouse button on each account you want to select.
- Select a range of user names by holding down the Shift key, selecting the first account name, and then clicking the last account in the range.

Note   When you delete a user account, Windows Server 2003 doesn't delete the user's profile, personal files, or home directory. If you want to delete these files and directories, you'll have to do it manually. If this is a task you perform routinely, you might want to create a Windows script that performs the necessary procedures for you. However, don't forget to back up files or data that might be needed before you do this.

Changing and Resetting Passwords

As an administrator, you'll often have to change or reset user passwords. This usually happens when users forget their passwords or when their passwords expire.

To change or reset a password, complete the following steps:

1. Access Active Directory Users And Computers or Local Users And Groups, whichever is appropriate for the type of account you're renaming.

2. Right-click the account name, and then select Reset Password or Set Password, as appropriate.

3. Type a new password for the user and confirm it. The password should conform to the password complexity policy set for the computer or domain.

4. Double-click the account name and then clear Account Is Disabled and Account Is Locked Out, whichever is appropriate and necessary. In Active Directory Users And Computers, these check boxes are in the Account tab.

Enabling User Accounts

User accounts can become disabled for several reasons. If a user forgets the password and tries to guess it, the user might exceed the account policy for bad logon attempts. Or another administrator could have disabled the account while the user was on vacation. Or the account could have expired. What to do when an account is disabled, locked out, or expired is described in the following sections.

Account Disabled

When an account is disabled, complete the following steps:

1. Access Active Directory Users And Computers or Local Users And Groups, whichever is appropriate for the type of account you're restoring.

2. Double-click the user's account name and then clear the Account Is Disabled check box. In Active Directory Users And Computers, this check box is in the Account tab.

Tip   To quickly search the current domain for disabled accounts, type **dsquery user –disabled** at a command prompt.

Account Locked Out

When an account is locked out, complete the following steps:

1. Access Active Directory Users And Computers or Local Users And Groups, whichever is appropriate for the type of account you're restoring.

2. Double-click the user's account name, and then clear the Account Is Locked Out check box. In Active Directory Users And Computers, this check box is in the Account tab.

Note   If users frequently get locked out of their accounts, consider adjusting the account policy for the domain. Here, you might want to increase the value for acceptable bad logon attempts and reduce the duration for the associated counter. For more information on setting account policy, see the section of Chapter 9 entitled "Configuring Account Policies."

Account Expired

Only domain accounts have an expiration date. Local user accounts don't have an expiration date.

When a domain account is expired, complete the following steps:

1. Access Active Directory Users And Computers.

2. Double-click the user's account name, and then click the Account tab.

3. In the Account Expires panel, select End Of and then click the down arrow on the related field. This displays a calendar that you can use to set a new expiration date.

Managing Multiple User Accounts

You can use Active Directory Users And Computers to modify the properties of multiple accounts simultaneously. Any changes you make to the property settings are made for all the selected accounts.

You can select multiple accounts by doing the following:

- Select multiple user names for editing by holding down the Ctrl key and clicking the left mouse button on each account you want to select.

- Select a range of user names by holding down the Shift key, selecting the first account name, and then clicking the last account in the range.

When you're finished selecting accounts for management, right-click to display a shortcut menu. The options available include:

Add To A Group   Displays the Select Group dialog box that you can use to designate the groups of which the selected users should be members.

Disable Account   Disables all the selected accounts.

Enable Account   Enables all the selected accounts.

Move   Moves the selected accounts to a new container or organizational unit.

Properties   Allows you to configure a limited set of properties for multiple accounts.

The Properties option is the one we'll look at in the sections that follow. As shown in Figure 10-10, the Properties On Multiple Objects dialog box has a different interface than the standard user Properties dialog box. You should note the following changes:

- Account name and password fields are no longer available. You can, however, set the Domain Name System (DNS) domain name (user principal name [UPN] suffix), logon hours, computer restrictions, accounts options, account expiration, and profiles.

- You must specifically select fields that you want to work with by clicking their associated check boxes. After you do this, the value you enter in the field is applied to all the selected accounts.

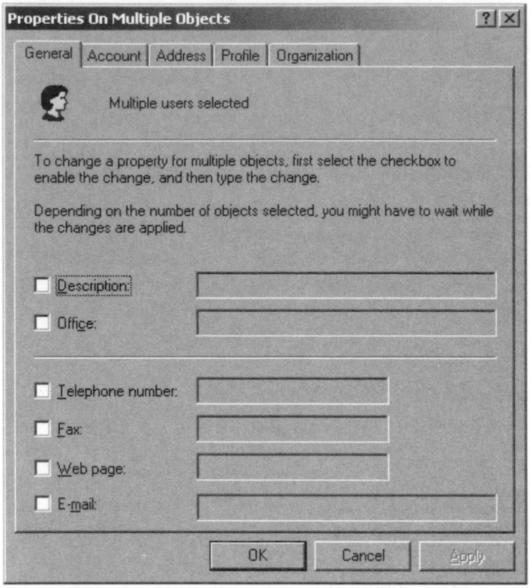

Figure 10-10   The Properties dialog box has a different interface when you work with multiple accounts.

Setting Profiles for Multiple Accounts

You set the profile information for multiple accounts using the options in the Profile tab. One of the best reasons to work with multiple accounts in Active Directory Users And Computers is to set all their environment profiles using a single interface. To do this, you will usually rely on the %UserName% environment variable, which lets you assign paths and file names that are based on individual user names. For example, if you assign the logon script name as %UserName%.cmd, Windows replaces this value with the user name—and it does so for each user you're managing. Thus, bobs, janew, and ericl would all be assigned unique logon scripts and those scripts would be named Bobs.cmd, Janew.cmd, and Ericl.cmd.

An example of setting environment profile information for multiple accounts is shown in Figure 10-11. Note that the %UserName% variable is used to assign the user profile path, the user logon script name, and the home folder.

Although you might want all users to have unique files and paths, sometimes you want users to share this information. For example, if you're using mandatory profiles for users, you might want to assign a specific user profile path rather than one that's dynamically created.

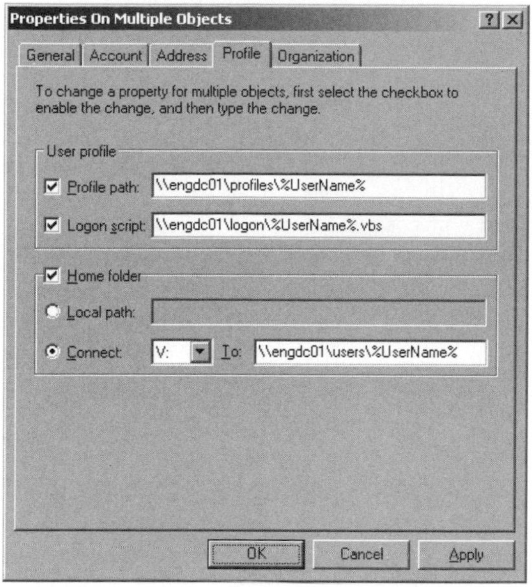

Figure 10-11   Use the %UserName% environment variable to assign paths and file names that are based on individual user names.

Setting Logon Hours for Multiple Accounts

When you select multiple user accounts in Active Directory Users And Computers, you can manage their logon hours collectively. To do this, follow these steps:

1. Select the accounts you want to work with in Active Directory Users And Computers.

2. Right-click and then select Properties. In the Properties dialog box, click the Account tab.

3. Choose the Logon Hours check box and then click Logon Hours. You can then set the logon hours as discussed in the section entitled "Configuring Logon Hours," earlier in this chapter.

    Note   Active Directory Users And Computers doesn't tell you the previous logon hour designations for the selected accounts, and it doesn't warn you if the logon hours for the accounts are different.

Setting Permitted Logon Workstations for Multiple Accounts

You set the permitted logon workstations for multiple accounts using the Logon Workstations dialog box. To access this dialog box, follow these steps:

1. Select the accounts you want to work with in Active Directory Users And Computers.

2. Right-click and then select Properties. In the Properties dialog box, click the Account tab.

3. Choose Computer Restrictions and then click Log On To.

4. If you want to allow the users to log on to any workstation, select All Computers. Otherwise, if you want to specify which workstations users are permitted to use, select The Following Computers option button and then enter the names of up to eight workstations. When you click OK, these settings are applied to all the selected user accounts.

Setting Logon, Password, and Expiration Properties for Multiple Accounts

Users accounts have many options that control logon, passwords, and account expiration. You set these values in the Account tab of the Properties dialog box. When you work with multiple accounts, you must enable the option you want to work with by selecting the corresponding check box in the leftmost column. You now have two options:

■ Set the option by selecting its check box. This enables the option. For example, if you were working with the Password Never Expires option, a flag is set so that the password for the selected users won't expire when you click OK.

■ Don't set the option, which effectively clears the option. For example, if you were working with the Account Is Disabled option, the accounts for the selected users are reenabled when you click OK.

If you want to set the expiration date of the selected accounts, you start by selecting Account Expires and then you select the appropriate expiration value. The Never option removes any existing account expiration values. You use the End Of option to set a specific expiration date.

Troubleshooting Logon Problems

The previous section listed ways in which accounts can become disabled. Beyond the typical reasons for an account being disabled, some system settings can also cause access problems. Specifically, you should look for the following:

User gets a message that says that the user can't log on interactively   The user right to log on locally isn't set for this user and the user isn't a member of a group that has this right.

The user might be trying to log on to a server or domain controller. If so, keep in mind that the right to log on locally applies to all domain controllers in the domain. Otherwise, this right only applies to the single workstation.

If the user should have access to the local system, configure the Logon Locally user right as described in the section of Chapter 9 entitled "Configuring User Rights Policies."

User gets a message that the system could not log the user on   If you've already checked the password and account name, you might want to check the account type. The user might be trying to access the domain with a local account. If this isn't the problem, the global catalog server might be unavailable, and, as a result, only users with administrator privileges can log on to the domain.

User has a mandatory profile and the computer storing the profile is unavailable   When a user has a mandatory profile, the computer storing the profile must be accessible during the logon process. If the computer is shut down or otherwise unavailable, users with mandatory profiles may not be able to logon. See the section titled "Local, Roaming, and Mandatory Profiles," earlier in this chapter.

User gets a message saying the account has been configured to prevent the user from logging on to the workstation   The user is trying to access a workstation that isn't defined as a permitted logon workstation. If the user should have access to this workstation, change the logon workstation information as described in the section of this chapter entitled "Setting Permitted Logon Workstations."

Setting Advanced Active Directory Permissions

As you know from previous discussions, user, group, and computer accounts are represented in Active Directory as objects. Active Directory objects have standard and advanced security permissions. These permissions grant or deny access to the objects. You can view advanced security permissions for objects by completing the following steps:

1. Start Active Directory Users And Computers, and then display advanced options by selecting Advanced Features from the View menu. Next, right-click the user, group, or computer account with which you want to work.

2. Select Properties from the shortcut menu, and then click the Security tab in the Properties dialog box.

3. Select the user, computer, or group whose permissions you want to view in the Name list box. If the permissions are dimmed, it means the permissions are inherited from a parent object.

Understanding Advanced User, Group, and Computer Permissions

Advanced permissions for Active Directory objects aren't as straightforward as other permissions. Different types of objects can have sets of permissions that are specific to the type of object. They can also have general permissions that are specific to the container in which they're defined.

To set advanced permissions for Active Directory objects, follow these steps:

1. Start Active Directory Users And Computers and then right-click the user, group, or computer account with which you want to work.

   Caution   Only those administrators with a solid understanding of Active Directory and Active Directory permissions should manipulate advanced object permissions. Incorrectly setting advanced object permissions can cause problems that are very difficult to track down.

2. Select Properties from the shortcut menu, and then click the Security tab in the Properties dialog box, as shown in Figure 10-12.

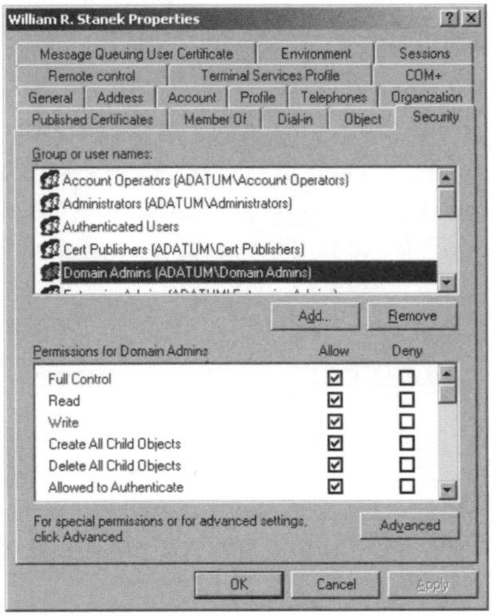

Figure 10-12   Use the Security tab to configure object permissions.

3. Users or groups with access permissions are listed in the Name list box. You can change permissions for these users and groups by doing the following:

   ❑   Select the user or group you want to change.

   ❑   Use the Permissions list box to grant or deny access permissions.

   ❑   When inherited permissions are dimmed, override inherited permissions by selecting the opposite permissions.

4. To set access permissions for additional users, computers, or groups, click Add. Then use the Select Users, Computers, Or Groups dialog box to add users, computers, or groups.

5. Select the user, computer, or group you want to configure in the Name list box, click Add, and then click OK. Then use the fields in the Permissions area to allow or deny permissions. Repeat for other users, computers, or groups. Click OK when you're finished.

Chapter 11

Managing File Systems and Drives

A hard disk drive is the most common storage device used on network workstations and servers. Users depend on hard disk drives to store their word-processing documents, spreadsheets, and other types of data. Drives are organized into file systems that users can access either locally or remotely as follows:

Local file systems   Installed on a user's computer and don't require remote network connections to access. An example of a local file system is the C drive available on most workstations and servers. You access the C drive using the file path C:\.

Remote file systems   Accessed, on the other hand, through a network connection to a remote resource. You can connect to a remote file system using the Map Network Drive feature of Windows Explorer.

Wherever disk resources are located, it's your job as a system administrator to manage them. The tools and techniques you use to manage file systems and drives are discussed in this chapter. Chapter 12, "Administering Volume Sets and RAID Arrays," looks at volume sets and fault tolerance. Chapter 13, "Managing Files and Folders," tells you how to manage files and directories.

Adding Hard Disk Drives

Before you make a hard disk drive available to users, you'll need to configure it and consider the way it'll be used. Microsoft Windows Server 2003 makes it possible to configure hard disk drives in a variety of ways. The technique you choose depends primarily on the type of data you're working with and the needs of your network environment. For general user data stored on workstations, you might want to configure individual drives as stand-alone storage devices. In that case, user data is stored on a workstation's hard disk drive, where it can be accessed and stored locally.

Although storing data on a single drive is convenient, it isn't the most reliable way to store data. To improve reliability and performance, you might want a set of drives to work together. Windows Server 2003 supports drive sets and arrays using redundant array of independent disks (RAID) technology, which is built into the operating system.

Physical Drives

Whether you use individual drives or drive sets, you'll need physical drives. Physical drives are the actual hardware devices that are used to store data. The amount of data a drive can store depends on its size and whether it uses compression. Typical drives have capacities of 20 gigabytes (GB) to 300 GB. Many drive types are available for use with Windows Server 2003, including Small Computer Systems Interface (SCSI) Ultra SCSI, Parallel ATA (PATA), and Serial ATA (SATA).

The terms SCSI, Ultra SCSI, PATA, and SATA designate the interface type used by the hard disk drives. This interface is used to communicate with a drive controller. SCSI drives use SCSI controllers, Ultra SCSI drives use Ultra SCSI controllers, and so on. When setting up a new server, you should give considerable thought to the drive configuration. Start by choosing drives or storage systems that provide the appropriate level of performance. There really is a substantial difference in speed and performance among various drive specifications.

You should consider not only the capacity of the drive but also its:

Rotational speed   A measurement of how fast the disk spins

Average seek time   A measurement of how long it takes to seek between disk tracks during sequential input/output (I/O) operations

Generally speaking, when comparing drives that conform to the same specification, such as Ultra320 SCSI or SATA II, the higher the rotational speed (measured in thousands of rotations per minute) and the lower the average seek time (measured in milliseconds), the better. As an example, a drive with a rotational speed of 15,000 RPM will give you 45 percent to 50 percent more I/O per second than the average 10,000 RPM drive, all other things being equal. A drive with a seek time of 3.5 msec will give you a 25 percent to 30 percent response time improvement over a drive with a seek time of 4.7 msec.

Other factors to consider include:

Maximum sustained data transfer rate   A measurement of how much data the drive can continuously transfer

Mean time to failure (MTTF)   A measurement of how many hours of operation you can expect to get from the drive before it fails

Nonoperational temperatures   Measurements of the temperatures at which the drive fails

Most drives of comparable quality will have similar transfer rates and MTTF. For example, if you compare Ultra320 SCSI drives with a 15,000 RPM rotational speed, you will probably find similar transfer rates and MTTF. As an example, the Maxtor Atlas 15K II has a maximum sustained data transfer rate of up to 98 megabytes per second (MBps). The Seagate Cheetah 15K.4 has a maximum sustained data transfer rate of up to 96 MBps. Both have a MTTF of 1.4 million hours. Transfer rates can also be expressed in gigabits per second (Gbps). A rate of 1.5 Gbps is equivalent to a data rate of 188 MBps, and 3.0 Gbps is equivalent to 375 MBps. Sometimes you'll see a maximum external transfer rate (per the specification to which the drive complies) and an average sustained transfer rate. The average sustained transfer rate is the most important factor. The Seagate Barracuda 7200 SATA II drive has a rotational speed of 7,200 RPM and an average sustained transfer rate of 58 MBps. With an average seek time of 8.5 msec and an MTTF of 1 million hours, the drive performs comparably to other 7,200 RPM SATA II drives. However, most Ultra320 SCSI drives perform better.

Temperature is another important factor to consider when you're selecting a drive—but it's a factor few administrators take into account. Typically, the faster a drive rotates, the hotter it will run. This is not always the case, but it is certainly something you should consider when making your choice. For example, 15K drives tend to run hot, and you must be sure to carefully regulate temperature. Both the Maxtor Atlas 15K II and the Seagate Cheetah 15K.4 can become nonoperational at temperatures of 70°C or higher (as would most other drives).

Preparing a Drive for Use

After you install a drive, you'll need to configure it for use. You configure the drive by partitioning it and creating file systems in the partitions, as needed. A partition is a section of a physical drive that functions as if it were a separate unit. After you create a partition, you can create a file system in the partition.

Two partition styles are used for disks: Master Boot Record (MBR) and globally unique identifier (GUID) Partition Table (GPT). x86-based computers use the MBR partition style. MBR contains a partition table that describes where the partitions are located on the disk. With this partition style, the first sector on a hard disk contains the master boot record and a binary code file called the master boot code that's used to boot the system. This sector is unpartitioned and hidden from view to protect the system.

With the MBR partitioning style, disks support volumes of up to 4 terabytes and use one of two types of partitions—primary and extended. Each MBR drive can have up to four primary partitions or three primary partitions and one extended partition. Primary partitions are drive sections that you can access directly for file storage. You make a primary partition accessible to users by creating a file system on it. Unlike primary partitions, you can't access extended partitions directly. Instead, you can configure extended partitions with one or more logical drives that are used to store files. Being able to divide extended partitions into logical drives allows you to divide a physical drive into more than four sections.

Itanium-based computers running 64-bit versions of Windows use the GPT partition style. The key difference between the GPT partition style and the MBR partition style has to do with how partition data is stored. With GPT, critical partition data is stored in the individual partitions and there are redundant primary and backup partition tables for improved structure integrity. Additionally, GPT disks support volumes of up to 18 exabytes and up to 128 partitions. Although there are underlying differences between the GPT and MBR partitioning styles, most disk-related tasks are performed in the same way.

Using Disk Management

You'll use the Disk Management snap-in for the Microsoft Management Console (MMC) to configure drives. Disk Management makes it easy to work with the internal and external drives on a local or remote system. Disk Management is included as part of the Computer Management console and can also be added to custom MMCs.

Windows Server 2003 R2 includes two additional consoles for working with disks and file systems: File Server Management and File Server Resource Management. File Server Management includes an extended form of the Disk Management snap-in called the Disk And Volume Management snap-in. The Disk And Volume Management snap-in includes Storage Manager for storage area networks (SANs), a component that uses the Virtual Disk Service (VDS) and VDS hardware providers installed on a computer to configure SANs.

To start Disk Management and connect to a local or remote system in Computer Management, follow these steps:

1. Run Computer Management by going to Start, selecting Programs or All Programs as appropriate, then Administrative Tools, and then Computer Management.

2. You're automatically connected to the local computer on which you're running Computer Management. To manage hard disk drives on another computer, right-click the Computer Management (Local) entry in the console tree and select Connect To Another Computer on the shortcut menu. You can now choose the system whose drives you want to manage.

3. In Computer Management, expand Storage and then select Disk Management. You can now manage the drives on the local or remote system.

   Tip   If you receive an error message from the Logical Disk Manager, read the message and click OK. A failed connection to the Logical Disk Manager Service usually means that this service or the related administrative service isn't started on the local or remote system. If necessary, start Logical Disk Manager and Logical Disk Manager Administrative Service as described in the section entitled "Starting, Stopping, and Pausing Services" in Chapter 3, "Monitoring Processes, Services, and Events." Network policies and trusts can affect your ability to administer computers remotely as well.

The steps for accessing Disk Management in File Server Management are similar. Regardless of whether you are using Computer Management or File Server Management, Disk Management has three views: Disk List, Graphical View, and Volume List. With remote systems, you're limited in the tasks you can perform with Disk Management. Remote management tasks you can peform include viewing drive details, changing drive letters and paths, and converting disk types. With removable media drives, you can also eject media remotely. To perform more advanced manipulation of remote drives, you can use the DISKPART command-line utility as discussed in Chapters 8–10 of the *Microsoft Windows Command-Line Administrator's Pocket Consultant* (Microsoft Press, 2004).

Note   Before you work with Disk Management, you should know several things. If you create a partition but don't format it, the partition will be labeled as Free Space. If you haven't assigned a portion of the disk to a partition, this section of the disk is labeled Unallocated.

In Figure 11-1, the Volume List view is in the upper-right corner and the Graphical View is in the lower-right corner. This is the default configuration. You can change the view for the top or bottom pane as follows:

- To change the top view, select View, choose Top, and then select the view you want to use.

- To change the bottom view, select View, choose Bottom, and then select the view you want to use.

- To hide the bottom view, select View, choose Bottom, and then select Hidden.

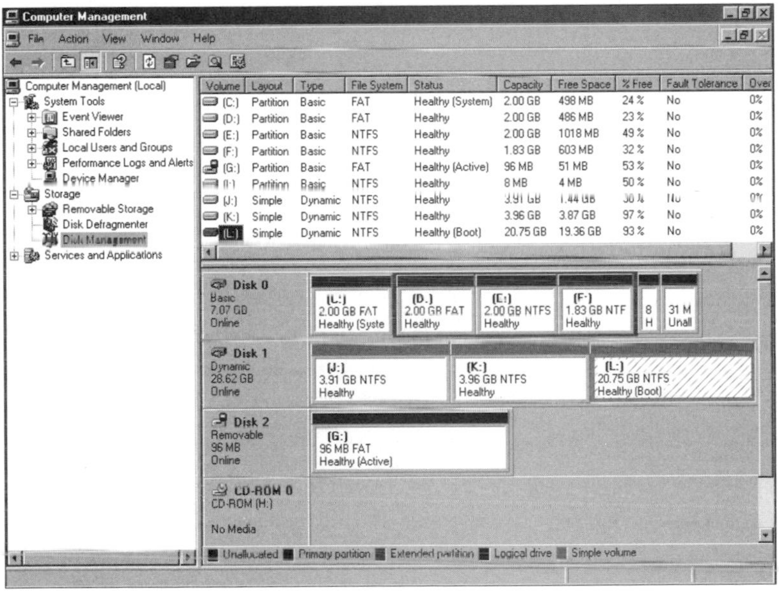

Figure 11-1   In Disk Management, the upper view provides a detailed summary of all the drives on the computer and the lower view provides an overview of the same drives by default.

More Detailed Drive Information

From the Disk Management window, you can get more detailed information on a drive section by right-clicking it and then selecting Properties from the shortcut menu. When you do this, you see a dialog box much like the one shown in Figure 11-2. This is the same dialog box that you can access from Windows Explorer (by selecting the top-level folder for the drive and then selecting Properties from the File menu).

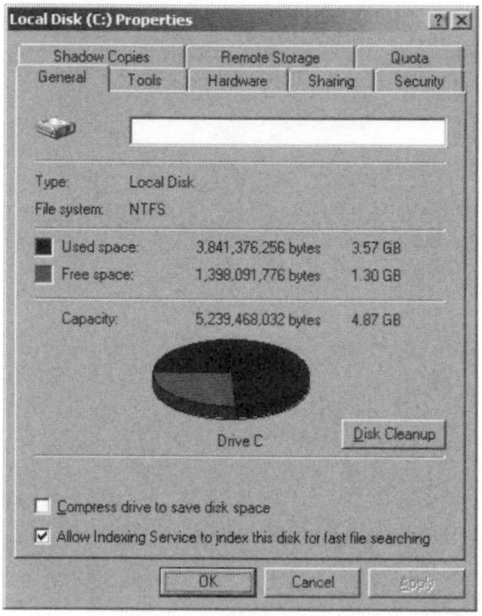

Figure 11-2   The General tab of the Properties dialog box provides detailed information about a drive.

Installing and Checking for a New Drive

Hot swapping is a feature that allows you to remove devices without shutting off the computer. Typically, hot-swappable drives are installed and removed from the front of the computer. If your computer supports hot swapping of drives, you can install drives to the computer without having to shut down. After you do this, access Disk Management, and, from the Action menu, select Rescan Disks. New disks that are found are added as basic disks. If a disk that you've added isn't found, reboot.

If the computer doesn't support hot swapping of drives, you must turn the computer off and then install the new drives. Afterward, you can scan for new disks as described previously.

Understanding Drive Status

Knowing the drive status is useful when you install new drives or troubleshoot drive problems. Disk Management shows the drive status in the Graphical View and Volume List views. Table 11-1 summarizes the most common status values.

Table 11-1   Common Drive Status Values and Their Meanings

Status	Description	Resolution
Online	The normal disk status. It means the disk is accessible and doesn't have problems. Both dynamic disks and basic disks display this status.	The drive doesn't have any known problems.
Online (Errors)	I/O errors have been detected on a dynamic disk.	You can try to correct temporary errors using the Reactivate Disk command.
Offline	The dynamic disk isn't accessible and might be corrupted or temporarily unavailable. If the disk name changes to Missing, the disk can no longer be located or identified on the system.	Check for problems with the drive, its controller, and cables. Make sure that the drive has power and is connected properly. Use the Reactivate Disk command to bring the disk back online (if possible).
Foreign	The dynamic disk has been moved to your computer but hasn't been imported for use. A failed drive brought back online might sometimes be listed as Foreign.	Use the Import Foreign Disks command to add the disk to the system.
Unreadable	The disk isn't currently accessible, which can occur when rescanning disks. Both dynamic and basic disks display this status.	If the drives aren't being scanned, the drive might be corrupt or have I/O errors. Use the Rescan Disk command to correct the problem (If possible). You might also want to reboot the system.
Unrecognized	The disk is of an unknown type and can't be used on the system. A drive from a non-Windows system might display this status.	You can't use the drive on the computer. Try a different drive.
No Media	No media have been inserted into the CD-ROM or removable drive. Only CD-ROM and removable disk types display this status.	Insert a CD-ROM, floppy disk, or removable disk to bring the disk online.

Working with Basic and Dynamic Disks

Windows Server 2003 supports two types of disk configurations:

Basic   The standard disk type used in previous versions of Windows. Basic disks are divided into partitions and can be used with previous versions of Windows.

Dynamic   An enhanced disk type for Windows Server 2003 that can be updated without having to restart the system (in most cases). Dynamic disks are divided into volumes and can be used only with Windows 2000 and Windows Server 2003.

> **Note**   You can't use dynamic disks on portable computers or with removable media.

Using Basic and Dynamic Disks

When you convert to Windows Server 2003, disks with partitions are initialized as basic disks. When you install Windows Server 2003 on a new system with unpartitioned drives, you have the option of initializing the drives as either basic or dynamic.

Basic drives support all the fault-tolerant features found in Microsoft Windows NT 4.0. You can use basic drives to maintain existing spanning, mirroring, and striping configurations and to delete these configurations. However, you can't create new fault-tolerant drive sets using the basic disk type. You'll need to convert to dynamic disks and then create volumes that use mirroring or striping. The fault-tolerant features and the ability to modify disks without having to restart the computer are the key capabilities that distinguish basic and dynamic disks. Other features available on a disk depend on the disk formatting.

You can use both basic and dynamic disks on the same computer. The catch is that volume sets must use the same disk type. For example, if you have mirrored drives C and D that were created under Windows NT 4.0, you can use these drives under Windows Server 2003. If you want to convert C to the dynamic disk type, you must also convert D. To learn how to convert a disk from basic to dynamic, see the section of this chapter entitled "Changing Drive Types."

Disk configuration tasks that you can perform with basic and dynamic disks are different. With basic disks, you can:

- Format partitions and mark them as active.
- Create and delete primary and extended partitions.
- Create and delete logical drives within extended partitions.
- Convert from a basic disk to a dynamic disk.

With dynamic disks, you can:

- Create and delete simple, striped, spanned, mirrored, and RAID-5 volumes.
- Remove a mirror from a mirrored volume.

- Extend simple or spanned volumes.
- Split a volume into two volumes.
- Repair mirrored or RAID-5 volumes.
- Reactivate a missing or offline disk.
- Revert to a basic disk from a dynamic disk (requires deleting volumes and reload).

With either disk type, you can:

- View properties of disks, partitions, and volumes.
- Make drive letter assignments.
- Configure security and drive sharing.

Special Considerations for Basic and Dynamic Disks

Whether you're working with basic or dynamic disks, you need to keep in mind three special types of drive sections:

System   The system partition or volume contains the hardware-specific files needed to load the operating system.

Boot   The boot partition or volume contains the operating system and its support files. The system and boot partition or volume can be the same.

Active   The active partition or volume is the drive section from which the computer starts.

> **Note**   On multiboot systems with pre–Windows 2000 operating systems, the active drive section might need to contain the startup files for all operating systems loaded on the computer and might also need to be a primary partition on a basic disk. You can't mark an existing dynamic volume as the active volume, but you can convert a basic disk containing the active partition to a dynamic disk. Once the update is complete, the partition becomes a simple volume that's active.

Marking an Active Partition

Windows Server 2003 supports two key central processing unit (CPU) architectures: x86 and Itanium. On an x86-based computer, you can mark a partition as active by completing the following steps:

1. Make sure that the necessary startup files are on the primary partition that you want to make the active partition. For Windows NT, Windows 2000 Server, and Windows Server 2003, these files are Boot.ini, Ntdetect.com, Ntldr, and Bootsect.dos. You might also need Ntbootdd.sys.

2. Access Disk Management.

3. Right-click the primary partition you want to mark as active, and then select Mark Partition As Active.

Note You can't mark dynamic disk volumes as active. When you convert a basic disk containing the active partition to a dynamic disk, this partition becomes a simple volume that's active automatically.

Changing Drive Types

Basic disks are designed to be used with previous versions of Windows. Dynamic disks are designed to let you take advantage of the latest Windows features. Only computers running Windows 2000 or Windows Server 2003 can use dynamic disks. However, you can use dynamic disks with other operating systems, such as UNIX. To do this, you need to create a separate volume for the non-Windows operating system. You can't use dynamic disks on portable computers.

Windows Server 2003 provides the tools you need to convert a basic disk to a dynamic disk and to change a dynamic disk back to a basic disk. When you convert to a dynamic disk, partitions are changed to volumes of the appropriate type automatically. You can't change these volumes back to partitions. Instead, you must delete the volumes on the dynamic disk and then change the disk back to a basic disk. Deleting the volumes destroys all the information on the disk.

Converting a Basic Disk to a Dynamic Disk

Before you convert a basic disk to a dynamic disk, you should make sure that you don't need to boot the computer to other versions of Windows. Only computers running Windows 2000 or Windows Server 2003 can use dynamic disks.

With MBR disks, you should also make sure that the disk has 1 MB of free space at the end of the disk. Although Disk Management reserves this free space when creating partitions and volumes, disk management tools on other operating systems might not. Without the free space at the end of the disk, the conversion will fail.

With GPT disks, you must have contiguous, recognized data partitions. If the GPT disk contains partitions that Windows doesn't recognize, such as those created by another operating system, you can't convert to a dynamic disk.

With either type of disk:

- You can't convert drives that use sector sizes larger than 512 bytes. If the drive has large sector sizes, you'll need to reformat before converting.

- You can't use dynamic disks on portable computers or with removable media. You can only configure these drives as basic drives with primary partitions.

- You can't convert a disk if the system or boot partition is part of spanned, striped, mirrored, or RAID-5 volume. You'll need to stop the spanning, mirroring, or striping before you convert.

- You shouldn't convert a disk if it contains multiple installations of the Windows operating system. If you do, you might be able to start the computer only using Windows Server 2003.

- You can convert disks with other types of partitions that are part of spanned, striped, mirrored, or RAID-5 volumes. These volumes become dynamic volumes of the same type. However, you must convert all drives in the set together.

To convert a basic disk to a dynamic disk, complete the following steps:

1. In Disk Management, right-click a basic disk that you want to convert, either in the Disk List view or in the left pane of the Graphical View. Then select Convert To Dynamic Disk.

2. In the Convert To Dynamic Disk dialog box, select the check boxes for the disks you want to convert. If you're converting a spanned, striped, mirrored, or RAID-5 volume, be sure to select all the basic disks in this set. You must convert the set together. Click OK when you're ready to continue.

3. The Disks To Convert dialog box shows the disks you're converting. The buttons and columns on this dialog box contain the following information:

   Name   Shows the disk number.

   Disk Contents   Shows the type and status of partitions, such as boot, active, or in use.

   Will Convert   Specifies whether the drive will be converted. If the drive doesn't meet the criteria, it won't be converted, and you might need to take corrective action, as described previously.

   Details   Shows the volumes on the selected drive.

   Convert   Starts the conversion.

4. If you're ready to begin the conversion, click Convert. Disk Management warns you that after you finish the conversion you won't be able to boot previous versions of Windows from volumes on the selected disks. Click Yes to continue.

5. Disk Management will restart the computer if a selected drive contains the boot partition, system partition, or a partition in use.

Changing a Dynamic Disk Back to a Basic Disk

Before you can change a dynamic disk back to a basic disk, you must delete all dynamic volumes on the disk. After you do this, right-click the disk and select the Convert To Basic Disk command. This changes the dynamic disk to a basic disk and you can then create new partitions and logical drives on the disk.

Reactivating Dynamic Disks

If the status of a dynamic disk displays as Online (Errors) or Offline, you can often reactivate the disk to correct the problem. You reactivate a disk by completing the following steps:

1. In Disk Management, right-click the dynamic disk you want to reactivate, and then select Reactivate Disk. Confirm the action when prompted.

2. If the drive status doesn't change, you might need to reboot the computer. If this still doesn't resolve the problem, check for problems with the drive, its controller, and the cables. Also, make sure that the drive has power and is connected properly.

Rescanning Disks

Rescanning all drives on a system updates the drive configuration information on the computer. It can sometimes resolve a problem with drives that show a status of Unreadable. Because the drive configuration might change as a result of the rescan, you might need to update the Boot.ini file for the computer, as discussed later in this chapter in the section entitled "Updating the Boot Disk."

You rescan disks on a computer by selecting Rescan Disk from Disk Management's Action menu.

Real World   Take a screenshot of the disk configuration in Disk Management before scanning and after scanning to double-check the configuration for changes. On my primary server, the original configuration had a floppy disk drive on A; logical drives on C, D, E, and F; a removable drive on G; and a CD-ROM drive on H. After rescanning, the removable drive was on B, and, as a result, the number of the boot partition changed (and Windows Server 2003 gave no notification of this change).

During reboot of the system, Windows Server 2003 stated incorrectly that the Ntoskrnl.exe file needed to be restored on the Windows Server 2003 root folder. Using the emergency repair disk created as explained in Chapter 15, "Data Backup and Recovery," you could modify the Boot.ini file and recover the system. Without the emergency repair disk, you'd need to repair the Windows Server 2003 installation using the Windows Server 2003 CD and the Recovery Console. Installing the Windows Server 2003 Recovery Console is also covered in Chapter 15.

Moving a Dynamic Disk to a New System

Windows Server 2003 makes the task of moving drives to a new system a lot easier. If you want to move a dynamic drive to a new computer, follow these steps:

1. Access Disk Management on the system where the dynamic drives are currently installed.

2. Check the status of the drives and ensure that they're marked as healthy. If the status isn't healthy, you should repair partitions and volumes, as necessary, before you move the disk drives.

3. Remove drive letters and drive paths that reference the drives, as described in the section of this chapter entitled "Assigning Drive Letters and Paths."

4. If the drives are hot-swappable and this feature is supported on both systems, remove the drives, and then install them on the destination computer. Otherwise, turn off both computers. Remove the drives from the original system and then install them on the new system. When you're finished, turn the computers back on.

5. On the destination computer, from the Action menu select Rescan Disks. When the scan finishes, right-click any disk marked Foreign, and then click Import Foreign Disks.

Using Basic Disks and Partitions

When you install a new computer or update an existing computer, you'll often need to partition the drives on the computer. You partition drives using Disk Management.

Partitioning Basics

On Windows Server 2003, a physical drive using MBR partition style can have up to four primary partitions and up to one extended partition. This allows you to configure MBR drives in one of two ways: using one to four primary partitions or using one to three primary partitions and one extended partition. Drives with GPT partition style can have up to 128 partitions.

After you partition a drive, you format the partitions to assign drive letters. This is a high-level formatting that creates the file system structure rather than a low-level formatting that sets up the drive for initial use. You're probably very familiar with the C drive used by Windows Server 2003. Well, the C drive is simply the designator for a disk partition. If you partition a disk into multiple sections, each section can have its own drive letter. You use the drive letters to access file systems in various partitions on a physical drive. Unlike MS-DOS, which assigns drive letters automatically starting with the letter C, Windows Server 2003 lets you specify drive letters. Generally, the drive letters C through Z are available for your use.

Note The drive letter A is usually assigned to the system's floppy disk drive. If the system has a second floppy disk drive, the letter B is assigned to it, so you can use only the letters C through Z. Don't forget that CD-ROMs, Zip drives, and other types of media drives need drive letters as well. The total number of drive letters you can use at one time is 24. If you need additional volumes, you can create them using drive paths.

In Windows NT 4.0 you could have only 24 active volumes. To get around this limitation, Windows 2000 and Windows Server 2003 allow you to mount disks to drive paths. A drive path is set as a folder location on another drive. For example, you could mount additional drives as E:\Data1, E:\Data2, and E:\Data3. You can use drive paths with basic and dynamic disks. The only restriction for drive paths is that you mount them on empty folders that are on NTFS drives.

To help you differentiate between primary partitions and extended partitions with logical drives, Disk Management color-codes the partitions. For example, primary partitions might be color-coded with a dark blue band and logical drives in extended partitions might be color-coded with a light blue band. The key for the color scheme is shown at the bottom of the Disk Management window. You can change the colors using the View Settings dialog box. From the Disk Management View menu, select the Settings option.

Creating Partitions

In Disk Management, you create partitions and logical drives by completing the following steps:

1. In the Disk Management Graphical View, right-click an area marked Unallocated and then choose New Partition. Or right-click a free space in an extended partition and select New Logical Drive. This starts the New Partition Wizard.

2. Click Next. As shown in Figure 11-3, you can now select a partition type as follows:

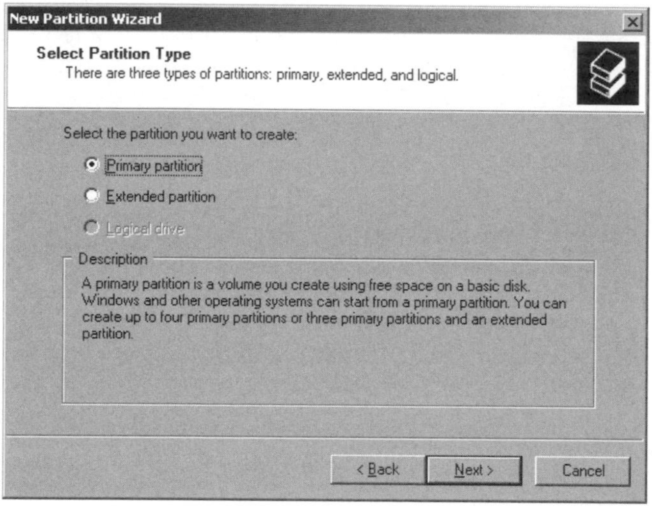

Figure 11-3   Use the New Partition Wizard to select a partition type.

Primary Partition   To create a primary partition. A primary partition can fill an entire disk, or you can size it as appropriate for the workstation or server you're configuring.

Extended Partition   To create an extended partition. Each physical drive can have one extended partition. This extended partition can contain one or more logical drives, which are simply sections of the partition with their own file system. If a drive already contains an extended partition, the Extended Partition option won't be available. Note also that you can't create extended partitions on removable drives.

Logical Drive   To create a logical drive within an extended partition. Although you can size the logical drive any way you want, you might want to take a moment to consider how you'll use logical drives on the current workstation or server. Generally, you use logical drives to divide a large drive into manageable sections. With this in mind, you might want to divide a 21-GB extended partition into three logical drives of 7 GB each.

3. You should see the Specify Partition Size page. This page specifies the minimum and maximum size for the partition in megabytes and lets you size the partition within these limits. Size the partition using the Amount Of Disk Space To Use field.

4. Specify whether you want to assign a drive letter or path, as shown in Figure 11-4. You use these options as follows:

Assign The Following Drive Letter   To assign a drive letter, choose this option, and then select an available drive letter in the selection list provided.

Mount In The Following Empty NTFS Folder   To assign a drive path, choose this option, and then type the path to an existing folder or click Browse to search for or create a folder.

Do Not Assign A Drive Letter Or Drive Path   To create the partition without assigning a drive letter or path, choose this option. You can assign a drive letter or path later, if necessary.

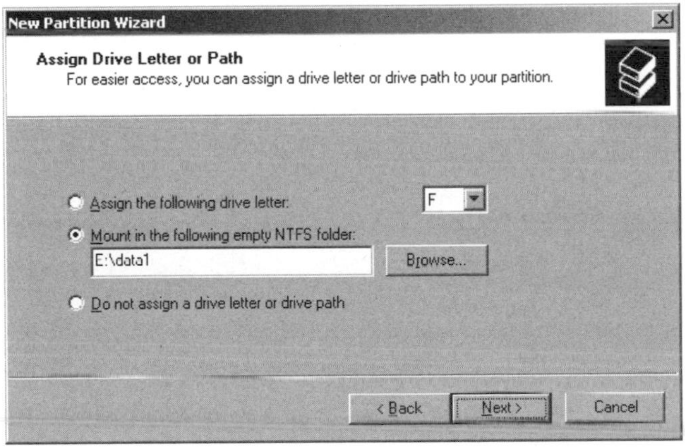

Figure 11-4   Use the Assign Drive Letter Or Path page to assign a drive letter, mount to an empty folder, or create the partition without assigning a driver letter or path.

5. Determine whether the partition should be formatted in the Format Partition page, shown in Figure 11-5. If you elect to format the partition, follow the steps described in the following section, "Formatting Partitions."

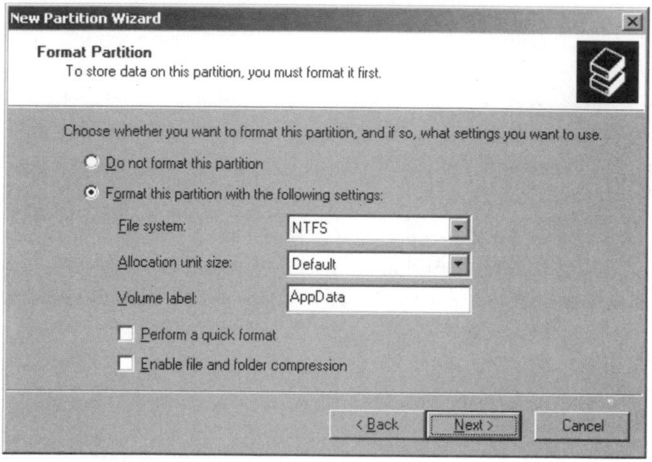

Figure 11-5 You can format a partition by specifying its file system type and volume label.

6. Click Next and then click Finish. If you add partitions to a physical drive that contains the Windows Server 2003 operating system, you might inadvertently change the number of the boot partition. Windows Server 2003 will display a prompt warning you that the number of the boot partition will change. Click Yes.

7. Disk Management then creates the partition, assigns a drive letter or path as appropriate, and formats the partition as appropriate. If you saw a warning prompt previously, you might see another warning prompt telling you to edit the Boot.ini file. Edit the Boot.ini file and update the designator for the boot partition as described in the section of this chapter entitled "Updating the Boot Disk." Then immediately reboot the computer.

Formatting Partitions

Formatting creates a file system in a partition and permanently deletes any existing data. This is a high-level formatting that creates the file system structure rather than a low-level formatting that initializes a drive for use. To format a partition, right-click the partition, and then chose Format. This opens the Format dialog box shown in Figure 11-6.

You use the formatting fields as follows:

Volume Label   Specifies a text label for the partition. This label is the partition's volume name.

File System   Specifies the file system type as FAT, FAT32, or NTFS. FAT is the file system type supported by MS-DOS and Microsoft Windows 3.1, Windows 95, Windows 98, and Windows Me. NTFS is the native file system type for Microsoft Windows NT, Windows 2000, and Windows Server 2003. The section of Chapter 13 entitled "Windows Server 2003 File Structures" tells you more about NTFS and the advantages of using it with Windows Server 2003.

Allocation Unit Size   Specifies the cluster size for the file system. This is the basic unit in which disk space is allocated. The default allocation unit size is based on the size of the volume and is set dynamically prior to formatting. To override this feature, you can set the allocation unit size to a specific value. If you use lots of small files, you might want to use a smaller cluster size, such as 512 or 1024 bytes. With these settings, small files use less disk space.

Perform A Quick Format   Tells Windows Server 2003 to format without checking the partition for errors. With large partitions this option can save you a few minutes. However, it's more prudent to check for errors, which allows Disk Management to mark bad sectors on the disk and lock them out.

Enable File And Folder Compression   Turns on compression for the disk. Built-in compression is available only for NTFS. Under NTFS, compression is transparent to users and compressed files can be accessed just like regular files. If you select this option, files and directories on this drive are compressed automatically. For more information on compressing drives, files, and directories, see the section of this chapter entitled "Compressing Drives and Data."

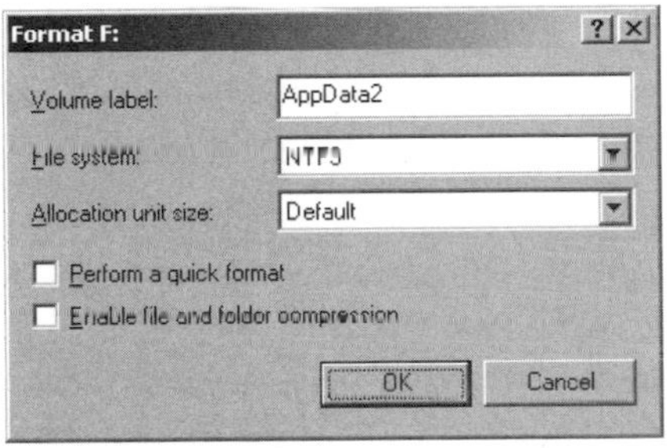

Figure 11-6   Use the Format dialog box to format a partition by specifying its file system type and volume label.

When you're ready to proceed, click OK. Because formatting a partition destroys any existing data, Disk Management gives you one last chance to abort the procedure. Click OK to start formatting the partition. Disk Management changes the drive's status to reflect the formatting and the percentage of completion. When formatting is complete, the drive status will change to reflect this.

Updating the Boot Disk

When you add partitions to a physical drive that contains the Windows Server 2003 operating system, the number of the boot partition might change. If this happens, you'll need to update the system's Boot.ini file. Normally, this file is located on the C drive.

The Boot.ini file contains entries that look like this:

```
[boot loader ]
timeout=30
default=multi(0)disk(0)rdisk(0)partition(3)\WINNT
[operating systems ]
multi(0)disk(0)rdisk(0)partition(3)\WINNT="Microsoft Windows Server 2003"
/fastdetect
multi(0)disk(0)rdisk(0)partition(2)\WIN2000="Microsoft Windows 2000
Server" /fastdetect
multi(0)disk(0)rdisk(0)partition(1)\WINXP="Microsoft Windows XP
Professional" /fastdetect
```

Tip The Boot.ini file might be hidden from view on the system with which you're working. To see Boot.ini and other system files in Windows Explorer, select Folder Options from the Tools menu. Afterward, in the Folder Options properties dialog box, click the View tab. Clear Hide Protected Operating System Files and then click OK.

Entries like this tell Windows Server 2003 where to find the operating system files:

```
multi(0)disk(0)rdisk(0)partition(3)\WINNT
```

The designators for this entry are used as follows:

multi(0) Designates the controller for the drive, which in this case is controller 0. If the secondary mirror is on a different controller, enter the number of the controller. Controllers are numbered from 0 to 3.

Note The format for the Boot.ini entries is the Advanced RISC Computer (ARC) name format. On SCSI systems that don't use SCSI basic input/output system (BIOS), the first field in the entry is scsi(n), where n is the controller number.

disk(0) Designates the SCSI bus adapter, which in this case is adapter 0. On most systems, this is always 0. The exception is for systems with multiple bus SCSI adapters. These systems use the scsi(n) syntax.

rdisk(0) Designates the ordinal number of the disk on the adapter, which in this case is drive 0. With SCSI drives that use SCSI BIOS, you'll see numbers from 0 to 6. With other SCSI drives this is always 0. With Integrated Device Electronics (IDE) you'll see either 0 or 1. In most cases, you'll need to change this field—so be sure to enter the number of the secondary mirror drive.

partition(3) Designates the partition that contains the operating system, which in this case is 3.

If the boot partition for Window Server 2003 changed from 3 to 4, you'd update the Boot.ini file shown earlier as follows:

```
[boot loader ]
timeout=30
default=multi(0)disk(0)rdisk(0)partition(4)\WINNT
[operating systems ]
multi(0)disk(0)rdisk(0)partition(4)\WINNT="Microsoft Windows Server 2003"
/fastdetect
multi(0)disk(0)rdisk(0)partition(2)\WIN2000="Microsoft Windows 2000
Server" /fastdetect
multi(0)disk(0)rdisk(0)partition(1)\WINXP="Microsoft Windows XP
Professional" /fastdetect
```

Managing Existing Partitions and Drives

Disk Management provides many ways to manage existing partitions and drives. Use these features to assign drive letters, delete partitions, set the active partition, and more. In addition, Windows Server 2003 provides other utilities to carry out common tasks such as converting a volume to NTFS, checking a drive for errors, and cleaning up unused disk space.

Assigning Drive Letters and Paths

You can assign drives one drive letter and one or more drive paths, provided the drive paths are mounted on NTFS drives. Drives don't have to be assigned a drive letter or path. A drive with no designators is considered to be unmounted, and you can mount it by assigning a drive letter or path at a later date. You need to unmount a drive before moving it to another computer.

To manage drive letters and paths, right-click the drive you want to configure in Disk Management, and then choose Change Drive Letter And Paths. This opens the dialog box shown in Figure 11-7. You can now:

Add a drive path   Click Add, select Mount In The Following Empty NTFS Folder, and then type the path to an existing folder or click Browse to search for or create a folder.

Remove a drive path   Select the drive path to remove, click Remove, and then click Yes.

Assign a drive letter   Click Add, select Assign A Drive Letter, and then choose an available letter to assign to the drive.

Change the drive letter   Select the current drive letter, and then click Change. Select Assign A Drive Letter, and then choose a different letter to assign to the drive.

Remove a drive letter   Select the current drive letter, click Remove, and then click Yes.

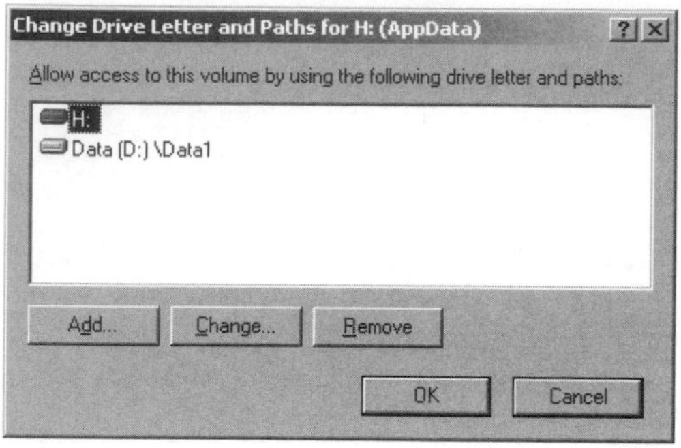

Figure 11-7   Use this dialog box to change the drive letter and path assignment.

Note   If you try to change the letter of a drive that's in use, Windows Server 2003 displays a warning. You'll need to exit programs that are using the drive and try again or allow Disk Management to force the change by clicking Yes when prompted.

Changing or Deleting the Volume Label

The volume label is a text descriptor for a drive. Because this label is displayed when the drive is accessed in various Windows Server 2003 utilities, such as Windows Explorer, you can use the label to help provide information about a drive's contents. You can change or delete a volume label using Disk Management or Windows Explorer.

Using Disk Management, you can change or delete a label by following these steps:

1. Right-click the partition, and then choose Properties.

2. In the General tab of the Properties dialog box, use the Label text box to type a new label for the volume or delete the existing label. Click OK.

Using Windows Explorer, you can change or delete a label by following these steps:

1. Right-click the drive icon and then choose Properties.

2. In the General tab of the Properties dialog box, use the Label text box to type a new label for the volume or delete the existing label. Click OK.

Deleting Partitions and Drives

To change the configuration of an existing drive that's fully allocated, you might need to delete existing partitions and logical drives. Deleting a partition or a drive removes the associated file system, and all data in the file system is lost. So, before you delete a partition or a drive, you should back up any files and directories that the partition or drive contains.

You can delete a primary partition or logical drive by following these steps:

1. In Disk Management, right-click the partition or drive you want to delete, and then choose Delete Partition or Delete Logical Drive, as appropriate.

2. Confirm that you want to delete the partition by clicking Yes.

3. If you delete a partition on a physical drive that contains the Windows Server 2003 operating system, the number of the boot partition might change. If so, you'll need to update the Boot.ini file as described in the section of this chapter entitled "Updating the Boot Disk." Be sure to note the new partition number to use.

To delete an extended partition, follow these steps:

1. Delete all the logical drives on the partition following the steps listed above.

2. You should now be able to select the extended partition area itself and delete it.

Converting a Volume to NTFS

Windows Server 2003 provides a utility for converting file allocation tables (FAT) volumes to NTFS. This utility, called Convert (Convert.exe), is located in the %SystemRoot% folder. When you convert a volume using this tool, the file and directory structure is preserved and no data is lost. Keep in mind, however, that Windows Server 2003 doesn't provide a utility for converting NTFS to FAT. The only way to go from NTFS to FAT is to delete the partition by following the steps listed in the previous section and then to recreate the partition as a FAT volume.

The Convert Utility Syntax

Convert is a command-line utility run at the Command prompt. If you want to convert a drive, use the following syntax:

```
convert volume /FS:NTFS
```

where *volume* is the drive letter followed by a colon, drive path, or volume name. For example, if you wanted to convert the D drive to NTFS, you'd use the following command:

```
convert D: /FS:NTFS
```

The complete syntax for Convert is shown below:

```
convert volume /FS:NTFS [/V] [/X] [/CvtArea:filename] [/NoSecurity]
```

The options and switches for Convert are used as follows:

volume	Sets the volume to work with
/FS:NTFS	Converts to NTFS
/V	Sets verbose mode
/X	Forces the volume to dismount before the conversion (if necessary)
/CvtArea: *filename*	Sets name of a contiguous file in the root directory to be a placeholder for NTFS system files
/NoSecurity	Removes all security attributes and makes all files and directories accessible to the group Everyone

A sample statement using convert is:

```
convert C: /FS:NTFS /V
```

Using the Convert Utility

Before you use the Convert utility, double-check to see if the partition is being used as the active boot partition or a system partition containing the operating system. With Intel x86 systems, you can convert the active boot partition to NTFS. Doing so requires that the system gain exclusive access to this partition, which can be obtained only during startup. Thus, if you try to convert the active boot partition to NTFS, Windows Server 2003 displays a prompt asking if you want to schedule the drive to be converted the next time the system starts. If you click Yes, you can restart the system to begin the conversion process.

Tip   Often it'll take several restarts of a system to completely convert the active boot partition. Don't panic. Let the system proceed with the conversion.

Before the Convert utility actually converts a drive to NTFS, the utility checks to see if the drive has enough free space to perform the conversion. Generally, Convert needs a block of free space that's roughly equal to 25 percent of the total space used on the drive. For example, if the drive stores 2 GB of data, Convert needs about 500 MB of free space. If there isn't enough free space, Convert aborts and tells you that you need to free up some space. On the other hand, if there is enough free space, Convert initiates the conversion. Be patient. The conversion process takes several minutes (longer for large drives). Don't access files or applications on the drive while the conversion is in progress.

Checking a Drive for Errors and Bad Sectors

The Windows Server 2003 utility for checking the integrity of a disk is Check Disk (Chkdsk.exe). You'll find this utility in the %SystemRoot% folder. Use Check Disk to check for and optionally repair problems found on FAT, FAT32, and NTFS volumes.

Although Check Disk can check for and correct many types of errors, the utility primarily looks for inconsistencies in the file system and its related metadata. One of the ways Check Disk locates errors is by comparing the volume bitmap to the disk sectors assigned to files in the file system. But beyond this, the usefulness of Check Disk is rather limited. For example, Check Disk can't repair corrupted data within files that appear to be structurally intact.

Running Check Disk from the Command Line

You can run Check Disk from the command line or within other utilities. At the Command prompt, you can test the integrity of the E drive by typing the command

```
chkdsk E:
```

To find and repair errors that are found in the E drive, use the command:

```
chkdsk /f E:
```

Note   Check Disk can't repair volumes that are in use. If the volume is in use, Check Disk displays a prompt that asks if you want to schedule the volume to be checked the next time you restart the system. Answer Yes to the prompt to schedule this.

The complete syntax for Check Disk is shown below:

```
chkdsk [volume[[path]filename]]] [/F] [/V] [/R] [/X] [/I] [/C] [/L[:size]]
```

The options and switches for Check Disk are used as follows:

volume	Sets the volume to work with.
filename	FAT/FAT32 only: Specifies files to check for fragmentation.
/F	Fixes errors on the disk.
/V	On FAT/FAT32: Displays the full path and name of every file on the disk. On NTFS: Displays cleanup messages, if any.
/R	Locates bad sectors and recovers readable information (implies /F).
/L:*size*	NTFS only: Changes the log file size.
/X	Forces the volume to dismount first if necessary (implies /F).
/I	NTFS only: Performs a minimum check of index entries.
/C	NTFS only: Skips checking of cycles within the folder structure.

Running Check Disk Interactively

You can also run Check Disk interactively by using either Windows Explorer or Disk Management. To do that, follow these steps:

1. Right-click the drive and then choose Properties.

2. In the Tools tab of the Properties dialog box, click Check Now.

3. As shown in Figure 11-8, you can now:

   ❑ Check for errors without repairing them. Click Start without selecting either of the check boxes.

   ❑ Check for errors and fix them. Make the appropriate selections in the check boxes to fix file system errors or to recover bad sectors, or both. Then click Start.

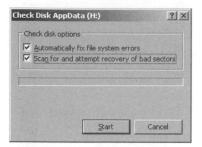

Figure 11-8   Check Disk is available by clicking the Check Now button in the Properties dialog box. Use it to check a disk for errors and repair them, if you wish.

Defragmenting Disks

Anytime you add files to or remove files from a drive, the data on the drive can become fragmented. When a drive is fragmented, large files can't be written to a single continuous area on the disk. As a result, the operating system must write the file to several smaller areas on the disk, which means more time is spent reading the file from the disk. To reduce fragmentation, you should periodically analyze and defragment disks using Disk Defragmenter.

You can analyze a disk to determine the level of fragmentation and defragment a disk by completing the following steps:

1. In Computer Management, expand Storage, and then select Disk Defragmenter.

2. Select the logical drive or volume that you want to work with by clicking it, as shown in Figure 11-9.

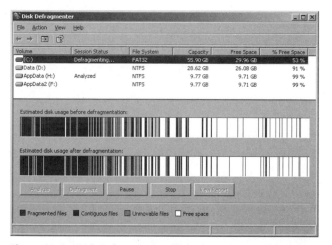

Figure 11-9   Disk Defragmenter efficiently analyzes and defragments disks. The more frequently data is updated on drives, the more often you'll need to run this utility.

3. To analyze the amount of fragmentation on a partition or volume, click Analyze. The progress of the analysis is shown in the Analysis Display area. Fragmented files, contiguous files, system files, and free space are highlighted in different colors using the color code shown at the bottom of the display area. You can pause or stop the analysis if necessary.

4. When the analysis is complete, Disk Defragmenter recommends a course of action based on the amount of fragmentation. If there's a lot of fragmentation, you'll be prompted to defragment the disk. Otherwise, you'll be told the disk doesn't need to be defragmented.

5. To defragment the disk, click Defragment. The progress of the defragment operation is shown in the Defragmentation Display area. You can pause or stop the operation, if necessary.

6. To view a report of the analysis or defragmentation, click View Report.

Compressing Drives and Data

When you format a drive for NTFS, Windows Server 2003 allows you to turn on the built-in compression feature. With compression, all files and directories stored on a drive are automatically compressed when they're created. Because this compression is transparent to users, compressed data can be accessed just like regular data. The difference is that you can store more information on a compressed drive than you can on an uncompressed drive.

Real World   Although compression is certainly a useful feature when you want to save disk space, you can't encrypt compressed data. Compression and encryption are mutually exclusive alternatives for NTFS volumes, which means you have the choice of either using compression or using encryption. You can't use both techniques. For more information on encryption, see the section later in this chapter entitled "Encrypting Drives and Data." If you try to compress encrypted data, Windows Server 2003 automatically decrypts the data and then compresses it. Likewise, if you try to encrypt compressed data, Windows Server 2003 uncompresses the data and then encrypts it.

Compressing Drives

To compress a drive and all its contents, complete these steps:

1. In Windows Explorer or Disk Management, right-click the drive that you want to compress, and then select Properties.

2. Select Compress Drive To Save Disk Space and then click OK.

Compressing Directories and Files

If you decide not to compress a drive, Windows Server 2003 lets you selectively compress directories and files. To compress a file or directory, complete these steps:

1. In Windows Explorer, right-click the file or directory that you want to compress, and then select Properties.

2. In the General tab of the related property dialog box, click Advanced. In the Advanced Attributes dialog box, select the Compress Contents To Save Disk Space check box, as shown in Figure 11-10. Click OK twice.

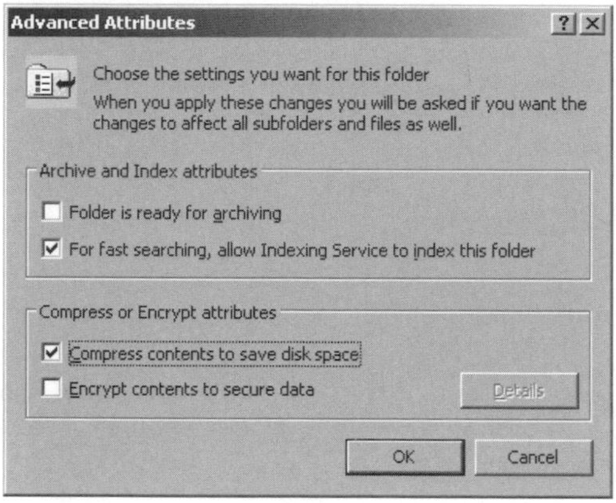

Figure 11-10   With NTFS, you can compress a file or directory by selecting the Compress Contents To Save Disk Space check box in the Advanced Attributes dialog box.

For an individual file, Windows Server 2003 marks the file as compressed and then compresses it. For a directory, Windows Server 2003 marks the directory as compressed and then compresses all the files in it. If the directory contains subfolders, Windows Server 2003 displays a dialog box that allows you to compress all the subfolders associated with the directory. Simply select Apply Changes To This Folder, Subfolders, And Files and then click OK. Once you compress a directory, any new files added or copied to the directory are compressed automatically.

Note   If you move an uncompressed file from a different drive, the file is compressed. However, if you move an uncompressed file to a compressed folder on the same NTFS drive, the file isn't compressed. Note also that you can't encrypt compressed files.

Expanding Compressed Drives

You can remove compression from a drive as follows:

1. In Windows Explorer or Disk Management, right-click the drive that contains the data you want to expand, and then select Properties.

2. Clear the Compress Drive To Save Disk Space check box and then click OK.

Tip   Windows always checks the available disk space before expanding compressed data. You should too. If there's less free space available than used space, you might not be able to complete the expansion. For example, if a compressed drive uses 1 GB of space and has 700 MB of free space available, there won't be enough free space to expand the drive.

Expanding Compressed Directories and Files

If you decide later that you want to expand a compressed file or directory, reverse the process by completing the following steps:

1. Right-click the file or directory in Windows Explorer.

2. In the General tab of the related property dialog box, click Advanced. Clear the Compress Contents To Save Disk Space check box. Click OK twice.

With files, Windows Server 2003 removes compression and expands the file. With directories, Windows Server 2003 expands all the files within the directory. If the directory contains subfolders, you'll also have the opportunity to remove compression from the subfolders. To do this, select Apply Changes To This Folder, Subfolders, And Files when prompted, and then click OK.

Tip   Windows Server 2003 also provides command-line utilities for compressing and decompressing your data. The compression utility is called Compact (Compact.exe). The decompression utility is called Expand (Expand.exe).

Encrypting Drives and Data

NTFS has many advantages over other file systems that you can use with Windows Server 2003. One of the major advantages is the capability to automatically encrypt and decrypt data using the Encrypting File System (EFS). When you encrypt data, you add an extra layer of protection to sensitive data—and this extra layer acts as a security blanket, blocking all other users from reading the contents of the encrypted files. Indeed, one of the great benefits of encryption is that only the designated user can access the data. This benefit is also a disadvantage, in that the user must remove encryption before authorized users can access the data.

Note   As discussed previously, you can't compress encrypted files. The encryption and compression features of NTFS are mutually exclusive. You can use one feature or the other, but not both.

Understanding Encryption and the Encrypting File System

File encryption is supported on a per-folder or per-file basis. Any file placed in a folder marked for encryption is automatically encrypted. Files in encrypted format can be read only by the person who encrypted the file. Before other users can read an encrypted file, the user must decrypt the file.

Every file that's encrypted has a unique encryption key. This means that an encrypted file can be copied, moved, and renamed just like any other file—and, in most cases, these actions don't affect the encryption of the data (for details, see the section later in this chapter entitled "Working with Encrypted Files and Folders"). The user who encrypted the file always has access to the file, provided the user's public-key certificate is available on the computer that he or she is using. For this user the encryption and decryption process is handled automatically and is transparent.

EFS is the process that handles encryption and decryption. The default setup for EFS allows users to encrypt files without needing special permission. Files are encrypted using a public/private key that EFS automatically generates on a per-user basis. The encryption algorithm used is the expanded Data Encryption Standard (DES), which is enforced using 56-bit encryption by default.

Security   For stricter security, North American users can order the Enhanced CryptoPAK from Microsoft. The Enhanced CryptoPAK provides 128-bit encryption. Files that use 128-bit encryption can be used only on a system that supports 128-bit encryption.

Encryption certificates are stored as part of the data in user profiles. If a user works with multiple computers and wants to use encryption, an administrator will need to configure a roaming profile for that user. A roaming profile ensures that the user's profile data and public-key certificates are accessible from other computers. Without this, users won't be able to access their encrypted files on another computer.

Security   An alternative to a roaming profile is to copy the user's encryption certificate to the computers that the user uses. You can do this using the certificate backup and restore process discussed in the section of Chapter 15 entitled "Backing Up and Restoring Encrypted Data and Certificates." Simply back up the certificate on the user's original computer and then restore the certificate on each of the other computers the user logs on to.

EFS has a built-in data recovery system to guard against data loss. This recovery system ensures that encrypted data can be recovered in the event that a user's public-key certificate is lost or deleted. The most common scenario for this is when a user leaves the company and the associated user account is deleted. Although a manager might have been able to log on to the user's account, check files, and save important files to other folders, if the user account has been deleted, encrypted files will be accessible only if the encryption is removed or if the files are moved to a FAT or FAT32 volume (where encryption isn't supported).

To access encrypted files after the user account has been deleted, you'll need to use a recovery agent. Recovery agents have access to the file encryption key necessary to unlock data in encrypted files. To protect sensitive data, however, recovery agents don't have access to a user's private key or any private key information.

Windows Server 2003 won't encrypt files without designated EFS recovery agents. For this reason, recovery agents are designated automatically and the necessary recovery certificates are generated automatically as well. This ensures that encrypted files can always be recovered.

EFS recovery agents are configured at two levels:

Domain   The recovery agent for a domain is configured automatically when the first Windows Server 2003 domain controller is installed. By default, the recovery agent is the domain administrator. Through Group Policy, domain administrators can designate additional recovery agents. Domain administrators can also delegate recovery agent privileges to designated security administrators.

Local computer   When a computer is part of a workgroup or in a stand-alone configuration, the recovery agent is the administrator of the local computer by default. Additional recovery agents can be designated. Further, if you want local recovery agents in a domain environment rather than domain-level recovery agents, you must delete the recovery policy from the group policy for the domain.

You can delete recovery agents if you don't want them to be used. However, if you delete all recovery agents, EFS will no longer encrypt files. One or more recovery agents must be configured for EFS to function.

Encrypting Directories and Files

With NTFS volumes, Windows Server 2003 lets you select files and folders for encryption. When you encrypt files, the file data is converted to an encrypted format that can be read only by the person who encrypted the file. Users can encrypt files only if they have the proper access permissions. When you encrypt folders, the folder is marked as encrypted, but actually only the files within it are encrypted. All files that are created in or added to a folder marked as encrypted are encrypted automatically.

To encrypt a file or directory, complete the following steps:

1. Right-click the file or directory that you want to encrypt, and then select Properties.

2. In the General tab of the related property dialog box, click Advanced. Then select the Encrypt Contents To Secure Data check box. Click OK twice.

> **Note**   You can't encrypt compressed files, system files, or read-only files. If you try to encrypt compressed files, the files are automatically uncompressed and then encrypted. If you try to encrypt system files, you'll get an error.

For an individual file, Windows Server 2003 marks the file as encrypted and then encrypts it. For a directory, Windows Server 2003 marks the directory as encrypted and then encrypts all the files in it. If the directory contains subfolders, Windows Server 2003 displays a dialog box that allows you to encrypt all the subfolders associated with the directory. Simply select Apply Changes To This Folder, Subfolders, And Files and then click OK.

Note On NTFS volumes, files remain encrypted even when they're moved, copied, and renamed. If you copy or move an encrypted file to a FAT or FAT32 drive, the file is automatically decrypted before being copied or moved. Thus, you must have proper permissions to copy or move the file.

Working with Encrypted Files and Folders

Previously, I said that you can copy, move, and rename encrypted files and folders just like any other files, which is true, but I qualified this by saying "in most cases." When you work with encrypted files, you'll have few problems as long as you work with NTFS volumes on the same computer. When you work with other file systems or other computers, you might run into problems. Two of the most common scenarios are:

Copying between volumes on the same computer When you copy or move an encrypted file or folder from one NTFS volume to another NTFS volume on the same computer, the files remain encrypted. However, if you copy or move encrypted files to a FAT or FAT32 volume, the files are decrypted before transfer and then transferred as standard files. FAT and FAT32 don't support encryption.

Copying between volumes on a different computer When you copy or move an encrypted file or folder from one NTFS volume to another NTFS volume on a different computer, the files remain encrypted as long as the destination computer allows you to encrypt files and the remote computer is trusted for delegation. Otherwise, the files are decrypted and then transferred as standard files. The same is true when you copy or move encrypted files to a FAT or FAT32 volume on another computer. FAT and FAT32 don't support encryption.

After you transfer a sensitive file that has been encrypted, you might want to confirm that the encryption is still applied. Right-click the file and then select Properties. In the General tab of the related property dialog box, click Advanced. The Encrypt Contents To Secure Data option should be selected.

Configuring Recovery Policy

Recovery policies are configured automatically for domain controllers and workstations. By default, domain administrators are the designated recovery agents for domains and the local administrator is the designated recovery agent for a stand-alone workstation.

Through the Group Policy console, you can view, assign, and delete recovery agents. To do that, follow these steps:

1. Access the Group Policy console for the local computer, site, domain, or organizational unit you want to work with. For details on working with Group Policy, see the section entitled "Group Policy Management" in Chapter 4, "Automating Administrative Tasks, Policies, and Procedures."

2. Access the Encrypted Data Recovery Agents node in Group Policy. To do this, expand Computer Configuration, Windows Settings, Security Settings, and Public Key Policies and then select Encrypting File System.

3. As shown in Figure 11-11, the right-hand pane lists the recovery certificates currently assigned. Recovery certificates are listed according to whom they are issued, who issued them, expiration data, purpose, and more. In the figure, the administrator self-issued the certificate for the purpose of file recovery (it's a recovery certificate for the local administrator).

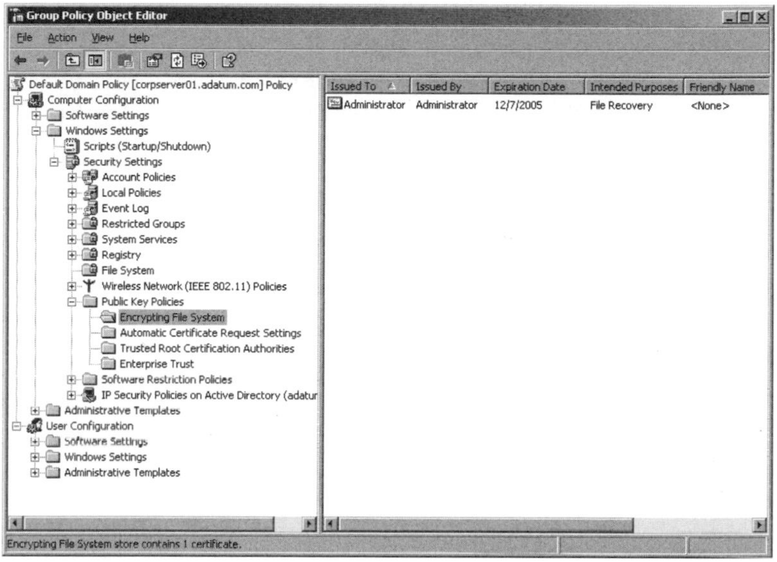

Figure 11-11   You use the Encrypting File System node to view, assign, and delete recovery agents in Group Policy.

4. To designate an additional recovery agent, right-click Encrypting File System and then select Add Data Recovery Agent. This starts the Add Recovery Agent Wizard, which you can use to select a previously generated certificate that has been assigned to a user and mark it as a designated recovery certificate. Click Next.

5. In the Select Recovery Agents page, click Browse Directory and then use the Find Users, Contacts, And Groups dialog box to select the user you want to work with.

Security   Before you can designate additional recovery agents, you must set up a root Certificate Authority (CA) in the domain. Afterward, you must use the Certificates snap-in to generate a personal certificate that uses the EFS Recovery Agent template. The root CA must then approve the certificate request so that the certificate can be used.

6. To delete a recovery agent, select the recovery agent's certificate in the right pane and then press Delete. When prompted to confirm the action, click Yes to permanently and irrevocably delete the certificate. If the recovery policy is empty (meaning that it has no other designated recovery agents), EFS will be turned off so that files can no longer be encrypted.

Decrypting Files and Directories

If you decide later that you want to decrypt a file or directory, reverse the process by completing the following steps:

1. Right-click the file or directory in Windows Explorer.

2. In the General tab of the related property dialog box, click Advanced. Clear the Encrypt Contents To Secure Data check box. Click OK twice.

With files, Windows Server 2003 decrypts the file and restores it to its original format. With directories, Windows Server 2003 decrypts all the files within the directory. If the directory contains subfolders, you'll also have the opportunity to remove encryption from the subfolders. To do this, select Apply Changes To This Folder, Subfolders, And Files when prompted and then click OK.

> **Tip**   Windows Server 2003 also provides a command-line utility for encrypting and decrypting your data. This utility is called Cipher (Cipher.exe). Typing **cipher** at the command prompt by itself shows you the encryption status of all folders in the current directory.

Recovering Disk Space

Disk Cleanup is a utility that examines disk drives for files that aren't needed or that could be compressed. By default, Disk Cleanup examines temporary files, the Recycle Bin, and catalogs used by the Content Indexer to see if there are files that can be deleted. Disk Cleanup also examines files that haven't been used in a while and recommends that they be compressed. Compressing old files can save a considerable amount of disk space.

You can work with Disk Cleanup by completing the following steps:

1. In Windows Explorer or Disk Management, right-click the drive that you want to clean up, and then select Properties.

2. Click Disk Cleanup. Disk Cleanup then examines the selected drive, looking for temporary files that can be deleted and for files that are candidates for compression. The more files on the drive, the longer the search process takes.

3. When Disk Cleanup finishes, you'll see a report detailing data that can be possibly cleaned up.

4. Use the check boxes provided in the Files To Delete list to choose the files that you want to clean up, and then click OK. When prompted to confirm the action, click Yes.

Chapter 12

Administering Volume Sets and RAID Arrays

When you work with Microsoft Windows Server 2003, you'll often need to perform advanced disk setup procedures, such as creating a volume set or setting up a redundant array of independent disks (RAID) array.

- With a *volume set*, you can create a single volume that spans multiple drives. Users can access this volume as if it were a single drive, regardless of how many drives the actual volume is spread over. A volume that's on a single drive is referred to as a *simple volume*. A volume that spans multiple drives is referred to as a *spanned volume*.

- With *RAID arrays*, you can protect important business data and, sometimes, improve the performance of drives. Windows Server 2003 supports three levels of RAID: 0, 1, and 5. RAID arrays are implemented as mirrored, striped, and striped with parity volumes.

You create volumes sets and RAID arrays on dynamic drives, which are accessible only by Windows 2000 Server and Windows Server 2003. Because of this, if you dual boot a computer to a different or previous version of Windows, the dynamic drives are unavailable. However, computers running previous versions of Windows can access the drives over the network—just like any other network drive.

Using Volumes and Volume Sets

You create and manage volumes in much the same way as partitions. A volume is a drive section that you can use to store data directly.

Note With spanned and striped volumes on basic disks, you can delete the volume but you can't create or extend volumes. With mirrored volumes on basic disks, you can delete, repair, and resync the mirror. You can also break the mirror. With striped with parity volumes (RAID 5) on basic disks, you can delete or repair the volume but you can't create new volumes.

Understanding Volume Basics

Disk Management color-codes volumes by type, much like partitions. As Figure 12-1 shows, volumes also have a specific:

Layout   Volume layouts include simple, spanned, mirrored, striped, and striped with parity.

Type   Volumes always have the type dynamic.

File System   As with partitions, each volume can have a different file system type, such as FAT, FAT32, or NTFS file system.

Status   The state of the drive. In Graphical View, the state is shown as Healthy, Failed Redundancy, and so on. The next section, "Understanding Volume Sets," discusses volume sets and the various states you might see.

Capacity   Total storage size of the drive.

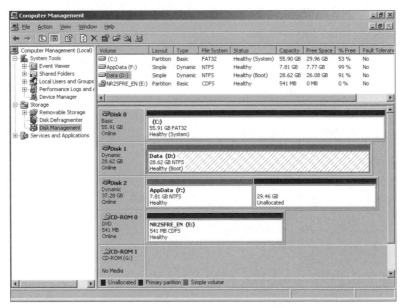

Figure 12-1   Disk Management displays volumes much like partitions.

An important advantage of dynamic volumes over basic volumes is that they let you make changes to volumes and drives without having to restart the system (in most cases). Volumes also let you take advantage of the fault tolerance enhancements of

Windows Server 2003. Although you can't use dynamic drives with previous versions of Windows, you can install other operating systems and dual boot a Windows Server 2003 system. To do this, you must create a separate volume for the other operating system. For example, you could install Windows Server 2003 on volume C and Linux on volume D.

With volumes, you can:

- Assign drive letters as discussed in the section entitled "Assigning Drive Letters and Paths" in Chapter 11, "Managing File Systems and Drives."

- Assign drive paths as discussed in the section of Chapter 11 entitled "Assigning Drive Letters and Paths."

- Create any number of volumes on a disk as long as you have free space.

- Create volumes that span two or more disks and, if necessary, configure fault tolerance.

- Extend volumes to increase the volume's capacity.

- Designate Active, System, and Boot volumes as described in the section of Chapter 11 entitled "Special Considerations for Basic and Dynamic Disks."

Understanding Volume Sets

With volume sets, you can create volumes that span several drives. To do this, you use free space on different drives to create what users see as a single volume. Files are stored on the volume set segment by segment, with the first segment of free space being used to store files before others. When this segment fills up, the second segment is used, and so on.

You can create a volume set using free space on up to 32 hard disk drives. The key advantage to volume sets is that they let you tap into unused free space and create a usable file system. The key disadvantage is that if any hard disk drive in the volume set fails, the volume set can no longer be used—which means that essentially all the data on the volume set is lost.

Understanding the volume status is useful when you install new volumes or are trying to troubleshoot problems. Disk Management shows the drive status in the Graphical View and Volume List views. Table 12-1 summarizes status values for dynamic volumes.

Table 12-1 Understanding and Resolving Volume Status Issues

Status	Description	Resolution
Data Incomplete	Spanned volumes on a foreign disk are incomplete. You must have forgotten to add the other disks from the spanned volume set.	Add the disks that contain the rest of the spanned volume and then import all the disks at one time.
Data Not Redundant	Fault-tolerant volumes on a foreign disk are incomplete. You must have forgotten to add the other disks from a mirror or RAID-5 set.	Add the remaining disk(s) and then import all the disks at one time.
Failed	An error disk status. The disk is inaccessible or damaged.	Ensure that the related dynamic disk is online. If necessary, reactivate the volume.
Failed Redundancy	An error disk status. One of the disks in a mirror or RAID-5 set is offline.	Ensure that the related dynamic disk is online. If necessary, reactivate the volume. Next, you might need to replace a failed mirror or repair a failed RAID-5 volume.
Formatting	A temporary status that indicates that the volume is being formatted.	The progress of the formatting is indicated as the percent complete.
Healthy	The normal volume status.	The volume doesn't have any known problems.
Regenerating	A temporary status that indicates that data and parity for a RAID-5 volume are being regenerated.	Progress is indicated as the percent complete. The volume should return to Healthy status.
Resynching	A temporary status that indicates that a mirror set is being resynchronized.	Progress is indicated as the percent complete. The volume should return to Healthy status.
Stale Data	Data on foreign disks that are fault tolerant are out of sync.	Rescan the disks or restart the computer, and then check the status. A new status should be displayed, such as Failed Redundancy.

Creating Volumes and Volume Sets

You create volumes and volume sets by completing the following steps:

1. In the Disk Management Graphical View, right-click an area marked Unallocated on a dynamic disk and then choose New Volume. This starts the New Volume Wizard. Read the Welcome To The New Volume Wizard page and then click Next.

2. As shown in Figure 12-2, select Simple to create a volume on a single disk or Spanned to create a volume set on multiple disks. You can format simple volumes as FAT, FAT32, or NTFS. To make management easier, you should format volumes that span multiple disks as NTFS. NTFS formatting allows you to expand the volume set if necessary. Click Next.

> **Tip** If you find that you need more space on a volume, you can extend simple and spanned volumes. You do this by selecting an area of free space and adding it to the volume. You can extend a simple volume within the same disk. You can also extend a simple volume onto other disks. When you do this, you create a spanned volume, which you must format as NTFS.

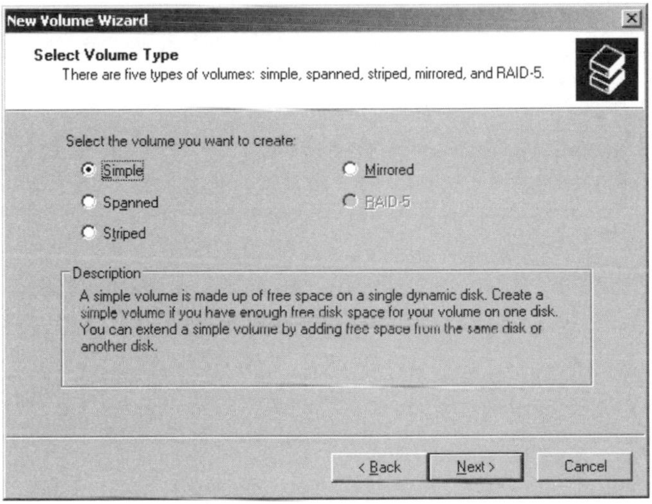

Figure 12-2   Use the New Volume Wizard to select a volume type.

3. You should see the Select Disks page shown in Figure 12-3. Use this page to select dynamic disks that are a part of the volume and to size the volume segments on those disks.

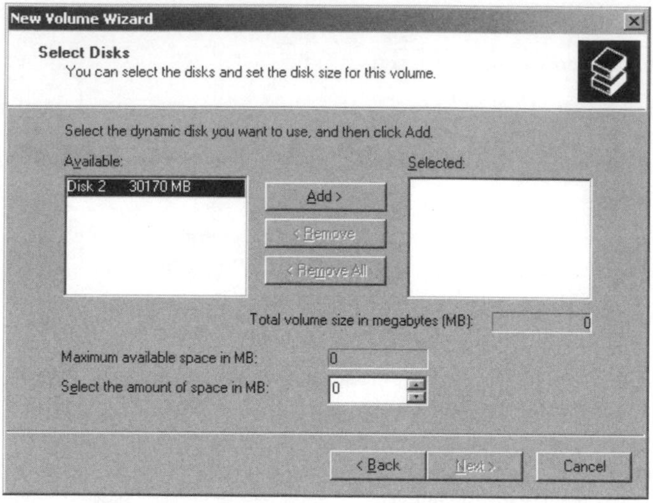

Figure 12-3   Use the Select Disks page to select disks to be a part of the volume and then size the volume on each disk.

4. Available dynamic disks are shown in the Available list box. If necessary, select a disk in this list box, and then click Add to add the disk to the Selected list box. If you make a mistake, you can remove disks from the Selected list box by selecting the disk and then clicking Remove.

5. Select a disk in the Selected list box and then use the Select The Amount Of Space In MB combo box to specify the size of the volume on the selected disk. The Maximum field shows you the largest area of free space available on the selected disk. The Total Volume Size field shows you the total disk space selected for use with the volume. Click Next.

> **Tip**   Although you can size the volume set any way you want, you might want to take a moment to consider how you'll use volume sets on the system. Simple and spanned volumes aren't fault tolerant, and rather than creating one monstrous volume with all the available free space, you might want to create several smaller volumes to help ensure that losing one volume doesn't mean losing all your data.

6. Specify whether you want to assign a drive letter or path to the volume, and then click Next. You use these options as follows:

Assign The Following Drive Letter   To assign a drive letter, choose this option, and then select an available drive letter in the selection list provided.

Mount In The Following Empty NTFS Folder   To assign a drive path, choose this option and then type the path to an existing folder on an NTFS drive or click Browse to search for or create a folder.

Don't Assign A Drive Letter Or Drive Path   To create the volume without assigning a drive letter or path, choose this option. You can assign a drive letter or path later, if necessary.

7. As shown in Figure 12-4, determine whether the volume should be formatted. If you elect to format the volume, use the following fields to set the formatting options:

File System   Specifies the file system type. The NTFS file system is the only option within Disk Management.

Allocation Unit Size   Specifies the cluster size for the file system. This is the basic unit in which disk space is allocated. The default allocation unit size is based on the volume's size and is set dynamically prior to formatting. To override this feature, you can set the allocation unit size to a specific value. If you use lots of small files, you might want to use a smaller cluster size, such as 512 or 1024 bytes. With these settings, small files use less disk space.

Volume Label   Specifies a text label for the partition. This label is the partition's volume name.

Perform A Quick Format   Tells Windows to format without checking the partition for errors. With large partitions, this option can save you a few minutes. However, it's more prudent to check for errors, which allows Disk Management to mark bad sectors on the disk and lock them out.

Enable File And Folder Compression   Turns on compression for the disk. Compression is transparent to users and compressed files can be accessed just like regular files. If you select this option, files and directories on this drive are compressed automatically. For more information on compressing drives, files, and directories, see the section of Chapter 11 entitled "Compressing Drives and Data."

8. Click Next and then click Finish. If you add volumes to a physical drive that contains the Windows Server 2003 operating system, you might inadvertently change the boot volume's number. Read the warning prompts and then make any necessary changes to the Boot.ini file as described in the section of Chapter 11 entitled "Updating the Boot Disk."

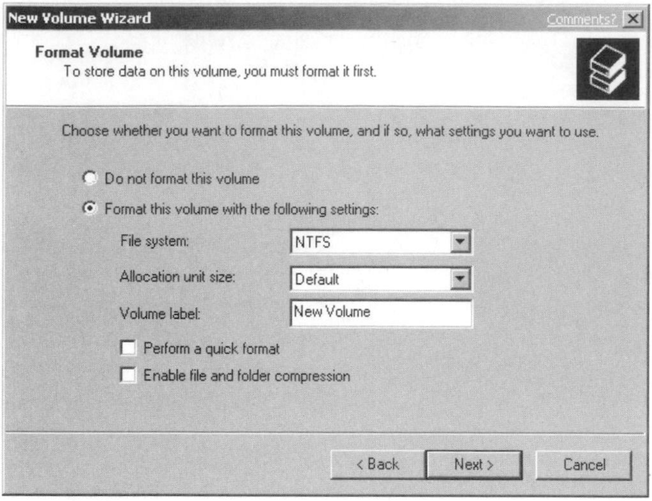

Figure 12-4   Format a volume by specifying its file system type and volume label.

Deleting Volumes and Volume Sets

You delete all volumes using the same technique, whether they're simple, spanned, mirrored, striped, or RAID 5 (striped with parity). Deleting a volume set removes the associated file system and all associated data is lost. So before you delete a volume set you should back up any files and directories that the volume set contains.

You can't delete a volume that contains the system, boot, or active paging files for Windows Server 2003.

To delete volumes, follow these steps:

1. In Disk Management, right-click any volume in the set and then choose Delete Volume. You can't delete a portion of a spanned volume without deleting the entire volume.

2. Confirm that you want to delete the volume by clicking Yes.

Extending a Simple or Spanned Volume

Windows Server 2003 provides several ways to extend NTFS volumes that aren't part of a mirror set or striped set. You can extend a simple volume and you can extend existing volume sets. When you extend volumes, you add free space to them.

> **Caution**   When extending volume sets, there are many things you can't do. You can't extend boot or system volumes. You can't extend volumes that use mirroring or striping. You can't extend a volume onto more than 32 disks, either. Additionally,

you can't extend FAT or FAT32 volumes—you must first convert them to NTFS. You can't extend simple or spanned volumes that were upgraded from basic disks, either. As you work with volume sets, please keep these exceptions in mind.

To extend an NTFS volume, complete the following steps:

1. In Disk Management, right-click the simple or spanned volume that you want to extend, and then select Extend Volume. This starts the Extend Volume Wizard. Read the Welcome To The Extended Volume Wizard page, and then click Next.

2. You can now select dynamic disks that are a part of the volume and size the volume segments on those disks as described in Steps 3–5 of the section of this chapter entitled "Creating Volumes and Volume Sets." The size you set for Select The Amount of Space In MB is the amount of space that you want to add to the volume, which is reflected in the Total Volume Size In Megabytes field. For example, if you created a 200-megabyte (MB) volume and then set the Select The Amount Of Space In MB field to 800, the total volume size would be 1000 MB.

    Note   A volume set that spans multiple drives can't be mirrored or striped. Only simple volumes can be mirrored or striped.

3. Click Next and then click Finish.

Managing Volumes

You manage volumes much like you manage partitions. Follow the techniques outlined in the section of chapter 11 entitled "Managing Existing Partitions and Drives."

Improving Performance and Fault Tolerance with RAIDs

You'll often want to give important data increased protection from drive failures. To do this, you can use RAID technology to add fault tolerance to your file systems. With RAID, you increase data integrity and availability by creating redundant copies of the data. You can also use RAID to improve your disks' performance.

Different implementations of RAID technology are available. These implementations are described in terms of levels. Currently, RAID levels 0 to 5 are defined. Each RAID level offers different features. Windows Server 2003 supports RAID levels 0, 1, and 5.

- You can use RAID 0 to improve the performance of your drives.

- You can use RAID 1 and 5 to provide fault tolerance for data.

Table 12-2 provides a brief overview of the supported RAID levels. This support is completely software-based.

Table 12-2 Windows Server 2003 Support for RAID

RAID Level	RAID Type	Description	Major Advantages
0	Disk striping	Two or more volumes, each on a separate drive, are configured as a striped set. Data is broken into blocks, called stripes, and then written sequentially to all drives in the striped set.	Speed/performance.
1	Disk mirroring	Two volumes on two drives are configured identically. Data is written to both drives. If one drive fails, there's no data loss because the other drive contains the data. (Doesn't include disk striping.)	Redundancy. Better write performance than disk striping with parity.
5	Disk striping with parity	Uses three or more volumes, each on a separate drive, to create a striped set with parity error checking. In the case of failure, data can be recovered.	Fault tolerance with less overhead than mirroring. Better read performance than disk mirroring.

The most common RAID levels in use on servers running Windows Server 2003 are level 1 disk mirroring and level 5 disk striping with parity. Disk mirroring is the least expensive way to increase data protection with redundancy. Here, you use two identically sized volumes on two different drives to create a redundant data set. If one of the drives fails, you can still obtain the data from the other drive.

On the other hand, disk striping with parity requires more disks—a minimum of three—but offers fault tolerance with less overhead than disk mirroring. If any of the drives fail, you can recover the data by combining blocks of data on the remaining disks with a parity record. Parity is a method of error checking that uses an exclusive OR operation to create a checksum for each block of data written to the disk. This checksum is used to recover data in case of failure.

Real World Although it's true that the upfront costs for mirroring should be less than the upfront costs for disk striping with parity, the actual cost per megabyte might be higher with disk mirroring. With disk mirroring, you have an overhead of 50 percent. For example, if you mirror two 36-gigabyte (GB) drives (a total storage space of 72 GB), the usable space is only 36 GB. With disk striping with parity, on the other hand, you have an overhead of around 33 percent. For example, if you create a RAID-5 set using three 36-GB drives (a total storage space of 108 GB), the usable space (with one-third lost for overhead) is 72 GB.

Implementing RAID on Windows Server 2003

Windows Server 2003 supports disk mirroring, disk striping, and disk striping with parity. Implementing these RAID techniques is discussed in the sections that follow.

Caution   Some operating systems, such as MS-DOS, don't support RAID. If you dual boot your system to one of these noncompliant operating systems, your RAID-configured drives will be unusable.

Implementing RAID 0: Disk Striping

RAID level 0 is disk striping. With disk striping, two or more volumes—each on a separate drive—are configured as a striped set. Data written to the striped set is broken into blocks that are called *stripes*. These stripes are written sequentially to all drives in the striped set. You can place volumes for a striped set on up to 32 drives, but in most circumstances, sets with two to five volumes offer the best performance improvements. Beyond this, the performance improvement decreases significantly.

The major advantage of disk striping is speed. Data can be accessed on multiple disks using multiple drive heads, which improves performance considerably. However, this performance boost comes with a price tag. As with volume sets, if any hard disk drive in the striped set fails, the striped set can no longer be used, which essentially means that all data in the striped set is lost. You'll need to re-create the striped set and restore the data from backups. Data backup and recovery is discussed in Chapter 15, "Data Backup and Recovery."

Caution   The boot and system volumes shouldn't be part of a striped set. Don't use disk striping with these volumes.

When you create striped sets, you'll want to use volumes that are approximately the same size. Disk Management bases the overall size of the striped set on the smallest volume size. Specifically, the maximum size of the striped set is a multiple of the smallest volume size. For example, if the smallest volume is 50 MB, the maximum size for the striped site is 150 MB.

To maximize performance of the striped set, you can do several things:

- Use disks that are on separate disk controllers. This allows the system to simultaneously access the drives.

- Don't use the disks containing the striped set for other purposes. This allows the disk to dedicate its time to the striped set.

You can create a striped set by doing the following:

1. In the Disk Management Graphical View, right-click an area marked Unallocated on a dynamic disk and then choose New Volume. This starts the New Volume

Wizard. Read the Welcome To The New Volume Wizard page, and then click Next.

2. Select Striped as the volume type and then click Next. Create the volume as described previously in this chapter under "Creating Volumes and Volume Sets." The key difference is that you need at least two dynamic disks to create a striped volume.

3. After you create a striped volume, you can use the volume just like any other volume. You can't extend a striped set once it's created. Because of this, you should carefully consider the setup before you implement it.

Implementing RAID 1: Disk Mirroring

RAID level 1 is disk mirroring. With disk mirroring you use identically sized volumes on two different drives to create a redundant data set. Here, the drives are written with identical sets of information and, if one of the drives fails, you can still obtain the data from the other drive.

Disk mirroring offers about the same fault tolerance as disk striping with parity. Because mirrored disks don't need to write parity information, they can offer better write performance in most circumstances. However, disk striping with parity usually offers better read performance because read operations are spread out over multiple drives.

The major drawback to disk mirroring is that it effectively cuts the amount of storage space in half. For example, to mirror a 5-GB drive, you need another 5-GB drive. That means you use 10 GB of space to store 5 GB of information.

> **Tip**   If possible, it's a good idea to mirror boot and system volumes. Mirroring these volumes ensures that you'll be able to boot the server in case of a single drive failure.

As with disk striping, you'll often want the mirrored disks to be on separate disk controllers. This provides increased protection against failure of the disk controller. If one of the disk controllers fails, the disk on other controller is still available. Technically, when you use two separate disk controllers to duplicate data, you're using a technique known as *disk duplexing*. Figure 12-5 shows the difference between the two techniques. Where disk mirroring typically uses a single drive controller, disk duplexing uses two drive controllers.

If one of the mirrored drives in a set fails, disk operations can continue. Here, when users read and write data, the data is written to the remaining disk. You'll need to break the mirror before you can fix it. To learn how, see the section entitled "Managing RAIDs and Recovering from Failures," later in this chapter.

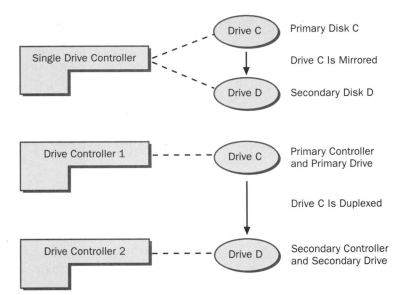

Figure 12-5   Although disk mirroring typically uses a single drive controller to create a redundant data set, disk duplexing uses two drive controllers. Otherwise, the two techniques are essentially the same.

Creating a Mirror Set in Disk Management

You create a mirror set by completing the following steps:

1. In the Disk Management Graphical View, right-click an area marked Unallocated on a dynamic disk and then choose New Volume. This starts the New Volume Wizard. Read the Welcome To The New Volume Wizard page, and then click Next.

2. Select Mirrored as the volume type. Create the volume as described previously under "Creating Volumes and Volume Sets." The key difference is that you must create two identically sized volumes and these volumes must be on separate dynamic drives. You won't be able to continue past the Selected Disks window until you've selected the two disks that you want to work with.

3. As with other RAID techniques, mirroring is transparent to users. Users see the mirrored set as a single drive that they can access and use like any other drive.

   Note   The status of a normal mirror is Healthy. During the creation of a mirror, you'll see a status of Resynching. This tells you that Disk Management is creating the mirror.

Mirroring an Existing Volume

Rather than creating a new mirrored volume, you can use an existing volume to create a mirrored set. To do this, the volume you want to mirror must be a simple volume and you must have an area of unallocated space on a second dynamic drive of equal or larger space than the existing volume.

In Disk Management you mirror an existing volume by completing the following steps:

1. Right-click the simple volume you want to mirror and then select Add Mirror. This displays the Add Mirror dialog box.

2. Use the Disks list to select a location for the mirror and then click Add Mirror. Windows Server 2003 begins the mirror creation process and you'll see a status of Resynching on both volumes.

Implementing RAID 5: Disk Striping with Parity

RAID level 5 is disk striping with parity. With this technique, you need a minimum of three hard disk drives to set up fault tolerance. Disk Management sizes the volumes on these drives identically.

RAID 5 is essentially an enhanced version of RAID 1—with the key addition of fault tolerance. Fault tolerance ensures that the failure of a single drive won't bring down the entire drive set. Instead, the set continues to function with disk operations directed at the remaining volumes in the set.

To allow for fault tolerance, RAID 5 writes parity checksums with the blocks of data. If any of the drives in the striped set fails, the parity information can be used to recover the data. (This process, called regenerating the striped set, is covered in the section of this chapter entitled "Managing RAIDs and Recovering from Failures.") If two disks fail, however, the parity information isn't sufficient to recover the data and you'll need to rebuild the striped set from backup.

Creating a Striped Set with Parity in Disk Management

In Disk Management you can create a striped set with parity by completing the following steps:

1. In the Disk Management Graphical View, right-click an area marked Unallocated on a dynamic disk and then choose New Volume. This starts the New Volume Wizard. Read the Welcome To The New Volume Wizard page, and then click Next.

2. Select RAID-5 as the volume type. Create the volume as described previously under "Creating Volumes and Volume Sets." The key difference is that you must select free space on three separate dynamic drives.

3. After you create a striped set with parity (RAID-5), users can use the set just like they would a normal drive. Keep in mind that you can't extend a striped set with parity after you create it. Because of this, you should carefully consider the setup before you implement it.

Managing RAIDs and Recovering from Failures

Managing mirrored drives and striped sets is somewhat different from managing other drive volumes, especially when it comes to recovering from failure. The techniques you'll need to manage RAID arrays and to recover from failure are covered in this section.

Breaking a Mirrored Set

You might want to break a mirror for two reasons:

- If one of the mirrored drives in a set fails, disk operations can continue. Here, when users read and write data, these operations use the remaining disk. Still, at some point, you'll need to fix the mirror, and to do this you must first break the mirror and then reestablish it.

- If you no longer want to mirror your drives, you might also want to break a mirror. This allows you to use the disk space for other purposes.

Best Practices   Although breaking a mirror doesn't delete the data in the set, you should always back up the data before you perform this procedure. This ensures that if you have problems, you can recover your data.

In Disk Management, you can break a mirrored set by following these steps:

- Right-click one of the volumes in the mirrored set and then choose Break Mirrored Volume.

- Confirm that you want to break the mirror by clicking Yes. If the volume is in use, you'll see another warning dialog box. Confirm that it's okay to continue by clicking Yes.

- Windows Server 2003 breaks the mirror, creating two independent volumes.

Resynchronizing and Repairing a Mirrored Set

Windows Server 2003 automatically synchronizes mirrored volumes on dynamic drives. However, data on mirrored drives can get out of sync. For example, if one of the drives goes offline, data is written only to the drive that's online.

You can resynchronize and repair mirrored sets on basic and dynamic disks, but you must rebuild the set using the same disk type. Follow these steps to resolve problems with a mirrored set:

1. You need to get both drives in the mirrored set online. The mirrored set's status should read Failed Redundancy. The corrective action you take depends on the failed volume's status.

2. If the status is Missing or Offline, make sure that the drive has power and is connected properly. Afterward, start Disk Management, right-click the failed volume,

and select Reactivate Disk. The drive status should change to Regenerating and then to Healthy. If the volume doesn't return to the Healthy status, right-click the volume and then click Resynchronize Mirror.

3. If the status is Online (Errors), right-click the failed volume and select Reactive Volume. The drive status should change to Regenerating and then to Healthy. If the volume doesn't return to the Healthy status, right-click the volume and then click Resynchronize Mirror.

4. If one of the drives shows as Unreadable, you might need to rescan the drives on the system by selecting Rescan Disks from Disk Management's Action menu. If the drive status doesn't change, you might need to reboot the computer.

5. If one of the drives still won't come back online, right-click the failed volume and then select Remove Mirror. Next, right-click the remaining volume in the original mirror and then select Add Mirror. You'll now need to mirror the volume on an unallocated area of free space. If you don't have free space, you'll need to create space by deleting other volumes or replacing the failed drive.

Repairing a Mirrored System Volume to Enable Boot

The failure of a mirrored drive might prevent your system from booting. Typically, this happens when you're mirroring the system or boot volume, or both, and the primary mirror drive has failed. In previous versions of the Windows operating system, you often had to go through several procedures to get the system back up and running. With Windows Server 2003, the failure of a primary mirror is usually much easier to resolve.

When you mirror a system volume, an entry that allows you to boot to the secondary mirror should be added to the system's Boot.ini file. The entry will look similar to the following:

```
multi(0)disk(0)rdisk(2)partition(2)\WINNT="Boot Mirror D: - secondary
plex"
```

Resolving a primary mirror failure is much easier with this entry in the Boot.ini file than without it because all you need to do is select the entry to boot to the secondary mirror. If you mirror the boot volume and a secondary mirror entry is not created for you, you should modify the Boot.ini file to create one.

To correct a failed mirror, follow these steps:

1. If a system fails to boot to the primary system volume, restart the system and select the Boot Mirror - Secondary Plex option for the operating system you want to start.

2. The system should start up normally.

After you successfully boot the system to the secondary drive, you can schedule the maintenance necessary to rebuild the mirror, if desired. You'll need to complete the following steps:

1. Shut down the system and replace the failed volume or add a hard disk drive. Afterward, restart the system.

2. Break the mirror set and then re-create the mirror on the drive you replaced, which is usually drive 0. Right-click the remaining volume that was part of the original mirror and then select Add Mirror. Next, follow the technique outlined in the section of this chapter entitled "Mirroring an Existing Volume."

3. If you want the primary mirror to be on the drive you added or replaced, use Disk Management to break the mirror again. Make sure that the primary drive in the original mirror set has the drive letter that was previously assigned to the complete mirror. If it doesn't, assign the appropriate drive letter.

4. Right-click the original system volume and then select Add Mirror. Now re-create the mirror.

5. Check Boot.ini and ensure that the original system volume is used during startup. You may need to modify Boot.ini to ensure this.

Removing a Mirrored Set

In Disk Management, you can remove one of the volumes from a mirrored set. When you do this, all data on the removed mirror is deleted and the space it used is marked as Unallocated.

To remove a mirror, complete the following steps:

1. In Disk Management, right-click one of the volumes in the mirrored set and then choose Remove Mirror. This displays the Remove Mirror dialog box.

2. In the Remove Mirror dialog box, select the disk from which to remove the mirror.

3. Confirm the action when prompted. All data on the removed mirror is deleted.

Caution   If the mirror contains a boot or system partition, you should check the settings in the Boot.ini file and then remove the mirror from the drive that isn't needed for system startup. For example, if rdisk(1) is used for startup and you have the choice of removing the mirror from Disk 1 or Disk 2, you'll usually want to remove the mirror from Disk 2. Removing the mirror from Disk 2 erases the redundant data.

Repairing a Striped Set Without Parity

A striped set without parity doesn't have fault tolerance. If a drive that's part of a striped set fails, the entire striped set is unusable. Before you try to restore the striped set, you should repair or replace the failed drive. Afterward, you need to re-create the striped set and then recover the data contained on the striped set from backup.

Regenerating a Striped Set with Parity

With RAID 5, you can recover the striped set with parity if a single drive fails. You'll know that a striped set with parity drive has failed because the set's status changes to Failed Redundancy and the individual volume's status changes to Missing, Offline, or Online (Errors).

You can repair RAID 5 on basic and dynamic disks, but you must rebuild the set using the same disk type. Follow these steps to resolve problems with the RAID-5 set:

1. You need to get all drives in the RAID-5 set online. The set's status should read Failed Redundancy. The corrective action you take depends on the failed volume's status.

   Best Practices   If possible, you should back up the data before you perform this procedure. This ensures that if you have problems, you can recover your data.

2. If the status is Missing or Offline, make sure that the drive has power and is connected properly. Afterward, start Disk Management, right-click the failed volume, and select Reactivate Disk. The drive's status should change to Regenerating and then to Healthy. If the drive's status doesn't return to Healthy, right-click the volume and select Regenerate Parity.

3. If the status is Online (Errors), right-click the failed volume and select Reactivate Disk. The drive's status should change to Regenerating and then to Healthy. If the drive's status doesn't return to Healthy, right-click the volume and select Regenerate Parity.

4. If one of the drives shows as unreadable, you might need to rescan the drives on the system by selecting Rescan Disks from Disk Management's Action menu. If the drive status doesn't change, you might need to reboot the computer.

5. If one of the drives still won't come back online, you need to repair the failed region of the RAID-5 set. Right-click the failed volume and then select Remove Volume. You now need to select an unallocated space on a separate dynamic disk for the RAID-5 set. This space must be at least as large as the region to repair, and it can't be on a drive that the RAID-5 set is already using. If you don't have enough space, the Repair Volume command is unavailable and you'll need to free space by deleting other volumes or by replacing the failed drive.

Chapter 13
Managing Files and Folders

Microsoft Windows Server 2003 provides a robust environment for working with files and folders. At the core of this environment are the two basic file system types:

- FAT (file allocation table), available in 16-bit and 32-bit versions

- NTFS file system (NTFS), available in 4.0 and 5.0 versions

When you work with files and folders on a Windows Server 2003 system, you'll usually work with one of these file system types. To help you better administer FAT and NTFS volumes, this chapter explains how to perform common file and folder tasks. The chapter also discusses techniques for combating malware, using file screening, and configuring storage reporting.

Windows Server 2003 File Structures

This section covers the essential information you'll need to work with files. An understanding of file basics can make your job as an administrator a lot easier.

Major Features of FAT and NTFS

What you can or can't do with files and folders in Windows Server 2003 depends on the file system type. Windows Server 2003 provides direct support for FAT and NTFS.

FAT Volumes

FAT volumes rely on an allocation table to keep track of the status of files and folders. Although FAT is adequate for most file and folder needs, it's rather limited. Two versions of FAT are supported on Windows Server 2003:

FAT16   FAT16 is the version of FAT widely used on Microsoft Windows NT 4.0. FAT16 supports a 16-bit file allocation table and is usually referred to as FAT. You'll have optimal performance with volumes that are smaller than 2 gigabytes (GB).

FAT32   FAT32 is the version of FAT introduced with Windows 95 OEM Service Release 2 (OSR2) and Windows 98. FAT32 supports a 32-bit file allocation table and is usually referred to as FAT32. FAT32 supports smaller cluster sizes than FAT and can more efficiently allocate space. On Windows Server 2003, FAT32 supports volumes up to 32 GB.

Table 13-1 provides a brief summary of FAT and FAT32 features.

Table 13-1   FAT and FAT32 Features Comparison

Feature	FAT	FAT32
File allocation table size	16-bit	32-bit
Maximum volume size	4 GB; best at 2 GB or less	2 terabytes; limited in Windows Server 2003 to 32 GB
Maximum file size	2 GB	4 GB
Operating systems supported	MS-DOS, all versions of Windows	Windows 95 OSR2, Windows 98, Windows Millennium Edition (Windows Me), Windows XP, Windows 2000, and Windows Server 2003
Supports small cluster size	No	Yes
Supports NTFS 4.0 features	No	No
Supports NTFS 5.0 features	No	No
Use on floppy disks	Yes	Yes
Use on removable disks	Yes	Yes

Using NTFS

NTFS offers a robust environment for working with files and folders. Two versions of NTFS have been implemented:

NTFS 4.0   NTFS 4.0 is the version used with Windows NT 4.0. It features full support for local and remote access controls on files and folders as well as support for Windows compression. It doesn't support most Windows 2000 and Windows Server 2003 file system features.

NTFS 5.0   NTFS 5.0 is the version used with Windows 2000 and Windows Server 2003. It features full support for Active Directory directory service, disk quotas, compression, encryption, and other enhancements. NTFS 5.0 is fully supported by Windows 2000 and Windows Server 2003 and minimally supported by Windows NT 4.0 with Service Pack 4 or later.

Note   If you created NTFS volumes on Windows NT 4.0 and upgraded to Windows 2000 or Windows Server 2003, the volumes aren't upgraded automatically to NTFS 5.0. You must specifically choose to upgrade the volumes during installation of the operating system or when you install Active Directory.

Table 13-2 provides a brief summary of NTFS 4.0 and NTFS 5.0. Windows NT 4.0 systems with Service Pack 4 or later can access NTFS 5.0 files and folders, provided they don't use any of the new NTFS features.

Table 13-2   NTFS 4.0 and NTFS 5.0 Features Comparison

Feature	NTFS 4.0	NTFS 5.0
Maximum volume size	32 GB	2 terabytes on Master Boot Record (MBR) disks; 18 exabytes on globally unique identifier (GUID) Partition Table (GPT) disks
Maximum file size	32 GB	Only limited by volume size
Operating systems supported	Windows NT 4.0, Windows 2000, Windows Server 2003	Windows 2000, Windows Server 2003, and Windows NT 4.0 SP 4
Advanced file access permissions	Yes	Yes
Supports Windows compression	Yes	Yes
Supports Windows encryption	No	Yes
Supports Active Directory structures	No	Yes
Supports sparse files	No	Yes
Supports remote storage	No	Yes
Supports disk quotas	No	Yes
Use on floppy disks	No	No
Use on removable disks	Yes	Yes

File Naming

Windows Server 2003 file naming conventions apply to both files and folders. For simplicity, the term file naming is often used to refer to both files and folders. Although Windows Server 2003 file names are case-aware, they aren't case-sensitive. This means you can save a file named MyBook.doc and the file name will be displayed in the correct case. However, you can't save a file called mybook.doc to the same folder.

Both NTFS and FAT support long file names—up to 255 characters. You can name files using just about any of the available characters, including spaces. However, there are some characters you can't use. They are:

? * / \ : " < > |

Tip   Using spaces in file names can cause access problems. Any time you reference the file name, you might need to enclose the file name within quotation marks.
Also, if you plan to publish the file on the Web, you might need to remove the
spaces from the file name or convert them to the underscore character (_) to ensure
that Web browsers have easy access to the file.

The following file names are all acceptable:

- My Favorite Short Story.doc

- My_Favorite_Short_Story.doc

- My..Favorite..Short..Story.doc

- My Favorite Short Story!!!.doc

Accessing Long File Names Under MS-DOS

Under MS-DOS and 16-bit FAT file systems, file and directory names are restricted to
eight characters with a three-character file extension, such as chapter4.txt. This naming convention is often referred to as the 8.3 file-naming rule or the standard MS-DOS
file-naming rule. Because of it, when you work with files at the command prompt you
might have problems accessing files and folders.

To support access to long file names, abbreviated file names are created for all files and
folders on a system. These file names conform to the standard MS-DOS file-naming
rule. You can see the abbreviated file names using the command:

`dir /X`

A typical abbreviated file name looks like this:

`PROGRA~1.DOC`

How Windows Server 2003 Creates an Abbreviated File Name

When Windows Server 2003 creates an abbreviated file name from a long file name, it
uses the following rules:

- Any spaces in the file name are removed. The file name My Favorite Short
Story.doc becomes MyFavoriteShortStory.doc.

- All periods in the file name are removed (with the exception of the period sepa-
rating the file name from the file extension). The file name My..Favor-
ite..Short..Story.doc becomes MyFavoriteShortStory.doc.

- Invalid characters under the standard MS-DOS naming rule are replaced with
the underscore character (_). The file name My[Favorite]ShortStory.doc becomes
My_Favorite_Short_Story.doc.

- All remaining characters are converted to uppercase. The file name My Favorite
Short Story.doc becomes MYFAVORITESHORTSTORY.DOC.

The Rules of Truncation

To make the file conform to the 8.3 naming convention, the file name and file extension are truncated, if necessary. The rules for truncation are as follows:

- The file extension is truncated to the first three characters. The file name Mary.text becomes MARY.TEX.

- The file name is truncated to the first six characters (this is the file's root name) and a unique designator is appended. The unique designator follows the convention ~n, where n is the number of the file with the six-character file name. Following this, the file name, My Favorite Short Story.doc, becomes MYFAVO~1.DOC. The second file in this folder that's truncated to MYFAVO becomes MYFAVO~2.DOC.

Note   The file name truncation rule described here is the one you'll usually see, and you won't often have to worry about anything else. However, if you have a lot of files with similar names, you might see another convention used to create the short file name.

Note   Specifically, if more than four files use the same six-character root, additional file names are created by combining the first two characters of the file name with a four-character hash code and then appending a unique designator. A folder could have files named MYFAVO~1.DOC, MYFAVO~2.DOC, MYFAVO~3.DOC, and MYFAVO~4.DOC. Additional files with this root could be named MY3140~1.DOC, MY40C7~1.DOC, and MYEACC~1.DOC.

Combating Malware

Firewall, virus, and spyware software are your first lines of defense in keeping malicious programs off the organization's workstations and servers. However, these programs alone aren't enough to stop malware in its tracks. I regularly and routinely encounter malware that finds its way around the best firewall and virus software that McAfee and Symantec have to offer. Additional spyware software can often detect and block these malware programs, but this isn't always the case. Case in point: my computer was infected recently with a malware program that activated every time I clicked the Back button in Microsoft Internet Explorer. This program redirected me to a Web page for a product that I supposedly couldn't live without.

Having to run separate firewall, virus, and spyware programs can be frustrating for both users and administrators, especially when these combined efforts fail to stop certain types of malicious programs. To fill in the gaps, I recommend:

- Combating malware through Internet security configurations.

- Combating malware through add-on management.

Note   Chapter 15 of *Microsoft Windows XP Professional Administrator's Pocket Consultant*, 2nd Edition, goes into detail about secure browsing, local machine lockdown, security zones, and add-ons. If you're unfamiliar with these features, I recommend referring to this discussion before reading the following sections.

Combating Malware Through Internet Security Configurations

One of the easiest but most restrictive ways to combat malware is to configure the Security Zone settings for the Internet zone to prevent most types of active content from executing and to configure other zones as appropriate for your organization. The High security setting might suffice in this case because it disables or restricts usage of many types of active content. However, this setting also limits Web site functionality and might cause certain sites not to work properly.

To configure security zones on a per-computer basis, follow these steps:

1. Access the Internet Options utility in Control Panel and then click the Security tab.

2. Select the zone you want to work with and then click Custom Level. If you want to reset the zone security level, select the security level using the Reset To selection list and then click Reset.

3. Make any necessary changes to the security configuration and then click OK.

After you configure the security settings for the Internet, Local Intranet, Trusted Sites, and Restricted Sites zones, you can import the settings into Group Policy for a site, domain, or organizational unit to apply the settings to all computers in that site, domain, or organizational unit. You import the settings by completing the following steps:

1. In Group Policy, access User Configuration\Windows Settings\Internet Explorer Maintenance\Security and then double-click Security Zones And Content Ratings.

2. Select Import The Current Security Zone And Privacy Settings.

3. Click Modify Settings and then check the settings you previously defined to confirm that they're as expected.

4. Click OK twice to apply the policy.

Best Practices   Internet Explorer has two security configurations: standard and enhanced. To import enhanced settings, you must install the enhanced security configuration and then import the enhanced security settings. If you don't do this, you will see a warning prompt stating that standard settings will be ignored on computers using the enhanced configuration.

Combating Malware Through Add-on Management

A proper Internet security configuration, combined with good firewall, virus, and spyware software, will keep your organization's computers safe from malware and viruses the vast majority of the time. Sometimes, however, programs like the one I mentioned will sneak through. Most of the time these programs attach themselves as Internet Explorer add-ons. To determine if this is the case, follow these steps:

1. On the infected computer, exit any running instances of Internet Explorer.

2. Access the Internet Options utility in Control Panel and then click the Programs tab.

3. Click Manage Add-ons. This displays the Manage Add-ons dialog box.

4. Look for adds-ons that are suspicious, such as those listed by class identifier (CLSID; a string of numbers enclosed in parentheses) or those that have an unlisted or unverified publisher.

5. To disable a suspect add-on, select its name in the list and then, under Settings, select Disable.

6. Click OK twice to apply the changes. If you start Internet Explorer and browse the Internet without the malware triggering, you've probably disabled the malware and this should prevent it from running again.

Note Most malware programs that successfully bypass protections will attempt to install themselves again using the same security hole they've previously exploited. Typically, when they do this, they will attempt to do so using a new add-on name or identifier.

Restricting add-on attachment on a domain-wide or organizational unit–wide basis is the preferred technique for combating add-on malware. Policies for managing add-ons are found in Group Policy under User Configuration\Administrative Templates\Windows Components\Internet Explorer\Security Features\Add-on Management. Specifically, you should enable Deny All Add-Ons Unless Specifically Allowed In The Add-On List and then use Add-On List policy settings to define the add-ons that you specifically want to allow.

Understanding File Screening and Storage Reporting

When you're working with Windows Server 2003 R2, file screening is another tool you can use in the effort to keep networks safe from malicious programs and to block unauthorized types of content. You can use file screening in conjunction with quotas and storage reports as discussed in Chapter 14, "Data Sharing, Security, and Auditing."

Using file screening, you can monitor and block the usage of certain types of files. You can configure file screening in one of two modes:

Active Screening   Does not allow users to save unauthorized files

Passive Screening   Allows users to save unauthorized files but monitors or warns about usage (or both).

You actively or passively screen files by defining a file screen. All file screens have a *file screen path*, which is a folder that defines the base file path to which the screening is applied. Screening applies to the designated folder and all subfolders of the designated folders. The particulars of how screening works and what is screened are derived from a source template that defines the file screen properties.

Windows Server 2003 R2 includes the file screen templates listed in Table 13-3. Using the File Server Resource Manager, you can easily define additional templates that would then be available whenever you define file screens or you can set single-user custom file screen properties when defining the file screen.

Table 13-3   File Screen Templates

File Screen Template Name	Screening Type	File Group Action
Block Audio And Video Files	Active	Block: Audio and Video files
Block E-Mail Files	Active	Block: E-Mail files
Block Executable Files	Active	Block: Executable files
Block Image Files	Active	Block: Image files
Monitor Executable And System Files	Passive	Warn: Executable files, System files

File screen templates or custom properties define:

- Screening type: active or passive
- File groups to which screening is applied
- Notifications: e-mail, event log, or both

The standard file groups for screening are listed in Table 13-4. Each file group has a predefined set of files to which it applies. You can modify the included file types and create additional file groups as necessary using File Server Resource Manager or File Server Management.

You can configure exception paths as well to designate specifically allowed save locations for blocked file types. You can use this feature to allow specific users to save blocked file types to designated locations or to allow all users to save blocked file types to designated locations. As an example, you might want to deter illegal downloading of music and movies within the organization. To do this, you might want to prevent users from saving audio and video files and thereby prevent them from downloading music and movies. However, if your organization has an audio/video department that needs to be able to save audio and video files, you could configure an exception to allow files to be saved on a folder accessible only to members of this group.

Table 13-4   File Screen Groups and the File Types To Which They Apply

File Group	Applies To...
Audio and Video Files	.aac, .aif, .aiff, .asf, .asx, .au, .avi, .m3u, .mid, .midi, .mov, .mp1, .mp2, .mp3, .mp4, .mpe, .mpeg, .mpeg2, .mpeg3, .mpg, .qt, .qtw, .ram, .rm, .rmi, .rmvb, .snd, .swf, .wav, .wax, .wma, .wmv, .wvx
Backup Files	.bak, .bck, .bkf, .old
Compressed Files	.ace, .arc, .arj, .bhx, .bz2, .cab, .gz, .gzip, .hpk, .hqx, .lha, .lzh, .lzx, .pak, .pit, .rar, .sea, .sit, .sqz, .tar, .tgz, .uu, .uue, .z, .zip, .zoo
E-Mail Files	.eml, .idx, .mbx, .msg, .ost, .otf, .pab, .pst
Executable Files	.bat, .cmd, .com, .cpl, .exe, .inf, .js, .jse, .msi, .msp, .ocx, .pl, .reg, .vb, .vbs, .wsf, .wsh
Image Files	.bmp, .dib, .gif, .img, .jfif, .jpe, .jpeg, .jpg, .pcx, .png, .psd, .raw, .rif, .spiff, .tif, .tiff
Office Files	.doc, .dot, .mad, .maf, .mda, .mdb, .mdm, .mdt, .mdw, .mdz, .mpd, .mpp, .mpt, .pot, .ppa, .pps, .ppt, .pwz, .rqy, .rtf, .rwz, .slk, .vdx, .vsd, .vsl, .vss, .vst, .vsu, .vsw, .vsx, .vtx, .wbk, .xla, .xlb, .xlc, .xld, .xlk, .xll, .xlm, .xls, .xlt, .xlv, .xlw
System Files	.acm, .dll, .ocx, .sys, .vxd
Temporary Files	.temp, .tmp, ~*
Text Files	.asc, .text, .txt, .wri
Web Page Files	.asp, .aspx, .css, .dhtml, .hta, .htm, .html, .mht, .shtml, .url

You can generate storage reports as part of quota and file screening management. Table 13-5 provides a summary of the available standard storage reports and their purposes. The three general types of storage reports that can be generated based on one of the standard storage reports are:

Incident Reports   Generated automatically when a user tries to save an unauthorized file or when a user exceeds a quota

Scheduled Reports   Generated periodically based on a scheduled report task

On-Demand Reports   Generated manually upon request

Table 13-5 Standard Storage Reports

Report Name	Description
Duplicate Files	Lists files that appear to be duplicates based on the file size and last modification time. Helps reclaim wasted space due to duplication.
File Screening Audit	Lists file screening audit events on the server for a specified period. Helps identify users and applications that violate screening policies. Report parameters can be set to filter events based on the minimum days since screening event occurred and user.
Files By File Group	Lists files by file group. Helps identify usage patterns and types of files that are using large amounts of disk space. Report parameters can be set to include or exclude specific file groups.
Files By Owner	Lists files by users who own them. Helps identify users who use large amounts of disk space. Report parameters can be set to include or exclude specific users as well as specific files by name pattern.
Large Files	Lists files that are of a specified size or larger. Helps identify files that are using large amounts of disk space. Report parameters can be set to define the minimum file size that is considered as a large file. The default parameters are set so that size 5 MB or larger are considered to be large files. You can include and exclude files only by name pattern.
Least Recently Accessed Files	Lists files that haven't been accessed recently. Helps identify files that you might be able to delete or archive. Report parameters can be set to define what constitutes a least recently used file. By default, any file that hasn't been accessed in the last 90 days is considered to be a least recently used file. You can also include or exclude specific files by name pattern.
Most Recently Accessed Files	Lists files that have been accessed recently. Helps identify frequently used files. Report parameters can be set to define what constitutes a most recently used file. By default, any file that has been accessed within the last seven days is considered to be a most recently used file. You can also include or exclude specific files by name pattern.
Quota Usage	Lists the quotas that exceed a minimum quota usage value. Helps identify file usage according to quotas. Report parameters can be set to define the quotas that should be included according to the percentage of the quota limit used.

You manage file screening and storage reporting using the File Server Resource Manager snap-in, which is available in the File Server Resource Management and File Server Management consoles as well as custom consoles you create. When you select the File Server Resource Manager node in any of these consoles, you'll see three additional nodes, as shown in Figure 13-1:

Quota Management Used to manage the quota features of Windows Server 2003 R2 and discussed in Chapter 14

File Screening Management   Used to manage the file screening features of Windows Server 2003 R2 and discussed in this chapter

Storage Reports Management   Used to manage the storage reporting features of Windows Server 2003 R2 and discussed in this chapter

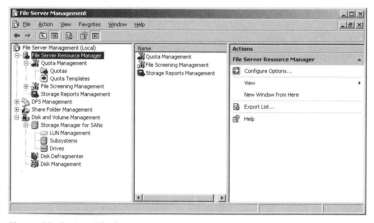

Figure 13-1   Use File Server Resource Manager to manage quotas, file screening, and storage reports.

Managing File Screening and Storage Reporting

File screening and storage reporting management can be divided into these key areas:

Global options   Control global settings for file server resources, including e-mail notification, storage report default parameters, report locations, and file screen auditing

File groups   Control the types of file to which screens are applied

File screen templates   Control screening properties (screening type: active or passive, file groups to which screening is applied; notifications: e-mail, event log, or both)

File screens   Control file paths that are screened

File screen exceptions   Control file paths that are screening exceptions

Report generation   Controls whether and how storage reports are generated

Each of these management areas is discussed in the sections that follow.

Managing Global File Resource Settings

You use global file resource options to configure e-mail notification, storage report default parameters, report locations, and file screen auditing. You should configure these global settings prior to configuring quotas, file screens, and storage reporting.

Configuring E-mail Notifications

Notifications and storage reports are e-mailed through a Simple Mail Transfer Protocol (SMTP) server. For this process to work, you must designate which organizational SMTP server to use, default administrative recipients, and the From address to be used in mailing notifications and reports. To configure these settings, follow these steps:

1. In File Server Management, select the File Server Resource Manager node. On the Action menu or in the Actions pane, click Configure Options. This displays the File Server Resource Manager Options dialog box with the Email Notifications tab selected by default, as shown in Figure 13-2.

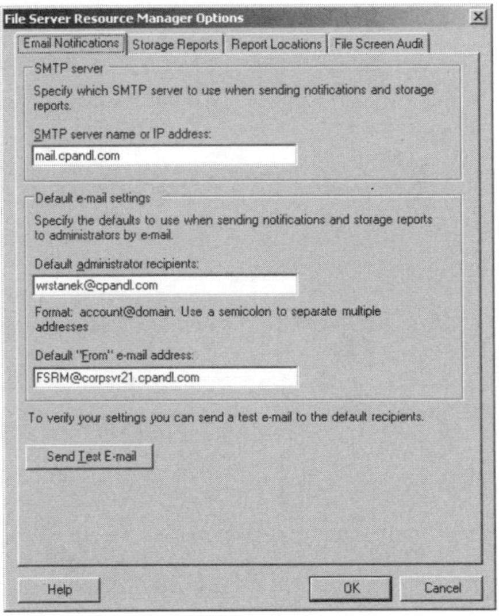

Figure 13-2   Use the Email Notifications tab to set e-mail notification and other global file resource settings.

2. In the SMTP Server Name Or IP Address text box, type the fully qualified domain name (FQDN) of the organization's mail server, such as mail.cpandl.com, or the Internet Protocol (IP) address of this server, such as 192.168.10.52.

3. In the Default Administrator Recipients field, type the name-mail address of the default administrator for notification, such as filescreens@cpandl.com. Typically, you'll want this to be a separate mailbox that is monitored by an administrator or a distribution list that goes to the specific administrators responsible for file server resource management. You can also enter multiple e-mail addresses. Be sure to separate each e-mail address with a semicolon.

4. In the Default "From" E-Mail Address field, type the e-mail address you want the server to use in the From field of notification messages. Remember, users as well as administrators may receive notifications.

5. To test the settings, click Send Test E-Mail. The test e-mail should be delivered to the default administrator recipients almost immediately. If it isn't, check to ensure that the e-mail addresses used are valid and that the From e-mail address is acceptable to the SMTP server as a valid sender. Click OK.

Reviewing Reports and Configuring Storage Report Parameters

Each storage report has a default configuration that you can review and modify using File Server Resource Manager Options. Default parameter changes apply to all future incident reports and any existing report tasks that use the default configuration. You're able to override the default settings as necessary if you subsequently schedule a report task or generate a report on demand.

You can access the standard storage reports and change their default parameters by completing the following steps:

1. In File Server Management, select the File Server Resource Manager node. On the Action menu or in the Actions pane, click Configure Options. This displays the File Server Resource Manager Options dialog box.

2. Click the Storage Reports tab.

3. To review a report's current settings, select the report name in the Reports list and then click Review Reports.

4. To modify a report's default parameters, select the report name in the Reports list and then click Edit Parameters.

5. When you're finished, click Close or OK as appropriate.

Configuring Report Locations

By default, incident, scheduled, and on-demand reports are stored on the server on which notification is triggered in separate subfolders under %SystemDrive% \StorageReports. You can review or modify this configuration by completing the following steps:

1. In File Server Management, select the File Server Resource Manager node. On the Action menu or in the Actions pane, click Configure Options. This displays the File Server Resource Manager Options dialog box.

2. Click the Report Locations tab.

3. The report folders currently in use are listed under Report Locations. To specify a different local folder for a particular report type, type a new folder path or click Browse to search for the folder path you want to use. Click OK.

Note   You can use only local paths for report storage. Nonlocal folder paths will be considered invalid.

Configuring File Screen Auditing

All file screening activity can be recorded in an auditing database for later review by running a File Screen Auditing Report. This auditing data is tracked on a per server basis, so that the server on which the activity occurs is the one where the activity is audited. To enable or disable file screen auditing, follow these steps:

1. In File Server Management, select the File Server Resource Manager node. On the Action menu or in the Actions pane, click Configure Options. This displays the File Server Resource Manager Options dialog box.

2. Click the File Screen Audit tab.

3. To enable auditing, select the Record File Screening Activity In Auditing Database check box.

4. To disable auditing, clear the Record File Screening Activity In Auditing Database check box. Click OK.

Managing the File Groups to Which Screens Are Applied

You use file groups to designate sets of similar file types to which screening can be applied. In File Server Management, you can view the currently defined screening file groups by expanding the File Server Resource Manager and File Screening Management nodes and then selecting File Groups. Table 13-4, shown previously, lists the default file groups and the included file types.

You can modify existing file groups by completing the following steps:

1. In File Server Management, expand the File Server Resource Manager and File Screening Management nodes and then select File Groups.

2. Currently defined file groups are listed along with included and excluded files.

3. To modify file group properties, double-click the file group name. This displays a related properties dialog box similar to the one shown in Figure 13-3.

4. In the Files To Include text box, type the file extension of an additional file type to screen, such as .pdf, or the file name pattern, such as **Archive*.***. Click Add. Repeat this step to specify other file types to screen.

5. In the Files To Exclude text box, type the file extension of a file type to exclude from screening, such as .doc, or the file name pattern, such as **Report*.***. Click Add. Repeat this step to specify other file types to exclude from screening.

6. Click OK to save the changes.

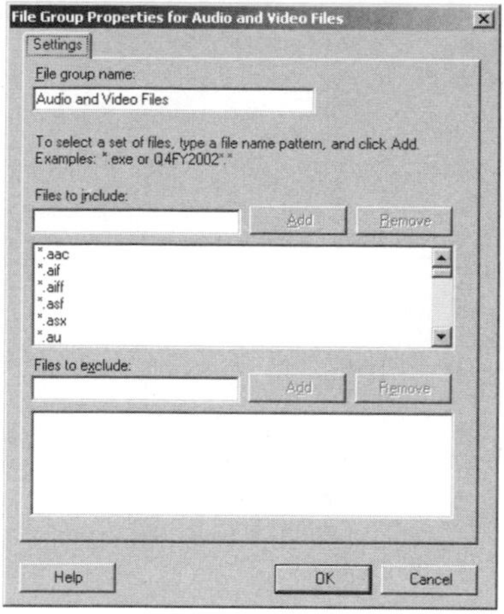

Figure 13-3   Include and exclude file types by modifying file group properties.

You can specify additional file groups to screen by completing the following steps:

1. In File Server Management, expand the File Server Resource Manager and File Screening Management nodes and then select File Groups.

2. On the Action menu or in the Actions pane, click Create File Group. This displays the Create File Group Properties dialog box.

3. In the File Group Name text box, type the name of the file group you're creating.

4. In the Files To Include field, type the file extension to screen, such as **.pdf**, or the file name pattern, such as **Archive*.***. Click Add. Repeat this step to specify other file types to screen.

5. In the Files To Exclude text box, type the file extension to exclude from screening, such as **.doc**, or the file name pattern, such as **Report*.***. Click Add. Repeat this step to specify other file types to exclude from screening.

6. Click OK to create the file group.

Managing File Screen Templates

You use file screen templates to define screening properties, including the screening type, the file groups to which screen is applied, and notification. In File Server Management, you can view the currently defined file screen templates by expanding the File Server Resource Manager and File Screening Management nodes and then selecting File Screen Templates. Table 13-3, shown previously, provides a summary of the default file screen templates.

You can modify existing file screen templates by completing the following steps:

1. In File Server Management, expand the File Server Resource Manager and File Screening Management nodes and then select File Screen Templates.

2. Currently defined file screen templates are listed by name, screening type, and file groups affected.

3. To modify file screen template properties, double-click the file screen template name. This displays a related properties dialog box (shown in Figure 13-4).

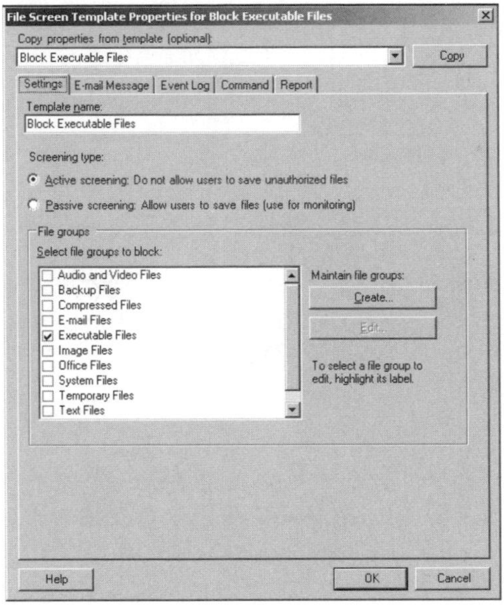

Figure 13-4 Use file screen properties to configure the screening type, the file groups to which screen is applied, and notification.

4. In the Settings tab, you can set the template name, screen type, and file groups affected using the text boxes provided.

5. In the E-Mail Message tab, you can configure notification:

   ❑ To notify an administrator when the file screen is triggered, select the Send E-Mail To The Following Administrators check box and then type the e-mail address or addresses to use. Be sure to separate multiple e-mail addresses with a semicolon. Use the value [Admin Email] to specify the default administrator as configured previously under the global options.

   ❑ To notify users, select the Send E-Mail To The User Who Attempted To Save An Unauthorized File check box .

   ❑ To specify the contents of the notification message, use the Subject and Message Body text boxes. Table 13-6 lists available variables and their meaning.

6. In the Event Log tab, you can configure event logging. Select Send Warning To Event Log to enable logging and then use the Log Entry field to specify the text of the log entry. Table 13-6 lists available variables and their meaning.

7. In the Report tab, select the Generate Report check box to enable incident reporting and then select the check boxes for the types of reports you want to generate. Incident reports are stored under %SystemDrive%\StorageReports\Incident by default and can also be sent to designated administrators. Use the value [Admin Email] to specify the default administrator as configured previously under the global options.

8. Click OK when you're finished modifying the template.

You can create a new file screen template by completing the following steps:

1. In File Server Management, expand the File Server Resource Manager and File Screening Management nodes and then select File Screen Templates.

2. On the Action menu or in the Actions pane, click Create File Screen Template. This displays the Create File Screen Template dialog box.

3. Follow Steps 4–8 of the previous procedure.

Creating File Screens

You use file screens to designate file paths that are screened. In File Server Management, you can view current file screens by expanding the File Server Resource Manager and File Screening Management nodes and then selecting File Screens. Before you define file screens, you should specify screening file groups and file screen templates that you will use, as discussed in the sections of this chapter entitled "Managing the File Groups to Which Screens Are Applied" and "Managing File Screen Templates."

After you've defined the necessary file groups and file screen templates, you can create a file screen by completing the following steps:

1. In File Server Management, expand the File Server Resource Manager and File Screening Management nodes and then select File Screens.

Table 13-6 File Screen Variables and Their Meaning

Variable Name	Description
[Admin Email]	Inserts the e-mail addresses of the administrators defined under the global options
[File Screen Path]	Inserts the local file path where the user attempted to save the file, such as C:\data
[File Screen Remote Path]	Inserts the remote file path where the user attempted to save the file, such as \\server\share
[File Screen System Path]	Inserts the canonical file path where the user attempted to save the file, such as \\?\VolumeGUID

Table 13-6   File Screen Variables and Their Meaning

Variable Name	Description
[Server Domain]	Inserts the domain of the server on which the notification occurred
[Server]	Inserts the server on which the notification occurred
[Source File Owner Email]	Inserts the e-mail address of the owner of the unauthorized file
[Source File Owner]	Inserts the user name of the owner of the unauthorized file
[Source File Path]	Inserts the source path of the unauthorized file
[Source Io Owner Email]	Inserts the e-mail address of the user who caused notification
[Source Io Owner]	Inserts the name of the user who caused notification
[Source Process Id]	Inserts the process ID (PID) of the process that caused notification
[Source Process Image]	Inserts the executable for the process that caused notification
[Violated File Group]	Inserts the name of the file group in which the file type is defined as unauthorized

2. Click Create File Screen on the Action menu or in the Actions pane.

3. In the Create File Screen dialog box, set the local computer path to screen by clicking Browse and then using the Browse For Folder dialog box to select the path to screen, such as C:\Data.

4. Use the Derive Properties selection list to choose the file screen template that defines the screening properties you want to use.

5. Click Create.

Defining File Screening Exceptions

You use exception paths to specifically designate folder locations where it's permitted to save blocked file types. Based on the NTFS permissions on the excepted file path, you can use this feature to allow specific users to save blocked file types to designated locations or to allow all users to save blocked file types to designated locations.

You can create a file screen exception by completing the following steps:

1. In File Server Management, expand the File Server Resource Manager and File Screening Management nodes and then select File Screens.

2. Click Create File Screen Exception on the Action menu or in the Actions pane.

3. In the Create File Screen Exception dialog box, set the local path to exclude from screening by clicking Browse and then using the Browse For Folder dialog box to select the path to exclude from screening, such as C:\Data\Images.

4. Select the file groups to exclude from screening on the designated path. Click OK.

Scheduling and Generating Storage Reports

Incident reports are generated automatically when triggered, as defined in the Reports tab properties of a file screen template (for details, see the section of this chapter entitled "Managing File Screen Templates"). Scheduled and on-demand reports are configured separately. In File Server Management, you can view currently scheduled reports by expanding the File Server Resource Manager node and then selecting Storage Reports Management.

You can schedule reports on a per volume or folder basis by completing the following steps:

1. In File Server Management, expand the File Server Resource Manager node and then select Storage Reports Management.

2. On the Action menu or in the Actions pane, click Schedule A New Report Task. This displays the Storage Reports Task Properties dialog box shown in Figure 13-5.

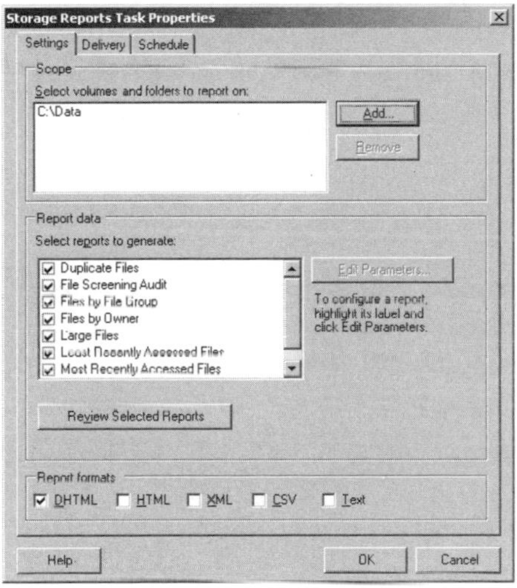

Figure 13-5 Schedule reports for delivery on a per volume or folder basis.

3. In the Settings tab under Scope, click Add. Use the Browse For Folder dialog box to select the volume or folder on which you want to generate scheduled storage reports. Repeat to add other volumes or folders.

4. Under Report Data, select the types of reports to generate.

5. Under Report Formats, select the format for the report, such as Dynamic HTML (DHTML).

6. By default, Windows Server 2003 R2 stores scheduled storage reports as they're generated in the %SystemDrive%\StorageReports\Scheduled folder. If you'd also like to deliver reports by e-mail to administrators, click the Delivery tab and then select the Send Reports To The Following Administrators check box. Enter the e-mail address or addresses to which reports should be delivered, making sure to separate each e-mail address with a semicolon.

7. In the Schedule tab, click Create Schedule. In the Schedule dialog box, click New and then define the run schedule for reporting.

8. Click OK twice to schedule the report task.

You can generate an on-demand report by following these steps:

1. In File Server Management, expand the File Server Resource Manager node and then select Storage Reports Management.

2. On the Action menu or in the Actions pane, click Generate Reports Now. This displays the Storage Reports Task Properties dialog box.

3. In the Settings tab under Scope, click Add. Use the Browse For Folder dialog box to select the volume or folder on which you want to generate the on-demand storage reports. Repeat to add other volumes or folders.

4. Under Report Data, select the types of reports to generate.

5. Under Report Formats, select the format for the report, such as DHTML.

6. Windows Server 2003 stores on-demand storage reports in the %SystemDrive% \StorageReports\Interactive folder. If you'd also like to deliver reports by e-mail to administrators, click the Delivery tab and then select the Send Reports To The Following Administrators check box. Enter the e-mail address or addresses to which reports should be delivered, making sure to separate each e-mail address with a semicolon.

7. Click OK. When prompted, specify whether to wait for the reports to be generated and then display them or to generate the reports in the background for later access. Click OK.

Chapter 14

Data Sharing, Security, and Auditing

Data sharing allows remote users to access network resources, such as files, folders, and drives. When you share a folder or a drive, you make all its files and subfolders available to a specified set of users. If you want to control access to specific files and subfolders within a shared folder, you can do it only with NTFS volumes. On NTFS volumes, you use access control lists to grant or deny access to files and folders.

Object security applies to all resources on NTFS volumes. It includes files, folders, and Active Directory directory service objects. Normally, only administrators have the right to manage Active Directory objects, but you can delegate to users the authority to manage Active Directory objects. When you do, you make information in Active Directory available for viewing and modification by designated users. You control these users' permissions through access control lists. By auditing access to objects, you can closely monitor network activity and ensure that only authorized users are accessing resources.

Sharing Folders on Local and Remote Systems

You use shares to control access for remote users. Permissions on shared folders have no effect on users who log on locally to a server or to a workstation that has shared folders.

- To grant remote users access to files across the network, you use standard folder sharing.

- To grant remote users access to files from the Web, you use Web sharing. This is available only if the system has Internet Information Services (IIS) installed.

Viewing Existing Shares

You can use both Computer Management and File Server Management to work with shares. You can also view current shares on a computer by typing **net share** at a command prompt.

In Computer Management, you can view the shared folders on a local or remote computer by completing the following steps:

1. You're connected to the local computer by default. If you want to connect to a remote computer, right-click the Computer Management node and select Connect To Another Computer. Choose Another Computer, type the name or Internet Protocol (IP) address of the computer to which you want to connect, and then click OK.

2. In the console tree, expand System Tools and Shared Folders, and then select Shares. The current shares on the system are displayed, as shown in Figure 14-1.

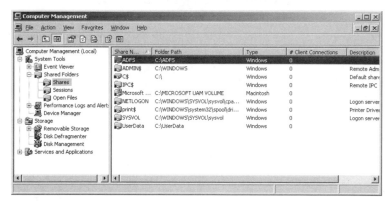

Figure 14-1   Available shares are listed in the Shared Folders node.

In File Server Management, you can view the shared folders on a local or remote computer by completing the following steps:

1. You're connected to the local computer by default. To connect to a remote computer, right-click the File Server Management node and select Connect To Another Computer. Choose Another Computer, type the name or IP address of the computer to which you want to connect, and then click OK.

2. In the console tree, expand Shared Folder Management and Shared Folders, and then select Shares. The current shares on the system are displayed, as shown previously in Figure 14-1.

The columns of the Shares node provide the following information:

Share Name   Name of the shared folder

Folder Path   Complete path to the folder on the local system

Type   What kind of computers can use the share, such as Macintosh or Windows

 # Client Connections   Number of clients currently accessing the share

Description   Description of the share

> **Note**   An entry of "Windows" in the Type column means that all clients can use the share, including those running Windows or Macintosh operating systems. An entry of "Macintosh" in the Type column means that only Macintosh clients can use the share.

Creating Shared Folders

Microsoft Windows Server 2003 provides several ways to share folders: you can share local folders using Windows Explorer, and you can also share local and remote folders using Computer Management and File Server Management.

Because Computer Management and File Server Management allow you to work with and manage shared resources on any of your network computers, they're usually the best tools to use. Which of the two consoles you use is a matter of preference, and the techniques for creating and working with shared folders are nearly identical.

To share folders on a server running Windows Server 2003, you must be a member of the Administrators or the Server Operators group. In Computer Management, you share a folder by completing the following steps:

1. If necessary, connect to a remote computer.

2. In the console tree, expand System Tools and Shared Folders, and then select Shares. The current shares on the system are displayed.

3. Right-click Shares and then select New Share. This starts the Share A Folder Wizard. Click Next.

4. In the Folder Path text box, type the local file path to the folder you want to share. The file path must be exact, such as C:\Data\CorpDocuments. If you don't know the full path, click Browse and then use the Browse For Folder dialog box to find the folder you want to share and then click OK. Click Next.

> **Tip**   If the file path doesn't exist, the wizard can create the necessary path for you. Click Yes when prompted to create the necessary folders.

5. In the Share Name text box, type a name for the share, as shown in Figure 14-2. This is the name of the folder to which users will connect. Share names must be unique for each system.

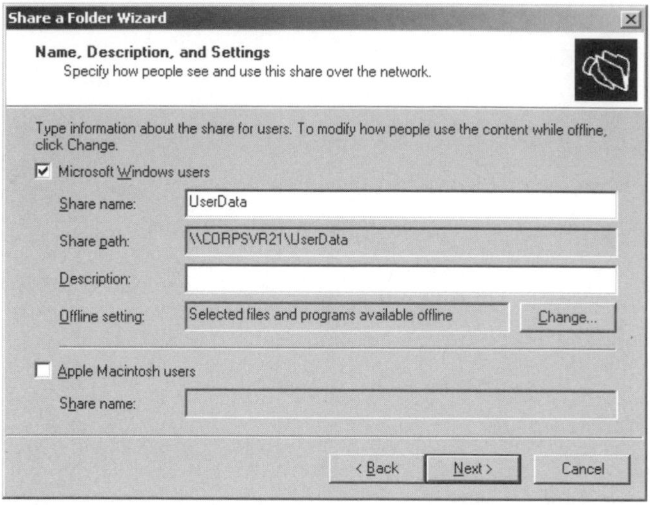

Figure 14-2 Use the Share A Folder Wizard to configure the essential share properties, including name, description, and offline resource usage.

6. If you've configured Macintosh services, the standard Name, Description, And Settings page is modified, as shown in Figure 14-2, to include Microsoft Windows Users and Apple Macintosh Users check boxes. By selecting Microsoft Windows Users (the default), you allow Windows users to access the share. By selecting Apple Macintosh Users and typing a share name in the field provided, you allow Macintosh users to access the share.

> **Tip** If you want to hide a share from users (which means that they won't be able to see the shared resource when they try to browse to it in Windows Explorer or at the command line), type **$** as the last character of the shared resource name. For example, you could create a share called **PrivEngData$**, which would be hidden from Windows Explorer, Net View, and other similar utilities. Users can still connect to the share and access its data, provided that they've been granted access permission and that they know the share's name. Note that the $ must be typed as part of the share name when mapping to the shared resource.

7. If you like, you can type a description of the share in the Description text box. Then, when you view shares on a particular computer, the description is displayed in Computer Management.

8. By default, the share is configured so that only files and programs that users specify are available for offline use. If you want to prohibit the offline use of files

or programs in the share or specify that all files and programs in the share are available for offline use, click Change, and then select the appropriate options in the Offline Settings dialog box.

9. Click Next and then set basic permissions for the share. You'll find helpful pointers in the "Managing Share Permissions" section of this chapter. As shown in Figure 14-3, the available options are as follows:

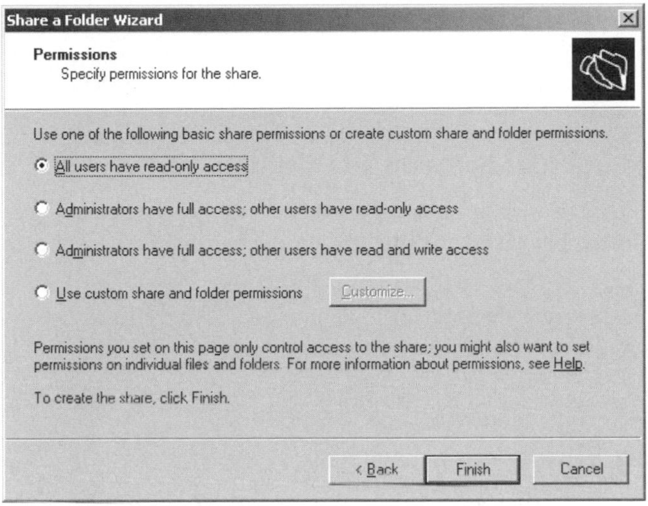

Figure 14-3   Use the Permissions page to set permissions for the share.

All Users Have Read-Only Access   Gives users access to view files and read data. They can't create, modify, or delete files and folders.

Administrators Have Full Access; Other Users Have Read-Only Access   Gives administrators complete control over the share. Full access allows administrators to create, modify, and delete files and folders. On NTFS, it also gives administrators the right to change permissions and to take ownership of files and folders. Other users can only view files and read data. They can't create, modify, or delete files and folders.

Administrators Have Full Access; Other Users Have Read And Write Access   Gives administrators complete control over the share and allows other users to create, modify, or delete files and folders.

Use Custom Share And Folder Permissions   Allows you to configure access for specific users and groups, which is usually the best technique to use. Setting share permissions is discussed fully later in this chapter in the section entitled "Managing Share Permissions."

10. When you click Finish, the wizard displays a status report, which should state "Sharing Was Successful." Click Close.

Note   If you view the shared folder in Windows Explorer, you'll see that the folder icon now includes a hand to indicate a share. Through Computer Management, you can also view shared resources. To learn how, see the section of this chapter entitled "Sharing Folders on Local and Remote Systems."

Best Practices   If you're creating a share that's for general use and general access, you should publish the shared resource in Active Directory. Publishing the resource in Active Directory makes it easier for users to find the share. To publish a share in Active Directory, right-click the share in Computer Management and then select Properties. On the Publish tab, select the Publish This Share In Active Directory check box, add an optional description and owner information, and then click OK.

Creating Additional Shares on an Existing Share

Individual folders can have multiple shares. Each share can have a different name and a different set of access permissions. To create additional shares on an existing share, simply follow the steps for creating a share outlined in the previous section—with these changes:

In Step 5: When you name the share, make sure that you use a different name.

In Step 6: When you add a description for the share, use a description that explains what the share is used for—and how it's different from the other share(s) for the same folder.

Managing Share Permissions

Share permissions set the maximum allowable actions available within a shared folder. By default, when you create a share, everyone with access to the network has read access to the share's contents. This is an important security change—in previous editions, the default permission was full control.

With NTFS volumes you can use file and folder permissions and ownership to further constrain actions within the share as well as share permissions. With file allocation table (FAT) volumes, share permissions provide the only access controls.

The Different Share Permissions

Share permissions available, from the most restrictive to the least restrictive, are:

No Access   No permissions are granted for the share.

Read   With this permission, users can:

1. View file and subfolder names.

2. Access the subfolders of the share.

3. Read file data and attributes.

4. Run program files.

Change   Users have Read permissions and the additional ability to:

1. Create files and subfolders.

2. Modify files.

3. Change attributes on files and subfolders.

4. Delete files and subfolders.

Full Control   Users have Read and Change permissions, as well as the following additional capabilities on NTFS volumes:

1. Change file and folder permissions.

2. Take ownership of files and folders.

You can assign share permissions to users and groups. You can even assign permissions to implicit groups. For details on implicit groups, see the section entitled "Implicit Groups and Special Identities" in Chapter 8, "Understanding User and Group Accounts."

Viewing Share Permissions

To view share permissions, follow these steps:

1. In Computer Management, connect to the computer on which the share is created.

2. In the console tree, expand System Tools and Shared Folders, and then select Shares.

3. Right-click the share you want to view, and then select Properties.

4. In the Properties dialog box, click the Share Permissions tab, shown in Figure 14-4. You can now view the users and groups that have access to the share and the type of access they have.

Configuring Share Permissions

In Computer Management, you can add user, computer, and group permissions to shares by completing the following steps:

1. Right-click the share you want to manage and then select Properties.

2. In the Share Properties dialog box, click the Share Permissions tab.

3. Click Add. This opens the Select Users, Computers, Or Groups dialog box shown in Figure 14-5.

4. Type the name of a user, computer, or group in the current domain and then click Check Names.

   ❑ If a single match is found, the dialog box is automatically updated as appropriate and the entry is underlined.

   ❑ If no matches are found, you've either entered an incorrect name part or you're working with an incorrect location. Modify the name and try again, or click Locations to select a new location.

❑   If multiple matches are found, select the name(s) you want to use and then click OK. To assign permissions to other users, computers, or groups, type a semicolon (;), and then repeat this step.

Note   The Locations button allows you to access account names from other domains. Click Locations to see a list of the current domain, trusted domains, and other resources that you can access. Because of the transitive trusts in Windows Server 2003, you can usually access all the domains in the domain tree or forest.

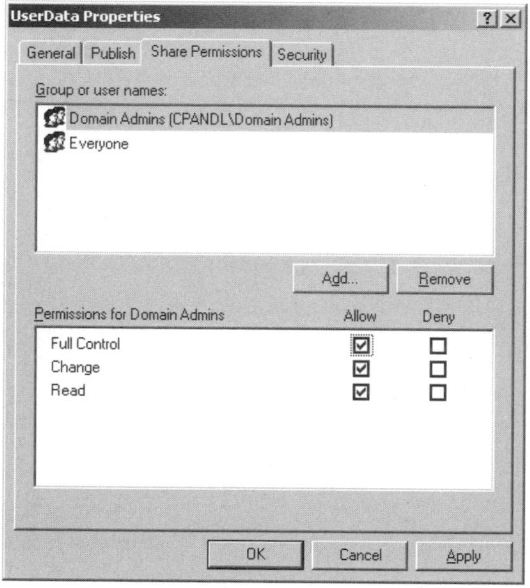

Figure 14-4   The Share Permissions tab shows which users and groups have access to the share and what type of access they have.

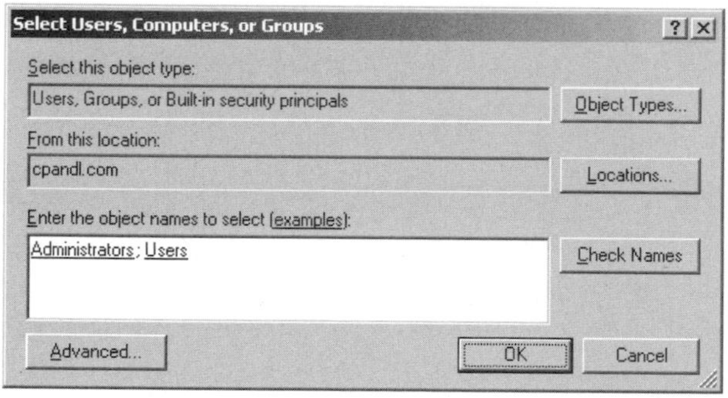

Figure 14-5   Add users and groups to the share using the Select Users, Computers, Or Groups dialog box.

5. Click OK. The users and groups are added to the Name list for the share.

6. Configure access permissions for each user, computer, and group by selecting an account name and then allowing or denying access permissions. Keep in mind that you're setting the maximum allowable permissions for a particular account.

7. Click OK when you're finished. To assign additional security permissions for NTFS, see the section of this chapter entitled "File and Folder Permissions."

Modifying Existing Share Permissions

You can change the share permissions you assign to users, computers, and groups by using the Share Properties dialog box. In Computer Management, follow these steps:

1. Right-click the share you want to manage, and then select Properties.

2. In the Share Properties dialog box, click the Share Permissions tab.

3. In the Name list box, select the user, computer, or group you want to modify.

4. Use the check boxes in the Permissions area to allow or deny permissions.

5. Repeat for other users, computers, or groups, and then click OK when you're finished.

Removing Share Permissions for Users and Groups

You also remove share permissions assigned to users, computers, and groups with the Share Permissions dialog box. In Computer Management, follow these steps:

1. Right-click the share you want to manage and then select Properties.

2. In the Share Properties dialog box, click the Share Permissions tab.

3. In the Name list box, select the user, computer, or group you want to remove, and then click Remove.

4. Repeat for other users or groups, as necessary, and then click OK when you're finished.

Managing Existing Shares

As an administrator, you'll often have to manage shared folders. The common administrative tasks of managing shares are covered in this section.

Understanding Special Shares

When you install Windows Server 2003, the operating system creates special shares automatically. These shares are also known as *administrative shares* and *hidden shares*. These shares are designed to help make system administration easier. You can't set access permissions on automatically created special shares; Windows Server 2003 assigns access permissions. (You can create your own hidden shares by typing $ as the last character of the resource name.)

You can delete special shares temporarily if you're certain the shares aren't needed. However, the shares are recreated automatically the next time the operating system starts. To permanently disable the administrative shares change the following registry values to 0 (zero):

- HKLM\SYSTEM\CurrentControlSet\Services\lanmanserver\parameters \AutoShareServer

- HKLM\SYSTEM\CurrentControlSet\Services\lanmanserver\parameters \AutoShareWks

Which special shares are available depends on your system configuration. Table 14-1 lists special shares you might see and how they're used.

Table 14-1   Special Shares Used by Windows Server 2003

Special Share Name	Description	Usage
ADMIN$	A share used during remote administration of a system. Provides access to the operating system %SystemRoot%.	On workstations and servers, administrators and backup operators can access these shares. On domain controllers, server operators also have access.
FAX$	Supports network faxes.	Used by fax clients when sending faxes.
IPC$	Supports named pipes during remote interprocess communications (IPC) access.	Used by programs when performing remote administration and when viewing shared resources.
NETLOGON	Supports the Net Logon service.	Used by the Net Logon service when processing domain logon requests. Everyone has Read access.
Microsoft UAM Volume	Supports Macintosh file and printer services.	Used by File Server For Macintosh and Print Server For Macintosh.
PRINT$	Supports shared printer resources by providing access to printer drivers.	Used by shared printers. Everyone has Read access. Administrators, server operators, and printer operators have full control.
SYSVOL	Supports Active Directory.	Used to store data and objects for Active Directory.
Driveletter$	A share that allows administrators to connect to a drive's root folder. These shares are shown as C$, D$, E$, and so on.	On workstations and servers, administrators and backup operators can access these shares. On domain controllers, server operators also have access.

Connecting to Special Shares

Special shares end with the $ symbol. Although these shares aren't displayed in Windows Explorer, administrators and certain operators can connect to them. To connect to a special share, follow these steps:

1. In Windows Explorer, from the Tools menu, select Map Network Drive. This opens the page shown in Figure 14-6.

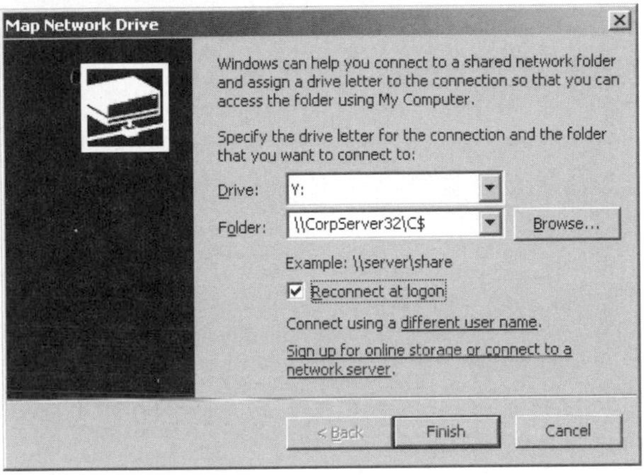

Figure 14-6   Connect to special shares by mapping them with the Map Network Drive page.

2. From the Drive drop-down list, select a free drive letter. This drive letter is used to access the special share.

3. In the Folder text box, type the Universal Naming Convention (UNC) path to the desired share. For example, to access the C$ share on a server called Twiddle, you'd use the path **\\TWIDDLE\C$**. Click Finish.

After you connect to a special share, you can access it as you would any other drive. Because special shares are protected, you don't have to worry about ordinary users accessing these shares. The first time you connect to the share, you might be prompted for a user name and password. If you are, provide that information.

Viewing User and Computer Sessions

You can use Computer Management to track all connections to shared resources on a Windows Server 2003 system. Whenever a user or computer connects to a shared resource, Windows Server 2003 lists a connection in the Sessions node.

To view connections to shared resources, type **net session** at a command prompt or follow these steps:

1. In Computer Management, connect to the computer on which you created the shared resource.

2. In the console tree, expand System Tools and Shared Folders, and then select Sessions.

3. As shown in Figure 14-7, you can now view connections to shares for users and computers.

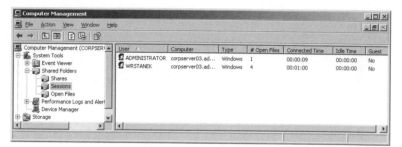

Figure 14-7   Use the Sessions node to view user and computer connections.

The Sessions node provides important information about user and computer connections. The columns of this node provide the following information:

User   The names of users or computers connected to shared resources. Computer names are shown with a $ suffix to differentiate them from users.

Computer   The name of the computer being used.

Type   The type of network connection being used.

 # Open Files   The number of files with which the user is actively working. For more detailed information, access the Open Files node.

Connected Time   The time that has elapsed since the connection was established.

Idle Time   The time that has elapsed since the connection was last used.

Guest   Whether the user is logged on as a guest.

Managing Sessions and Shares

Managing sessions and shares is a common administrative task. Before you shut down a server or an application running on a server, you might want to disconnect users from shared resources. You might also need to disconnect users when you plan to change access permissions or delete a share entirely. Another reason to disconnect users is to break locks on files. You disconnect users from shared resources by ending the related user sessions.

Ending Individual Sessions   To disconnect individual users from shared resources, type **net session \\ComputerName /delete** at a command prompt or follow these steps:

1. In Computer Management, connect to the computer on which you created the share.

2. In the console tree, expand System Tools and Shared Folders, and then select Sessions.

3. Right-click the user sessions you want to end and then choose Close Session.

4. Click Yes to confirm the action.

Ending All Sessions   To disconnect all users from shared resources, follow these steps:

1. In Computer Management, connect to the computer on which you created the share.

2. In the console tree, expand System Tools and Shared Folders, and then right-click Sessions.

3. Choose Disconnect All Sessions and then click Yes to confirm the action.

Note   Keep in mind that you're disconnecting users from shared resources and not from the domain. You can only force users to log off once they've logged on to the domain through logon hours and Group Policy. Thus, disconnecting users doesn't log them off the network. It simply disconnects them from the shared resource.

Managing Open Resources

Any time users connect to shares, the individual file and object resources with which they're actively working are displayed in the Open Files node. The Open Files node might show the files the user has open but isn't currently editing.

You can access the Open Files node by completing the following steps:

1. In Computer Management, connect to the computer on which you created the share.

2. In the console tree, expand System Tools and Shared Folders, and then select Open Files. This displays the Open Files node, shown in Figure 14-8. The Open Files node provides the following information about resource usage:

   Open File   The file or folder path to the open file on the local system. It might also be a named pipe, such as \PIPE\spools, which is used for printer spooling.

   Accessed By   The name of the user accessing the file.

   Type   The type of network connection being used.

   # Locks   The number of locks on the resource.

   Open Mode   The access mode used when the resource was opened, such as read, write, or write+read mode.

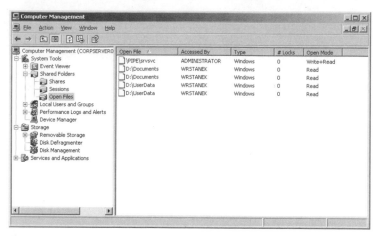

Figure 14-8   You can manage open resources using the Open Files node.

Close an Open File   To close an open file on a computer's shares, follow these steps:

1. In Computer Management, connect to the computer with which you want to work.

2. In the console tree, expand System Tools and Shared Folders, and then select Open Files.

3. Right-click the open file you want to close, and then choose Close Open File.

4. Click Yes to confirm the action.

Close All Open Files   To close all open files on a computer's shares, follow these steps:

1. In Computer Management, connect to the computer on which the share is created.

2. In the console tree, expand System Tools and Shared Folders and then right-click Open Files.

3. Choose Disconnect All Open Files and then click Yes to confirm the action.

Stopping File and Folder Sharing

To stop sharing a folder, follow these steps:

1. In Computer Management, connect to the computer on which you created the share and then access the Shares node.

2. Right-click the share you want to remove and then choose Stop Sharing. Click Yes to confirm the action.

Caution   You should never delete a folder containing shares without first stopping the shares. If you fail to stop the shares, Windows Server 2003 attempts to reestablish the shares the next time the computer is started, and the resulting error is logged in the System event log.

Using Shadow Copies

Any time your organization uses shared folders you might want to consider creating shadow copies of these shared folders as well. Shadow copies are point-in-time backups of data files that users can access directly in shared folders. These point-in-time backups can save you and the other administrators in your organization a lot of work, especially if you routinely have to retrieve lost, overwritten, or corrupted data files from backup. The normal procedure for retrieving shadow copies is to use the Previous Versions or Shadow Copy client. Windows Server 2003 R2 includes a feature enhancement that allows you to revert an entire (nonsystem) volume to a previous shadow copy state.

Understanding Shadow Copies

You can create shadow copies only on NTFS volumes. On NTFS volumes, you use the Shadow Copy feature to create automatic backups of the files in shared folders on a per volume basis. For example, if a file server has three NTFS volumes, each containing shared folders, you'd need to configure this feature for each volume separately.

If you enable this feature in the default configuration, shadow copies are created twice each weekday (Monday–Friday) at 7:00 A.M. and 12:00 P.M. You need at least 100 megabytes (MB) of free space to create the first shadow copy on a volume. The total disk space used beyond this depends on the amount of data in the volume's shared folders. You can restrict the total amount of disk space used by Shadow Copy by setting the allowable maximum size of the point-in-time backups.

You configure and view current Shadow Copy settings using the Shadow Copies tab of the disk properties dialog box. Right-click the icon for the disk you want to work with in Windows Explorer or Computer Management, select Properties, and then click the Shadow Copies tab. The Select A Volume panel shows:

Volume   Volume label of NTFS volumes on the selected disk drive

Next Run Time   The status of Shadow Copy as Disabled or the next time a Shadow Copy of the volume will be created

Shares   Number of shared folders on the volume

Used   Amount of disk space used by Shadow Copy

Individual shadow copies of the currently selected volume are listed in the Shadow Copies Of Selected Volume panel by date and time.

Creating Shadow Copies

To create a shadow copy on an NTFS volume with shared folders, follow these steps:

1. Start Computer Management. If necessary, connect to a remote computer.

2. In the console tree, expand Storage and then select Disk Management. The volumes configured on the selected computer are displayed in the details pane.

3. Right-click Disk Management, point to All Tasks, and then select Configure Shadow Copies.

4. In the Shadow Copies tab, select the volume with which you want to work in the Select A Volume list.

5. Click Settings to configure the maximum size of all shadow copies for this volume and to change the default schedule. When you're finished, click OK twice.

6. If necessary, click Enable after you've configured the volume for shadow copying. When prompted to confirm this action, click Yes. This creates the first shadow copy and sets the schedule for later shadow copies.

Note   If you create a run schedule when configuring the shadow copy settings, shadow copying is enabled automatically for the volume when you click OK to close the Settings dialog box.

Restoring a Shadow Copy

Users on client computers access shadow copies of individual shared folders using the Previous Versions or Shadow Copy client. The Previous Versions client is stored in the %SystemRoot%\System32\Clients\Twclient\X86 folder and its installer is named Twcli32.msi. The Shadow Copy client can be downloaded from the Microsoft Web site and its installer is named ShadowCopyClient.msi. After you install these clients, the best way to access shadow copies on a client computer is to follow these steps:

1. In My Network Places, expand Entire Network and Microsoft Windows Network to display the available domains, and then expand the domain node to display servers on the network.

2. When you expand a server node, any publicly shared resources on that server are listed. Right-click the share for which you want to access previous file versions, choose Properties, and then click the Previous Versions tab.

3. After you access the Previous Versions tab, select the folder version that you want to work with. Each folder has a date and time stamp. Then click the button corresponding to the action you want to perform:

    ❑   Click View to open the shadow copy in Windows Explorer.

    ❑   Click Copy to display the Copy Items dialog box, which lets you copy the snapshot image of the folder to the location you specify.

    ❑   Click Restore to roll back the shared folder to its state as of the snapshot image you selected.

Reverting An Entire Volume to a Previous Shadow Copy

Windows Server 2003 R2 features a shadow copy enhancement that allows you to revert an entire volume to the state it was in when a particular shadow copy was created.

As volumes containing operating system files can't be reverted, the volume you want to revert must not be a system volume.

To revert an entire volume to a previous state, follow these steps:

1. Start Computer Management. If necessary, connect to a remote computer.

2. In the console tree, expand Storage. Right-click Disk Management, point to All Tasks, and then select Configure Shadow Copies.

3. In the Shadow Copies tab, select the volume you want to work with in the Select A Volume list.

4. Individual shadow copies of the currently selected volume are listed in the Shadow Copies Of Selected Volume panel by date and time. Select the shadow copy with the date and timestamp to which you want to revert and then click Revert. To confirm this action, select the Check Here If You Want To Revert This Volume check box and then click Revert Now. Click OK to close the Shadow Copies dialog box.

Deleting Shadow Copies

Each point-in-time backup is maintained separately. You can delete individual shadow copies of a volume as necessary. This recovers the disk space used by the shadow copies.

To delete a shadow copy, follow these steps:

1. Start Computer Management. If necessary, connect to a remote computer.

2. In the console tree, expand Storage. Right-click Disk Management, point to All Tasks, and then select Configure Shadow Copies.

3. In the Shadow Copies tab, select the volume you want to work with in the Select A Volume list.

4. Individual shadow copies of the currently selected volume are listed in the Shadow Copies Of Selected Volume panel by date and time. Select the shadow copy you want to delete and then click Delete Now.

Disabling Shadow Copies

If you no longer want to maintain shadow copies of a volume, you can disable the Shadow Copy feature. Disabling this feature turns off the scheduling of automated point-in-time backups and removes any existing shadow copies.

To disable shadow copies of a volume, follow these steps:

1. Start Computer Management. If necessary, connect to a remote computer.

2. In the console tree, expand Storage. Right-click Disk Management, point to All Tasks, and then select Configure Shadow Copies.

3. In the Shadow Copies tab, select the volume you want to work with in the Select A Volume list and then click Disable.

4. When prompted, confirm the action by clicking Yes. Click OK to close the Shadow Copies dialog box.

Connecting to Network Drives

Users can connect to a network drive and to shared resources available on the network. This connection is shown as a network drive that users can access like any other drive on their systems.

Note When users connect to network drives, they're subject not only to the permissions set for the shared resources, but also to Windows Server 2003 file and folder permissions. Differences in these permission sets are usually the reason users might not be able to access a particular file or subfolder within the network drive.

Mapping a Network Drive

In Windows Server 2003, you connect to a network drive by mapping to it using NET USE and the following syntax:

```
net use Device \\ComputerName\ShareName
```

where Device specifies the drive letter or * to use the next available drive letter and \\ComputerName\ShareName is the UNC path to the share, such as:

```
net use g: \\ROMEO\DOCS
```

Or

```
net use *  \\ROMEO\DOCS
```

Note To ensure the mapped drive is available each time the user logs in, make the mapping persistent by adding the /Persistent:Yes option.

Another way to map network drives is to follow these steps:

1. While the user is logged on, start Windows Explorer on the user's computer.

2. From the Tools menu, select Map Network Drive. This opens the Map Network Drive page.

3. Using the Drive drop-down list, you can now create a network drive for a shared resource. Select a free drive letter to create a network drive that can be accessed in Windows Explorer and My Computer. Select (None) to create a network drive without assigning a drive letter. This drive is opened in its own Windows Explorer window and can't be accessed from My Computer.

4. In the Folder text box, type the UNC path to the desired share. For example, to access a share called DOCS on a server called ROMEO, you'd use the path

\\ROMEO\DOCS. If you don't know the share location, click Browse to search for available shares. After selecting the appropriate share, click OK to close the Browse For Folder dialog box.

5. If you want the network drive to be automatically connected in subsequent sessions, select the Reconnect At Logon check box. Otherwise, clear this check box to later establish a connection whenever you double-click the network drive.

6. To connect using a different user name from the logon name, click Different User Name, and then type a user name and password for the connection. Click OK to close the Connect As dialog box.

7. Click Finish to map the network drive.

Disconnecting a Network Drive

To disconnect a network drive, follow these steps:

1. While the user is logged on, start Windows Explorer on the user's computer.

2. From the Tools menu, select Disconnect Network Drive. This opens the Disconnect Network Drive dialog box.

3. Select the drive you want to disconnect, and then click OK.

Object Management, Ownership, and Inheritance

Windows Server 2003 takes an object-based approach to describing resources and managing permissions. Objects that describe resources are defined on NTFS volumes and in Active Directory. With NTFS volumes, you can set permissions for files and folders. With Active Directory, you can set permissions for other types of objects, such as users, computers, and groups. You can use these permissions to control access with precision.

Objects and Object Managers

Whether defined on an NTFS volume or in Active Directory, each type of object has an object manager and primary management tools. The object manager controls object settings and permissions. The primary management tools are the tools of choice for working with the object. Objects, their managers, and management tools are summarized in Table 14-2.

Table 14-2   Windows Server 2003 Objects

Object Type	Object Manager	Management Tool
Files and folders	NTFS	Windows Explorer
Shares	Server service	Windows Explorer; Computer Management
Registry keys	Windows registry	Registry Editor

Table 14-2   Windows Server 2003 Objects

Object Type	Object Manager	Management Tool
Services	Service controllers	Security Configuration Tool Set
Printers	Print spooler	Printers in Control Panel

Object Ownership and Transfer

It's important to understand the concept of object ownership. In Windows Server 2003, the object owner isn't necessarily the object's creator. Instead, the object owner is the person who has direct control over the object. Object owners can grant access permissions and give other users permission to take ownership of the object.

As an administrator, you can take ownership of objects on the network. This ensures that authorized administrators can't be locked out of files, folders, printers, and other resources. After you take ownership of files, however, you can't return ownership to the original owner (in most cases). This prevents administrators from accessing files and then trying to hide the fact.

The way ownership is assigned initially depends on the location of the resource being created. In most cases, however, the Administrators group is listed as the current owner and the object's actual creator is listed as a person who can take ownership.

Ownership can be transferred in several ways:

- If Administrators is initially assigned as the owner, the creator of the object can take ownership, provided he or she does this before someone else takes ownership.

- The current owner can grant the Take Ownership permission to other users, allowing those users to take ownership of the object.

- An administrator can take ownership of an object, provided the object is under his or her administrative control.

To take ownership of an object, follow these steps:

1. Start the management tool for the object. For example, if you want to work with files and folders, start Windows Explorer.

2. Right-click the object of which you want to take ownership.

3. From the shortcut menu, select Properties, and then, in the Properties dialog box, click the Security tab.

4. Display the Access Security Settings dialog box by clicking Advanced. Then click the Owner tab, shown in Figure 14-9.

5. Select the new owner in the Change Owner To list box, and then click OK.

> **Tip**   If you're taking ownership of a folder, you can take ownership of all subfolders and files within the folder by selecting the Replace Owner On Sub-containers And Objects check box. This option also works with objects that contain other objects. Here, you'd take ownership of all child objects.

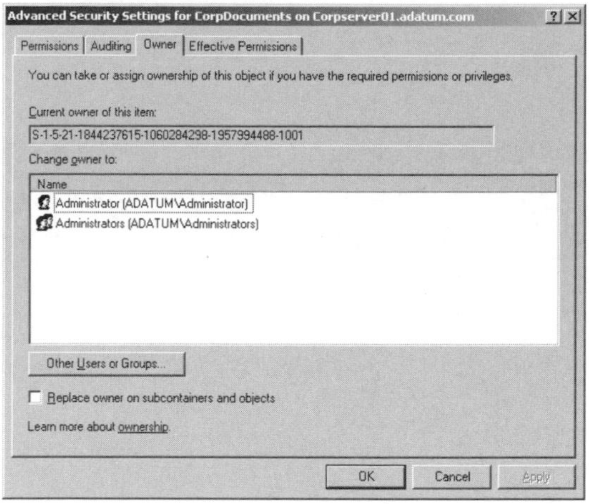

Figure 14-9   Use the Owner tab to change ownership of a file.

Object Inheritance

Objects are defined using a parent-child structure. A parent object is a top-level object. A child object is an object defined below a parent object in the hierarchy. For example, the folder C:\ is the parent of the folders C:\data and C:\backups. Any subfolders created in C:\data or C:\backups are children of these folders and grandchildren of C:\.

Child objects can inherit permissions from parent objects. In fact, all Windows Server 2003 objects are created with inheritance enabled by default. This means that child objects automatically inherit the permissions of the parent. Because of this, the parent object permissions control access to the child object. If you want to change permissions on a child object, you must:

- Edit the permissions of the parent object.

- Stop inheriting permissions from the parent object, and then assign permissions to the child object.

- Select the opposite permission to override the inherited permission. For example, if the parent allows the permission, you'd deny it on the child object.

To start or stop inheriting permissions from a parent object, follow these steps:

1 Start the management tool for the object. For example, if you want to work with files and folders, start Windows Explorer.

2. Right-click the object with which you want to work.

3. From the shortcut menu, select Properties, and then, in the Properties dialog box, click the Security tab.

4. Display the Advanced Security Settings dialog box by clicking Advanced.

5. In the Permissions tab, select or clear the Allow Inheritable Permissions From The Parent To Propagate To This Object And All Child Objects check box as appropriate. Click OK.

File and Folder Permissions

On NTFS volumes, you can set security permissions on files and folders. These permissions grant or deny access to the files and folders. You can view security permissions for files and folders by completing the following steps:

1. In Windows Explorer, right-click the file or folder with which you want to work.

2. From the shortcut menu, select Properties, and then, in the Properties dialog box, click the Security tab.

3. In the Name list box, select the user, computer, or group whose permissions you want to view. If the permissions are dimmed, it means the permissions are inherited from a parent object.

Understanding File and Folder Permissions

The basic permissions you can assign to files and folders are summarized in Table 14-3. File permissions include Full Control, Modify, Read & Execute, Read, and Write. Folder permissions include Full Control, Modify, Read & Execute, List Folder Contents, Read, and Write.

Table 14-3   File and Folder Permissions Used by Windows Server 2003

Permission	Meaning for Folders	Meaning for Files
Read	Permits viewing and listing files and subfolders	Permits viewing or accessing the file's contents
Write	Permits adding files and subfolders	Permits writing to a file
Read & Execute	Permits viewing and listing files and subfolders as well as executing files; inherited by files and folders	Permits viewing and accessing the file's contents as well as executing the file
List Folder Contents	Permits viewing and listing files and subfolders as well as executing files; inherited by folders only	N/A
Modify	Permits reading and writing of files and subfolders; allows deletion of the folder	Permits reading and writing of the file; allows deletion of the file
Full Control	Permits reading, writing, changing, and deleting files and subfolders	Permits reading, writing, changing, and deleting the file

Anytime you work with file and folder permissions, you should keep the following in mind:

- Read is the only permission needed to run scripts. Execute permission doesn't matter.

- Read access is required to access a shortcut and its target.

- Giving a user permission to write to a file but not to delete it doesn't prevent the user from deleting the file's contents. A user can still delete the contents.

- If a user has full control over a folder, the user can delete files in the folder regardless of the permission on the files.

The basic permissions are created by combining special permissions in logical groups. Table 14-4 shows special permissions used to create the basic permissions for files. Using advanced permission settings, you can assign these special permissions individually, if necessary. As you study the special permissions, keep the following in mind:

- By default, if no access is specifically granted or denied, the user is denied access.

- Actions that users can perform are based on the sum of all the permissions assigned to the user and to all the groups of which the user is a member. For example, if the user GeorgeJ has Read access and is a member of the group Techies that has Change access, GeorgeJ will have Change access. If Techies is in turn a member of Administrators, which has Full Control, GeorgeJ will have complete control over the file.

Table 14-4   Special Permissions for Files

Special Permissions	Basic Permissions				
	Full Control	Modify	Read & Execute	Read	Write
Traverse Folder/Execute File	Yes	Yes	Yes		
List Folder/Read Data	Yes	Yes	Yes	Yes	
Read Attributes	Yes	Yes	Yes	Yes	
Read Extended Attributes	Yes	Yes	Yes	Yes	
Create Files/Write Data	Yes	Yes			Yes
Create Folders/Append Data	Yes	Yes			Yes
Write Attributes	Yes	Yes			Yes
Write Extended Attributes	Yes	Yes			Yes
Delete Subfolders and Files	Yes				

Table 14-4   Special Permissions for Files

Special Permissions	Basic Permissions				
	Full Control	Modify	Read & Execute	Read	Write
Delete	Yes	Yes			
Read Permissions	Yes	Yes	Yes	Yes	Yes
Change Permissions	Yes				
Take Ownership	Yes				

Table 14-5 shows special permissions used to create the basic permissions for folders. As you study the special permissions, keep the following in mind:

- When you set permissions for parent folders, you can force all files and subfolders within the folder to inherit the permissions. You do this by selecting Reset Permissions On All Child Objects And Enable Propagation Of Inheritable Permissions.

- When you create files in folders, these files inherit certain permission settings. These permission settings are shown as the default file permissions.

Table 14-5   Special Permissions for Folders

Special Permissions	Basic Permissions					
	Full Control	Modify	Read & Execute	List Folder Contents	Read	Write
Traverse Folder/Execute File	Yes	Yes	Yes	Yes		
List Folder/Read Data	Yes	Yes	Yes	Yes	Yes	
Read Attributes	Yes	Yes	Yes	Yes	Yes	
Read Extended Attributes	Yes	Yes	Yes	Yes	Yes	
Create Files/Write Data	Yes	Yes				Yes
Create Folders/ Append Data	Yes	Yes				Yes
Write Attributes	Yes	Yes				Yes
Write Extended Attributes	Yes	Yes				Yes
Delete Subfolders And Files	Yes					
Delete	Yes	Yes				

Table 14-5   Special Permissions for Folders

Special Permissions	Basic Permissions					
	Full Control	Modify	Read & Execute	List Folder Contents	Read	Write
Read Permissions	Yes	Yes	Yes	Yes	Yes	Yes
Change Permissions	Yes					
Take Ownership	Yes					

Setting File and Folder Permissions

To set permissions for files and folders, follow these steps:

1. In Windows Explorer, right-click the file or folder with which you want to work.

2. From the shortcut menu, select Properties, and then, in the Properties dialog box, click the Security tab, shown in Figure 14-10.

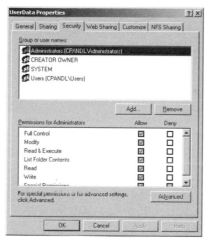

Figure 14-10   Use the Security tab to configure basic permissions for the file or folder.

3. Users or groups that already have access to the file or folder are listed in the Name list box. You can change permissions for these users and groups by doing the following:

   a.   Select the user or group you want to change.

   b.   Use the Permissions list box to grant or deny access permissions.

   Tip   Inherited permissions are shaded. If you want to override an inherited permission, select the opposite permission.

4. To set access permissions for additional users, computers, or groups, click Add. This displays the Select Users, Computers, Or Groups dialog box shown in Figure 14-11.

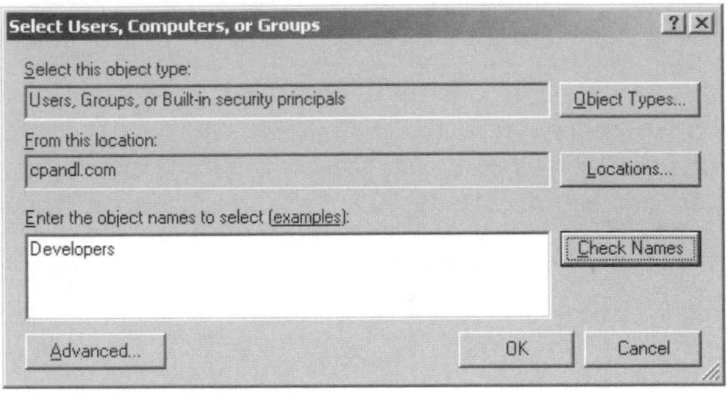

Figure 14-11   Use the Select Users, Computers, Or Groups dialog box to select users, computers, and groups that should be granted or denied access.

5. Type the name of a user, computer, or group in the current domain and then click Check Names.

   ❑ If a single match is found, the dialog box is automatically updated as appropriate and the entry is underlined.

   ❑ If no matches are found, you've either entered an incorrect name part or you're working with an incorrect location. Modify the name and try again, or click Locations to select a new location.

   ❑ If multiple matches are found, select the name(s) you want to use and then click OK. To add more users, computers, or groups, type a semicolon (;) and then repeat this step.

   Note   The Locations button allows you to access account names from other domains. Click Locations to see a list of the current domain, trusted domains, and other resources that you can access. Because of the transitive trusts in Windows Server 2003, you can usually access all the domains in the domain tree or forest.

6. In the Name list box, select the user, computer, or group you want to configure, and then use the check boxes in the Permissions area to allow or deny permissions. Repeat for other users, computers, or groups. Click OK when you're finished.

Auditing System Resources

Auditing is the best way to track what's happening on your Windows Server 2003 systems. You can use auditing to collect information related to resource usage, such as file access, system logon, and system configuration changes. Any time an action occurs that you've configured for auditing, the action is written to the system's security log, where it's stored for your review. The security log is accessible from Event Viewer.

Note   For most auditing changes, you'll need to be logged on using an account that's a member of the Administrators group or be granted the Manage Auditing And Security Log right in Group Policy.

Setting Auditing Policies

Auditing policies are essential to ensure the security and integrity of your systems. Just about every computer system on the network should be configured with some type of security logging. You configure auditing policies for individual machines with local Group Policy and for all machines in domains with Active Directory Group Policy. Through Group Policy, you can set auditing policies for an entire site, domain, or organizational unit. You can also set policies for an individual workstation or server.

After you access the Group Policy container with which you want to work, you can set auditing policies by completing the following steps:

1. As shown in Figure 14-12, access the Audit Policy node by working your way down through the console tree. Expand Computer Configuration, Windows Settings, Security Settings, and Local Policies. Then select Audit Policy.

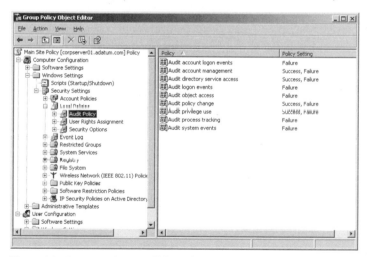

Figure 14-12   Set auditing policies using the Audit Policy node in Group Policy.

2. The auditing options are as follows:

   Audit Account Logon Events   Tracks events related to user logon and logoff.

   Audit Account Management   Tracks account management by means of Active Directory Users And Computers. Events are generated any time user, computer, or group accounts are created, modified, or deleted.

Audit Directory Service Access   Tracks access to Active Directory. Events are generated any time users or computers access the directory.

Audit Logon Events   Tracks events related to user logon, logoff, and remote connections to network systems.

Audit Object Access   Tracks system resource usage for files, directories, shares, printers, and Active Directory objects.

Audit Policy Change   Tracks changes to user rights, auditing, and trust relationships.

Audit Privilege Use   Tracks the use of user rights and privileges, such as the right to back up files and directories.

> **Note**   The Audit Privilege Use policy doesn't track system access–related events, such as the use of the right to log on interactively or the right to access the computer from the network. You track these events with Logon and Logoff auditing.

Audit Process Tracking   Tracks system processes and the resources they use.

Audit System Events   Tracks system startup, shutdown, and restart, as well as actions that affect system security or the security log.

3. To configure an auditing policy, double-click its entry or right-click and select Properties. This opens a properties dialog box for the policy.

4. Select the Define These Policy Settings check box, and then select either the Success check box or the Failure check box, or both. Success logs successful events, such as successful logon attempts. Failure logs failed events, such as failed logon attempts.

5. Click OK when you're finished.

When auditing is enabled, the Security Event log will reflect the following:

- Event ID of 560 and 562 detailing User audits
- Event ID of 592 and 593 detailing Process audits

Auditing Files and Folders

If you configure a group policy to enable the Audit Object Access option, you can set the level of auditing for individual folders and files. This allows you to control precisely how folder and file usage is tracked. Auditing of this type is available only on NTFS volumes.

You can configure file and folder auditing by completing the following steps:

1. In Windows Explorer, right-click the file or folder to be audited, and then, from the shortcut menu, select Properties.

2. Click the Security tab and then click Advanced.

3. In the Access Control Settings dialog box, click the Auditing tab, shown in Figure 14-13.

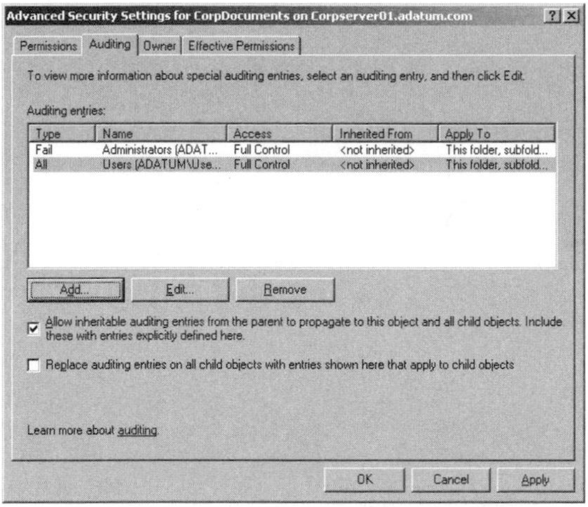

Figure 14-13   After you audit object access, you can use the Auditing tab to set auditing policies on individual files and folders.

4. If you want to inherit auditing settings from a parent object, ensure that the Allow Inheritable Permissions From The Parent To Propagate To This Object And All Child Objects check box is selected.

5. If you want child objects of the current object to inherit the settings, select the Replace Auditing Entries On All Child Objects With Entries Shown Here That Apply To Child Objects check box.

6. Use the Auditing Entries list box to select the users, groups, or computers whose actions you want to audit. To remove an account, select the account in the Auditing Entries list box, and then click Remove.

7. To add specific accounts, click Add, and then use the Select User, Computer, Or Group dialog box to select an account name to add. When you click OK, you'll see the Auditing Entry For ... dialog box, shown in Figure 14-14.

> **Tip**   If you want to audit actions for all users, use the special group Everyone. Otherwise, select the specific user groups or users, or both, that you want to audit.

8. As necessary, use the Apply Onto drop-down list to specify where objects are audited.

9. Select the Successful or Failed check boxes, or both, for each of the events you want to audit. Successful logs successful events, such as successful file reads.

Failed logs failed events, such as failed file deletions. The events you can audit are the same as the special permissions listed in Table 14-5—except you can't audit synchronizing of offline files and folders. For essential files and folders, you'll typically want to track:

❑   Write Attributes – Successful

❑   Write Extended Attributes – Successful

❑   Delete Subfolders and Files – Successful

❑   Delete – Successful

❑   Change Permissions – Successful

10.   Clear the Allow Inheritable Auditing Entries From Parent To Propagate To This Object checkbox.

11.   Click OK when you're finished. Repeat this process to audit other users, groups, or computers.

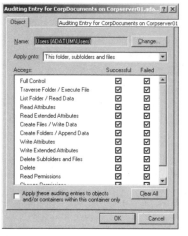

Figure 14-14   Use the Auditing Entry For... dialog box to set auditing entries for a user, computer, or group.

Auditing the Registry

If you configure a group policy to enable the Audit Object Access option, you can set the level of auditing for keys within the Registry. This allows you to track when key values are set, when subkeys are created, and when keys are deleted.

You can configure Registry auditing by completing the following steps:

1.   At a command prompt, type **regedit**.

2.   Browse to a key you want to audit. On the Edit menu, select Permissions.

3. Click Advanced. In the Advanced Security Settings For ... dialog box, select the Auditing tab.

4. Click Add. In the Select User, Computer, Or Group dialog box, type **Everyone**, click Check Names, and then click OK.

5. In the Auditing Entries For ... dialog box, choose the actions you want to audit. Typically, you'll want to track:

   ❑ Set Value – Successful and Failed

   ❑ Create Subkey – Successful and Failed

   ❑ Delete – Successful and Failed

6. Click OK.

7. Clear the Allow Inheritable Auditing Entries From Parent To Propagate To This Object check box.

8. Click OK twice to close all open dialog boxes and apply the auditing settings.

Auditing Active Directory Objects

If you configure a group policy to enable the Audit Directory Service Access option, you can set the level of auditing for Active Directory objects. This allows you to control precisely how object usage is tracked.

To configure object auditing, follow these steps:

1. In Active Directory Users And Computers, access the container for the object.

2. Right-click the object to be audited, and then, from the shortcut menu, select Properties.

3. Click the Security tab, and then click Advanced.

4. In the Access Security Settings dialog box, click the Auditing tab. To inherit auditing settings from a parent object, make sure that the Allow Inheritable Permissions From The Parent To Propagate To This Object And All Child Objects check box is selected.

5. Use the Auditing Entries list box to select the users, groups, or computers whose actions you want to audit. To remove an account, select the account in the Auditing Entries list box and then click Remove.

6. To add specific accounts, click Add, and then use the Select User, Computer, Or Group dialog box to select an account name to add. When you click OK, the Auditing Entry For dialog box is displayed.

7. Use the Apply Onto drop-down list to specify where objects are audited.

8. Select the Successful or Failed check boxes, or both, for each of the events you want to audit. Successful logs successful events, such as a successful attempt to

modify an object's permissions. Failed logs failed events, such as a failure to modify an object's owner.

9. Click OK when you're finished. Repeat this process to audit other users, groups, or computers.

Using, Configuring, and Managing NTFS Disk Quotas

Windows Server 2003 supports two different types of disk quotas:

NTFS Disk Quotas   NTFS disk quotas are supported with all versions of Windows Server 2003 and allow you to manage disk space usage by users. You configure quotas on a per volume basis. Although users who exceed limits will see warnings, administrator notification is primarily through the event logs.

Storage Resource Manager Disk Quotas   Storage Resource Manager disk quotas are supported in Windows Server 2003 R2 and allow you to manage disk space usage by folder and by volume. Users who are approaching or have exceeded a limit can be automatically notified by e-mail. The notification system also allows for notifying administrators by e-mail, triggering incident reporting, running commands, and logging related events.

The sections that follow discuss NTFS disk quotas.

Note   Regardless of the quota system being used, you can configure quotas only for NTFS volumes. You can't create quotas for FAT or FAT32 volumes.

Understanding NTFS Disk Quotas and How NTFS Quotas Are Used

Administrators use NTFS disk quotas to manage disk space usage for critical volumes, such as those that provide corporate data shares or user data shares. When you enable NTFS disk quotas, you can configure two values:

Disk quota limit   Sets the upper boundary for space usage, which you can use to prevent users from writing additional information to a volume and to log events regarding the user exceeding the limit, or both.

Disk quota warning   Warns users and logs warning events when users are getting close to their disk quota limit.

Tip   You can set disk quotas but not enforce them, but you might be wondering why you'd do this. Sometimes you want to track disk space usage on a per-user basis and know when they've exceeded some predefined limit, but instead of denying them additional disk space, you log an event in the application log to track the overage. You can then send out warning messages or figure out other ways to reduce the space usage.

NTFS disk quotas apply only to end users. NTFS disk quotas don't apply to administrators. Administrators can't be denied disk space even if they exceed enforced disk quota limits.

In a typical environment, you'll restrict disk space usage in MB or GB. For example, on a corporate data share that's used by multiple users in a department, you might want to limit disk space usage to 20 to 100 GB. For a user data share, you might want to set the level much lower, such as 5 to 20 GB, which would restrict the user from creating large amounts of personal data. Often you'll set the disk quota warning as a percentage of the disk quota limit. For example, you might set the warning to 90 to 95 percent of the disk quota limit.

Because NTFS disk quotas are tracked on a per-volume, per-user basis, disk space used by one user doesn't affect the disk quotas for other users. Thus, if one user exceeds his or her limit, any restrictions applied to this user don't apply to other users. For example, if a user exceeds a 1 GB disk quota limit and the volume is configured to prevent writing over the limit, the user can no longer write data to the volume. Users can, however, remove files and folders from the volume to free up disk space. They could also move files and folders to a compressed area on the volume, which might free up space, or they could elect to compress the files themselves. Moving files to a different location on the volume doesn't affect the quota restriction. The amount of file space will be the same unless the user is moving uncompressed files and folders to a folder with compression. In any case, the restriction on a single user doesn't affect other users' ability to write to the volume (as long as there's free space on the volume).

You can enable NTFS disk quotas on the following:

Local volumes   To manage disk quotas on local volumes, you work with the local disk itself. When you enable disk quotas on a local volume, the Windows systems files are included in the volume usage for the user who installed those files. Sometimes this might cause the user to go over the disk quota limit. To prevent this, you might want to set a higher limit on a local workstation volume.

Remote volumes   To manage disk quotas on remote volumes, you must share the root directory for the volume and then set the disk quota on the volume. Remember, quotas are set on a per volume basis, so if a remote file server has separate volumes for different types of data—that is, a corporate data volume and a user data volume—these volumes have different quotas.

Only members of the domain Administrators group or the local system Administrators group can configure disk quotas. The first step in using quotas is to enable quotas in Group Policy. You can do this at two levels.

Local   Through local group policy, you can enable disk quotas for an individual computer.

Enterprise   Through site, domain, and organizational unit policy you can enable disk quotas for groups of users and computers.

Having to keep track of disk quotas does cause some overhead on computers. This overhead is a function of the number of disk quotas being enforced, the total size of volumes and their data, and the number of users to which the disk quotas apply.

Although on the surface disk quotas are tracked per user, behind the scenes Windows Server 2003 manages disk quotas according to security identifiers (SIDs). Because SIDs track disk quotas, you can safely modify user names without affecting the disk quota configuration. Tracking by SIDs does cause some additional overhead when viewing disk quota statistics for users. That's because Windows Server 2003 must correlate SIDs to user account names so that the account names can be displayed in dialog boxes. This means contacting the local user manager and the Active Directory domain controller as necessary.

After Windows Server 2003 looks up names, it caches them to a local file so that they can be available immediately the next time they're needed. The query cache is infrequently updated, and if you notice a discrepancy between what's displayed and what's configured, you'll need to refresh the information. Usually, this means selecting Refresh or pressing F5 in the current window.

Setting NTFS Disk Quota Policies

The best way to configure NTFS disk quotas is through Group Policy. When you configure disk quotas through local policy or through unit, domain, and site policy, you define general policies that are set automatically when you enable quota management on individual volumes. Thus, rather than having to configure each volume separately, you can use the same set of rules and apply them to each volume you want to manage in turn.

Policies that control NTFS disk quotas are applied at the system level. You access these policies through Computer Configuration\Administrative Templates\System\Disk Quotas. Table 14-6 summarizes the available policies.

Table 14-6   Policies for Setting NTFS Disk Quotas

Policy Name	Description
Enable Disk Quotas	Turns disk quotas on or off for all NTFS volumes of the computer and prevents users from changing the setting.
Enforce Disk Quota Limit	Specifies whether quota limits are enforced. If quotas are enforced, users will be denied disk space if they exceed the quota. This overrides settings in the Quota tab on the NTFS volume.
Default Quota Limit And Warning Level	Sets a default quota limit and warning level for all users. This setting overrides other settings and affects only new users.
Log Event When Quota Limit Exceeded	Determines whether an event is logged when users reach their limit and prevents users from changing their logging options.
Log Event When Quota Warning Level Exceeded	Determines whether an event is logged when users reach the warning level.

Table 14-6   Policies for Setting NTFS Disk Quotas

Policy Name	Description
Apply Policy To Removable Media	Determines whether quota policies apply to NTFS volumes on removable media. If you don't enable this policy, quota limits apply only to fixed media drives.

Whenever you work with quota limits, you'll want to use a standard set of policies on all systems. Typically, you won't want to enable all the policies. Instead, you'll selectively enable policies and then use the standard NTFS features to control quotas on various volumes. If you want to enable quota limits, use the following technique:

1. Access Group Policy for the system with which you want to work, such as a file server. Then, access the Disk Quotas node by expanding Computer Configuration \Administrative Templates\System and then selecting Disk Quotas.

2. Double-click Enable Disk Quotas, and then, in the Setting tab, choose Enabled. Click Next Setting. This displays the Enforce Disk Quota Limit policy.

3. If you want to enforce disk quotas on all NTFS volumes residing on this computer, click Enabled. Otherwise, click Disabled and then set specific limits on a per volume basis.

4. Click Next Setting. This displays the Default Quota Limit And Warning Level Properties dialog box. Select Enabled.

5. Under Default Quota Limit, set a default limit that's applied to users when they first write to the quota-enabled volume. The limit doesn't apply to current users or affect current limits in place. On a corporate share, such as a share used by all members of a team, a good limit is between 500 and 1000 MB. Of course, this depends on the size of the data files that the users routinely work with. Graphic designers and data engineers might need much more disk space.

6. If you scroll down in the subwindow provided in the Setting tab, you'll be able to set a warning limit as well. A good warning limit is about 90 percent of the default quota limit, which means that if you set the default quota limit to 1000 MB, you'd set the warning limit to 900 MB.

7. Click Next Setting. This displays the Log Event When Quota Limit Exceeded policy. Select Enabled so that limit events are recorded in the Application log.

8. Click Next Setting. This displays the Log Event When Quota Warning Level Exceeded policy. Select Enabled so that warning events are recorded in the Application log.

9. Click Next Setting. This displays the Apply Policy To Removable Media policy. Select Disabled so that the quota limits apply only to fixed media volumes on the computer. Click OK.

> **Tip**   To ensure that the policies are enforced immediately, access the Computer Configuration\Administrative Templates\System\Group Policy node and

then double-click Disk Quota Policy Processing. Next, select Enabled and then select the Process Even If The Group Policy Objects Have Not Changed check box. Click OK.

Enabling NTFS Disk Quotas on NTFS Volumes

You can set NTFS disk quotas on a per-volume basis. Only NTFS volumes can have disk quotas. After you've configured the appropriate group policies, you can set disk quotas for local and remote volumes using Computer Management.

Note   If quotas are enforced using the Enforce Disk Quota Limit policy setting, users will be denied disk space if they exceed the quota. This overrides settings in the Quota tab on the NTFS volume.

To enable NTFS disk quotas on an NTFS volume, follow these steps:

1. Start Computer Management. If necessary, connect to a remote computer.

2. In the console tree, expand Storage and then select Disk Management. The volumes configured on the selected computer are displayed in the details pane.

3. Using the Volume List or Graphical View, right-click the volume you want to work with and then select Properties.

4. Click the Quota tab and then select the Enable Quota Management check box, as shown in Figure 14-15. If you've already set quota management values through Group Policy, the options are dimmed and you can't change them. You must modify options through Group Policy instead.

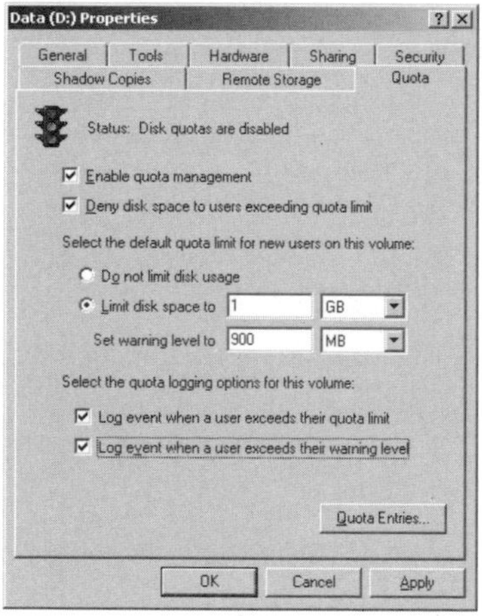

Figure 14-15   After you enable quota management, you can configure a quota limit and quota warning for all users. If you've already set these values through Group Policy, the options are dimmed and you can't change them.

Best Practices   Whenever you work with the Quota tab, pay particular attention to the Status text and the associated traffic light icon. Both change based on the state of quota management. If quotas aren't configured, the traffic light icon shows a red light and the status shows as inactive or not configured. If the operating system is working or updating the quotas, the traffic light icon shows a yellow light and the status shows the activity being performed. If quotas are configured, the traffic light icon shows a green light and the status text states that the quota system is active.

5. To set a default disk quota limit for all users, select Limit Disk Space To and then use the text boxes provided to set a limit in KB, MB, GB, TB, PB, or EB. Afterward, use the Set Warning Level To text boxes to set the default warning limit. Again, you'll usually want the disk quota warning limit to be 90–95 percent of the disk quota limit.

> **Tip**   Although the default quota limit and warning applies to all users, you can configure different levels for individual users. You do this through the Quota Entries dialog box. If you create many unique quota entries and don't want to recreate them on a volume with similar characteristics and usage, you can export the quota entries and import them on a different volume.

6. To enforce the disk quota limit and prevent users from going over the limit, select the Deny Disk Space To Users Exceeding Quota Limit check box. Keep in mind that this creates an actual physical limitation for users (but not administrators).

7. To configure logging when users exceed a warning limit or the quota limit, select the Log Event check boxes. Click OK to save your changes.

8. If the quota system isn't currently enabled, you'll see a prompt asking you to enable the quota system. Click OK to allow Windows Server 2003 to rescan the volume and update disk usage statistics. Actions might be taken against users who exceed the current limit or warning levels. These actions can include preventing additional writing to the volume, notifying them the next time they access the volume, and logging applicable events in the Application log.

Viewing Disk Quota Entries

Disk space usage is tracked on a per user basis. When disk quotas are enabled, each user storing data on a volume has an entry in the disk quota file. This entry is updated periodically to show the current disk space used, the applicable quota limit, the applicable warning level, and the percentage of allowable space being used. As an administrator, you can modify disk quota entries to set different limits and warning levels for particular users. You can also create disk quota entries for users who haven't yet saved data on a volume. The key reason for creating entries is to ensure that when a user does make use of a volume, the user has an appropriate limit and warning level.

To view the current disk quota entries for a volume, follow these steps:

1. Start Computer Management. If necessary, connect to a remote computer.

2. In the console tree, expand Storage and then select Disk Management. The volumes configured on the selected computer are displayed in the details pane.

3. Using the Volume List or Graphical View, right-click the volume with which you want to work and then select Properties.

4. In the Quota tab, click Quota Entries. This displays the Quota Entries dialog box. Each quota entry is listed according to a status. The status is meant to quickly depict whether a user has gone over a limit. A status of OK means the user is working within the quota boundaries. Any other status usually means the user has reached the warning level or the quota limit.

Creating Disk Quota Entries

You can create disk quota entries for users who haven't yet saved data on a volume. This allows you to set custom limits and warning levels for a particular user. You'll usually use this feature when a user frequently stores more information than other users and you want to allow the user to go over the normal limit or when you want to set a specific limit for administrators. As you might recall, administrators aren't subject to disk quota limits, so if you want to enforce limits for individual administrators, you must create disk quota entries for each administrator you want to limit.

> **Real World**   You shouldn't create individual disk quota entries haphazardly. You need to track individual entries carefully. Ideally, you'll keep a log that details any individual entries so that other administrators understand the policies in place and how those policies are applied. When you modify the base rules for quotas on a volume, you should reexamine individual entries to see if they're still applicable or need to be updated as well. I've found that certain types of users are exceptions more often than not and that it's sometimes better to put different classes of users on different volumes and then apply disk quotas to each volume. In this way, each class or category of user has a quota limit that's appropriate for its members' typical usage and you have fewer (perhaps no) exceptions. For example, you might use separate volumes for executives, managers, and users, or you might have separate volumes for management, graphic designers, engineers, and all other users.

To create a quota entry on a volume, follow these steps:

1. Access the Quota Entries dialog box as discussed in the section of this chapter entitled "Viewing Disk Quota Entries." Current quota entries for all users are listed. To refresh the listing, press F5 or select Refresh from the View menu.

2. If the user doesn't have an existing entry on the volume, you can create it by selecting New Quota Entry from the Quota menu. This opens the Select Users dialog box.

3. In the Select Users dialog box, type the name of a user you want to use in the Name text box and then click Check Names. If matches are found, select the account you want to use and then click OK. If no matches are found, update the

name you entered and try searching again. Repeat this step as necessary and then click OK when you're finished.

4. After you've selected a user, the Add New Quota Entry dialog box is displayed as shown in Figure 14-16. You have several options. You can remove all quota restrictions for this user by selecting Do Not Limit Disk Usage. Or you can set a specific limit and warning level by selecting Limit Disk Space To and then entering the appropriate values in the fields provided. Click OK.

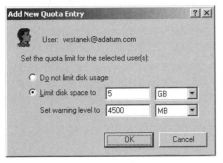

Figure 14-16   Use the Add New Quota Entry dialog box to customize the user's quota limit and warning level or remove quota restrictions altogether.

Deleting Disk Quota Entries

When you've created disk quota entries on a volume and a user no longer needs to use the volume, you can delete the associated disk quota entry. When you delete a disk quota entry, all files owned by the user are collected and displayed in a dialog box so that you can permanently delete the files, take ownership of the files, or move the files to a folder on a different volume.

To delete a disk quota entry for a user and manage the user's remaining files on the volume, follow these steps:

1. Access the Quota Entries dialog box as discussed in the section of this chapter entitled "Viewing Disk Quota Entries." Current quota entries for all users are listed. To refresh the listing, press F5 or select Refresh from the View menu.

2. Select the disk quota entry that you want to delete and then press the Delete key or select Delete Quota Entry from the Quota menu. You can select multiple entries using the Shift and Ctrl keys.

3. When prompted to confirm the action, click Yes. This displays the Disk Quota dialog box with a list of current files owned by the selected user or users.

4. Use the List Files Owned By selection list to display files for a user whose quota entry you're deleting. You must now specify how the files for the user are to be handled. You can handle each file separately by selecting individual files and

then choosing an appropriate option. You can select multiple files using the Shift and Ctrl keys. The options available are as follows:

Permanently Delete Files   Select the files to delete and then press Delete. When prompted to confirm the action, click Yes.

Take Ownership Of Files   Select the files of which you want to take ownership and then click Take Ownership.

Move Files To   Select the files that you want to move and then enter the path to a folder on a different volume in the field provided. If you don't know the path that you want to use, click Browse to display the Browse For Folder dialog box, which you can use to find the folder. Once you find the folder, click Move.

5. Click Close when you're finished managing the files. If you've appropriately handled all user files, the disk quota entries will be deleted.

Exporting and Importing NTFS Disk Quota Settings

Rather than recreating custom disk quota entries on individual volumes, you can export the settings from a source volume and then import the settings on another volume. You must format both volumes using NTFS. The steps you follow to export and then import disk quota entries are the following:

1. Access the Quota Entries dialog box as discussed in the section of this chapter entitled "Viewing Disk Quota Entries." Current quota entries for all users are listed. To refresh the listing, press F5 or select Refresh from the View menu.

2. Select Export from the Quota menu. This displays the Export Quota Settings dialog box. Use the Save In drop-down list to choose the save location for the file containing the quota settings and then set a name for the file using the File Name text box. Afterward, click Save.

> **Note**   If you save the settings file to a mapped drive on the target volume, you'll have an easier time importing the settings. Quota files are usually fairly small, so you won't need to worry about disk space usage.

3. On the Quota menu, select Close to exit the Quota Entries dialog box.

4. Right-click Computer Management in the console tree. On the shortcut menu, select Connect To Another Computer. In the Select Computer dialog box, choose the computer containing the target volume. The target volume is the one that you want to use the exported settings.

5. As explained previously, access the Properties dialog box for the target volume. Then click Quota Entries in the Quota tab. This displays the Quota Entries dialog box for the target volume.

6. Select Import on the Quota menu. Then, in the Import Quota Settings dialog box, select the quota settings file that you saved previously. Click Open.

7. If the volume had previous quota entries, you'll have the opportunity to replace existing entries or keep existing entries. When prompted about a conflict, click Yes to replace an existing entry or click No to keep the existing entry. You can apply the option to replace or keep existing entries to all entries on the volume by selecting the Do This For All Quota Entries check box prior to clicking Yes or No.

Disabling NTFS Disk Quotas

You can disable quotas for individual users or all users on a volume. When you disable quotas for a particular user, the user is no longer subject to the quota restrictions but disk quotas are still tracked for other users. When you disable quotas on a volume, quota tracking and management are completely removed. To disable quotas for a particular user, follow the technique outlined in the section of this chapter entitled "Creating Disk Quota Entries." To disable quota tracking and management on a volume, follow these steps:

1. Start Computer Management. If necessary, connect to a remote computer.

2. Display the Properties dialog box for the volume on which you want to disable NTFS quotas.

3. In the Quota tab, clear the Enable Quota Management check box. Click OK. When prompted to confirm, click OK again.

Using, Configuring, and Managing Storage Resource Manager Disk Quotas

Windows Server 2003 R2 supports an enhanced quota management system called Storage Resource Manager Disk Quotas. Using Storage Resource Manager Disk Quotas, you can manage disk space usage by folder and by volume.

> **Tip** Because you manage Storage Resource Manager disk quotas separately from NTFS disk quotas, you can in fact configure a single volume to use both quota systems. However, it's recommended that you use one quota system or the other rather than both. Alternately, if you've already configured NTFS disk quotas, you might want to continue using NTFS disk quotas on a per volume basis and supplement this quota management with Storage Resource Manager disk quotas for important folders.

Understanding Storage Resource Manager Disk Quotas

When you're working with Windows Server 2003 R2, Storage Resource Manager disk quotas are another tool you can use to manage disk usage. You can configure Storage Resource Manager disk quotas on a per-volume basis and on a per-folder basis. You can set disk quotas with a specific limit as a hard limit, meaning a limit can't be exceeded, or a soft limit, meaning a limit can be exceeded.

Generally, you'll use hard limits when you want to prevent users from exceeding a specific disk usage limitation. You'll use soft limits when you want to monitor usage and simply warn users who exceed or are about to exceed usage guidelines. All quotas have a quota path, which designates the base file path on the volume or folder to which the quota is applied. The quota applies to the designated volume or folder and all subfolders of the designated volume or folder. The particulars of how quotas work and how users are limited or warned are derived from a source template that defines the quota properties.

Windows Server 2003 R2 includes the quota templates listed in Table 14-7. Using the File Server Resource Manager, you can easily define additional templates that would then be available whenever you define quotas or you can set single-use custom quota properties when defining a quota.

Table 14-7   Disk Quota Templates

Quota Template	Limit	Quota Type	Description
100 MB Limit	100 MB	Hard	Sends warnings to users as the limit is approached and exceeded.
200 MB Limit Reports to User	200 MB	Hard	Sends storage reports to the users who exceed the threshold.
200 MB Limit With 50 MB Extension	200 MB	Hard	Uses the DIRQUOTA command to grant an automatic one-time 50 MB extension to users who exceed the quota limit.
250 MB Extended Limit	250 MB	Hard	Meant to be used by those whose limit has been extended from 200 MB to 250 MB.
Monitor 200 GB Volume Usage	200 GB	Soft	Monitors volume usage and warns when the limit is approached and exceeded.
Monitor 500 MB Share	500 MB	Soft	Monitors share usage and warns when the limit is approached and exceeded.

Quota templates or custom properties define the following:

Limit   The disk space usage limit

Quota type   Hard or soft

Notification thresholds   The types of notification that occur when usage reaches a specific percentage of the limit

Although each quota has a specific limit and type, you can define multiple notification thresholds as either a warning threshold or a limit threshold. Warning thresholds are considered to be any percentage of the limit that is less than 100 percent. Limit thresholds occur when the limit reached is 100 percent. For example, you could define warning thresholds that were triggered at 85 percent and 95 percent of the limit and a limit threshold that is triggered when 100 percent of the limit is reached.

Users who are approaching or have exceeded a limit can be automatically notified by e-mail. The notification system also allows for notifying administrators by e-mail, triggering incident reporting, running commands, and logging related events.

Managing Disk Quota Templates

You use disk quota templates to define quota properties, including the limit, quota type, and notification thresholds. In File Server Management, you can view the currently defined disk quota templates by expanding the File Server Resource Manager and Quota Management nodes and then selecting Quota Templates. Table 14-7 provided a summary of the default disk quota templates.

You can modify existing disk quota templates by completing the following steps:

1. In File Server Management, expand the File Server Resource Manager and Quota Management nodes and then select Quota Templates.

2. Currently defined disk quota templates are listed by name, limit, and quota type.

3. To modify disk quota template properties, double-click the disk quota template name. This displays a related properties dialog box, as shown in Figure 14-17.

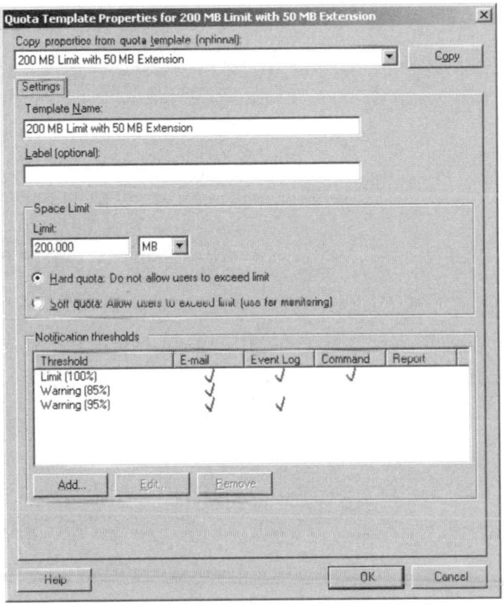

Figure 14-17 Use disk quota properties to configure the limit, quota type, and notification thresholds.

4. In the Settings tab, you can set the template name, limit, and quota type. Current notification thresholds are listed. To modify an existing threshold, select it and then click Edit. To define a new threshold, click Add.

5. When you're finished modifying the quota template, click OK to save the changes.

You can create a new disk quota template by completing the following steps:

1. In File Server Management, expand the File Server Resource Manager and Disk Management nodes and then select Quota Templates.

2. On the Action menu or in the Actions pane, select Create Quota Template. This displays the Create Quota Template dialog box.

3. In the Settings tab, set the template name, limit, and quota type.

4. A limit threshold is already created. You should edit this threshold first and then create additional warning thresholds as necessary. Select Limit and then click Edit to define the limit threshold.

5. Click Add to add warning thresholds. In the Add Threshold dialog box, enter a percentage value under Generate Notifications When Usage Reaches (%).Warning thresholds are considered to be any percentage of the limit that is less than 100 percent. Limit thresholds occur when the limit reached is 100 percent.

6. In the E-mail Message tab, you can configure notification as follows:

   ❑ To notify an administrator when the disk quota is triggered, select the Send E-Mail To The Following Administrators check box and then type the e-mail address or addresses to use. Be sure to separate multiple e-mail addresses with a semicolon. Use the value [Admin Email] to specify the default administrator as configured previously under the global options.

   ❑ To notify users, select the Send E-Mail To The User Who Attempted To Save An Unauthorized File check box.

   ❑ To specify the contents of the notification message, use the Subject and Message Body text boxes. Table 13-6, "File Screen Variables and Their Meaning," in Chapter 13, "Managing Files and Folders," lists available variables and their meaning.

7. In the Event Log tab, you can configure event logging. Select the Send Warning To Event Log check box to enable logging and then use the Log Entry text box to specify the text of the log entry. Table 13-6 in Chapter 13 lists available variables and their meaning.

8. In the Report tab, select the Generate Reports check box to enable incident reporting and then select the types of reports to generate. Incident reports are stored under %SystemDrive%\StorageReports\Incident by default, and they can

also be sent to designated administrators. Use the value [Admin Email] to specify the default administrator as configured previously under the global options.

9. Repeat Steps 5–8 to define additional notification thresholds. Click OK when you're finished creating the template.

Creating Disk Quotas

You use disk quotas to designate file paths that have specific usage limits. In File Server Management, you can view current disk quotas by expanding the File Server Resource Manager and Quota Management nodes and then selecting Quotas. Before you define disk quotas, you should specify screening file groups and disk quota templates that you will use, as discussed in Chapter 13 under "Managing the File Groups to Which Screens Are Applied" and in this chapter under "Managing Disk Quota Templates," respectively.

After you've defined the necessary file groups and disk quota templates, you can create a disk quota by completing the following steps:

1. In File Server Management, expand the File Server Resource Manager and Quota Management nodes and then select Quotas.

2. Select Create Quota on the Action menu or in the Actions pane.

3. In the Create Quota dialog box, set the local computer path for the quota by clicking Browse and then using the Browse For Folder dialog box to select the desired path, such as C:\Data. Click OK.

4. Use the Derive Properties From This Quota Template drop-down list to choose the disk quota template that defines the quota properties you want to use. Click Create.

Data Backup and Recovery

Because data is the heart of the enterprise, it's crucial for you to protect it. And to protect your organization's data, you need to implement a data backup and recovery plan. Backing up files can protect against accidental loss of user data, database corruption, hardware failures, and even natural disasters. It's your job as an administrator to make sure that backups are performed and that backup tapes are stored in a secure location.

Creating a Backup and Recovery Plan

Data backup is an insurance plan. Important files are accidentally deleted all the time. Mission-critical data can become corrupt. Natural disasters can leave your office in ruin. With a solid backup and recovery plan, you can recover from any of these. Without one, you're left with nothing to fall back on.

Figuring Out a Backup Plan

It takes time to create and implement a backup and recovery plan. You'll need to figure out what data needs to be backed up, how often the data should be backed up, and more. To help you create a plan, consider the following:

How important or sensitive is the data on your systems? The importance of data can go a long way in helping you determine if you need to back it up—as well as when and how it should be backed up. For critical data, such as a database, you'll want to have redundant backup sets that extend back for several backup periods. For sensitive data, you'll want to ensure backup data is physically secure or encrypted.

For less important data, such as daily user files, you won't need such an elaborate backup plan, but you'll need to back up the data regularly and ensure that the data can be recovered easily.

What type of information does the data contain?   Data that doesn't seem important to you might be very important to someone else. Thus, the type of information the data contains can help you determine if you need to back up the data—as well as when and how the data should be backed up.

How often does the data change?   The frequency of change can affect your decision on how often the data should be backed up. For example, data that changes daily should be backed up daily.

Can you supplement backups with shadow copies?   *Shadow copies* are point-in-time copies of documents in shared folders. These point-in-time copies make it easy to recover documents, as you can quickly go back to an older version in case a document is deleted or overwritten accidentally. You should use shadow copies in addition to standard backup—and not to replace backup procedures.

How quickly do you need to recover the data?   Time is an important factor in creating a backup plan. For critical systems, you might need to get back online swiftly. To do this, you might need to alter your backup plan.

Do you have the equipment to perform backups?   You must have backup hardware to perform backups. To perform timely backups, you might need several backup devices and several sets of backup media. Backup hardware includes tape drives, optical drives, and removable disk drives. Generally, tape drives are less expensive but slower than other types of drives.

Who will be responsible for the backup and recovery plan?   Ideally, someone should be a primary contact for the organization's backup and recovery plan. This person might also be responsible for performing the actual backup and recovery of data.

What's the best time to schedule backups?   Scheduling backups when system use is as low as possible will speed the backup process. However, you can't always schedule backups for off-peak hours. So you need to carefully plan when key system data is backed up.

Do you need to store backups off-site?   Storing copies of backup tapes off-site is essential to recovering your systems in the case of a natural disaster. In your off-site storage location, you should also include copies of the software you might need to install to reestablish operational systems.

The Basic Types of Backup

There are many techniques for backing up files. The techniques you use will depend on the type of data you're backing up, how convenient you want the recovery process to be, and more.

If you view the properties of a file or directory in Windows Explorer, you'll note an attribute called Archive. You often use this attribute to determine whether a file or directory should be backed up. If the attribute is on, the file or directory might need to be backed up. The basic types of backups you can perform include:

Normal/full backups   All files that have been selected are backed up, regardless of the archive attribute's setting. When a file is backed up, the archive attribute is cleared. If the file is later modified, this attribute is set, which indicates that the file needs to be backed up.

Copy backups   All files that have been selected are backed up, regardless of the archive attribute's setting. Unlike a normal backup, the archive attribute on files isn't modified. This allows you to perform other types of backups on the files at a later date.

Differential backups   Designed to create backup copies of files that have changed since the last normal backup. The presence of the archive attribute indicates that the file has been modified and only files with this attribute are backed up. However, the archive attribute on files isn't modified. This allows you to perform other types of backups on the files at a later date.

Incremental backups   Designed to create backups of files that have changed since the most recent normal or incremental backup. The presence of the archive attribute indicates that the file has been modified and only files with this attribute are backed up. When a file is backed up, the archive attribute is cleared. If the file is later modified, this attribute is set, which indicates that the file needs to be backed up.

Daily backups   Designed to back up files using the modification date on the file itself. If a file has been modified on the same day as the backup, the file will be backed up. This technique doesn't change the archive attributes of files.

In your backup plan, you'll probably want to perform full backups on a weekly basis and supplement this with daily, differential, or incremental backups. You might also want to create an extended backup set for monthly and quarterly backups that includes additional files that aren't being backed up regularly.

> **Tip**   You'll often find that weeks or months can go by before anyone notices that a file or data source is missing. This doesn't mean the file isn't important. Although some types of data aren't used often, they're still needed. So don't forget that you might also want to create extra sets of backups for monthly or quarterly periods, or both, to ensure that you can recover historical data over time.

In previous editions of the Backup utility for Microsoft Windows, Backup would write errors to the log for any files that were in read+write or write mode. Files in these modes are in use. In Microsoft Windows Server 2003, Backup uses the Shadow Copy feature to create automatic point-in-time backups of files that are in use. As an administrator, you probably know how frustrating it can be to try to get a complete backup set, and this feature goes a long way toward ensuring that the Backup utility is a viable option for backing up data in a wide variety of conditions.

Differential and Incremental Backups

The difference between differential and incremental backups is extremely important. To understand the distinction, examine Table 15-1. As it shows, with differential backups, you back up all the files that have changed since the last full backup (which means that the size of the differential backup grows over time). With incremental backups, you back up only files that have changed since the most recent full or incremental backup (which means the size of the incremental backup is usually much smaller than a full backup).

Table 15-1   Incremental and Differential Backup Techniques

Day of Week	Weekly Full Backup with Daily Differential Backup	Weekly Full Backup with Daily Incremental Backup
Sunday	A full backup is performed.	A full backup is performed.
Monday	A differential backup contains all changes since Sunday.	An incremental backup contains changes since Sunday.
Tuesday	A differential backup contains all changes since Sunday.	An incremental backup contains changes since Monday.
Wednesday	A differential backup contains all changes since Sunday.	An incremental backup contains changes since Tuesday.
Thursday	A differential backup contains all changes since Sunday.	An incremental backup contains changes since Wednesday.
Friday	A differential backup contains all changes since Sunday.	An incremental backup contains changes since Thursday.
Saturday	A differential backup contains all changes since Sunday.	An incremental backup contains changes since Friday.

After you determine what data you're going to back up and how often, you can select backup devices and media that support these choices. These are covered in the next section.

Selecting Backup Devices and Media

Many tools are available for backing up data. Some are fast and expensive. Others are slow but very reliable. The backup solution that's right for your organization depends on many factors, including:

Capacity   The amount of data that you need to back up on a routine basis. Can the backup hardware support the required load given your time and resource constraints?

Reliability   The reliability of the backup hardware and media. Can you afford to sacrifice reliability to meet budget or time needs?

Extensibility   The extensibility of the backup solution. Will this solution meet your needs as the organization grows?

Speed   The speed with which data can be backed up and recovered. Can you afford to sacrifice speed to reduce costs?

Cost   The cost of the backup solution. Does it fit into your budget?

Common Backup Solutions

Capacity, reliability, extensibility, speed, and cost are the issues driving your backup plan. If you understand how these issues affect your organization, you'll be on track to select an appropriate backup solution. Some of the most commonly used backup solutions include:

Tape drives   Tape drives are the most common backup devices. Tape drives use magnetic tape cartridges to store data. Magnetic tapes are relatively inexpensive but aren't highly reliable. Tapes can break or stretch. They can also lose information over time. The average capacity of tape cartridges ranges from 24 gigabytes (GB) to 72 GB. Compared with other backup solutions, tape drives are fairly slow. Still, the selling point is the low cost.

Digital audio tape (DAT) drives   DAT drives are quickly replacing standard tape drives as the preferred backup devices. Many DAT formats are available. The most commonly used format is Digital Linear Tape (DLT) or Super DLT (SDLT). With SDLT 320 and 600, tapes have a capacity of either 160 GB or 300 GB uncompressed (320 GB or 600 GB compressed). Large organizations might want to look at Linear Tape Open (LTO) tape technologies. LTO-3 tapes have a capacity of 400 GB uncompressed (800 GB compressed).

Autoloader tape systems   Autoloader tape systems use a magazine of tapes to create extended backup volumes capable of meeting the enterprise's high-capacity needs. With an autoloader system, tapes within the magazine are automatically changed as needed during the backup or recovery process. Most autoloader tape systems use DAT tapes formatted for DLT, SDLT, or LTO. Typical DLT drives can record up to 45 GB per hour, and you can improve that speed by purchasing a type library system with multiple drives. In this way, you can record on multiple tapes simultaneously. In contrast, most SDLT and LTO drives record over 100 GB per hour, and by using multiple drives in a system, you can record hundreds of GB per hour.

Disk drives   Disk drives provide one of the fastest ways to back up and restore files. With disk drives, you can often accomplish in minutes what takes a tape drive hours. So when business needs mandate a speedy recovery, nothing beats a disk drive. The drawbacks to disk drives, however, are relatively high costs compared to tape library systems.

Disk-based backup systems   Disk-based backup systems provide complete backup and restore solutions using large arrays of disks to achieve high performance. High reliability can be achieved when you use redundant array of independent disks (RAID) to build in redundancy and fault tolerance. Typical disk-based backup systems use virtual library technology so that Windows sees them as autoloader tape library systems. This makes them easier to work with. A typical 20-drive system can record up to 500 GB per hour; a typical 40-drive system can record up to 2 terabytes (TB) per hour.

Note   Disks and disk-based backup systems are usually used between the servers to backup and an enterprise autoloader. Servers are backed up to disk first because disks are very fast compared to tape, and then later backed up to an enterprise autoloader. Having data on tapes also makes it easier to rotate backup sets to offsite storage.

Before you can use a backup device, you must install it. When you install backup devices other than standard tape and DAT drives, you need to tell the operating system about the controller card and drivers that the backup device uses. For detailed information on installing devices and drivers, see the section entitled "Managing Hardware Devices and Drivers" in Chapter 2, "Managing Servers Running Microsoft Windows Server 2003."

Buying and Using Tapes

Selecting a backup device is an important step toward implementing a backup and recovery plan. But you also need to purchase the tapes or disks, or both, that will allow you to implement your plan. The number of tapes you need depends on how much data you'll be backing up, how often you'll be backing up the data, and how long you'll need to keep additional data sets.

The typical way to use backup tapes is to set up a rotation schedule whereby you rotate through two or more sets of tapes. The idea is that you can increase tape longevity by reducing tape usage and, at the same time, reduce the number of tapes you need to ensure that you have historic data on hand when necessary.

One of the most common tape rotation schedules is the 10-tape rotation. With this rotation schedule, you use 10 tapes divided into two sets of 5 (one for each weekday). The first set of tapes is used one week and the second set of tapes is used the next week. On Fridays, full backups are scheduled. On Mondays through Thursdays, incremental backups are scheduled. If you add a third set of tapes, you can rotate one of the tape sets to an off-site storage location on a weekly basis.

The 10-tape rotation schedule is designed for the 9 to 5 workers of the world. If you're in a 24 x 7 environment, you'll definitely want extra tapes for Saturday and Sunday. In this case, use a 14-tape rotation with two sets of 7 tapes. On Sundays, schedule full backups. On Mondays through Saturdays, schedule incremental backups.

Backing Up Your Data

Windows Server 2003 provides a backup utility, called Backup, for creating backups on local and remote systems. You use Backup to archive files and folders, restore archived files and folders, access media pools reserved for Backup, access remote resources through My Network Places, create snapshots of the system state for backup and restore, schedule backups through the Task Scheduler, and create emergency repair disks.

Getting Started with the Backup Utility

You can access Backup in several ways, including:

- Click the Start menu, and then click Run. In the Run dialog box, type **ntbackup**, and then click OK.

- Click the Start menu, choose Programs or All Programs as appropriate, choose Accessories, choose System Tools, and then select Backup.

The first time you use the Backup utility, it starts in basic wizard mode. As an administrator, you'll want to use advanced mode, as it gives you more options. Clear the Always Start In Wizard Mode check box and then click the Advanced Mode link. You should now see the main Backup utility interface. As shown in Figure 15-1, the standard interface has four tabs that provide easy access to key features. These tabs are the following:

Welcome   Introduces Backup and provides buttons for starting the Backup Wizard, the Restore Wizard, and the Automated System Recovery Wizard.

Backup   Provides the main interface for selecting data to back up. You can back up data on local drives and mapped network drives.

Restore And Manage Media   Provides the main interface for restoring archived data. You can restore data to the original location or to an alternate location anywhere on the network.

Schedule Jobs   Provides a month-by-month job schedule for backups. You can view executed jobs as well as jobs scheduled for future dates.

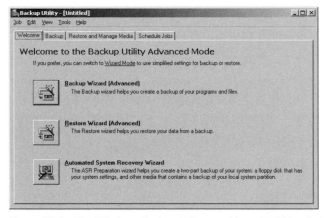

Figure 15-1   The Windows Backup utility provides a user-friendly interface for backup and restore.

To perform backup and recovery operations, you must have certain permissions and user rights. Members of the Administrators and the Backup Operators groups have full authority to back up and restore any type of file, regardless of who owns the file and the permissions set on it. File owners and those who have been given control over files can also back up files, but only those files that they own or those for which they have Read, Read & Execute, Modify, or Full Control permissions.

> **Note**   Keep in mind that although local accounts can work only with local systems, domain accounts have domain-wide privileges. Therefore, a member of the local administrators group can work only with files on the local system, but a member of the domain administrators group could work with files throughout the domain.

Backup provides extensions for working with special types of data, including:

System state data   Includes essential system files needed to recover the local system. All computers have system state data, which must be backed up in addition to other files to restore a complete working system.

Exchange server data   Includes the Exchange information store and data files. You must back up this data if you want to be able to recover Exchange server. Only systems running Microsoft Exchange Server have this type of data.

Removable Storage data   Is stored in %SystemRoot%\System32\Ntmsdata. If you back up this data, you can use the advanced restore option Restore Removable Storage Database to recover the Removable Storage configuration.

Remote Storage data   Is stored in %SystemRoot%\System32\Remotestorage. If you back up this data, you can restore Remote Storage by copying the data back to this directory.

Setting Default Options for Backup

You create backups using the Backup utility's Backup tab or the Backup Wizards. Both techniques make use of default options set for the Backup utility. You can view or change the default options by completing the following steps:

1. Click the Advanced Mode link on the first Backup Or Restore Wizard page or start the utility with the wizard mode disabled (by clearing the Always Start In Wizard Mode check box).

2. Click Tools and then select Options.

    As Figure 15 2 shows, there are five categories of default options: General, Restore, Backup Type, Backup Log, and Exclude Files. Each of these option categories is examined in the sections that follow.

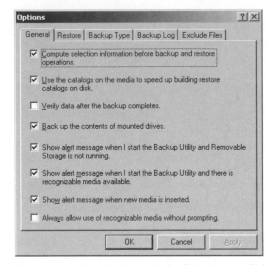

Figure 15-2   Use the General tab of the Options dialog box to set default options for the Backup utility.

General Backup Options

General options control the default behavior of Backup. You can work with these options using the fields in the General tab of the Options dialog box. The available options are summarized in Table 15-2.

Table 15-2   General Backup Options

Option	Description
Always Allow Use Of Recognizable Media Without Prompting	Allows Removable Storage to move new media to the backup pool automatically. Select this option if you use Removable Storage and you want new media to be available to Backup.
Back Up The Contents Of Mounted Drives	Allows you to back up data on mounted network drives. Otherwise, only the path information for mounted drives will be backed up.
Compute Selection Information Before Backup And Restore Operations	Calculates the number of files and bytes involved prior to the backup/restore procedure and displays this information. Otherwise, this data isn't displayed and the progress bar won't function.
Show Alert Message When I Start The Backup Utility And Removable Storage Is Not Running	Displays an alert if you start Backup and the Removable Storage service isn't running. It's a good option to use if you work with removable media.

Table 15-2   General Backup Options

Option	Description
Show Alert Message When I Start The Backup Utility And There Is Recognizable Media Available	Displays an alert if you start Backup and new media is available in the import media pool. It's useful if you work with removable media.
Show Alert Message When New Media Is Inserted	Displays an alert when Removable Storage detects new media. It's useful if you work with removable media.
Use The Catalogs On The Media To Speed Up Building Restore Catalogs On Disk	Allows you to use archive logs on the media rather than scan the entire archive to determine what files are included. Clear this option only when the catalog is missing, damaged, or otherwise unavailable.
Verify Data After The Backup Completes	Checks the archive data against the original data to ensure that the data is the same. If the data isn't the same, there might be a problem with the backup media and you should run the backup again using different media.

Setting Restore and Backup Options

The list of general options is quite extensive but, for the most part, the list doesn't control the behavior of the actual backup or restore operation. Table 15-3 summarizes options for controlling backup and restore behavior.

Table 15-3   Restore, Backup Type, and Backup Log Options

Tab	Option	Description
Restore	Do Not Replace The Files On My Computer (Recommended)	Select this option if you don't want to copy over existing files.
	Replace The File On Disk Only If the File On Disk Is Older	Select this option to replace older files on disk with newer files from the backup.
	Always Replace The File On My Computer	Select this option to replace all files on disk with files from the backup.
Backup Type	Default Backup Type	Select this option to set the default backup type. Available types are Normal, Copy, Differential, Incremental, and Daily.
Backup Log	Detailed	Select this option to log all operations, including the names of files.
	Summary	Select this option to log only key information and backup failure.
	None	Select this option to disable logging.

Viewing and Setting Backup Exclusions

Many types of system files are excluded from backups by default. You manage exclusions in the Options dialog box, which you access by selecting Options from the Tools menu in the Backup utility.

Viewing Exclusions   In the Backup utility, you can view file exclusions by clicking the Exclude Files tab in the Options dialog box. File exclusions are based on file ownership, and you can set them for all users as well as for the user currently logged on to the system (see Figure 15-3).

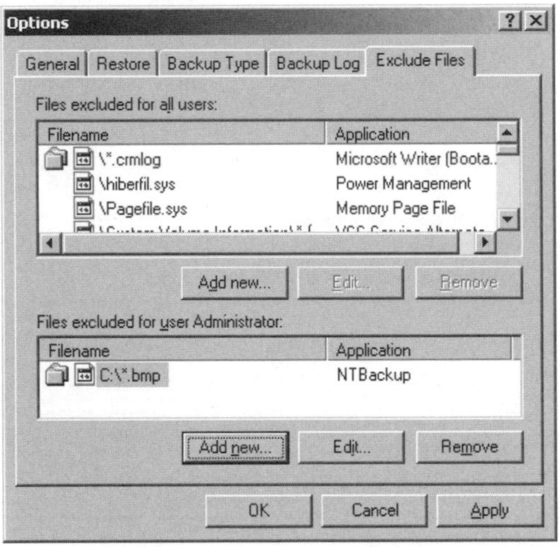

Figure 15-3   Use the Exclude Files tab to view existing file exclusions for users.

Creating Exclusions   To exclude additional files, follow these steps:

1. In the Options dialog box, click the Exclude Files tab.

2. If you want to exclude files that are owned by any user, click Add New under the Files Excluded For All Users list. This displays the Add Excluded Files dialog box shown in Figure 15-4.

3. If you want to exclude only files that you own, click Add New under the Files Excluded For User ... list. This displays the Add Excluded Files dialog box.

4. You can exclude files by registered file type by clicking a file type in the Registered File Type list box. Or you can exclude files by custom file type by typing a period and then the file extension in the Custom File Mask box. For example, you could choose .doc or type the custom type **wbk**.

5. Enter a drive or file path in Applies To Path text box. Files are then restricted from all subfolders of that path unless you clear the Applies To All Subfolders check box. For example, if you use C:\ and select Applies To All Subfolders, all

files ending with the designated file extension are excluded wherever they occur on the C drive. Click OK.

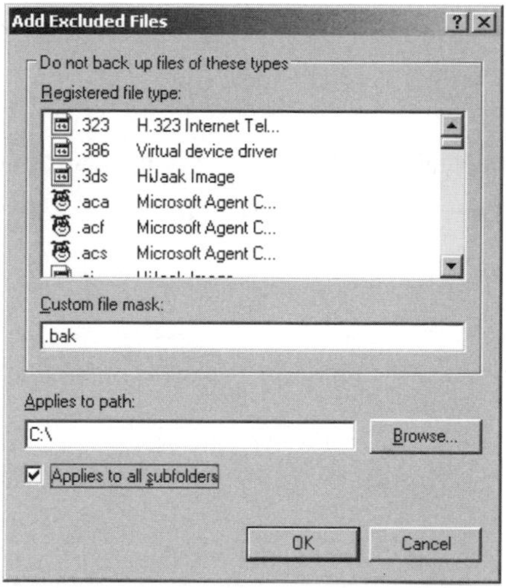

Figure 15-4   Use the Add Excluded Files dialog box to set file exclusions for users.

Tip   Type \ as the path to specify matching files on any file system. For example, if the system had C, D, and F hard disk drives and you wanted to exclude all files of a certain type on all three drives, you'd type \ in the Applies To Path field.

Changing Exclusions   To change existing exclusions, follow these steps:

1. In the Options dialog box, click the Exclude Files tab.

2. Select an existing exclusion you want to edit and then click Edit. You can now edit the file exclusion.

3. Select an existing exclusion you want to remove and then click Remove. The exclusion is removed. Click Apply when you're finished.

Backing Up Data with the Backup Wizard

The procedures you use to work with the Backup Wizard are similar to those you use to back up data manually. You start and work with the wizard by completing the following steps:

1. Start the Backup utility in advanced mode and then click Backup Wizard in the Welcome tab. If wizard mode is enabled, click the Advanced Mode link and then click Backup Wizard.

    Note   You can select files in the Backup tab and then start the Backup Wizard. If you do this, you'll be given the opportunity to back up the selected files only. Clicking Yes takes you directly to the Items To Backup dialog box. Clicking No clears the selected files and starts the wizard as usual.

2. Click Next. Select what you want to back up. The options are:

   Back Up Everything On This Computer   Back up all data on the computer, including the system state data

   Back Up Selected Files, Drives, Or Network Data   Only back up data you select

   Only Back Up The System State Data   Create a backup of the system state data

   > **Note**   For servers running Windows Server 2003 that aren't domain controllers, system state data includes essential boot files, key system files, the Windows registry, and the COM+ class registration database. For domain controllers, system state data includes Active Directory directory service data and files stored on the system volume (Sysvol) as well.

3. Click Next. If you wanted to select data to back up, choose the items you want to back up as shown in Figure 15-5:

   ❑ You make selections by selecting or clearing the check boxes associated with a particular drive or folder. When you select a drive's check box, all the files and folders on the drive are selected. When you clear a drive's check box, all the files and folders on the drive are cleared.

   ❑ If you want to work with individual files and folders on a drive, click the plus sign (+) to the right of the drive icon. You can now select and clear individual directories and files by clicking their associated check boxes. When you do this, the drive's check box shows a shaded checkmark. This indicates that you haven't selected all the files on the drive.

4. Click Next and then select the Backup Media Type. Choose File if you want to back up to a file. Choose a storage device if you want to back up files and folders to a tape or removable disk.

   > **Tip**   When you write backups to a file, the backup file normally has the .bkf file extension. However, you can use another file extension if you want. Also, keep in mind that Removable Storage is used to manage tapes and removable disks. If no media are available, you'll be prompted to allocate media to the Backup media pool. Follow the instructions given in the section of this chapter entitled "Managing Media Pools."

5. Select the backup file or media you want to use. If you're backing up to a file, select a location from those available or click Browse to specify a file location and name. If you're backing up to a tape or removable disk, choose the tape or disk you want to use.

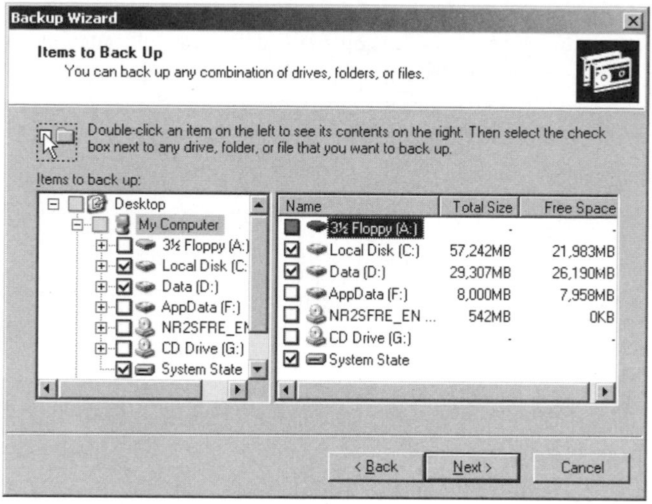

Figure 15-5   If you're backing up selected data, choose the drives, folders, and files to back up.

6. Click Next. Click Advanced if you want to override default options or schedule the backup to be run as a job. Important advanced options that you'll be able to set include:

Verify Data After Backup   Instructs Backup to verify data after the backup procedure is completed. If selected, every file on the backup tape is compared to the original file. Verifying data can protect against write errors or failures.

Use Hardware Compression, If Available   Allows Backup to compress data as it's written to the storage device. The option is available only if the device supports hardware compression, and only compatible drives can read the compressed information, which might mean that only a drive from the same manufacturer can recover the data.

Disable Volume Shadow Copy   Tells the Backup utility not to perform volume shadow copies. Volume shadow copies are used to back up files that are being written to. Thus, if you disable this feature, the Backup utility will skip files that are locked for writing.

7. Click Next and then click Finish to start the backup using the default backup options. This starts the backup operation. You can cancel the backup by clicking Cancel in the Set Information and Backup Progress dialog boxes.

> **Note**   The Backup Progress dialog box displays the backup operation's current status. Note the number of files processed and the total byte size of these files. With tape library units, you'll want to allocate additional media to the Free Media pool as necessary during the backup operation.

8. During backup operations, the Backup utility behaves differently depending on the type and status of a file. If a file is open, the utility generally attempts to back up the last saved version. If the file is locked by an exclusive lock, such as when the file is being written to, it's backed up only if volume snapshots are enabled. The utility also doesn't back up any files on the exclusion list and backs up system state data only if you've elected to do so.

9. When the backup is completed, click Close to complete the process or click Report to view the backup log.

Backing Up Files Without the Wizard

You don't have to use a wizard to back up files. You can configure backups manually by completing the following steps:

1. Start the Backup utility. If wizard mode is enabled, click the Advanced Mode button and then click the Backup tab as shown in Figure 15-6. Otherwise, just click the Backup tab.

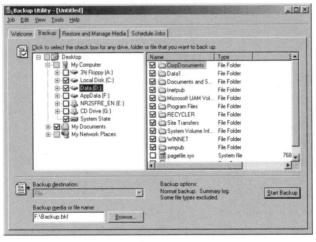

Figure 15-6 Use the Backup tab to configure backups by hand, and then click Start Backup.

2. Clear any existing selections in the Backup tab by selecting New from the Job menu and clicking Yes if prompted.

3. Choose the data you want to back up:

   ❑ You make selections by selecting or clearing the check boxes associated with a particular drive or folder. When you select a drive's check box, all files and folders on the drive are selected. When you clear a drive's check box, all files and folders on the drive are cleared.

❑   If you want to work with individual files and folders on a drive, click the plus sign (+) to the right of the drive icon. You can now select and clear individual directories and files by clicking their associated check boxes. When you do this, the drive's check box shows a shaded checkmark. This indicates that you haven't selected all the files on the drive.

❑   If you want to back up system state data, select System State below the My Computer node. For servers that aren't domain controllers, system state data includes essential boot and system files, the Windows registry, and the COM+ class registration database. For domain controllers, system state data includes Active Directory data and Sysvol files as well.

❑   If you're backing up an Exchange server, be sure to select the Microsoft Exchange icon below the My Computer node. When you do this, you'll be prompted to type the Universal Naming Convention (UNC) name of the Microsoft Exchange server you want to back up, such as **CorpMail**.

4. Use the Backup Destination selection list to choose the media type for the backup. Choose File if you want to back up to a file. Choose a storage device if you want to back up files and folders to a tape or removable disk.

> **Tip**   When you write backups to a file, the backup file normally has the .bkf file extension. However, you can use another file extension if you want. Also, keep in mind that Removable Storage is used to manage tapes and removable disks. If no media are available, you'll be prompted to allocate media to the Backup media pool. Follow the instructions given in the section of this chapter entitled "Managing Media Pools."

5. In the Backup Media Or File Name text box, select the backup file or media you want to use. If you're backing up to a file, type a path and file name for the backup file or click Browse to find a file. If you're backing up to a tape or removable disk, choose the tape or disk you want to use.

6. Click Start Backup. This displays the Backup Job Information dialog box shown in Figure 15-7. You use the options in this dialog box as follows:

Backup Description   Sets the backup label, which applies to the current backup only.

Append This Backup To The Media   Adds the backup after existing data.

Replace The Data On The Media With This Backup   Overwrites existing data.

If The Media Is Overwritten, Use This Label To Identify The Media   Sets the media label, which is changed only when you're writing to a blank tape or overwriting existing data.

Allow Only The Owner And Administrator Access To The Backup Data   If you're overwriting data, you can select this option to specify that only the owner and an administrator can access the archive file. This restricts the backup set so Backup Operators and Server Operators cannot restore the data. It does not, however, secure the data on the tape.

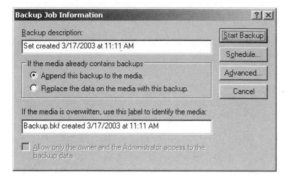

Figure 15-7   Use the Backup Job Information dialog box to configure backup options and information as necessary, and then click Start Backup.

7. Click Advanced if you want to override default options. After you select the advanced options to use, click OK.

8. Click Schedule if you want to schedule the backup for a later date. When prompted to save the backup settings, click Yes. Next, type a name for the backup selection script, and then click Save. Afterward, set the user name and password under which the scheduled job should run. In the Scheduled Job Options dialog box, type a job name, click Properties, and then set a run schedule. Skip the remaining steps.

> **Note**   Backup selection scripts and backup logs are stored in %Userprofile% \Local Settings\Application Data\Microsoft\Windows NT\NTBackup\Data. Backup selection scripts are saved with the .bks extension. Backup logs are saved with the .log extension. You can view these files with any standard text editor.

9. Click Finish to start the backup. Later, if you need to, you can cancel the backup by clicking Cancel in the Set Information and Backup Progress dialog boxes.

10. When the backup is completed, click Close to complete the process or click Report to view the backup log.

Recovering Data Using the Restore Wizard

You can restore files with the Backup utility using the Restore Wizard or the Restore tab. To recover data with the Restore Wizard, follow these steps:

1. As necessary, make sure that the backup set you want to work with is loaded into the tape library system.

2. Start the Backup utility in advanced mode and then click Restore Wizard in the Welcome tab. If wizard mode is enabled, click the Advanced Mode link and then click Restore Wizard.

> **Note**   You can select files in the Restore tab and then start the Restore Wizard. If you do this, you'll be given the opportunity to restore the selected files only. Click Yes. Clicking No clears the selected files and starts the wizard as usual.

3. Click Next. As shown in Figure 15-8, you can now choose the data you want to restore. The left view displays files organized by volume. The right view displays media sets. To restore data, complete any or all of the following actions:

   ❑ Select the check box next to any drive, folder, or file that you want to restore. If the media set with which you want to work isn't shown, click Import File, and then type the path to the catalog for the backup.

   ❑ To restore system state data, select the check box for System State as well as other data you want to restore. If you're restoring to the original location, the system state data you're restoring will replace the current system state. If you restore to an alternate location, only the registry, Sysvol, and system boot files are restored. You can restore system state data only on a local system.

> **Tip**   When you select a system state restore on a domain controller, you have to be in the Directory Services Restore Mode. To learn how to restore Active Directory, see the "Restoring Active Directory" section of this chapter.

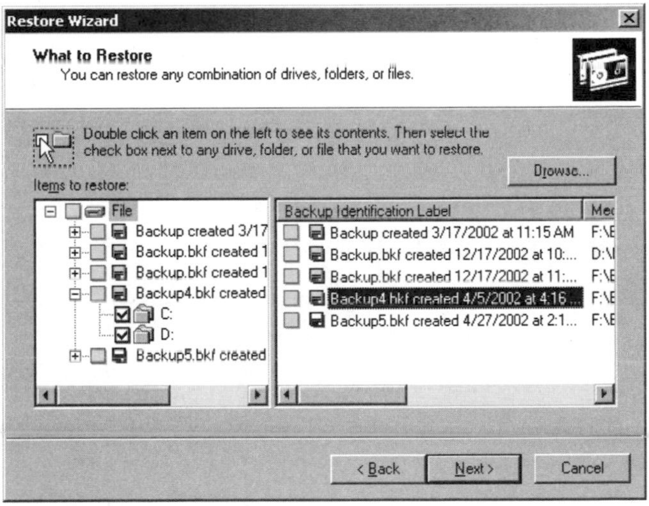

Figure 15-8   Use the Restore Wizard to select the files and folders to restore.

❑   If you're restoring Microsoft Exchange, select the Microsoft Exchange data to restore. Before the restore starts, you'll see the Restoring Microsoft Exchange dialog box. If you're restoring the Information Store, type the UNC name of the Microsoft Exchange server you want to restore, such as **\\CorpMail**. If you're restoring to a different server, select Erase All Existing Data. This destroys all existing data and creates a new Information Store.

4.   Click Next. Click Advanced if you want to override default options. Important advanced options that you'll be able to set include the restore location. The restore location options are:

Original Location   Restores data to the folder or files it was in when it was backed up.

Alternate Location   Restores data to a folder that you designate, preserving the directory structure. After selecting this option, enter the folder path to use or click Browse to select the folder path.

Single Folder   Restores all files to a single folder without preserving the directory structure. After selecting this option, enter the folder path to use or click Browse to select the folder path.

> **Tip**   If you aren't entirely sure that you want to overwrite the files in the original location, select Alternate Path and then specify a new location for the files, such as C:\temp. After the files are in the temp directory, you can compare them to the existing files and determine if you want to recover them. Keep in mind that you should always restore files backed up from NTFS drives to NTFS drives. This ensures that you can restore security permissions and retain NTFS compression and encryption.

5.   Click Next and then click Finish. If prompted, type the path and name of the backup set to use. You can cancel the backup by clicking Cancel in the Operation Status and Restore Progress dialog boxes.

6.   When the restore is completed, click Close to complete the process or click Report to view a backup log containing information about the restore operation.

Recovering Data Without the Wizard

You don't have to use the Restore Wizard to recover data. You can recover archives manually by completing the following steps:

1.   As necessary, load the backup set you want to work with in the library system.

2.   Start the Backup utility. If wizard mode is enabled, click the Advanced Mode link and then click the Restore And Manage Media tab as shown in Figure 15-9. Otherwise, just click the Restore And Manage Media tab.

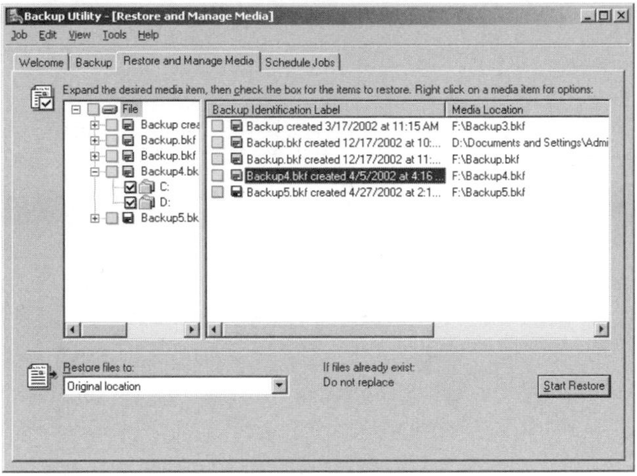

Figure 15-9   Use the Restore And Manage Media tab to specify the files and folders to restore.

3. Choose the data you want to restore. The left view displays files organized by volume. The right view displays media sets. To do this, complete any or all of the following actions:

   ❏ Select the check box next to any drive, folder, or file that you want to restore. If the media set you want to work with isn't shown, right-click File in the left view, select Catalog, then type the name and path of the catalog you want to use.

   ❏ To restore system state data, select the check box for System State as well as other data you want to restore. If you're restoring to the original location, the system state data you're restoring will replace the current system state. If you restore to an alternate location, only the registry, Sysvol, and system boot files are restored. You can restore system state data only on a local system.

   > **Tip**   When you select a system state restore on a domain controller, you have to be in the Directory Services Restore Mode. To learn how to restore Active Directory, see the section of this chapter entitled "Restoring Active Directory."

   ❏ If you're restoring Microsoft Exchange, select the Microsoft Exchange data to restore. Before the restore starts, you'll see the Restoring Microsoft Exchange dialog box. If you're restoring the Information Store, type the UNC name of the Microsoft Exchange server you want to restore, such as **\\CorpMail**. If you're restoring to a different server, select Erase All Existing Data. This destroys all existing data and creates a new Information Store.

> **Note**   On the Exchange server, the Information Store and Directory services are stopped prior to running the restore. After the restore is finished, you might need to restart these services.

4. Use the Restore Files To drop-down list to choose the restore location. The options are:

   Original Location   Restores data to the folder or files it was in when it was backed up.

   Alternate Location   Restores data to a folder that you designate, preserving the directory structure. After you select this option, enter the folder path to use or click Browse to select the folder path.

   Single Folder   Restores all files to a single folder without preserving the directory structure. After you select this option, enter the folder path to use or click Browse to select the folder path.

5. Specify how you want to restore files. Click Tools and then select Options. In the Options dialog box, click the Restore tab. Select one of the following options and then click OK:

   Do Not Replace The Files On My Computer (Recommended)   Select this option if you don't want to copy over existing files.

   Replace The File On Disk Only If The File On Disk Is Older   Select this option to replace older files on disk with newer files from the backup.

   Always Replace The File On My Computer   Select this option to replace all files on disk with files from the backup.

6. In the Restore And Manage Media tab, click Start Restore. This displays the Confirm Restore dialog box.

7. If you want to set advanced restore options, click Advanced and then set additional options as necessary.

8. In the Confirm Restore dialog box, click OK to start the restore operation. If prompted, enter the path and name of the backup set to use. You can cancel the backup by clicking Cancel in the Operation Status and Restore Progress dialog boxes.

9. When the restore is completed, you can click Close to complete the process or click Report to view a backup log containing information about the restore operation.

Restoring Active Directory

When restoring system state data to a domain controller, you must choose whether you want to perform an authoritative or nonauthoritative restore. The default is nonauthoritative. In this mode, Active Directory and other replicated data are restored from backup and any changes are replicated from another domain controllers. Thus, you can safely restore a failed domain controller without overwriting the latest Active Directory information. On the other hand, if you're trying to restore Active Directory throughout the network using archived data, you must use authoritative restore. With authoritative restore, the restored data is restored on the current domain controller and then replicated to other domain controllers.

Caution   An authoritative restore overwrites all Active Directory data throughout the domain. Before you perform an authoritative restore, you must be certain that the archive data is the correct data to propagate throughout the domain and that the current data on other domain controllers is inaccurate, outdated, or otherwise corrupted.

To restore Active Directory on a domain controller and enable the restored data to be replicated throughout the network, follow these steps:

1. Make sure the domain controller server is shut down.

2. Restart the domain controller server. When you see the prompt Please Select The Operating System To Start, press F8 to display the Advanced Options Menu.

3. Select Directory Services Restore Mode.

4. When the system starts, use the Backup utility to restore the system state data and other essential files.

5. After restoring the data, but before restarting the server, use the Ntdsutil tool to mark objects as authoritative. Be sure to check the Active Directory data thoroughly.

6. Restart the server. When the system finishes startup, the Active Directory data should begin to replicate throughout the domain.

Backing Up and Restoring Data on Remote Systems

You can use the Backup utility to back up data on remote systems. To do this, you must create network drives for the remote file systems before you begin the backup procedure. When backing up data on network drives, be sure to select the General option Back Up The Contents Of Mounted Drives. If you don't, only folder references are backed up and not the actual data.

You can also use Backup to restore data on remote systems. When you do this, you can select restore locations in My Network Places. If you're restoring to a volume containing junction points, such as a volume containing the Sysvol, be sure to select the advanced restore option Restore Junction Points, And Restore File And Folder Data Under Junction Points To The Original Location. See Microsoft Knowledge Base article 205524 for more information on junction points (*http://support.microsoft.com/default.aspx?scid =kb;en-us; 205524*).

Viewing Backup Logs

Backup logs are written as Unicode text files and are stored in %Userprofile% \Local Settings\Application Data\Microsoft\Windows NT\NTBackup\Data. The %Userprofile % variable is the profile path for the user who created or scheduled that backup. Backup logs are named in the format backup##.log, where backup01.log is the initial log created by the Backup utility.

Although you can view backup logs in any text editor, including Microsoft Notepad, the Backup utility provides direct access to logs through the advanced mode interface. Complete the following steps:

1. In advanced mode, select Report from the Tools menu. This displays the Backup Reports dialog box.

2. To view a log, select it and then click View. This opens the log in the default text editor for the system.

3. To print a log, select it and then click Print. This prints the log to the default printer for the system.

Managing Encryption Recovery Policy

If you're an administrator for an organization that uses the Encrypting File System (EFS), your disaster recovery planning must include additional procedures and prep-arations. You'll need to consider how to handle issues related to personal encryption certificates, EFS recovery agents, and EFS recovery policy. These issues are discussed in the sections that follow.

Understanding Encryption Certificates and Recovery Policy

File encryption is supported on a per-folder or per-file basis. Any file placed in a folder marked for encryption is automatically encrypted. Files in encrypted format can be read only by the person who encrypted the file. Before other users can read an encrypted file, the user must decrypt the file.

Every file that's encrypted has a unique encryption key. This means that encrypted files can be copied, moved, and renamed just like any other file—and in most cases these actions don't affect the encryption of the data. The user who encrypted the file always has access to the file, provided the user's private key is available in the user profile on the computer or the user has credential roaming with digital identification management service. For this user the encryption and decryption process is handled automatically and is transparent.

The process that handles encryption and decryption is called the Encrypting File Sys-tem (EFS). The default setup for EFS allows users to encrypt files without needing spe-cial permission. Files are encrypted using a public/private key that EFS generates automatically on a per-user basis. By default, Windows XP SP1 or later and Windows Server 2003 use the Advanced Encryption Standard (AES) algorithm for encrypting files with EFS. AES is not supported on Windows 2000 or Windows XP versions prior to SP1, and AES encrypted files viewed on these computers can appear to be corrupted when in fact they are not.

Encryption certificates are stored as part of the data in user profiles. If a user works with multiple computers and wants to use encryption, an administrator will need to configure a roaming profile for that user. A roaming profile ensures that the user's profile data and public-key certificates are accessible from other computers. Without this, users won't be able to access their encrypted files on another computer.

> **Tip**   An alternative to a roaming profile is to copy the user's encryption certificate to the computers the user uses. You can do this using the certificate backup and restore process discussed later in this chapter under "Backing Up and Restoring Encrypted Data and Certificates." Simply back up the certificate on the user's original computer and then restore the certificate on each of the other computers to which the user logs on.

EFS has a built-in data recovery system to guard against data loss. This recovery system ensures that encrypted data can be recovered if a user's public-key certificate is lost or deleted. The most common scenario in which this occurs is when a user leaves the company and the associated user account is deleted. Although a manager might have been able to log on to the user's account, check files, and save important files to other folders, encrypted files will be accessible afterward only if the encryption is removed or by the user that encrypted them to a FAT or FAT32 volume (where encryption isn't supported).

To access encrypted files after the user account has been deleted, you'll need to use a recovery agent. Recovery agents have access to the file encryption key that's necessary to unlock data in encrypted files. To protect sensitive data, recovery agents don't, however, have access to a user's private key or any private key information.

Recovery agents are designated automatically and the necessary recovery certificates are generated automatically as well. This ensures that encrypted files can always be recovered.

EFS recovery agents are configured at two levels:

Domain   The recovery agent for a domain is configured automatically when the first Windows Server 2003 domain controller is installed. By default, the recovery agent is the domain administrator. Through Group Policy, domain administrators can designate additional recovery agents. Domain administrators can also delegate recovery agent privileges to designated security administrators.

Local computer   When a computer is part of a workgroup or in a stand-alone configuration, the recovery agent is the administrator of the local computer by default. You can designate additional recovery agents. Further, if you want local recovery agents in a domain environment rather than domain-level recovery agents, you must delete the recovery policy from the Group Policy for the domain.

You can delete recovery policies if you don't want them to be available.

Configuring the EFS Recovery Policy

Recovery policies are configured automatically for domain controllers and workstations. By default, domain administrators are the designated recovery agents for domains and the local administrator is the designated recovery agent for a stand-alone workstation.

Through Group Policy, you can view, assign, and delete recovery agents. Follow these steps:

1. Access the Group Policy console for the local computer, site, domain, or organizational unit with which you want to work. For details on working with Group Policy, see the section entitled "Group Policy Management" in Chapter 4, "Automating Administrative Tasks, Policies, and Procedures."

2. Access the Encrypted Data Recovery Agents node in Group Policy. To do this, expand Computer Configuration, Windows Settings, Security Settings, and Public Key Policies, and then click Encrypting File System.

3. As shown in Figure 15-10, the right-hand pane lists the recovery certificates currently assigned. Recovery certificates are listed according to whom they're issued to, whom they're issued by, expiration data, purpose, and more. In the figure, the administrator self-issued the certificate for the purpose of file recovery (it's a recovery certificate for the local administrator).

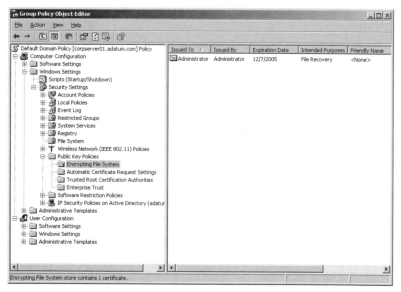

Figure 15-10 Use the Encrypted Data Recovery Agents node in Group Policy to view, assign, and delete recovery agents.

4. To designate an additional recovery agent, right-click Encrypting File System and then select Add Data Recovery Agent. This starts the Add Recovery Agent Wizard, which you can use to select a previously generated certificate that has been assigned to a user and mark it as a designated recovery certificate. Click Next. In the Select Recovery Agents window, click Browse Directory and then use the Finds Users, Contacts, And Groups dialog box to select the user you want to work with. Click OK, and then click Next. Click Finish to add the recovery agent.

> **Note**   Before you can designate additional recovery agents, you should set up a root Certificate Authority (CA) in the domain. Afterward, you must use the Certificates snap-in to generate a personal certificate that uses the EFS Recovery Agent template. The root CA must then approve the certificate request so that the certificate can be used. You can also use Cipher.exe to generate the EFS recovery agent key and certificate.

5. To delete a recovery agent, select the recovery agent's certificate in the right pane and then press Delete. When prompted to confirm the action, click Yes to permanently and irrevocably delete the certificate. If the recovery policy is empty (meaning it has no other designated recovery agents), EFS is turned off so that users can no longer encrypt files.

Backing Up and Restoring Encrypted Data and Certificates

You can back up and restore encrypted data just as you do any other data. The key thing to remember is that you must use backup software that understands EFS, such as the built-in Backup and Restore tools. There are lots of ways to go wrong, however.

The backup or restore process doesn't necessarily back up or restore the certificate needed to work with the encrypted data. The user's profile data contains the certificate needed to work with the encrypted data. If the user's account exists and the profile still contains the necessary certificate, then, yes, the user can still work with the encrypted data.

If the user's account exists and you previously backed up the user's profile and then restored the profile to recover a deleted certificate, then, yes, the user can still work with the encrypted data. Otherwise, however, there's no way to work with the data and you'll need to have a designated recovery agent access the files and then remove the encryption.

Being able to back up and restore certificates is an important part of any disaster recovery planning. The next sections examine the techniques you can use to perform these tasks.

Backing Up Encryption Certificates

You can use the Certificates snap-in to back up and restore personal certificates. Personal certificates are saved with the Personal Information Exchange (.pfx) format.

The steps you follow to back up personal certificates are as follows:

1. Log on to the computer where the personal certificate you want to work with is stored as the user. Open the Run dialog box by clicking Start and then selecting Run.

2. Type **mmc** in the Open field and then click OK. This opens the Microsoft Management Console (MMC).

3. In the MMC, select File, and then select Add/Remove Snap-In. This opens the Add/ Remove Snap-In dialog box.

4. In the Standalone tab, click Add. In the Add Snap-In dialog box, select Certificates, and then click Add. This displays the Certificates Snap-in dialog box.

5. Select My User Account and then click Finish.

6. Click Close and then click OK.

7. Expand Certificates - Current User, Personal, and then select Certificates. Right-click the certificate you want to save, choose All Tasks, and then select Export. This starts the Certificate Export Wizard.

8. Click Next and then select Yes, Export The Private Key. Click Next.

9. Click Next, accepting the default values, and then type a password for the certificate.

10. Specify a file location for the certificate file. Be sure that this location is secure, because you don't want to compromise system security. The file is saved with the .pfx extension.

11. Click Next and then click Finish. If the export process is successful, you'll see a message box confirming this. Click OK to close the message box.

Restoring Encryption Certificates

When you have a backup of a certificate, you can restore the certificate to any computer on the network—not just the original computer. The backup and restore process is, in fact, how you move certificates from one computer to another.

The steps you follow to restore a personal certificate are as follows:

1. Copy the Personal Information Exchange (.pfx) file onto a floppy disk and then log on to the computer where you want to use the personal certificate as the user.

> **Note**   Log on to the target computer as the user whose certificate you're restoring. If you don't do this, the user won't be able to work with his or her encrypted data.

2. Access the Certificates snap-in for My User Account as described previously.

3. Expand Certificates - Current User and then right-click Personal. Choose All Tasks and then select Import. This starts the Certificate Import Wizard.

4. Click Next and then insert the floppy disk.

5. Click Browse and then use the Open dialog box to locate the personal certificate on the floppy disk. Be sure to select Personal Information Exchange as the file type. After you locate the file, select it and then click Open.

6. Click Next. Type the password for the personal certificate and then click Next again.

7. The certificate should be placed in the Personal store by default, so accept the default by clicking Next. Click Finish. If the import process is successful, you'll see a message box confirming this. Click OK.

Disaster Recovery and Preparation

Backups are only one part of a comprehensive disaster recovery plan. You also need to have emergency repair disks and boot disks on hand to ensure that you can recover systems in a wide variety of situations. You might also need to install the Recovery Console.

When you set out to recover a system, you should follow these steps:

1. Try to start the system in safe mode, as described in the section of this chapter entitled "Starting a System in Safe Mode."

2. Try to recover the system using the System Recovery Data (if available). See the section of this chapter entitled "Using the Recovery Data to Restore a System."

3. Try to recover the system using the Recovery Console. See the section of this chapter entitled "Working with the Recovery Console."

4. Restore the system from backup. Be sure to restore the system state data as well as any essential files.

Creating System Recovery Data

Automated System Recovery (ASR) data can often help you recover a system that won't boot. The recovery data includes essential system files, partition boot sector information, and the startup environment for a particular system. You should create recovery data for each computer on the network, starting with servers running Windows Server 2003. Normally, you'll want to update the recovery data when you install service packs, manipulate the boot drive, or modify the startup environment. Recovery data does not include user data files.

You can create ASR data using the Backup utility. ASR data is stored in two different forms: primary data and secondary data. The primary data is stored on the backup media you choose, such as a tape backup or disk drive. The secondary data is stored on a floppy disk and contains the files needed to boot the operating system and access the primary data.

> **Tip** When you completed the installation of the operating system, basic recovery information was saved in the %SystemRoot%\Repair folder on the system partition. The Repair folder contains a copy of the local Security Account Manager (SAM) data and other essential system files. It doesn't contain a backup of the Windows registry. You should create a registry backup when you create the recovery data.

You can create a system recovery data snapshot by completing the following steps:

1. Insert a blank 3.5-inch, 1.44-MB disk into the floppy drive.

2. Start the Backup utility. If wizard mode is enabled, click Next, select Prepare An Automated System Recovery Backup, and then click Next again. If wizard mode is disabled, click Automated System Recovery Wizard in the Welcome tab and then click Next.

3. On the Backup Destination page, specify where the primary data should be stored. Select the backup media type and then specify the location of the backup media. Click Browse to search for a save location.

4. Click Next and then click Finish.

5. Click OK. When prompted, remove the ASR disk and label it for the system.

> **Note** On member servers, the primary data is approximately 1 GB in size. On domain controllers, the primary data is approximately 2 GB in size. If you backup the primary data to a network path, this network path may not be available when you are trying to recover a server.

Starting a System in Safe Mode

If a system won't boot normally, you can use safe mode to recover or troubleshoot system problems. In safe mode, Windows Server 2003 loads only basic files, services, and drivers. The drivers loaded include the mouse, monitor, keyboard, mass storage, and base video. No networking services or drivers are started—unless you choose the Safe Mode With Networking option. Because safe mode loads a limited set of configuration information, it can help you troubleshoot problems. You'll usually want to use safe mode before trying to use the emergency repair disk or the Recovery Console.

You start a system in safe mode by completing the following steps:

1. Start (or restart) the problem system.

2. During startup you should see a prompt labeled Please Select The Operating System To Start. Press F8.

3. Use the arrow keys to select the safe mode you want to use, and then press Enter. The safe mode option you use depends on the type of problem you're experiencing. The key options you might see are:

    Safe Mode   Loads only basic files, services, and drivers during the initialization sequence. The drivers loaded include the mouse, monitor, keyboard, mass storage, and base video. No networking services or drivers are started.

    Safe Mode With Command Prompt   Loads basic files, services, and drivers and then starts a command prompt instead of the Windows Server 2003 graphical interface. No networking services or drivers are started.

    Safe Mode With Networking   Loads basic files, services, and drivers, as well as services and drivers needed to start networking.

    Enable Boot Logging   Allows you to create a record of all startup events in a boot log.

    Enable VGA Mode   Allows you to start the system in Video Graphics Adapter (VGA) mode, which is useful if the system display is set to a mode that can't be used with the current monitor.

    Last Known Good Configuration   Starts the computer in safe mode using registry information that Windows Server 2003 saved at the last successful logon.

    Directory Services Recovery Mode   Starts the system in safe mode and allows you to restore the directory service. This option is available on Windows Server 2003 domain controllers.

    Debugging Mode   Starts the system in debugging mode, which is useful only for troubleshooting operating system bugs.

4. If a problem doesn't reappear when you start in safe mode, you can eliminate the default settings and basic device drivers as possible causes. If a newly added device or updated driver is causing problems, you can use safe mode to remove the device or reverse the update.

Using the Recovery Data to Restore a System

When you can't start or recover a system in safe mode, your next step is to try to recover the system using the last system recovery data snapshot you made (if available). The recovery data comes in handy in two situations. If the boot sector or essential system files are damaged, you might be able to use the recovery data to restore the system. If the startup environment is causing problems on a dual or multiboot system, you might be able to recover the system as well. You can't recover a damaged registry, however. To do that, you must use the Recovery Console.

You can repair a system using the recovery data by completing the following steps:

1. Insert the Windows Server 2003 CD or the first setup boot disk into the appropriate drive, and then restart the computer. When booting from a floppy disk, you'll need to remove and insert disks when prompted.

2. When the Setup program begins, follow the prompts, and then choose the Repair Or Recover option by pressing R.

3. If you haven't already done so, insert the Windows Server 2003 CD into the appropriate drive when prompted.

4. Choose emergency repair by pressing R and then do one of the following:

    Press M For Manual Repair   Select this option to choose whether you want to repair system files, the partition boot sector, or the startup environment. Only advanced users or administrators should use this option.

    Press F For Fast Repair   Select this option to have Windows Server 2003 attempt to repair problems related to system files, the partition boot sector, and the startup environment.

5. Insert the System Recovery floppy disk when prompted. Damaged or missing files are replaced with files from the Windows Server 2003 CD or from the %SystemRoot%\Repair folder on the system partition. These replacement files won't reflect any configuration changes made after setup, and you might need to reinstall service packs and other updates.

6. If the repair is successful, the system is restarted and should boot normally. If you still have problems, you might need to use the Recovery Console.

Working with the Recovery Console

The Recovery Console is one of your last lines of defense in recovering a system. The Recovery Console operates much like the command prompt and is ideally suited to resolving problems with files, drivers, and services. Using the Recovery Console, you can fix the boot sector and master boot record; enable and disable device drivers and services; change the attributes of files on FAT, FAT32, and NTFS volumes; read and write files on FAT, FAT32, and NTFS volumes; copy files from floppy or CD to hard disk drives; run Check Disk; and format drives.

The sections that follow discuss techniques you can use to work with the Recovery Console. As you'll learn, you can start the Recovery Console from the setup boot disks or you can install the Recovery Console as a startup option.

Installing the Recovery Console as a Startup Option

On a system with frequent or recurring problems, you might want to install the Recovery Console as a startup option. In this way, you don't have to go through the setup boot disks to access the Recovery Console. You can use this option only if the system is running. If you can't start the system, see the section of this chapter entitled "Starting the Recovery Console."

You install the Recovery Console as a startup option by completing the following steps:

1. Insert the Windows Server 2003 CD into the CD-ROM drive.

2. Click the Start menu and then click Run. This displays the Run dialog box.

3. Type **h:\i386\winnt32.exe /cmdcons** in the Open field, where h is the CD-ROM drive letter.

4. Click OK, and then when prompted, click Yes. The Recovery Console is then installed as a startup option.

Note   Normally, only administrators can install and run the Recovery Console. If you want normal users to be able to run the Recovery Console, you must enable the Auto Admin Logon policy for the local computer policy (Computer Configuration\Windows Settings\Security Settings\Local Policies\Security Options\Recovery Console: Allow Automatic Administrative Logon). This, however, is not recommended, as it represents a major security vulnerability.

Starting the Recovery Console

If a computer won't start and you haven't installed the Recovery Console as a startup option, you can start the computer and the Recovery Console by completing the following steps:

1. Insert the Windows Server 2003 CD or the first setup boot disk into the appropriate drive and then restart the computer. When booting from a floppy disk, you'll need to remove and insert disks when prompted.

2. When the Setup program begins, follow the prompts, and then choose the Repair Or Recover option by pressing R.

3. If you haven't already done so, insert the Windows Server 2003 CD into the appropriate drive when prompted.

4. Choose Recovery Console by pressing C. When prompted, type the local administrator password.

5. When the system starts, you'll see a command prompt into which you can type Recovery Console commands. Exit the console and restart the computer by typing **exit**.

Recovery Console Commands

The Recovery Console is run in a special command prompt. At this command prompt, type **HELP** to list all available commands.

The commands you'll use most often are ATTRIB, NET, FIXBOOT, FIXMBR, and EXIT. ATTRIB changes the attributes of files. You could, for example, change a read-only file to read/write. Windows Server 2003 allows you to map to a shared folder on another system using the NET command. You could then transfer files to or from the remote system. The FIXBOOT and FIXMBR commands can get you out of real jams. These commands can resolve problems with the boot sector and the master boot record on Master Boot Record drives. After you've made any necessary changes or repairs, use the EXIT command to exit the console and restart the computer.

Deleting the Recovery Console

If you installed Recovery Console as a startup option and no longer want this option to be available, you can delete the Recovery Console. To do that, follow these steps:

1. Start Windows Explorer, and then select the hard disk drive on which you installed the Recovery Console. This is normally the boot drive.

2. From the Tools menu, select Folder Options.

3. In the View tab, select Show Hidden Files And Folders, and then clear the Hide Protected Operating System Files check box. Click OK.

4. The right pane should show the root directory for the boot drive. Delete the Cmdcons folder and the Cmldr file.

5. Right-click the Boot.ini file, and then click Properties.

6. In the Properties dialog box, clear the Read-only check box. Then click OK.

7. Open Boot.ini in Notepad. Then remove the startup entry for the Recovery Console. The entry looks like this:

   ```
   C:\CMDCONS \BOOTSECT.DAT="Microsoft Windows Server 2003 Recovery
   Console " //cmdcons
   ```

8. Save the Boot.ini file and then change its property settings back to read-only. Once deleted, the Recovery Console is no longer listed as a startup option. You can reinstall the console if you need to at a later date or run the console as described in the "Starting the Recovery Console" section of this chapter.

Managing Media Pools

Collections of tapes are organized into media pools. The tasks you use to work with media pools are explained in the following sections.

Understanding Media Pools

You manage media pools through the Removable Storage node in Computer Management, shown in Figure 15-11. With Removable Storage all media belongs to a pool of a specific media type. The concept of a media pool is very dynamic. Libraries can have multiple media pools, and some media pools can span multiple libraries.

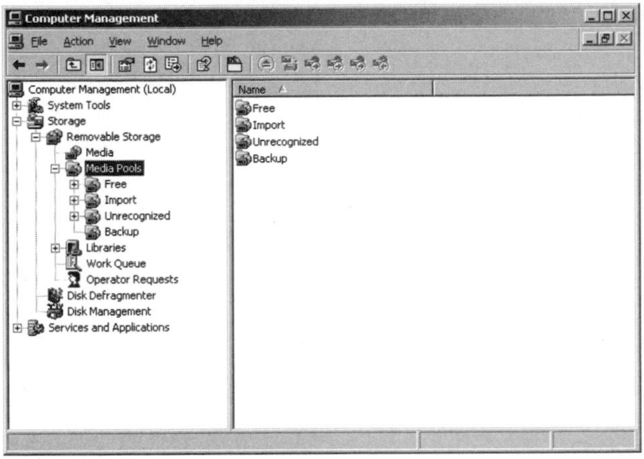

Figure 15-11 When you manage media using Removable Storage, keep in mind that each media pool has a specific purpose. The Backup utility uses media allocated to the Backup application pool and the Free Media pool.

You can also use media pools to establish a hierarchy in which top-level media pools contain lower-level media pools and these media pools in turn contain collections of tapes or disks.

Removable Storage categorizes media pools into types. The different types of media pools are:

Unrecognized Media pools containing media that Removable Storage doesn't recognize, as well as new media that hasn't been written to yet. To make Unrecognized media available for use, move the media to the Free media pool. If you eject the media before doing this, the media are automatically deleted from the Removable Storage database and no longer tracked.

Free Media pools containing media that aren't currently in use and don't contain useful data. These media are available for use by applications.

Import Media pools containing media that Removable Storage recognizes but that haven't been used before in a particular Removable Storage system. For example, if you're transferring media from one office to another, the media might be listed as Import. To reuse the media at the new location, move the media to Free media or Application media pools.

Application Media pools containing media that are allocated to and controlled by an application, such as the Backup utility. Members of the Administrators and the Backup Operators groups can control Application media pools as well. You can configure Application media pools to automatically draw media from Free media pools, as necessary. Once they're allocated, you can't move Application media between media pools.

Free, Unrecognized, and Import media pools are referred to as *system media pools*. Unlike Application media pools that you can delete, you can't delete system media pools.

Preparing Media for Use in the Free Media Pool

If media have information that you don't need anymore, you can initialize the media and prepare them for use in the Free media pool. When you do this, you destroy the information on the media and move the media to the Free media pool.

To prepare media for the Free media pool, follow these steps:

1. In Computer Management, access Removable Storage, and then double-click Libraries.

2. Expand the library and the library's Media folder by double-clicking them.

3. Right-click the media you want to prepare and then click Prepare.

4. Confirm the action by clicking Yes.

Moving Media to a Different Media Pool

You can move media to a different media pool to make it available for use or to allocate it to an application. To do that, follow these steps:

1. In Computer Management, access Removable Storage. Afterward, expand the Libraries and Media Pools folders by double-clicking them.

2. Select the media pool that contains the media you want to move.

3. In the details pane, drag the media you want to the applicable media pool in the console tree.

> **Caution**   Moving media to the Free media pool destroys the data on the media. Additionally, you can't move read-only media to the Free media pool.

Creating Application Media Pools

The only type of media pool you can create is an Application media pool. To do this, follow these steps:

1. In Removable Storage, right-click Media Pools, and then click Create Media Pool. Or right-click an existing Application media pool and then click Create Media Pool.

2. In the Create A New Media Pool Properties dialog box, type a name and description of the media pool as shown in Figure 15-12.

3. If the media pool will contain other media pools, select Contains Other Media Pools. Otherwise, click Contains Media Of Type and select an appropriate media type from the list.

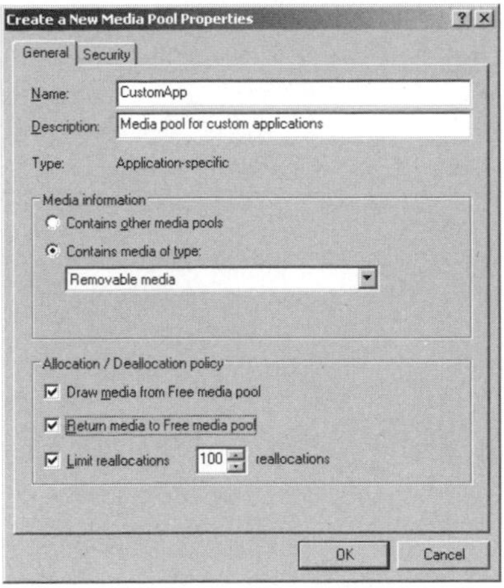

Figure 15-12 When you create a media pool for applications, be sure to specify the appropriate media type. You should also specify how media will be allocated or deallocated from the media pool.

4. Complete the process by clicking OK. As necessary, allocate media and configure security. These procedures are described in the "Setting Allocation and Deallocation Policies" and "Working with Access Permissions for Removable Storage" sections of this chapter.

Changing the Media Type in a Media Pool

Each media pool can contain only one type of media. The media type is normally assigned when you create the media pool, but you can change the media type provided no media is currently assigned to the media pool.

To change the media type, follow these steps:

1. In Removable Storage, double-click Media Pools.

2. Right-click the media pool you want to work with, and then select Properties.

3. In the General tab, select Contains Media Of Type, and then select an appropriate media type from the list. Click OK.

Setting Allocation and Deallocation Policies

You can configure Application media pools to automatically allocate and deallocate Free media. By enabling this process, you ensure that when an application needs media, the application can obtain it. Then, when the media is no longer needed, it can be returned to the Free media pool.

You configure allocation and deallocation of media by completing the following steps:

1. In Removable Storage, double-click Media Pools.

2. Right-click the media pool you want to work with and then select Properties. This media pool must contain media of a specific type and can't be a container for other media pools.

3. In the General tab, use the following check boxes under Allocation/Deallocation Policy to control media allocation:

    Draw Media From Free Media Pool   Select this option to automatically draw unused media from a Free media pool when needed.

    Return Media To Free Media Pool   Select this option to automatically return media to a Free media pool when no longer needed.

    Limit Reallocations   Select this option if you want to limit the number of times that tapes or disks can be reused. Then use the Reallocations field to set a specific limit.

4. Click OK.

Working with Access Permissions for Removable Storage

Like other objects in Windows Server 2003, Removable Storage has specific access permissions. You can set access permissions for all of Removable Storage as well as individual media pools, libraries, and media. Table 15-4 summarizes the available user permissions from lowest to highest. Higher-level permissions inherit the capabilities of lower-level permissions.

Note   Keep in mind that these permissions apply to the Removable Storage system and not to the files that might be stored in media. NTFS access permissions still apply to files on NTFS formatted media.

Table 15-4   Access Permissions for Removable Storage

Permission	Meaning for Removable Storage	Meaning for Media, Media Pools, or Libraries
Use	Grants read access to Removable Storage but not necessarily to media, media pools, or libraries.	Grants read access to the individual media, media pool, or library. Allows user to insert/eject media and take inventory in a library.
Modify	Grants read/write access. User can create media pools and manage the work and requests queues.	User can change properties of the media, media pool, or library.

Table 15-4   Access Permissions for Removable Storage

Permission	Meaning for Removable Storage	Meaning for Media, Media Pools, or Libraries
Control	Grants all Use and Modify permissions. In addition, user can delete media pools and delete libraries.	User can insert/eject media, take inventory in a library, and delete media pools or libraries.
Modify Permissions	Grants user the right to change permissions for media, media pools, and libraries.	User can change permissions for media, media pools, and libraries.
View Permissions	Grants user the right to change permissions for media, media pools, and libraries.	User can review but not change permissions for media, media pools, and libraries.

Initially, Removable Storage is configured to be managed by the operating system, Administrators, and Backup Operators. Normal users are granted only limited access, which might be necessary when they're working with both Removable Storage and Remote Storage. If you use Removable Storage for purposes other than backup and recovery operations, you might want to grant access to other users and groups. However, only Administrators and Backup Operators have the necessary permissions to back up and restore files on computers. Thus, even if you grant an operator control, that person might not be able to back up and restore files.

You can set access permissions for Removable Storage, media pools, libraries, and media. The available permissions are Use, Modify, Control, Modify Permissions, and View Permissions. These permissions were summarized earlier in the chapter.

You set or view permissions by completing the following steps:

1. In Removable Storage, right-click the element with which you want to work.

2. Select Properties from the pop-up menu and then click the Security tab, as shown in Figure 15-13.

3. Users or groups that already have access to the element are listed in the Group Or User Names list box. Change permissions by selecting a group or user and then using the Permissions For ... list box to grant or deny access permissions.

4. To set access permissions for additional users, computers, or groups, click the Add button. Then use Select Users, Computers, Or Groups to add users, computers, or groups. Afterward, set permissions for the groups or users you've added.

5. Click OK when you're finished.

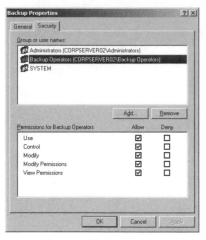

Figure 15-13   Use the Security tab to configure access permissions.

Deleting Application Media Pools

In Removable Storage, you delete Application media pools by right-clicking them and selecting Delete. Do this only if you no longer need the media pool.

Note   You shouldn't delete Application media pools created by Windows Server 2003, such as Backup and Remote Storage. The operating system uses these.

Managing Work Queues, Requests, and Operators

Whenever you work with removable media, you'll need to keep a close eye on the work queues, operator requests, and security.

Using Work Queue

Work Queue is the area where Removable Storage displays the status of operations. You access Work Queue by expanding Removable Storage and then clicking Work Queue in the console tree.

Operations are tasks that administrators, backup operators, and other authorized users initiate. Each operation listed in the queue has a specific state, which indicates the operation's status. Operation states include:

Waiting   Operation is waiting to execute.

In Progress   Operation is executing.

Completed   Operation has completed successfully.

Cancelled   An administrator or other operator cancelled the operation.

Failed   Operation failed to complete.

By default, completed, cancelled, and failed requests stay in the queue for 72 hours. Waiting or in-progress operations stay in the queue until their status changes. If waiting or in-progress operations are causing problems, such as delaying priority operations, you can manage the requests in one of these ways:

Reorder mount operations   Changing the mount order can allow priority operations to execute before lower priority operations. For example, if you're backing up a database, you can make your mount operation the next one in the queue, pushing it ahead of others. You change the mount order as described in the section of this chapter entitled "Changing Mount Operations."

Cancel operations   Canceling an operation can free up drives and media when operations are waiting for another operation to complete. For example, processes that are waiting to be executed can often be holding up other processes, and in this case you might need to cancel the process to allow other processes to execute. You cancel a waiting operation by right-clicking it and then selecting Cancel Operation.

Deleting operations   You can delete completed, canceled, or failed operations manually or automatically. You configure when operations are deleted as described in the section of this chapter entitled "Controlling When Operations Are Deleted."

Troubleshooting Waiting Operations

If operations have a status of Waiting, it can be an indicator that something has gone wrong. For example, the operation might be waiting because the resource isn't in the correct state. If the operation has been waiting for a long time, this can mean that the resource isn't mounted, enabled, or otherwise working properly and that you might need to dismount, enable, or correct a problem with the resource.

To correct the problem you might need to cancel the operation, perform a corrective action, and then issue a new operation. You cancel a waiting operation by right-clicking it and then selecting Cancel Operation.

Changing Mount Operations

When two or more mount operations are waiting, you can change the order of the operations to allow priority operations to proceed ahead of other operations. To do this, follow these steps:

1. Right-click the waiting mount operation you want to manipulate, and then select Re-Order Mounts. This displays the Change Mount Order dialog box.

2. The current order of the mount operation is shown. The options available allow you to:

   ❑ Move the mount operation to the front of the queue, which ensures that it's the next mount operation executed.

❑ Move the mount operation to the back of the queue, which ensures that it's executed after existing mount operations.

❑ Move the mount operation to a specific location in the queue, which allows you to move the operation ahead of or behind other operations without making it the highest or lowest priority.

3. Click OK.

Controlling When Operations Are Deleted

By default, completed, canceled, and failed operations are deleted from the work queue after 72 hours. You can control when operations are deleted by:

Deleting individual operations   To delete operations individually, right-click them and then select Delete.

Deleting all operations   To delete all completed, canceled, and failed operations, right-click Work Queue, select Properties, and then click Delete All Now.

Reconfiguring automatic deletion times   To change the automatic deletion time, follow these steps:

1. Right-click Work Queue, and then select Properties. This displays the dialog box shown in Figure 15-14.

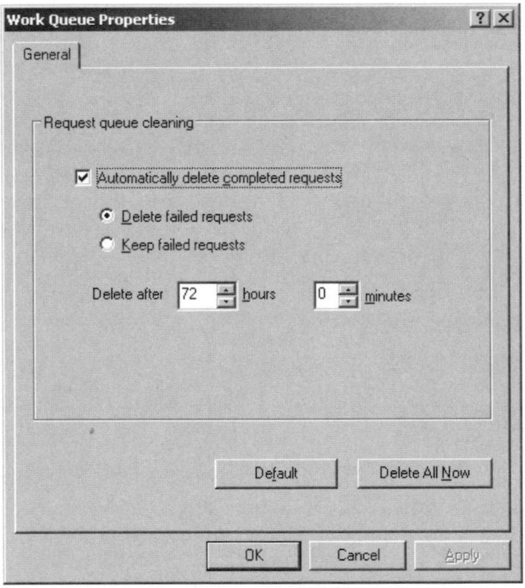

Figure 15-14   You can control when operations are deleted from the queue by using the Work Queue Properties dialog box.

2. To stop automatic deletion of all operations, clear the Automatically Delete Completed Requests check box and complete the process by clicking OK.

3. To enable automatic deletion, select the Automatically Delete Completed Requests check box. Completed requests are now deleted automatically.

4. Select Delete Failed Requests to automatically delete failed requests as well. Or, to save failed requests, select Keep Failed Requests.

5. In Delete After, change the deletion interval using the Hours and Minutes combo boxes.

6. Click OK.

Using the Operator Requests Queue

Operator Requests is the area where Removable Storage displays the status of requests that need the attention of administrators or backup operators. You access Operator Requests by expanding Removable Storage and then clicking Operator Requests in the console tree.

Each entry in the queue represents a task that you or another operator needs to perform. These requests are issued by Removable Storage or a compliant application for operations that are performed manually, such as inserting a cleaning cartridge, inserting offline tapes, or servicing a library. Each request has a specific state, which indicates the request's status. You can respond to requests by either completing or refusing the request. By default, completed or refused requests stay in the queue for 72 hours.

To help you track the status of requests, all requests are listed according to their current state. Request states include:

Completed   Request was completed as specified by an operator or detected by Removable Storage. To mark a request as completed, right-click it and select Complete.

Refused   Request was refused by an operator and won't be performed. To mark a request as refused, right-click it and select Refuse.

Submitted   Removable Storage or a compliant application submitted the request and is waiting for an operator to handle the request.

Chapter 16

Managing TCP/IP Networking

As an administrator, you enable networked computers to communicate by using the basic networking protocols built into Microsoft Windows Server 2003. The key protocol you'll use is Transmission Control Protocol/Internet Protocol (TCP/IP). TCP/IP is actually a collection of protocols and services used for communicating over a network. It's the primary protocol used for internetwork communications. Compared to configuring other networking protocols, configuring TCP/IP communications is fairly complicated, but TCP/IP is the most versatile protocol available.

In this chapter, you'll learn about configuring and managing TCP/IP networking. Whenever you work with TCP/IP networking, you must tell the computer about the network. You do this by telling the computer how to route information on the network and how to access other computers. After you configure TCP/IP, you also need to make the computer a member of the network so it can access network resources.

> **Note** Group policy settings can affect your ability to install and manage TCP/IP networking. Key policies you'll want to examine are those in User Configuration \Administrative Templates\Network\Network Connections and Computer Configuration\Administrative Templates\System\Group Policy. Group policy is discussed in Chapter 4, "Automating Administrative Tasks, Policies, and Procedures."

Installing TCP/IP Networking

TCP/IP networking relies on network adapters and the TCP/ IP protocol. To access the network using TCP/IP, you need to install one or more network adapters on the computer and then set up the TCP/IP protocol.

Installing Network Interface Cards

Network interface cards (NICs), also known as network adapters, are hardware devices that are used to communicate on networks. You can install and configure NICs by completing the following steps:

1. Configure the NIC following the manufacturer's instructions. For example, you might need to modify the card's Interrupt setting or Port setting by using the software provided by the manufacturer.

2. Disconnect the computer from the network, turn it off, unplug it, and then install the adapter in the appropriate slot on the computer. When you're finished, boot the system.

3. Windows Server 2003 should detect the new adapter during startup. If you have a separate driver disk for the adapter, you should insert it now. Otherwise, you might be prompted to insert a driver disk.

4. If Windows Server 2003 doesn't detect the adapter automatically, follow the installation instructions in the section entitled "Managing Hardware Devices and Drivers" in Chapter 2, "Managing Servers Running Microsoft Windows Server 2003."

5. If networking services aren't installed on the system, install them as described in the next section.

Installing the TCP/IP Protocol

TCP/IP networking is normally installed during Windows Server 2003 installation. You can also install TCP/IP networking through Network Connections. If you're installing TCP/IP after installing Windows Server 2003, log on to the computer using an account with Administrator privileges and then follow these steps:

1. Access Network Connections in Control Panel.

2. Select or double-click the connection you want to work with.

   Note   Local area network (LAN) connections are created automatically if the computer has a network adapter and is connected to a network. If a computer has multiple adapter cards and is connected to a network, you'll see one LAN connection for each adapter card. If no network connection is available, you should connect the computer to the network or create a different type of connection, as explained in the section of this chapter entitled "Managing Network Connections."

3. In the Status dialog box, click Properties. This displays the Local Area Connection Properties dialog box shown in Figure 16-1. If Internet Protocol (TCP/IP) isn't shown in the list of installed components, you'll need to install it. Click Install, select Protocol, and then click Add. In the Select Network Protocol dialog box, select Internet Protocol (TCP/IP), and then click OK.

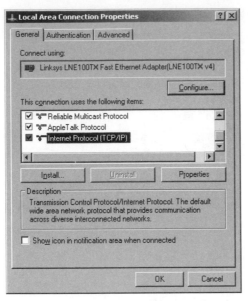

Figure 16-1   Use the Local Area Connection Properties dialog box to install and configure TCP/IP.

4. In the Local Area Connection Properties dialog box, make sure that the Internet Protocol (TCP/IP) check box is selected, and then click OK.

5. As necessary, follow the instructions in the next section for configuring TCP/IP for the computer.

Configuring TCP/IP Networking

Computers use IP addresses to communicate over TCP/IP. Windows Server 2003 provides several ways to configure IP addressing:

Manually   IP addresses that are assigned manually are called *static* IP addresses. Static IP addresses are fixed and don't change unless you change them. You'll usually assign static IP addresses to servers running Windows Server 2003, and when you do this, you'll need to configure additional information to help the server navigate the network.

Dynamically   A Dynamic Host Configuration Protocol (DHCP) server (if one is installed on the network) assigns dynamic IP addresses at startup, and the addresses might change over time. Dynamic IP addressing is the default configuration and in most cases is set up automatically on Windows workstations.

Alternatively   When a computer is configured to use DHCP and no DHCP server is available, Windows Server 2003 assigns an alternate private IP address automatically. This alternate IP address is referred to as an Automatic Private IP Address (APIPA). By default, this address is in the range from 169.254.0.1 to 169.254.255.254 with a subnet mask of 255.255.0.0. You can also specify a user-configured alternate IP address, which is particularly useful for laptop users who need one IP configuration in the office and another at home.

Configuring Static IP Addresses

When you assign a static IP address, you need to tell the computer the IP address you want to use, the subnet mask for this IP address, and, if necessary, the default gateway to use for internetwork communications. An IP address is a numeric identifier for a computer. IP addressing schemes vary according to how your network is configured, but they're normally assigned from a range of addresses for a particular network segment. For example, if you're working with a computer on the network segment 192.168.10.0, the address range you have available for computers is usually from 192.168.10.1 to 192.168.10.254. The address 192.168.10.255 normally is reserved for network broadcasts.

If the network is connected directly to the Internet and you've reserved a range of IP addresses, you can use the IP addresses you've been assigned. If you're on a private network that's indirectly connected to the Internet, you should use private IP addresses. Private network addresses are summarized in Table 16-1.

Table 16-1   Private Network Addresses

Private Network ID	Subnet Mask	IP Address Range
10.0.0.0	255.0.0.0	10.0.0.1 – 10.255.255.254
172.16.0.0	255.240.0.0	172.16.0.1 – 172.31.255.254
192.168.0.0	255.255.0.0	192.168.0.1 – 192.168.255.254

All other network addresses are public and must be leased or purchased.

Using Ping to Check an Address

Before you assign a static IP address, you should make sure that the address isn't already in use or reserved for use with DHCP. You can use the Ping utility to find out if an address is in use. Open a command prompt and type **ping**, followed by the IP address you want to check. To test the IP address 192.168.10.12, you would use the following command:

```
ping 192.168.10.12
```

If you receive a successful reply from the ping test, the IP address is in use and you should try another IP address. If the request times out for all ping attempts, the IP address isn't active on the network at this time and probably isn't in use. Your company's network administrator would be able to confirm this for you as well.

Assigning a Static IP Address

You assign a static IP address by doing the following:

1. Access Network Connections in Control Panel.

2. Select or double-click the connection with which you want to work.

3. Click Properties and then open the Internet Protocol (TCP/ IP) Properties dialog box shown in Figure 16-2 by double-clicking Internet Protocol (TCP/IP). Or select Internet Protocol (TCP/IP) and then click Properties.

> **Note**   LAN connections are created automatically when you start a computer that's attached to a network; you don't need to create a connection. One LAN connection is shown for each network adapter installed. If you use a dial-up or other type of connection, you must create the connection as described in the "Managing Network Connections" section of this chapter.

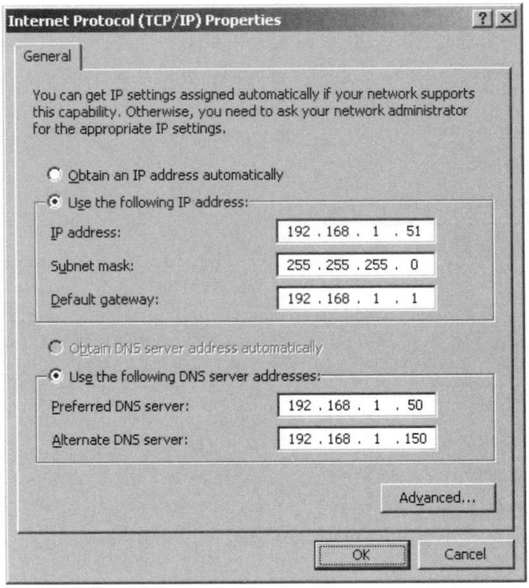

Figure 16-2   Use the Internet Protocol (TCP/IP) Properties dialog box to configure dynamic and static IP addressing.

4. Select Use The Following IP Address, and then type the IP address in the IP Address field. The IP address you assign to the computer must not be used anywhere else on the network.

5. The Subnet Mask field ensures that the computer communicates over the network properly. Windows Server 2003 should insert a default value for the subnet mask into the Subnet Mask field. If the network doesn't use subnets, the default

value should suffice. But if it does use subnets, you'll need to change this value as appropriate for your network.

6. If the computer needs to access other TCP/IP networks, the Internet, or other subnets, you must specify a default gateway. Type the IP address of the network's default router in the Default Gateway field.

7. Domain name services are needed for domain name resolution. Type a preferred and alternate Domain Name System (DNS) server address in the fields provided.

8. When you're finished, click OK. Repeat this process for other network adapters you want to configure. Keep in mind that each network adapter must have a unique IP address.

9. Configure Windows Internet Name Service (WINS) as necessary. You might also need to set advanced options for DNS.

Configuring Dynamic IP Addresses

DHCP gives you centralized control over IP addressing and TCP/IP default settings. If the network has a DHCP server, you can assign a dynamic IP address to any of the network adapter cards on a computer. Afterward, you rely on the DHCP server to supply the basic information necessary for TCP/IP networking. Because the dynamic IP address can change, you shouldn't use a dynamic IP address for servers running Windows Server 2003. You configure dynamic IP addressing by completing the following steps:

1. Access Network Connections in Control Panel, and then select or double-click the connection with which you want to work.

   Note   One LAN connection is shown for each network adapter installed. These connections are created automatically.

2. Click Properties and then open the Internet Protocol (TCP/ IP) Properties dialog box by double-clicking Internet Protocol (TCP/IP). Or you could select Internet Protocol (TCP/IP) and then click Properties.

3. Select Obtain An IP Address Automatically. If desired, select Obtain DNS Server Address Automatically. Or select Use The Following DNS Server Addresses and then type a preferred and alternate DNS server address in the text boxes provided.

4. When you're finished, click OK. Afterward, configure alternate private IP addresses, DNS, and WINS as necessary.

Configuring Alternate Private IP Addresses

When you use DHCP, don't forget that Windows Server 2003 automatically assigns an alternate IP address when it can't reach the DHCP server during startup or when the current IP address lease expires. By default, the alternate IP address is in the range from 169.254.0.1 to 169.254.255.254 with a subnet mask of 255.255.0.0. Because the automatic private IP address configuration doesn't include default gateway, DNS, or WINS server settings, a computer using the alternate IP addressing is essentially isolated on its own network segment.

If you want to ensure that a computer uses a specific IP address when no DHCP server is available, you need to specify an alternate configuration manually. One of the key reasons for setting an alternate configuration is to accommodate portable computer users who take their computers home. In this way, the user's portable computer could be configured to use a dynamically assigned IP address at work and an alternate IP address configuration at home.

You can specify an alternate private IP address by completing the following steps:

1. Access Network Connections in Control Panel and then select or double-click the connection with which you want to work.

2. Click Properties and then open the Internet Protocol (TCP/ IP) Properties dialog box by double-clicking Internet Protocol (TCP/IP). Or you could select Internet Protocol (TCP/IP) and then click Properties.

3. Provided that you've already configured the adapter to obtain an IP address automatically, you should be able to click the Alternate Configuration tab shown in Figure 16-3.

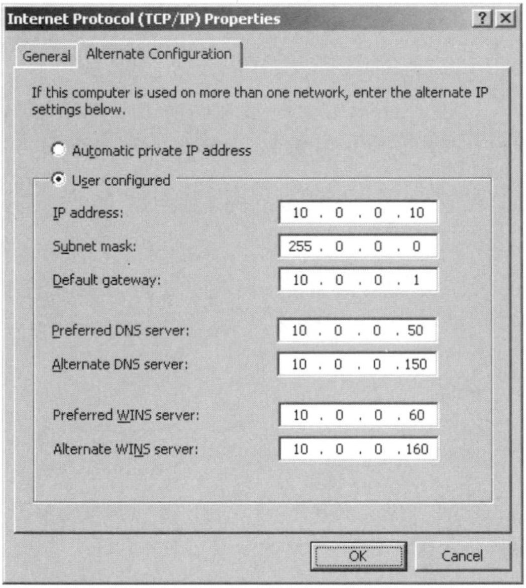

Figure 16-3   Use the Alternate Configuration tab to configure a private IP address for the computer.

4. Select User Configured in the Alternate Configuration tab and then type the IP address you want to use in the IP Address text box. The IP address you assign to the computer should be a private IP address as shown in Table 16-1, and it must not be in use anywhere else at the time the settings are applied.

5. The Subnet Mask text box ensures that the computer communicates over the network properly. Windows Server 2003 should insert a default value for the subnet mask into the Subnet Mask text box. If the network doesn't use subnets, the default value should suffice. But if it does use subnets, you'll need to change this value as appropriate for your network.

6. If the computer needs to access other TCP/IP networks, the Internet, or other subnets, you must specify a default gateway address. Type the IP address of the network's default router in the Default Gateway text box.

7. Domain name services are needed for domain name resolution. Type a preferred and alternate DNS server address in the text boxes provided.

8. If you use WINS on the network for backward compatibility with previous versions of Windows, configure a preferred and alternate WINS server using the text boxes provided. When you're finished, click OK.

Configuring Multiple IP Addresses and Gateways

Computers running Windows Server 2003 can have multiple IP addresses—even if the computers only have a single network adapter card. Multiple IP addresses are useful in several situations:

- You want a single computer to appear to be several computers. For example, if you're installing an intranet server, you might also want the server to provide Web, File Transfer Protocol (FTP), and Simple Mail Transfer Protocol (SMTP) services. You can use a different IP address for each service, and you can use different IP addresses for the intranet and the FTP services.

- If your network is divided into multiple logical IP networks (subnets), and the computer needs access to these subnets to route information or provide other internetworking services, you might want a single network adapter card to have multiple IP addresses. For example, the address 192.168.10.8 could be used for workstations accessing a server from the 192.168.10.0 subnet, and the address 192.168.11.8 could be used for workstations accessing a server from the 192.168.11.0 subnet.

When you use a single network adapter, IP addresses must be assigned to the same network segment or segments that are part of a single logical network. If your network is divided into multiple physical networks, you must use multiple network adapters, with each network adapter being assigned an IP address in a different physical network segment.

Real World If you're looking for a simple cost-effective solution for connecting multiple networks, you might want to take advantage of the IP routing or network bridging features of Windows Server 2003. With IP routing, you configure a server with two adapters (one configured for one network and another configured for another network) to route traffic between the networks. You use Routing And Remote Access Services to configure routing using an appropriate routing protocol, such as RIP Version 2 for Internet Protocol. IP routing is designed for medium and large enterprises and is fairly complex to configure. With network bridging, you create a logical bridge between two networks that's managed by Windows. Bridges are designed for small enterprises and are available only on Windows Server 2003. You won't find this feature in the Windows Server 2003 Advanced Server or Datacenter Server editions.

Assigning Addresses and Gateways

If you've configured a computer with a static IP address, each network adapter installed on the computer can have one or more IP addresses. You can associate both static and dynamic IP addresses with one or more default gateways. You assign multiple IP addresses and gateways to a single network adapter card by doing the following:

1. Access Network Connections in Control Panel and then select or double-click the connection you want to work with.

2. Click Properties and then open the Internet Protocol (TCP/IP) Properties dialog box by double-clicking Internet Protocol (TCP/IP). Or you could select Internet Protocol (TCP/IP) and then click Properties.

3. Click Advanced to open the dialog box shown in Figure 16-4.

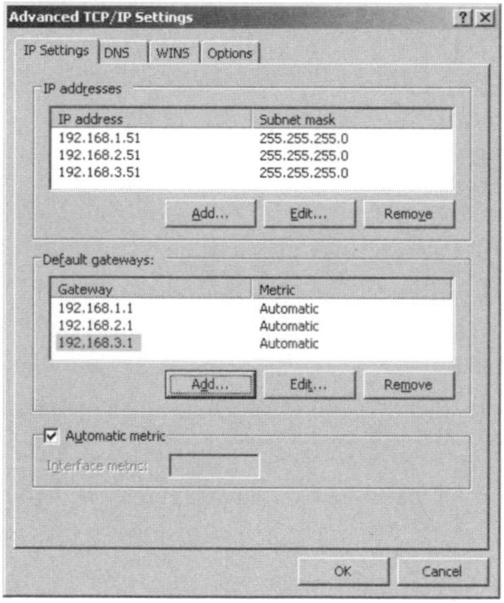

Figure 16-4 Use the Advanced TCP/IP Settings dialog box to configure multiple IP addresses and gateways.

4. In the IP Settings tab, click Add in the IP Addresses area, and then type the IP address in the IP Address text box and the subnet mask in the Subnet Mask text box. Repeat this step for each IP address you want to add to the network adapter card.

5. You can enter additional default gateways, as necessary. Click Add and then type the gateway address in the Gateway text box.

6. The gateway metric indicates the relative cost of using a gateway. If multiple default routes are available for a particular IP address, Windows Server 2003 uses the gateway with the lowest cost first. If the computer can't communicate with the initial gateway, Windows Server 2003 tries to use the gateway with the next lowest metric. By default, Windows Server 2003 automatically assigns a metric to the gateway. You can assign the metric manually, however. To do this, clear the Automatic Metric check box and then enter a metric in the text box provided.

7. Click Add and then repeat Steps 5–6 for each gateway you want to add.

Configuring DNS Resolution

DNS is a host name resolution service. You use DNS to determine a computer's IP address from its host name. This allows users to work with host names, such as *http://www.msn.com* or *http://www.microsoft.com*, rather than an IP address, such as 192.168.5.102 or 192.168.12.68. DNS is the primary name service for Windows Server 2003 and the Internet.

> **Tip**   In order for DNS to function properly, a DNS server must be installed on the network (or be available to the network). Managing DNS servers is covered in Chapter 20, "Optimizing DNS."

Basic DNS Settings

You can configure basic DNS settings by completing the following steps:

1. Access Network Connections in Control Panel. Afterward, select or double-click the connection with which you want to work.

2. Click Properties and then open the Internet Protocol (TCP/ IP) Properties dialog box by double-clicking Internet Protocol (TCP/IP). Or you could select Internet Protocol (TCP/IP) and then click Properties.

3. If the computer is using DHCP and you want DHCP to specify the DNS server address, select Obtain DNS Server Address Automatically. Otherwise, select Use The Following DNS Server Addresses and then type a primary and alternate DNS server address in the text boxes provided.

Advanced DNS Settings

You configure advanced DNS settings by using the DNS tab in the Advanced TCP/IP Settings dialog box shown in Figure 16-5. You use the fields of the DNS tab as follows:

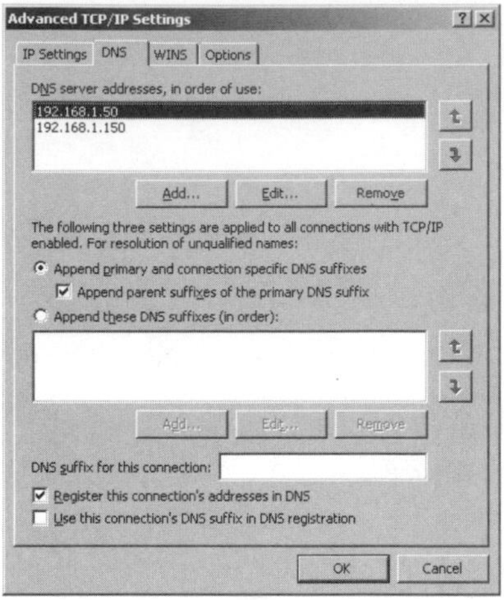

Figure 16-5   Use the DNS tab of the Advanced TCP/IP Settings dialog box to configure advanced DNS settings.

DNS Server Addresses, In Order Of Use   Use this area to specify the IP address of the DNS servers that are used for domain name resolution. Use the Add button to add a server IP address to the list. Use the Remove button to remove a server from the list. Use the Edit button to edit the selected entry. You can specify multiple servers to use for DNS resolution. These servers are used in priority order. If the first server isn't available to respond to a host name resolution request, the next DNS server on the list is accessed, and so on. It's important to note that TCP/ IP doesn't go to the next server if the first server can't resolve the name, only if the first server doesn't respond. To change the position of a server in the list box, click it and then use the Up or Down arrow button.

Append Primary And Connection Specific DNS Suffixes   Select this option to resolve unqualified computer names in the primary domain. For example, if the computer name "Rage" were used and the parent domain were microsoft.com, the computer name would resolve to rage.microsoft.com. If the fully qualified computer name doesn't exist in the parent domain, the query fails. The parent domain used is the one set in the Network Identification tab of the System Properties dialog box. Normally, this option is selected by default.

Append Parent Suffixes Of The Primary DNS Suffix   Select this option to resolve unqualified computer names using the parent-child domain hierarchy. If a query fails in the immediate parent domain, the suffix for the parent of the parent domain is used to try to resolve the query. This process continues until the top of the DNS domain hierarchy is reached. For example, if the computer name "Rage" were used in the dev.microsoft.com domain, DNS would attempt to resolve the computer name to rage.dev.microsoft.com. If this didn't work, DNS would attempt to resolve the computer name to rage.microsoft.com. Normally, this option is selected by default.

Append These DNS Suffixes (In Order)   Select this option to set specific DNS suffixes to use rather than resolving through the parent domain. Use the Add button to add a domain suffix to the list. Use the Remove button to remove a domain suffix from the list. Use the Edit button to edit the selected entry. You can specify multiple domain suffixes. These suffixes are used in priority order. If the first suffix doesn't resolve properly, DNS attempts to use the next suffix in the list. If this fails, the next suffix is used, and so on. To change the order of the domain suffixes, select the suffix, and then use the Up or Down arrow buttons to change its position.

DNS Suffix For This Connection   Sets a specific DNS suffix for the connection that overrides DNS names already configured for use on this connection. You'll usually want to set the DNS domain name through the Network Identification tab in the System Properties dialog box instead.

Register This Connection's Addresses In DNS   Select this option if you want all IP addresses for this connection to be registered in DNS under the computer's fully qualified domain name. This option is selected by default.

Use This Connection's DNS Suffix In DNS Registration   Select this option if you want all IP addresses for this connection to be registered in DNS under the parent domain.

Configuring WINS Resolution

You use WINS to resolve NetBIOS computer names to IP addresses. You can use WINS to help computers on a network determine the addresses of other computers on the network. If a WINS server is installed on the network, you can use the server to resolve computer names. Although WINS is supported on all versions of Windows, Windows Server 2003 uses WINS primarily for backward compatibility.

You can also configure computers running Windows Server 2003 to use the local file LMHOSTS to resolve NetBIOS computer names. However, LMHOSTS is consulted only if normal name resolution methods fail. In a properly configured network, these files are rarely used. Thus, the preferred method of NetBIOS computer name resolution is WINS in conjunction with a WINS server.

You can configure WINS by completing the following steps:

1. Access the Advanced TCP/IP Settings dialog box, and then click the WINS tab. This displays the dialog box shown in Figure 16-6.

2. The box named WINS Addresses, In Order Of Use allows you to specify the IP address of the WINS servers that are used for NetBIOS name resolution. Use the Add button to add a server IP address to the list. Use the Remove button to remove a server from the list. Use the Edit button to edit the selected entry.

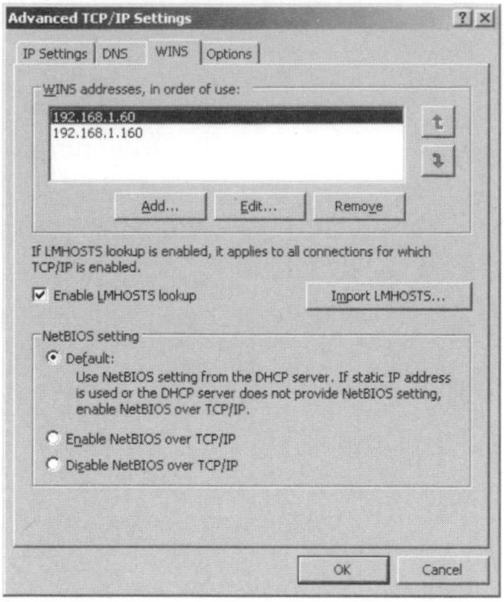

Figure 16-6   Use the WINS tab of the Advanced TCP/IP Settings dialog box to configure WINS resolution for NetBIOS computer names.

3. You can specify multiple servers to use for WINS resolution. These servers are used in priority order. If the first server isn't available to respond to a NetBIOS name resolution request, the computer accesses the next WINS server on the list, and so on. It's important to note that TCP/IP doesn't go to the next server if the first server can't resolve the name, only if the first server doesn't respond. To change the position of a server in the list box, select it and then use the Up or Down arrow button to move the server in this list.

4. To enable LMHOSTS lookups, select the Enable LMHOSTS Lookup check box. If you want the computer to use an existing LMHOSTS file defined somewhere on the network, retrieve this file with the Import LMHOSTS button. You generally use LMHOSTS only when other name resolution methods fail.

> **Best Practices**   LMHOSTS files are maintained locally on a computer-by-computer basis, which can eventually make them unreliable. Rather than relying on LMHOSTS, ensure that your DNS and WINS servers are configured properly and are accessible to the network. This way, you can ensure centralized administration of name resolution services.

5. NetBIOS Over TCP/IP services are required for WINS name resolution. Choose one of the following options to configure WINS name resolution using NetBIOS:

   ❑ If you use DHCP and dynamic addressing, you can get the NetBIOS setting from the DHCP server. Select Default, Use NetBIOS Setting From The DHCP Server.

   ❑ If you use static IP addressing or the DHCP server doesn't provide NetBIOS settings, select Enable NetBIOS Over TCP/IP.

❑   If WINS and NetBIOS aren't used on the network, select Disable NetBIOS Over TCP/IP. This eliminates the NetBIOS broadcasts that the computer would otherwise send.

6. Repeat this process for other network adapters, as necessary.

Configuring Additional Networking Components

You can configure Windows Server 2003 systems to use additional networking clients, services, and protocols. You install these networking components through the Network Connection Properties dialog box or through the Windows Optional Networking Components Wizard. Each one offers different components.

Installing and Uninstalling Networking Components

You use the Network Connection Properties dialog box to install networking clients, services, and protocols. Table 16-2 provides a brief overview of the various network components you can install using this dialog box.

Table 16-2   Network Components Available on Windows Server 2003

Component	Description
AppleTalk Protocol	Allows other computers to communicate with the computer through the AppleTalk protocol. Allows servers running Windows Server 2003 to be AppleTalk routers.
Client For Microsoft Networks	Allows the computer to access resources on Windows networks.
Client Service For NetWare	Allows the computer to access NetWare networks.
File And Printer Sharing For Microsoft Networks	Allows other computers to access resources on the computer.
Microsoft TCP/IP V6	Provides network layer protocols that support IP version 6 (IPv6). IPv6 provides a 128-bit address space and is the next generation of IP addressing. You should have a thorough understanding of IPv6 before trying to install or use this protocol.
Network Load Balancing	Provides TCP/IP load balancing functions for the server.
Network Monitor Driver	Driver that allows Netmon to capture network packets. Netmon is the network monitor utility.
NWLink IPX/SPX/NetBIOS Compatible Transport Protocol	Enables the computer to communicate with NetWare Servers running Internetwork Packet Exchange/Sequenced Packet Exchange (IPX/SPX).
QoS Packet Scheduler	Quality of Service packet scheduler, which provides network traffic control services.

Table 16-2   Network Components Available on Windows Server 2003

Component	Description
Reliable Multicast Protocol	Allows the computer to be configured for multicast broadcasting. With multicasting, transmissions are broadcast to multiple clients in a single data stream. For example, QoS Admission Control hosts send multicast broadcasts notifying clients that the host is active and ready to receive requests.
Service Advertising Protocol	Installs Service Advertising Protocol Agent, which advertises servers and addresses on the network. Netware servers running IPX/SPX to locate servers and services use this protocol.

You install and uninstall these network components by completing the following steps:

1. Access Network Connections in Control Panel. Afterward, select or double-click the connection with which you want to work.

2. Click Properties.

3. The Local Area Connection Properties dialog box shows a list of components currently installed. You can perform the following actions:

    Disable Component   To disable a component, clear its related check box.

    Uninstall Component   To uninstall a component, select it, and then click Uninstall. Confirm the action by clicking Yes when prompted.

    Install Component   To install additional components, click Install. This displays the Select Network Component Type dialog box. Select the type of network component by choosing Client, Protocol, or Service and then clicking Add. Select the component to add.

Installing Optional Networking Components

You can install additional networking components through the Windows Optional Networking Components Wizard. When you install these components, Windows Server 2003 might also install utilities that the components need in order to operate. These utilities are installed in the Administrative Tools (Common) folder.

Table 16-3 provides a brief overview of optional network components you can install. The component package is the name of the component shown in the Windows Components dialog box. The individual component names are the components you can select individually through the Details button.

Table 16-3   Optional Network Components Available on Windows Server 2003

Component Package	Individual Component Name	Description
Management and Monitoring Tools	Connection Manager Administration Kit	Installs tool for creating custom remote access connections that can be distributed to users
	Connection Point Services	Installs the Phone Book Service, which allows you to distribute phone books
	Network Monitor Tools	Installs network monitoring tools for analyzing network traffic
	Simple Network Management Protocol (SNMP)	Installs SNMP and SNMP agents
	WMI Providers And Components	Components used to access Windows Management Instrumentation (WMI)
Networking Services	Domain Name System (DNS)	Allows the computer to be configured as a DNS server
	Dynamic Host Configuration Protocol (DHCP)	Allows the computer to be configured as a DHCP server
	Internet Authentication Service	Allows authentication, authorization, and accounting of dial-up and virtual private network (VPN) users
	Remote Procedure Call (RPC) Over HTTP Proxy	Allows distributed COM objects to travel over Hypertext Transfer Protocol (HTTP)
	Simple TCP/IP Services	Installs the basic TCP/IP services Character Generator, Daytime, Discard, Echo, and Quote of the Day
	Windows Internet Name Service (WINS)	Allows the computer to be configured as a WINS server
Other Network File and Print Services	File Services For Macintosh	Enables Macintosh users to work with files on a server running Windows Server 2003
	Print Services For Macintosh	Enables Macintosh users to send print jobs to a print spooler on a server running Windows Server 2003
	Print Services For Unix	Enables Unix users to send print jobs to a print spooler on a server running Windows Server 2003

To install optional networking components, complete the following steps:

1. Select or double-click Add Or Remove Programs in Control Panel.

2. Click Add/Remove Windows Components. This starts the Windows Components Wizard.

3. As shown in Figure 16-7, you can now select component packages to install. The networking components with which you might want to work are found within Management And Monitoring Tools, Networking Services, or Other Network File And Print Services.

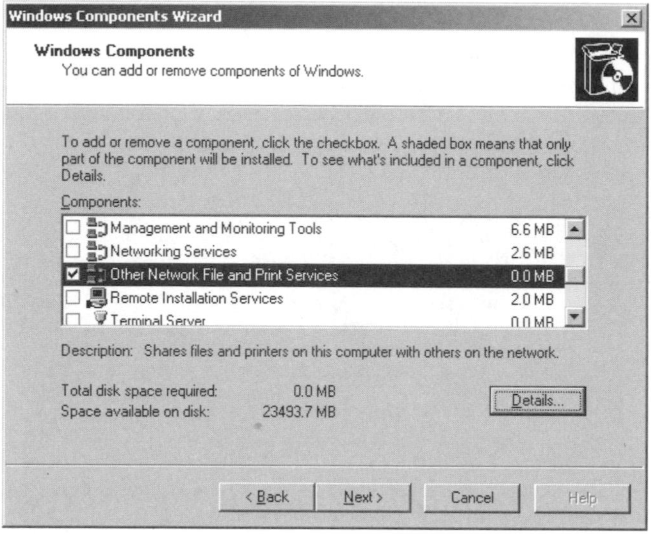

Figure 16-7   Use the Windows Components page to select the components to add. Click Details to select individual components.

4. To select or cancel individual components, select a component category and then click Details. Then, select or clear the check boxes for the individual components you want to install or remove from the computer.

5. Click OK and then click Next. The selected components are then installed.

Managing Network Connections

Network connections make it possible for computers to access remote resources. This section examines techniques you can use to create and manage network connections. Keep in mind that local area connections are created automatically when you start a computer that's attached to a network; you don't need to create this type of connection.

Creating Network Connections

You can configure many types of network connections. You create connections by completing the following steps:

1. Access Network Connections in Control Panel. Afterward, click New Connection Wizard or select New Connection from the File menu.

2. Click Next and then select the type of connection you want to make (see Figure 16-8). The available options are:

   Connect To The Internet   Enables a computer to connect to the Internet over a dial-up or high-speed connection. After you set up a connection to an Internet service provider (ISP), you can share the connection, which allows one computer to provide access for other computers.

   Connect To The Network At My Workplace   Enables a computer to connect to a corporate network over the Internet. The connection can be a standard dial-up connection or a VPN connection. The advantage of a VPN connection over a standard connection is that the data transferred over the connection is encrypted.

   Set Up An Advanced Connection   Enables a computer to connect directly to another computer through a serial, parallel, or infrared port. This type of link is commonly used to synchronize a handheld computer with a PC. It can also enable a computer to access incoming calls through remote access services. If a computer accepts VPN, direct, or dial-up connections, you need to configure incoming connections as well.

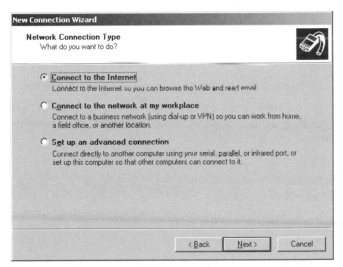

Figure 16-8   Use the Network Connection Type page to select the type of connection and then create it.

3. The dialog boxes you see depend on the type of connection you select. Follow the onscreen prompts. When you're done, click Finish and the connection is created.

Managing Security for Remote Access Connections

Sometimes you'll need to configure servers so that they can access networks at branch offices or other distant locations. Any time you configure a server for this type of access, you'll want to ensure that the identities used are validated using a secure authentication technique. Secure authentication ensures that the logon password and other vital information aren't passed as clear text and are instead encrypted using public key encryption or another technique. With remote access connections, you can validate the logon information for connections using the following options:

Allow Unsecured Password   Allows the logon information to be passed in clear text over the connection. You can think of this as basic authentication.

Require Secured Password   Forces Windows Server 2003 to attempt to pass logon information using a secure technique, such as Windows Authentication, rather than clear text.

Use Smart Card   Tells Windows Server 2003 to validate the logon using a smart card.

With dial-up and broadband connections you can use any of these options. With VPN connections, you can use only the secure techniques. When you require a secured password, you can also automatically pass the Windows logon name, password, and domain specified in the configuration. Passing the Windows logon information automatically is useful when users connect to the office and must be authenticated in the Windows domain.

With both secure validation techniques you can also require data encryption and force Windows Server 2003 to disconnect if data encryption can't be used. This setting protects the data sent over the remote connection so that it can't be monitored.

To configure security for remote connections, follow these steps:

1. Access Network Connections in Control Panel. Afterward, right-click the icon for the remote connection you want to work with and then select Properties. This displays a properties dialog box.

2. Click the Security tab.

3. In the Security Options panel, you can select typical or advanced validation options. The typical options are Allow Unsecured Password (excluding VPN connections), Require Secure Password, and Use Smart Card.

4. If you require secure passwords, you can also set automatic logon and require data encryption. Both options are useful when logging on to a Windows domain. However, the settings must be supported. If they aren't, users won't be able to validate their logons and connections will fail.

If you use smart cards, you should require data encryption. Data encryption is essential to ensuring the integrity and security of the data passed between the smart card and the authenticating computer.

Checking the Status, Speed, and Activity of Local Area Connections

To check the status of a local area connection, access Network Connections in Control Panel, right-click the connection, and then select Status. This displays the Local Area Connection Status dialog box. If the connection is disabled or the media is unplugged, you won't be able to access this dialog box. Enable the connection or connect the network cable to resolve the problem and then try to display the status dialog box again.

The General tab of this dialog box, shown in Figure 16-9, provides useful information regarding the following:

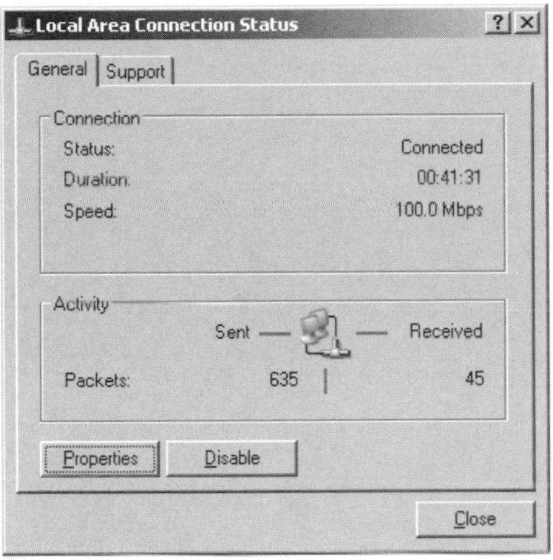

Figure 16-9   The General tab of the Local Area Connection Status dialog box provides access to summary information regarding connections, properties, and support.

Status   The current connection state. You'll typically see the status as Connected because if the state should change, Windows Server 2003 usually closes the status dialog box.

Duration   The amount of time the connection has been established. If the duration is fairly short, the user either recently connected to the network or the connection was recently reset.

Speed   The speed of the connection. This should read 10.0 Mbps for 10-Mbps connections and 100.0 Mbps for 100-Mbps connections. An incorrect setting can affect the user's performance.

Packets   The number of TCP/IP packets sent and received by the connection. As the computer sends or receives packets, you'll see the computer icons light up to indicate the flow of traffic.

Viewing Network Configuration Information

In Windows Server 2003, you can view the current configuration for network adapters in several ways. To view configuration settings using the Local Area Connection Status dialog box, follow these steps:

1. Access Network Connections in Control Panel. Afterward, right-click the connection you want to examine and then select Status.

2. Click the Support tab, shown in Figure 16-10. The fields of the Internet Protocol (TCP/IP) panel provide basic information about the connection, including address type (Manually Configured, Assigned By DHCP, or Autoconfigured), IP address, subnet mask, and default gateway.

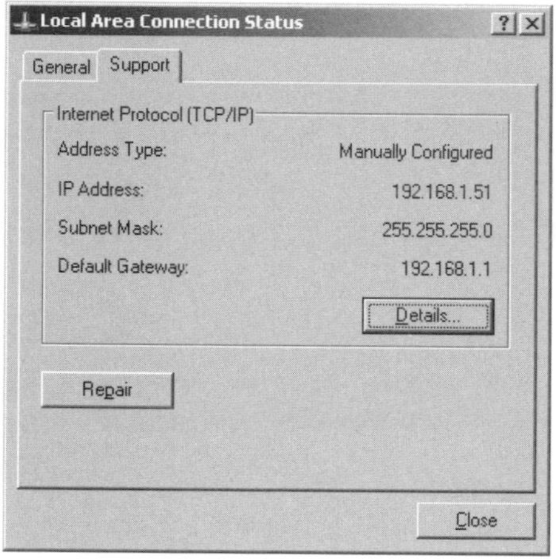

Figure 16-10   Use the Support tab to obtain information on the current configuration of a local area connection.

3. For more detailed information, click Details. This displays the Network Connection Details dialog box in which you'll find the basic information fields and the following information:

   Physical Address   The machine or Media Access Control (MAC) address of the network adapter. This address is unique for each network adapter.

   DHCP Server   The IP address of the DHCP server from which the current lease was obtained.

   DNS Servers   The DNS server IP addresses.

   Primary WINS Server   The IP address for the primary WINS server.

Secondary WINS Server   The IP address for the secondary WINS server.

Lease Obtained   A date and time stamp for when the DHCP lease was obtained.

Lease Expires   A date and time stamp for when the DHCP lease expires.

You can also use the Ipconfig command-line utility to view detailed configuration settings. To do so, follow these steps:

1. Click Start and select Run. In the Run dialog box, type **cmd** in the Open text box and then click OK. This starts a command prompt.

2. At the command line, type **ipconfig /all** to see detailed configuration information for all network adapters configured on the computer.

Duplicating Network Connections

Before you make changes that might invalidate a connection, you might want to create a copy of the existing connection. Right-click the connection and then select Create Copy. You can create copies only of connections you create and not LAN connections.

Enabling and Disabling Network Connections

Windows Server 2003 creates and connects LAN connections automatically. If you want to disconnect from the network or start another connection, you can complete the following steps:

1. Access Network Connections in Control Panel.

2. Right-click the connection you want to disable and then select Disconnect or Disable to deactivate the connection.

3. Later, if you want to activate the connection, you can right-click it and then select Connect or Enable.

Deleting Network Connections

If they aren't needed anymore, you can delete network connections that you created. To do that, follow these steps:

1. Access Network Connections in Control Panel.

2. Right-click the connection you want to remove and then select Delete. When prompted, confirm the action by clicking Yes.

Note   You can't delete a LAN connection. Windows Server 2003 manages this connection.

Renaming Local Area Connections

Windows Server 2003 assigns default names for local area connections initially. You can rename the connections at any time by right-clicking the connection, selecting

Rename, and then typing a new connection name in the Rename text box. If a computer has multiple local area connections, proper naming can help users better understand the purpose of a particular connection.

Repairing Local Area Connections

Occasionally, network cables can get unplugged or the network adapter might experience a problem that temporarily prevents it from working. After you plug the cable back in to solve the adapter problem, the connection should automatically reconnect. If it doesn't, right-click the connection and select Repair. Repairing the connection can sometimes resolve connection problems.

Note   If the repair operation doesn't work, see the next section of this chapter, "Troubleshooting and Testing Network Settings."

Troubleshooting and Testing Network Settings

Windows Server 2003 includes many tools for troubleshooting and testing TCP/IP connectivity. This section looks at a few basic tests that you should perform every time you install or modify a computer's network settings. It then goes on to examine techniques for performing more thorough troubleshooting.

Performing Basic Network Tests

Whenever you install a new computer or make configuration changes to the computer's network settings, you should test the configuration. The most basic TCP/IP test is to use the Ping utility to test the computer's connection to the network. Ping is a command-line utility and is used as follows:

```
ping host
```

where host is the host computer you're trying to reach.

On Windows Server 2003, there are several ways to test the configuration using Ping:

Try to ping IP addresses   If the computer is configured correctly and the host you're trying to reach is accessible to the network, Ping should receive a reply. If it can't reach the host, Ping will time out.

On domains that use WINS, try to ping NetBIOS computer names   If NetBIOS computer names are resolved correctly, the NetBIOS facilities, such as WINS, are correctly configured for the computer.

On domains that use DNS, try to ping DNS host names   If fully qualified DNS host names are resolved correctly, DNS name resolution is configured properly.

You might also want to test network browsing for the computer. If the computer is a member of a Windows Server 2003 domain and computer browsing is enabled throughout the domain, log on to the computer and then use the Windows Explorer or

My Network Places to browse other computers in the domain. Afterward, log on to a different computer in the domain and try to browse the computer you just configured. These tests tell you if the DNS resolution is being handled properly in the local environment. If you can't browse, check the configuration of the DNS services and protocols.

Releasing and Renewing DHCP Settings

DHCP servers can assign many network configuration settings automatically. These include IP addresses, default gateways, primary and secondary DNS servers, primary and secondary WINS servers, and more. When computers use dynamic addressing, they're assigned a lease on a specific IP address. This lease is good for a specific time period and must be renewed periodically. When the lease needs to be renewed, the computer contacts the DHCP server that provided the lease. If the server is available, the lease is renewed and a new lease period is granted. You can also renew leases manually as necessary on individual computers or using the DHCP server itself.

Problems can occur during the lease assignment and renewal process that prevent network communications. If the server isn't available and can't be reached before a lease expires, the IP address can become invalid. If this happens, the computer might use the alternate IP address configuration to set an alternate address, which usually has settings that are inappropriate and prevent proper communications. To resolve this problem, you'll need to release and then renew the DHCP lease.

Another type of problem occurs when users move around to various offices and subnets within the organization. While moving from location to location, their computers might obtain DHCP settings from the wrong server. When the users return to their offices, the computer might seem sluggish or might perform incorrectly due to the settings assigned by the DHCP server at another location. If this happens, you'll need to release and then renew the DHCP lease.

You can use the Ipconfig command-line utility to renew and release settings by following these steps:

1. Click Start and select Run. Type **cmd** in the Open text box of the Run dialog box and then click OK. This starts a command prompt.

2. To release the current settings, type **ipconfig /release** at the command line. Then renew the lease by typing **ipconfig /renew**.

3. To renew a DHCP lease, type **ipconfig /renew** at the command line.

4. You can check the updated settings by typing **ipconfig /all** at the command line.

Registering and Flushing DNS

The DNS resolver cache maintains a history of DNS lookups that have been performed when a user accesses network resources using TCP/IP. This cache contains forward lookups, which provide host name to IP address resolution, and reverse lookups, which provide IP address to host name resolution. Once a DNS entry is stored in the resolver cache for a particular DNS host, the local computer no longer has to query external servers for DNS information on that host. This allows the computer to resolve DNS requests locally, which provides a quicker response.

How long entries are stored in the resolver cache depends on the Time to Live (TTL) value assigned to the record by the originating server. To view current records and see the remaining TTL value for each record, type **ipconfig /displaydns** at the command line. These values are given as the number of seconds that a particular record can remain in the cache before it expires. The local computer is continually counting down these values. When the TTL value reaches zero, the record expires and is removed from the resolver cache.

Occasionally, you'll find that the resolver cache needs to be cleared out to remove old entries and allow computers to check for updated DNS entries before the normal expiration and purging process takes place. Typically, this happens because server IP addresses have changed and the current entries in the resolver cache point to the old addresses rather than the new ones. Sometimes the resolver cache itself can get out of sync, particularly when DHCP has been misconfigured.

> **Real World**   Skilled administrators know that they should start to decrease the TTL values for DNS records that are going to be changed several weeks in advance of the actual change. Typically, this means reducing the TTL from a number of days (or weeks) to a number of hours, which allows for quicker propagation of the changes to computers that have cached the related DNS records. Once the change is completed, administrators should restore the original TTL value to reduce renewal requests.

You can usually resolve problems with the DNS resolver cache by either flushing the cache or reregistering DNS. When you flush the resolver cache, all DNS entries are cleared out of the cache and new entries aren't created until the next time the computer performs a DNS lookup on a particular host or IP address. When you reregister DNS, Windows Server 2003 attempts to refresh all current DHCP leases and then performs a lookup on each DNS entry in the resolver cache. By looking up each host or IP address again, the entries are renewed and reregistered in the resolver cache. You'll generally want to flush the cache completely and allow the computer to perform lookups as needed. Reregister DNS only when you suspect that there are problems with DHCP and the DNS resolver cache.

To flush or register DNS entries using Ipconfig, complete the following tasks:

1. Click Start and select Run. Type **cmd** in the Open text box of the Run dialog box and then click OK. This starts a command prompt.

2. To clear out the resolver cache, type **ipconfig /flushdns** at the command line.

3. To renew DHCP leases and reregister entries, type **ipconfig /registerdns** at the command line.

4. When the tasks are complete, you can check your work by typing **ipconfig /displaydns** at the command line.

Performing Detailed Network Diagnostics

Few things are more complicated than trying to troubleshoot network problems. Because there are so many interdependencies between services, protocols, and configuration settings, finding the problem area can be difficult. Fortunately, Windows Server 2003 includes a powerful network diagnostics toolkit for pinpointing network problems that relate to the following:

- General network connectivity problems

- Internet service settings for e-mail, newsgroups, and proxies

- Settings for modems, network clients, and network adapters

- DNS, DHCP, and WINS configuration

- Default gateways and IP addresses

You can, for example, use the network diagnostics toolkit to find out quickly that a network adapter has failed or that another computer is using the IP address you've configured for the current system. To run the diagnostics tests using the default setup, follow these steps:

1. Click Start and then select Help And Support. This starts the Help And Support Center.

2. Under Support Tasks, click Tools. Afterward, in the left pane, expand the Help And Support Center Tools node and then select Network Diagnostics.

3. Click Scan Your System to start the testing.

During testing, the Help And Support Services console is displayed with a progress bar showing the progress and status of the diagnostics tests. Default tests that are conducted include:

- Ping tests to determine if the network is reachable

- Connectivity tests over the configured modems and network adapters

- Internet service tests for e-mail, newsgroups, and proxies

The tests also return information about the computer system, operating system configuration, and operating system version.

When complete, you'll see the results of the testing, as shown in Figure 16-11. As you examine the results, look for items that are labeled Not Configured or Failed, as these might point to problem areas. If you see items with these or other labels that indicate problems, click the plus sign (+) to the left of the entry to examine the related diagnostics information.

Continue to navigate through the information provided until you find the problem area. For example, on a test system, the DNS server entries were misconfigured and the servers were unreachable. The failure to ping the DNS servers showed up as a failure of the primary network adapter. When I expanded the adapter entry, the

DNSServerSearchOrder entry was flagged as Failed. By continuing to expand the entries, I found that the computer was unable to send packets to the DNS servers because the primary and secondary DNS server IP addresses were set incorrectly on the DHCP server. After updating the settings on the DHCP server and renewing the DHCP lease, the computer was again able to resolve DNS properly.

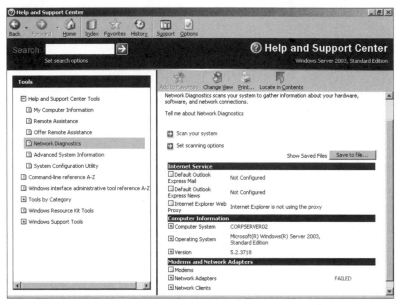

Figure 16-11   Use network diagnostics to pinpoint network configuration problems.

If you want to conduct more extensive testing, click Set Scanning Options and then select the check boxes for additional test actions and categories, such as Domain Name System, Dynamic Host Configuration Protocol, and Default Gateways. Then rerun the diagnostics tests by clicking Start. Note any problems and resolve them as necessary. At a command line, you can use NETSH DIAG to get detailed diagnostic output of the networking configuration as well. Be sure to use the /V parameter and redirect the output to a file for easy review as shown here:

```
netsh diag show all /v > netconfig.txt
```

When troubleshooting networking configurations of domain controllers, I also recommended running DCDIAG, a tool for diagnosing a variety of common problems on domain controllers. This tool is available when you install the Windows Support tools on a computer. To run this tool from a command prompt while logged on to the domain controller you are troubleshooting, simply type **dcdiag**.

Chapter 17

Administering Network Printers and Print Services

As an administrator, you need to do two main things so users throughout a network can access print devices connected to Microsoft Windows Server 2003: you need to set up a print server and you need to use the print server to share print devices on the network.

This chapter covers the basics of setting up shared printing and accessing it from the network. You'll also find advice on administering printers and troubleshooting printer problems, which is where we'll begin. The chapter doesn't examine Internet printing.

Troubleshooting Printer Problems

An understanding of how printing works can go a long way when you're trying to troubleshoot printer problems. Many processes, drivers, and devices work together to print documents. If you use a printer connected to a printer server, the key operations are as follows:

Printer driver   When you print a document in an application, your computer loads a printer driver. If the print device is attached to your computer physically, the printer driver is loaded from a local disk drive. If the print device is located on a remote computer, the printer driver might be downloaded from the remote computer. The availability of printer drivers on the remote computer is configurable by operating system and chip architecture. If the computer can't obtain the latest printer driver, it's probably because an administrator hasn't enabled the driver for the computer's operating system. For more information, see the section of this chapter entitled "Managing Printer Drivers."

Local print spool and print processor   The application you're printing from uses the printer driver to translate the document into a file format understandable to the selected print device. Then your computer passes the document off to the local print spooler. The local spooler in turn passes the document to a print processor, which creates the raw print data necessary for printing on the print device.

Print router and print spooler on the print server   The raw data is passed back to the local print spooler. If you're printing to a remote printer, the raw data is then routed to the print spooler on the print server. On Windows Server 2003 systems, the printer router, Winspool.exe, handles the tasks of locating the remote printer, routing print jobs, and downloading printer drivers to the local system, if necessary. If any one of these tasks fails, the print router is usually the culprit. See the sections of this chapter entitled "Solving Spooling Problems" and "Setting Printer Access Permissions" to learn possible fixes for this problem. If these procedures don't work, you might want to replace or restore Winspool.exe.

The main reason for downloading printer drivers to clients is to provide a single location for installing driver updates. This way, instead of having to install a new driver on all the client systems, you install the driver on the print server and allow clients to download the new driver. For more information on working with printer drivers, see the section of this chapter entitled "Managing Printer Drivers."

Printer (print queue)   The document goes from the print spooler into the printer stack—which, in some operating systems, is called the print queue—for the selected print device. Once in the queue, the document is referred to as a *print job*—a task for the print spooler to handle. The length of time the document waits in the printer stack is based on its priority and position within the printer stack. For more information, see the section of this chapter entitled "Scheduling and Prioritizing Print Jobs."

Print monitor   When the document reaches the top of the printer stack, the print monitor sends the document to the print device, where it's actually printed. If the printer is configured to notify users that the document has been printed, you see a message confirming this.

The specific print monitor used by Windows Server 2003 depends on the print device configuration and type. The default monitor is Localmon.dll. You might also see monitors from the print device manufacturer, such as Hpmon.dll, which is used with most Hewlett-Packard print devices. This dynamic-link library (DLL) is required to print to the print device. If it's corrupted or missing, you might need to reinstall it.

Print device   The print device is the physical device that prints documents on paper. Common print device problems and display errors include:

- ❑ Insert Paper Into Tray X
- ❑ Low Toner
- ❑ Out Of Paper
- ❑ Out Of Toner; Out Of Ink

❑   Paper Jam

❑   Printer Offline

Group Policy can affect your ability to install and manage printers. If you're having problems and believe they're related to Group Policy, the key policies you'll want to examine are those in:

■   Computer Configuration\Administrative Templates\Printers

■   User Configuration\Administrative Templates\Control Panel\Printers

■   User Configuration\Administrative Templates\Start Menu And Taskbar

Installing Printers

The following sections examine techniques you can use to install printers. Windows Server 2003 allows you to install and manage printers anywhere on the network. You install and manage printers through the Printers And Faxes folder. On a local system you can access this folder by selecting Printers And Faxes from the Start Menu or by clicking Printers And Faxes in Control Panel. On a remote system you can access this folder through My Network Places. In My Network Places, access a domain, select a computer whose printer settings you want to manage, and then double-click Printers. Windows Server 2003 R2 introduces the Print Management console, which you can also use to work with printers and print servers. Print Management is designed to centralize and automate many printer and print server management tasks.

Using Local and Network Printers

Two types of print devices are used on a network:

Local print device   A print device that's physically attached to the user's computer and employed only by the user who's logged on to that computer.

Network print device   A print device that's set up for remote access over the network. This can be a print device attached directly to a print server or a print device attached directly to the network through a network interface card (NIC).

> **Note**   The key difference between a local printer and a network printer is that a local printer isn't shared. A local printer can easily be made a network printer. To learn how to do this, see the section of this chapter entitled "Starting and Stopping Printer Sharing."

You install new network printers on print servers or as separate print devices attached to the network. A *print server* is a workstation or server that's configured to share one or more printers. These printers can be physically attached to the computer or the network.

You can configure any Windows Server 2003 system as a print server. The print server's primary job is to share the print device out to the network and to handle print spooling. The main advantages of print servers are that the printer will have a centrally managed print queue and you don't have to install printer drivers on client systems.

You don't have to use a print server, however. You can connect users directly to a network-attached printer. When you do this, the network printer is handled much like a local printer attached directly to the user's computer. The key differences are that multiple users can connect to the printer and that each user has a different print queue. Each individual print queue is managed separately, which can make administration and problem resolution difficult.

To install or configure a new printer on Windows Server 2003, you must be a member of the Administrators, Print Operators, or Server Operators group. To connect to and print documents to the printer, you must have the appropriate access permissions. See the section in this chapter entitled "Setting Printer Access Permissions" for details.

Using the Autoinstall Feature of Print Management

Print Management can automatically detect all network printers located on the same subnet as the computer on which the console is running. After detection, print management can automatically install the appropriate printer drivers, set up print queues, and share the printers. To automatically install network printers and configure a print server, follow these steps:

1. Log on to the computer you want to configure as a print server. You can log on locally at the keyboard or remotely by using Remote Desktop.

2. Start Print Management by clicking Start, Programs or All Programs, Administrative Tools and then selecting Print Management.

3. In Print Management, expand the Print Servers node by double-clicking it and then right-click the entry for the server to which you are either locally or remotely logged on. The entry should have the server name followed by (local).

4. Select Automatically Add Network Printers. This displays the Automatically Add Network Printers dialog box.

5. Click Start to start the detection process for network printers on the current subnet. Printers found are listed by Internet Protocol (IP) address, status, and printer model. If a printer can't be installed or configured, there will be an error status for the printer. If there are multiple possible drivers for a detected printer, you'll be prompted to select the driver to use. Click Close.

Installing Physically Attached Print Devices

Physically attached print devices are connected to a computer directly through a serial cable, a parallel cable, a universal serial bus (USB) cable, or an infrared (IR) port. You can configure physically attached printers as local print devices or as network print devices. The key difference is that a local device is accessible only to users logged on to the computer and a network device is accessible to any network users as a shared print device. Remember that the workstation or server you're logged on to becomes the print server for the device you're configuring.

You can install physically attached print devices locally by logging on to the print server you want to configure or remotely through My Network Places. If you're configuring a local plug and play printer and are logged on to the print server, installing a print device is a snap. To install a print device, follow these steps:

1. Connect the print device to the server using the appropriate serial, parallel, or USB cable, and then turn the printer on.

2. If Windows Server 2003 automatically detects the print device, Windows begins installing the device and the necessary drivers. If the necessary drivers aren't found, you might need to insert the Windows Server 2003 CD into the CD-ROM drive or a driver disk into the floppy disk drive.

3. If Windows Server 2003 doesn't detect the print device automatically, you'll need to install the print device manually as described in the next set of instructions. Skip the remaining steps in this section.

4. Windows Server 2003 automatically shares the printer for network access. The share name is set to the first eight characters of the printer name—not including spaces. Any spaces in the printer name are omitted. Thus, the printer name HP DeskJet 890C is set to the printer share HPDeskJe.

5. If you want to rename the print share, right-click the printer icon in the Printers And Faxes folder and then select Sharing. Then type a name for the printer share in the Share Name field. In a large organization, you'll want the share name to be logical and helpful in locating the printer. For example, you might want to name the printer that points to a print device in the northeast corner of the twelfth floor TwelveNE.

Sometimes Windows won't detect your printer or you'll need to install the print device remotely. In this case, follow these steps to install the print device:

1. Access the Printers And Faxes folder on the computer you want to configure as a print server.

    ❑ On a local system, you can access this folder by selecting Printers And Faxes from the Start menu or by clicking Printers And Faxes in Control Panel.

    ❑ On a remote system, you can access this folder through My Network Places. In My Network Places, access a domain, select a computer whose printer settings you want to manage, and then select Printers And Faxes.

2. Select or double-click Add Printer to start the Add Printer Wizard. Click Next.

3. If you're accessing the computer through a local logon, you'll see a page similar to the one shown in Figure 17-1. Select Local Printer Attached To This Computer, clear Automatically Detect And Install My Plug And Play Printer, and then click Next.

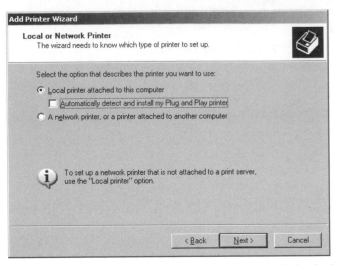

Figure 17-1   If you're logged on locally and want to install a local print device, select Local Printer Attached To This Computer.

4. If you're accessing the computer remotely, the Add Printer Wizard doesn't try to detect local printers and the wizard goes directly to the Select A Printer Port page. You need to configure the port used by the printer. Select Use The Following Port and then choose the appropriate LPT, COM, or IR port. LPT1 is the recommended printer port. You can also print to a file. If you do, Windows Server 2003 prompts users for a file name each time they print. Click Next.

5. As shown in Figure 17-2, you must now specify the print device manufacturer and model. This allows Windows Server 2003 to assign a printer driver to the print device. After you choose a print device manufacturer, choose a printer model. If the print device manufacturer and model you're using isn't displayed in the list, click Have Disk to install a new driver. For example, if you have an HP LaserJet 8150 PCL printer, you'd choose HP as the manufacturer and HP LaserJet 8150 Series PCL as the printer.

    Note   If a driver for the specific printer model you're using isn't available, you can usually select a generic driver or a driver for a similar print device. Consult the print device documentation for pointers.

6. Click Next. If a printer driver is already installed, you can choose to keep the existing driver or replace it. Click Next.

7. Assign a name to the printer. This is the name you'll see in the Printers And Faxes folder of Control Panel. On a local system, you can also set the printer as the local default, if you like. Click Next.

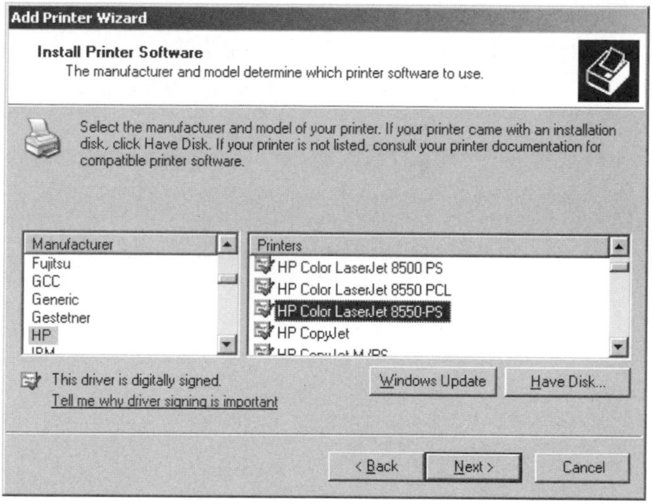

Figure 17-2   Select a print device manufacturer and printer model with the Add Printer Wizard.

8. Specify whether the printer is available to remote users (see Figure 17-3). To create a printer that's accessible to remote users, select the Share Name option button and enter a name for the shared resource. In a large organization, you'll want the share name to be logical and helpful in locating the printer. For example, you might want to name the printer that points to the print device in the northeast corner of the twelfth floor TwelveNE.

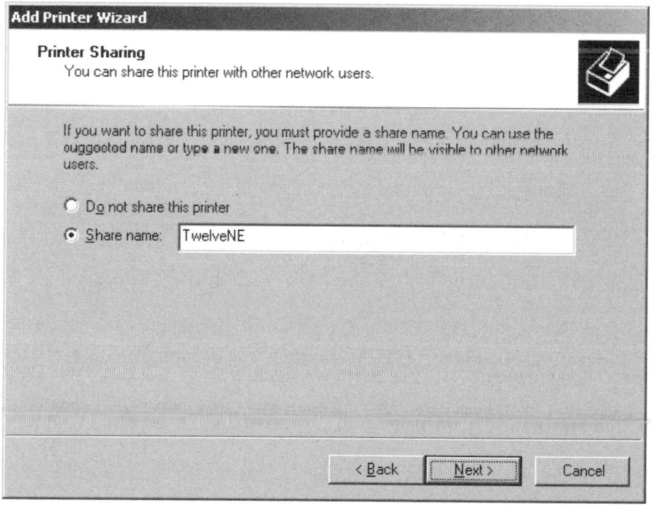

Figure 17-3   Use the Add Printer Wizard to share the network printer and assign it a name.

9. If you like, you can enter a location description and comment. This information can help users find a printer and determine its capabilities.

10. The final page lets you test the installation by printing a test page to the print device. If you want to do this, select Yes. Otherwise, select No. When you're ready to complete the installation, click Finish.

When the Add Printer Wizard finishes installing the new printer, the Printers And Faxes folder will have an additional icon with the name set the way you specified. You can change the printer properties and check printer status at any time. For more information, see the section of this chapter entitled "Configuring Printer Properties."

Tip   If you repeat this process, you can create additional printers for the same print device. All you need to do is change the printer name and share name. Having additional printers for a single print device allows you to set different properties to serve different needs. For example, you could have a high priority printer for print jobs that need to be printed immediately and a low priority printer for print jobs that aren't as urgent.

Installing Network-Attached Print Devices

A network-attached print device is a print device that's attached directly to the network through a network adapter card. Network-attached printers are configured as network print devices so that they're accessible to network users as shared print devices. Remember that the server on which you configure the print device becomes the print server for the device you're configuring.

Install a network-attached print device by completing these steps:

1. Access the Printers And Faxes folder on the computer you want to configure as a print server.

   ❑ On a local system, you can access this folder by selecting Printers And Faxes from the Start Menu or by clicking Printers And Faxes in Control Panel.

   ❑ On a remote system, you can access this folder through My Network Places. In My Network Places, access a domain, select a computer whose printer settings you want to manage, and then select Printers And Faxes.

2. Double-click Add Printer to start the Add Printer Wizard. Click Next.

3. If you're accessing the computer through a local logon, select Local Printer, clear Automatically Detect And Install My Plug And Play Printer, and then click Next.

4. If you're accessing the computer remotely, the Add Printer Wizard doesn't try to detect local printers and you jump directly to the Select A Printer Port page.

5. As shown in Figure 17-4, select Create A New Port and then set the type of port to Standard TCP/IP Port. Click Next to start the Add Standard TCP/IP Printer Port Wizard.

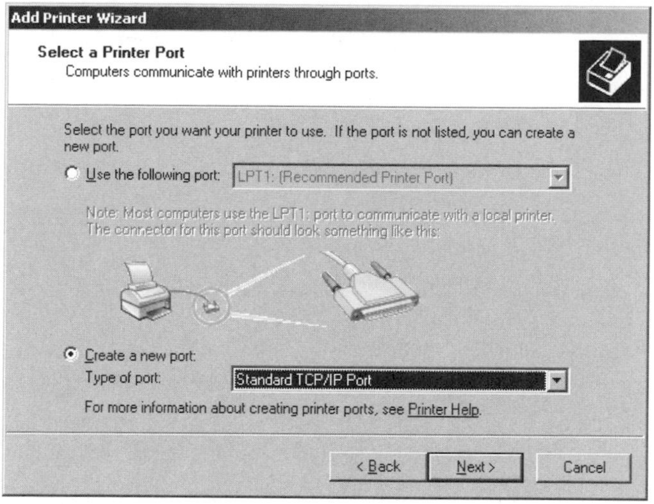

Figure 17-4   Use the Select A Printer Port page to configure a TCP/IP port for the network-attached printer.

6. Click Next. As shown in Figure 17-5, type the printer name or IP address for the printer device. A port name is filled in for you automatically. For example, if you type the IP address 192.168.12.8, the port name is entered as IP_192.168.12.8.

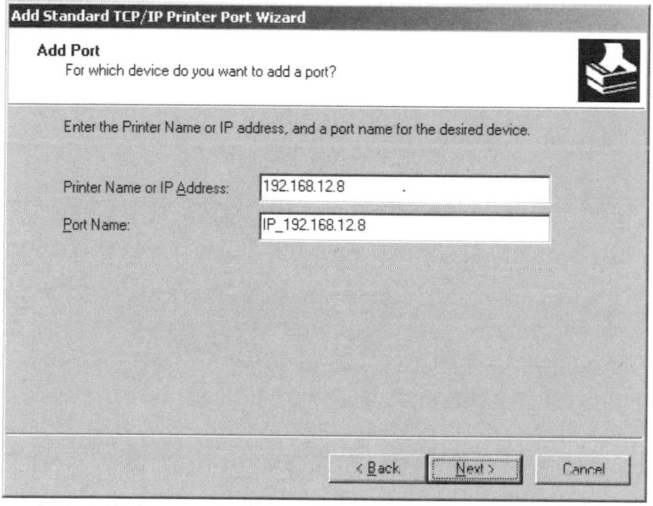

Figure 17-5   Use the Add Port page to enter the IP address of the network printer.

Tip   The port name doesn't matter as long as it's unique on the system. If you're configuring multiple printers on the print server, be sure to write down the port to printer mapping.

7. Click Next and the wizard attempts to automatically detect the print device. If the wizard is unable to detect the print device, make sure that:

    ❑ The print device is turned on and connected to the network.

    ❑ The printer is configured properly.

    ❑ You typed the correct IP address or printer name in the previous page.

8. If the IP address or printer name is incorrect, click Back and then retype this information.

9. If the information is correct, you might need to identify the device further. In the Device Type area, click Standard, and then select the printer or network adapter used by the printer. Or click Custom and then click Settings to define custom settings for the printer, such as protocol and Simple Network Management Protocol (SNMP) status.

10. Click Next and then click Finish. This completes the configuration of the new port. You now need to continue with the printer installation in the Add Printer Wizard.

11. You must now specify the print device manufacturer and model. This allows Windows Server 2003 to assign a printer driver to the print device. After you choose a print device manufacturer, choose a printer model. If the print device manufacturer and model you're using isn't displayed in the list, click Have Disk to install a new driver.

12. Click Next. If a printer driver is already installed, you can choose to keep the existing driver or replace it. Click Next.

    Note   If a driver for the specific printer model you're using isn't available, you can usually select a generic driver or a driver for a similar print device. Consult the print device documentation for pointers.

13. Assign a name to the printer. This is the name you'll see in the Printers And Faxes folder of Control Panel. On a local system, you can also set the printer as the local default, if you like. Click Next.

14. Check the share name for the printer. By default, the share name is set to the first eight characters of the printer name—not including spaces. Any spaces in the printer name are omitted. Thus, the printer name Canon LBP-8IV is set to the printer share CanonLBP. In a large organization, you'll want the share name to be logical and helpful in locating the printer. For example, you might want to name the printer that points to the print device in the northeast corner of the twelfth floor TwelveNE.

15. Click Next. If you like, you can enter a location description and comment. This information can help users find a printer and determine its capabilities.

16. The final window lets you test the installation by printing a test page to the print device. If you want to do this, select Yes. Otherwise, select No. When you're ready to complete the installation, click Finish.

When the Add Printer Wizard finishes installing the new printer, the Printers And Faxes folder will have an additional icon with the name set the way you specified. You can change the printer properties and status at any time. For more information, see the section of this chapter entitled "Configuring Printer Properties."

> **Tip**   If you repeat this process, you can create additional printers for the same print device. All you need to do is change the printer name and share name. Having additional printers for a single print device allows you to set different properties to serve different needs. For example, you could have a high priority printer for print jobs that need to be printed immediately and a low priority printer for print jobs that aren't as urgent.

Connecting to Printers Created on the Network

After you create a network printer, remote users can connect to it and use it much like any other printer. You'll need to set up a connection on a user-by-user basis or have users do this themselves. To create the connection to the printer on a Windows Server 2003 system, follow these steps:

1. With the user logged on, access the Printers And Faxes folder.

2. Select or double-click Add Printer to start the Add Printer Wizard. Afterward, select A Network Printer, and then click Next.

    In the Specify A Printer dialog box, choose a method for finding the network printer. The available options are:

    Find A Printer In The Directory   Choose this option if you want to search Active Directory directory service for the printer. All printers configured for sharing on Windows Server 2003 systems are automatically listed in Active Directory. Printers can be removed from the directory, however.

    Type The Printer Name, Or Click Next To Browse For A Printer   Choose this option if you want to browse the network for shared printers just as you'd browse in My Network Places.

    Connect To A Printer On The Internet Or On Your Intranet   Choose this option if you want to enter the Uniform Resource Locator (URL) of an Internet printer.

3. When the printer is selected, click OK.

4. Determine whether the printer is the default used by Windows applications. Select Yes or No, and then click Next.

5. Choose Finish to complete the operation.

The user can now print to the network printer by selecting the printer in an application. The Printers And Faxes folder on the user's computer shows the new network printer. You can configure local property settings using this icon. By default, the printer name is set to *Printer* On *Computer*, such as HP DeskJet On ENGSVR01.

Solving Spooling Problems

Windows Server 2003 uses the Print Spooler service to control the spooling of print jobs. If this service isn't running, print jobs can't be spooled. You can check the status of the Print Spooler using the Services utility. Follow these steps to check and restart the Print Spooler service:

1. In Administrative Tools, click or double-click Computer Management.

2. If you want to connect to a remote computer, right-click the Computer Management entry in the console tree and select Connect To Another Computer from the shortcut menu. You can now choose the system whose services you want to manage.

3. Expand the Services And Applications node by clicking the plus sign (+) next to it, and then choose Services.

4. Select the Print Spooler service. The Status should be Started. If it isn't, right-click Print Spooler and then select Start. The Startup Type should be Automatic. If it isn't, double-click Print Spooler and then set Startup Type to Automatic.

5. If this doesn't resolve the problem, you might want to check other related services, including:

    ❑ TCP/IP Print Server (if installed)

    ❑ Print Server for Macintosh (if installed)

    ❑ Print Server for UNIX (if installed)

Tip   Spoolers can become corrupted. Symptoms include a frozen printer or one that doesn't send jobs to the print device. Sometimes the print device might print pages of garbled data. In most of these cases, stopping and starting the Print Spooler service resolves the problem. Other spooling problems might be related to permissions. See the section of this chapter entitled "Setting Printer Access Permissions" for details.

Configuring Printer Properties

The sections that follow explain how to set commonly used printer properties. After you install network printing, you can use the Properties dialog box to set its properties. You access the Properties dialog box by doing the following:

1. Access the Printers And Faxes folder on the computer with which you want to work. Or select the Printers node in Print Management.

2. Right-click the icon of the printer you want to configure and then, from the pop-up menu, select Properties.

3. This opens the dialog box shown in Figure 17-6. You can now set the printer properties.

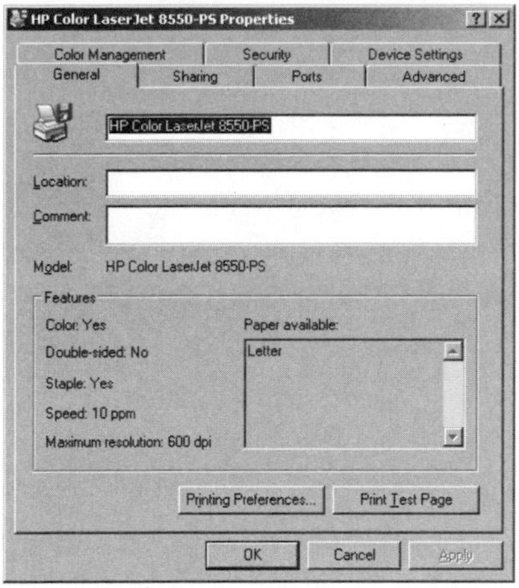

Figure 17-6   Set printer properties with the Properties dialog box for the printer you want to configure.

Adding Comments and Location Information

To make it easier to determine which printer to use when, you can add comments and location information to printers. Comments provide general information about the printer, such as the type of print device and who is responsible for it. Location describes the actual site of the print device. Once set, applications can display these fields. For example, Microsoft Word displays this information when you select Print from the File menu in the Comment and Where fields, respectively.

You can add comments and location information to a printer by using the fields in the General tab of the printer's Properties dialog box. Type your comments in the Comment field. Type the printer location in the Location field.

Managing Printer Drivers

In a Windows Server 2003 domain, you should configure and update printer drivers only on your print servers. You don't need to update printer drivers on Windows clients. Instead, you configure the network printer to provide the drivers to client systems, as necessary.

Updating a Printer Driver

You can update a printer's driver by doing the following:

1. Open the printer's Properties dialog box and click the Advanced tab.

2. The Driver field lets you select the driver from a list of currently installed drivers. Use the Driver drop-down list to select a new driver from a list of known drivers.

3. If the driver you need isn't listed or if you obtained a new driver, click New Driver. This starts the Add Printer Driver Wizard. Click Next. Choose Have Disk to install the new driver from a file or disk.

4. Click Next and then click Finish.

Configuring Drivers for Network Clients

After you install a printer or change drivers, you might want to select the operating systems that should download the driver from the print server. By allowing clients to download the printer driver, you provide a single location for installing driver updates. This way, instead of having to install a new driver on all the client systems, you install the driver on the print server and allow clients to download the new driver.

You can allow clients to download the new driver by doing the following:

1. Right-click the icon of the printer you want to configure and then select Properties.

2. Click the Sharing tab and then click Additional Drivers.

3. Use the Additional Drivers dialog box to select operating systems that can download the printer driver. As necessary, insert the Windows Server 2003 CD or printer driver disks, or both, for the selected operating systems. The Windows Server 2003 CD has drivers for most Windows operating systems.

Setting a Separator Page and Changing Print Device Mode

Separator pages have two uses on Windows Server 2003 systems:

- They can be used at the beginning of a print job to make it easier to find a document on a busy print device.

- They can be used to change the print device mode, such as whether the print device uses PostScript or Printer Control Language (PCL).

To set a separator page for a print device, follow these steps:

1. Access the Advanced tab of the printer's Properties dialog box and then click Separator Page.

2. In the Separator Page dialog box, click Browse, and then select one of the three available separator pages:

   Pcl.sep   Switches the print device to PCL mode and prints a separator page before each document.

   Pscript.sep   Sets the print device to PostScript mode but doesn't print a separator page.

   Sysprint.sep   Sets the print device to PostScript mode and prints a separator page before each document.

To stop using the separator page, access the Separator Page dialog box and remove the filename.

Changing the Printer Port

You can change the port used by a print device at any time by using the Properties dialog box for the printer you're configuring. Open the Properties dialog box and then click the Ports tab. You can now either add a port for printing by selecting its check box or remove a port by clearing its check box. To add a new port type, click Add Port. Afterward, select the port type and then click New Port. To remove a port permanently, select it and then click Delete Port.

Scheduling and Prioritizing Print Jobs

You use the Properties dialog box for the printer you're configuring to set default settings for print job priority and scheduling. Open the dialog box and then click the Advanced tab. You can now set the default schedule and priority settings using the fields shown in Figure 17-7. Each of these fields is discussed in the sections that follow.

Figure 17-7   You configure print job scheduling and priority using the Advanced tab.

Scheduling Printer Availability

Printers are either always available or available only during the hours specified. You set printer availability using the Advanced tab. Access the Advanced tab, and then select Always Available to make the printer available at all times or select Available From to set specific hours of operation.

Setting Printer Priority

Use the Priority box of the Advanced tab to set the default priority for print jobs. Print jobs always print in order of priority. Jobs with higher priority print before jobs with lower priority.

Configuring Print Spooling

For print devices attached to the network, you'll usually want the printer to spool files rather than print files directly. Print spooling makes it possible to use a printer to manage print jobs.

Enabling Spooling   To enable spooling, use one of the following options:

Spool Print Documents So Program Finishes Printing Faster   Select this option to spool print jobs.

Start Printing After Last Page Is Spooled   Select this option if you want the entire document to be spooled before printing begins. This option ensures that the entire document makes it into the print queue before printing. If for some reason printing is canceled or not completed, the job won't be printed.

Start Printing Immediately   Select this option if you want printing to begin immediately when the print device isn't already in use. This option is preferable when you want print jobs to be completed faster or when you want to ensure that the application returns control to users as soon as possible.

Other Spooling Options   You can disable spooling by selecting the Print Directly To The Printer option button. Additional check boxes let you configure other spooling options. You use these check boxes as follows:

Hold Mismatched Documents   If selected, the spooler holds print jobs that don't match the setup for the print device. Selecting this option is a good idea if you frequently have to change printer form or tray assignments.

Print Spooled Documents First   If selected, jobs that have completed spooling will print before jobs in the process of spooling—regardless of whether the spooling jobs have higher priority.

Keep Printed Documents   Normally, documents are deleted from the queue after they're printed. To keep a copy of documents in the printer, select this option. Use this option if you're printing files that can't easily be recreated. In this way, you can reprint the document without having to recreate it. For details, see the section of this chapter entitled "Pausing, Resuming, and Restarting Individual Document Printing."

Enable Advanced Printing Features   When this option is enabled, you can use advanced printing options (if available), such as Page Order and Pages Per Sheet. If you note compatibility problems when using advanced options, you should disable the advanced printing features by clearing this check box.

Starting and Stopping Printer Sharing

You use the Properties dialog box of the printer you're configuring to set printer sharing. Right-click the icon of the printer you want to configure and then select Sharing.

You can use this tab to change the name of a network printer as well as to start sharing or stop sharing a printer. Printer sharing tasks that you can perform include:

Sharing a local printer (thus making it a network printer)   To share a printer, select Share This Printer and then specify a name for the shared resource in the Share Name field. Click OK when you're finished.

Changing the shared name of a printer   To change the shared name, simply type a new name in the Share Name field and click OK.

Stopping the sharing of a printer   To quit sharing a printer, select the Do Not Share This Printer option button. Click OK when you're finished.

Setting Printer Access Permissions

Network printers are a shared resource, and, as such, you can set access permissions for them. You use the Properties dialog box of the printer you're configuring to set access permissions. Open the dialog box and then click the Security tab.

Permissions that can be granted or denied for printers are Print, Manage Documents, and Manage Printers. Table 17-1 summarizes the capabilities of these permissions.

Table 17-1   Printer Permissions Used by Windows Server 2003

Permission	Print	Manage Documents	Manage Printers
Print documents	X	X	X
Pause, restart, resume, and cancel own documents	X	X	X
Connect to printers	X	X	X
Control settings for print jobs		X	X
Pause, restart, and delete print jobs		X	X
Share printers			X
Change printer properties			X
Change printer permissions			X
Delete printers			X

The default settings of the Printer Permissions dialog box are used for any new network printer you create. These settings are as follows:

1. Administrators, Print Operators, and Server Operators have full control over printers by default. This allows you to administer a printer and its print jobs.

2. Creator or Owner of the document can manage his or her own document. This allows the person who printed a document to change its settings and to delete it.

3. Everyone can print to the printer. This makes the printer accessible to all users on the network.

As with other permission sets, you create the basic permissions for printers by combining special permissions into logical groups. Table 17-2 shows special permissions used to create the basic permissions for printers. Using Advanced permission settings, you can assign these special permissions individually, if necessary.

Table 17-2   Special Permissions for Printers

Special Permissions	Print	Manage Documents	Manage Printers
Print	X		X
Manage Documents		X	
Manage Printers			X
Read Permissions	X	X	X
Change Permissions		X	X
Take Ownership		X	X

Auditing Print Jobs

Windows Server 2003 lets you audit common printer tasks. To do this, follow these steps:

1. Open the printer's Properties dialog box and then click the Security tab. Open the Access Security Settings dialog box by clicking Advanced.

   Note   Actions aren't audited by default. You must first enable auditing by establishing a group policy to audit the printer.

2. In the Auditing tab, add the names of users or groups you want to audit with the Add button and remove names of users or groups with the Remove button.

3. Select the events you want to audit by selecting the check boxes under the Successful and Failed headings, as appropriate. Click OK when you're finished.

Setting Document Defaults

Document default settings are used only when you print from non-Windows applications, such as when you print from the MS-DOS prompt. You can set document defaults by doing the following:

1. Access the Printers And Faxes folder on the computer with which you want to work. Or select the Printers node in Print Management.

2. Right-click the printer's icon and select Properties. Click Printing Preferences in the General tab of the Properties dialog box.

3. Use the fields in the Layout tab and the Paper/Quality tab to configure the default settings.

Configuring Print Server Properties

Windows Server 2003 allows you to control global settings for print servers by using the Print Server Properties dialog box. You can access this dialog box by doing either of the following:

- Access the Printers And Faxes folder on the print server. In the Printers And Faxes window, select Server Properties from the File menu. Or right-click in an open area of the window and select Server Properties from the shortcut menu.

- In Print Management, right-click the server entry for the print server with which you want to work and then select Properties. If the print server isn't listed, you can add it using the Add/Remove Servers dialog box, which you can display by right-clicking Print Servers and then selecting Add/Remove Servers.

The sections that follow examine some of the print server properties that you can configure.

Locating the Spool Folder and Enabling Printing on NTFS

The Spool folder holds a copy of all documents in the printer spool. By default, this folder is located at %SystemRoot%\system32\spool\PRINTERS. On the NTFS file system (NTFS), all users who access the printer must have Change permission on this directory. If they don't, they won't be able to print documents.

To check the permission on this directory if you're experiencing problems, follow these steps:

1. Access the Print Server Properties dialog box.

2. Click the Advanced tab. The location of the Spool folder is shown in the Spool Folder field. Note this location.

3. Right-click the Spool folder in Windows Explorer, and then, from the pop-up menu, select Properties.

4. Click the Security tab. Now you can verify that the permissions are set appropriately.

Managing High Volume Printing

Printers used in corporate environments can print hundreds or thousands of documents daily. This heavy load puts a high burden on print servers, which can cause printing delays, document corruption, and other problems. To alleviate some of this burden, you should do the following:

- Use network-attached printers rather than printers attached through serial, parallel, USB, or IR ports. Network-attached printers use fewer system resources (namely CPU time) than do other printers.

- Dedicate the print server to handle print services only. If the print server is handling other network duties, it might not be very responsive to print requests and management. To increase responsiveness, you can move other network duties to other servers.

- Move the Spool folder to a drive dedicated to printing. By default, the Spool folder is on the same file system as the operating system. To further improve disk input/output (I/O), use a drive that has a separate controller.

Logging Printer Events

You can use the Print Server Properties dialog box to configure the logging of printer events. Access this dialog box and then click the Advanced tab. Use the check boxes provided to determine which spooler events are logged.

Removing Print Job Completion and Notification

Print servers can notify users when a document has finished printing. By default, this feature is turned off since it can become annoying. If you want to activate or remove notification, access the Advanced tab of the Print Server Properties dialog box. Then select or clear the check box labeled Notify When Remote Documents Are Printed. You might also want to select or clear the check box labeled Notify Computer, Not User, When Remote Documents Are Printed.

Managing Print Jobs on Local and Remote Printers

You manage print jobs and printers using the print management window. If the printer is configured on your system, you can access the print management window by using one of the following techniques:

- Access the Printers And Faxes folder on the print server you want to manage. Double-click the icon of the printer with which you want to work. If the printer isn't configured on your system, you can manage the printer remotely by starting Windows Explorer and then using My Network Places to access the print server. Access the Printers And Faxes folder on the print server and then double-click the icon of the printer you want to work with.

- In Print Management, expand the Print Servers node by double-clicking it and the entry for the printer server itself. Select Printers. Right-click the printer with which you want to work and then select Open Printer Queue.

Using the Print Management Window

You can now manage print jobs and printers using the print management window shown in Figure 17-8. The print management window shows information about documents in the printers. This information tells you the following:

Document Name   The document file name, which can include the name of the application that printed it.

Status   The status of the print job, which can include the document's status as well as the printer's status. Document status entries you'll see include Printing, Spooling, Paused, Deleting, and Restarting. Document status can be preceded by the printer status, such as Printer Off-Line.

Owner   The document's owner.

Pages   The number of pages in the document.

Size   The document size in kilobytes or megabytes.

Submitted   The time and date the print job was submitted.

Port   The port used for printing, such as LPT1, COM3, or File (if applicable).

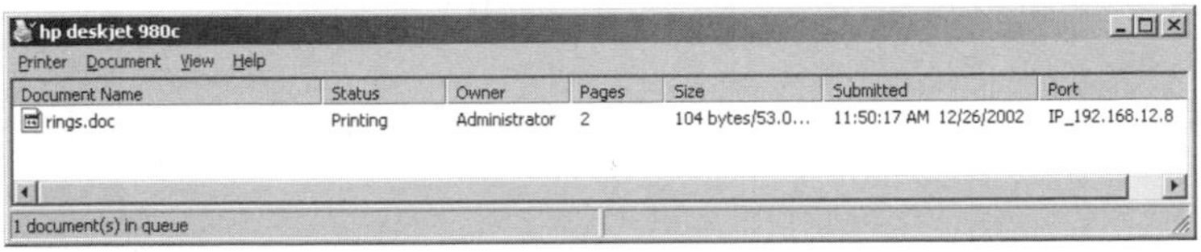

Figure 17-8   You manage print jobs and printers using the print management window.

Pausing the Printer and Resuming Printing

Sometimes you need to pause a printer. Using the print management window, you do this by selecting the Pause Printing option from the Printer menu (a check mark indicates that the option is selected). When you pause printing, the printer completes the current job and then puts all other jobs on hold.

To resume printing, select the Pause Printing option a second time. This should remove the check mark next to the option.

Emptying the Print Queue

You can use the print management window to empty the print queue and delete all its contents. To do this, from the Printer menu select the Cancel All Documents option.

Pausing, Resuming, and Restarting Individual Document Printing

You set the status of individual documents using the Document menu in the print management window. To change the status of a document, follow these steps:

1. Select the document in the print management window.

2. Use the Pause, Resume, and Restart options on the Document menu to change the status of the print job:

   Pause   Puts the document on hold and lets other documents print.

   Resume   Tells the printer to resume printing the document from where it left off.

   Restart   Tells the printer to start printing the document again from the beginning.

Removing a Document and Canceling a Print Job

To remove a document from the printer or cancel a print job, follow these steps:

1. Select the document in the print management window.

2. Select Cancel from the Document menu or press Delete.

Note When you cancel a print job that's currently printing, the print device might continue to print part or all of the document. This is because most print devices cache documents in an internal buffer and the print device might continue to print the contents of this cache.

Checking the Properties of Documents in the Printer

Document properties can tell you many things about documents that are in the printer, such as the page source, orientation, and size. You can check the properties of a document in the printer by doing either of the following:

- Select the document in the print management window and then, from the Document menu, select Properties.

- Double-click the document name in the print management window.

Setting the Priority of Individual Documents

Scheduling priority determines when documents print. Documents with higher priority print before documents with lower priority. You can set the priority of individual documents in the printer by doing the following:

1. Select the document in the print management window and then, from the Document menu, select Properties.

2. In the General tab, use the Priority slider to change the document's priority. The lowest priority is 1 and the highest is 99.

Scheduling the Printing of Individual Documents

In a busy printing environment, you might need to schedule the printing of documents in the printer. For example, you might want large print jobs of low priority to print at night. To set the printing schedule, follow these steps:

1. Select the document in the print management window and then, from the Document menu, select Properties.

2. In the General tab, select the Only From option button and then specify a time interval. The time interval you set determines when the job is allowed to print. For example, you can specify that the job can print only between the hours of midnight and 5:00 a.m.

Chapter 18
Running DHCP Clients and Servers

You can use Dynamic Host Configuration Protocol (DHCP) to simplify administration of Active Directory directory service domains, and in this chapter you'll learn how to do that. You use DHCP to dynamically assign Transmission Control Protocol/Internet Protocol (TCP/IP) configuration information to network clients. This not only saves time during system configuration but also provides a centralized mechanism for updating the configuration. To enable DHCP on the network, you need to install and configure a DHCP server. This server is responsible for assigning the necessary network information.

Understanding DHCP

DHCP gives you centralized control over Internet Protocol (IP) addressing and more. If the network has a DHCP server, you can assign a dynamic IP address to any of the network interface cards (NICs) on a computer. Once DHCP is installed, you rely on the DHCP server to supply the basic information necessary for TCP/IP networking, which can include the following: IP address, subnet mask, and default gateway; primary and secondary Domain Name System (DNS) servers; primary and secondary Windows Internet Name Service (WINS) servers; and the DNS domain name.

Using Dynamic Addressing

A computer that uses dynamic addressing is called a DHCP client. When you boot a DHCP client, an IP address is retrieved from a pool of IP addresses defined for the network's DHCP server and assigned for a specified time period known as a lease. When the lease is approximately 50 percent expired, the client tries to renew it. If the client can't renew the lease, it'll try again before the lease expires. If this attempt fails, the client will try to contact a new DHCP server. IP addresses that aren't renewed are returned to the address pool. If the client is able to contact the DHCP server but the current IP address can't be reassigned, the DHCP server assigns a new IP address to the client.

The availability of a DHCP server doesn't affect startup or logon (in most cases). DHCP clients can start and users can log on to the local machine even if a DHCP server isn't available.

During startup, the client looks for a DHCP server. If a DHCP server is available, the client gets its configuration information from the server. If a DHCP server isn't available and the client's previous lease is still valid, the client pings the default gateway listed in the lease. A successful ping tells the client that it's probably on the same network it was on when it was issued the lease, and the client will continue to use the lease as described previously. A failed ping tells the client that it might be on a different network. In this case the client uses IP autoconfiguration. The client also uses IP autoconfiguration if a DHCP server isn't available and the previous lease has expired.

IP autoconfiguration works like this:

1. The client computer selects an IP address from the Microsoft-reserved class B subnet 169.254.0.0 and uses the subnet mask 255.255.0.0. Before using the IP address, the client performs an Address Resolution Protocol (ARP) test to make sure that no other client is using this IP address.

2. If the IP address is in use, the client repeats Step 1, testing up to 10 IP addresses before reporting failure.

   Note   When a client is disconnected from the network, the ARP test always succeeds. As a result, the client uses the first IP address it selects.

3. If the IP address is available, the client configures the NIC with this address. The client then attempts to contact a DHCP server, sending out a broadcast every five minutes to the network. When the client successfully contacts a server, the client obtains a lease and reconfigures the network interface.

Checking IP Address Assignment

You can use Ipconfig to check the currently assigned IP address and other configuration information. To obtain information for all network adapters on the computer, type the command **ipconfig /all** at the command prompt. If the IP address has been assigned automatically, you'll see an entry for Autoconfiguration IP Address. In this example, the autoconfiguration IP address is 169.254.98.59:

```
Windows IP Configuration
        Host Name ................: DELTA
        Primary DNS Suffix ........: microsoft.com
        Node Type ................: Hybrid
        IP Routing Enabled.........: No
```

```
·  WINS Proxy Enabled.........: No
   DNS Suffix Search List.....: microsoft.com
Ethernet adapter Local Area Connection:
   Connection-specific DNS Suffix...:
   Description ...............: NDC ND5300 PnP Ethernet Adapter
   Physical Address............: 23-17-C6-F8-FD-67
   DHCP Enabled...............: Yes
   Autoconfiguration Enabled...: Yes
   Autoconfiguration IP Address: 169.254.98.59
   Subnet Mask ...............: 255.255.0.0
   Default Gateway ...........:
   DNS Servers ...............:
```

Understanding Scopes

Scopes are pools of IP addresses that you can assign to clients through leases and reservations. A reservation differs from a lease in that an IP address is assigned to a particular computer until you remove the reservation. This allows you to set semi-permanent addresses for a limited number of DHCP clients.

You'll create scopes to specify IP address ranges that are available for DHCP clients. For example, you could assign the IP address range 192.168.12.2 – 192.168.12.250 to a scope called Enterprise Primary. Scopes can use public or private IP addresses on:

Class A networks   IP addresses from 1.0.0.0 to 126.255.255.255

Class B networks   IP addresses from 128.0.0.0 to 191.255.255.255

Class C networks   IP addresses from 192.0.0.0 to 223.255.255.255

Class D networks   IP addresses from 224.0.0.0 to 239.255.255.255

> **Note**   The IP address 127.0.0.1 is used for local loopback.

A single DHCP server can manage multiple scopes. Three types of scopes are available.

Normal scopes   Used to assign IP address pools for class A, B, and C networks.

Multicast scopes   Used to assign IP address pools for class D networks. Computers use multicast IP addresses as secondary IP addresses in addition to a standard IP address assigned from a class A, B, or C network.

Superscopes   These are containers for other scopes and are used to simplify management of multiple scopes.

> **Tip**   Although you can create scopes on multiple network segments, you'll usually want these segments to be in the same network class, such as all class C IP addresses. Don't forget that you must configure DHCP relays to relay DHCP broadcast requests between network segments. You can configure relay agents with the Routing and Remote Access Service (RRAS) and the DHCP Relay Agent Service. You can also configure some routers as relay agents.

Installing a DHCP Server

Dynamic IP addressing is available only if a DHCP server is installed on the network. You install the DHCP components through the Windows Components Wizard, and then you use the DHCP console to start and authorize the server in Active Directory. Only authorized DHCP servers can provide dynamic IP addresses to clients.

Installing DHCP Components

On a server running Microsoft Windows Server 2003, you complete the following steps to allow it to function as a DHCP server:

1. Click Start, choose Programs or All Programs, Administrative Tools, and then select Configure Your Server Wizard.

2. Click Next twice. The server's current roles are shown. Select DHCP Server and then click Next.

3. On the Summary Of Selections page, click Next to begin the installation.

4. The wizard installs DHCP and begins configuring the server. When this task is finished, the wizard launches the New Scope Wizard. If you want to create the initial scope for the DHCP server, click Next and follow the steps outlined in the section of this chapter entitled "Creating and Managing Scopes." Otherwise, click Cancel and create the necessary DHCP scope(s) later.

5. Click Finish. To use the server, you must authorize the server in the domain as described in the section of this chapter entitled "Authorizing a DHCP Server in Active Directory." Next, you must create and activate any DHCP scopes that the server will use, as discussed in section of this chapter entitled "Creating and Managing Scopes."

Starting and Using the DHCP Console

After you've installed a DHCP server, you use the DHCP console to configure and manage dynamic IP addressing. To start the DHCP console, click Start, choose Programs or All Programs, as appropriate, then Administrative Tools, and then click DHCP. The main window for the DHCP console is shown in Figure 18-1. As you see, the main window is divided into two panes. The left pane lists the DHCP servers in the domain by IP address as well as the local machine (if it's a DHCP server). You can expand the listing to show the scopes and options defined for each DHCP server by double-clicking an entry. The right pane shows the expanded view of the current selection.

Icons on the server and scope nodes show their current status. For servers, icons you might see are the following:

- A green up arrow indicates that the DHCP service is running and the server is active.

- A red X indicates that the console can't connect to the server. The DHCP service has been stopped or the server is inaccessible.

- A red down arrow indicates that the DHCP server hasn't been authorized.

- A blue warning icon indicates that the server's state has changed or a warning has been issued.

For scopes, icons you might see are the following:

- A red down arrow indicates that the scope hasn't been activated.

- A blue warning icon indicates that the scope's state has changed or a warning has been issued.

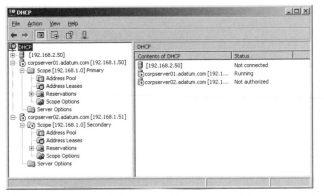

Figure 18-1   Use the DHCP console to create and manage DHCP server configurations.

Connecting to Remote DHCP Servers

When you start the DHCP console, you'll be connected directly to a local DHCP server but you won't see entries for remote DHCP servers. You can connect to remote servers by completing the following steps:

1. Right-click DHCP in the console tree, and then select Add Server. This opens the dialog box shown in Figure 18-2.

2. Select This Server, and then type the IP address or computer name of the DHCP server you want to manage. If you want to manage authorized DHCP servers only, select This Authorized DHCP Server, and then click the server you want to add. Keep in mind that you can manage only DHCP servers in trusted domains.

3. Click OK. An entry for the DHCP server is added to the console tree.

Note   You can also manage local and remote DHCP servers through Computer Management. Start Computer Management, and then connect to the server you want to manage. Afterward, expand Services And Applications, and then select DHCP.

Tip   When you work with remote servers, you might find that you can't select certain options. A simple refresh of the server information might resolve this. Right-click the server node and then select Refresh.

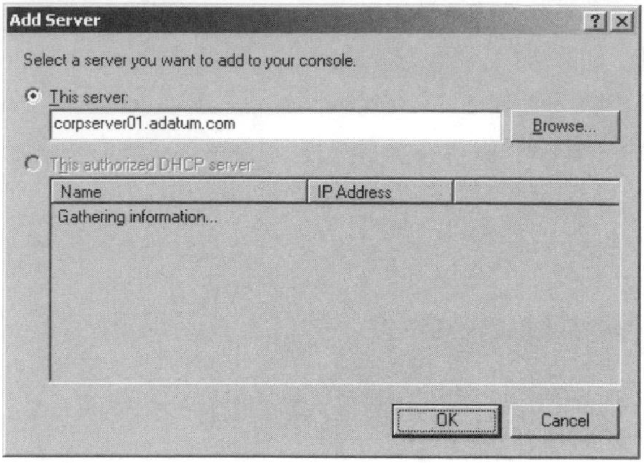

Figure 18-2 If your DHCP server isn't listed, you'll need to use the Add Server dialog box to add it to the DHCP console.

Starting and Stopping a DHCP Server

You manage DHCP servers through the DHCP Server service. Like any other service, you can start, stop, pause, and resume the DHCP Server service in the Services node of Computer Management or from the command line. You can also manage the DHCP service in the DHCP console. Right-click the server you want to manage in the DHCP console, choose All Tasks, and then select Start, Stop, Pause, Resume, or Restart, as appropriate.

> **Note**   To start and stop a DHCP server using Computer Management, expand DHCP, right-click the server, choose All Tasks, and then select Start, Stop, Pause, Resume, or Restart, as appropriate.

Authorizing a DHCP Server in Active Directory

Before you can use a DHCP server in the domain, you must authorize it in Active Directory. By authorizing the server, you specify that the server is authorized to provide dynamic IP addressing in the domain. Windows Server 2003 requires authorization to prevent unauthorized DHCP servers from serving domain clients. This in turn ensures that network operations can run smoothly.

In the DHCP console, you authorize a DHCP server by right-clicking the server entry in the tree view and then selecting Authorize. To remove the authorization, right-click the server and then select Unauthorize.

> **Note**   To authorize a DHCP server using Computer Management, expand DHCP, right-click the server, and then select Authorize. The authorization process can take several minutes, so be patient. Press F5 to refresh the view. When the DHCP server is authorized, the scope status should change to active and you should see a green up arrow in the console tree. To remove the authorization, expand DHCP, right-click the server, and then select Unauthorize.

Tip   You might need to log on or remotely connect to a domain controller in order to authorize the DHCP server in Active Directory. Once you access the domain controller, start the DHCP console, and connect to the server you want to authorize. Afterward, right-click the server and then select Authorize.

Configuring DHCP Servers

When you install a new DHCP server, configuration options are automatically optimized for the network environment. You don't normally need to change these settings unless you have performance problems that you need to resolve or you have options that you'd like to add or remove. With DHCP server, you change configuration options through the Properties dialog box shown in Figure 18-3. In the DHCP console, you access this dialog box by right-clicking the server in the console tree and then selecting Properties. To configure DHCP servers using Computer Management, expand DHCP, right-click the server, and then select Properties.

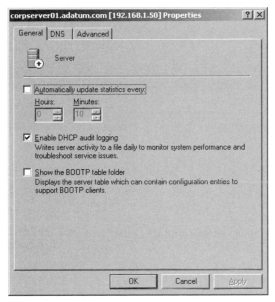

Figure 18-3   You can control statistics, auditing, DNS integration, and other options through the DHCP server Properties dialog box.

Binding a DHCP Server with Multiple Network Interface Cards to a Specific IP Address

A server with multiple NICs has multiple local area network (LANs) connections and can provide DHCP services on any of these network connections. Unfortunately, you might not want DHCP to be served over all available connections. For example, if the server has both a 10 megabit per second (Mbps) connection and a 100 Mbps connection, you might want all DHCP traffic to go over the 100 Mbps connection.

To bind DHCP to a specific network connection, follow these steps:

1. Start the DHCP console. Click Start, choose Programs or All Programs as appropriate, choose Administrative Tools, and then select DHCP.

2. In the DHCP console, right-click the server with which you want to work and then select Properties.

3. In the Advanced tab of the Properties dialog box, click Bindings.

4. The Bindings dialog box displays a list of available network connections for the DHCP server. If you want the DHCP Server service to use a connection to service clients, select the check box for the connection. If you don't want the service to use a connection, clear the related check box. Click OK when you're finished.

Updating DHCP Statistics

The DHCP console provides statistics concerning IP address availability and usage. By default, these statistics are updated only when you start the DHCP console or when you select the server and then click the Refresh button on the toolbar. If you monitor DHCP routinely, you might want these statistics to update automatically. To do that, follow these steps:

1. In the DHCP console, right-click the server with which you want to work and then select Properties.

2. In the General tab, select Automatically Update Statistics Every and then enter an update interval in hours and minutes. Click OK.

DHCP Auditing and Troubleshooting

Windows Server 2003 is configured to audit DHCP processes by default. Auditing tracks DHCP processes and requests in log files.

Understanding DHCP Auditing

You can use audit logs to help you troubleshoot problems with a DHCP server. The default location for DHCP logs is %SystemRoot%\system32\DHCP. In this directory, you'll find a different log file for each day of the week. The log file for Monday is named DhcpSrvLog-Mon.log. The log file for Tuesday is named DhcpSrvLog-Tue.log, and so on.

When you start the DHCP server or a new day arrives, a header message is written to the log file. This header provides a summary of DHCP events and their meanings. Stopping and starting the DHCP Server service doesn't necessarily clear out a log file. Log data is cleared only when a log hasn't been written to in the last 24 hours. You don't have to monitor space usage by DHCP Server. DHCP Server is configured to monitor itself and restricts disk space usage by default.

Enabling or Disabling DHCP Auditing

You can enable or disable DHCP auditing by completing the following steps:

1. In the DHCP console, right-click the server you want to work with and then select Properties.

2. In the General tab, select or clear the Enable DHCP Audit Logging check box. Click OK.

Changing the Location of DHCP Auditing Logs

By default, DHCP logs are stored in %SystemRoot%\system32\DHCP. You can change the location of DHCP logs by completing the following steps:

1. In the DHCP console, right-click the server with which you want to work with, and then select Properties.

2. Click the Advanced tab. The Audit Log File Path field shows the current folder location for log files. Enter a new folder location or click Browse to find a new location.

3. Click OK. Windows Server 2003 will need to restart the DHCP Server service. When prompted to confirm that this is OK, click Yes. The service will be stopped and then started.

Changing the Log Usage

DHCP Server has a self-monitoring system that checks disk space usage. By default, the maximum size of all DHCP server logs is 70 MB, with each individual log being limited to one-seventh of this space. If the server reaches the 70 MB limit or an individual log grows beyond the allocated space, logging of DHCP activity stops until log files are cleared out or space is otherwise made available. Normally, this happens when a new day is reached and the server clears out the previous week's log file.

Registry keys that control the log usage and other DHCP settings are located in the folder HKEY_LOCAL_MACHINE\SYSTEM\CurrentControlSet\Services \DHCPServer\Parameters.

The following keys control the logging:

DhcpLogFilesMaxSize   Sets the maximum file size for all logs. The default is 70 MB.

DhcpLogDiskSpaceCheckInterval   Determines how often DHCP checks disk space usage. The default interval is 50 minutes.

DhcpLogMinSpaceOnDisk   Sets the free space threshold for writing to the log. If the disk has less free space than the value specified, logging is temporarily disabled. The default value is 20 MB.

Only DhcpLogFilesMaxSize is created automatically. So, if you want to control logging, you'll need to create additional keys as necessary and set appropriate values for your network.

Integrating DHCP and DNS

DNS is used to resolve computer names in Active Directory domains and on the Internet. Thanks to the DNS dynamic update protocol, you don't need to register DHCP clients in DNS manually. The protocol allows either the client or the DHCP server to register the necessary forward lookup and reverse lookup records in DNS, as necessary. When configured using the default setup for DHCP, Windows Server 2003 DHCP clients automatically update their own DNS records after receiving an IP address lease, and DHCP server updates records for pre-Windows Server 2003 clients after issuing a lease.

Tip Microsoft Windows NT 4.0 DNS servers don't support the dynamic update protocol, and records aren't updated automatically. One workaround is to enable WINS lookup for DHCP clients that use NetBIOS. This allows the client to find other computers through WINS. A better long-term solution is to upgrade older DNS servers to Windows Server 2003.

You can view and change the DNS integration settings by completing the following steps:

1. In the DHCP console, right-click the server with which you want to work and then select Properties.

2. Click the DNS tab. Figure 18-4 shows the default DNS integration settings for DHCP. Because these settings are configured by default, you usually don't need to modify the configuration.

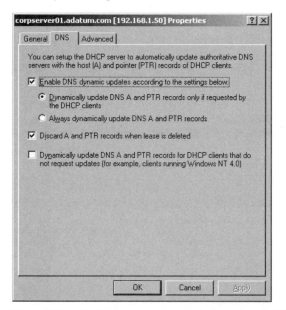

Figure 18-4   The DNS tab shows the default settings for DNS integration with DHCP.

Avoiding IP Address Conflicts

IP address conflicts are a common cause of problems with DHCP. No two computers on the network can have the same unicast IP address. If a computer is assigned the same unicast IP address as another, one or both of the computers might become disconnected from the network. To better detect and avoid potential conflicts, you might want to enable IP address conflict detection by completing the following steps:

1. In the DHCP console, right-click the server with which you want to work, and then select Properties.

2. In the Advanced tab, set Conflict Detection Attempts to a value other than zero. The value you enter determines the number of times DHCP server checks an IP address before leasing it to a client. DHCP server checks IP addresses by sending a ping request over the network.

Real World   A unicast IP address is a standard IP address for class A, B, and C networks. When a DHCP client requests a lease, a DHCP server checks its pool of available addresses and assigns the client a lease on an available IP address. By default, the server checks only the list of current leases to determine if an address is available. It doesn't actually query the network to see if an address is in use. Unfortunately, in a busy network environment, an administrator might have assigned this IP address to another computer or an offline computer might have been brought online with a lease that it believes hasn't expired, even though the DHCP server believes the lease has expired. Either way, you have an address conflict that will cause problems on the network. To reduce these types of conflicts, set the conflict detection to a value greater than zero.

Saving and Restoring the DHCP Configuration

After you configure all the necessary DHCP settings, you might want to save the DHCP configuration so that you can restore it on the DHCP server. To save the configuration, enter the following command at the command prompt:

```
netsh dump dchp >dhcpconfig.dmp
```

In this example, dhcpconfig.dmp is the name of the configuration script you want to create. Once you create this script, you can restore the configuration by entering the following command at the command prompt:

```
netsh exec dhcpconfig.dmp
```

Tip   You can also use this technique to set up another DHCP server with the same configuration. Simply copy the configuration script to a folder on the destination computer and then execute it.

Managing DHCP Scopes

After you install a DHCP server, you need to configure the scopes that the DHCP server will use. Scopes are pools of IP addresses that you can lease to clients. As explained earlier in this chapter in the section entitled "Understanding Scopes," you can create three types of scopes: superscopes, normal scopes, and multicast scopes.

Creating and Managing Superscopes

A superscope is a container for scopes in much the same way that an organizational unit is a container for Active Directory objects. Superscopes help you manage scopes available on the network. With a superscope you can activate or deactivate multiple scopes through a single action. You can also view statistics for all scopes in the superscope rather than having to check statistics for each scope.

Creating Superscopes

After you've created at least one normal or multicast scope, you can create a superscope by completing the following steps:

1. In the DHCP console, right-click the server with which you want to work and then select New Superscope. This starts the New Superscope Wizard. Click Next.

2. Type a name for the superscope and then click Next.

3. Select scopes to add to the superscope. Select individual scopes by clicking their entry in the Available Scopes list box. Select multiple scopes by clicking while holding down Shift or Ctrl.

4. Click Next and then click Finish.

Adding Scopes to a Superscope

You can add scopes to a superscope when you create it or you can do it later. To add a scope to an existing superscope, follow these steps:

1. Right-click the scope you want to add to an existing superscope and then select Add To Superscope.

2. In the Add Scope ... To A Superscope dialog box, select a superscope.

3. Click OK. The scope is then added to the superscope.

Removing Scopes from a Superscope

To remove a scope from a superscope, follow these steps:

1. Right-click the scope you want to remove from a superscope and then select Remove From Superscope.

· **2.** Confirm the action by clicking Yes when prompted. If this is the last scope in the superscope, the superscope is deleted automatically.

Activating and Deactivating a Superscope

When you activate or deactivate a superscope, you make all the scopes within the superscope active or inactive. To activate a superscope, right-click the superscope and then select Activate. To deactivate a superscope, right-click the superscope and then select Deactivate.

Deleting a Superscope

Deleting a superscope removes the superscope container but doesn't delete the scopes it contains. If you want to delete the member scopes, you'll need to do this after deleting the superscope. To delete a superscope, right-click the superscope and then select Delete. When prompted, click Yes to confirm the action.

Creating and Managing Scopes

Scopes provide a pool of IP addresses for DHCP clients. A normal scope is a scope with class A, B, or C network addresses. A multicast scope is a scope with class D network addresses. Although you create normal scopes and multicast scopes differently, you manage them in much the same way. The key differences are that multicast scopes can't use reservations and you can't set additional options for WINS, DNS, routing, and so forth.

Creating Normal Scopes

You can create a normal scope by completing the following steps:

1. In the DHCP console, right-click the server on which you want to create the scope. If you want to add the new scope to an existing superscope automatically, right-click the superscope instead.

2. From the shortcut menu, select New Scope. This starts the New Scope Wizard. Click Next.

3. Type a name and description for the scope, and then click Next.

4. The Start IP Address and End IP Address fields define the valid IP address range for the scope. Enter a start address and an end address in these fields.

   > **Note**   Generally, the scope doesn't include the x.x.x.0 and x.x.x.255 addresses, which are usually reserved for network addresses and broadcast messages, respectively. Accordingly, you would use a range of 192.168.10.1 to 192.168.10.254 rather than 192.168.10.0 to 192.168.10.255.

5. When you enter an IP address range, the bit length and subnet mask are filled in for you automatically (see Figure 18-5). Unless you use subnets, you should use the default values.

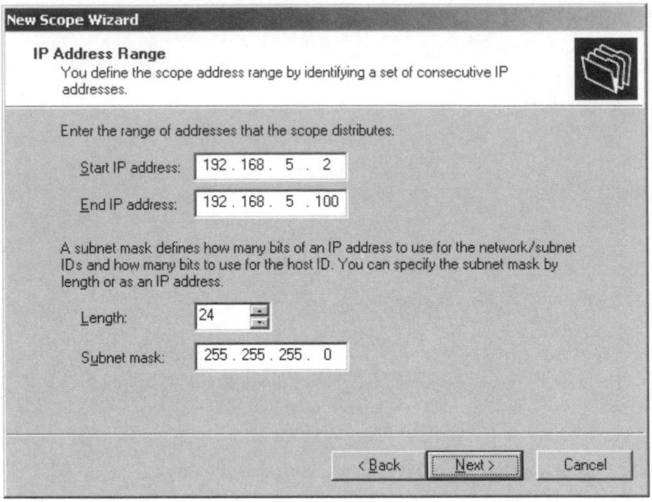

Figure 18-5   In the New Scope Wizard, enter the IP address range for the scope.

6. Click Next. If the IP address range you entered is on multiple networks, you'll have the opportunity to create a superscope that contains separate scopes for each network. Select the Yes option button to continue and then click Next. If you made a mistake, click Back and modify the IP address range you entered.

7. Use the Start IP Address and End IP Address fields on the Add Exclusions page to define IP address ranges that are to be excluded from the scope. You can exclude multiple address ranges as follows:

   ❑ To define an exclusion range, type a start address and an end address in the Exclusion Range's Start IP Address and End IP Address fields, respectively, and then click Add. To exclude a single IP address, use that address as both the start IP address and the end IP address.

   ❑ To track which address ranges are excluded, use the Excluded Address Range list box.

   ❑ To delete an exclusion range, select the range in the Excluded Address Range list box and click Remove.

8. Click Next. Specify the duration of leases for the scope using the Day(s), Hour(s), and Minute(s) fields. The default duration is eight days.

   Best Practices   Take a few minutes to plan the lease duration you want to use. A lease duration that's set too long can reduce the effectiveness of DHCP and might eventually cause you to run out of available IP addresses, especially on networks with mobile users or other types of computers that aren't fixed members of the network. A good lease duration for most networks is from one to three days.

9. You have the opportunity to set common DHCP options for DNS, WINS, gateways, and more. If you want to set these options now, select Yes, I Want To Configure These Options Now. Otherwise, select No, I Will Configure These Options Later and skip Steps 10–14.

10. Click Next. The first option you can configure is the default gateway. In the IP Address field, enter the IP address of the primary default gateway. Click Add. Repeat this process for other default gateways.

11. The first gateway listed is the one clients try to use first. If the gateway isn't available, clients try to use the next gateway, and so on. Use the Up and Down buttons to change the order of the gateways, as necessary.

12. Click Next, and then, as shown in Figure 18-6, configure default DNS settings for DHCP clients. Enter the name of the parent domain to use for DNS resolution of computer names that aren't fully qualified.

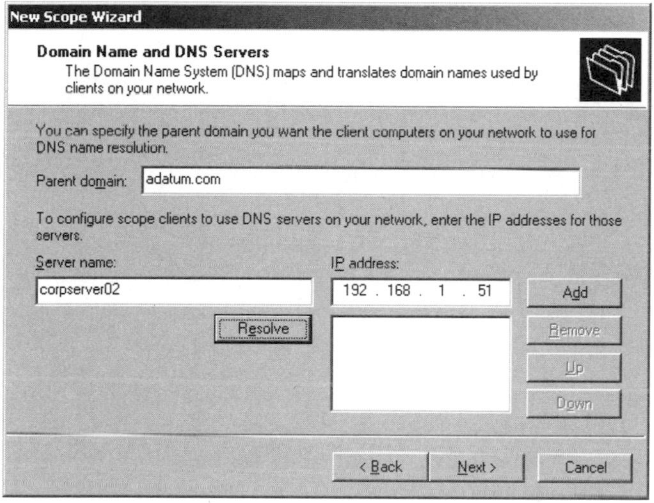

Figure 18-6   Use the Domain Name And DNS Servers page to configure default DNS settings for DHCP clients.

13. In the IP Address field, enter the IP address of the primary DNS. Click Add. Repeat this process to specify additional DNS servers. Again, the order of the entries determines which IP address is used first. Change the order as necessary using the Up and Down buttons. Click Next.

> **Tip**   If you know the name of a server instead of its IP address, enter the name in the Server Name field and then click Resolve. The IP address is then entered in the IP Address field, if possible. Add the server by clicking Add.

14. Configure default WINS settings for the DHCP clients. The techniques you use are the same as those previously described. Click Next.

15. If you want to activate the scope, select Yes, I Want To Activate This Scope Now and then click Next. Otherwise, select No, I Will Activate This Scope Later and then click Next.

16. Complete the process by clicking Finish.

Creating Multicast Scopes

To create a multicast scope, follow these steps:

1. In the DHCP console, right-click the server on which you want to create the scope. If you want to add the new scope to an existing superscope, right-click the superscope instead.

2. From the shortcut menu, select New Multicast Scope. This starts the New Multicast Scope Wizard. Click Next.

3. Enter a name and description for the scope and then click Next.

4. The Start IP Address and End IP Address fields define the valid IP address range for the scope. Enter a start address and an end address in these fields. Multicast scopes must be defined using Class D IP addresses. This means the valid IP address range is 224.0.0.0 to 239.255.255.255.

5. Messages sent by computers using multicast IP addresses have a specific Time to Live (TTL) value. The TTL value specifies the maximum number of routers the message can go through. The default value is 32, which is sufficient on most networks. If you have a large network, you might need to increase this value to reflect the actual number of routers that might be used.

6. Click Next. If you made a mistake, click Back and modify the IP address range you entered.

7. Use the Exclusion Range fields to define IP address ranges that are to be excluded from the scope. You can exclude multiple address ranges. To define an exclusion range, enter a start address and an end address in the Exclusion Range's Start IP Address and End IP Address fields, respectively, and then click Add.

   ❑ To track which address ranges are excluded, use the Excluded Addresses list box.

   ❑ To delete an exclusion range, select the range in the Excluded Addresses list box and then click Remove.

8. Click Next. Specify the duration of leases for the scope using the Day(s), Hour(s), and Minute(s) fields. The default duration is 30 days. Click Next.

   Tip   If you haven't worked a lot with multicast, you shouldn't change the default value. Multicast leases aren't used in the same way as normal leases. Multiple computers can use a multicast IP address, and all of these computers can have a lease on the IP address. A good multicast lease duration for most networks is from 30 to 60 days.

9. If you want to activate the scope, select Yes and then click Next. Otherwise, select No and then click Next. Complete the process by clicking Finish.

Setting Scope Options

Scope options allow you to precisely control a scope's functioning and to set default TCP/IP settings for clients that use the scope. For example, you can use scope options to enable clients to automatically find DNS servers on the network. You can also define settings for default gateways, WINS, and more. Scope options only apply to normal scopes, not to multicast scopes.

You can set scope options in any of the following ways:

- Globally, for all scopes, by setting default server options
- On a per scope basis, by setting scope options
- On a per client basis, by setting reservation options
- On a client class basis, by configuring user-specific or vendor-specific classes

Scope options use a hierarchy to determine when certain options apply. This hierarchy's order is as shown in the previous list. Basically, this means that:

- Per scope options override global options.
- Per client options override per scope and global options.
- Client class options override all other options.

Viewing and Assigning Server Options   Server options are applied to all scopes configured on a particular DHCP server. You can view and assign server options by completing the following steps:

1. Start the DHCP console, and then double-click the server with which you want to work to expand its folder in the tree view.

2. To view current settings, select Server Options. Currently configured options are displayed in the right pane.

3. To assign new settings, right-click Server Options and then select Configure Options. This opens the Server Options dialog box. Under Available Options, select the check box for the first option you want to configure. Then, with the option selected, enter any required information in the fields of the Data Entry panel. Repeat this step to configure other options. Click OK to save your changes.

Viewing and Assigning Scope Options   Scope options are specific to an individual scope and override the default server options. You can view and assign scope options by completing the following steps:

1. Expand the entry for the scope you want to work with in the DHCP console.

2. To view current settings, select Scope Options. Currently configured options are displayed in the right pane.

3. To assign new settings, right-click Scope Options and then select Configure Options. This opens the Scope Options dialog box. Under Available Options, select the check box for the first option you want to configure. Then, with the option selected, enter any required information in the fields of the Data Entry panel, as shown in Figure 18-7. Repeat this step to configure other options. Click OK.

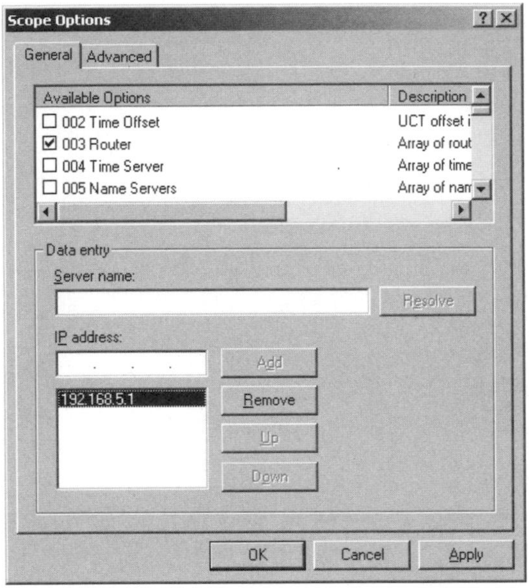

Figure 18-7   Each scope option has different settings. Use the Scope Options dialog box to select the option you want to configure and then enter the required information using the fields of the Data Entry panel.

Viewing and Assigning Reservation Options   You can assign reservation options to a client that has a reserved IP address. These options are specific to an individual client and override server-specific and scope-specific options. To view and assign reservation options, complete the following steps:

1. Expand the entry for the scope with which you want to work in the DHCP console.

2. Double-click the Reservations folder for the scope.

3. To view current settings, click the reservation you want to examine. Currently configured options are displayed in the right pane.

4. To assign new settings, right-click the reservation and then select Configure Options. This opens the Reservation Options dialog box. Under Available Options, select the check box for the first option you want to configure. Then, with the option selected, enter any required information in the fields of the Data Entry panel. Repeat this step to configure other options.

Modifying Scopes

You can modify an existing scope by doing the following:

1. Start the DHCP console and then double-click the entry for the DHCP server you want to configure. This should display the currently configured scopes for the server.

2. Right-click the scope you want to modify and then choose Properties.

3. When you modify normal scopes, you have the option of setting an unlimited lease expiration time. If you do, you create permanent leases that reduce the effectiveness of pooling IP addresses with DHCP. Permanent leases aren't released unless you physically release them or deactivate the scope. As a result, you might eventually run out of addresses, especially as your network grows. A better alternative to unlimited leases is to use address reservations—and then only for specific clients that need fixed IP addresses.

4. When you modify multicast scopes, you have the option of setting a lifetime for the scope. The scope lifetime determines the amount of time the scope is valid. By default, multicast scopes are valid as long as they're activated. To change this setting, click the Lifetime tab, select Multicast Scope Expires On, and then set an expiration date.

5. Finish modifying the scope as necessary, and then close the Scope Properties dialog box by clicking OK. The changes are saved in the DHCP console.

Activating and Deactivating Scopes

In the DHCP console, inactive scopes are displayed with an icon showing a red arrow pointing down. Active scopes display a normal folder icon.

Activating a Scope   You can activate an inactive scope by right-clicking it in the DHCP console and then selecting Activate.

Deactivating a Scope   You can deactivate an active scope by right-clicking it in the DHCP console and then selecting Deactivate.

> **Tip**   Deactivating turns off a scope but doesn't terminate current client leases. If you want to terminate leases, follow the instructions in the section of this chapter entitled "Releasing Addresses and Leases."

Enabling the Bootstrap Protocol

Bootstrap Protocol (BOOTP) is a dynamic IP addressing protocol that predates DHCP. Normal scopes don't support BOOTP. To enable a scope to support BOOTP, follow these steps:

1. Right-click the scope you want to modify, and then choose Properties.

2. In the Advanced tab, click Both to support DHCP and BOOTP clients.

3. As necessary, set a lease duration for BOOTP clients, and then click OK.

Removing a Scope

Removing a scope permanently deletes the scope from the DHCP server. To remove a scope, follow these steps:

1. Right-click the scope you want to remove in the DHCP console and then choose Delete.

2. When prompted to confirm that you want to delete the scope, click Yes.

Configuring Multiple Scopes on a Network

You can configure multiple scopes on a single network. A single DHCP server or multiple DHCP servers can serve these scopes. However, anytime you work with multiple scopes, it's extremely important that the address ranges used by different scopes don't overlap. Each scope must have its own unique address range. If it doesn't, the same IP address might be assigned to different DHCP clients, which can cause severe problems on the network.

To understand how you can use multiple scopes, consider the following scenario, in which each server has its respective DHCP scope IP address ranges on the same subnet.

	DHCP Scope IP Address Range
Server A	192.168.10.1 to 192.168.10.99
Server B	192.168.10.100 to 192.168.10.199
Server C	192.168.10.200 to 192.168.10.254

Each of these servers will respond to DHCP discovery messages, and any of them can assign IP addresses to clients. If one of the servers fails, the other servers can continue to provide DHCP services to the network.

Managing the Address Pool, Leases, and Reservations

Scopes have separate folders for address pools, leases, and reservations. By accessing these folders, you can view current statistics for the related data and manage existing entries.

Viewing Scope Statistics

Scope statistics provide summary information on the address pool for the current scope or superscope. To view statistics, right-click the scope or superscope and then select Display Statistics.

The primary fields of this dialog box are used as follows:

Total Scopes Shows the number of scopes in a superscope.

Total Addresses Shows the total number of IP addresses assigned to the scope.

In Use   Shows the total number of addresses being used, as a numerical value and as a percentage of the total available addresses. If the total reaches 85 percent or more, you might want to consider assigning additional addresses or freeing up addresses for use.

Available   Shows the total number of addresses available for use, as a numerical value and as a percentage of the total available addresses.

Setting a New Exclusion Range

You can exclude IP addresses from a scope by defining an exclusion range. Scopes can have multiple exclusion ranges. To define an exclusion range, follow these steps:

1. In the DHCP console, expand the scope you want to work with, and then right-click the Address Pool folder. On the shortcut menu, select New Exclusion Range.

2. Enter a start address and an end address in the Exclusion Range's Start IP Address and End IP Address fields, respectively, and then click Add. The range specified must be a subset of the range set for the current scope and must not be currently in use. Repeat this step to add other exclusion ranges. Click Close when you're finished.

Deleting an Exclusion Range

If you don't need an exclusion any more, you can delete it. Right-click the exclusion, select Delete, and then click Yes in response to the confirmation message.

Reserving DHCP Addresses

DHCP provides several ways to assign permanent addresses to clients. One way is to use the Unlimited setting in the Scope dialog box to assign permanent addresses to all clients that use the scope. Another way is to reserve DHCP addresses on a per client basis. When you reserve a DHCP address, the DHCP server always assigns the client the same IP address, and you can do so without sacrificing the centralized management features that make DHCP so attractive.

To reserve a DHCP address for a client, follow these steps:

1. In the DHCP console, expand the scope with which you want to work and then right-click the Reservations folder. On the shortcut menu, select New Reservation. This opens the dialog box shown in Figure 18-8.

2. In the Reservation Name field, type a short but descriptive name for the reservation. This field is used only for identification purposes.

3. In the IP Address field, enter the IP address you want to reserve for the client.

> **Note**   Note that this IP address must be within the valid range of addresses for the currently selected scope.

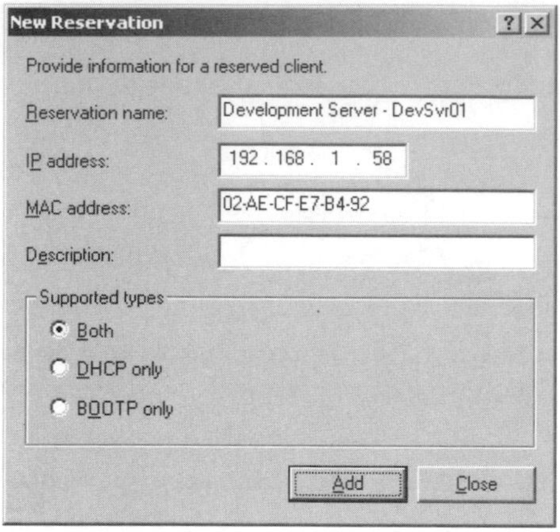

Figure 18-8   Use the New Reservation dialog box to reserve an IP address for a client.

4. The MAC Address field specifies the Media Access Control (MAC) address for the client computer's NIC. You can obtain the MAC address by typing the command **ipconfig /all** at the command prompt on the client computer. The Physical Address entry shows the client's MAC address. You must type this value exactly for the address reservation to work.

5. Enter an optional comment in the Description field if you like.

6. By default, both DHCP and BOOTP clients are supported. This option is fine, and you need to change it only if you want to exclude a particular type of client.

7. Click Add to create the address reservation.

Releasing Addresses and Leases

When you work with reserved addresses, you should heed a couple of caveats:

- Reserved addresses aren't automatically reassigned. So, if the address is already in use, you'll need to release the address to ensure that the appropriate client can obtain it. You can force a client to release an address by terminating the client's lease or by logging on to the client and typing the command **ipconfig /release** at the command prompt.

- Clients don't automatically switch to the reserved address. So, if the client is already using a different IP address, you'll need to force the client to release the current lease and request a new one. You can do this by terminating the client's lease or by logging on to the client and typing the command **ipconfig /renew** at the command prompt.

Modifying Reservation Properties

You can modify the properties of reservations by doing the following:

1. In the DHCP console, expand the scope with which you want to work and then click the Reservations folder.

2. Right-click a reservation, and then select Properties. You can now modify the reservation properties. You can't modify fields that are shaded, but you can modify other fields. These fields are the same fields described in the previous section.

Deleting Leases and Reservations

You can delete active leases and reservations by completing the following steps:

1. In the DHCP console, expand the scope with which you want to work, and then click the Address Leases or Reservations folder, as appropriate.

2. Right-click the lease or reservation you want to delete and then choose Delete.

3. Confirm the deletion by clicking Yes.

4. The lease or reservation is now removed from DHCP. However, the client isn't forced to release the IP address. To force the client to release the IP address, log on to the client that holds the lease or reservation and type the command **ipconfig /release** at the command prompt.

Backing Up and Restoring the DHCP Database

DHCP servers store DHCP lease and reservation information in database files. By default, these files are stored in the %SystemRoot%\System32\dhcp directory. The key files in this directory are used as follows:

Dhcp.mdb   Primary database file for the DHCP server

J50.log   Transaction log file used to recover incomplete transactions in case of a server malfunction

J50.chk   Checkpoint file used in truncating the transaction log for the DHCP server

Res1.log   Reserved log file for the DHCP server

Res2.log   Reserved log file for the DHCP server

Tmp.edb   Temporary working file for the DHCP server

Backing Up the DHCP Database

The backup directory in the %SystemRoot%\System32\dhcp folder contains backup information for the DHCP configuration and the DHCP database. By default, the

DHCP database is backed up every 60 minutes automatically. To manually back up the DHCP database at any time, follow these steps:

1. In the DHCP console, right-click the server you want to back up and then choose Backup.

2. In the Browse For Folder dialog box, select the folder that will contain the backup DHCP database and then click OK.

Registry keys that control the location and timing of DHCP backups, as well as other DHCP settings, are located in the folder:

`HKEY_LOCAL_MACHINE\SYSTEM\CurrentControlSet\Services\DHCPServer\Parameters`

The following keys control the DHCP database and backup configuration:

BackupDatabasePath   Sets the location of the DHCP database. You should set this option through the DHCP Properties dialog box. Click the Advanced tab and then set the Database Path field as appropriate.

DatabaseName   Sets the name of the primary DHCP database file. The default value is DHCP.mdb.

BackupInterval   Sets the backup interval in minutes. The default value is 60 minutes.

DatabaseCleanupInterval   Sets the interval for cleaning entries in the database. The default value is 60 minutes.

Restoring the DHCP Database from Backup

In the case of a server crash and recovery, you might need to restore and then reconcile the DHCP database. To force DHCP to restore the database from backup, follow these steps:

1. If necessary, restore a good copy of the %SystemRoot%\System32\ dhcp\backup directory from a tape or other archive source. Afterward, start the DHCP console, right-click the server you want to restore, and then choose Restore.

2. In the Browse For Folder dialog box, select the folder that contains the backup you want to restore and then click OK.

3. During restoration of the database, the DHCP Server service is stopped. As a result, DHCP clients will temporarily be unable to contact the DHCP server to obtain IP addresses.

Using Backup and Restore to Move the DHCP Database to a New Server

If you need to rebuild a server providing DHCP services you might want to move the DHCP services to another server prior to rebuilding the server. To do this, you need to perform several tasks on the source and destination servers. On the destination server, do the following:

1. Install the DHCP Server service on the destination server and then restart the server.

2. Stop the DHCP service in the Services utility.

3. Delete the contents of the %SystemRoot%\System32\dhcp folder.

On the source server, do the following:

1. Stop the DHCP service in the Services utility.

2. After the DHCP service is stopped, disable the service so that it can no longer be started.

3. Copy the entire contents of the %SystemRoot%\System32\dhcp folder to the %SystemRoot%\System32\dhcp folder on the destination server.

Now all the necessary files are on the destination server. Start the DHCP Server service on the destination server to complete the migration.

Repairing the DHCP Database

Sometimes DHCP databases can become corrupt. When this happens, you'll see error messages in the System event log. These error messages have DHCPServer as the source and reference JET database errors, such as:

```
The JET database returned the following Error: -510.
```

To use the Jetpack.exe utility to detect and repair the database consistency problems, complete the following steps:

1. Start a command prompt by clicking Start, choosing Programs or All Programs as appropriate, choosing Accessories, and then selecting Command Prompt.

2. Stop the DHCP Server service by entering **net stop dhcpserver** at the command prompt.

3. Afterward, change to the DHCP database directory. By default, this is %SystemRoot%\System32\dhcp.

4. Type the following command:

   ```
   jetpack dhcp.mdb dhcptemp.mdb
   ```

   where dhcp.mdb is the name of the DHCP database and dhcptemp.mdb is the name of a temporary file that the Jetpack utility can use.

5. The Jetpack utility will do the following:

   ❑ Examine the database for inconsistencies and other problems.

❑   Fix any consistency errors, writing all changes to the temporary database file.

❑   Compact the database, writing all changes to the temporary database file.

❑   Overwrite the original database file with the temporary file, completing the operation.

6. On successful completion, restart the DHCP Server service by typing **net start dhcpserver**. If the Jetpack utility fails to repair the database, you'll need to restore the database from backup or force the DHCP Server service to recreate the database.

Forcing the DHCP Server Service to Regenerate the DHCP Database

If the DHCP database becomes corrupt, you might be unable to repair the database using the Jetpack.exe program. If this happens, you should attempt to restore the database as described in the section of this chapter entitled "Restoring the DHCP Database from Backup." If this fails or you'd rather start with a fresh copy of the DHCP database, complete these steps:

1. Stop the DHCP Server service in the Services utility.

2. Delete the contents of the %SystemRoot%\System32\dhcp folder. If you want to force a complete regeneration of the database and not allow the server to restore from a previous backup, you should also delete the contents of the backup folder.

    Caution   Don't delete DHCP files if the DHCPServer registry keys aren't intact. These keys must be available to restore the DHCP database.

3. Restart the DHCP Server service.

4. No active leases or other information for scopes are displayed in the DHCP console. To regain the active leases for each scope, you must reconcile the server scopes as discussed in the following section of this chapter, "Reconciling Leases and Reservations."

5. To prevent conflicts with previously assigned leases, you should enable address conflict detection for the next few days, as discussed in the section of this chapter entitled "Avoiding IP Address Conflicts."

Reconciling Leases and Reservations

Reconciling checks the client leases and reservations against the DHCP database on the server. If inconsistencies are found between what is registered in the Windows registry and what is recorded in the DHCP server database, you can select and reconcile any inconsistent entries. Once reconciled, DHCP either restores the IP address to the original owner or creates a temporary reservation for the IP address. When the lease time expires, the address is recovered for future use.

You can reconcile scopes individually or you can reconcile all scopes on a server. To reconcile a scope individually, follow these steps:

1. In the DHCP console, right-click the scope with which you want to work and then choose Reconcile All Scopes.

2. In the Reconcile All Scopes dialog box, click Verify.

3. Inconsistencies found are reported in the status window. Select the displayed addresses and then click Reconcile to repair inconsistencies.

4. If no inconsistencies are found, click OK.

To reconcile all scopes on a server, follow these steps:

1. In the DHCP console, right-click the server entry and then choose Reconcile All Scopes.

2. In the Reconcile All Scopes dialog box, click Verify.

3. Inconsistencies found are reported in the status window. Select the displayed addresses and then click Reconcile to repair inconsistencies.

4. If no inconsistencies are found, click OK.

Chapter 19
Maintaining WINS

Microsoft Windows Internet Name Service (WINS) is a name resolution service that resolves computer names to Internet Protocol (IP) addresses. Using WINS, the computer name OMEGA, for example, could be resolved to an IP address that enables computers on a Microsoft network to find one another and transfer information.

WINS is needed to support pre-Windows 2000 systems and older applications that use Network Basic Input/Output System (NetBIOS) over Transmission Control Protocol/Internet Protocol (TCP/IP), such as the NET command-line utilities. If you don't have pre-Windows 2000 systems or applications on the network, you don't need to use WINS.

The underlying application programming interface (API) that enables WINS name resolution and information transfers between computers is NetBIOS. The NetBIOS API contains a set of commands that applications can use to access session-layer services. Commonly used extensions for NetBIOS are NetBIOS Enhanced User Interface (NetBEUI) and NetBIOS over TCP/IP (NBT). This chapter focuses on WINS and NBT.

In Windows Server 2003, WINS isn't automatically installed. To install WINS, you'll need to perform the following tasks:

1. Click Start, choose Programs or All Programs, Administrative Tools, and then select Configure Your Server Wizard.

2. Click Next, and then click Next again. The current server roles are shown.

3. Select WINS Server from the Server Role list box, and then click Next.

4. Click Next. The wizard installs WINS and begins configuring the server. As necessary, insert the Windows Server 2003 CD when prompted.

5. Click Finish and then close the Manage Your Server console.

From now on, the WINS service should start automatically each time you reboot the server. If it doesn't start, you'll need to start it manually. See the section of this chapter entitled "Starting and Stopping a WINS Server."

Note   WINS servers should have static IP addresses. This ensures that WINS clients can consistently connect to the server.

Understanding WINS and NetBIOS Over TCP/IP

WINS works best in client-server environments where WINS clients send queries to WINS servers for name resolution and WINS servers resolve the query and respond. To transmit WINS queries and other information, computers use NetBIOS. NetBIOS provides an API that allows computers on a network to communicate. When you install TCP/IP networking on a Microsoft client or server, NBT is also installed. NBT is a session-layer service that enables NetBIOS applications to run over the TCP/IP protocol stack.

NetBIOS applications rely on WINS or the local LMHOSTS file to resolve computer names to IP addresses. On pre-Windows 2000 networks, WINS is the primary name resolution service available. On Windows 2000 and Windows Server 2003 networks, Domain Name System (DNS) is the primary name resolution service and WINS has a different role. This new role is to allow pre-Windows 2000 systems to browse lists of resources on the network and to allow Windows 2000, Windows XP, and Windows Server 2003 systems to locate NetBIOS resources.

Configuring WINS Clients and Servers

To enable WINS name resolution on a network, you need to configure WINS clients and servers. When you configure WINS clients, you tell the clients the IP addresses of WINS servers on the network. Using the IP address, clients can communicate with WINS servers anywhere on the network, even if the servers are on different subnets. WINS clients can also communicate using a broadcast method in which clients broadcast messages to other computers on the local network segment requesting their IP addresses. Because messages are broadcast, the WINS server isn't used. Any non-WINS clients that support this type of message broadcasting can also use this method to resolve computer names to IP addresses.

When clients communicate with WINS servers, they establish sessions that have three key parts:

Name registration   During name registration, the client gives the server its computer name and its IP address and asks to be added to the WINS database. If the specified computer name and IP address aren't already in use on the network, the WINS server accepts the request and registers the client in the WINS database.

Name renewal   Name registration isn't permanent. Instead, the client has use of the name for a specified period, which is known as a *lease*. The client is also given a time period within which the lease must be renewed, which is known as the *renewal interval*. The client must reregister with the WINS server during the renewal interval.

Name release   If the client can't renew the lease, the name registration is released, allowing another system on the network to use the computer name or IP address, or both. The names are also released when you shut down a WINS client.

> **Note**   Configuring a WINS client is described in the section entitled "Configuring WINS Resolution" in Chapter 16, "Managing TCP/IP Networking." Configuring a WINS server is described later in this chapter in the section entitled "Configuring WINS Servers."

Name Resolution Methods

After a client establishes a session with a WINS server, the client can request name resolution services. Which method is used to resolve computer names to IP addresses depends on how the network is configured. Four name resolution methods are available:

B-node (broadcast)   Uses broadcast messages to resolve computer names to IP addresses. Computers that need to resolve a name broadcast a message to every host on the local network, requesting the IP address for a computer name. On a large network with hundreds or thousands of computers, these broadcast messages can use up valuable network bandwidth.

P-node (peer-to-peer)   Uses WINS servers to resolve computer names to IP addresses. As explained earlier, client sessions have three parts: name registration, name renewal, and name release. In this mode, when a client needs to resolve a computer name to an IP address, the client sends a query message to the server and the server responds with an answer.

M-node (mixed)   Combines b-node and p-node. With it, a WINS client first tries to use b-node for name resolution. If the attempt fails, the client then tries to use p-node. Because b-node is used first, this method has the same problems with network bandwidth usage as b-node.

H-node (hybrid)   Also combines b-node and p-node. With it, a WINS client first tries to use p-node for peer-to-peer name resolution. If the attempt fails, the client then tries to use broadcast messages with b-node. Because peer-to-peer is the primary method, h-node offers the best performance on most networks. H-node is also the default method for WINS name resolution.

If WINS servers are available on the network, Windows clients use the p-node method for name resolution. If no WINS servers are available on the network, Windows clients use the b-node method for name resolution. Windows computers can also use DNS and the local files LMHOSTS and HOSTS to resolve network names. Working with DNS is covered in the next chapter, "Optimizing DNS."

Tip   When you use Dynamic Host Configuration Protocol (DHCP) to dynamically assign IP addresses, you should set the name resolution method for DHCP clients. To do this, you need to set DHCP scope options for the 046 WINS/NBT Node Type as specified in the section entitled "Setting Scope Options" in Chapter 18, "Running DHCP Clients and Servers." The best method to use is h-node. You'll get the best performance and have reduced traffic on the network.

Using the WINS Console

When you install a new WINS server, it's configured with default settings. You can view and change these settings at any time using the WINS console.

Getting to Know the WINS Console

To manage WINS servers on a network, you'll use the WINS console. This console is found in the Administrative Tools folder. The main window for the WINS console is shown in Figure 19-1. As you see, the main window is divided into two panes. The left pane lists the WINS servers in the domain by IP address, as well as the local machine, if it's a WINS server.

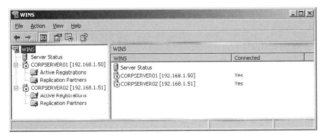

Figure 19-1   Use the WINS console to manage WINS server configurations.

By double-clicking a server entry in the left pane, you can expand the listing to display the Active Registrations and Replication Partners folders. The Active Registrations folder displays information about the status of registered computer names. The Replication Partners folder shows summary information for WINS servers, with which the server replicates registration information.

Adding a WINS Server to the WINS Console

If the WINS console doesn't list the WINS server you want to configure, you can add the server by completing the following steps:

1. Right-click WINS in the console tree and then select Add Server.

2. Enter the IP address or computer name of the WINS server you want to manage.

3. Click OK. An entry for the WINS server is added to the console tree.

Note   You can also manage local and remote WINS servers through Computer Management. Start Computer Management and then connect to the server you want to manage. Afterward, expand Services And Applications and then select WINS.

Starting and Stopping a WINS Server

You manage WINS servers using Windows Internet Name Service (WINS). Like any other service, you can start, stop, pause, and resume WINS in the Services node of Computer Management as well as from the command line. To manage WINS servers using the Services node of Computer Management, right-click WINS, choose All Tasks, and then select Start, Stop, Pause, Resume, or Restart, as appropriate. You can also manage WINS in the WINS console. Right-click the server you want to manage in the WINS console, choose All Tasks, and then select Start, Stop, Pause, Resume, or Restart, as appropriate.

Viewing Server Statistics

Server statistics provide summary information for WINS that can be helpful in monitoring and troubleshooting WINS. To view server statistics, right-click the server in the WINS console and then select Display Server Statistics. The statistics are displayed in a summary format and provide the following information:

Server Start Time   The time that WINS started on the server.

Database Initialized   The time the server's WINS database was initialized.

Statistics Last Cleared   The time the server's statistics were last cleared.

Last Periodic Replication   The time the WINS database was last replicated based on the replication interval set in the Pull Partner Properties dialog box.

Last Manual Replication   The time an administrator last replicated the WINS database.

Last Net Update Replication   The time the WINS database was last replicated based on a push notification message that requested propagation.

Last Address Change Replication   The time the WINS database was last replicated based on an address change message.

Total Queries   The total number of queries received by the server since it was last started. Records Found indicates the number of queries successfully resolved. Records Not Found indicates the number of queries that failed.

Total Releases   The total number of messages received that indicate that a NetBIOS application has released its name registration and shut itself down. Records Found indicates the number of successful releases. Records Not Found indicates the number of failed releases.

Unique Registrations   The total number of name registration messages received and accepted from WINS clients. Conflicts indicate the number of name conflicts encountered for each unique computer name. Renewals indicate the number of renewals received for each unique computer name.

Group Registrations   The total number of name registration messages received and accepted from groups. Conflicts indicate the number of name conflicts encountered for group names. Renewals indicate the number of renewals received for group names.

Total Registrations   The total number of name registration messages received from WINS clients.

Last Periodic Scavenging   The last time a cleaning took place because of the renewal interval set in the WINS Server Configuration dialog box.

Last Manual Scavenging   The last time an administrator initiated a cleaning.

Last Extinction Scavenging   The last time a cleaning took place because of the extinction interval set in the WINS Server Configuration dialog box.

Last Verification Scavenging   The last time a cleaning took place because of the verification interval set in the WINS Server Configuration dialog box.

WINS Partner   The number of successful replications with WINS partners as well as the number of failed communications with WINS partners.

Configuring WINS Servers

When you install a WINS server, the server is configured with default settings. You can change these settings by completing the following steps:

1. Right-click the server with which you want to work in the WINS console and then select Properties. This displays the dialog box shown in Figure 19-2.

2. Change property values in the General, Intervals, Database Verification, and Advanced tabs as explained in the sections that follow. Click OK when you're finished making changes.

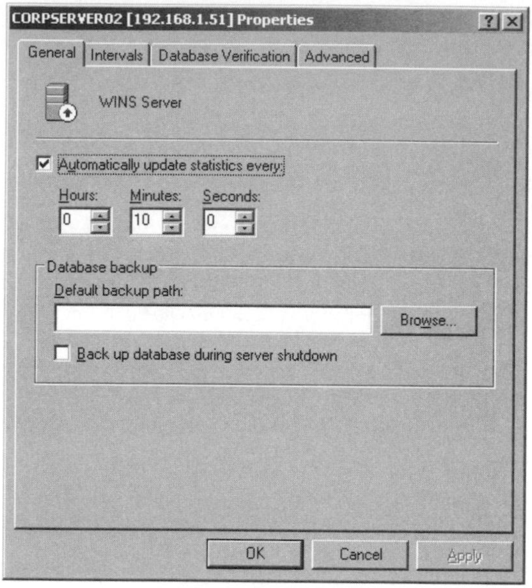

Figure 19-2   Use the Properties dialog box to configure settings for the WINS server.

Updating WINS Statistics

The WINS console provides statistics on address registrations and replication. By default, these statistics are updated every 10 minutes. If you want, you can change the update interval or stop automatic updates altogether. To do this, follow these steps:

1. In the WINS console, right-click the server with which you want to work and then select Properties.

2. If necessary, click the General tab.

3. To set an update interval, select the Automatically Update Statistics Every check box and then type an update interval in hours, minutes, and seconds. Click OK.

4. To stop automatic updates, clear the Automatically Update Statistics Every check box. Click OK.

Managing Name Registration, Renewal, and Release

Computer names are registered in the WINS database for a specified amount of time known as a lease. By setting renewal, extinction, and verification intervals, you can control many aspects of the lease.

1. In the WINS console, right-click the server with which you want to work and then select Properties.

2. Click the Intervals tab shown in Figure 19-3 and then use the following fields to configure the WINS server:

    Renewal Interval   Sets the interval during which a WINS client must renew its computer name. It's also known as the *lease period*. Generally, clients attempt to renew when they reach 50 percent of the lease. The minimum value is 40 minutes. The default value is six days, which means that clients attempt to renew their lease every three days. A computer name that isn't renewed is marked as released.

    Extinction Interval   Sets the interval during which a computer name can be marked as extinct. Once a computer name has been released, the next step is to mark it as extinct. This value must be greater than or equal to the renewal interval or four days, whichever is smaller.

    Extinction Timeout   Sets the interval during which a computer name can be purged from the WINS database. Once a computer name has been marked as extinct, the next step is to purge it from the database. The default value is four days.

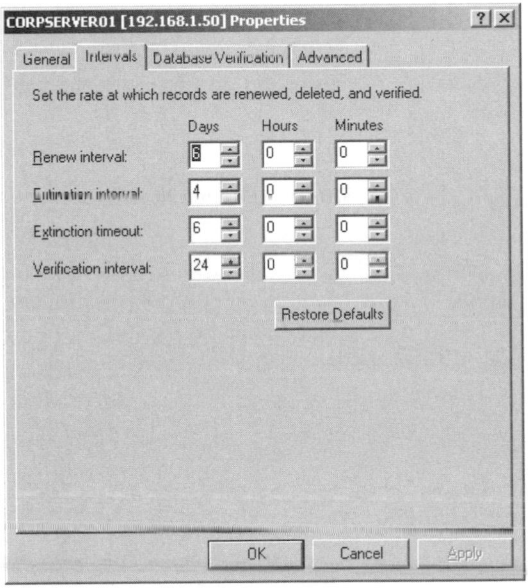

Figure 19-3   In the Intervals tab, configure intervals to customize server operation for your network needs.

Verification Interval   Sets the interval after which a WINS server must verify old names it doesn't own. If the names aren't active, they can be removed. The minimum value is 24 days. Generally, computer names registered in a different WINS server have a different owner, and thus they fall into this category.

Tip   Think of these intervals as giving you a timeline for names listed in the WINS database. Renewal Interval affects when leases are renewed. Extinction Interval affects when names that aren't renewed are marked as extinct. Extinction Timeout affects when extinct names are purged from the database. If you set Renewal Interval to 24 hours, Extinction Interval to 48 hours, and Extinction Timeout to 24 hours, it could take as long as 96 hours for a record to clear out of the WINS database.

Logging WINS Events in the Windows Event Logs

WINS events are logged in the System event log automatically. Although you can't turn this feature off, you can temporarily turn on detailed logging to help troubleshoot WINS problems. To turn on detailed logging, follow these steps:

1. In the WINS console, right-click the server with which you want to work and then select Properties.

2. Click the Advanced tab and then select the Log Detailed Events To Windows Event Log check box. Click OK to save your changes.

Note   Detailed logging on a busy network can cause a heavy load on the WINS server. Because of this, you should use detailed logging only during testing, troubleshooting, or optimizing.

Setting the Version ID for the WINS Database

The version ID for the WINS database is updated automatically when changes are made to the database. If the WINS database becomes corrupt and you need to restore the database throughout the network, you'll need to access the primary WINS server and then set the version ID to a value higher than the version number counter on all remote partners. Setting a higher version number ensures that the latest information is replicated to replication partners.

You can view and change the current version ID number by completing the following steps:

1. In the WINS console, expand the node for the server with which you want to work. Right-click Active Registrations and then select Display Records.

2. In the Record Owners tab, the Highest ID column shows the highest version ID number being used on each server.

Tip   The value shown is in decimal format. However, you set version ID in hexadecimal format, and the maximum value is 2^31. To convert the decimal value to hexadecimal value, you can use the Calculator. Start Calculator from Accessories. Select Scientific from the View menu. Click the Dec button (which stands for Decimal) and then type the ID value. Click the Hex button (which stands for Hexadecimal) and the previously entered value is automatically converted to Hexadecimal. Note the value.

3. Note the highest version ID value and then click Cancel.

4. Right-click the entry for the primary WINS server in the console tree and then select Properties.

5. In the Advanced tab, type a new value in the Starting Version ID field. This value must be entered in hexadecimal format, such as E8B, and should be higher than the value you noted previously. Click OK.

Configuring Burst Handling of Name Registrations

Multiple WINS clients often try to register with a WINS server at the same time. Sometimes this can overload a WINS server, especially if hundreds of computers are all trying to register at the same time. Rather than being unresponsive to new requests, the WINS server can switch to a burst-handling mode. In this mode, the server sends a positive response to client requests before the server processes and enters the requests in the WINS database.

You can modify the threshold at which burst handling occurs to fit your network's size and the server's capacity. The default threshold occurs when more than 500 registration and name requests are in the burst queue. You can set this threshold to a different value by completing the following steps:

1. In the WINS console, right-click the server with which you want to work and then select Properties.

2. In the Advanced tab, make sure that the Enable Burst Handling check box is selected and then use the following fields to set a new threshold:

   Low   Sets the threshold to 300 registration and name requests.

   Medium   Sets the threshold to 500 registration and name requests. This is the default value.

   High   Sets the threshold to 1000 registration and name requests.

   Custom   Allows you to set a threshold value between 50 and 5000.

3. Click OK when you're finished.

Note   The maximum number of registration and name requests that WINS can handle at any one time is 25,000. The WINS server will drop requests if this limit is exceeded.

Saving and Restoring the WINS Configuration

After you configure all the necessary WINS settings, you might want to save the WINS configuration so that you can restore it on the WINS server. To save the configuration, type **netsh dump WINS > winsconfig.dmp** at the command prompt.

In this example, winsconfig.dmp is the name of the configuration script you want to create. After you create this script, you can restore the configuration by typing **netsh exec winsconfig.dmp** at the command prompt.

> **Tip**   You can also use this technique to set up another WINS server with the same configuration. Simply copy the configuration script to a folder on the destination computer and then execute it.

Configuring WINS Database Replication

You can configure WINS servers to replicate their databases with one another. This ensures that each server's database is current and reflects changes on the network. As an administrator, you have many options for controlling when replication occurs. You can also force replication at any time.

Replication is handled with push partners and pull partners. A *push partner* is a WINS server that notifies other WINS servers of changes on the network. A *pull partner* is a WINS server that requests replicas from a push partner. You can configure any WINS server as a push partner or pull partner, or both.

To increase the reliability of replication, you can configure persistent connections between replication partners. With persistent connections, replication partners keep connections open even when they're idle. This allows the WINS servers to replicate changes throughout the network quickly and efficiently.

Setting Default Replication Parameters

Before you create replication partners, you'll want to set default parameters. These parameters are used to configure new push and pull partners.

Assigning General Parameters

General parameters control replication and migration. You can set general parameters by completing the following steps:

1. Expand the view for the server with which you want to work in the WINS console.

2. Right-click Replication Partners in the tree view and then choose Properties.

3. In the General tab, select or clear the Replicate Only With Partners check box. If it's selected, this option ensures that WINS information is replicated only with designated replication partners. If it's cleared, you can manually replicate WINS information with any WINS server on the network.

4. Static mappings are created for non-WINS clients on the network, which allows their computer names to be registered in WINS. If multiple computers may use the same IP addresses, you might want WINS to overwrite existing entries with information from new registrations. To do this, select the Overwrite Unique Static Mappings At This Server check box. Click OK.

Assigning Default Push Replication Parameters

By default, replication partners are configured to use both push and pull replication. In this scenario, you usually don't want push replication to occur automatically. Instead, you want it to rely primarily on pull replication for automatic updates. Additionally, because partners are configured for both push and pull replication, you can still initiate push replication manually if you need to.

If you want push replication to occur automatically or you want to change the default settings, follow these steps:

1. Expand the view for the server with which you want to work in the WINS console.

2. Right-click Replication Partners in the tree view and then choose Properties.

3. Click the Push Replication tab shown in Figure 19-4.

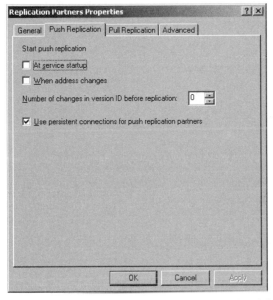

Figure 19-4   Use the Push Replication tab to assign default parameters to manage push replication in the enterprise.

4. Push replication can be initiated when WINS starts and when address changes occur. By default, these options aren't selected. To change this behavior, select the At Service Startup check box or When Address Changes check box, or both.

5. Number Of Changes In Version ID Before Replication specifies the number of registrations and changes that must take place before pull partners are notified, which triggers database replication. This counter is for local changes only and doesn't tally changes pulled from other partners. If the field is set to zero, no push replication takes place.

6. By default, push replication partners use persistent connections. If you don't want to use persistent connections, clear the Use Persistent Connections For Push Replication Partners check box. Click OK.

Assigning Default Pull Replication Parameters

Pull replication is the default replication technique for replication partners. Because of this, most of the default pull replication parameters are enabled automatically. If you'd rather use push replication as the primary replication technique, you should enable automatic push replication using the options in the Push Replication tab and then disable pull replication defaults using the Pull Replication tab.

To change pull replication settings, follow these steps:

1. Expand the view for the server with which you want to work in the WINS console.

2. Right-click Replication Partners in the tree view and then choose Properties.

3. Click the Pull Replication tab, shown in Figure 19-5.

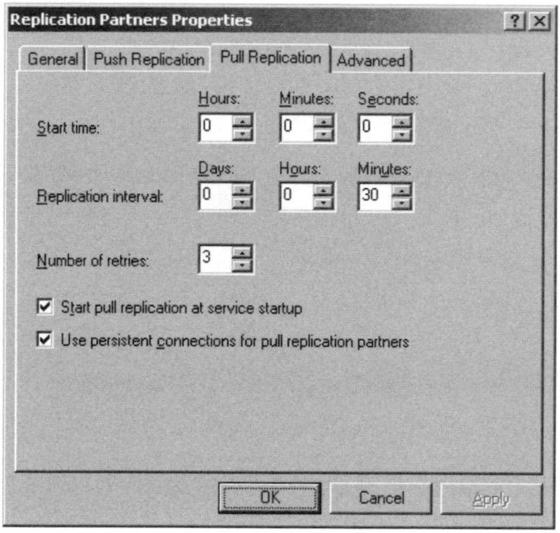

Figure 19-5   Pull replication is the primary replication technique you should use.

4. Start Time sets the hour of the day when replication should begin. The time is set using a 24-hour clock.

5. Replication Interval sets the intervals at which scheduled replication should occur, such as every 30 minutes.

6. Number Of Retries sets the number of times the WINS server will retry a connection to a pull partner in the event of a failed connection.

7. By default, pull replication starts when the WINS server starts. To change this behavior, clear the Start Pull Replication At Service Startup check box. When it's cleared, pull replication starts only at the specified Start Time.

8. By default, pull replication partners use persistent connections. If you don't want to use persistent connections, clear the Use Persistent Connections For Pull Replication Partners check box. Click OK.

Creating Push and Pull Partners

Push and pull partners are needed to replicate WINS databases whenever multiple WINS servers are on a network. Replication partners get their initial settings from the default replication parameters you've configured for a server. You must configure replication separately for each WINS server on the network.

To designate WINS servers as push and pull partners, follow these steps:

1. Expand the entry for the server with which you want to work in the WINS console. This server is the one for which you'll configure replication partners.

2. Right-click Replication Partners in the console tree and then select New Replication Partner.

3. Type the name or IP address of the replication partner in the WINS Server text box. Or click Browse and, in the Select Computer dialog box, search for a computer with which to work.

4. Click OK. If the server can be contacted, the replication entry is created automatically using the default settings. The server is configured as a push and pull replication partner.

Changing Replication Type and Settings for Partners

Default settings are used to initialize the parameters for replication partners. You can change these parameters on a per partner basis at any time by completing the following steps:

1. Expand the entry for the server with which you want to work in the WINS console. This server is the one for which you'll configure replication partners.

2. In the console tree, select Replication Partners. This displays current replication partners for the server in the right pane.

3. In the right pane, right-click the replication partner with which you want to work, and then select Properties.

4. Click the Advanced tab, shown in Figure 19-6.

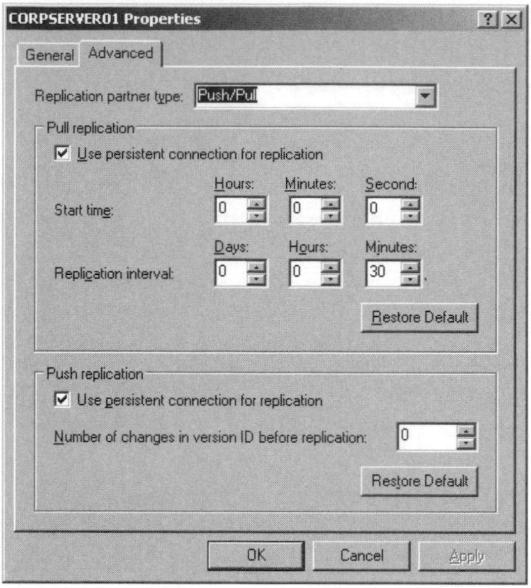

Figure 19-6   Use the Advanced tab to change the default replication settings for each replication partner, if necessary.

5. The Replication Partner Type drop-down list shows what type of replication is configured for the partner. By default, most clients are set to use both push and pull replication. You can change this behavior by selecting the Push option or the Pull option.

6. The remaining settings are the same as those discussed previously in the sections of this chapter entitled "Assigning Default Push Replication Parameters" and "Assigning Default Pull Replication Parameters." Note that you can configure only some of the options through the Replication Partners Properties dialog box. Click OK when you're finished.

Triggering Database Replication

Sometimes you might want to immediately update the WINS databases on replication partners. You can do this by forcing immediate database replication with partners or by triggering replication among partners. You can also specify the type of replication to initiate:

Forcing replication with all partners   To force replication with all partners, right-click the Replication Partners folder for the server whose database you want to replicate, and then select Replicate Now.

Triggering push replication with all partners   To start push replication with all partners, right-click the server whose database you want to replicate, and then select Start Push Replication.

Triggering pull replication with all partners   To start pull replication with all partners, right-click the server whose database you want to replicate, and then select Start Pull Replication.

Triggering push or pull replication with an individual partner   To start push or pull replication with an individual partner, go to the WINS console and click the Replication Partners folder for the server whose database you want to replicate. Currently configured partners are displayed in the right pane. Right-click the partner with which you want to replicate the database, and then select Start Push Replication or Start Pull Replication, as appropriate.

Managing the WINS Database

You should actively manage the WINS database to maintain the health of WINS name resolution on the network. The sections that follow examine common management tasks.

Examining WINS Database Mappings

When the Active Registrations folder is selected in the console tree, the WINS console's right pane displays the records that you've selected for viewing. Each entry represents a record in the WINS databases. At the left side of the entry, you'll see one of two icons. An icon of a single computer shows that the mapping is for a unique name. An icon with multiple computers shows that the mapping is for a group, domain, Internet group, or multihomed entry. Mappings also show the following:

Record Name   The complete NetBIOS name of the computer, group, or service registered in the database.

Type   The record type associated with this mapping, such as 00h WorkStation.

IP Address   The IP address associated with the mapping.

State   The state of the record, such as active or released.

Static   An X in this column indicates a static mapping.

Owner   The IP address of the WINS server that owns the record.

Version   The database version ID from which the record originates.

Expiration   The time and date the mapping expires. Static mappings have an expiration date of Infinite, which means that they don't expire (unless they're overwritten or deleted).

Cleaning and Scavenging the WINS Database

You should periodically clean the WINS database to ensure that old computer names are removed. The process of cleaning the database, called scavenging, is initiated automatically according to the relationship between the Extinction Interval and the Extinction Timeout set in the Server Properties dialog box.

You can also initiate scavenging manually. To do this, right-click the server with which you want to work in the WINS console, and then choose Scavenge Database. When prompted to confirm, click Yes.

Verifying the Consistency of the WINS Database

On a large network with multiple WINS servers, the databases on different servers can sometimes get out of sync with one another. To help maintain the integrity of the databases, you might want to verify their consistency periodically. You can perform two types of consistency checking: database consistency and version ID consistency.

When you verify database consistency, WINS checks the integrity of database records on WINS servers. To verify database consistency, select the server with which you want to work in the WINS console and then, from the Action menu, select Verify Database Consistency.

When you verify version ID consistency, WINS checks the local records with records on other WINS servers to ensure that the correct record versions are being maintained. To verify version ID consistency, select the server with which you want to work in the WINS console and then, from the Action menu, select Verify Version ID Consistency.

To configure automatic database consistency checks, complete the following steps:

1. Right-click the server with which you want to work in the WINS console and then select Properties.

2. In the Database Verification tab, select the Verify Database Consistency Every check box, as shown in Figure 19-7. Then, in the text box provided, type a time interval for the checks, such as every 24 hours or every 48 hours.

3. Using the Begin Verifying At options, enter the time when you want verification to start. You set the time with a 24-hour clock.

4. As necessary, set the Maximum Number Of Records Verified Each Period. The default value is 30,000.

5. You can verify records against servers designated as owners or against randomly selected partners. Random selection works best if you have a very large network and can't check all the records at any one time. Otherwise, select Owner Servers to verify records on the servers designated as record owners. Click OK when you're finished.

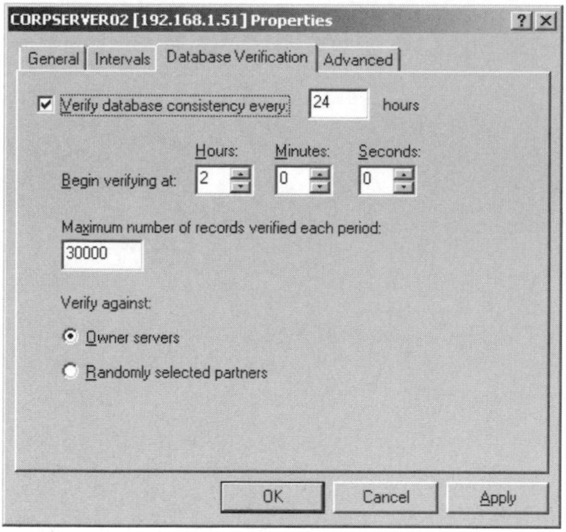

Figure 19-7   Rather than manually verifying data, you can configure automatic consistency checks.

Best Practices   Don't forget that consistency checks can use considerable system and network resources. To gain better control over when checks occur, you'll usually want to check the WINS database in 24-hour increments and then use the Begin Verifying At fields to set a time that occurs after hours. For example, if you set the database checks on a 24-hour cycle and then enter a begin time of 2 hours, 0 minutes, and 0 seconds, WINS will verify the database at 2 A.M. every 24 hours.

Backing Up and Restoring the WINS Database

Two WINS server tasks that administrators often overlook are backup and restore.

Configuring WINS for Automatic Backups

The WINS database isn't backed up by default. If you have problems with the database, you won't be able to recover it. To protect against database failure, you should configure automatic backups or run manual backups periodically. To prepare WINS to perform automatic backups, follow these steps:

1. Right-click the server with which you want to work in the WINS console and then select Properties.

2. In the General tab, enter the folder path that you want to use for backups in Default Backup Path. Click Browse if you want to search for a folder.

3. To ensure that backups are created whenever the WINS server is stopped, select the Back Up Database During Server Shutdown check box.

4. Click OK. Automatic backups will then be performed every three hours. The default location for database backups is %WinDir%\System32\Wins.

Restoring the Database

If you have a good backup of the WINS database, you can restore it by completing the following steps:

1. Select the server with which you want to work in the WINS console.

2. On the Action menu, select All Tasks, and then select Stop.

3. On the Action menu, select Restore Database.

4. In the Browse For Folder dialog box, select the wins_bak subdirectory containing the most recent backup and then click OK.

5. If the restore is successful, the WINS database is restored to its state at the time of the backup. WINS should be started automatically.

6. If the restore is unsuccessful, you might need to clear out all WINS files and then start with a fresh database.

Clearing Out WINS and Starting with a Fresh Database

If WINS won't restore using a backup or won't start normally, you might need to clear out all WINS records and logs and then start with a fresh database. To do this, follow these steps:

1. Right-click the server with which you want to work in the WINS console and then select Properties.

2. In the Advanced tab, note the folder path set in Database Path and then click OK to close the Properties dialog box.

3. Stop the server by selecting the Action menu, All Tasks, and then selecting Stop.

4. Using Windows Explorer, delete all files in the WINS database folder.

5. In the WINS console, right-click the server you're recovering, choose All Tasks, and then select Start. This starts the WINS servers.

Optimizing DNS

This chapter discusses the techniques you'll use to set up and manage Domain Name System (DNS) on a network. DNS is a name resolution service that resolves computer names to Internet Protocol (IP) addresses. Using DNS, the fully qualified host name omega.microsoft.com, for example, could be resolved to an IP address, which enables computers to find one another. DNS operates over the Transmission Control Protocol/ Internet Protocol (TCP/IP) protocol stack and can be integrated with Windows Internet Name Service (WINS), Dynamic Host Configuration Protocol (DHCP), and Active Directory directory service. Full integration with these Microsoft Windows networking features allows you to optimize DNS for Microsoft Windows Server 2003 domains.

Understanding DNS

DNS organizes groups of computers into domains. These domains are organized into a hierarchical structure, which can be defined on an Internet-wide basis for public networks or on an enterprise-wide basis for private networks (also known as intranets and extranets). The various levels within the hierarchy identify individual computers, organizational domains, and top-level domains. For the fully qualified host name omega.microsoft.com, omega represents the host name for an individual computer, microsoft is the organizational domain, and com is the top-level domain.

Top-level domains are at the root of the DNS hierarchy and are therefore also called *root domains*. These domains are organized geographically, by organization type, and by function. Normal domains, such as microsoft.com, are also referred to as *parent domains*. They're called parent domains because they're the parents of an organizational structure. Parent domains can be divided into subdomains, which can be used for groups or departments within an organization.

Subdomains are often referred to as *child domains*. For example, the fully qualified domain name (FQDN) for a computer within a human resources group could be designated as jacob.hr.microsoft.com. Here, *jacob* is the host name, *hr* is the child domain, and *microsoft.com* is the parent domain.

Integrating Active Directory and DNS

As stated in Chapter 6, "Using Active Directory," Active Directory domains use DNS to implement their naming structure and hierarchy. Active Directory and DNS are tightly integrated, so much so that you must install DNS on the network before you can install Active Directory.

During installation of the first domain controller on an Active Directory network, you'll have the opportunity to automatically install DNS if a DNS server can't be found on the network. You'll also be able to specify whether DNS and Active Directory should be integrated fully. In most cases, you should respond affirmatively to both requests. With full integration, DNS information is stored directly in Active Directory. This allows you to take advantage of Active Directory's capabilities. The difference between partial integration and full integration is very important:

Partial integration With partial integration, the domain uses standard file storage. DNS information is stored in text-based files that end with the .dns extension, and the default location of these files is %SystemRoot%\System32\Dns. Updates to DNS are handled through a single authoritative DNS server. This server is designated as the primary DNS server for the particular domain or area within a domain called a zone. Clients that use dynamic DNS updates through DHCP must be configured to use the primary DNS server in the zone. If they aren't, their DNS information won't be updated. Likewise, dynamic updates through DHCP can't be made if the primary DNS server is offline.

Full integration With full integration, the domain uses directory-integrated storage. DNS information is stored directly in Active Directory and is available through the container for the dnsZone object. Because the information is part of Active Directory, any domain controller can access the data and a multimaster approach can be used for dynamic updates through DHCP. This allows any domain controller running the DNS Server service to handle dynamic updates. Furthermore, clients that use dynamic DNS updates through DHCP can use any DNS server within the zone. An added benefit of directory integration is the ability to use directory security to control access to DNS information.

When you look at the way DNS information is replicated throughout the network, you see more advantages to full integration with Active Directory. With partial integration, DNS information is stored and replicated separately from Active Directory. By having two separate structures, you reduce the effectiveness of both DNS and Active Directory and make administration more complex. Because DNS is less efficient than Active Directory at replicating changes, you might also increase network traffic and the amount of time it takes to replicate DNS changes throughout the network.

Enabling DNS on the Network

To enable DNS on the network, you need to configure DNS clients and servers. When you configure DNS clients, you tell the clients the IP addresses of DNS servers on the network. Using these addresses, clients can communicate with DNS servers anywhere on the network, even if the servers are on different subnets.

When the network uses DHCP, you should configure DHCP to work with DNS. To do this, you need to set the DHCP scope options 006 DNS Servers and 015 DNS Domain Name as specified in the section entitled "Setting Scope Options" in Chapter 18, "Running DHCP Clients and Servers."

Additionally, if computers on the network need to be accessible from other Active Directory domains, you need to create records for them in DNS. DNS records are organized into zones, where a zone is simply an area within a domain.

> **Note**   Configuring a DNS client is explained in the section entitled "Configuring DNS Resolution" in Chapter 16, "Managing TCP/IP Networking." Configuring a DNS server is explained in the following section of this chapter.

Installing DNS Servers

You can configure any Windows Server 2003 system as a DNS server. Four types of DNS servers are available:

Active Directory–integrated primary server   A DNS server that's fully integrated with Active Directory. All DNS data is stored directly in Active Directory.

Primary server   The main DNS server for a domain that uses partial integration with Active Directory. This server stores a master copy of DNS records and the domain's configuration files. These files are stored as text with the .dns extension.

Secondary server   A DNS server that provides backup services for the domain. This server stores a copy of DNS records obtained from a primary server and relies on zone transfers for updates. Secondary servers obtain their DNS information from a primary server when they're started, and they maintain this information until the information is refreshed or expired.

Forwarding-only server   A server that caches DNS information after lookups and always passes requests to other servers. These servers maintain DNS information until it's refreshed or expired or until the server is restarted. Unlike secondary servers, forwarding-only servers don't request full copies of a zone's database files. This means that when you start a forwarding-only server, its database contains no information.

Before you configure a DNS server, you must install the DNS Server service. Afterward, you can configure the server to provide integrated, primary, secondary, or forwarding-only DNS services.

Installing the DNS Server Service

All domain controllers can act as DNS servers, and you might be prompted to install and configure DNS during installation of the domain controller. If you responded affirmatively to the prompts, DNS is already installed and the default configuration is set automatically. You don't need to reinstall.

If you're working with a member server instead of a domain controller or if you haven't installed DNS, complete the following steps to install DNS:

1. Click Start, choose Programs or All Programs, Administrative Tools, and then select Configure Your Server Wizard. Click Next.

2. Click Next. All the possible server roles are shown with an indication of which roles have already been configured. Select DNS Server and then click Next.

3. Click Next. The wizard installs DNS and begins configuring the server. As necessary, insert the Windows Server 2003 CD when prompted.

4. The Configure A DNS Server Wizard starts. Click Next.

5. Select Configure Root Hints Only to specify that only the base DNS structures should be created at this time.

6. Click Next. The wizard searches for existing DNS structures and modifies them as necessary.

7. Click Finish twice. Close the Manage Your Server console.

From now on, DNS should start automatically each time you reboot the server. If it doesn't start, you'll need to start it manually. See the section of this chapter entitled "Starting and Stopping a DNS Server."

Configuring a Primary DNS Server

Every domain should have a primary DNS server. This server can be integrated with Active Directory or it can act as a standard primary server. Primary servers should have forward lookup zones and reverse lookup zones. Forward lookups are used to resolve domain names to IP addresses. Reverse lookups are needed to authenticate DNS requests by resolving IP addresses to domain names or hosts.

After you install the DNS Server service on the server, you can configure a primary server by completing the following steps:

1. Start the DNS console. Click the Start menu, select Programs or All Programs as appropriate, choose Administrative Tools, and then select DNS. This displays the DNS console shown in Figure 20-1.

2. If the server you want to configure isn't listed in the tree view, you'll need to connect to the server. Right-click DNS in the tree view and then choose Connect To DNS Server. Now do one of the following:

❑ If you're trying to connect to a local server, select This Computer and click OK.

❑ If you're trying to connect to a remote server, select The Following Computer and then type the server's name or IP address. Then click OK.

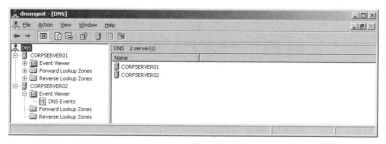

Figure 20-1   Use the DNS console to manage DNS servers on the network.

3. An entry for the DNS server should be listed in the tree view window of the DNS console. Right-click the server entry and then, from the shortcut menu, select New Zone. This starts the New Zone Wizard. Click Next.

    Note   An alternative to the DNS console is to use the Services And Applications node in Computer Management. Access this node and then click DNS.

4. As Figure 20-2 shows, you can now select the zone type. If you're configuring a primary server integrated with Active Directory (domain controller), select Primary Zone and ensure that the Store The Zone In Active Directory check box is selected. If you don't want to integrate DNS with Active Directory, select Primary Zone and then clear the Store The Zone In Active Directory check box. Click Next.

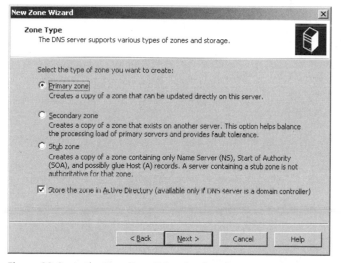

Figure 20-2   In the New Zone Wizard, select the zone type.

5. If you're integrating the zone with Active Directory, choose a replication strategy; otherwise, proceed to Step 6.

   To All DNS Servers In The Active Directory Forest   Choose this strategy if you want the widest replication strategy. Remember, the Active Directory forest includes all domain trees that share the directory data with the current domain.

   To All DNS Servers In The Active Directory Domain   Choose this strategy if you want to replicate DNS information within the current domain and child domains of the current domain.

   To All Domain Controllers In The Active Directory Domain   Choose this strategy if you want to replicate DNS information to all domain controllers within the current domain and child domains of the current domain. Although this strategy gives wider replication for DNS information within the domain, not every domain controller is a DNS server as well (and you don't need to configure every domain controller as a DNS server either).

6. Click Next. Select Forward Lookup Zone and then click Next.

7. Type the full DNS name for the zone. The zone name should help determine how the server or zone fits into the DNS domain hierarchy. For example, if you're creating the primary server for the microsoft.com domain, you should type **microsoft.com** as the zone name. Click Next.

8. If you're configuring a primary zone that isn't integrated with Active Directory, you need to set the zone file name. A default name for the zone's DNS database file should be filled in for you. You can use this name or type a new file name. Click Next.

9. Specify whether dynamic updates are allowed. You have three options:

   Allow Only Secure Dynamic Updates   When the zone is integrated with Active Directory, you can use access control lists (ACLs) to restrict which clients can perform dynamic updates. With this option selected, only clients with authorized computer accounts and approved ACLs can dynamically update their resource records in DNS when changes occur.

   Allow Both Nonsecure And Secure Dynamic Updates   Choose this option to allow any client to update its resource records in DNS when changes occur. Clients can be secure or nonsecure.

   Do Not Allow Dynamic Updates   Choosing this option disables dynamic updates in DNS. You should use this option only when the zone isn't integrated with Active Directory.

10. Click Next and then click Finish to complete the process. The new zone is added to the server and basic DNS records are created automatically.

11. A single DNS server can provide services for multiple domains. If you have multiple parent domains, such as *microsoft.com* and *msn.com*, you can repeat this process to configure other forward lookup zones. You also need to configure reverse lookup zones. Follow the steps listed later in the chapter in the section entitled "Configuring Reverse Lookups."

12. You need to create additional records for any computers you want to make accessible to other DNS domains. To do this, follow the steps listed later in this chapter in the section entitled "Managing DNS Records."

Real World   Most organizations have private and public areas of their network. The public network areas might be where Web, File Transfer Protocol (FTP), and external e-mail servers reside. Your organization's public network areas shouldn't allow unrestricted access. Instead, they should be configured as a part of perimeter networks (also known as DMZs, demilitarized zones, and screened subnets) and refer to areas protected by your organization's firewall that have restricted external access and no access to the internal network or be in a completely separate and firewall-protected area.

The private network areas are where the organization's internal servers and workstations reside. On the public network areas, your DNS settings are in the public Internet space. Here, you might use a .com, .org, or .net DNS name that you've registered with an Internet registrar and public IP addresses that you've purchased or leased. On the private network areas, your DNS settings are in the private network space. Here, you might use adatum.com as your organization's DNS name and private IP addresses as discussed in the section of Chapter 16 entitled "Configuring TCP/IP Networking."

Configuring a Secondary DNS Server

Secondary servers provide backup DNS services on the network. If you're using full Active Directory integration, you don't really need to configure secondaries. Instead, you should configure multiple domain controllers to handle DNS services. Active Directory replication will then handle replicating DNS information to your domain controllers. On the other hand, if you're using partial integration, you might want to configure secondaries to lessen the load on the primary server. On a small or medium-sized network, you might be able to use the name servers of your Internet service provider (ISP) as secondaries; in this case, you should contact your ISP to configure secondary DNS services for you.

Because secondary servers use forward lookup zones for most types of queries, reverse lookup zones might not be needed. But reverse lookup zone files are essential for primary servers, and they must be configured for proper domain name resolution.

If you want to set up your own secondaries for backup services and load balancing, follow these steps:

1. Start the DNS console and connect to the server you want to configure, as described previously.

2. Right-click the server entry and then, from the shortcut menu, select New Zone. This starts the New Zone Wizard. Click Next.

3. For Zone Type, select Secondary Zone. Click Next.

4. Secondary servers can use both forward and reverse lookup zone files. You'll create the forward lookup zone first, so select Forward Lookup Zone and then click Next.

5. Type the full DNS name for the zone then click Next.

6. Type the IP address of the primary server for the zone and then click Add. If you want to copy zone data from other servers in case the first server isn't available, repeat this step.

7. Click Next and then click Finish.

8. On a busy or large network, you might need to configure reverse lookup zones on secondaries. If so, follow the steps listed in the following section of this chapter, "Configuring Reverse Lookups."

Configuring Reverse Lookups

Forward lookups are used to resolve domain names to IP addresses. Reverse lookups are used to resolve IP addresses to domain names. Each segment on your network should have a reverse lookup zone. For example, if you have the subnets 192.168.10.0, 192.168.11.0, and 192.168.12.0, you should have three reverse lookup zones.

The standard naming convention for reverse lookup zones is to type the network ID in reverse order and then use the suffix in-addr.arpa. With the previous example, you'd have reverse lookup zones named 10.168.192.in-addr.arpa, 11.168.192.in-addr.arpa, and 12.168.192.in-addr.arpa. Records in the reverse lookup zone must be in sync with the forward lookup zone. If the zones get out of sync, authentication might fail for the domain.

You create reverse lookup zones by doing the following:

1. Start the DNS console and connect to the server you want to configure in the way described previously.

2. Right-click the server entry and then, from the shortcut menu, select New Zone. This starts the New Zone Wizard. Click Next.

3. If you're configuring a primary server integrated with Active Directory (domain controller), select Primary Zone and ensure that Store The Zone In Active Directory is selected. If you don't want to integrate DNS with Active Directory, select Primary Zone and then clear the Store The Zone In Active Directory check box. Click Next.

4. If you're configuring a reverse lookup zone for a secondary server, select Secondary Zone and then click Next.

5. If you're integrating the zone with Active Directory, choose a replication strategy:

To All DNS Servers In The Active Directory Forest   Choose this strategy if you want the widest replication strategy. Remember, the Active Directory forest includes all domain trees that share the directory data with the current domain.

To All DNS Servers In The Active Directory Domain   Choose this strategy if you want to replicate DNS information within the current domain and child domains of the current domain.

To All Domain Controllers In The Active Directory Domain   Choose this strategy if you want to replicate DNS information to all domain controllers within the current domain and child domains of the current domain. Although this strategy gives wider replication for DNS information within the domain, not every domain controller is a DNS server as well (and you don't need to configure every domain controller as a DNS server either).

6. Select Reverse Lookup Zone. Click Next.

7. Type the network ID for the reverse lookup zone. The values you enter set the default name for the reverse lookup zone. Click Next.

> **Note**   If you have multiple subnets on the same network, such as 192.168.10 and 192.168.11, you can enter only the network portion for the zone name. That is, you'd use 168.192.in-addr.arpa and allow the DNS console to create the necessary subnet zones when needed.

8. If you're configuring a primary or secondary server that isn't integrated with Active Directory, you need to set the zone file name. A default name for the zone's DNS database file should be filled in for you. You can use this name or type a new file name. Click Next.

9. Specify whether dynamic updates are allowed. You have three options:

Allow Only Secure Dynamic Updates   When the zone is integrated with Active Directory, you can use ACLs to restrict which clients can perform dynamic updates. With this option selected, only clients with authorized computer accounts and approved ACLs can dynamically update their resource records in DNS when changes occur.

Allow Both Nonsecure And Secure Dynamic Updates   Choose this option to allow any client to update its resource records in DNS when changes occur. Clients can be secure or nonsecure.

Do Not Allow Dynamic Updates   Choosing this option disables dynamic updates in DNS. You should use this option only when the zone isn't integrated with Active Directory.

10. Click Next and then click Finish to complete the process. The new zone is added to the server and basic DNS records are created automatically.

After you set up the reverse lookup zones, you need to ensure that delegation for the zone is handled properly. Contact your Information Services department or your ISP to ensure that the zones are registered with the parent domain.

Managing DNS Servers

The DNS console is the tool you'll use to manage local and remote DNS servers. As shown in Figure 20-3, the DNS console's main window is divided into two panes. The left pane allows you to access DNS servers and their zones. The right pane shows the details for the currently selected item. You can work with the DNS console in three ways:

- Double-click an entry in the left pane to expand the list of files for the entry.

- Select an entry in the left pane to display details such as zone status and domain records in the right pane.

- Right-click an entry to display a context menu with available options.

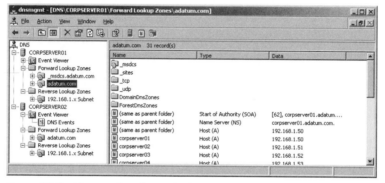

Figure 20-3   Manage domains and subnets through the Forward Lookup Zones and Reverse Lookup Zones folders.

The Forward Lookup Zones and Reverse Lookup Zones folders provide access to the domains and subnets configured for use on this server. When you select domain or subnet folders in the left pane, you can manage DNS records for the domain or subnet.

Adding Remote Servers to the DNS Console

You can manage servers running DNS from the DNS console by completing the following steps:

1. Right-click DNS in the console tree and then select Connect To DNS Server. This opens the dialog box shown in Figure 20-4.

2. If you're trying to connect to the local computer, select This Computer. Otherwise, select The Following Computer and then type the IP address or fully qualified host name of the remote computer to which you want to connect.

Figure 20-4   Connect to a local or remote server through the Connect To DNS Server dialog box.

3. Click OK. Windows Server 2003 attempts to contact the server, and if it does, it adds the server to the console.

Note   If a server is offline or otherwise inaccessible due to security restrictions or problems with the Remote Procedure Call (RPC) service, the connection will fail. You can still add the server to the console by clicking Yes when prompted.

Removing a Server from the DNS Console

In the DNS console, you can delete a server by selecting its entry and then pressing the Delete key. When prompted, click OK to confirm the deletion. Deleting a server only removes it from the server list in the console tree. It doesn't actually delete the server.

Starting and Stopping a DNS Server

To manage DNS servers, you use the DNS Server service. You can start, stop, pause, resume, and restart the DNS Server service in the Services node of Computer Management or from the command line. You can also manage the DNS Server service in the DNS console. Right-click the server you want to manage in the DNS console, choose All Tasks, and then select Start, Stop, Pause, Resume, or Restart, as appropriate.

Note   In the Computer Management console, under the Services And Applications node, right-click DNS, choose All Tasks, and then select Start, Stop, Pause, Resume, or Restart, as appropriate.

Creating Child Domains Within Zones

Using the DNS console, you can create child domains within a zone. For example, if you created the primary zone microsoft.com, you could create hr.microsoft.com and mis.microsoft.com subdomains for the zone. You create child domains by completing the following steps:

1. In the DNS console, expand the Forward Lookup Zones folder for the server with which you want to work.

2. Right-click the parent domain entry, and then, from the shortcut menu, select New Domain.

3. Enter the name of the new domain, and then click OK. For hr.microsoft.com, enter **hr**. For mis.microsoft.com, enter **mis**.

Creating Child Domains in Separate Zones

As your organization grows, you might want to organize the DNS name space into separate zones. At the corporate headquarters, you could have a zone for the parent domain microsoft.com. At branch offices you could have zones for each office, such as memphis.microsoft.com, newyork.microsoft.com, and la.microsoft.com.

You create child domains in separate zones by completing the following steps:

1. Install a DNS server in each child domain, and then create the necessary forward and reverse lookup zones for the child domain as described earlier in this chapter in the section entitled "Installing DNS Servers."

2. On the authoritative DNS server for the parent domain, you delegate authority to each child domain. Delegating authority allows the child domain to resolve and respond to DNS queries from computers inside and outside the local subnet.

You delegate authority to a child domain by completing the following steps:

1. In the DNS console, expand the Forward Lookup Zones folder for the server with which you want to work.

2. Right-click the parent domain entry and then, from the shortcut menu, select New Delegation. This starts the New Delegation Wizard. Click Next.

3. As shown in Figure 20-5, type the name of the delegated domain, such as **ts**, and then click Next. The name you enter updates the value in the Fully Qualified Domain Name (FQDN) text box. Click Next.

4. Click Add. In the Server name text box, type the fully qualified host name of a DNS server for the child domain, such as **corpserver01.memphis.adatum.com**.

5. In the IP Address text box, type the primary IP address for the server. Click Add. Repeat this process to specify additional IP addresses for this server. The order of the entries determines which IP address is used first. Change the order as necessary using the Up and Down buttons.

> **Note** If the server is reachable on the network, you can type the name in the Server name text box and then click Resolve. If the server is reachable, the IP address is then entered in the IP Address text box and added automatically.

6. Click OK and then repeat steps 3–5 to specify other authoritative DNS servers for the child domain.

7. Click Next and then click Finish to complete the process.

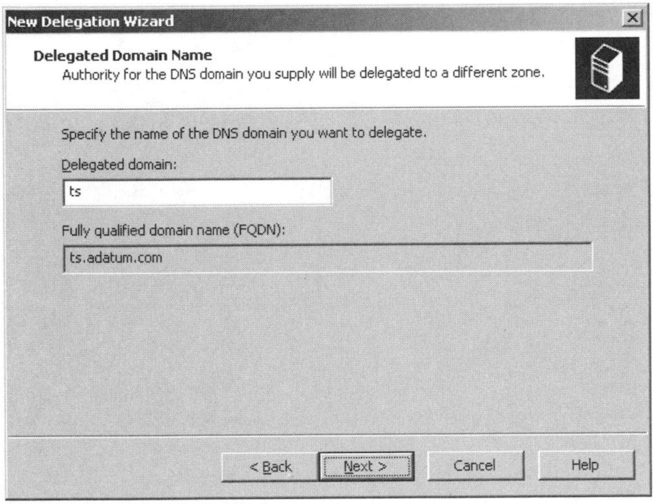

Figure 20-5   Entering the name of the delegated domain sets the FQDN.

Deleting a Domain or Subnet

Deleting a domain or subnet permanently removes it from the DNS server. To delete a domain or subnet, follow these steps:

1. In the DNS console, right-click the domain or subnet entry.

2. From the shortcut menu, select Delete, and then confirm the action by clicking Yes.

3. If the domain or subnet is integrated with Active Directory, you'll see a warning prompt. Confirm that you want to delete the domain or subnet from Active Directory by clicking Yes.

Note   Deleting a domain or subnet deletes all DNS records in a zone file but doesn't actually delete the zone file on a primary or secondary server that isn't integrated with Active Directory. You'll find that the actual zone file remains in the %SystemRoot% \System32\Dns directory. You can delete this file after you have deleted the zones from the DNS console.

Managing DNS Records

After you create the necessary zone files, you can add records to the zones. Computers that need to be accessed from Active Directory and DNS domains must have DNS records. Although there are many types of DNS records, most of these record types aren't commonly used. So, rather than focus on record types you probably won't use, let's focus on the ones you will use:

A (address)   Maps a host name to an IP address. When a computer has multiple adapter cards or IP addresses, or both, it should have multiple address records.

CNAME (canonical name)   Sets an alias for a host name. For example, using this record, zeta.microsoft.com can have an alias as www.microsoft.com.

MX (mail exchange)   Specifies a mail exchange server for the domain, which allows mail to be delivered to the correct mail servers in the domain.

NS (name server)   Specifies a name server for the domain, which allows DNS lookups within various zones. Each primary and secondary name server should be declared through this record.

PTR (pointer)   Creates a pointer that maps an IP address to a host name for reverse lookups.

SOA (start of authority)   Declares the host that's the most authoritative for the zone and, as such, is the best source of DNS information for the zone.

Each zone file must have a start of authority (SOA) record (which is created automatically when you add a zone).

Adding Address and Pointer Records

The A record maps a host name to an IP address, and the PTR record creates a pointer to the host for reverse lookups. You can create address and pointer records at the same time or separately.

You create a new host entry with A and PTR records by doing the following:

1. In the DNS console, expand the Forward Lookup Zones folder for the server with which you want to work.

2. Right-click the domain you want to update and then, from the shortcut menu, select New Host (A). This opens the dialog box shown in Figure 20-6.

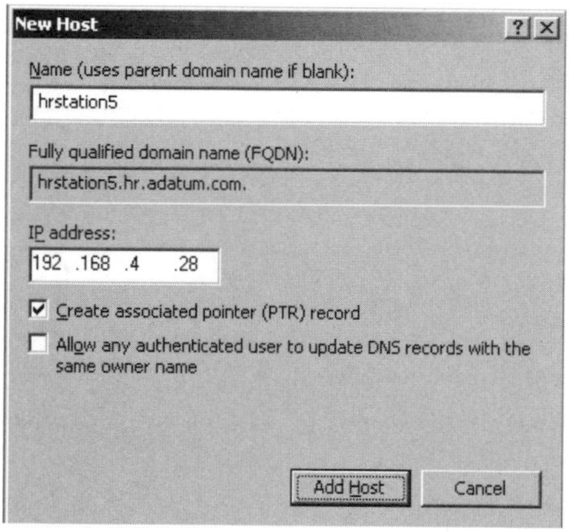

Figure 20-6   Create A records and PTR records simultaneously with the New Host dialog box.

3. Type the single-part computer name, such as **corpserver01**, and then the IP address, such as **192.168.1.50**.

4. Select the Create Associated Pointer (PTR) Record check box.

   Note   You can create PTR records only if the corresponding reverse lookup zone is available. You can create this file by following the steps listed earlier in this chapter in the section entitled "Configuring Reverse Lookups." The Allow Any Authenticated Users... option is only available when a DNS server is configured on a domain controller.

5. Click Add Host, and then click OK. Repeat as necessary to add other hosts. Click Done when you're finished.

Adding a PTR Record Later

If you need to add a PTR record later, you can do so by completing the following steps:

1. In the DNS console, expand the Reverse Lookup Zones folder for the server with which you want to work.

2. Right-click the subnet you want to update and then, from the shortcut menu, select New Pointer (PTR). This opens the dialog box shown in Figure 20-7.

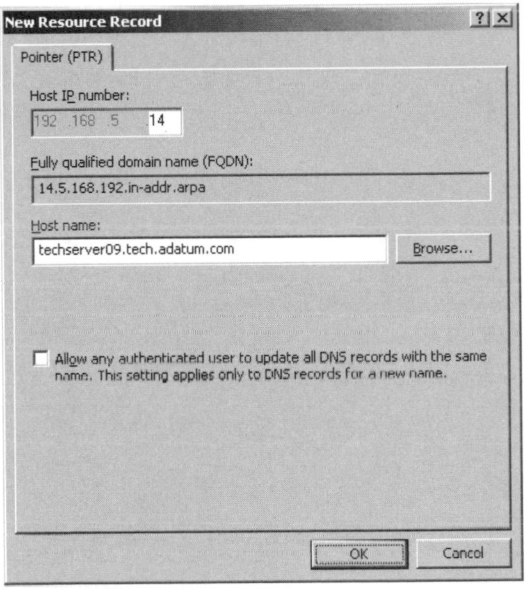

Figure 20-7   You can add a PTR record later, if necessary, with the New Resource Record dialog box.

3. Type the Host IP Number, such as **14**, and then type the Host Name, such as **techserver09.tech.adatum.com**. Click OK.

Adding DNS Aliases with CNAME

You specify host aliases using CNAME records. Aliases allow a single host computer to appear to be multiple host computers. For example, the host gamma.microsoft.com can be made to appear as www.microsoft.com and ftp.microsoft.com.

To create a CNAME record, follow these steps:

1. In the DNS console, expand the Forward Lookup Zones folder for the server with which you want to work.

2. Right-click the domain you want to update and then, from the shortcut menu, select New Alias (CNAME). This opens the dialog box shown in Figure 20-8.

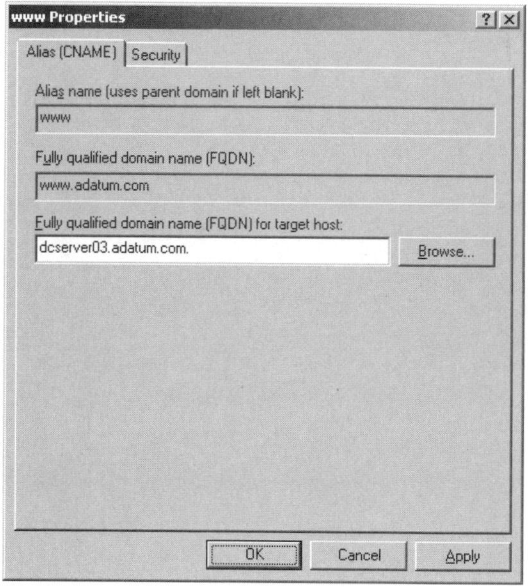

Figure 20-8 When you create the CNAME record, be sure to use the single-part host name and then the fully qualified host name.

3. Type the alias in the Alias Name text box. The alias is a single-part host name, such as www or ftp.

4. In the Fully Qualified Domain Name (FQDN) For Target Host text box, type the full host name of the computer for which the alias is to be used. Click OK.

Adding Mail Exchange Servers

MX records identify mail exchange servers for the domain. These servers are responsible for processing or forwarding mail within the domain. When you create an MX record, you must specify a preference number for the mail server. A preference number is a value from

0 to 65,535 that denotes the mail server's priority within the domain. The mail server with the lowest preference number has the highest priority and is the first to receive mail. If mail delivery fails, the mail server with the next lowest preference number is tried.

You create an MX record by doing the following:

1. In the DNS console, expand the Forward Lookup Zones folder for the server with which you want to work.

2. Right-click the domain you want to update and then, from the shortcut menu, select New Mail Exchanger (MX). This opens the dialog box shown in Figure 20-9.

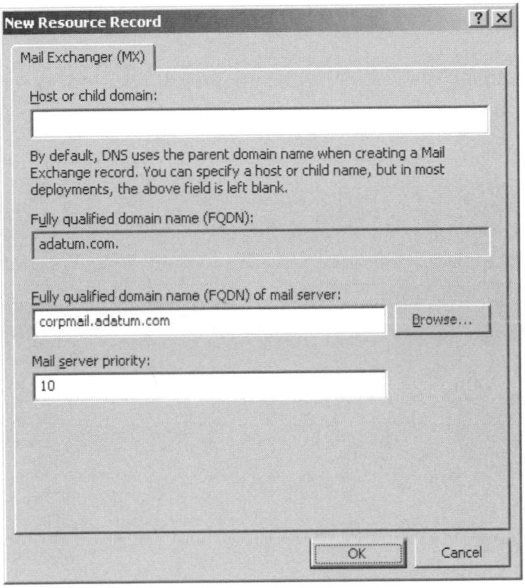

Figure 20-9   Mail servers with the lowest preference number have the highest priority.

3. You can now create a record for the mail server by filling in these text boxes:

Host Or Child Domain   Enter the single-part name for the mail exchanger if desired. In most cases, you'll want to leave this blank, which specifies that the mail exchanger name is the same as the parent domain name.

Fully Qualified Domain Name (FQDN)   Enter the FQDN of the domain to which this mail exchanger record should apply, such as **tech.adatum.com**.

Fully Qualified Domain Name (FQDN) Of Mail Server   Enter the FQDN of the mail server that should handle mail receipt and delivery, such as **corp-mail.tech .adatum.com**. E-mail for the previously specified domain is routed to this mail server for delivery.

Mail Server Priority   Enter a preference number for the host from 0 to 65,535.

> **Note** Assign preference numbers that leave room for growth. For example, use 10 for your highest priority mail server, 20 for the next, and 30 for the one after that.

4. Click OK.

Adding Name Servers

NS records specify the name servers for the domain. Each primary and secondary name server should be declared through this record. If you obtain secondary name services from an ISP, be sure to insert the appropriate Name Server records.

You create an NS record by doing the following:

1. In the DNS console, expand the Forward Lookup Zones folder for the server with which you want to work.

2. Display the DNS records for the domain by selecting the domain folder in the tree view.

3. Right-click an existing Name Server record in the view pane and then select Properties. This opens the Properties dialog box for the domain with the Name Servers tab selected, as shown in Figure 20-10.

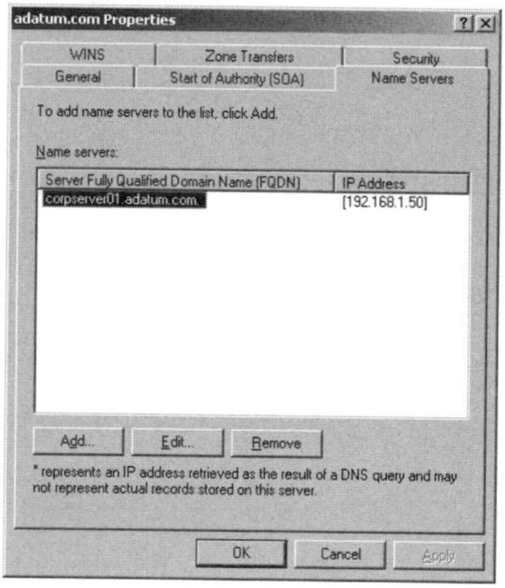

Figure 20-10   Configure name servers for the domain through the domain's Properties dialog box.

4. Click Add.

5. In the Server Fully Qualified Domain Name (FQDN) text box, type the fully qualified host name of the DNS server you're adding, such as **corpserver01 .adatum.com**.

6. In the IP Address text box, type the primary IP address for the server. Click Add. Repeat this process to specify additional IP addresses for the server. The order of the entries determines which IP address is used first. Change the order as necessary using the Up and Down buttons.

7. Click OK. Repeat Steps 5–7 to specify other DNS servers for the domain.

Viewing and Updating DNS Records

To view or update DNS records, follow these steps:

1. Double-click the zone with which you want to work. Records for the zone should be displayed in the right pane.

2. Double-click the DNS record you want to view or update. This opens the record's Properties dialog box. Make the necessary changes and click OK.

Updating Zone Properties and the SOA Record

Each zone has separate properties that you can configure. These properties set general zone parameters by using the SOA record, change notification, and WINS integration. In the DNS console, you set zone properties by doing the following:

■ Right-click the zone you want to update and then, from the shortcut menu, select Properties.

■ Or, select the zone and then, from the Action menu, select Properties.

Properties dialog boxes for forward and reverse lookup zones are identical except for the WINS and WINS-R tabs. In forward lookup zones, you use the WINS tab to configure lookups for NetBIOS computer names. In reverse lookup zones, you use the WINS-R tab to configure reverse lookups for NetBIOS computer names.

Modifying the SOA Record

An SOA record designates the authoritative name server for a zone and sets general zone properties, such as retry and refresh intervals. You can modify this information by doing the following:

1. In the DNS console, right-click the zone you want to update and then, from the shortcut menu, select Properties.

2. Click the SOA tab and then update the text boxes shown in Figure 20-11.

   You use the text boxes in the SOA tab as follows:

   Serial Number   A serial number that indicates the version of the DNS database files. The number is updated automatically whenever you make changes to zone files. You can also update the number manually. Secondary servers use this number to determine if the zone's DNS records have changed. If the primary server's serial number is larger than the secondary server's serial number, the records have changed and the secondary server can request the DNS records for the zone. You can also configure DNS to notify secondary servers of changes (which might speed up the update process).

Primary Server   The FQDN for the name server, followed by a period. The period is used to terminate the name and ensure that the domain information isn't appended to the entry.

Responsible Person   The e-mail address of the person in charge of the domain. The default entry is hostmaster followed by a period, meaning hostmaster @your_domain.com. If you change this entry, substitute a period in place of the @ symbol in the e-mail address and terminate the address with a period.

Refresh Interval   The interval at which a secondary server checks for zone updates. If it's set to 60 minutes, NS record changes might not get propagated to a secondary server for up to an hour. You reduce network traffic by increasing this value.

Retry Interval   The time the secondary server waits after a failure to download the zone database. If it's set to 10 minutes and a zone database transfer fails, the secondary server waits 10 minutes before requesting the zone database once more.

Expires After   The period of time for which zone information is valid on the secondary server. If the secondary server can't download data from a primary server within this period, the secondary server lets the data in its cache expire and stops responding to DNS queries. Setting Expires After to seven days allows the data on a secondary server to be valid for seven days.

Minimum (Default) TTL   The minimum Time to Live (TTL) value for cached records on a secondary server. The value is set in the format Days : Hours : Minutes : Seconds. When this value is reached, the secondary server causes the associated record to expire and discards it. The next request for the record will need to be sent to the primary server for resolution. Set the minimum TTL to a relatively high value, such as 24 hours, to reduce traffic on the network and increase efficiency. However, keep in mind that a higher value slows down the propagation of updates through the Internet.

TTL For This Record   The TTL value for this particular SOA record. The value is set in the format Days : Hours : Minutes : Seconds and generally should be the same as the minimum TTL for all records.

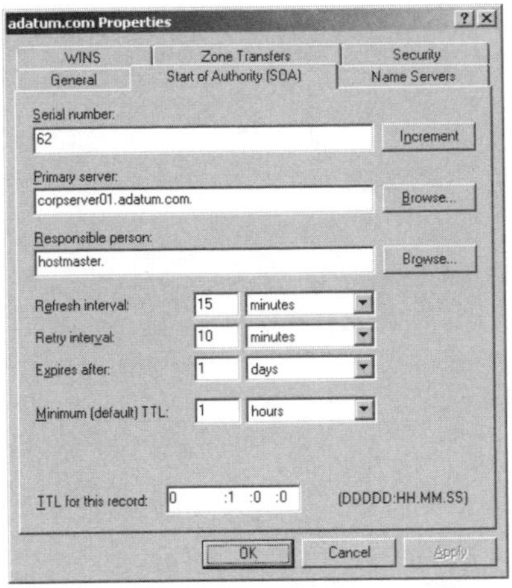

Figure 20-11   Use the zone's Properties dialog box to set general properties for the zone and to update the SOA record.

Allowing and Restricting Zone Transfers

Zone transfers send a copy of zone information to other DNS servers. These servers can be in the same domain or in other domains. For security reasons, Windows Server 2003 disables zone transfers. To enable zone transfers for secondaries you've configured internally or with ISPs, you'll need to permit zone transfers and then specify the types of server to which zone transfers can be made.

Although you can allow zone transfers with any server, this opens the server up to possible security problems. Instead of opening the floodgates, you should restrict access to zone information so that only servers that you've identified can request updates from the zone's primary server. This allows you to funnel requests through a select group of secondary servers, such as your ISP's secondary name servers, and to hide the details of your internal network from the outside world.

To allow zone transfers and restrict access to the primary zone database, follow these steps:

1. In the DNS console, right-click the domain or subnet you want to update and then, from the shortcut menu, select Properties.

2. Click the Zone Transfers tab as shown in Figure 20-12.

3. To restrict transfers to name servers listed in the Name Servers tab, select the Allow Zone Transfers check box and then choose Only To Servers Listed On The Name Servers Tab.

4. To restrict transfers to designated servers, select the Allow Zone Transfers check box and then choose Only To The Following Servers. Afterward, type the IP addresses for the servers that should receive zone transfers and click Add. Click OK.

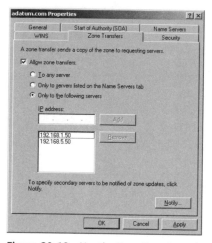

Figure 20-12   Use the Zone Transfers tab to allow zone transfers to any server or to designated servers.

Notifying Secondaries of Changes

You set properties for a zone with its SOA record. These properties control how DNS information is propagated on the network. You can also specify that the primary server should notify secondary name servers when changes are made to the zone database. To do this, follow these steps:

1. In the DNS console, right-click the domain or subnet you want to update and then, from the shortcut menu, select Properties.

2. In the Zone Transfers tab, click Notify. This displays the dialog box shown in Figure 20-13.

3. To notify secondary servers listed in the Name Servers tab, select the Automatically Notify check box and then choose Servers Listed On The Name Servers Tab.

4. If you want to designate specific servers to notify, select the Automatically Notify check box and then choose The Following Servers. Afterward, type the IP addresses of a secondary server to notify and then click Add. You can repeat this process to configure notification for multiple servers. Click OK twice.

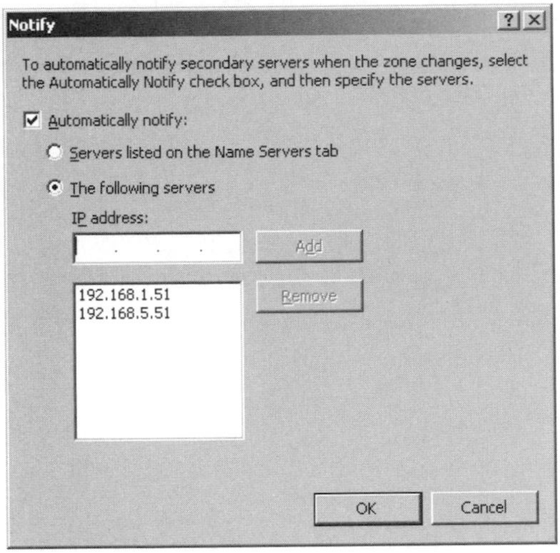

Figure 20-13   Use the Notify dialog box to notify all secondaries listed in the Name Servers tab or specific servers that you designate.

Setting the Zone Type

When you create zones, they're designated as having a specific zone type and Active Directory integration mode. You can change the type and integration mode at any time by completing the following steps:

1. In the DNS console, right-click the domain or subnet you want to update and then, from the shortcut menu, select Properties.

2. Under Type in the General tab, click Change. In the Change Zone Type dialog box, select the new type for the zone.

3. To integrate the zone with Active Directory, select the Store The Zone In Active Directory check box.

4. To remove the zone from Active Directory, clear the Store The Zone In Active Directory check box. Click OK twice.

Enabling and Disabling Dynamic Updates

Dynamic updates allow DNS clients to register and maintain their own address and pointer records. This is useful for computers dynamically configured through DHCP. By enabling dynamic updates, you make it easier for dynamically configured computers to locate one another on the network. When a zone is integrated with Active Directory, you have the option of requiring secure updates. With secure updates, you use ACLs to control which computers and users can dynamically update DNS.

You can enable and disable dynamic updates by completing the following steps:

1. In the DNS console, right-click the domain or subnet you want to update and then, from the shortcut menu, select Properties.

2. Use the following options of the Dynamic Updates drop-down list to enable or disable dynamic updates:

   None   Disable dynamic updates.

   Nonsecure And Secure   Enable nonsecure and secure dynamic updates.

   Secure Only   Enable dynamic updates with Active Directory security. This is available only with Active Directory integration.

3. Click OK.

Note   DNS integration settings must also be configured for DHCP. See the section of Chapter 18 entitled "Integrating DHCP and DNS."

Managing DNS Server Configuration and Security

You use the Server Properties dialog box to manage the general configuration of DNS servers. Through it, you can enable and disable IP addresses for the server and control access to DNS servers outside the organization. You can also configure monitoring, logging, and advanced options.

Enabling and Disabling IP Addresses for a DNS Server

By default, multihomed DNS servers respond to DNS requests on all available network interfaces and the IP addresses they're configured to use.

Through the DNS console, you can specify that the server can answer requests only on specific IP addresses. To do this, follow these steps:

1. In the DNS console, right-click the server you want to configure and then, from the shortcut menu, select Properties.

2. In the Interfaces tab, select Only The Following IP Addresses, type an IP address that should respond to DNS requests, and then click Add. Repeat this step as necessary. Only these IP addresses will be used for DNS. All other IP addresses on the server will be disabled for DNS.

3. Click Add. Repeat Steps 2 and 3 to specify additional IP addresses. Click OK.

Controlling Access to DNS Servers Outside the Organization

Restricting access to zone information allows you to specify which internal and external servers can access the primary server. For external servers, this controls which servers can get in from the outside world. You can also control which DNS servers within your organization can access servers outside it. To do this, you need to set up DNS forwarding within the domain.

With DNS forwarding, you configure DNS servers within the domain as:

Nonforwarders   Servers that must pass DNS queries they can't resolve on to designated forwarding servers. These servers essentially act like DNS clients to their forwarding servers.

Forwarding-only   Servers that can only cache responses and pass requests on to forwarders. This is also known as a caching-only DNS server.

Forwarders   Servers that receive requests from nonforwarders and forwarding-only servers. Forwarders use normal DNS communication methods to resolve queries and to send responses back to other DNS servers.

Conditional forwarders   Servers that forward requests based on the DNS domain. Conditional forwarding is useful if your organization has multiple internal domains.

> **Note**   You can't configure the root server for a domain for forwarding (except for conditional forwarding used with internal name resolution). You can configure all other servers for forwarding.

Creating Nonforwarding DNS Servers

To create a nonforwarding DNS server, follow these steps:

1. In the DNS console, right-click the server you want to configure and then, from the shortcut menu, select Properties.

2. In the Forwarders tab, select All Other DNS Domains in the DNS Domain list.

3. Enter the IP addresses of the network's forwarders.

4. Click Add. Repeat this process to specify additional IP addresses.

5. Set the Forward Time Out. This value controls how long the nonforwarder tries to query the current forwarder if it gets no response. When the Forward Time Out interval passes, the nonforwarder tries the next forwarder on the list. The default is five seconds. Click OK.

Creating Forwarding-Only Servers

To create a forwarding-only server, follow these steps:

1. In the DNS console, right-click the server you want to configure and then, from the shortcut menu, select Properties.

2. In the Forwarders tab, select All Other DNS Domains in the DNS Domain list and then select Do Not Use Recursion For This Domain.

3. Enter the IP addresses of the network's forwarders.

4. Click Add. Repeat this process to specify additional IP addresses.

5. Set the Forward Time Out. This value controls how long the server tries to query the server if it gets no response. When the Forward Time Out interval passes, the server tries the next forwarder on the list. The default is five seconds. Click OK.

Creating Forwarding Servers

Any DNS server that isn't designated as a nonforwarder or a forwarding-only server will act as a forwarder. Thus, on the network's designated forwarders you should make sure that Do Not Use Recursion For This Domain is not selected and that you haven't configured the server to forward requests to other DNS servers in the domain.

Configuring Conditional Forwarding

If you have multiple internal domains, you might want to consider configuring conditional forwarding, which allows you to direct requests for specific domains to specific DNS servers for resolution. Conditional forwarding is useful if your organization has multiple internal domains and you need to resolve requests between these domains.

To configure conditional forwarding, follow these steps:

1. In the DNS console, right-click the server you want to configure and then, from the shortcut menu, select Properties.

2. In the Forwarders tab, click New. In the New Forwarder dialog box enter the name of domain to which queries should be forwarded, such as adatum.com, and then click OK.

3. With the domain you previously entered selected in the DNS Domain list, enter the IP address of an authoritative DNS server in the specified domain. Click Add. Repeat this process to specify additional IP addresses.

4. Repeat Steps 2 and 3 to configure conditional forwarding for other domains. Click OK.

Enabling and Disabling Event Logging

By default, the DNS service tracks all events for DNS in the DNS event log. This means all informational, warning, and error events are recorded. You can change the logging options by completing the following steps:

1. In the DNS console, right-click the server you want to configure and then, from the shortcut menu, select Properties.

2. Use the options in the Event Logging tab to configure DNS logging. To disable logging altogether, choose No Events. Click OK.

Using Debug Logging to Track DNS Activity

You normally use the DNS Server event log to track DNS activity on a server. This log records all applicable DNS events and is accessible through the Event View node in Computer Management. If you're trying to troubleshoot DNS problems, it's sometimes useful to configure a temporary debug log to track certain types of DNS events. To do this, follow these steps:

1. In the DNS console, right-click the server you want to configure and then, from the shortcut menu, select Properties.

2. In the Debug Logging tab, select the Log Packets For Debugging check box and then select the check boxes for the events you want to track temporarily. Don't forget to clear these events after you've finished debugging.

3. In the File Path And Name text box, enter the name of the log file, such as dns.log. Logs are stored in the %SystemRoot%\System32\Dns directory by default.

4. Click OK. When you're finished debugging, turn off logging by clearing Log Packets For Debugging.

Monitoring DNS Server

Windows Server 2003 has built-in functionality for monitoring DNS server. You can configure monitoring to occur manually or automatically by completing the following steps:

1. In the DNS console, right-click the server you want to configure and then, from the shortcut menu, select Properties.

2. Click the Monitoring tab, shown in Figure 20-14. You can perform two types of tests. To test DNS resolution on the current server, select the A Simple Query Against This DNS Server check box. To test DNS resolution in the domain, select the A Recursive Query To Other DNS Servers check box.

3. You can perform a manual test by clicking Test Now or schedule the server for automatic monitoring by selecting the Perform Automatic Testing At The Following Interval check box and then setting a time interval in seconds, minutes, or hours.

4. The results of testing are shown in the Test Results panel. You'll see a date and time stamp indicating when the test was performed and a result, such as Pass or Fail. Although a single failure might be the result of a temporary outage, multiple failures normally indicate a DNS resolution problem.

> **Note**   If all recursive query tests fail, the advanced server option Disable Recursion might be selected. Click the Advanced tab and check the server options.

> **Real World**   If you're actively troubleshooting a DNS problem, you might want to configure testing to occur every 10–15 seconds. This will provide a rapid succession of test results. If you're monitoring DNS for problems as part of your daily administrative duties, you'll want a longer time interval, such as two or three hours.

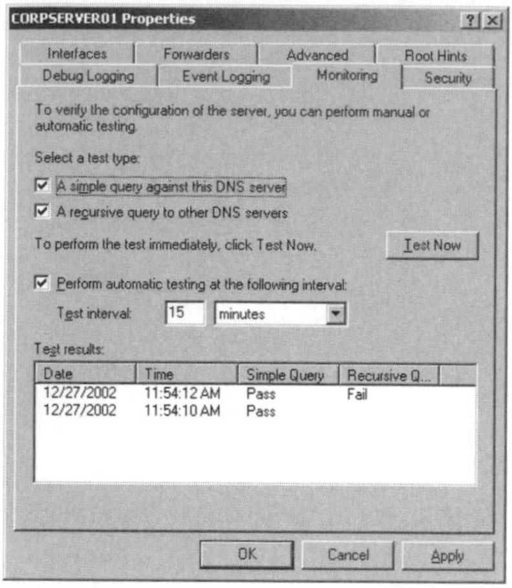

Figure 20-14 Use the Monitoring tab to configure a DNS server for manual or automatic monitoring. Monitoring is useful to ensure that DNS resolution is configured properly.

Integrating WINS with DNS

You can integrate DNS with WINS. WINS integration allows the server to act as a WINS server or to forward WINS requests to specific WINS servers. When you configure WINS and DNS to work together, you can configure forward lookups using NetBIOS computer names, reverse lookups using NetBIOS computer names, caching and time-out values for WINS resolution, and full integration with NetBIOS scopes.

Configuring WINS Lookups in DNS

When you configure WINS lookups in DNS, the leftmost portion of the FQDN can be resolved using WINS. The procedure works in the following manner. The DNS server looks for an address record for the FQDN. If a record is found, the server uses the record to resolve the name using only DNS. If a record isn't found, the server extracts the leftmost portion of the name and uses WINS to try to resolve the name (as a NetBIOS computer name). You configure WINS lookups in DNS by doing the following:

1. In the DNS console, right-click the domain you want to update and then, from the shortcut menu, select Properties.

2. In the WINS tab, select the Use WINS Forward Lookup check box and then type the IP addresses of the network's WINS servers. You must specify at least one WINS server.

3. If you want to ensure that the WINS record on this server isn't replicated to other DNS servers in zone transfers, select the Do Not Replicate This Record check box. Selecting this option is useful to prevent errors and transfer failures to non-Windows DNS servers. Click OK.

Configuring Reverse WINS Lookups in DNS

When you configure reverse WINS lookups in DNS, the host's IP address can be resolved to a NetBIOS computer name. The procedure works in the following manner. The DNS server looks for a pointer record for the specified IP address. If a record is found, the server uses the record to resolve the FQDN. If a record isn't found, the server sends a request to WINS, and, if possible, WINS returns the NetBIOS computer name for the IP address and the host domain is appended to this computer name.

You configure reverse WINS lookups in DNS by doing the following:

1. In the DNS console, right-click the subnet you want to update and then, from the shortcut menu, select Properties.

2. In the WINS-R tab, select the Use WINS-R Lookup check box, and then, if you wish, select the Do Not Replicate This Record check box. As with forward lookups, you usually don't want to replicate the WINS-R record to non-Windows DNS servers.

3. In the Domain To Append To Returned Name text box, type the DNS parent domain information. This domain is appended to the computer name returned by WINS. For example, if you use seattle.adatum.com and WINS returns the NetBIOS computer name gamma, the DNS server will combine the two values and return gamma.seattle.adatum.com. Click OK.

Setting Caching and Time-Out Values for WINS in DNS

When you integrate WINS and DNS, you should also set WINS caching and time-out values. The caching value determines how long records returned from WINS are valid. The time-out value determines how long DNS should wait for a response from WINS before timing out and returning an error. These values are set for both forward and reverse WINS lookups.

You set caching and time-out values for WINS in DNS by doing the following:

1. In the DNS console, right-click the reverse lookup zone subnet you want to update and then, from the shortcut menu, select Properties.

2. Click the WINS or WINS-R tab, as appropriate, and then click Advanced. This opens the dialog box shown in Figure 20-15.

3. Set the caching and time-out values using the Cache Time-Out text box and the Lookup Time-Out text box. By default, DNS caches WINS records for 15 minutes and times out after 2 seconds. For most networks you should increase these values. Sixty minutes for caching and 3 seconds for time-outs might be better choices.

4. Click OK. Repeat this process for other domains and subnets, as necessary.

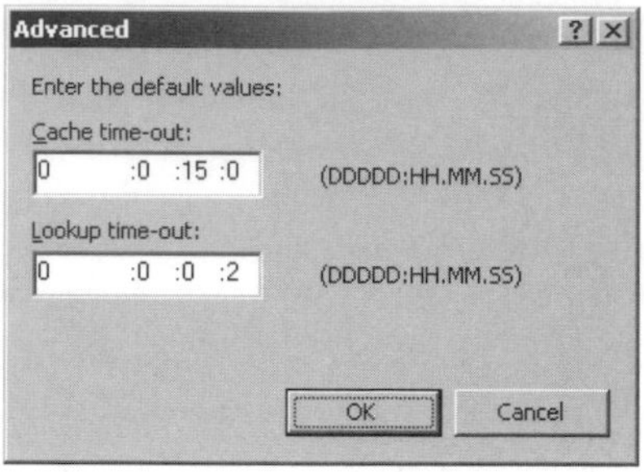

Figure 20-15   In the Advanced dialog box, set caching and time-out values for DNS.

Configuring Full Integration with NetBIOS Scopes

When you configure full integration, lookups can be resolved using NetBIOS computer names and NetBIOS scopes. Here, a forward lookup works in the following manner. The DNS server looks for an address record for the FQDN. If it finds a record, the server uses the record to resolve the name using only DNS. If it doesn't find a record, the server extracts the leftmost portion of the name as the NetBIOS computer name and the remainder of the name as the NetBIOS scope. These values are then passed to WINS for resolution.

You configure full integration of WINS and DNS by doing the following:

1. After you enable WINS lookups for all the appropriate zones, you should enable reverse WINS lookups as well. When you access the Advanced dialog box from the WINS-R tab, you'll see an additional option that allows you to Submit DNS Domain As NetBIOS Scope. Select this check box to enable full integration

2. Click OK. Repeat this process for other domains and subnets, as necessary.

Before you use this technique, make sure that the NetBIOS scope is properly configured on the network. You should also make sure that a consistent naming scheme is used for all network computers. Because NetBIOS is case-sensitive, queries resolve only if the case matches exactly. Note also that if the domain has subdomains, the subdomains must be delegated the authority for name services in order for WINS and DNS integration to work properly.

Index

546

About the Author

William R. Stanek (*http://www.williamstanek.com*) has more than 20 years of hands-on experience with advanced programming and development. He is a leading technology expert, an award-winning author, and a pretty darn good instructional trainer. Over the years, his practical advice has helped millions of programmers, developers, and network engineers all over the world. He has written more than 50 books. Current or forthcoming books include *Microsoft Windows Command-Line Administrator's Pocket Consultant, Microsoft SQL Server 2005 Administrator's Pocket Consultant,* and *Windows Server 2003 Inside Out.* He is codeveloper and series editor of the *Administrator's Pocket Consultant* series.

Mr. Stanek has been involved in the commercial Internet community since 1991. His core business and technology experience comes from more than 11 years of military service. He has substantial experience in developing server technology, encryption, and Internet solutions. He has written many technical white papers and training courses on a wide variety of topics. He is widely sought after as a subject matter expert.

Mr. Stanek has an M.S. in information systems, with distinction, and a B.S. in computer science, magna cum laude. He is proud to have served in the Persian Gulf War as a combat crew member on an electronic warfare aircraft. He flew on numerous combat missions into Iraq and was awarded nine medals for his wartime service, including one of the United States of America's highest flying honors, the Air Force Distinguished Flying Cross. Currently, he resides in the Pacific Northwest with his wife and children.

What do you think of this book? We want to hear from you!

Do you have a few minutes to participate in a brief online survey? Microsoft is interested in hearing your feedback about this publication so that we can continually improve our books and learning resources for you.

To participate in our survey, please visit:
www.microsoft.com/learning/booksurvey

And enter this book's ISBN, 0-7356-2245-0. As a thank-you to survey participants in the United States and Canada, each month we'll randomly select five respondents to win one of five $100 gift certificates from a leading online merchant.* At the conclusion of the survey, you can enter the drawing by providing your e-mail address, which will be used for prize notification *only*.

Thanks in advance for your input. Your opinion counts!

Sincerely,

Microsoft Learning

Microsoft | Learning

Learn More. Go Further.